Volkswagen Beetle 1200 Owners Workshop Manual

by J H Haynes
Member of the Guild of Motoring Writers
and D H Stead

Models covered:
All 1200 Volkswagen Beetle models, 1192 cc (72.7 cu in)

ISBN 978 0 85733 616 3

© Haynes Group Limited 1974, 1979, 1986, 1987, 1989

(036-11P3)

Haynes Group Limited
Haynes North America, Inc

www.haynes.com

The manufacturer's authorised representative in the EU for product safety is:

HaynesPro BV
Stationsstraat 79 F, 3811MH Amersfoort,
The Netherlands
gpsr@haynes.co.uk

Acknowledgements

Thanks are due to the VW Organization for the supply of technical information and certain illustrations, to Castrol Limited who supplied lubrication data, and to the Champion Sparking Plug Company who supplied the illustrations showing the various sparking plug conditions. The bodywork repair photographs used in this Manual were provided by Lloyds Industries Limited who supply 'Turtle Wax', 'Dupli-color Holts', and other Holts range products.

A special mention must go to those people who were so forth-coming with help and information; Swallowdale Garages of Seaton, Devon - particularly Bill Longman and Ken Holmwood; Mead Motors of Mudford, Somerset - particularly Tony Pearce; Kittwhistle Garage in Dorset - particularly Doug Hibberd and son.

Lastly, special thanks are due to all those people at Sparkford who helped in the production of this Manual, particularly Bill Kinchin, John Austin and Stanley Randolph.

About this manual

Its aims

The aim of this Manual is to help you get the best value from your car. It can do so in several ways. It can help you decide what work must be done (even should you choose to get it done by a garage), provide information on routine maintenance and servicing, and give a logical course of action and diagnosis when random faults occur. However, it is hoped that you will use the Manual by tackling the work yourself. On simpler jobs it may even be quicker than booking the car into a garage, and going there twice to leave and collect it. Perhaps most important, a lot of money can be saved by avoiding the costs the garage must charge to cover its labour and overheads.

The Manual has drawings and descriptions to show the function of the various components so that their layout can be understood. Then the tasks are described and photographed in a step-by-step sequence so that even a novice can do the work.

Its arrangement

The Manual is divided into thirteen Chapters, each covering a logical sub-division of the vehicle. The Chapters are each divided into Sections, numbered with single figures, eg 5; and the Sections into paragraphs (or sub-sections), with decimal numbers following on from the Section they are in, eg 5.1, 5.2, 5.3 etc.

It is freely illustrated, especially in those parts where there is a detailed sequence of operations to be carried out. There are two forms of illustration: figures and photographs. The figures are numbered in sequence with decimal numbers, according to their position in the Chapter: eg Fig.6.4 is the 4th drawing/illustration in Chapter 6. Photographs are numbered (either individually or in related groups) the same as the Section or sub-section of the text where the operation they show is described.

There is an alphabetical index at the back of the Manual as well as a contents list at the front.

References to the 'left' or 'right' of the vehicle are in the sense of a person in the driver's seat facing forwards.

Whilst every care is taken to ensure that the information in this Manual is correct, no liability can be accepted by the authors or publishers for loss, damage or injury caused by any errors in, or omissions from, the information given.

1971 Volkswagen Beetle — 1200 basic saloon (UK)

Introduction to the VW Beetle 1200

The VW Beetle 1200 was first introduced in the UK in 1954. It used an engine of 1192 cc capacity producing 30 bhp. The following year saw the engine power being increased to 34 bhp, and in 1958 the windscreen and rear window were increased in size for better visibility. In 1959 the chassis was strengthened and in 1961 the engine power output was again increased, this time to 40 bhp. This coincided with the replacement of the split-casing type gearbox by a single-piece casing, all-synchromesh gearbox.

In 1965 the glass area was again increased, and an improved braking system was fitted. 1967 saw modifications to suspension and in 1969 a dual-circuit braking system was fitted. In 1971 the rear window was again enlarged and in 1973 the rear lights were modified.

In late 1975 imports to the UK were confined to the 1200L model with de-luxe trim and equipment, this being discontinued in late 1977, when Beetle production in Europe ceased.

This is just a brief outline of the history of the Beetle 1200. It will be appreciated that it is impossible to list every last modification made, as in a production run of well over twenty years these have been many and varied.

Buying spare parts and vehicle identification numbers

Buying spare parts

Spare parts are available from many sources. VW have many dealers throughout the UK and the USA, and other dealers, accessory stores and motor factors will also stock VW spare parts.

Our advice regarding spare part sources is as follows:

Officially appointed vehicle main dealers — This is the best source of parts which are peculiar to your vehicle and are otherwise not generally available (eg complete cylinder heads, internal transmission components, badges, interior trim etc). It is also the only place at which you should buy parts if your vehicle is still under warranty. To be sure of obtaining the correct parts it will always be necessary to give the storeman your vehicle's engine and chassis number, and if possible, to take the 'old' part along for positive identification. Remember that many parts are available on a factory exchange scheme — any parts returned should always be clean! It obviously makes good sense to go straight to the specialists on your vehicle for this type of part, for they are best equipped to supply you.

Other dealers and auto accessory stores — These are often very good places to buy materials and components needed for the maintenance of your vehicle (eg oil filters, sparking plugs, bulbs, fan belts, oils and greases, touch-up paint, filler paste etc). They also sell general accessories, usually have convenient opening hours, charge lower prices and can often be found not far from home.

Motor factors — Good factors will stock all of the more important components which wear out relatively quickly (eg clutch components, pistons, valves, exhaust systems, brake cylinders/pipes/hoses/seals/shoes and pads etc). Motor factors will often provide new or reconditioned components on a part exchange basis — this can save a considerable amount of money.

Vehicle identification numbers

Modifications are a continuing and unpublicised process in vehicle manufacture. Spare parts manuals and lists are compiled on a numerical basis, the individual vehicle numbers being essential to identify correctly the component required.

Chassis number — The chassis number is stamped on the frame tunnel under the back seat.

Engine number — The engine number is stamped on the crankcase at the base of the generator pedestal.

Contents

Routine maintenance

Volkswagen routine maintenance for the various parts of the car is given in detail at the beginning of each chapter. A general summary is given here for ease of reference. It must be borne in mind that for those cars requiring an annual roadworthiness test certificate inspection may reveal the need for repairs and renewals. These become necessary in time even though the necessary maintenance has been carried out.

250 miles

EVERY 250 MILES (or weekly)

Check and top up/adjust as necessary the following:

Engine oil level
Fan belt tension
Battery electrolyte
Tyre pressures (including spare) and tyre condition
Brake fluid reservoir
Windscreen washer reservoir
All light bulbs

3000 miles

EVERY 3000 miles (or every three months, whichever comes first)

ENGINE
Drain engine oil (hot), remove and clean filter screen, replenish with fresh oil - 4½ pints. (New gaskets and washers required).
Remove air cleaner, clean filter mesh and bowl and refill with fresh oil.

Checking engine oil level

Check and adjust distributor contact breaker points.
Lubricate distributor cam.
Adjust valve clearances. (New cover gaskets required).
Remove and clean spark plugs and reset gap.
General inspection underneath with attention to:

Oil leaks — engine
　　　　　transmission
　　　　　axle shaft inner boots
　　　　　axle shaft oil seals
　　　　　steering box

Control cables — heater flaps
　　　　　　　handbrake
　　　　　　　clutch

Exhaust manifold and connections - holes - looseness
Heater hoses and connections - splits - looseness
Steering track rods
Bodyframe - damage and signs of rust

TRANSMISSION AND CLUTCH
Check transmission oil level and top up.
Check and adjust clutch pedal free play.

STEERING AND SUSPENSION
Grease torsion bar bearings (4 nipples).
Grease king pins (4 nipples) and check for play in link pins. On cars fitted with ball joints rather than king pins inspect the seals for condition and the ball joints for wear.
Check steering box oil level where applicable.

BRAKES
Examine all brake lines for signs of corrosion or fracture.
Adjust brakes.

6000 miles

EVERY 6000 miles (or every 6 months, whichever comes first)

ENGINE
In addition to 3000 mile service operations fit new contact points and new plugs.

STEERING AND SUSPENSION
Check steering box adjustment.
Check and adjust front wheel bearings.

BRAKES
Remove all brake drums and examine linings for wear.

30000 miles

EVERY 30000 miles (or every three years)

TRANSMISSION
Drain and refill with fresh oil.
Clean the drain plugs.

STEERING AND SUSPENSION
Repack front wheel bearings with grease.

BRAKES
Renew all hydraulic seals and replenish the system with new fluid.

Checking fan belt tension. A = 1.5 cm (0.6 inch)

Checking hydraulic fluid level in reservoir

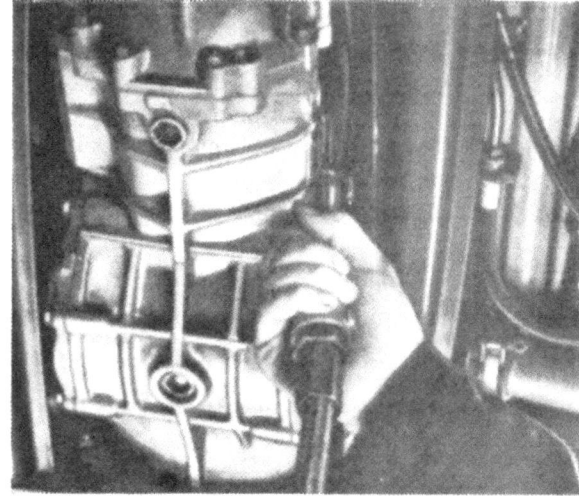

Topping up transmission unit oil level

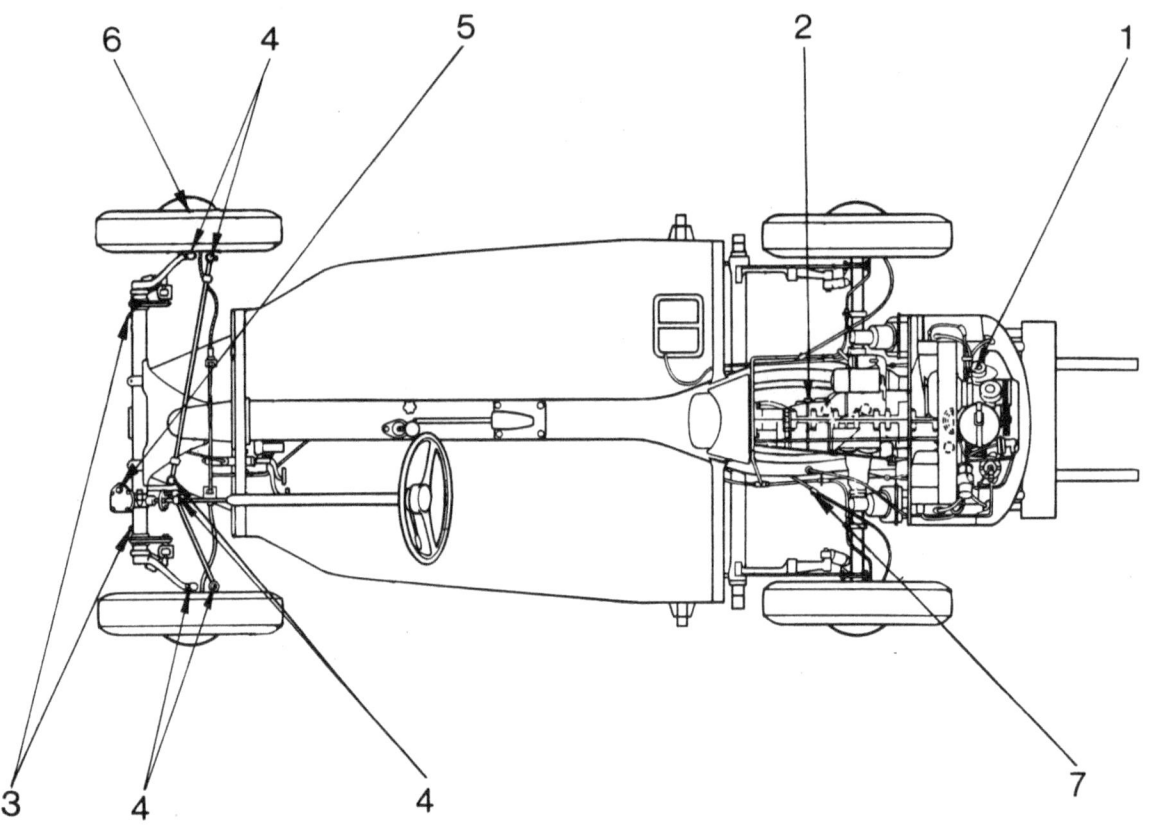

Recommended lubricants

Component	Castrol product
Engine — (1)	... Castrol GTX*
Transmission — (2)	... Castrol Hypoy (90 EP)
Front axle tubes (2 nipples each side) — (3)	... Castrol LM grease
King pins (2 nipples each side) and ball joints (4 nipples) — where applicable — (4)	... Castrol LM grease
Steering gear — early models only — (5)	... Castrol Hypoy (90 EP)
Front wheel bearings — (6)	... Castrol LM grease
Oil bath air cleaner	... Castrol GTX
Brake fluid reservoir	... Castrol Girling Universal Brake and Clutch fluid
Handbrake cables — early models only (1 nipple each side) — (7) ...	... Castrol LM grease

*Alternatively, use Castrol CRI 20 in winter, or Castrol CRI 30 in summer. Note that where engines have been run exclusively on non-detergent oil, caution should be exercised if changing to detergent oil. Dislodged sediment particles could cause restrictions in the oil cooler tubes. This would apply especially to engines where oil changes have been irregular.

Note: The above are general recommendations only. Lubrication requirements vary from territory to territory and depend on vehicle usage. If in doubt, consult your local dealer, or the operator's handbook supplied with the vehicle.

Use of English

As this book has been written in England, it uses the appropriate English component names, phrases, and spelling. Some of these differ from those used in America. Normally, these cause no difficulty, but to make sure, a glossary is printed below. In ordering spare parts remember the parts list may use some of these words:

English	American	English	American
Accelerator	Gas pedal	Locks	Latches
Aerial	Antenna	Methylated spirit	Denatured alcohol
Anti-roll bar	Stabiliser or sway bar	Motorway	Freeway, turnpike etc
Big-end bearing	Rod bearing	Number plate	License plate
Bonnet (engine cover)	Hood	Paraffin	Kerosene
Boot (luggage compartment)	Trunk	Petrol	Gasoline (gas)
Bulkhead	Firewall	Petrol tank	Gas tank
Bush	Bushing	'Pinking'	'Pinging'
Cam follower or tappet	Valve lifter or tappet	Prise (force apart)	Pry
Carburettor	Carburetor	Propeller shaft	Driveshaft
Catch	Latch	Quarterlight	Quarter window
Choke/venturi	Barrel	Retread	Recap
Circlip	Snap-ring	Reverse	Back-up
Clearance	Lash	Rocker cover	Valve cover
Crownwheel	Ring gear (of differential)	Saloon	Sedan
Damper	Shock absorber, shock	Seized	Frozen
Disc (brake)	Rotor/disk	Sidelight	Parking light
Distance piece	Spacer	Silencer	Muffler
Drop arm	Pitman arm	Sill panel (beneath doors)	Rocker panel
Drop head coupe	Convertible	Small end, little end	Piston pin or wrist pin
Dynamo	Generator (DC)	Spanner	Wrench
Earth (electrical)	Ground	Split cotter (for valve spring cap)	Lock (for valve spring retainer)
Engineer's blue	Prussian blue	Split pin	Cotter pin
Estate car	Station wagon	Steering arm	Spindle arm
Exhaust manifold	Header	Sump	Oil pan
Fault finding/diagnosis	Troubleshooting	Swarf	Metal chips or debris
Float chamber	Float bowl	Tab washer	Tang or lock
Free-play	Lash	Tappet	Valve lifter
Freewheel	Coast	Thrust bearing	Throw-out bearing
Gearbox	Transmission	Top gear	High
Gearchange	Shift	Torch	Flashlight
Grub screw	Setscrew, Allen screw	Trackrod (of steering)	Tie-rod (or connecting rod)
Gudgeon pin	Piston pin or wrist pin	Trailing shoe (of brake)	Secondary shoe
Halfshaft	Axleshaft	Transmission	Whole drive line
Handbrake	Parking brake	Tyre	Tire
Hood	Soft top	Van	Panel wagon/van
Hot spot	Heat riser	Vice	Vise
Indicator	Turn signal	Wheel nut	Lug nut
Interior light	Dome lamp	Windscreen	Windshield
Layshaft (of gearbox)	Countershaft	Wing/mudguard	Fender
Leading shoe (of brake)	Primary shoe		

Chapter 1 Engine

Contents

Specifications

Engine specifications and data 1192 c.c. 1954 on 30 and 34 DIN b.h.p.

Engine - General

Type	4 cylinder horizontally opposed flat. Pushrod o.h.v.
Weight	237 lbs. (108 kgs)
Bore	77 mm
Stroke	64 mm
Cubic capacity	1192 c.c.
Compression ratio	30 DIN b.h.p. 6.6:1
	34 DIN b.h.p. 7.0:1
Power output	30 DIN b.h.p. at 3400 r.p.m. (up to 1960)
	34 DIN b.h.p. at 3600 r.p.m. (1960 on)
Torque (30 DIN b.h.p.)	55.7 ft/lb at 2000 r.p.m.
(34 DIN b.h.p.)	60.76 ft/lb at 2000 r.p.m.
Compression pressure	100 - 128 lb/in^2
Location of No. 1 cylinder	Right hand pair - front
Firing order	1 (R. Front) 4 (L. Rear) 3 (L. Front) 2 (R. Rear)
Engine mountings	Bolted direct to transmission casing 2 bolts, 2 studs

Camshaft and Camshaft Bearings

Camshaft drive	Lightweight alloy gear direct from crankshaft.
Camshaft bearings - Until 1965	Machined in crankcase
1965 on	Steel backed white metal shells

Camshaft journal diameters...	24.99 - 25.00 mm (.9837 - .9842 inch)
Journal/bearing radial clearance	.02 - .12 mm (.0008 - .0047 inch)
End float	.04 - .16 mm (.0016 - .0063 inch)
Gear backlash	.00 - .05 mm (.00 - .0019 inch)

Connecting Rods and Bearings

Type	Steel forging I section shaft
Big end bearings	Three layer thin wall shells
Crankpin (big end) diameter	54.97 - 54.99 mm (2.164 - 2.1648 inch)
Small end bush	Pressed in steel bush with lead/bronze coating
Undersize big end bearings available	3. - .25 mm, .50 mm and .75 mm
Crankpin to bearing clearance limits	.02 - .15 mm (.0008 - .006 inch)
Crankpin end float	0.1 - 0.7 mm (.004 - .028 inch)
Gudgeon pin/bush radial clearance limit	.01 - .04 mm (.0004 - .0016 inch)
Gudgeon pin diameter	19.996 - 20.000 mm (.7871 - .7874 inch)
Connecting rod weights - brown/white	487 - 495 grams
grey/black	507 - 515 grams
Maximum crankpin ovality	.03 mm (.0011 inch)

Crankshaft and Main Bearings

Number of bearings	4
Main bearing journal diameters - Nos. 1, 2, & 3...	54.97 - 54.99 mm (2.164 - 2.1648 inch)
No. 4	39.98 - 40.00 mm (1.5739 - 1.5748 inch)
Regrind diameters	.25 mm, .50 mm, .75 mm
Bearing shells type - Nos. 1, 3 & 4...	Aluminium - lead coated
No. 2	Split shell, 3 layer steel backed
Journal/bearing radial clearance limits - Nos. 1, 3	.04 - .18 mm (.0016 - .007 inch)
No. 2	.03 - .17 mm (.0011 - .0066 inch)
No. 4	.05 - .19 mm (.0019 - .0074 inch)
Crankshaft end float	Taken by flange of No. 1 main bearing and adjusted by shims
End float limits	.07 - .15 mm (.0027 - .006 inch)
Main bearing maximum ovality	.03 mm (.0011 inch)

Crankcase

Main bearing bore diameters - Nos. 1, 2 & 3...	65.00 - 65.03 mm (2.559 - 2.5601 inch)
No. 4	50.00 - 50.04 mm (1.9685 - 1.9700 inch)
Oil seal bore diameter (flywheel end)...	90.00 - 90.05 mm (3.5433 - 3.5452 inch)
Camshaft bearing bore diameter (direct)	25.02 - 25.12 mm (.9850 - .9889 inch)
(split shells)	27.5 - 27.52 mm (1.0825 - 1.0852 inch)
Oil pump housing bore diameter	70.00 - 70.03 mm (2.756 - 2.758 inch)
Tappet (cam follower) bore diameters	19.00 - 19.05 mm (.748 - .750 inch)

Cylinders

Type	Single barrels - finned - cast iron
Distance between centres	112 mm (4.41 inch)

Cylinder Heads

Type	Aluminium - 1 per pair of cylinders
Port arrangement	Single inlet port per pair of cylinders. One exhaust port for each cylinder.

Gudgeon Pins

Type ... ... ,..	Fully floating, machined steel tube retained by circlips
Diameter	19.996 - 20.000 mm (.7871 - .7874 inch)

Lubrication System

Type	Wet sump - pressure and splash
Oil filter	Gauze suction strainer in sump
Sump capacity	2½ litres (4.4 Imp. pints)
Oil pump type	Twin gear
Oil pressure (SAE 30, 70°C @ 2500 r.p.m.)	42 p.s.i.
Oil pressure warning switch...	Comes on between 2.1 - 6.3 p.s.i. (.15 - .45 kg/cm²)
Oil cooler	Pressure fed tube type in fan housing

Oil Pump

Gear/body end clearance (no gasket)	0.1 mm (.004 inch) maximum
Gears backlash	0.0 - 0.2 mm (.008 inch)

Oil Pressure Regulating Valve

Spring length loaded at 7.75 kg (17 lbs)	23.6 mm (.928 inch)

Pistons

Type	Light alloy with steel inserts and flat crown
Clearance in cylinder limits	.04 - 0.20 mm (.0015 - .008 inch)
Number of rings	3 - Two compression, one oil control
Ring groove side clearances - Top compression	.07 - .12 mm (.0027 - .0047 inch)
Lower compression	.05 - .10 mm (.0019 - .0039 inch)
Oil control	.03 - .10 mm (.0012 - .0039 inch)
Piston oversizes available	2 - .5 mm and 1.00 mm (.020 and .040 inch)
Piston pin bore offset	1.5 mm (.060 inch)

Piston Rings

Top compression ring:	
Thickness	2.5 mm (0.100 inch)
Gap limit	0.30 - 0.90 mm (.012 - .035 inch)
Bearing face	Bevelled, angle facing top of piston
Lower compression ring:	
Thickness	2.5 mm (0.100 inch)
Gap limit	.030 - .090 mm (.012 - .035 inch)
Bearing face	Parallel, lower edge cut back
Oil control ring	
Gap	0.25 - 0.95 mm (.010 - .037 inch)

Tappets (Cam Followers)

Type	Cylindrical, flat based
Diameter (early type with pushrod)	14.967 - 15.12 mm (.5893 - .5899 inch)
(later type)	18.96 - 18.89 mm (.7463 - .7471 inch)

Pushrods & Rocker Arms

Pushrod type - (early)	Tube incorporating cam follower
(later)	Tube with hemispherical ends
Length (later type)	272.5 mm
Rocker arm bore size limits (later)	18.00 - 18.04 mm (.7086 - .7093 inch)
Rocker shaft diameter size limits (later)	17.97 - 17.95 mm (.7073 - .7066 inch)

Valves

	30 DIN b.h.p.	34 DIN b.h.p.
Inlet - head diameter	30 mm (1.18 in.)	31.5 mm (1.24 in.)
stem diameter	6.94 mm (.2740 in.)	7.95 mm (.3129 in.)
seat width	1.3 - 1.6 mm (.05 - .06 in.)	1.3 - 1.6 mm (.05 - .06 in.)
seat angle	45º	45º
guide bore diameter	7.00 mm (.2756 in.)	8.00 mm (.3149 in.)
maximum rock in guide	0.8 mm (.031 in.)	0.8 mm (.031 in.)
Exhaust - head diameter	28 mm (1.102 in.)	30.0 mm (1.181 in.)
stem diameter	6.94 mm (.2740 in.)	7.92 mm (.3118 in.)
seat width	1.7 - 2.00 mm (.066 - .08 in.)	1.7 - 2.00 mm (.066 - .08 in.)
seat angle	45º	45º
guide bore diameter	7.00 mm (.2756 in.)	8.00 mm (.3149 in.)
maximum rock in guide	0.8 mm (.031 in.)	0.8 mm (.031 in.)
Seat width correction angles - all valves	Inner 75º Outer 15º	
Timing - Inlet opens	2½º BTDC	6º BTDC
Inlet closes	37½º ABDC	35½º ABDC
Exhaust opens	37½º BBDC	42½º BBDC
Exhaust closes	2½º ATDC	3º ATDC

Note: 34 b.h.p. figures are the latest models - variations occurred with early versions. Rocker clearances are set at 1 mm (.040 inch) for the purpose of valve timing settings only.

Rocker clearances:

Pre 1960 - 30 DIN b.h.p.	.1 mm (.004 inch) exhaust and inlet
1961 - 65 - 34 DIN b.h.p.	.2 mm (.008 inch) inlet
	.3 mm (.012 inch) exhaust
1966 on	.1 mm (.004 inch) exhaust and inlet * See Appendix

Note: When the change was made in 1966 stickers indicating the new clearances were fixed to the fan housings of the engines concerned.

Valve springs

Type	Single coil spring
Loaded length	28 mm @ 33.5 kg (1.1 in. @ 74 lbs) 30 DIN b.h.p.
	33.5 mm @ 45 kg (1.31 in @ 96 lbs) 34 DIN b.h.p.

Torque Wrench Settings

Crankshaft pulley nut	33 lb/ft. (4.5 mkg)
Oil pump nuts	14 lb/ft. (2.0 mkg)
Oil drain plug	33 lb/ft. (4.5 mkg)
Oil strainer cover nuts	5 lb/ft. (0.7 mkg)
Rocker shaft nuts	18 lb/ft. (2.5 mkg)
Cylinder head nuts 34 DIN b.h.p.	23 lb/ft. (3.2 mkg) See text
Flywheel screw	217 lb/ft. (30.0 mkg)
Crankcase nuts and screws M8	14 lb/ft. (2.0 mkg)) 34 DIN b.h.p.
Crankcase nuts and screws M12	25 lb/ft. (3.5 mkg))
Connecting rod big end cap nuts/screws	24 lb/ft. (3.3 mkg)
Engine mounting nuts	22 lb/ft. (3.0 mkg)
Crankcase nuts and screws M10	22 lb/ft. (3.0 mkg)) 30 DIN b.h.p.
Cylinder head nuts 30 DIN b.h.p.	26-27 lb/ft. (3.6-3.8 mkg))

1. Engine - General Description, Changes and Engine Numbers

The Volkswagen Beetle engine is an air-cooled horizontally opposed flat four cylinder design. The short crankshaft runs in aluminium alloy shell bearings located between the two halves of a magnesium alloy crankcase which join vertically. The camshaft runs centrally below the crankshaft and is gear driven from the rear end of the crankshaft. The camshaft is also located between the crankcase halves and in early models the bearings consisted of the crankcase material itself. Later, shell bearings were introduced.

The distributor is driven by a removable shaft from a gear mounted on the rear end of the crankshaft. The same shaft incorporates a cam which operates the fuel pump operating plunger rod.

The gear type oil pump is mounted in the rear of the crankcase, held between the two halves and driven by a horizontal shaft. A tongue on the inner end of the shaft engages in a slot in the end of the camshaft.

The four, finned cylinder barrels are separately mounted and each pair has a common cylinder head containing the valves and rocker gear. The push rods locate in cylindrical flat faced cam followers at the camshaft end and pass through sealed cylindrical tubes clamped between the head and crankcase outside the cylinder barrels. Each rocker cover is held to the head by spring hoops locating in a recess in the cover.

The flywheel is located on the front of the crankshaft by four dowel pegs and secured by a single central bolt which also incorporates needle roller bearings for the gearbox input shaft. The front crankcase oil seal bears on the centre hub land of the flywheel. The rear end of the crankshaft has an oil thrower plate and a helical groove machined in the pulley wheel hub to contain the oil. An oil filter screen is mounted in the bottom centre of the crankcase and the oil suction pipe for the pump comes from the centre of it. There is no other form of oil filter incorporated. The generator, which is mounted on a pedestal above the engine, is driven by a V-belt from the crankshaft pulley. On the forward end of the generator shaft the cooling fan is mounted. This runs in a sheet steel housing which ducts air down to the cylinder barrels.

There is no separate oil sump - the crankcase acting as an oil reservoir of just under 4½ pints.

Engine cooling is regulated by a bellows type thermostat which is mounted in the air flow under the right hand pair of cylinders. This operates a choke ring in the front face of the fan housing, restricting the intake of cold air into the system when the engine is cold. As the engine warms up so the choke flap is opened allowing more cool air to be drawn into the circulation system. On later models the thermostat operates two linked control flaps in the fan housing lower ducting section at left and right.

The car heating system is integral with the engine cooling and is achieved by directing air through ducts which shroud the exhaust pipes. Early models directed air into the heater ducts after it had passed the cylinders. Later on, two separate hoses directed air from the fan housing straight to the heat exchangers - not via the cylinder barrel fins.

The cooling system also incorporates an oil cooler which is a multitube heat exchanger mounted vertically on the crankcase and projecting into the air stream inside the fan housing.

As a guide to some of the main changes made to the engine since 1954 the following should be of interest. It is most important to know your engine and chassis numbers when ordering spares.

1954 on Engine Nos. 695,355 - 3,912,903 30 DIN b.h.p.
Fuel pump mounted below and to the left of the distributor and the generator pedestal is cast as part of the crankcase.
N.B. Nos. 3,400,000-3,580,070 in this series were modified versions used in transporters.

1960 on Engine Nos. 5,000,001 - 9,800,000 34 DIN b.h.p.
Fuel pump mounted to the right of the distributor centrally and the generator pedestal is detachable. Valves were angled in the cylinder heads and separate push rod cam followers were introduced.
N.B. At engine No. 7,326,420 (1963) redesigned cooling and heating arrangements (identified by two large hoses coming out of the fan housing) were introduced. This is the 'clean air' system.

When the 1300 and 1500 engines came into production (in 1966 and 1967 respectively) the numbering system was revised and became very complex. It is not intended to detail it here. The chassis number identification is easier to use for determining the model year (see Page 7).

2. Routine Maintenance

1. At weekly intervals or every 300 miles check the oil level in the crankcase by removing the dipstick, wiping it clean and replacing it and noting the oil level on withdrawing it again. It is important that the car is standing level when this is done as the reservoir is relatively shallow in a Volkswagen. The indicator level mark is much more critical than on cars with a deep sump. Fill up to the level mark but do not overfill. Remember, the Volkswagen engine **uses** oil, from the day it is new, at a rate of ¾ to 2½ pints per 1,000 miles.

2. Every 3,000 miles undo the oil drain plug when the engine is hot and drain out the oil. Then remove the nuts holding the surrounding plate to the crankcase to remove the oil filter screen. Thoroughly clean this in paraffin or petrol and replace it using two new gaskets and new stud washers (copper). Replace the drain plug with a new washer and fill up once more with 4.4 pints (2.5 litres) of engine oil of the appropriate grade. Note: The 3,000 mile oil change interval is the absolute minimum and if the car is normally driven hard or in hot and dusty conditions or in stop/start heavy traffic conditions a 1,500 mile frequency would be preferable. As the quantity of oil in circulation is relatively small and in general runs at higher

temperatures and lower pressures than in a conventional water-cooled engine, the importance of maintaining its quantity and cleanliness cannot be over emphasised. It is recommended that the same type of oil be used at all times and not mixed. Changes of viscosity rating can be made seasonally as required. If non-detergent oils have been used for any length of time the change to detergent oils could well dislodge accumulations of deposits, particularly in the oil cooler. If such changes are made the oil should be changed again after 500 miles and the oil strainer cleaned.

3. Every 6,000 miles the valve clearances should be checked and adjusted as necessary. For details see the appropriate section in this Chapter.

3. Repair and Overhaul Procedures and Degree of Dismantling Necessary

Although it may be possible to do more than remove and replace items as stated below when the engine is installed no recommendations are made which are considered bad basic practice. Maintaining cleanliness is the main reason for limiting the amount of work done with the engine installed.

a) Engine in Car
   Rocker box covers.
   Oil cooler.
   Crankshaft pulley wheel.
   Oil pressure relief valve.
   Oil filter screen.
   Distributor drive shaft.

b) Engine removed but crankcase not split
   Cylinders.
   Piston rings.
   Pistons.
   Connecting rods.
   Big end bearing shells.
   Flywheel.
   Oil pump.
   Crankshaft oil seal.
   Cylinder heads and valves.

c) Crankcase split
   Camshaft.
   Cam followers.
   Crankshaft.
   Main bearings.
   Distributor drive worm gear.
   Camshaft bearings.

4. Engine Removal - General Preparation

Removal of the Beetle engine is quite straightforward and speedy provided that the correct tools and lifting tackle are assembled beforehand. The engine is held to the transmission unit by two studs and two bolts - nothing more. It has to be drawn back from these and lowered out of the car. If you have a pit or raised ramp, a firm stand or platform will be needed to support the engine as soon as it is detached. It weighs 200 lbs and attempts to draw it off without providing support under the ramp or in the pit will result in disaster.

Without a pit or ramp a method must be devised to support the engine as soon as it is detached so that the supports may then be removed and the engine readily lowered to ground level. The car body is then lifted up at the rear and the engine drawn out from under - or the car rolled forward over the engine. Four strong men can lift the car the required three feet to clear the engine. Alternatively a conventional hoist can be used to lift the car with the sling fastened between the rear bumper support brackets. If no hoist is available then at least two conventional scissor jacks or hydraulic

jacks will be needed together with suitable wooden or concrete blocks, to raise and support the car at each side near the jacking points.

A 17 mm ring spanner - of the non-cranked sort you get on a combination - is essential for undoing the mounting nuts and bolts as there is no space to get a socket on. A second 17 mm open-ended spanner will also be needed.

If the car is very dirty underneath it would be well worthwhile getting it thoroughly cleaned off away from the removal area first. The lower mounting stud nuts are exposed to the elements and the top bolts and nuts call for a certain amount of reaching around. If you are working on your back at floor level, dirt falling in the eyes can be a major irritation.

It is possible to get the engine out and clear single-handed if all the foregoing equipment is available but the trickiest part is lowering the engine to floor level, assistance is insurance against dropping it. Even a few inches fall could crack the aluminium crankcase - there being no conventional sump. The engine which was removed and dismantled for the purposes of writing this manual was an 1192 cc 34 b.h.p. of 1961 - No. 5,773,931 to be precise. There may be minor detail variations if your car is older or younger, but within the span 1954 - 1970 Beetle engines are all removed in the same basic manner. Note that the engine is back-to-front as compared with a conventional layout so that the flywheel is at the front. All references to front and rear of the engine will, therefore, be in relation to its position in the car.

5. Engine - Removal

1. Stand the car on a level hard surface with sufficient room to roll it forward about four to six feet if you wish to lift the car over the engine rather than drag the engine back from under the car. Disconnect the battery. Always disconnect the earth lead first and reconnect last. Now is the time to drain the engine oil into a container - whilst you are disconnecting the ancillaries described next.

2. Open the engine compartment cover and then remove the carburettor air cleaner by slackening the clamp, removing also the pre-heater hose from the air duct end and the oil breather pipe from the filler neck. The air cleaner, complete with hoses, is then lifted off.

3. Remove the cheese headed screws which hold the rear cover plate in position and then lift the cover plate out. On later models this is unnecessary.

4. Next disconnect the electrics. Starting at the right there are two heavy cables to a common screw clamp terminal on the voltage regulator on top of the generator. Disconnect these. Then disconnect the smaller gauge wire from the voltage regulator; then the wire from the automatic choke on the right side of the carburettor (not fitted on manual choke models). There may be a second lead to the carburettor underneath the auto choke which operates the electric pilot jet on later models. Remove this too. If the voltage regulator is mounted elsewhere (under the back seat in later models) remove the two leads from the generator that run down to it. Disconnect the lead from the coil (which is connected to the automatic choke lead) and finally remove the wire leading to the oil pressure gauge sender unit at the side of the crankcase. All leads to the engine are now detached and they can be pushed to one side or held to the sides of the engine compartment with sticky tape.

5. The accelerator cable connected to the carburettor is the next item to be detached. This is a somewhat unusual arrangement as the cable has to pass through the fan housing en route to the carburettor. First undo the locking screw which clamps the end of the cable to the link pin on the operating lever. Pull the cable out and do not lose the link. On the cable, behind the rigid end piece, there is a sleeve containing a spring and this is held in position by a dished washer with a slot in it. This washer should be pulled off the cable whilst holding the spring tension so that it does not fly off and get lost. The sleeve and spring can then be drawn off the end of the cable. This leaves the front of the guide tube projecting through the front of the fan housing and this can now be pulled out over the cable.

Battery removal (Section 5.4)

Removal of lead from the battery regulator (Section 5.4)

Removal of cables from voltage regulator (Section 5.4)

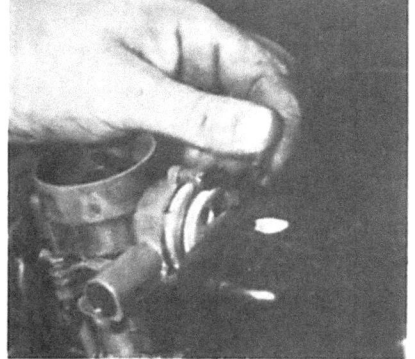

Removal of cable from auto choke (Section 5.4)

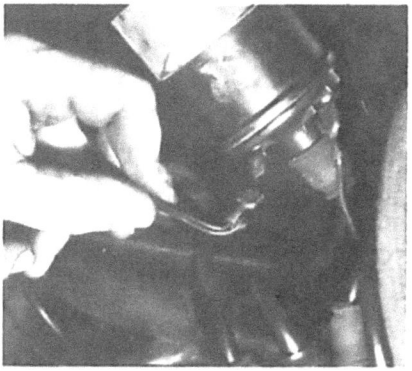

Removal of cable from ignition coil (Section 5.4)

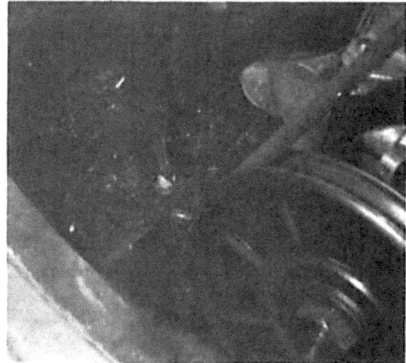

Removal of cheese headed screw for rear cover plate (Section 5.3)

Removal of rear cover plate (Section 5.3)

Drawing engine back for removal (Section 5.8)

Engine being lowered ready for removal (Section 5.8)

Engine on floor, jack removed (Section 5.8)

Car being lifted clear of engine (Section 5.9)

Mission complete. Engine clear of car. (Section 5.9)

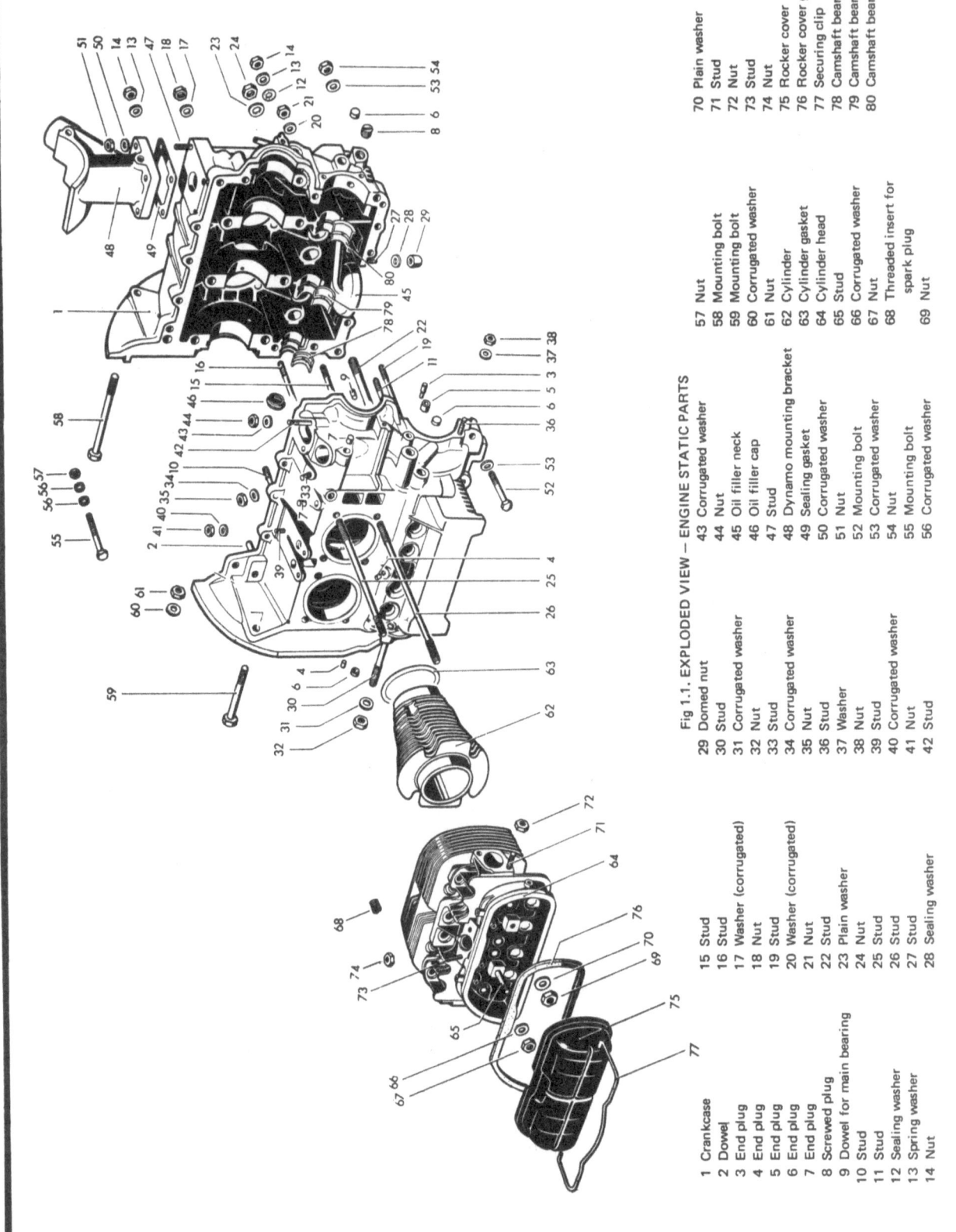

Fig 1.1. EXPLODED VIEW – ENGINE STATIC PARTS

1 Crankcase	15 Stud	29 Domed nut	43 Corrugated washer	57 Nut	70 Plain washer
2 Dowel	16 Stud	30 Stud	44 Nut	58 Mounting bolt	71 Stud
3 End plug	17 Washer (corrugated)	31 Corrugated washer	45 Oil filler neck	59 Mounting bolt	72 Nut
4 End plug	18 Nut	32 Nut	46 Oil filler cap	60 Corrugated washer	73 Stud
5 End plug	19 Stud	33 Stud	47 Stud	61 Nut	74 Nut
6 End plug	20 Washer (corrugated)	34 Corrugated washer	48 Dynamo mounting bracket	62 Cylinder	75 Rocker cover
7 End plug	21 Nut	35 Nut	49 Sealing gasket	63 Cylinder gasket	76 Rocker cover gasket
8 Screwed plug	22 Stud	36 Stud	50 Corrugated washer	64 Cylinder head	77 Securing clip
9 Dowel for main bearing	23 Plain washer	37 Washer	51 Nut	65 Stud	78 Camshaft bearing shell
10 Stud	24 Nut	38 Nut	52 Mounting bolt	66 Corrugated washer	79 Camshaft bearing shell
11 Stud	25 Stud	39 Stud	53 Corrugated washer	67 Corrugated washer	80 Camshaft bearing shell
12 Sealing washer	26 Stud	40 Corrugated washer	54 Nut	68 Threaded insert for spark plug	
13 Spring washer	27 Stud	41 Nut	55 Mounting bolt	69 Nut	
14 Nut	28 Sealing washer	42 Stud	56 Corrugated washer		

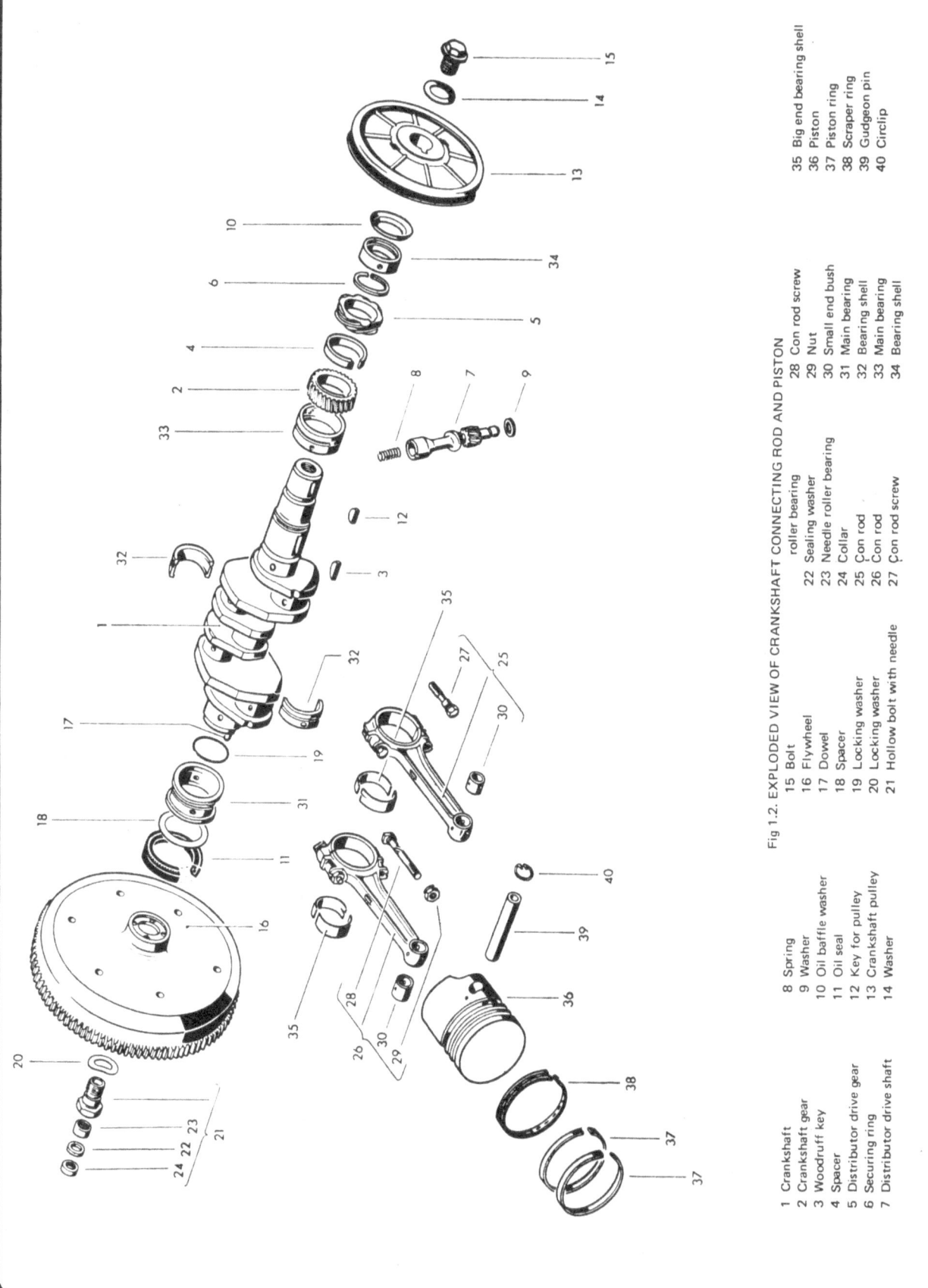

Fig 1.2. EXPLODED VIEW OF CRANKSHAFT CONNECTING ROD AND PISTON

1 Crankshaft	8 Spring	15 Bolt	roller bearing
2 Crankshaft gear	9 Washer	16 Flywheel	22 Sealing washer
3 Woodruff key	10 Oil baffle washer	17 Dowel	23 Needle roller bearing
4 Spacer	11 Oil seal	18 Spacer	24 Collar
5 Distributor drive gear	12 Key for pulley	19 Locking washer	25 Con rod
6 Securing ring	13 Crankshaft pulley	20 Locking washer	26 Con rod
7 Distributor drive shaft	14 Washer	21 Hollow bolt with needle	27 Con rod screw

28 Con rod screw	35 Big end bearing shell
29 Nut	36 Piston
30 Small end bush	37 Piston ring
31 Main bearing	38 Scraper ring
32 Bearing shell	39 Gudgeon pin
33 Main bearing	40 Circlip
34 Bearing shell	

The cable itself need not be pulled through from the back of the fan housing until the engine has been disengaged from the transmission. If the carburettor has a mechanical (as opposed to an electric automatic) choke, slacken the cable clamping screw and disengage the cable from the operating lever.

6. Now jack up the car, using the vehicle jack to enable you to get underneath the rear end comfortably but keep the tyres touching the ground. Replace the oil drain plug. From underneath, first disconnect the control wires that run to the heater flaps, one on each side. They are held to the flap control arms by cable clamps as used on the carburettor but are quite likely to be dirty and rusted up so be prepared with penetrating oil and suitable self-grip wrenches as necessary. If you have difficulty in identifying them get someone to operate the heater control while you are underneath. You will see them move. The fuel pipe runs along on the left side of the engine and if you feel around you will be able to locate the point where the flexible hose connection occurs. This should be pulled off at the end of the hose nearest the engine so that the end of the flexible pipe can be clamped, or plugged with a pencil stub, to prevent the fuel leaking out. If the fuel level in the tank is fairly low it may not be necessary to do this. Next unclip and pull off the flexible concertina hoses which fit onto the heat exchangers on the side of the engine.

7. The two lower mounting nuts can now be removed and this is where the 17 mm ring spanner mentioned earlier is needed. The nuts are positioned about four inches from each side of the engine centre line and about two inches up from the bottom of the flange where the engine joins the transmission unit. Remove the two nuts and washers (if any). Then lower the car and remove the vehicle jack. The ease or difficulty of removing the top two mounting bolts and nuts depends on whether they are rusted or not. The point is, you cannot see either the bolt head or the nut so you will have to feel for them. The nuts are behind (in front of!) the fan housing and you can get an arm round and put a 17 mm ring spanner on. Strictly speaking, it is safer to support the engine underneath now before the last two mounting bolts are removed although in fact the likelihood of the engine moving 3 to 4 inches rearward and falling down of its own accord is fairly remote. If the bolts turn when the nuts are being undone there are two ways to hold the bolt heads. The most sure way in the long run is to jack the car up a little way so that you can get underneath once more and get another 17 mm spanner on the bolt head. It is easier to do this with two people. If you are on your own an open ended spanner can be put on in such a way that it will jam against the car when the nut is turned. Alternatively, the bolts can be jammed by drawing the engine back now so that the bolt heads bind against the transmission casing. This will mean putting the engine support arrangements under the engine straight away. A stout piece of plank about 18" x 12" should be put under the crankcase so that the jacks can be placed to support the whole unit firmly and evenly. If a trolley jack with a large lifting head is used it can be placed centrally.

8. Pull the engine back. It may need jiggling a little to disengage it from the transmission. Grip it by the silencer unit and the fan housing for this purpose. As soon as the top nuts are undone the engine may be drawn off completely. Disconnect the accelerator cable from the fan housing before lowering the engine. The engine should then be lowered as far as the jacks will permit and then the jacks should be pulled out from underneath. To do this the engine should be tipped as carefully as possible and be prevented from any sharp knocks until it is resting flat on the ground.

9. All that remains is to raise the rear of the car sufficiently to enable it to be rolled forward over the engine or for the engine to be drawn out from underneath. This can be achieved by four strong men or by hoisting the rear of the car with a sling stretched between the two rear bumper support brackets. Alternatively the car can be raised on two jacks, one on each side and supported progressively on blocks near the body jacking points. Great care must be taken to chock the front wheels securely when using this latter method and the blocks used must be perfectly square and large enough to provide a stable 'pillar' when stacked up. Each support under the body at each side will have to be at least 2ft. 6 ins. high so collect sufficient blocks beforehand. Do **not** use odd bits and pieces. The base blocks should be at least 9" x 12" square. When the car is raised sufficiently the engine can be pulled out from the rear. It is a little more work to lower the car to the ground at this stage but if you are going to leave it then the extra effort is worthwhile. It is better to be sure than sorry, particularly if there are children about.

6. Engine Dismantling - General

1. Unlike the majority of conventional engines the Volkswagen is one which does not make it easy to carry out most tasks with the engine still in the car. In view of the relative ease with which it can be taken out and lifted on to a bench this manual does not, in general, recommend that engine repair work of any significance is carried out with the engine still in the car. If you have a pit or ramp that enables you to work conveniently under the car there are instances when it is justifiable. Otherwise the inconvenient 'flat on your back' method is far too risky in view of the likelihood of dirt getting into the wrong places and mistakes occurring.

2. For an engine which is obviously in need of a complete overhaul the economies against a replacement engine must also be carefully considered. The dismantling and reassembly of a Volkswagon engine is more complex than for a conventional four cylinder block. Each cylinder is separate and the crankshaft and camshaft run in bearings mounted between the two halves of a precision faced, split crankcase. The number of individual parts is far greater. It is not our intention to put you off - far from it - but we must, in fairness to the owner, point out that it is much easier to make an assembly mistake than on a conventional engine.

3. The dismantling, inspection, repair and reassembly as described in this Chapter follows the procedure as for a complete overhaul. Each section will indicate the practicability and method of any partial work to be carried out which may not justify the removal of the engine.

4. Before starting work on any part it is strongly recommended that time is spent in first reading the whole Chapter. It would be too cumbersome and confusing to cross reference the implications of each and every activity. So if you think that the big end bearings are your problem, for example, do not think that by turning to the heading 'Big end Bearings' all the implications of repairing them will be contained in that single section alone. Mention will be made in brief of the operations necessary which may lead up to it and the details of these should be read first.

7. Engine Ancillaries - Removal

Although the items listed may be removed separately with the engine installed (as described in the appropriate Chapters referred to) it is normal practice to take them off after the engine has been removed from the car when extensive dismantling is envisaged.

Fuel System
    Carburettor with inlet manifold.
    Exhaust silencer unit.
    Fuel pump.

Ignition System
    Sparking plugs.
    Distributor.

Cooling System and Electrical Components
    Fan belt.
    Generator with fan assembly.
    Fan housing.
    Engine cover plates.
    Heat exchangers.
    Generator pedestal.

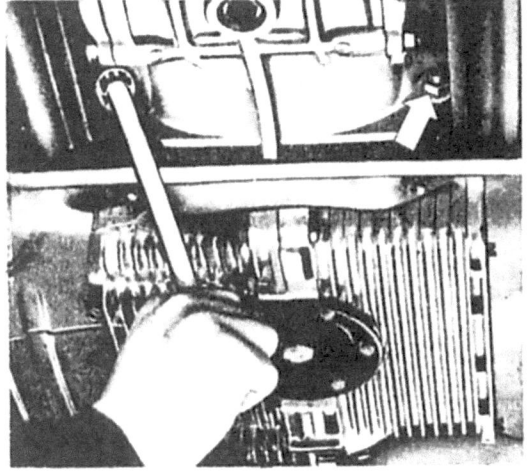

Fig 1.4. Removing two nuts from lower engine mounting screws

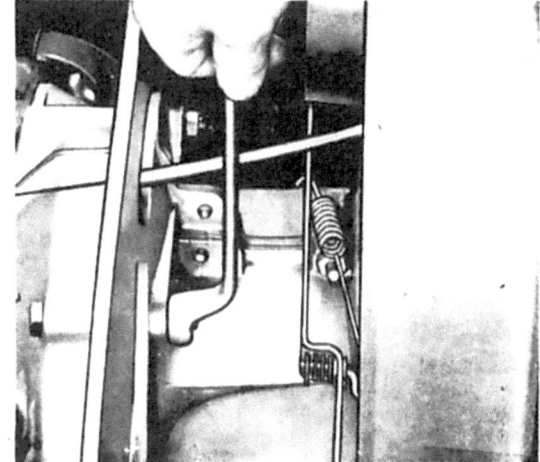

Fig. 1.5. Removing the upper mounting bolts

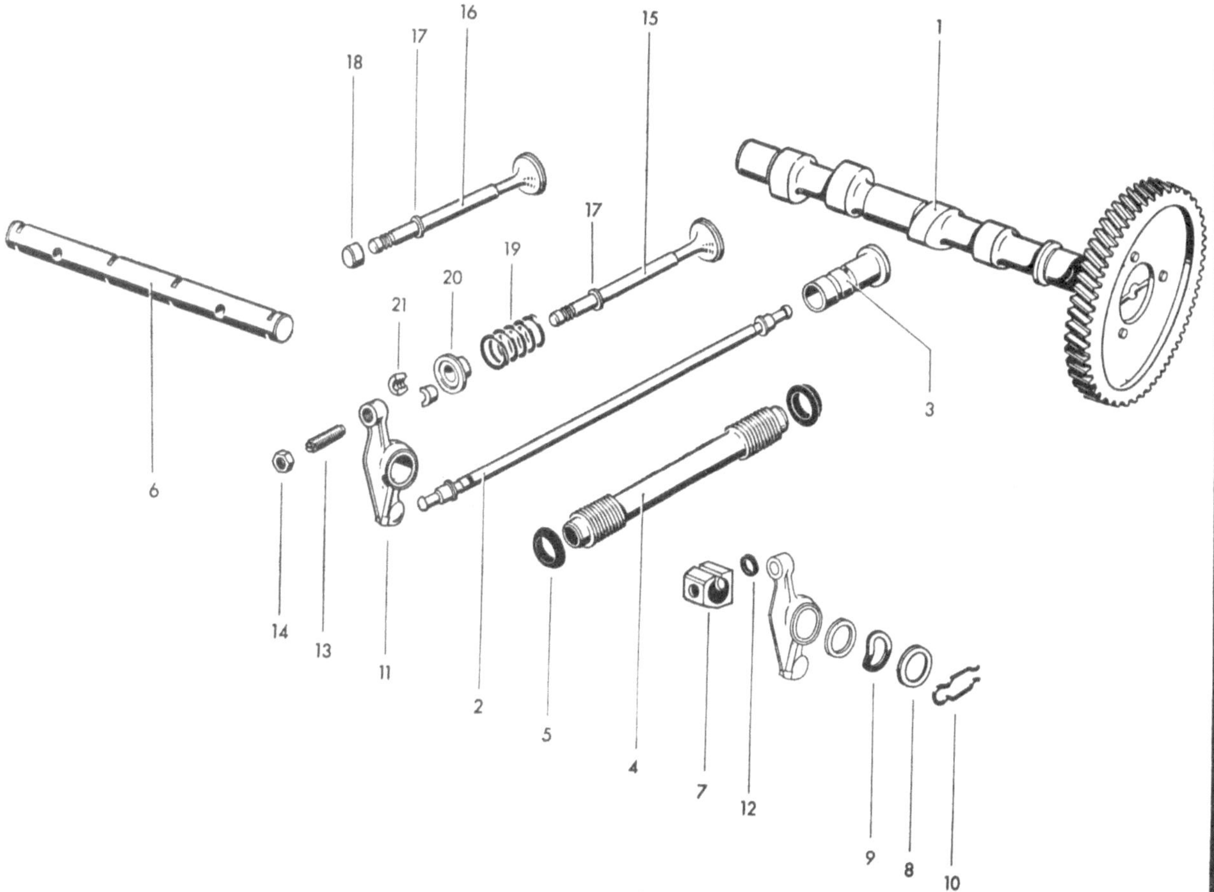

Fig. 1.3. EXPLODED VIEW OF CAMSHAFT AND VALVES

1 Camshaft and gear assembly
2 Pushrod
3 Tappet
4 Pushrod tube
5 Pushrod tube seal
6 Rocker shaft
7 Shaft support bracket
8 Thrust washer
9 Corrugated washer
10 Securing clip
11 Rocker arm
12 Sealing ring
13 Tappet adjusting screw
14 Locknut
15 Inlet valve
16 Exhaust valve
17 Oil wiper
18 Valve cap
19 Valve spring
20 Valve spring seat
21 Valve cotter halves

Note that the last item referred to the generator pedestal, is also the oil filler and crankcase vent tube. On early models it was cast integrally with the crankcase but later on it was made a separate item and is held in position by four studs. Ensure that there is a good gasket fitted between it and the crankcase.

8. Oil Cooler - Removal and Replacement

1. The oil cooler may be removed with the engine still in the car provided that the engine compartment lid, fan and fan housing are removed and that a suitable cranked spanner is available to gain access to the securing nuts. The details of the fan and fan housing removal may be found in Chapter 2.
2. The oil cooler is held in position by two downward pointing studs which locate on lugs on the crankcase and a third stud fixed into the crankcase. With the three nuts removed the cooler may be lifted off. The photographs show the cooler being removed with the left hand top cylinder cowl detached. Consequently a conventional spanner can be used. With the cowl in position access and spanner movement is restricted.
3. Replacement is a reversal of the removal procedure, making sure that two new seals are fitted between the base of the cooler and the crankcase oil passageway openings. Make sure you fit the correct pair of sealing rings. There are others in the gasket set (for the rocker shaft mounting studs) which could be fitted by mistake. When the correct ones are fitted it is necessary to compress them between the cooler and crankcase and this can be felt.

9. Oil Pressure Relief Valve - Removal and Replacement

1. When overhauling an engine the oil pressure relief valve should be examined. If it does not function properly it could cause oil starvation to the bearings when the engine is cold, and excessive pressure in the cooler (possibly causing it to leak). It could also cause, at the other extreme, overheating of the oil and inadequate oil pressure.
2. The valve is positioned in the underside of the crankcase to the left of the oil pump at the rear. A slotted retaining plug can be removed with a large screwdriver and the spring and piston should then fall out. If the engine is cold and the piston sticks it will be forced out if the engine is turned over (this assumes of course that the engine is in the car and has oil in it). If the piston is stuck because of dirt or seizure it may be necessary to drill and tap a hole in it to draw it from the bore in the crankcase. This is only likely in cases of extreme neglect. If the bore of the crankcase is also damaged then the crankcase may have to be scrapped.
3. Replacement of the piston and spring is a reversal of the removal procedure. When fitting the plug use a new compressible sealing washer and make sure that the spring sits snugly in the recess of the plug.

10. Oil Pump - Removal

1. The oil pump gears may be removed relatively easily because once the oil pump cover plate (situated on the end of the crankcase under the crankshaft pulley) has been released by removing the four retaining nuts, the gears may be drawn out of the pump body.
2. The pump body itself is mounted over the same four studs as the cover plate and is clamped between the two halves of the crankcase. To remove the pump body from the engine without splitting the crankcase it is best done with a special tool which fits over the studs, locks to the inside of the body and draws it out. If you do not have such a tool then the best way is first to slacken the crankcase clamping stud nuts above and below the pump. This relieves the pressure on the body. A suitable pointed tool can then be tapped against the edge of the pump body and, in easy stages, it can be eased out over the studs. Do not force a tool into the gap between

the pump body and the crankcase as this could damage the mating faces and upset the correct alignment of the pump on replacement.

11. Cylinder Heads - Removal

1. Remove the exhaust system, heat exchangers and upper cylinder cover plates as described in the Fuel and Cooling Chapters. The inlet manifold together with carburettor should also be taken off. See the Fuel System Chapter for details.
2. Prise off the spring clip, downwards, which clamps the rocker cover to the head. Take off the cover.
3. Undo the two nuts, evenly, which secure the rocker shaft standards and then pull off the standards, shaft and rockers as a complete assembly. Pull out the four push rods and push them through a piece of cardboard so that the location of each one is known and which is the top and bottom end.
4. Before starting to undo the eight nuts which hold the cylinder head down onto the cylinder barrels it must be appreciated that when the head is released the four push rod tubes will be freed and the cylinder barrels also. If the cylinder barrels are not being taken off the pistons they will rest in position but the engine must not be turned. If the engine is to be turned the barrels should be temporarily tied down to the crankcase with string or wire.
5. Using a socket spanner, the cylinder head stud nuts should be slackened ¼ to ½ turn each only, in the reverse order of the final tightening sequence as given in Fig. 1.18. Continue releasing each nut a little at a time until they are all slack. When all are removed the head may be drawn back a little way.
6. Remove the push rod tubes from between the head and crankcase and make sure the cylinders are disengaged from the head before pulling the head right off.

12. Cylinder Heads - Dismantling of Rocker Gear, Valves and Springs

1. To remove the rocker arms from the shaft the spring clips at each end should be removed and the thrust washers and wave washers taken off. The end rockers may then be removed. The rocker shaft support standards may need tapping off if they are tight in order to remove the two inner rocker arms, clips and washers. If possible lay out the parts in the order in which they were dismantled in a place where they need not be disturbed.
2. To remove the valves it is necessary to use a proper tool to compress the valve springs. The tops of the springs are almost level with the edge of the head casting. If you are unable to obtain a G-clamp with extended ends (to clear the edge of the head when the spring is compressed) it will be necessary to use a short piece of tube, with an aperture cut in the side, in conjunction with a conventional spring compressor. The aperture is to enable one to get at the split collars on the valve stem.
3. Compress the spring using the clamp and if the tubular spacer is being used make sure that the pressure is applied squarely and that the tube cannot slip. As soon as the two split conical collars round the valve stem are revealed, use a small screwdriver through the aperture to hook them off the valve stem. It is advisable to maintain one's hold on the spring clamp while doing this to prevent anything from slipping. When the collars are clear release the spring clamp.
4. The spring retainer collar and spring may then be lifted off. On later models there will be small sealing rings round the valve stems and these too should be taken off. The valve can now be pushed through the guide and taken out. If it tends to stick then it will be because of carbon or sludge deposits on the end of the valve stems and these should be cleaned off as necessary. The end of the valve stem could also be burred due to the 'hammering' action of the rocker arm; in which case the burrs should be carefully stoned off.

Be certain you get the correct sealing rings
(Section 8.3)

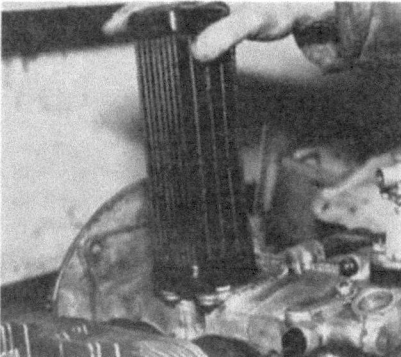

Placing the cooler in position (Section 8.3)

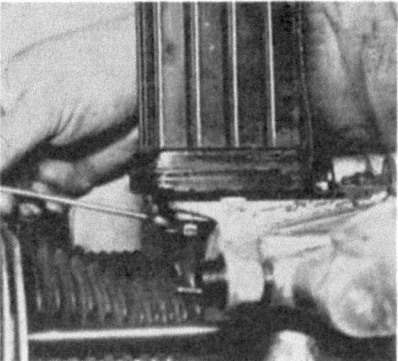

Tightening the oil cooler holding bolts (easy
with the cowl removed) (Section 8.3)

View of the piston and spring pressure relief
valve (Section 9)

Spring and piston in position, plug ready for
replacement (Section 9)

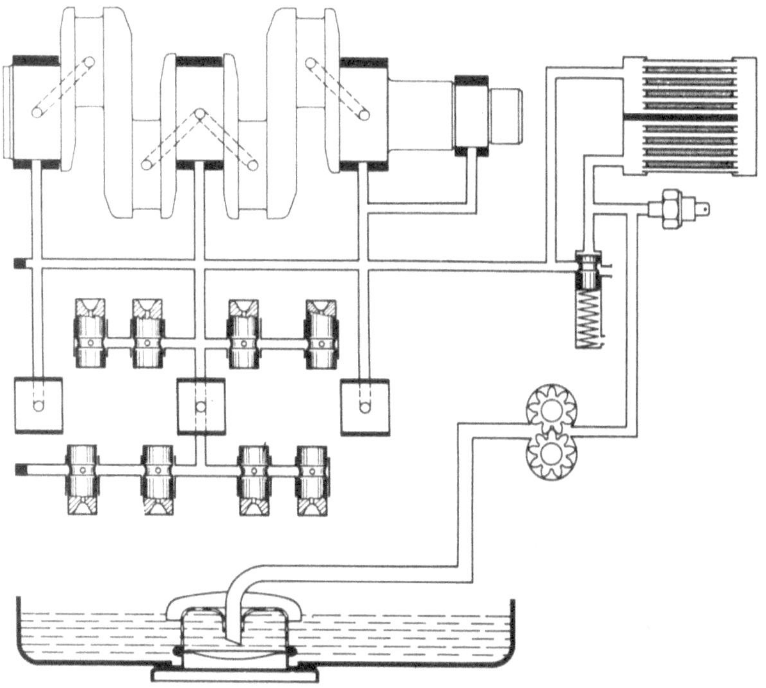

Fig. 1.6. LUBRICATION SYSTEM SCHEMATIC DIAGRAM OF
PRESSURISED OIL FLOW

Do not force the valve through the guide or you will damage the latter. Keep valves in order so that they may be replaced in the same port. Push them through a piece of cardboard to avoid getting them mixed up.

13. Cylinders - Removal

The cylinders may be removed, after the cylinder heads are off, simply by drawing them from over the pistons. Make sure that the piston and rings are not damaged after the cylinder has been removed. It must also be remembered that if the crankshaft is turned after removing the cylinder the piston skirts can foul the crankcase unless they are guided at the bottom of the stroke.

14. Crankshaft Pulley Wheel - Removal and Replacement

1. The crankshaft pulley wheel is keyed to the rear end of the crankshaft and is a straight keyed fit. It is secured by a single central bolt. To lock the pulley when undoing or tightening the bolt push a suitable article through one of the holes in the pulley and jam it against the crankcase flange.
2. If, when the nut has been removed, the pulley is a very tight fit, do not apply force at the edges or you are likely to distort it. Soak the boss with penetrating oil and hook something through the two holes if any leverage is necessary.
3. If the pulley has been removed during the course of an overhaul remember that the lower rear engine plate has to be re-fixed before the pulley. There is no access to the two securing screws after the pulley is in position.
4. The nut should be tightened to a torque of 33 ft/lbs. when the pulley has been replaced.

15. Piston Rings and Pistons - Removal

1. Remove first the cylinders. The piston rings may be removed from the pistons by carefully spreading the ends of each ring so that it comes out of its groove and then drawing it off over the top of the piston.
2. To remove the piston it is necessary to separate it from the connecting rod as it is not possible to get at the connecting rod bolts with the pistons fitted.
3. Remove the circlip from one side of the piston boss where the gudgeon pin is retained and it will be possible to push out the gudgeon pin. If it resists then warm up the piston with an electric light bulb held next to it for a while. Do not try and drive out the gudgeon pin from a cold piston. You will possibly bend a connecting rod. It is only necessary to push out the pin far enough to enable the connecting rod to be released from the piston. If the pistons are to be put back make sure that each one is marked suitably so that you know (a) which number cylinder it came from and (b) which way faces forward. A good way is to scratch the number and an arrow, pointing forward, on the crown before removal. If you do make a nonsense and forget how it came off then carefully clean the top of the crown and look for identifying marks which indicate the front or flywheel side. Volkswagen pistons are stamped with an arrow at the edge of the crown pointing towards the flywheel. British made pistons have the word 'flywheel' stamped on in that position.

16. Connecting Rods and Big End Bearings - Removal

1. Connecting rods may be removed only after the pistons have been taken off. It is not necessary to split the crankcase although if you are going to do so anyway it will be simpler to take the connecting rods off the crankshaft afterwards. Start with No. 1 and, using a socket with an extension, slacken the two connecting rod cap bolts by inserting the extension into the crankcase. It is important to have the crankshaft positioned so that the socket spanner fits squarely and completely onto the head of each bolt.
2. Once both bolts are loose, carefully undo each one and draw the connecting rod back at the same time so that you can bring them back with it. On later models, instead of a bolt going through the shoulder of the rod into the cap there are captive rod shoulders. Where nuts are used keep them captive in the socket when undoing them so as not to drop them in the crankcase. You can easily see what is fitted before starting dismantling. The cap will be left behind and may be awkward to retrieve. Tip the engine to shake it out if necessary. Retrieve both halves of the bearing shells also. Loosely refit the cap to the connecting rod noting the two matching numbers on the shoulders of the rod and cap which must line up on replacement. It is a good idea to note on a piece of paper which serial number applies to which cylinder number. This avoids the need to mark the connecting rods further. If the same rods and pistons are being put back it is very desirable that they should go back in the same position as they came out.
3. If you have by chance ignored our advice and decided to go as far as removing the connecting rods with the engine still in the car do not blame us if you find yourself unable to retrieve some big end bearing caps or shells from inside the crankcase!

17. Camshaft and Tappets - Removal

1. See under 'Crankshaft - Removal'.

18. Flywheel - Removal

1. With the engine removed from the car the flywheel may be removed once the clutch cover has been taken off (as described in Chapter 7).
2. The flywheel is held by a single centre bolt which is tightened up to 227 ft/lbs so do not think you can get it undone just like that. We found it necessary to obtain a piece of angle iron so that we could lock the flywheel by putting the angle iron across two of the clutch bolts which were put back into the flywheel and clamping the other end of this locking bar in the vice. This, of course, was done with the engine on the bench, the flywheel facing towards the front and lined up with the vice so that the angle iron was positioned firmly and squarely. A 36 mm socket was then put on the bolt with the longest handle from our socket set (do not under any circumstances try to use anything other than a correct sized socket - you could easily cause serious damage or even hurt yourself). A four foot piece of steel pipe was then put over the socket handle and leaned on with considerable weight. The bolt slackened with no fuss at all. It may cost you a little money to get the stuff to do this job properly but we cannot recommend any other way.
3. Remove the bolt and large washer and before going any further make an identifiable mark on the flywheel hub so that you can re-locate the flywheel in the same place. The matching mark on the crankshaft cannot be made until the flywheel is off, so remember not to move the flywheel when it has come off until you can make a corresponding line up mark on the crankshaft flange. This is important as there may be no other way of knowing the correct position of balance.
4. The flywheel is now located solely by four dowel pegs which fit into holes in the crankshaft flange and flywheel boss. Put a piece of wood under the edge of the flywheel starter teeth to support the weight and then use a soft mallet or block of wood to tap the edges of the flywheel and draw it off. Do not try and lever it off with anything against the crankcase or you are likely to crack the casting and that will be very expensive.
5. When the flywheel is free, hold it steady and remove the metal or paper gasket fitted over the four dowel pegs in the flange. Then make the second line-up mark on the crankshaft referred to in paragraph 3.

Replacing the pulley wheel on the crankshaft (Section 14.1)

Tightening the nut to a torque of 33 ft lbs Hold the wheel through the hole provided (Section 14.1)

Replacing the lower rear plate prior to fitting the pulley wheel (Section 14.3)

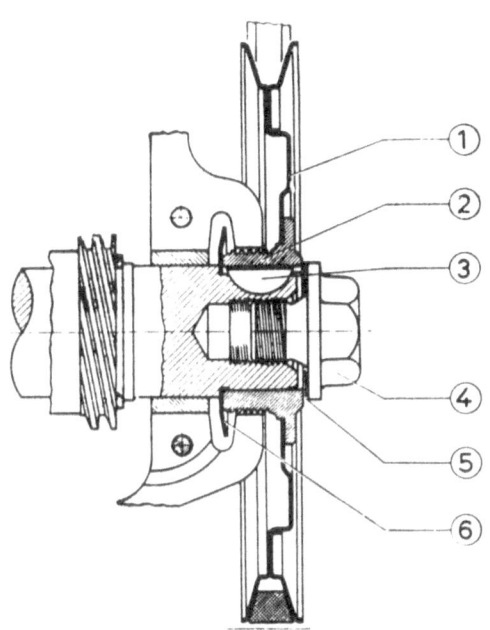

Fig. 1.7. CRANKSHAFT AND PULLEY WHEEL — CROSS SECTION DRAWING

1 Pulley	4 Securing bolt
2 Oil return scroll thread	5 Spring washer
3 Woodruff key	6 Crankshaft oil flinger

Fig. 1.8. Pushrods and tappets - early models. Showing adjust-adjustable guide plates in crankcase which locate cam followers at the end of the pushrods.

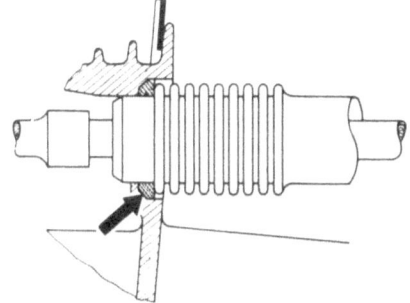

Fig 1.9. Cylinder head - pushrod tube seal position (arrowed)

19. Crankshaft Front Oil Seal - Removal

1. The crankshaft front oil seal may be removed after taking the engine from the car and removing the flywheel.

2. The oil seal may be levered out of the crankcase with a screwdriver or similar but great care must be taken to avoid damaging the crankcase where the seal seats. This means that the point of the tool used must not be allowed to dig into the crankcase.

3. When the oil seal is removed a number of shims which fit between the flywheel hub and the flange on the front main bearing will be observed. There should be three of them normally. These govern the amount of crankshaft end float. Make sure they are kept safely and not damaged.

4. If the crankcase is being split anyway it is simpler to wait until this is done when the oil seal may be easily lifted out.

20. Crankshaft - Removal

1. In order to remove the crankshaft, camshaft and cam followers (tappets) the two halves of the crankcase will need to be separated. Unless you are quite sure that this is essential do not do it. It is not worth opening the crankcase up just to 'have a look'. Remember also that the main bearing shells are much more expensive than on conventional cars (three of the four are not split) and before you can remove one of them two gears must be removed from the crankshaft. These gears are on very tight and are difficult to draw off.

2. Having decided to split the crankcase, remove the oil filler and generator pedestal casting (if detachable) and prop the crankcase on its left side. All pistons and cylinders should already have been removed as should the flywheel. If the flywheel is left on it will add to the difficulty of controlling the weight of the crankshaft when the two halves release it. It will also be much more difficult to remove from the crankshaft afterwards. The connecting rods may be left on as these will be easier to remove after the crankcase is split.

3. The two halves are held together by large and small studs and nuts and two bolts and nuts. Early models have studs all the same size. Slacken all the small nuts followed by the large nuts. Before starting to separate the two halves remember that the crankshaft and camshaft are held between them and you do not want either to fall out haphazardly. So if you keep the crankcase tilted to the left they will both rest in that half.

4. Separate the two halves by tapping lightly at the projecting lugs of the left half with a soft faced mallet or piece of wood. Do not hit anything hard. This progressive gentle tapping at the four corners will gradually increase the gap between the two until the right hand half will be free enough to lift off the studs. If you have a second pair of hands to help so much the better. When the right hand half has moved out a little way there will probably be a light clatter as one or more of the four cam followers in the right hand half fall out. If possible try and get hold of these and arrange them somewhere (in an egg box or numbered row on a shelf) so that they may be put back in the same bores.

5. Put the crankcase half in a safe place where it cannot fall or be damaged.

6. Lift out the camshaft from the other half of the crankcase. If it is one of the later engines with detachable bearing shells the shells should be left in position. If they should fall out note where they came from. If being renewed anyway take them out.

7. The tappets from the left hand half of the crankcase may now be taken out. Keep them in order like the others so they may be replaced in the same bores.

8. The crankshaft can now be lifted out and should be carefully put somewhere safe. The bearing shell halves for No. 2 main bearing should be removed from their locations in each half of the crankcase. Note that the location of each main bearing is by a dowel peg which locates each bearing shell. These normally remain in the crankcase but if any have come out with the bearings retrieve them now before

they get lost.

21. Distributor Drive Shaft - Removal

1. The procedure for removing and replacing the distributor drive shaft from an assembled engine is given in Chapter 4. It is mentioned here because it is in order to leave it in position right up until the time when the crankcase is divided. It should however now be removed before the crankcase is re-assembled.

22. Crankshaft Main Bearings - Removal

1. Three of the four main bearings may be removed as soon as the crankshaft is taken from the crankcase. No. 1 is a circular flanged shell which is drawn off the flywheel end, No. 2 is the split bearing and No. 4 is a narrow circular bearing which can be drawn off the crankshaft pulley end. No. 3, however, is trapped by the helical gear which drives the camshaft. In front of this gear is a spacer and the distributor drive shaft worm gear, an oil thrower disc and Woodruff key.

2. To remove No. 3 main bearing first tap the Woodruff key out of the shaft and keep it safe. Take off the oil thrower disc. The two gears are a tight keyed fit onto the shaft and the only way to get them off is by using a proper sprocket puller which has grips which will fit snugly and completely behind the helical gear so that both the gears and the spacer can be drawn off together. If you have difficulty in fitting the puller in the small gap between the bearing and gear do not try and pull off the gear gripping only against the gear teeth. You will either chip them or break them off. If you are committed to new bearings anyhow, cut the old bearing off to enable you to get the puller properly seated behind the gear.

3. If, when you start putting the pressure on it is obvious that considerable force is going to be needed it is best to clamp the legs of the puller to prevent them spreading and possibly flying off and causing damage to the gear. Some pullers have a clamp incorporated for such a purpose. If you have press facilities available so much the better but on no account should you try to hammer the gears off. It is virtually impossible to do this without damaging the gears.

4. With the two gears removed the bearing can be taken off the shaft.

23. Engine Components - Examination for Wear

Whatever degree of dismantling is carried out, components can only be examined properly after they have been thoroughly cleaned. This is best carried out using paraffin and a stiff bristled brush. Some engines can be particularly bad, with a stubborn coating of hard sludgy deposits - generally denoting neglect of regular oil changing - and it can take some time and effort to get this off. Afterwards, the paraffin can be hosed off with a water jet. Cleaning may sometimes seem to take a disproportionate amount of time but there is no doubt that it is time well spent.

24. Crankcase - Examination and Renovation

The crankcase should be free from cracks or any other form of damage and the two mating edges must be quite free from dents, scratches and burrs which could in any way affect their precise alignment when both are clamped together. The crankshaft bearing locations should also be examined for any signs of damage or distortion. In an engine which has been permitted to run on with worn out main bearings it is possible that the bearing shells themselves will have been 'hammered' by the vibration of the crankshaft into the crankcase. This will mean that new bearings will not be a tight fit in their crankcase locations. In such instances the crankcase must be scrapped. In these circumstances the best action

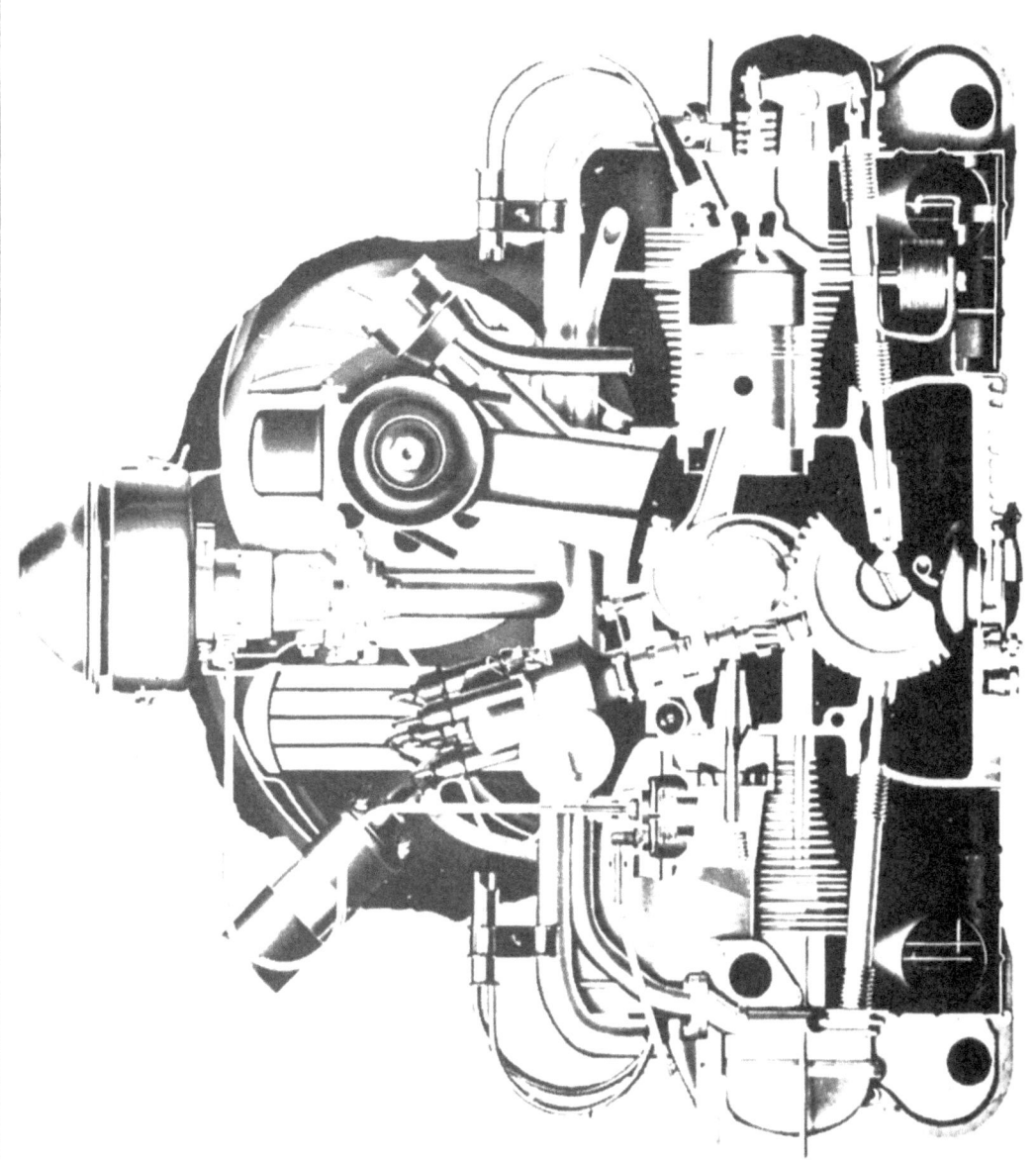

Fig 1.10. CROSS SECTION OF THE 30 DIN BHP ENGINE (EARLY MODEL)
(Compare this with the engine on Page 27)

would be to abandon ideas of renovating the engine and obtain a complete replacement. Make sure that the camshaft bearing surfaces are in good condition - particularly on those versions that do not have renewable shells.

The studs in the crankcase, both for attaching the cylinder heads and for the two halves must be tight in their threads. Any sign of looseness which may be due to worn threads in the alloy crankcase is removable. It will mean drilling and fitting a 'Helicoil' insert - which is a new thread in effect. This can be done at the Volkswagen agents for certain and at many other places where aluminium engines and castings are often being repaired. In any case check the economics before buying a lot of other parts.

25. Crankshaft - Examination and Renovation

1. It is possible to examine the connecting rod big end crankshaft journals after removing the pistons and connecting rods but without splitting the crankcase, but only visually. They cannot be measured satisfactorily. Provided there is no good reason to suspect that the big end bearings were seriously worn and that the surfaces of the journal are bright and smooth with no signs of pitting or scoring then there should be no need to proceed further.

2. The main crankshaft bearing journals may be examined only when the crankcase has been split and the crankshaft taken out. An indication of serious wear in these bearings can be obtained by checking the camshaft for signs of slackness in the bearings before the crankcase is split. A wooden lever put through one of the cylinder apertures can be used to test for any indications of rocking in the bearings. If there is any then the bearing shells will almost certainly need renewal, even though the crankshaft journals themselves may be serviceable. The journals should be perfectly smooth with a bright mirror finish. They should be measured with a micrometer across the diameter for signs of ovality. If any measurement should differ by more than .03 mm (.0011 inch) from any other the crankshaft should be reground. This means taking it to a specialist engineering firm who can grind it to the undersizes permissible and supply the matching new bearing shells. In view of the need to remove the two gears in order to examine No. 3 main bearing journal the condition of the gears should also be checked, in conjunction with their respective mating gears on the camshaft and distributor drive spindle. The bronze worm gear which drives the distributor drive spindle is the most likely to show signs of wear. Any noticeable ridging or 'feathering' and variations in thickness of each spiral tooth indicate wear and renewal is probably justifiable.

26. Main and Big End Bearings - Examination and Renovation

1. When connecting rods are removed from the crankshaft the bearing shells will be released and even though the crankshaft journals are in good condition the bearings may need renewal. Certainly if their bearing surfaces are anything other than an even, matt grey in colour they should be renewed. Any scores, pitting or discoloration is an indication of damage by metal particles or the top bearing surface wearing away. If there is any doubt it is always a good idea to replace them anyway unless there is a definite record that they have only been fitted for a small mileage. The backs of the shells are marked with serial numbers and an indication of whether or not they are undersized due to the crankshaft having been re-ground previously. If in doubt take them to your supplier who will be able to ensure that you are sold new ones of the correct type. If the crankshaft is being re-ground new bearings will be required anyhow and these are always available from the firm which does the re-grinding.

2. The same principles apply to renewal of the main bearings. If they are to be renewed it should be remembered that the No. 3 bearing will require removal of the helical and worm gears before it may be taken off. It should not be left and only the other three renewed.

27. Camshaft and Tappets - Examination and Renovation

1. The tappets should be checked in their respective bores in the crankcase and no excessive side-play should be apparent. The faces of the tappets which bear against the camshaft lobes should also have a clear, smooth shiny surface. If they show signs of pitting or serious wear they should be renewed. Re-facing is possible with proper grinding facilities but the economics of this need investigating first. Early (pre 1960) engines were fitted with one piece push rods and tappets and the bearing faces of these should be regarded in the same way. The lobes of the camshaft should be examined for any indications of flat spots, pitting or extreme wear on the bearing surfaces. If in doubt get the profiles checked against specification dimensions with a micrometer. Minor blemishes may be smoothed down with a 120 grain oil stone and polished with one of 300 grain. The bearing journals also should be checked in the same way as those on the crankshaft. In earlier models damage to the camshaft bearing journals may mean damaged bearing surfaces in the crankcase and these cannot be repaired. On later versions the camshaft bearings are renewable.

2. The gear wheel which is rivetted to the end of the camshaft must be perfectly tight and the teeth should be examined for any signs of breakage or excessive wear. It may be possible to have a new gear-wheel fitted to the existing camshaft - much depends on the facilities available in your area. It is not a job to be attempted by the owner driver.

28. Connecting Rods and Small End Bushes - Examination and Renovation

1. It is unlikely that a connecting rod will be bent except in cases of severe piston damage and seizure. It is not normally within the scope of the owner to check the alignment of a connecting rod with the necessary accuracy so if in doubt have it checked by someone with the proper facilities. It is in order to have slightly bent connecting rods straightened - the manufacturers provide special jigs for the purpose. If a rod needs replacement, care should be taken to ensure that it is within 10 grams in weight of the others. If too heavy, connecting rods may be lightened by removing metal from the shoulders near the big end or the wider parts where the bearing cap mates up to it.

2. The small end bushes are also subject to wear. At a temperature of 70ºF the piston (gudgeon) pin should be a push fit. No axial or rocking movement should be apparent. The fitting of new bushes is a specialist task and although the bushes themselves may be easily pressed in it is necessary to ream them to fit the gudgeon pins. Unless you have reamers readily available and the knowledge of how to use them this should be done by a firm (or individual) specialising in engine reconditioning. Remember that if you are fitting new pistons it may be necessary to fit new connecting rod bushes. If you are lucky the new gudgeon pins may fit the old bushes properly however. Make sure that the new bushes have been drilled to match the oil holes in the connecting rod. This should be done before reaming so that there are no burrs on the bush bore.

29. Pistons, Rings and Cylinders - Examination and Renovation

1. Piston and cylinder bore wear are contributory factors to excessive oil consumption (over 1 pint to 300 miles) and general engine noise. They also affect engine power output due to loss of compression. If you have been able to check the individual cylinder pressures before dismantling so much the better. They will indicate whether one or more is losing compression which may be due to cylinders and pistons if the valves are satisfactory.

2. The piston rings should be removed from the pistons first by carefully spreading the open ends and easing them from their grooves over the crown of the piston. Each one should then be pushed into

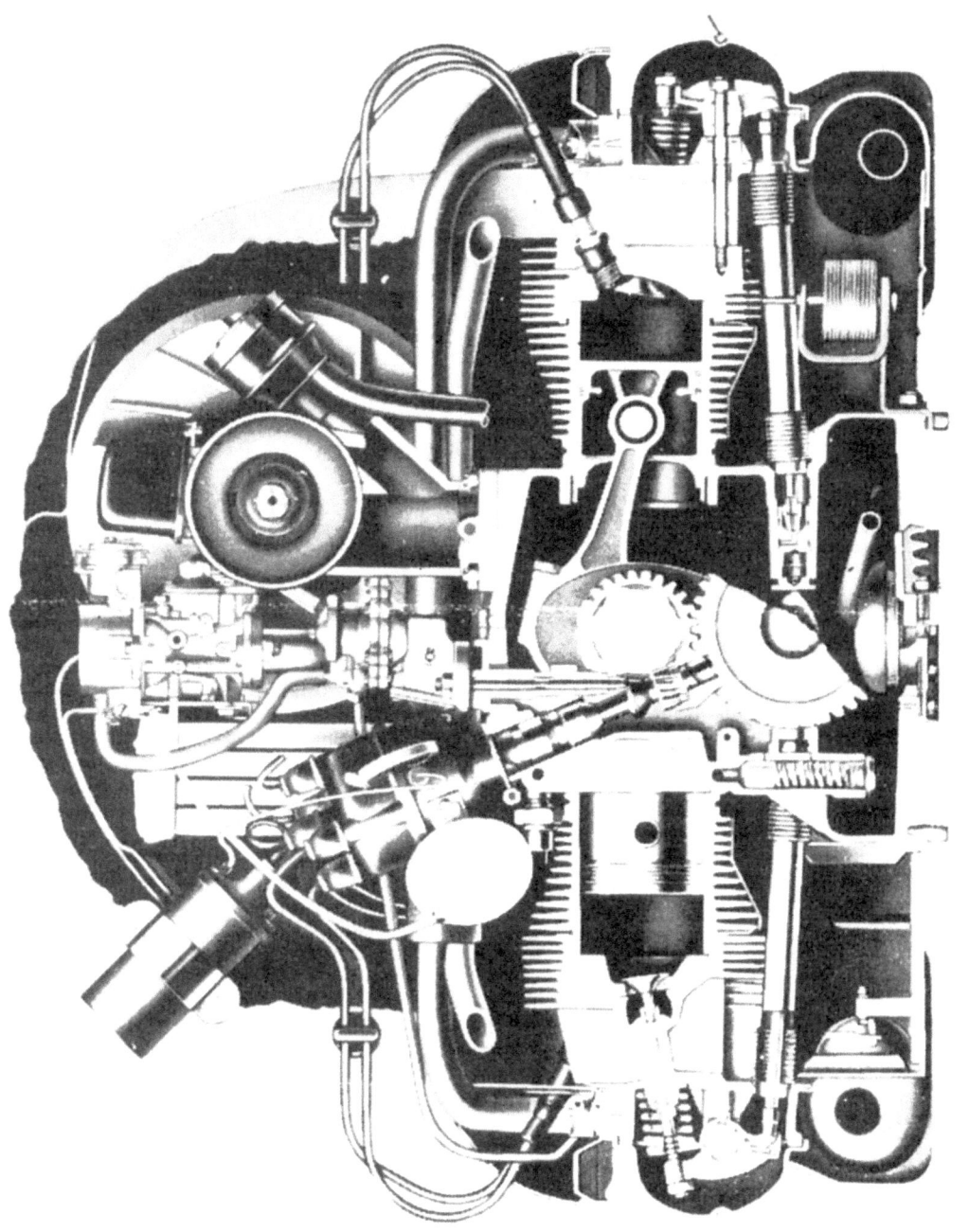

Fig 1.11. CROSS SECTION OF THE 34 DIN BHP ENGINE
(Note differences in the valve position, cam follower, fuel pump position and drive
and generator pedestal compared with the 30 DIN bhp engine on Page 25)

the cylinder bore from the bottom, using the head of the piston to make sure they rest square in position about 5 mm from the bottom edge. The gap between the ends of the ring can then be measured with a feeler gauge. For the two compression rings it should not exceed .90 mm (.035 inch) and for the oil scraper ring .95 mm (.037 inch). If the gaps are greater you know that new rings at least are required.

3. Determining the degree of wear on pistons and cylinders is complimentary. In some circumstances the pistons alone may need renewal - the cylinders not needing reboring. If the cylinders need reboring then new pistons must be fitted. First check the cylinders. A preliminary check can be done simply by feeling the inside walls about ½ inch down from the top edge. If a ridge can be felt at any point then the bores should be measured with an inside micrometer or callipers to see how far they vary from standard. The measurement should be taken across the bore of the cylinder about 15 mm (.6 inch) down from the top edge at right angles to the axis of the gudgeon pin. Depending on whether or not the cylinders have already been rebored once the measurement should be 77 mm, 77.5 mm or 78 mm. Then measure the piston, also at right angles to the gudgeon pin across the skirt at the bottom. The two measurements should not differ by more than .20 mm (.008 inch).

4. Further measurement of the cylinder across the bore will indicate whether or not the wear is mostly on the piston or not. If the cylinder bore is uniform in size it is conceivable that the fitting of new pistons in the original bore size is possible. However, it is a very short sighted policy. If new pistons are needed anyway the cost of reboring will add 20 - 25% to the cost of the pistons so it would be as well to get it done whilst the cylinders are off.

5. Another feature of the pistons to check is the piston ring side clearance in the grooves. This should not exceed .12 mm (.0047 inch) for the top ring and .10 mm (.004 inch) for the other two. Usually however this wear is proportionate to the rest on the piston and will not occur in a piston which is otherwise apparently little worn. If you think that only a new set of rings is required it would be a good idea to take your pistons to the supplier of the new rings and check the new rings in the gaps. You may change your mind about how worn the pistons really are! Once a cylinder has been rebored twice (to 78 mm diameter) it must not be rebored again and new cylinders must be obtained.

30. Cylinder Heads, Rocker Gear and Valves - Examination and Renovation

1. After the cylinder head has been removed and the valves taken out the head itself should be thoroughly cleaned of carbon in the combustion chambers and examined for cracks. If there are any visible cracks the head should be scrapped. Cracks are most likely to occur round the valve seats or spark plug holes. Bearing in mind that one head will cost (new) nearly 20% of the cost of a complete replacement engine economies should be considered as well as the likelihood of obtaining a used head from a breaker's yard. If the latter, make sure that the head you get is the same type as the old one - and in better condition! Early engines (pre 1960) had horizontally mounted valves and different rocker gear and heads so should not be mixed.

2. The valve seats should be examined for signs of burning away or pitting and ridging. If there is slight pitting the refacing of the seats by grinding in the valve with carborundum paste will probably cure the problem. If the seat needs re-cutting, due to severe pitting, then the seat width should not exceed specification. Fitting new valve seat inserts is a specialist task as they are chilled and shrunk in order to fit them. Check with the nearest Volkswagen dealer because you could have difficulty in getting this problem solved cheaply.

3. The rocker gear should be dismantled and thoroughly cleaned of the sludge deposits which normally tend to accumulate on it. The rocker arms should be a smooth fit on the shaft with no play. If there is any play it is up to the owner to decide whether it is worth the cost of renewal. The effects on engine performance and noise will

not be noticeable under normal circumstances although wear tends to accelerate once it is started. The valve clearance adjusting screws should also be examined. The domed ends that bear on the valve stems tend to get hammered out of shape. If bad, replacement is relatively cheap and easy.

4. The valves themselves must be thoroughly cleaned of carbon. The head should be completely free of cracks or pitting and must be perfectly circular. The edge which seats in to the cylinder head should also be unpitted and unridged although very minor blemishes may be ground out when re-seating the valve face.

5. Replace the valve into its guide in the head and note if there is any sideways movement which denotes wear between the stem and guide. Here again the degree of wear can vary. If excessive, the performance of the engine can be noticeably affected and oil consumption increased. The maximum tolerable sideways rock, measured at the valve head with the end of the valve stem flush with the end of the guide, is .8 mm (.031 inch). Wear is normally in the guide rather than on the valve stem but check a new valve in the guide if possible first. Valve guide renewal is a tricky operation in these cylinder heads and you may find it difficult to get it done. Check with the nearest Volkswagen dealer first. Do not attempt it yourself. One final part of the examination involves the end of the valve stem where the rocker arm bears. It should be flat but often gets 'hammered' into a concave shape or ridged. Special caps are available to put over the ends. Alternatively the ends can be ground off flat with a fine oil stone. Remember that it is difficult to set the valve clearances accurately with the adjusting screw and valve stem in a battered condition.

31. Flywheel - Inspection and Renovation

1. The flywheel is aligned to the crankshaft flange by means of four dowel pegs which are a precision fit into both the flange and flywheel. If any of these should be a slack fit there is considerable risk of the flywheel working loose, despite the tightness of the securing bolt. Where a flywheel has worked loose and caused the holes to become oval a new flywheel will be needed. (The precision work of boring and fitting oversize dowel pegs would cost more).

2. Another area of wear is in the starter teeth. These are machined into the flywheel itself so there is no question of fitting a new ring gear. If the teeth have become seriously chewed up it is in order to have up to 2 mm (.08 inch) machined off on the clutch side of the teeth. The teeth should then be chamfered and de-burred. Any good machine shop should be able to carry out this work.

3. Examine also the land on the flywheel boss where the oil seal runs. If this is severely ridged it may need cleaning up on a lathe also. Any such ridging is very exceptional.

32. Oil Cooler - Examination and Renovation

It will be fairly obvious if the cooler leaks severely but if there is no apparent damage it may be difficult to decide whether it functions correctly. If suspect it should be subjected to a pressure test by a Volkswagen agent equipped with the proper equipment. If there is any doubt about it the only sure remedy is a new one. If the cooler is found to be leaking the oil pressure relief valve should also be checked as it could have caused the failure of the cooler.

33. Oil Pressure Relief Valve - Examination and Renovation

1. The piston of the relief valve is perfectly plain and should be a free sliding fit in the bore of the crankcase. Minor signs of seizure may be cleaned up but if severe a new piston should be fitted. Other models of engine have a piston with a groove in it but this should not be used in the 1200 except in hot climates.

2. The spring should be cleaned and examined. The length of the spring under a load of 7.75 kgs. (17 lbs) should be 23.6 mm (0.9 ins.).

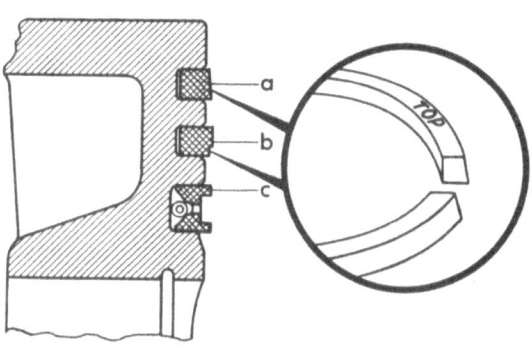

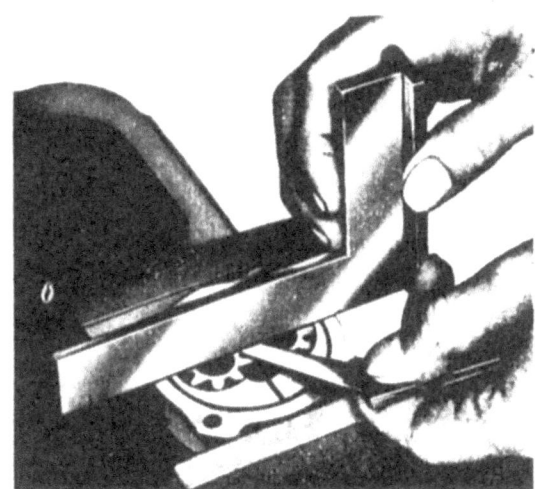

Fig. 1.12. PISTON RINGS

(a) Top compression ring with bevelled face
(b) Lower compression ring with stepped lower edge
(c) Oil scraper control ring

Fig 1.13. Oil pump, measuring gear end play

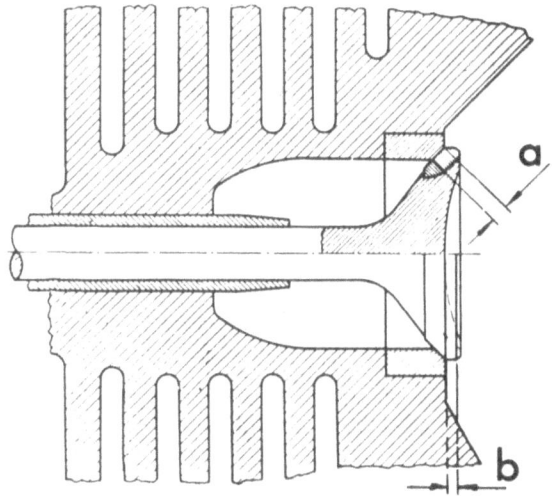

Fig 1.14. VALVES — CROSS SECTION OF
VALVE AND SEAT

Dimension 'A' is seat width   Dimension 'B' is margin required
above seat

'A' Exhaust 1.7 - 2 mm Inlet 1.25 - 1.65 mm

'B' Minimum 1 mm (all valves)

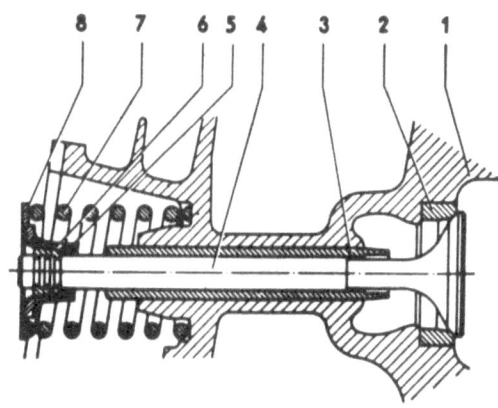

Fig 1.15. VALVE ASSEMBLY — CROSS SECTION OF
VALVE, SPRING AND GUIDE IN
ASSEMBLED POSITION

1 Cylinder head   5 Oil seal ring (later models)
2 Seat insert   6 Split collar
3 Guide   7 Valve spring
4 Valve   8 Spring retaining collar

If you have no way of conveniently measuring it then buy a new one.

34. Oil Pump - Examination and Renovation

1. It is possible to check the pump fairly comprehensively without removing the body from the crankcase but it is, of course, far less convenient and liable to cause measurement inaccuracies.

2. First check the cover plate. If it is very badly scored it should be renewed anyway. Light scoring can be ground out using carborundum paste on a piece of plate glass.

3. Check that the driving spindle is a good fit in the body. Any apparent rocking must indicate that the inside of the pump body is also worn. The driven gear spindle should be tight in the body. The gear should be a good fit on it also with no play.

4. Provided both gear spindles are in good shape refit the gears and measure the end clearance between them and the end of the pump body. This is done by putting a straight edge across the body and using a feeler gauge to measure the gap between the straight edge and the gears. Make sure no traces of gasket remain on the flange of the body when doing this. The gap should not exceed 0.1 mm (.004 inch) or inadequate oil pressure will result. The wear is most likely to be in the pump body in this case and will need renewal.

5. The backlash between the gear teeth can also be measured with a feeler blade and this should not exceed 0.2 mm (.008 inch).

6. Depending on the availability of individual parts any renewals to parts of the pump must be weighed against the advantages of having a complete unit. If only the body shows signs of scoring or wear take the gears along to the Volkswagen parts store and try them for fit in a new body. In most cases of sloppiness fitting a new body alone will cure the problem.

35. Engine Reassembly - General

1. As mentioned earlier, the Volkswagen engine is more complex in assembly than a conventional engine with a single cylinder block. It is therefore essential to get everything right first time and this means DO NOT RUSH IT. More than likely you will not have assembled an engine like this before so the order of assembly which is basically similar on other types cannot be relied upon for experience.

2. Before starting work clear the bench and arrange all the components nearby. The assembly surface must be particularly clean and it is a good idea to cover the working surface with sheets of strong paper. Have all the necessary gaskets and seals available together with clean oil in a can or convenient dispenser pack. If you are replacing bearing shells, cam followers and various other parts make sure the old parts are kept away from the assembly area in a carton or something. It is very easy to pick up an old cam follower for instance by mistake. At each stage, get the relevant batch of nuts and bolts ready - having cleaned the grit from them in a paraffin bath. A plentiful supply of clean clothes is the final requirement. Do not forget to clean the tools you will use as well. It is easy to transfer grit from a spanner to the engine with your hands and any small pieces of grit can ruin many hours and pounds worth of work. And again finally, take your time!

36. Crankshaft - Assembly of Gears and Nos. 3 and 4 Main Bearings

1. With the crankshaft thoroughly clean and the oilways blown out lubricate No. 3 journal with clean engine oil. No. 3 main bearing is one of the two largest one-piece circular shells. It does **not** have a flange on it. This bearing goes on to the journal **one way only** - that is with the small dowel peg hole (which is not central) towards the flywheel end of the crankshaft. Do not get this wrong or assembly will grind to a halt when you try and locate the bearing in the crankcase halves.

2. Next replace the camshaft drive gear. Before putting it on examine the surfaces of the crankshaft and key and the bore of the gear. If

there are signs of slight scoring as a result of seizure when the gear was drawn off, clean them up with a very fine file. This will avoid a tendency to bind on replacement. The gear keyway should be lined up with the key in the shaft and the chamfered edge of the gear bore must face the flywheel end - i.e. it goes on first. The gear may be difficult to start on the shaft so keep it square and make sure that the keyway is precisely lined up. It can then be drifted on with firm evenly spaced strikes around the gear (away from the teeth). Keep it square, particularly at the start, and drive it fully home. The crankshaft should be clamped between padded vice jaws for this operation.

3. Next the spacer ring followed by the spiral distributor drive gear are fitted. They can go on either way round and the gear should be carefully drifted up to the spacer without damaging the spiral teeth. Finally, fit the retaining circlip and make sure it fits snugly in its groove. If it will not go in the groove then one of the gears has not been fully driven onto the crankshaft and this must be rectified.

4. Next fit the small circular bearing over the end journal, once again making sure that the offset dowel peg hole is towards the flywheel end of the crankshaft. Do not confuse the dowel peg hole with the other circular groove machined in the outside of this bearing. Lubricate the journal.

5. Next fit the oil thrower disc with the concave face outwards. Fit the Woodruff key (for the crankshaft pulley wheel) into the keyway now as this will prevent the disc from falling off inadvertently.

37. Connecting Rods - Assembly to Crankshaft

1. If the crankcase has been split the connecting rods (without the pistons) should first be fitted to the crankshaft. Check that the gudgeon pins fit correctly in their respective small end bushes, otherwise difficulty will be encountered in fitting the pistons later. If you are refitting the connecting rods to the crankshaft in the assembled crankcase, note the additional information at the end of this section.

2. Lay the crankshaft down on the bench with the flywheel flange pointing away from you.

3. Arrange the connecting rods, two on each side of the crankshaft with Nos. 1 and 2 on the right, No. 1 nearest the flywheel end and No. 3 and 4 on the left with No. 3 nearest the flywheel end. The numbers on each connecting rod and cap must face downward for each cylinder. There is a forging mark on each rod on the opposite side which obviously faces upwards. If you are fitting new connecting rods check with the supplier first about any changes which may possibly have occurred in this principle of marking. Later rods are fitted with fixed bolts in the caps and nuts. These should not be mixed with earlier rods having bolts fitted through the rods into the caps. The first crank on the crankshaft, from the flywheel end, is No. 3, left. Pick up the connecting rod and after wiping the bearing surface perfectly clean, fit the bearing shell with the notch engaging in the corresponding notch in the rod. Fit the other half of the shell bearing to the cap in the same fashion. Next, liberally oil the bearing journal with clean oil and assemble the rod to the crankshaft. Match the two numbers on the shoulders and with the rod pointing to the left face them downwards. Replace the cap bolts (or nuts) finger tight so that the assembly is not loose on the crankshaft.

4. Repeat this for No. 1, right, which is the second crank from the flywheel end followed by No. 4, left, and No. 2, right. It is easy to get confused while doing this. If your crankshaft assembly does not look like the one in the photograph rotate the crankshaft 180° but keep the connecting rods pointing the same way. Then it should look familiar! Above all, think and do not rush.

5. Once the rods are correctly fitted to the crankshaft the bolts will need tightening to the correct torque of 3.3 mkg (24 ft lbs). The best way to do this is to mount the crankshaft vertically in the vice, clamping the No. 4 bearing journal firmly between two pieces of wood. All the connecting rod bolts can then be tightened. It is advisable to tap the shoulders of each rod with a hammer to relieve any pre-tension which can be set up between the mating surfaces of

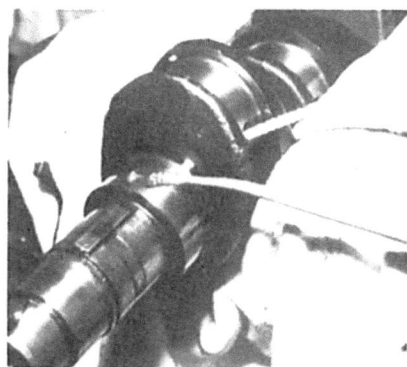
Clean out the oilways and lubricate No 3 journal (Section 36.1)

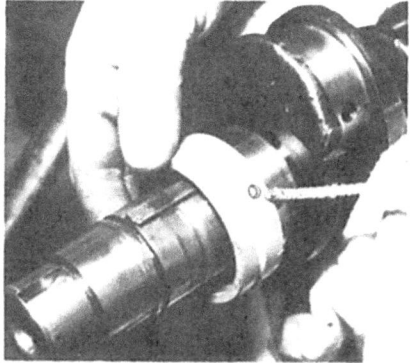
No 3 main bearing goes on one way only. The pipe cleaner is pointing to the small dowel peg hole (Section 36.1)

Replacing camshaft gear (Section 36.2)

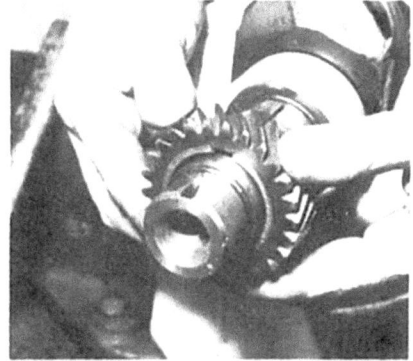
Lining up the camshaft gear keyway (Section 36.2)

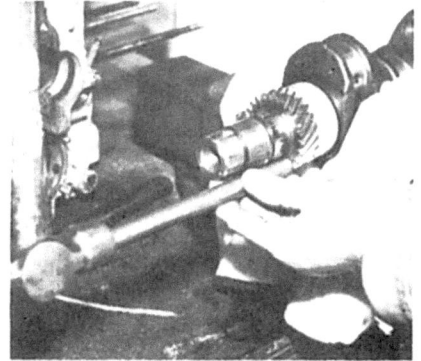
Drifting on the camshaft drive gear (Section 36.2)

Next fit the spacer ring and drift it up to the gear (Section 36.3)

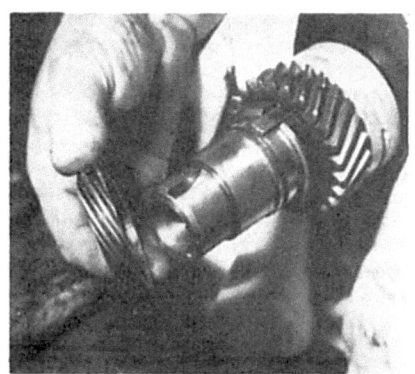
Fit the spiral distributor drive gear (Section 36.3)

Drift the spiral gear up to the spacer (Section 36.3)

Fitting the retaining circlip (Section 36.3)

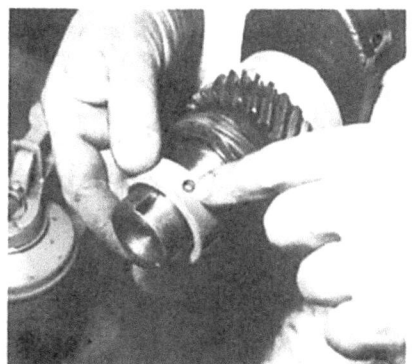
Fitting the small circular bearing over the end journal. Note the dowel hole position. (Section 36.4)

Fitting the oil thrower disc concave face outwards (Section 36.5)

Finally tap home the Woodruff key (Section 36.5)

the cap and the rod. When the cap bolts are fully tightened the connecting rods should be able to rotate around the journals under their own weight. There should be no tight or 'free' spots anywhere although if you are fitting new shells to an unreground crankshaft this is possible. If very noticeable however it indicates that the journal is out of round. If rods on a reground crankshaft are slightly too tight the engine will need running-in. If very tight then the regrinding tolerances are wrong and it should be returned to the machinists for correction.

6. Place the assembled crankshaft on the bench once more, as before, with each connecting rod facing its proper cylinder position.

7. If you are fitting the connecting rods to an assembled crankcase/crankshaft lay out the rods alongside their respective cylinder positions as already explained and fit the shells into the rods and caps. Turn the crankshaft so that the journal for the rod to be fitted is nearest its crankcase opening. The cap must then be placed on the journal and the rod fitted to it. This is easy if you have four hands and fingers ten inches long! It is helpful to have a piece of bent metal rod which can be put through from the opposite side of the crankcase to hold the cap on the journal whilst the rod and bolts are being fitted. A certain amount of patience is essential as it is more than likely that you will drop a bolt or bearing cap into the crankcase at some stage and have to shake it out. The most important thing to ensure is that a bearing shell/s does not drop out unnoticed while you are fiddling about and get trapped and damaged. So if a shell drops in the crankcase go easy on rotating the crankshaft until you get it out. Needless to say, this operation is made even more difficult if attempted with the engine in the car. This is why we do not recommend it. As soon as the first connecting rod is fitted tighten the bolts to the correct torque and check that it moves freely but without any clearance. You will be refitting new shells to the original journal sizes so if something seems amiss - bearing too tight or too loose - make sure you have bought the correct shells by comparing the numbers and oversize (if any) with the old ones removed.

38.   Crankcase, Crankshaft, Camshaft and Cam Followers - Re-assembly

1. The items in the section heading are grouped together for the very good reason that they all have to be assembled together. None may be omitted.

2. Both crankcase halves must be perfectly clean, inside and out. All traces of jointing compound must be removed from the mating faces and at the roots of the studs. It should also be removed from the chamfers in the stud hole mating faces. Use a solvent such as carbon tetrachloride to remove sealing compound and not a scraper which could damage the aluminium surfaces. The distributor drive gear should have been removed. The oil pump suction pipe must be tightly fitted. If loose it must be peened in position as necessary.

3. Place the left hand half of the crankcase on the bench with the flywheel end away from you and leaning over so that it rests on the cylinder head studs.

4. Oil the four cam followers for the left half and place them in their bores. On early engines the cam followers are integral with the push rods so the details about cam followers here do not apply. If new followers are being fitted it is possible that their heads may be slightly thicker than the originals so compare them. If they are thicker then it is essential to check the clearance between them and the crankcase with the cam lift at its highest point. So having placed the cam followers in position replace the camshaft temporarily, with its shell bearings if appropriate, and revolve it. If any of the cam lobes should jam the followers against the crankcase then clearance will have to be provided by relieving the crankcase by about 1-2 mm behind each cam follower head. This can be done by a small, end face grindstone in a power drill by a competent handyman. Great accuracy is not important provided that there is no damage to the actual cam follower bore and the resulting clearance is adequate to permit full unobstructed movement of the cam and follower. Be sure

to blow out all traces of metal after such work. Repeat this check for the four cam followers in the right hand half of the crankcase.

5. Fit the flanged No. 1 bearing shell at the flywheel end. Once again make sure that the off-centre locating dowel peg hole goes towards the flywheel end of the crankshaft. Look to see that the corresponding dowel pegs in the crankcase will mate up. The bearing surfaces of the journal should be well lubricated with clean oil but keep the outside surfaces of the bearing shell clean and dry.

6. Place one half of the split shell in position at No. 2 bearing in the crankcase, engaging the dowel pin in the hole. Lubricate the bearing with clean oil.

7. The crankshaft assembly should now be placed into position in the left hand crankcase half. The three dowel holes in the circular bearings will need lining up so that they will locate snugly and Nos. 3 and 4 connecting rods must pass through their respective apertures. It is a good idea to lift the assembly up by Nos. 1 and 2 connecting rods for this operation. Do not force anything into place. The circular bearings may need rotating a little until you can feel the pegs engage. Ensure the thrower disc locates within the oil thrower recess in the casting. Once all the bearing pegs are located a little pressure will ensure that the assembly and bearings are completely seated. If it is stubborn for any reason lift it out, pause, look, think and have another go.

8. Next fit the camshaft bearing shells into clean locations, if applicable, engaging the notches appropriately in the crankcase. Then oil the bearings. Otherwise oil the bearing surfaces in the crankcase in readiness for the camshaft.

9. Turn the crankshaft carefully until the two teeth, each marked with a centre punch, are visible and well clear of the edge of the crankcase. There is a single tooth on the camshaft gear similarly marked which must mesh between them. Engage the teeth and roll the camshaft round, in mesh still, into its bearing location. Then turn the gears again to check that the timing marks are still correctly aligned.

10 Now fit the four tappets (cam followers) into the right hand half of the crankcase and if it seems as though they might fall out when it is lifted and tilted then put a dab of grease behind the lip of each one to help stick it in position.

11 Fit the other half of No. 2 bearing shell into the crankcase, locating it over its dowel peg correctly.

12 Now thinly coat the two clean, smooth mating surfaces of the crankcase halves with aluminium alloy jointing compound. Use a good quality product such as Volkswagen themselves recommend or 'Hylomar'. Neither is cheap but then you do not want your crankcase to leak oil when it gets hot. Make sure the two surfaces are coated completely but thinly and evenly. Take care to cover round the base of the studs. Do not let any compound get into oilways or other places where it is not wanted and may cause obstruction or binding.

13 Place the right hand half of the crankcase over the studs of the left and carefully slide it down until it just touches the crankshaft bearings.

14 Coat the circular camshaft sealing plug with jointing compound and place it in position in its groove in the left hand half at the flywheel end of the camshaft, with the recess facing inwards.

15 Move the two halves together, tapping lightly with a block of wood if necessary. Use no force - none should be necessary.

16 Now stop and check:

1. Are all the connecting rods protruding from their proper holes? Cap bolts tight?

2. Are all four bearings, two gears and oil thrower disc fitted to the crankshaft?

3. Are all eight cam followers in position?

4. You did not forget the camshaft? (It has been known!). And did you mesh the timing properly?

5. Camshaft sealer plug?

All in order, replace all the nuts on the studs finger tight. Revolve the crankshaft just to make sure that everything moves freely at this

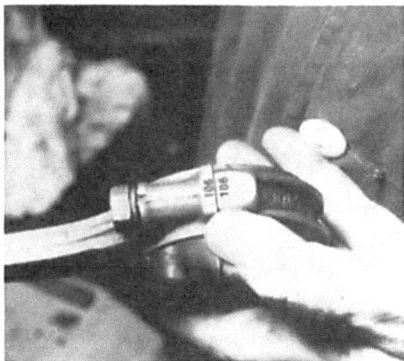

Check the numbers on the rod and cap (Section 37.3)

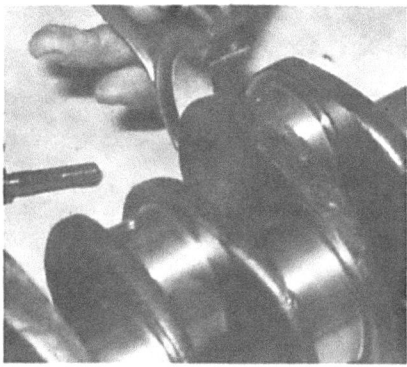

Fitting the connecting rod to the crankshaft (Section 37.3)

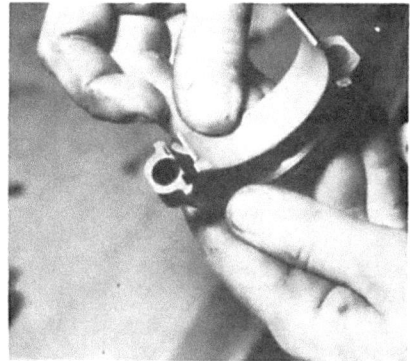

Fitting the shell to the bearing cap (Section 37.3)

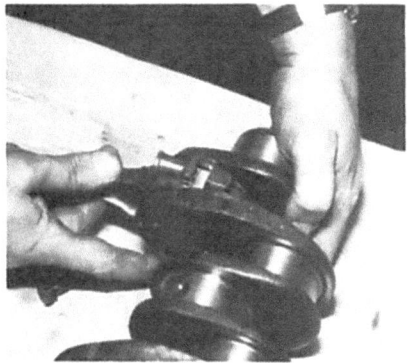

Fitting the cap to the rod (Section 37.3)

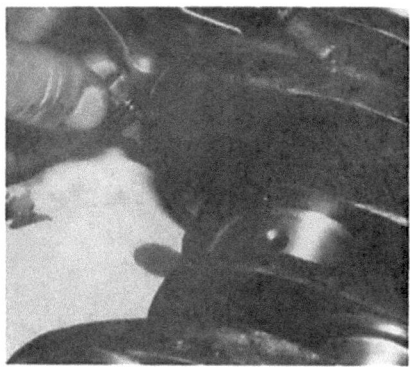

Tighten the bolts hand tight as you go. (Section 37.3)

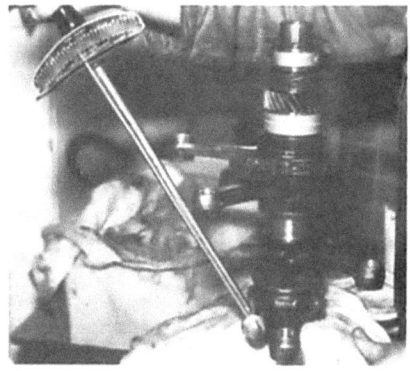

Tighten all bolts finally to a torque of 4.5 mkg (32 lb ft) (Section 37.5)

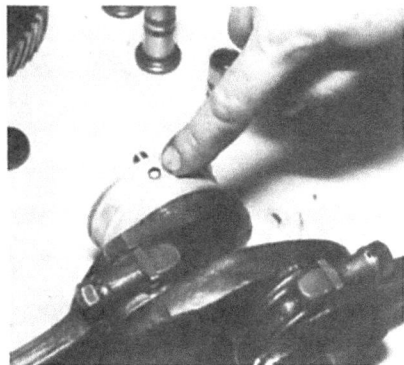

No 1 main bearing correctly positioned (Section 38.5)

One half of No 2 main bearing being positioned (Section 38.6)

Comparing tappets before assembly (Section 38.4)

Inserting tappets into cylinder block (Section 38.4)

Checking cam lobe clearance (Section 38.4)

Tappets in place. Note plain camshaft bearings in crankshaft casting (Section 38.4)

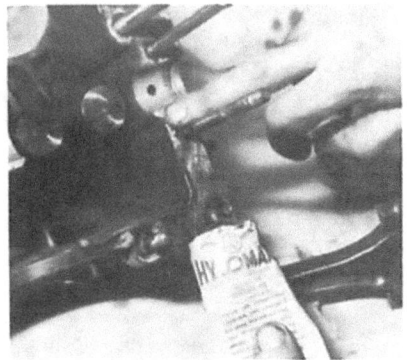

Preparing crankcase joint with sealing compound (Section 38.12)

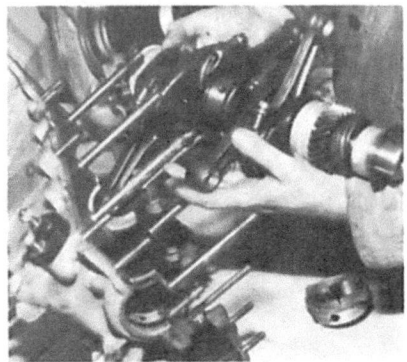

Placing crankshaft assembly into left half of crankcase 1st stage.

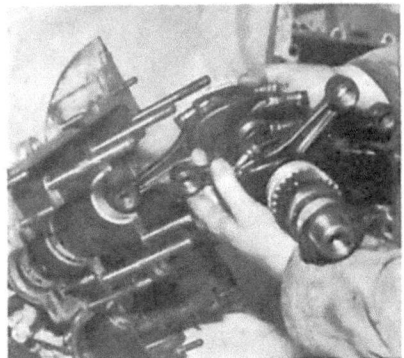

Placing crankshaft assembly into left half of crankcase 2nd stage (Section 38.7)

Meshing camshaft gear into crankshaft gear (Section 38.9)

Fitting right hand half of crankcase (Section 38.13)

Tapping the two halves together (Section 38.15)

Tighten down nuts evenly (Section 38.17)

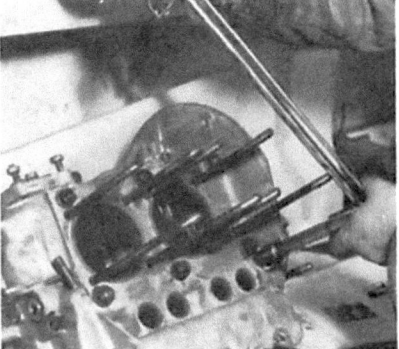

Go round steadily as shown in the text (Section 38.17)

Fig 1.16. Exploded view of all components with main bearings in position ready for crankcase assembly (Section 38)

Fig 1.17. Crankshaft in position in left hand half of crankcase (Section 38)

stage at least.

17 It is important to tighten down the stud nuts evenly and in the correct order. Tighten first the six large nuts to a torque of 1.5 mkg (11 ft/lbs) only, followed by all the smaller nuts to the same torques. Then tighten the small nut near the lower large stud clamping round No. 1 main bearing to its full torque of 2 mkg (14 ft/lbs). Earlier models with one size of nuts had all nuts finally torqued to 22 ft/lbs but the same principle applies with regard to the nut near No. 1 bearing and the same pattern and order should be followed.

18 For crankcases with two nut sizes tighten first the larger ones, progressively to a torque of 20 ft/lbs and then to 22 ft/lbs. Then tighten the smaller ones progressively to 14 ft/lbs. Where the nuts are all the same size tighten all progressively up to 20 ft/lbs.

19 On earlier models with the annular ring thermostat control you will have one blank hole on top where the pivot shaft fits. This can go in later.

20 Now rotate the crankshaft - it should revolve smoothly without any stiffness. If there is stiffness however slacken all the crankcase nuts. If it then turns freely then something is wrong and you should separate the crankcase again. Then check that all the bearings have been properly located on their dowel pegs and that the split bearings of the camshaft are seated properly. Any pressure spots on bearings will be visible. The cause is normally due to dirt or burrs behind them, particularly on the corners of the bearing bore corners and mating face edges. These can be chamfered lightly if necessary. Whatever happens do not press on until you have found the reason for any tightness. Start again from the beginning if necessary.

39. Pistons, Piston Rings and Connecting Rods - Reassembly

1. If you are only fitting new rings to existing pistons make sure you have examined the pistons properly as detailed in Section 25, and checked the new ring gaps in the cylinder bores.

2. The new rings should be fitted over the piston crown replacing the bottom ring first. If you do not have a proper ring expander tool spread the ends of the ring so that it goes over the top of the piston. Then carefully ease it down, over the other grooves a little at a time. The blade of a feeler gauge or some shim steel will be of great assistance in sliding it over the grooves. Do not bend the ring in any way more than necessary to move it. It breaks easily. The top two rings are difficult. The lower of the two has a cut-away lower edge and the top ring is chamfered on its outer face. Both rings will be marked 'oben' or 'top' which denotes which way up they go. The lower of the two is fitted first, followed by the upper.

3. When new pistons are supplied for rebored cylinders the rings are already fitted and the gaps should automatically be correct. It does no harm however to take the top ring off each piston and check it in the bore to make sure.

4. Assuming the small end bushes have been correctly sized for the gudgeon pins remove one circlip from each piston - if not already done - and push out the gudgeon pin until the piston boss is clear to permit the end of the connecting rod to be positioned. If the pins are too tight to push out do **not** force them. Warm up the pistons in front of the fire or on a radiator or next to an electric light bulb. Do **not** play over them with a blow-lamp or gas torch. They only need warming - not heating.

5. If new pistons are being fitted they can go to any connecting rod and all that matters is that the side of the piston marked on the crown 'flywheel' or with a pointing arrow goes towards the flywheel end of the engine. Push the gudgeon pin back into place and replace the circlip. Make sure that you use only the circlips supplied with the pistons. Do not use the old circlips just because they are easier to contract. (Volkswagen pistons have wire circlips with long legs. English pistons have spring steel clips with small eyes needing proper circlip pliers to release them).

6. As soon as one piston has been fitted **take care** because when the

crankshaft is rotated the skirt of the piston can foul the crankcase at bottom dead centre unless it is guided into the cylinder aperture. This could break it. Watch too that the piston rings do not get snagged up on anything which could break them.

40. Cylinders - Replacement

1. Cylinders should normally go back in their original locations unless new pistons are being fitted or they have been rebored, in which case it does not matter.

2. It is a good idea to turn the engine upside down for the fitting of the cylinders as this will make the next step of fitting the cylinder heads so much easier also.

3. Make sure that the mating faces at both top and bottom of the cylinders are perfectly clean and clear of old gaskets. Select the new thin, cylinder base gaskets from the set and separate them. It is easy for two to stick together. Hang one over each connecting rod now so you do not forget to put them on.

3. Cylinders will only go on one way, that is with the narrow fins at the base and the flat fin edges of a pair of cylinders facing each other. This should be remembered for the first cylinder of each pair. You could get it wrong and have to take it off again when the second one is ready to go on!

4. The piston ring gaps should be spaced equally round the circumference of each piston with the gap in the oil control ring facing the top of the engine. Remember that the engine is upside down when positioning it.

5. The rings must be compressed into the piston grooves in order to get the cylinder over them. The type of compressor used must be such that it will split and come off round the piston because once the cylinder is on it will not be possible to lift it off over the top of the piston. In the instance illustrated a 'Jubilee' hose clip was used quite satisfactorily. The cylinder bore is chamfered at the bottom which also facilitates assembly.

6. Fit the clip round the rings and tighten it so that all three are compressed. Take care to see that no ring slips out from under the clip. This can easily happen, particularly when first tightening up the clip screw.

7. Tighten the clip until the rings are flush with the piston but do not tighten it so much that the clip grips the piston tightly. Otherwise it will be difficult to slide the clip down the piston when the cylinder barrel takes over.

8. Not forgetting the lower cylinder gasket, place the cylinder over the piston head, narrow end first and with the fin flats facing the adjacent cylinder position and with the four studs aligned in the passages in the fins.

9. Press the base of the cylinder against the piston ring compressor or clip and tap it down with a wooden block or soft hammer. If the clip does not move slacken it a fraction and try again. Do not let the cylinder 'bounce' off the clip when tapping it otherwise you are likely to release an otherwise captive ring. If a ring does escape it will be necessary to start again. If you break a ring you will probably have to buy a set of three for that piston - rarely can you buy a single ring unless you are lucky and a supplier has a part set or is prepared to split a set.

10 Once all rings are inside the cylinder remove the compressor. With the 'Jubilee' clip this means unscrewing it until the end can be drawn out to release it.

11 Next, carefully position the base gasket onto the bottom of the cylinder barrel. Then move the barrel down and locate it into the crankcase. It will not be a straight fit. It is important to make sure that the gasket is not dislodged and trapped incorrectly. If it is the joint may leak and, worse, the cylinder tilted fractionally out of line.

12 It may be found convenient to rotate the crankshaft as each cylinder is fitted. When this is done, precautions must be taken to keep the other cylinders in position, otherwise you will have to keep checking the gasket seating. This can be done by holding them down with string or wire.

Positioning the piston over the small end bush (Section 39.5)

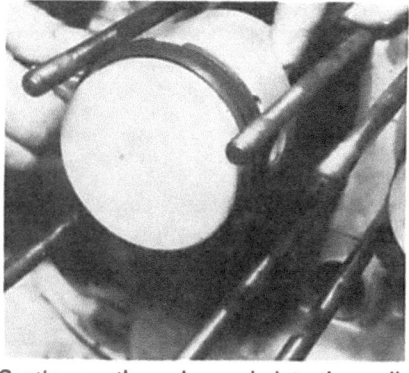
Gently ease the gudgeon pin into the small end bush (Section 39.5)

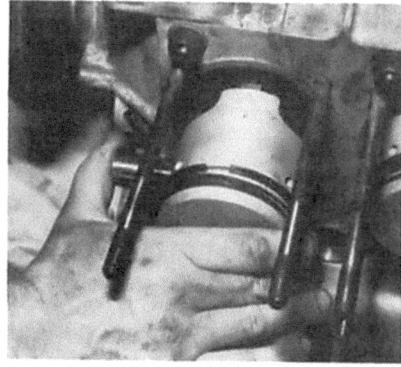
Push the gudgeon pin home gently but firmly (Section 39.5)

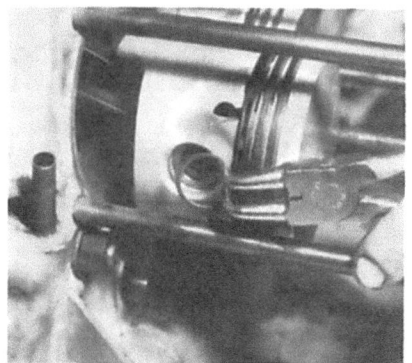
Fit the circlip (a new one) (Section 39.5)

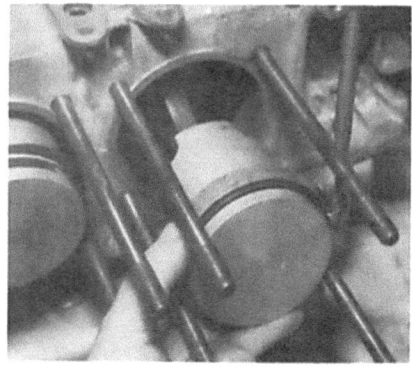
Fitting the piston ring clamp (Section 40.6)

Clean the base of the cylinder carefully (Section 40.3)

Fitting the new gasket to the cylinder (Section 40.3)

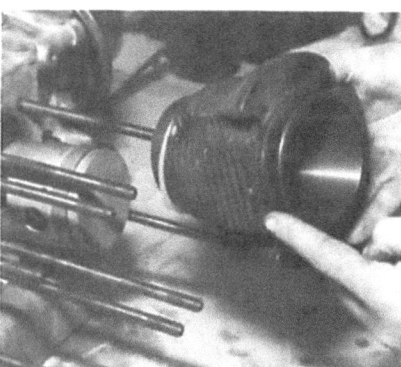
Line up the cylinder for assembly over the piston (Section 40.3)

Feed the cylinder onto the piston. Note the fin position (Section 40.3)

When all the rings are in the piston remove the clamp (Section 40.10)

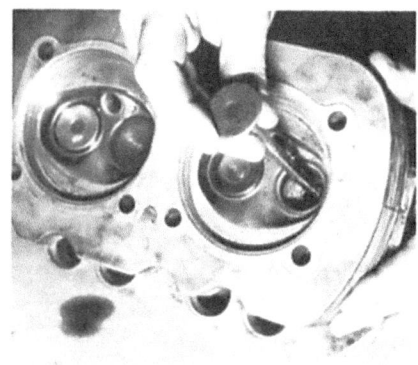
Fitting the valve to the guide (Section 41.3)

Fit the spring and cap over the valve stem (Section 41.3)

41. Cylinder Heads, Valve and Springs - Reassembly

1. The valves removed should be refitted in their original positions unless, of course, new ones are being fitted.

2. If possible treat the valve stem with molybdenum disulphide or some other form of anti-scuffing paste to prevent excessive initial wear in the guide.

3. Place the valve in the guide and put the spring and spring cap over the stem. Note that the close coils of the spring go against the head. On later engines which have an oil deflection ring round the valve stem fit this before the spring cap.

4. Next arrange the valve spring compressor with the spacer tube fitted as required and carefully compress the spring. Watch that there is no likelihood of the spring flying out. Often the spring tends to tilt on compression and this can impede the fitting of the split collars. If you can straighten the spring up without risk of releasing it all is well. Sometimes it may be necessary to find another spring compressor.

5. Compress the spring far enough to expose the grooves into which the split collars locate.

6. It will be necessary to fit the split collars through the slot in the tube if you have used this method. Fingers will be found to be too fat so put a blob of grease on the end of a screwdriver and use this to pick up the collett and put it in position with the narrow end downwards. You may have difficulty with the second half because of the spring not being centrally spaced round the valve stem. This can be overcome by carefully tapping the spring with the compressor or by a little extra compression.

7. When both split collars are properly located in the grooves in the valve stems slowly release the compressor tool making sure that neither of the split collars is pushed out of position. When the spring compressor is fully released the two halves of the split collar should be flush. If not, one is not properly bedded in the grooves of the valve stem.

8. Repeat the procedure for each valve in turn.

42. Cylinder Heads - Replacement

1. It is best for the engine to be inverted when fitting the cylinder heads as in this way the push rod tubes will be much easier to assemble between the head and crankcase.

2. First check the push rod tubes. They have compressible concertina ends and these should be stretched out a little by pulling them so that the distance between the outer ends of the concertina sections is no less than 181 mm. A new sealing ring should be fitted over each end so that the radiused face will go into the head or crankcase as appropriate. When stretching the tubes pull straight so as to avoid any possibility of cracking them. If they are fractured a positive oil leak will result so check their condition carefully.

3. Next fit the sheet steel air deflector plate, of which there is one to each pair of cylinders. It is a spring fit to the two centre studs and to make sure it is tight, the clip flanges may be bent out a little. Note that these deflectors (which guide air into the cooling fins) are on the lower side, i.e. the same side as the push rod tubes. They follow the contour of the cooling fins when installed so make sure they are the right way round. They cannot be fitted after putting the cylinder heads and tubes in position.

4. Locate the four copper/asbestos sealing ring gaskets, one on each cylinder and see that the slot in the copper sheath faces the cylinder head. Note that on the later versions of the 1200 these sealing rings were not fitted.

5. One head should now be put on to the eight head studs just far enough to be secure. Then place the four push rod tubes into position in their recesses in the crankcase and move the head further on so that the other ends of the tubes locate in the corresponding

holes in the head. Make sure that the push rod seals seat firm and square and that the recesses are clean.

6. The cylinder head studs should not be touching any of the cylinder barrel fins so if necessary turn the barrels a little to achieve this. A piece of postcard placed behind each stud will establish the presence of a gap.

7. Replace the stud washers and nuts and tighten them lightly and evenly as far as is possible with a socket and extension using no lever bar.

8. The tightening progression of the nuts is important and is in two stages. First tighten the nuts to 1 mkg (7 ft/lbs) in the order shown in fig 1.18 (a). Then tighten them to 3.2 mkg (23 ft/lbs) in the final diagonal pattern sequence as shown in fig 1.18 (b). There is a temptation to overtighten these head nuts. Resist it! Otherwise you will distort the head.

9. Repeat the operation for the second head.

43. Rocker Gear and Push Rods - Replacement

1. With the cylinder heads replaced, put the push rods into position making sure that the lower end engages in the recess in the cam follower.

2. Place a new seal over each rocker gear mounting stud and then place the rocker shaft support blocks over the studs so that the socketed ends of the rocker arms will line up with the push rods and the adjusters over the valve stems. On later models the support blocks were chamfered and slotted. These are fitted with the chamfers outwards and slots upwards.

3. Replace the washers and nuts and tighten the two nuts down evenly ensuring that the push rods are properly engaged in the rocker arms. Tightening torque is 2.5 mkg (18 ft/lbs). Slacken all the rocker adjuster screws for later adjustment.

44. Valve to Rocker Clearances - Adjustment

1. First check from the specifications that you know which clearances apply to your engine. Clearances are important. If they should be too great the valves will not open as fully as they should. They will also open late and close early. This will affect engine performance. Similarly, if the clearances are too small the valves may not close completely which would result in lack of compression and power. It will cause damage to valves and seatings.

2. The valve clearances should be set for each cylinder when the piston is at the top of its firing stroke. With the engine in the car this may be first found on No. 1 cylinder (right, front) by removing the distributor cap and turning the engine so that the middle of the three notches on the crankshaft pulley (or the left hand one of two) wheel lines up with the centre of the crankcase and the rotor arm points to the notch in the edge of the distributor body.

3. With the engine out of the car and distributor not yet installed the easiest method is to turn the camshaft pulley wheel clockwise up to the mark and at the same time keep a finger over No. 1 cylinder plug hole to check that there is compression. This indicates that you are on the firing stroke.

4. Both valves on No. 1 cylinder may then be adjusted. First slacken the locknut on each rocker arm adjusting screw. Then put a feeler blade of the appropriate thickness between the adjuster and the end of the valve stem and turn the adjusting screw until a light drag can be felt when the blade is moved. Tighten the locknut, holding the adjuster simultaneously with a screwdriver. Check the gap once again.

5. Continue with the subsequent cylinders; the order is 2, 3, 4 and the crankshaft pulley wheel should be rotated ½ turn (180°) anticlockwise. The distributor rotor arm will turn ¼ turn (90°). The valve clearances for No. 2 cylinder may then be set. Continue the

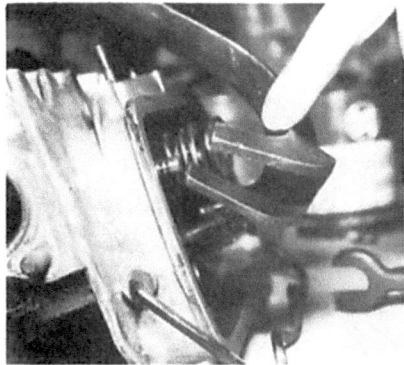

One type of valve spring compressor

Alternative type of valve spring compressor

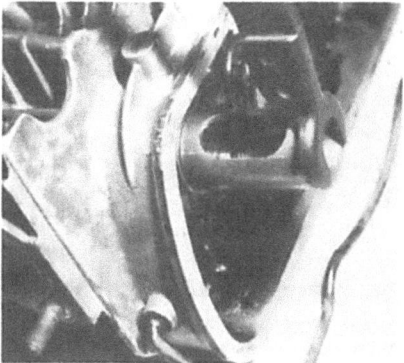

Spring compressor in position

Collet held with a blob of grease (Section 41.6)

Collet placed in position (Section 41.7)

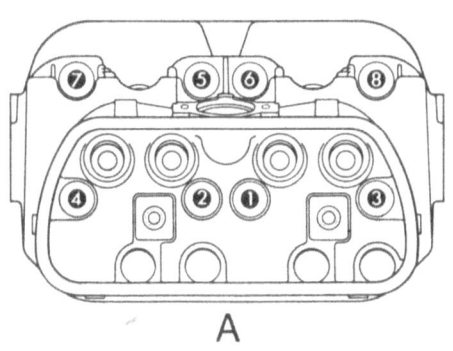

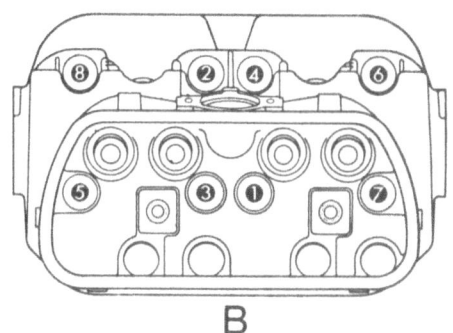

A   B

Fig 1.18. CYLINDER HEAD NUTS — TIGHTENING SEQUENCE (Section 42)
(a) up to 7 lb ft (1 m kg)   (b) up to 23 lb ft (3.2 m kg) or
26.5 lb ft (3.7 m kg) on earlier
30 bhp DIN engines

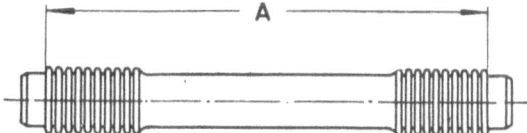

Fig 1.19. Pushrod tube: measurement 'a' not to be less than 181 mm (7.1 inches) prior to installation (Section 42)

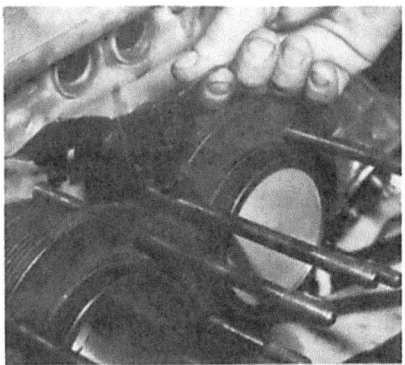

Fitting bottom air deflector plate (Section 42.3)

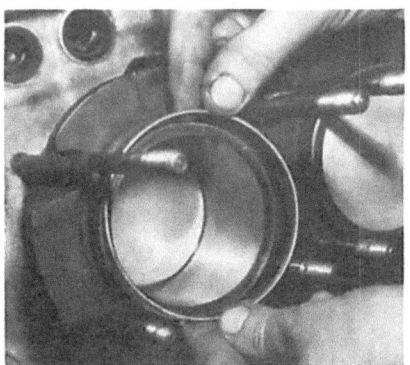

Fitting the copper asbestos sealing ring (Section 42.4)

Positioning the head ready for assembly (Section 42.5)

Feeding the head onto the studs

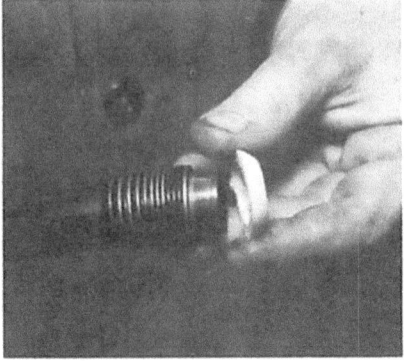

Fitting the pushrod tube seals (Section 42.5)

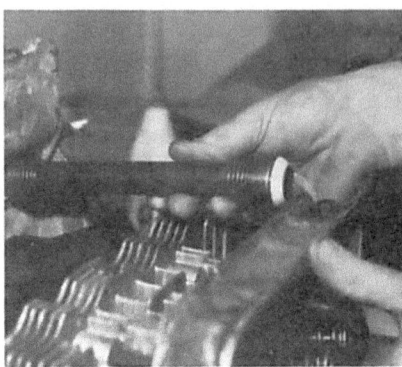

Positioning the pushrods tube for assembly (Section 42.5)

Pushrod tubes in position (Section 42.5)

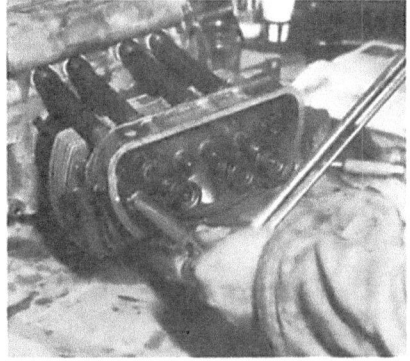

Tightening cylinder head nuts (Section 42.7)

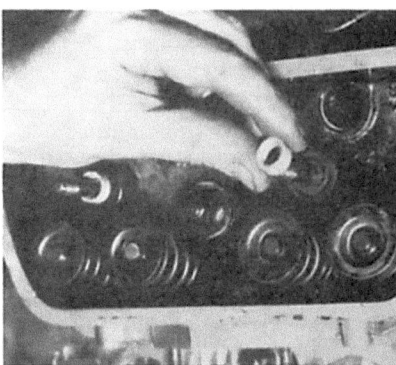

Fitting rocker stud seals (Section 43.2)

Fitting pushrods (Section 43.1)

Fitting rocker shaft assembly (Section 43.2)

Tightening down rocker shaft retaining nuts (Section 43.3)

Adjusting valve to rocker clearance (Section 44)

Clearances adjusted. Cover ready for assembly.

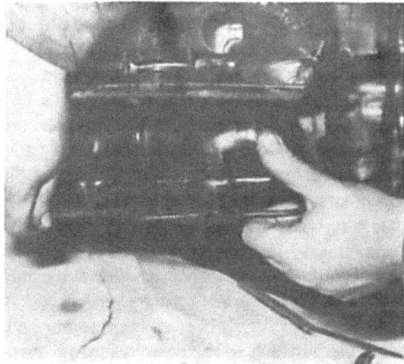

Cover replaced

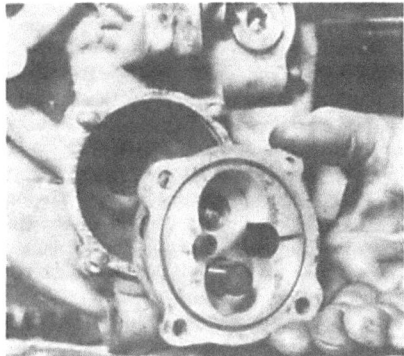

Checking the oil pump body (Section 45.1)

Fitting the 1st pump gear (Section 45.5)

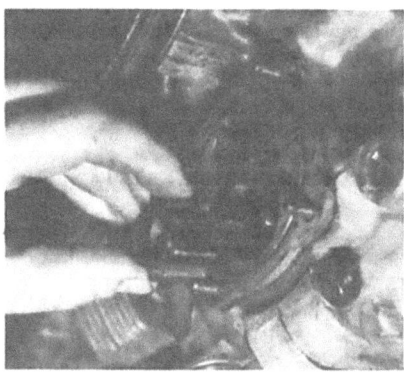

Fitting the 2nd pump gear (Section 45.5)

Fitting the cover plate (Section 45.5)

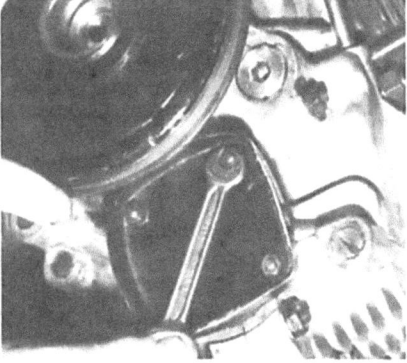

Tightening down the cover plate (Section 45.5)

Finally.do not forget the oil pressure switch

Crankshaft end float shims which must be calculated and inserted before the oil seal is fitted (Section 46.2)

Placing the oil seal (Section 46.3)

Driving the oil seal home (Section 46.3(

same way for cylinders 3 and 4 in that order.

45. Oil Pump - Replacement

1. Make sure that the mating faces of the crankcase and pump body are pefectly clean and unmarked.
2. Using a new gasket fit the pump body over the studs so that the fixed spindle is towards the bottom of the crankcase.
3. Carefully tap the body fully home over the studs, taking care that the gasket does not get trapped incorrectly.
4. When the body is fully home tighten the two crankcase stud nuts, above and below, to the correct torque.
5. Next fit the two gears, turning the driving spindle so that the tongue engages in the slot in the end of the camshaft. With both gears fully home the engine should now be turned through at least two complete revolutions. This ensures that the pump body is correctly centred by the revolving gears. The body should not be disturbed again after this has been done. Fit a new cover plate gasket followed by the cover plate. Replace the four nuts. Whilst tightening up the nuts to the recommended torque of 14 ft/lbs it is worthwhile rotating the engine once or twice more in case the pump body should inadvertently have moved during tightening.

46. Crankshaft Front Oil Seal - Replacement

1. The seal must be replaced (if it has been removed) before the flywheel is fitted. Do not fit it however until the crankshaft end-float has been checked as this involves temporary replacement of the flywheel and the movement of shims.
2. Before fitting the seal, place the necessary circular shims over the crankshaft flange and make sure they are perfectly clean and lightly oiled.
3. Coat the outer metal edge of the new oil seal with jointing compound and place it squarely in position into the crankcase with the inner lip of the seal facing inwards. It may then be tapped squarely home using a flat piece of wood.

47. Flywheel - Replacement

1. If you have taken the flywheel off you will presumably have the same equipment still available for replacing it. You will need it.
2. If you have overhauled the complete engine it will be advisable to check the crankshaft endfloat. This is governed by the gap between the inner face of the flywheel boss and the flange of the rear main bearing shell. Shims are introduced to reduce the gap and these shims need to be fitted before the oil seal. Although it is possible for them to be pushed in past the oil seal it is very difficult to get them out again without buckling or kinking them. If the main bearing shell has been renewed it is most likely that the shims originally fitted will be correct as the main wear takes place on the bearing shell flange. Three shims are always used to make up the required total thickness and they come in six thicknesses (0.24 mm, 0.30 mm, 0.32 mm, 0.34 mm, 0.36 mm, 0.38 mm). Fit two shims to start with, when the thickness of the third may then be calculated.
3. The four dowel pegs should all be placed in the crankshaft flange after having been checked for fitting in both the flange and the flywheel. If any of these should be slack there is considerable risk of the flywheel working loose, despite the tightness of the nut, and this could be disastrous.
4. Over the dowel pegs a metal or paper gasket is placed - fit a new one the same as the one you took off - both are provided in the gasket set. Note the position of your lining up mark made before removal before putting the gasket in position.
5. Grip the flywheel firmly and, with the marks lined up, locate it over the dowel pegs. It is most important for the flywheel to be kept square. If it proves a bit of a strain and a fiddle to get in position find a piece of wood of a thickness suitable to support it at the

right height. Once the flywheel is positively located on the pegs replace the centre bolt and washer and take it up as far as it will go finger tight. Then very carefully tighten the bolt to draw the flywheel on, at the same time keeping it perfectly square by tapping the rim as necessary with a soft faced mallet. If the bolt is tightened with the flywheel out of square the dowel pegs and holes will be seriously damaged.
6. It will be necessary to tighten the centre bolt to at least 75 ft/lbs in order that the crankshaft end float may be accurately read. To do this a clock gauge micrometer is used against the face of the flywheel. The crankshaft is then moved in and out and the float measured. The thickness of the third shim is the measured float less 0.10 mm. Any three shims will do of course provided they add up in total thickness to the sum of the two in position and the calculated third.
7. Once the correct shims have been selected the flywheel should be removed and the three shims put in position and the oil seal fitted as described in Section 46. The flywheel is then replaced in the same fashion.
8. Final tightening of the centre bolt involves a torque of 217 ft/lbs (30 mkg) and the locking of the flywheel for this purpose should be arranged in the same way as for removal. If you do not have a torque spanner capable of 217 ft/lbs, calculate the weight required on the end of the lever extension you have. For example, a 4 ft. (overall) leverage will require 50 lbs weight to give 200 ft/lbs of torque so 55 lbs will give 220 ft/lbs on 4 ft. which is near enough. You can calculate the weight by standing on some scales and applying the force on a 4 ft. lever until your weight has decreased by 55 lbs. It is important to get this torque as accurate as possible because the flywheel may vibrate loose if it is insufficient. Too much, on the other hand, could cause unwanted stresses to be built up.
9. It should also be remembered that the flywheel bolt has a built-in roller bearing which supports the transmission input shaft. This bearing should be in good condition and not over-greased.

48. Engine - Final Assembly

Before the engine is replaced into the car it is normal to replace all the ancillary components. However, as it is not essential and as these various items may be removed whilst the engine is still in the car, they are dealt with in the appropriate chapters. Thus, the replacement of the inlet manifold and exhaust manifold is detailed in Chapter 3 and the fan housing heat exchangers, thermostat and associated 'tinware' (as it is affectionately referred to it!) is covered in Chapter 2. However, various items should be fitted in the correct order otherwise a lot of time may be wasted taking things off again. The list below gives a summary of what that order is although each item is dealt with under the appropriate chapter heading. Assuming that the crankcase oil pump cylinders and heads have been assembled the order is:

Flywheel
Lower rear cover plate
Crankshaft pulley wheel
Oil cooler
Upper cylinder cover plates
Heat exchangers (do not tighten down)
Induction manifold (do not tighten down)
Generator pedestal (where detachable)
Fan housing (do not tighten)
Fan/generator assembly
Silencer assembly (connect up with heat exchangers and induction manifold)
Carburettor
Fuel pump *
Distributor *

*Sequence not important

Those items which are not tightened down immediately are

Fitting the dowel pegs (Section 47.3)

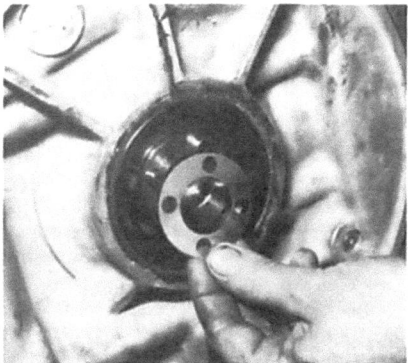

Fitting the gasket (Section 47.4)

Fitting the flywheel (Section 47.5)

Offer up the flywheel carefully (Section 47.5)

Flywheel locked by length of angle iron on two of the clutch mounting bolts

Tightening the flywheel centre bolt. Torque (217 ft lbs)

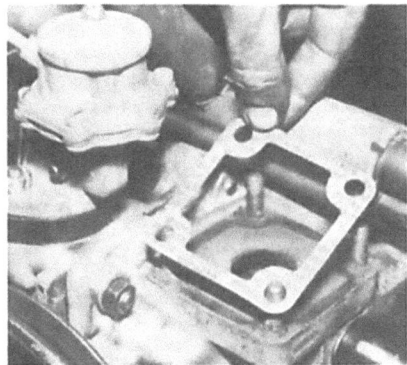

Gasket fitted before generator pedestal (Section 48)

Replace the pedestal (Section 48)

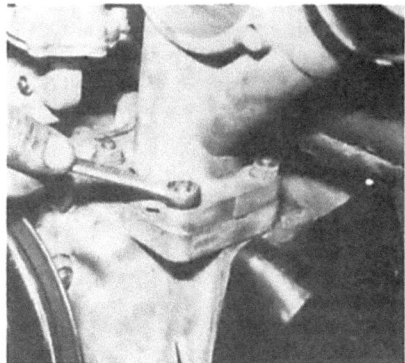

Tightening down the generator pedestal (Section 48)

Replacing the engine (Section 49)

assembled and connected to other components as well as the main body of the engine so it is important to get them all lined up first.

49. Engine - Replacement

1. Engine replacement is best done when the whole unit, including fan housing, has been assembled. However, it is possible to do the replacement before the ancillaries have been refitted. A slight advantage is that the car need be raised at the rear about a foot less. Also the top mounting bolts are more easily seen and accessible. If the starter motor has been taken out it is a good idea to connect the cables and put it in position with the top mounting bolt through the transmission casing before fitting the engine.

2. Note that if you put the engine back with the fan and fan housing off it will be necessary to remove the engine compartment cover to get them on afterwards. Details will be found in the section dealing with fan housing removal in Chapter 2.

3. It is much easier generally if you can raise the engine on a trolly jack as this permits easy forward and backward movement. Otherwise you will have to make a stable platform with conventional jacks as described in the removal procedure.

4. Make sure the clutch has been refitted and the friction disc centralised (see Chapter 5).

5. If the fan housing is already assembled do not forget to fit the front cover plate which clips to the main casing. You will not be able to get this on afterwards.

6. See that the clutch and accelerator cables are correctly in position where they will not get trapped. The accelerator cable should be in an unrestricted straight line and not caught round the clutch cable or anything else. It has to pass through the front cover plate and the fan housing in due course. It should be prevented from getting badly kinked or bent.

7. As soon as the engine has been raised sufficiently to line up the gearbox shaft with the centre of the clutch cover, move it forward into position. The two top mounting bolts should be placed loosely in position but make quite sure that their respective nuts are an easy run on the threads first. This will make tightening up a great deal easier.

8. If difficulty is encountered when trying to mate up the engine to the transmission unit check that it is not tilted out of alignment with the transmission input shaft. A certain amount of sideways juggling may be necessary but if the clutch plate has been centred with reasonable accuracy there should be no difficulty whatsoever.

9. When in position replace the nuts on the lower studs and on the upper bolts. For the latter you will have to feel around the fan housing and this is where preparation by cleaning the bolt threads will pay off. With luck you should be able to tighten the nut without the bolt itself needing to be held with another spanner.

10 Feed the accelerator cable (and choke cable if applicable) through the hole in the cover plate and small hole in the fan housing. (The large holes in the fan housing are for the rubber grommets which support the H.T. leads).

11 With the engine and all ancillaries refitted the following check list should be used as a final check to ensure a first-time start without problems:

    Fuel line connected to fuel pump inlet
    Fuel line connected - pump to carburettor
    Oil drain plug replaced and oil replenished
    L.T. wires connected to coil, automatic choke and regulator box
    H.T. leads connected to coil, distributor and spark plugs
    Spark plugs tight
    Rotor arm and contact points correct
    Throttle cable connected
    Starter motor leads connected (1 heavy, 1 light)
    Two main feed cables connected to clamp terminal on control box
    Battery leads securely and cleanly connected
    All 'tinware' cheese head screws tight
    Generator mounting strap and fan backplate bolts tight
    Fan belt correctly tensioned and pulley bolt tight

12 As soon as the engine fires watch it running for some time - at least until fully warmed up - to ensure nothing is leaking or loose. Check and adjust if necessary the clutch pedal free travel.

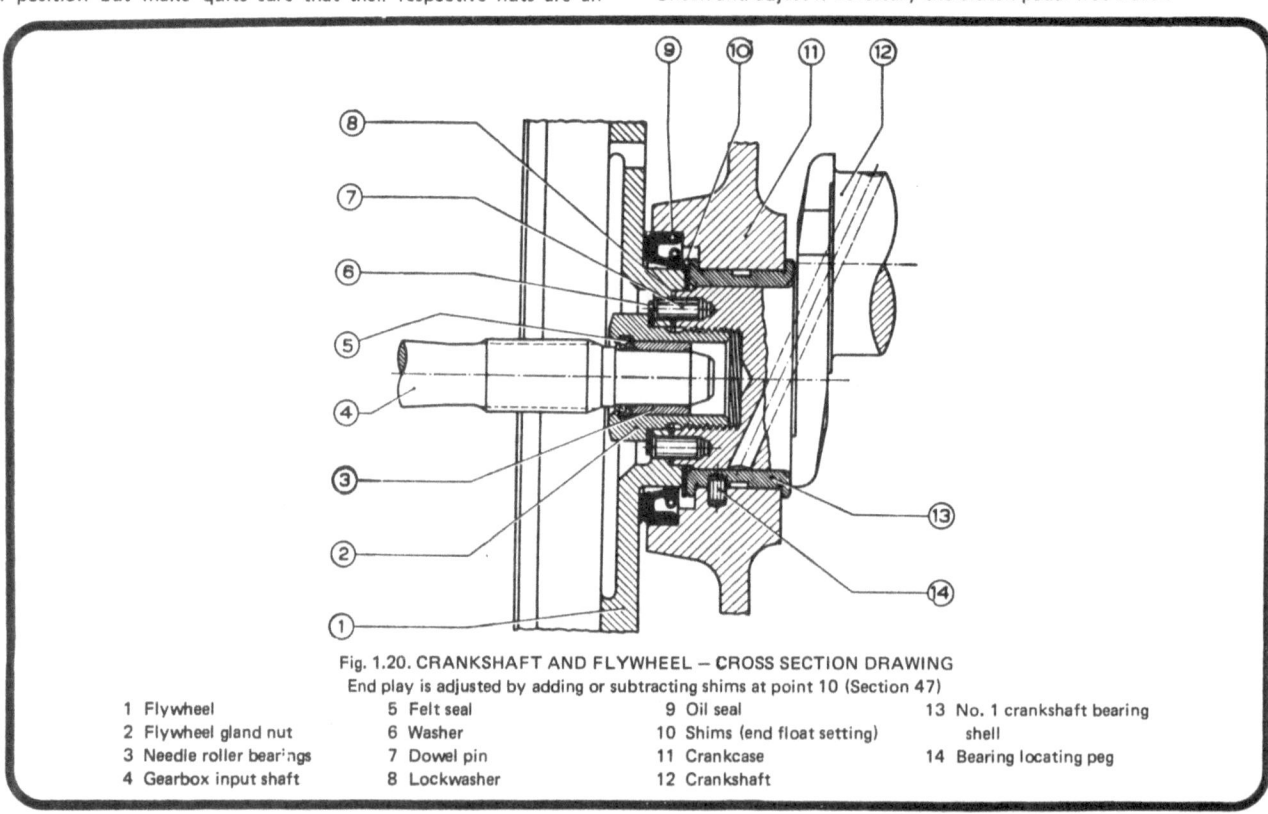

Fig. 1.20. CRANKSHAFT AND FLYWHEEL — CROSS SECTION DRAWING
End play is adjusted by adding or subtracting shims at point 10 (Section 47)

1 Flywheel	5 Felt seal	9 Oil seal	13 No. 1 crankshaft bearing
2 Flywheel gland nut	6 Washer	10 Shims (end float setting)	shell
3 Needle roller bearings	7 Dowel pin	11 Crankcase	14 Bearing locating peg
4 Gearbox input shaft	8 Lockwasher	12 Crankshaft	

Fault Finding Chart - Engine

Symptom	Reason/s	Remedy
Engine will not turn over when starter switch is operated	Flat battery Bad battery connections Bad connections at solenoid switch and/or starter motor	Check that battery is fully charged and that all connections are clean and tight.
	Starter motor jammed	Rock car back and forth with a gear engaged. If ineffective remove starter.
	Defective solenoid	Remove starter and check solenoid.
	Starter motor defective	Remove starter and overhaul.
Engine turns over normally but fails to fire and run	No spark at plugs	Check ignition system according to procedures given in Chapter 4.
	No fuel reaching engine	Check fuel system according to procedures given in Chapter 3.
	Too much fuel reaching the engine (flooding)	Check the fuel system as above.
Engine starts but runs unevenly and misfires	Ignition and/or fuel system faults	Check the ignition and fuel systems as though the engine had failed to start.
	Incorrect valve clearances	Check and reset clearances.
	Burnt out valves	Remove cylinder heads and examine and overhaul as necessary.
	Worn out piston rings	Remove cylinder heads and examine pistons and cylinder bores. Overhaul as necessary.
Lack of power	Ignition and/or fuel system faults	Check the ignition and fuel systems for correct ignition timing and carburettor settings.
	Incorrect valve clearances	Check and reset the clearances.
	Burnt out valves Blown cylinder head gasket	Remove cylinder heads and examine and overhaul as necessary.
	Worn out piston rings	Remove cylinder heads and examine pistons and cylinder bores. Overhaul as necessary.
Excessive oil consumption	Oil leaks from crankshaft oil seal, rocker cover gasket, oil pump, sump gasket, sump plug washer, oil cooler	Identify source of leak and renew seal as appropriate.
	Worn piston rings or cylinder bores resulting in oil being burnt by engine Smoky exhaust is an indication	Fit new rings or rebore cylinders and fit new pistons, depending on degree of wear.
	Worn valve guides and/or defective valve stem seals	Remove cylinder heads and recondition valve stem bores and valves and seals as necessary.
Excessive mechanical noise from engine	Wrong valve to rocker clearances	Adjust valve clearances.
	Worn crankshaft bearings Worn cylinders (piston slap)	Inspect and overhaul where necessary.
Unusual vibration	Misfiring on one or more cylinders	Check ignition system.
	Loose mounting bolts	Check tightness of bolts and condition of flexible mountings.

NOTE: When investigating starting and uneven running faults do not be tempted into snap diagnosis. Start from the beginning of the check procedure and follow it through. It will take less time in the long run. Poor performance from an engine in terms of power and economy is not normally diagnosed quickly. In any event the ignition and fuel systems must be checked first before assuming any further investigation needs to be made.

Chapter 2 Cooling, heating and exhaust systems

Contents

Specifications

Air volume	530 litres (19 cubic feet) per second at 3,800 r.p.m.
Thermostat opens at	65 - 70ºC (149 - 158ºF)
Fan to cover plate clearance	1.5 mm (.060 inch)

Torque Wrench Settings

Fan securing nut	43 lb/ft (6.0 mkg)
Fan/generator drive pulley nut	43 lb/ft (6.0 mkg)

1. General Description

One of the most famous and well known features of the Volkswagen engine throughout its life has been the fact that it is air-cooled. The advantages are obvious - none of the problems and cost of maintaining a water cooling system with the attendant problems of extreme temperatures. There are certain disadvantages of an air cooled system however - there is greater engine noise, more engine power used to drive the cooling fan and a less precise control of engine temperatures. Air cooled engines are not at their best in dense traffic in hot weather. Great care must also be taken to ensure that the lubrication system is not neglected as the engine oil plays a more significant part in engine cooling.

The Volkswagen system is neat and simple. A multibladed turbo fan is mounted on the shaft which drives the generator. It rotates in a sheet steel, semi-circular housing, drawing in air through the fan centre and directing it down to each pair of finned cylinders. The cylinders are shrouded above with carefully designed sheet steel covers. Below each pair of cylinders a contoured deflection plate is mounted centrally. Thus the air is directed over the full surface area of the cylinder cooling fins.

In order to shorten the warming up time a thermostat is mounted below the right hand pair of cylinders. This is a conventional bellows type and it operates a restriction on the through flow of air when the engine is cold. On early models (pre 1962) this consisted of an annular ring mounted in the fan housing air inlet. As the engine warms up, so the ring moves out permitting progressively more cold air to be drawn in. On later models this ring was superseded by control flaps within the fan housing.

The car heating system is linked with the cooling system. In addition to the cooling air circuit there are also two heat exchangers mounted one below each pair of cylinders. Basically these are sheet steel 'tanks' through which the exhaust pipe of each front cylinder passes. Air passing round the pipe inside the steel duct can be directed to the car interior.

Early models (those with the annular ring thermostat control) had heat exchangers which directed the warm air from the cylinders through them when two flaps were operated. This air then passed into the car. When the heater was not required the air passed straight out to the rear. Later models (flat thermostat control) were designed so that 'clean air' (i.e. air that had not passed round the cylinders first) was directed through the heat exchangers when required. This air was taken by two large hoses direct from the fan housing and these hoses are very obvious distinguishing marks for this kind of engine. On these engines the hot air from the cylinders always exhausts straight down to the road.

It will be appreciated that the condition of that part of the exhaust system within the heat exchangers must always be in excellent order. Any leaks will result in exhaust fumes being forced directly into the car when the heater is in operation. Also the condition and fit of all the covers and shrouds is important. Sealing strips and grommets must all be properly positioned. If air leaks out then the cooling capacity is reduced.

2. Routine Maintenance

1. The fan housing and cover plates are held in position by cheese head screws which should be checked for tightness each month. Replace missing screws without delay.
2. Check the heat exchangers for security and if one is inadvertently damaged (they are completely exposed) it should be put right without delay.
3. Each month check the fan belt tension. The fan it drives on this car is indispensible even for short distances (unlike a water cooled engine) and if it slips or breaks without being rectified severe damage will soon be caused. Always carry a spare fan belt in the car.
4. Check that the spark plug lead grommets are in good condition and correctly fitted. Air leaks reduce the cooling efficiency.

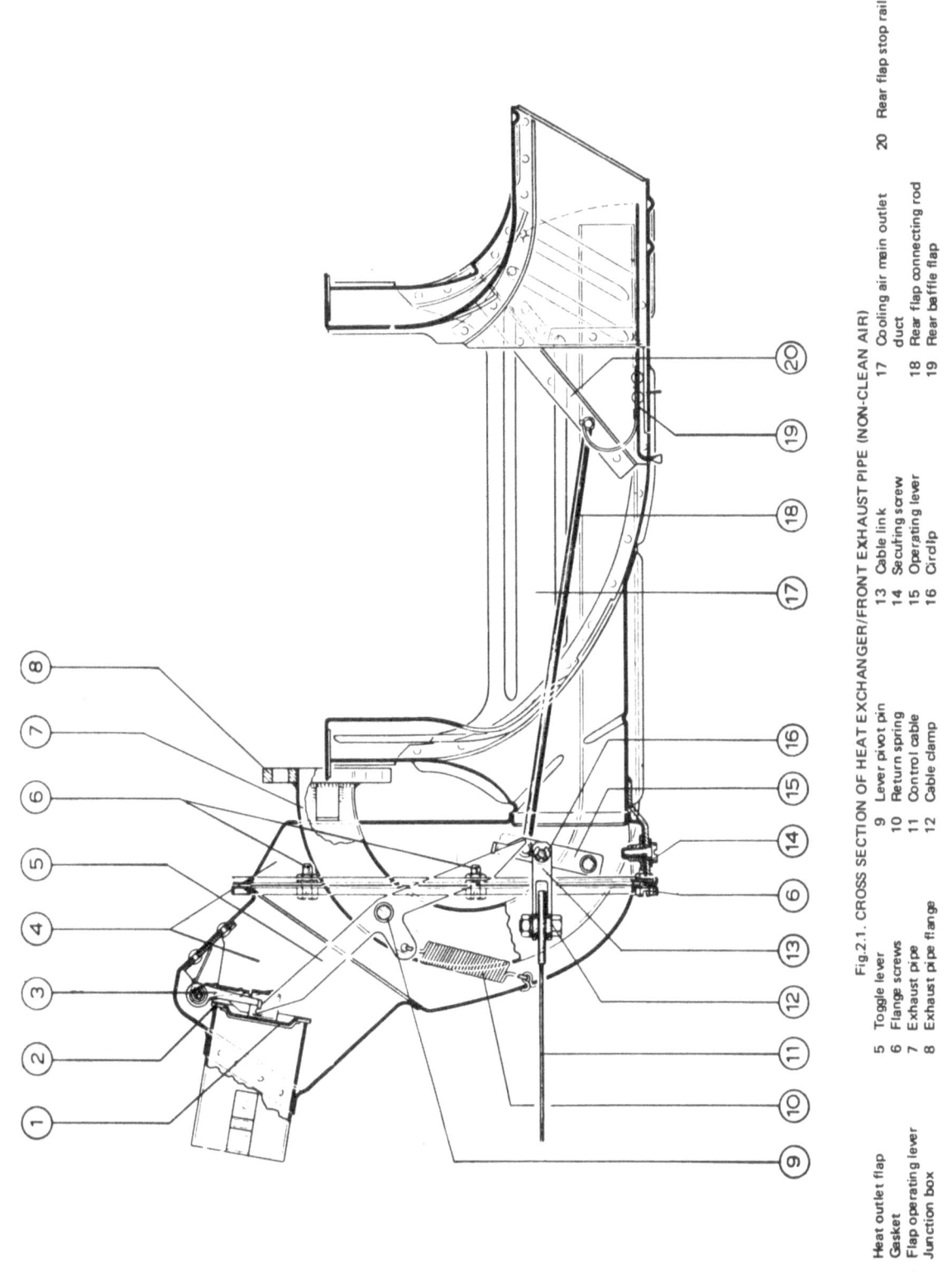

Fig.2.1. CROSS SECTION OF HEAT EXCHANGER/FRONT EXHAUST PIPE (NON-CLEAN AIR)

1 Heat outlet flap
2 Gasket
3 Flap operating lever
4 Junction box

5 Toggle lever
6 Flange screws
7 Exhaust pipe
8 Exhaust pipe flange

9 Lever pivot pin
10 Return spring
11 Control cable
12 Cable clamp

13 Cable link
14 Securing screw
15 Operating lever
16 Circlip

17 Cooling air main outlet duct
18 Rear flap connecting rod
19 Rear baffle flap
20 Rear flap stop rail

3. Removal of Cooling and Heating System Components - General

It is more difficult to dismantle the cooling and heating systems with the engine in the car than after the engine has been removed. Routine overhaul should coincide with engine overhaul but there may be occasions when it will be necessary to remove components from the system without disturbing the engine, for example:

    a) The fan and fan housing may be removed to service a damaged fan, for generator overhaul, or to give access to the oil cooler.

    b) The heat exchanger may be leaking and need renewal.

4. Fan Belt - Adjustment, Removal and Replacement

1. The Volkswagen fan belt needs more regular inspection than a water cooled engine fan belt usually gets because if it slips or breaks the consequences are more serious more quickly.

2. Adjustment takes a little more time than usual. There is no tension pulley. The pulley on the generator is split into two and the gap between the two halves governs the effective diameter. The gap is regulated by spacer rings. If the belt is too slack the gap between the two halves is decreased by removing one or more spacer rings. Spare spacers are fitted to the outside of the pulley.

3. The belt is correctly tensioned when firm thumb pressure on the belt midway between the two pulleys causes a deflection of 12-18 mm (½ - ¾ inch).

4. To remove the belt and split the pulley, lock the pulley first with a screwdriver in the edge of the inner flange against the top generator bolt. Remove the nut and clamp ring. The outer half of the pulley can then be separated from the inner half. To tighten the fan belt remove one spacer from between and then replace everything (with the moved spacer now on the outside of the pulley) and try the tension again. Take care when refitting the outer half of the pulley to get it square. It helps if the engine is rotated. This will get the bolt into its 'running' position. The engine is easily rotated with a spanner on the crankshaft pulley wheel. Continue removing spacers until the tension is correct. If all the spacers are out and the belt is still slack it is over-stretched and must be renewed.

5. Check the tension of a new belt after a few hundred miles running as initial stretch may need taking up.

5. Fan - Removal and Replacement

1. The fan is mounted on the generator shaft and in order to remove it the generator must first be taken off.

2. Remove the fan belt (Section 4).

3. Disconnect the battery to prevent accidental short circuits and then disconnect the wires from the control box mounted on the top of the generator. Tag the wires so that you know where to replace them.

4. The generator is clamped to the pedestal by means of a metal strap. Undo the clamping bolt at the right and disengage the strap. If the engine is out of the car it is a good idea to slacken the fan nut before undoing this strap. The locking notch in the fan belt pulley can then be used to hold the shaft whilst the nut is slackened off. Put the fan belt pulley back on if you have already taken it off.

5. Undo the four bolts holding the fan cover plate to the fan housing.

6. Remove the carburettor air cleaner and it should then be possible to lift the whole assembly out. If the carburettor prevents the fan from coming right out, undo the two carburettor mounting nuts so that it may be moved to one side. This may be necessary on some models. Do not disconnect the carburettor control connections as it will not be necessary to move it very far to one side. Whatever happens do not bend anything. On early models which have the intake ring on the front of the fan housing it is best to undo the clamp nut on the shaft so that the ring can be moved out of the way. If there is still difficulty undo the two side screws securing the

fan housing so that it may be juggled about to aid fan removal.

7. With the assembly out of the car, refit the fan belt pulley and clamp the generator body in a vice. The pulley is needed so that you can use the notch to lock the shaft whilst the fan nut is undone.

8. Once the nut has been removed the lock washer may be drawn off followed by the fan. Behind the fan is the thrust washer spacer washers and fan hub which is keyed to the shaft.

9. The fan cover plate is held to the generator by two nuts on the ends of the two generator through bolts.

10 When reassembling the fan to the generator shaft the procedure is reversed but there are several important points to watch.

    a) If the fan is being refitted after a generator overhaul be quite sure that the spacer collar on the generator shaft (behind the keyway) is in position. If it is missing there will be nothing to prevent the fan hub being forced right up to the end cover and jamming the shaft so that it will not turn.

    b) Make sure that the fan backplate is mounted to the two generator through bolts, together with the central reinforcing plate, the correct way round.

    c) Fit the Woodruff key followed by the fan hub with the flats on the hub away from the backplate.

    d) If you can remember the number fit the same quantity of shims onto the hub followed by the thrust washer, main fan, lock washer and nut.

    e) Tighten the nut sufficiently to ensure that the fan hub is fully home on the shaft and measure the gap between the fan and backplate which should be 1.5 - 1.8 mm (.060 - .070 ins.). If the gap is wrong remove or add shims on the hub as necessary. Spare shims should be kept behind the lockwasher of the main shaft nut.

    f) Tighten the fan nut to the correct torque of 43 lb/ft (6 mkg) using a screwdriver in the pulley slot to lock the shaft.

11 Replacement of the generator/fan assembly is a reversal of the removal procedure. Take care not to distort anything and get the clamp strap and fan backplate bolts all in position before any are tightened. See that the strap fits the contours of the pedestal bracket as before. When all is tightened spin the fan to ensure that nothing is touching. If it is it could be due to the generator not being set fully forward on the pedestal. Otherwise the fan housing is not seated correctly or something is bent.

12 Reset the thermostatically controlled fan inlet cowl if it has been disturbed for any reason.

6. Fan Housing - Removal and Replacement

1. With the engine installed the engine compartment cover must be removed before the fan housing can be lifted out. The hinges also must be taken off. It is easiest to remove the lid from the hinges first and then the hinges from the body. It may seem unnecessary work but it makes for much easier replacement later. Mark the hinge positions before slackening off the bolts. This saves a lot of fiddling about later.

2. On models fitted with the annular ring air control (pre 'clean-air') reach around to the front of the fan housing (front!) and there you will be able to feel the circular ring and, at the bottom the flange by which it is held to the thermostat link rod bracket. Two 10 mm bolts hold the ring in position and these should be slackened off (see Section 8).

3. On later models fitted with the control flaps inside the fan housing, it will be necessary to remove the two hoses running from the fan housing to the heat exchangers. On later models it will also be necessary to take off the lower warm air duct under the cylinders by removing the securing screws. This will reveal the thermostat which must be detached as the link rod is attached to the control flaps in the fan housing. To disconnect the thermostat undo the hexagon headed bolt holding it to the mounting bracket. Then grip the bellows and unscrew it from the rod which runs up between the cylinders.

View of left side cylinders upper air duct in relation to engine (Section 1)

Pulley split showing belt position and spacers (Section 4.2)

Pulley assembled (Section 4.4)

Tightening the pulley nut 43 lbs ft torque (Section 4.4)

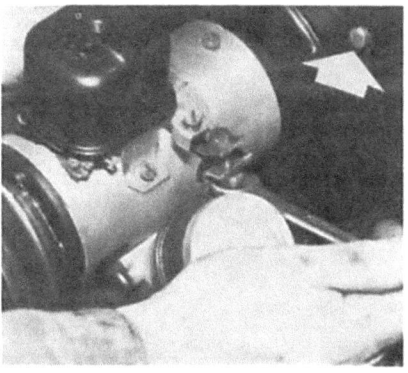

Tightening the generator securing strap. Arrow indicates fan cover plate securing bolt (Section 5)

Make sure the strap fits the generator contours (Section 5)

Fitting the fan assembly (Section 5)

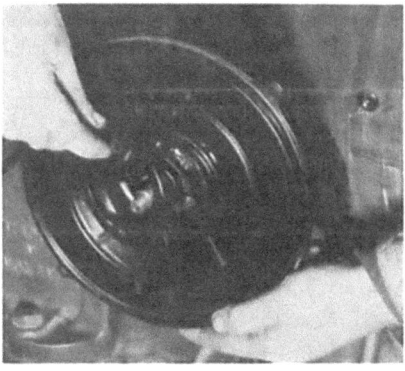

Replacing fan backplate (Section 5)

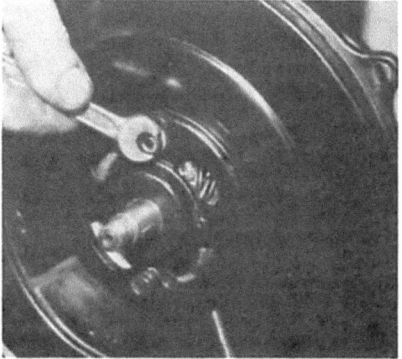

Tightening the bolts holding the backplate

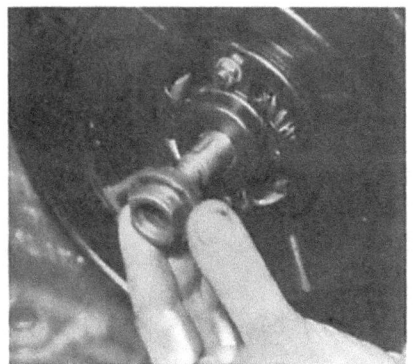

Fitting the fan hub (Section 5.9)

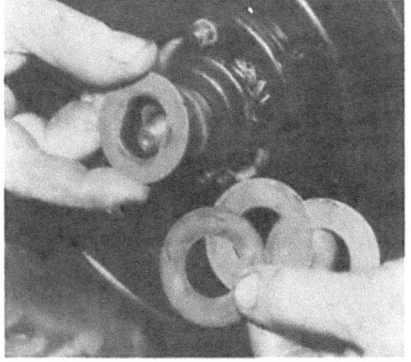

Positioning shims and thrust washer (Section 5.9)

Next fit the fan (Section 5.9)

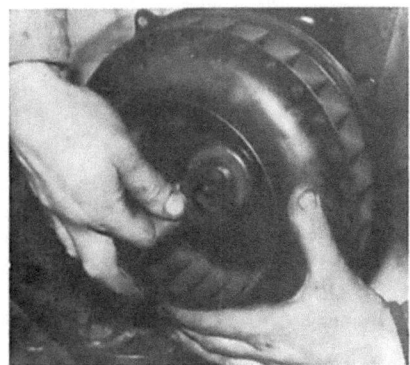

Fit the lock washer and nut and tighten the nut

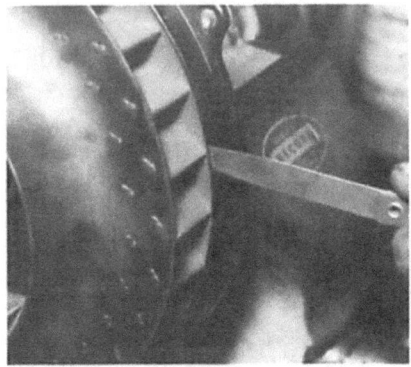

Measure the gap between the fan and the backplate. It should be 1.5 to 1.8 mm. (Section 5.10c)

Tighten the fan nut to a torque of 43 lb ft. (Section 5.10f)

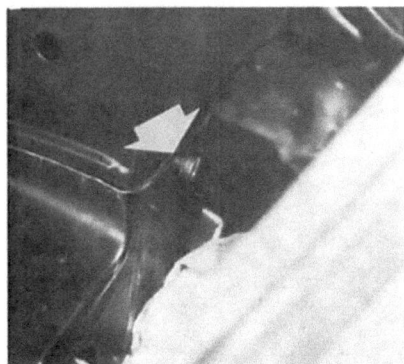

Right hand side securing screw for fan housing (Section 6.3)

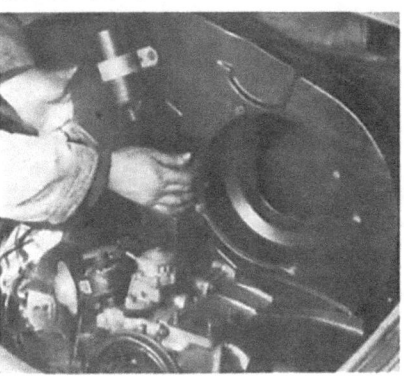

Removing the fan housing, engine in the car

Removing the fan housing, engine out of car. Generator and pedestal, carburettor and manifold not shown to give clearer picture

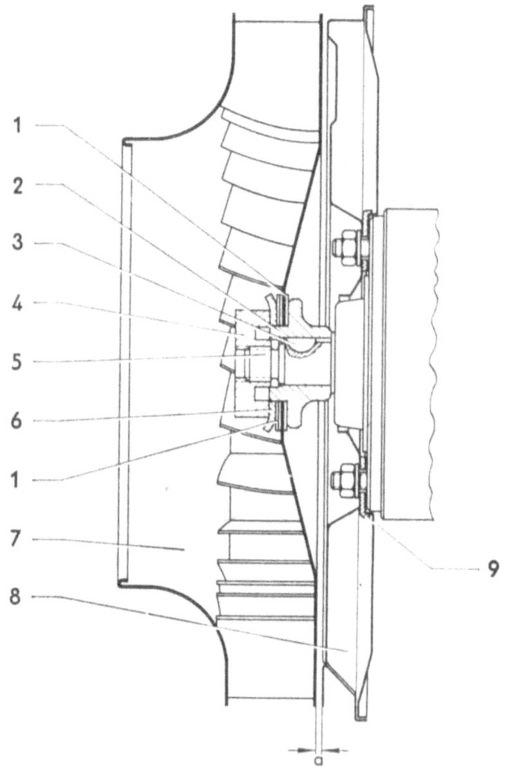

Fig. 2.2. CROSS SECTION DRAWING
OF COOLING FAN

1 Spacer shims   6 Dished washer
2 Fan hub   7 Fan
3 Woodruff key   8 Fan backplate
4 Securing nut   9 Reinforcing plate
5 Shaft

Dimension (A) = 1.8 mm (.070 inch) approx

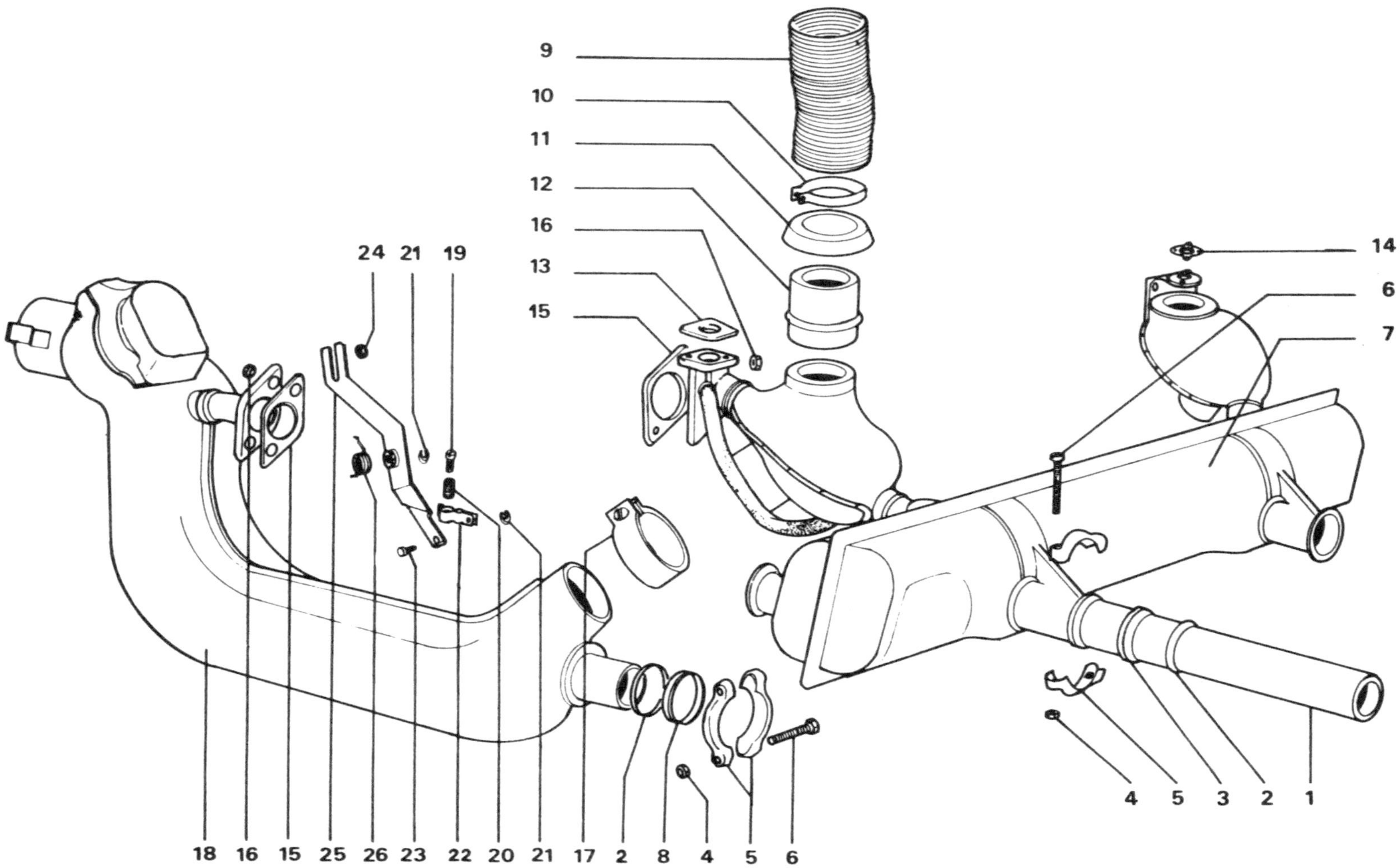

Fig. 2.3. HEATER EXCHANGER AND EXHAUST SYSTEM
('CLEAN-AIR' MODELS)

1 Tail pipe
2 Retaining ring
3 Seal
4 Self-locking nut
5 Clamp
6 Clamp bolt
7 Silencer
8 Seal
9 Air inlet hose
10 Hose clip
11 Grommet
12 Connecting pipe
13 Gasket - pre-heater pipe (left)
14 Gasket - pre-heater pipe (right)
15 Gasket - exhaust pipe flange
16 Self-locking nut
17 Clamp
18 Heat exchanger
19 Bolt
20 Pin
21 Circlip
22 Heater cable link
23 Pin
24 Clamp washer
25 Heater flap lever (left)
26 Lever return spring (left)

4. Remove the generator and fan assembly as described in the previous section.

5. There are two screws holding the fan housing to the upper cylinder covers - one at each side. Remove these and the housing can be lifted up and out.

6. Once the fan housing is loose the thermostat control ring (which was slackened off earlier) can be disengaged and lifted out. Do not force anything because the oil cobler projects up inside the housing and any strain could damage it.

7. Whenever the fan housing is removed - for whatever reason - the opportunity should be taken to examine the condition and operation of the air flaps inside. If these stick shut at any time the engine will overheat. If they are in a very poor condition and the expense of renewing them does not appeal, the best thing to do is remove them altogether. Their function is merely to shorten the warming up time and only in extremely low temperatures (well below freezing) is the engine likely to run over cold. The same applies to the annular ring air control on earlier models.

8 Replacement of the fan housing is a reversal of these procedures and all the joints of the ducting should fit neatly to prevent leakage of air. On later models which involved removal of the thermostat the air duct flaps must be reset as described in Section 9. The annular ring type should not need to be reset but it should be checked nevertheless. Make sure the annular ring is in position before the fan is finally secured. Otherwise you will not be able to get it between the fan housing and bulkhead.

---

7. Heat Exchangers - Removal and Replacement

1. On the early models particularly (pre 'clean air') deterioration of the outer shroud can lead only to rattles and inefficient heating but deterioration of the inner exhaust pipe section will be dangerous.

2. First disconnect the warm air duct hose from the front of the heat exchanger underneath the car. It can simply be pulled off.

3. Disconnect the control wire from the operating lever by undoing the clamping screw in the toggle. This will probably be rusty and dirty so use plenty of penetrating oil otherwise you could break something which would just add to your repair list.

4. On early models the heat exchanger and lower warm air duct are a single assembly but on the 'clean air' models the exchanger is to one side and attached to the warm air duct plate by two screws. These should be taken out.

5. The front exhaust pipe flange should then be released by undoing the two nuts; and the rear exhaust connection by undoing the clamp. On later models the heat exchanger inlet duct is clipped to the main exhaust silencer unit also as this has a small heat exchanger section on it too.

6. By moving the heat exchanger forward off the front exhaust studs it will then be possible to lower and remove it.

7. Before replacing a heat exchanger it should be examined carefully for signs of splits or severe corrosion or rusting. If it is damaged due to impact but otherwise sound it might be worthwhile having it straightened and/or welded. Otherwise fit a new one. Make sure also that the faces of the exhaust pipe flanges are perfectly flat. If they are distorted, steps must be taken to remedy the situation as any leak would be serious. Always fit new gaskets.

8. The replacement of the heat exchanger is a reversal of the removal procedure. Make sure that when it is offered up all the joints fit true and flush before the nuts and clamps are tightened. If the nuts and clamps have to be used to force the unit into position, rather than hold it in position, stresses will be set up and something will break sooner or later. Certainly sooner than it would normally.

---

8. Thermostat and Controls - Removal, Replacement and Adjustments

1. The thermostat controls flaps which restrict the air flow but do not completely obstruct it. If it should fail to operate therefore the engine will only be noticeably overheated in extreme conditions of high temperatures or hard use. The only indications of overheating are either a noticeable fall off in performance or the oil warning light indicating an exceptionally low oil pressure. It is essential to stop immediately either of these conditions appear as the engine will already have reached an undesirable state and will be seriously damaged if allowed to continue.

2. On the earlier models (pre 'clean air') with the air control ring in the front of the fan housing the position of the ring when the engine is hot will indicate whether there is anything wrong. The edge of the ring should be at least ¾ of an inch away from the fan housing at the top when the engine is warm. This gap can be judged by passing the hand round to the front of the housing and feeling it with the fingers. If the gap is wrong it can be altered by slackening the clamp nut and bolt which connects the operating lever to the regulator ring pivot shaft. This is also in front of the fan housing near the right hand lower edge. When the nut is slackened the regulator ring can be moved. The nut should then be tightened when the gap is correct. If the setting is done when the engine is cold the rubber buffer on the ring should just touch the fan housing. Having set the ring correctly, either at the warm of cold position, it is then necessary to see whether it moves as it should when the engine temperature changes. If it does not then the thermostat bellows must be at fault. If it is not possible to take immediate action then the regulator ring can be set in the open position so the engine will not overheat. It will merely take longer to warm up.

3. On the 'clean air' models, which have the flaps on each side at the base of the fan housing, any adjustment has to be made at the thermostat and mounting bracket.

4. Access to the thermostat is by removing the right hand heat exchanger on earlier models (explained in Section 7). Once this is done the bolt which secures the thermostat to the bracket can be removed. The thermostat itself may then be unscrewed from the operating rod. Refitting is the reverse of this procedure.

5. On the 'clean air' models the thermostat is accessible once the right hand lower air duct plate is removed. To adjust the flaps first remove the bolt securing the bellows to the bracket. Then make sure that the bellows is screwed fully on to the operating rod. Slacken the bolt which holds the bracket to the crankcase and then push the bellows unit upwards so that the flaps are fully open. The top of the bracket loop should now just touch the top of the bellows and the bracket bolt may be tightened. Then replace the bolt securing the bellows to the bracket (which will involve pulling the bellows down and closing the flaps if the engine is cold). If the thermostat is suspected of malfunctioning a check can be made on its length (excluding the projecting screwed bosses at each end) which should be at least 46 mm (1.8 inch) at a temperature (in water) of 65-70°C (150-158°F) or more. If you wish to set the thermostat so that the flaps are always open (i.e. if the bellows do not work and you have no immediate replacement) push the bellows and bracket up together into the 'flaps open' position and clamp the bracket at the raised position.

6. If the flaps themselves are suspected of jamming or being out of position on their spindles then the fan housing must first be taken off as described in Section 6. Both flap housings can be removed from the fan housing together once the eight securing screws are removed and the return spring unhooked. Examine the flaps and spindles for security and ability to stay in position. Once again, if there should be some doubt and the flaps are likely to jam shut they can be removed completely.

---

9. Heater Controls

1. As previously explained the car is heated by ducting hot air from exchangers surrounding the exhaust pipes. On the early models (pre 'clean air') each heat exchanger was equipped with two flaps. The two flaps were linked on a common control arm so that when operated the upper flap near the front outlet opened and the larger rear flap closed. Hot air from the engine and around the exhaust

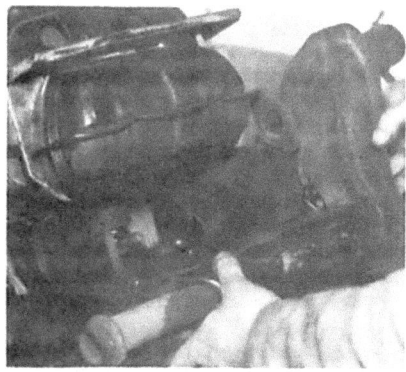

The right hand heat exchanger lowered away from the engine (early type). Note thermostat bellows. (Section 7)

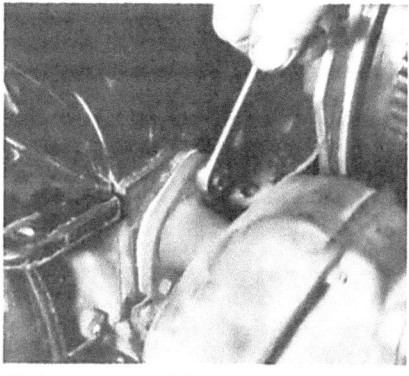

Tightening nut of front exhaust pipe flange (Section 7)

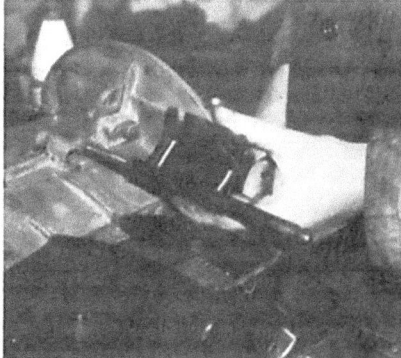

Fitting pivot for fan cowl (Section 8)

Tightening pivot of fan cowl shaft (Section 8)

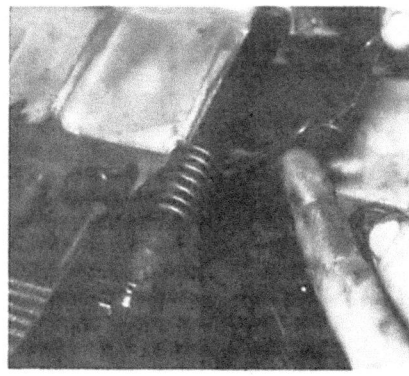

Return spring fitted (Section 8)

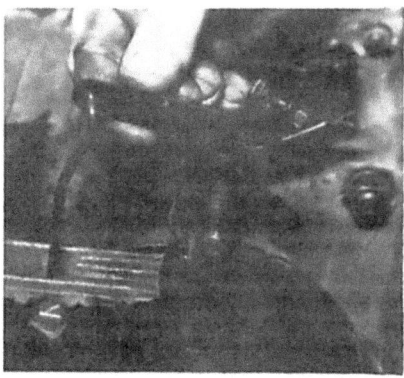

Fitting operating arms to shaft (Section 8)

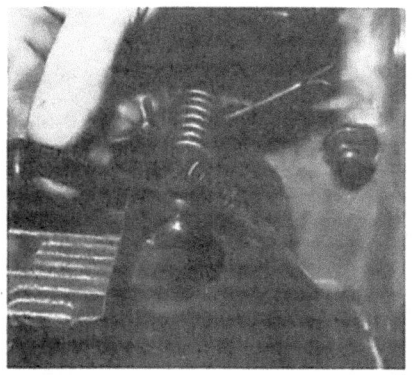

Operating arm fitted in correct position (Section 8)

Offering bellows to end of operating rod (Section 8)

Bellows positioned in bracket (early pre-clean air model) (Section 8)

Final assembly of bellows (Section 8)

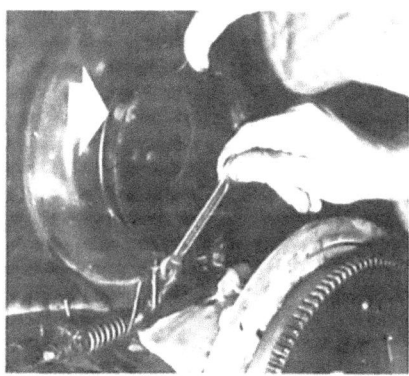

Mounting control cowl on bracket

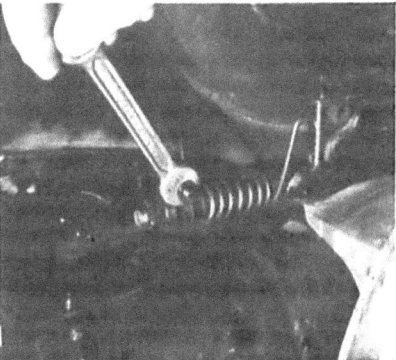

Tightening operating arm clamp bolt on shaft after setting cowl position. Must be done blind when engine is in the car

pipes was then directed straight into the car. The later 'clean air' type has only the single forward flap. When hot air from the exchanger is required the flap is opened so that the air pressure from the fan housing will carry it into the car. The cooling air from the engine is discharged separately and is no longer used for heating. To compensate for the reduced heat available there is a small section of heat exchanger also fitted to the rear cylinder exhaust pipes - unlike the early ones - which only took heat from the engine and pipes of the front cylinders alone.

2. Should the heater efficiency drop the first thing to check is the operation of the flap control wires and the flaps. This can be done on the early models by looking into the heat exchanger rear outlets to see if the flaps move when the control knob (or lever) is operated. If one (or both) does not move check the control wires. These are connected to the flap operating arm on the side of the heat exchanger by means of a ferrule on the end of the wire clamped into a clevis. If the wire is broken on either side undo both. The clevis pin clamp screws are usually rusty so lubricate them well beforehand.

3. Once slackened the wire ends may be pulled out from the pins. Inside the car unscrew the knurled screw under the control knob and when clear the whole assembly and the wires can be drawn out.

4. By pushing out the pin from the control knob cylinder the end loop of the old control wire may be disengaged and the new one fitted.

5. Feed the ends of the new cable into the tube - they will separate into two further tubes and can be readily pushed through. Make sure that they are greased well. Check when replacing the cylinder end that the slot engages in the internal peg and then slide the cylinder home and screw up the knurled cap.

6. It is a fiddle getting the ends of the wires reconnected at the heater end. This is due to the fact that they are not very flexible. It is much easier therefore if someone else is available to operate the control knob while you are doing this. The ends can then be guided easily into the holes in the clevis pins.

7. When both ends are in position but not clamped, turn the control knob to the fully closed (cold) position and then clamp them. Operate the control and see that the flaps operate properly.

---

10. Exhaust System - Removal, Inspection and Replacement

1. The Volkswagen exhaust and silencer unit is a complex unit made of heavy gauge material, which is an expensive item to replace. The silencer and tail pipe assembly is connected at three places on each side and on the later 'clean air' models (see Chapter 2) at five points on each side. These are (on each side):

a) to the exhaust pipe coming from the front cylinder through the heat exchanger (clamp)

b) to the exhaust port in the heat for the rear cylinder (flange)

c) the pre-heater pipe of the inlet manifold (flange) and additionally for the 'clean air' version

d) to the heat exchanger (clip)

e) to the air inlet hoses from the fan housing

The 'clean air' exhaust manifold has a small heat exchanger shrouding the upper pipes which were not incorporated in the earlier models.

2. To remove the exhaust/silencer unit first remove the rear engine cover plate, all the nuts, bolts and clamps which attach it at the six or ten locations. If some of the underside nuts and bolts are badly rusted buy new ones before attempting to get the old ones off. It is quite usual for them to break or need cutting. A complete set of the gaskets should also be acquired (two exhaust flange, two inlet manifold flange, two clamp rings) before disturbing the unit.

3. Once all the connections are loosened the silencer can be drawn backwards off the studs of the cylinder head rear exhaust port and lowered to the ground.

4. Depending on the reason for removal subsequent inspection and repair will have to be judged in the light of the seriousness of deterioration. The unit is made of heavier gauge material than more conventional exhaust systems. Thus small holes or cracks in the silencer may be patched and welded in the knowledge that the repair will last longer than on some other systems. This does not apply to the actual pipes leading into the silencer. If these are unserviceable repair is likely to be less successful. The flanges and connection to the other exhaust pipe must be examined for pitting, distortion or fractures. The mating faces of the flanges can be filed flat if necessary. The gaskets are thick enough to take up minor variations.

5. Before replacing the unit offer it up into position so that the line up of all the connecting points can be made without having to strain anything. If strain is necessary to make any connection then the likelihood of a fracture developing is greatly increased. It is worthwhile taking some trouble to heat and straighten any twisted parts.

6. Replacement of the system is a reversal of the removal procedure. First put new gaskets over the studs at the rear exhaust ports, offer up the unit and put the nuts on the studs enough to prevent it falling off. Then assemble the lower gasket rings and clamps loosely - but sufficiently tight to prevent them becoming dislodged. Then fit the pre-heater pipe gaskets in position and replace the bolts loosely. Finally where appropriate, assemble the heat exchanger connecting clips.

7. The pipe clamp and flange bolts and nuts should now be progressively tightened a little at a time until fully tight. Do not overdo the tightening on any of them. Finally tighten the heat exchanger clips (if fitted). After running the engine for some miles, so that it has had the opportunity to heat up and cool down a few times, recheck the connections for tightness.

Inserting the ends of the heater control wires (Section 9)

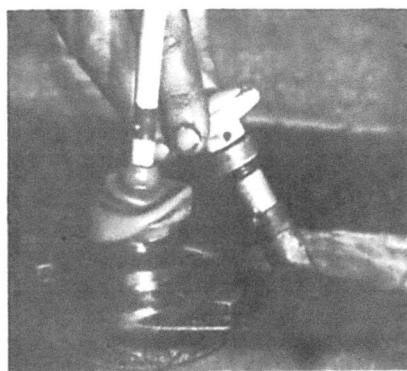
Refitting regulator sleeve and knobs (Section 9)

Exhaust system. Offering up the exhaust, engine in car (Section 10)

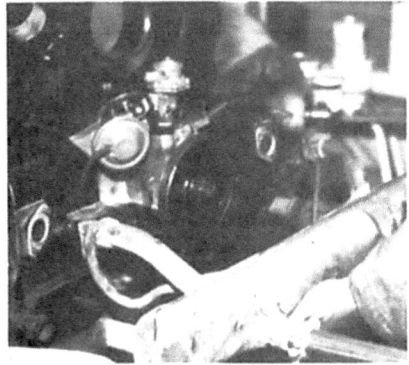
Offering up the exhaust, engine out of car (Section 10)

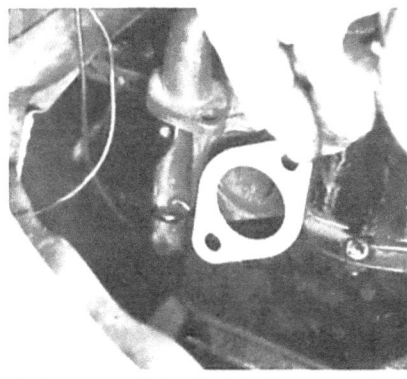
Exhaust manifold. Positioning rear exhaust flange gasket (Section 10)

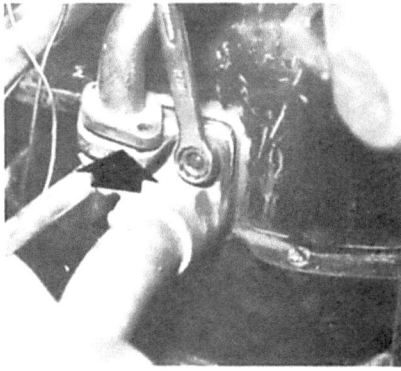
Tightening up securing nut. Pre-heater pipe gasket has yet to be positioned (Section 10)

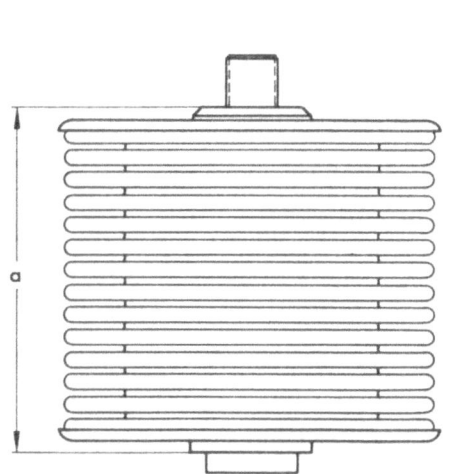
Fig. 2.4. THERMOSTAT BELLOWS
Dimension 'a' at 65°−70°C (149°−158°F) = 46 mm minimum (1.8 inches)

Fault Finding Chart - Cooling and Heating System

Symptom	Reason/s	Remedy
Overheating	Slack fan belt	Check fan belt.
	Insufficient engine oil	Check oil level and top up.
	Ignition timing incorrect	Retime ignition.
	Thermostat or flaps stuck shut	Check operation of thermostat and fan housing controls.
Overcooling	Thermostat or flaps stuck open	Check operation of thermostat and fan housing controls.
Heater ineffective	Thermostat or flaps stuck open	Check operation of thermostat and fan housing controls.
	Flexible hose ducts either to or from heat exchangers disconnected or broken	Check and renew as necessary.

Chapter 3 Fuel system and carburation

Contents

Specifications

Fuel Pump

Make and type	Pierburg mechanical
Delivery rate	VW3 300 cc
per min. at 3400 r.p.m.	VW7 400 cc
Delivery pressure (max.)...	3.5 lbs. per sq.in.

Carburettor

Make	Solex	Solex
Type	28 P.C.I.	28 P.C.I.T. & P.C.I.T.–1
Venturi dia. mm.	21.5	22.5
Main jet	117.5	122.5
Air correction jet	195	130g (incl. emulsion tube)
Pilot jet	g50	g55
Emulsion tube	29	–
Emulsion tube carrier dia. mm.	5.0	–
Float needle valve mm.	1.5	1.5
Float weight grams	5.7	5.7
Accelerator pump capacity cc/stroke	0.4–0.6	1.1–1.4

1. General Description

The Volkswagen fuel system is conventional in principle.

A fuel tank is mounted in the front luggage compartment and fuel is fed to the carburettor by a mechanically operated diaphragm pump which is driven by a push rod actuated by a cam on the distributor drive shaft.

The carburettor is a fixed single choke downdraught type which incorporates a strangler, electrically operated on later models, and an accelerator pump of the diaphragm type. The feed from the accelerator pump can also operate as a subsidiary fuel supply jet under certain conditions. On other, later models there is yet a third fuel supply source in the form of an additional feed from the float chamber into the venturi. This is referred to as the 'power fuel system'. On carburettors fitted with the automatic choke a diaphragm operated push rod overrides the choke spring slightly as soon as there is vacuum on the engine side of the throttle flap.

2. Routine Maintenance

Maintenance is concerned principally with keeping the air filter and fuel filter clean.

Every 1,000 miles or monthly remove the air cleaner and check the oil level in the bath. If it is dirty empty it out, wash out any sludge and refill with oil.

The fuel filter is mounted under the top cover of the pump on those types with a single central cover securing screw. Early and later models have the filter gauze funnel held by a hexagon headed plug in the upper pump body. When removed, both types should be flushed in petrol and blown free of any blockages in the mesh.

3. Air Filter - Removal and Servicing

1. To check the level of the oil in the filter bowl it is necessary only to undo the two clips securing the top cover and lift it off. The oil should be in line with the mark. At the same time the sludge deposits can be ascertained by dipping a suitable probe into the oil. The oil should be no less than 4 - 5 mm deep above any sludge.
2. To remove the sludge the lower half of the unit should be removed from the carburettor.
3. To do this slacken the clip at the base of the cleaner and pull off the air heater and crankcase breather hoses. Lift off the bowl carefully otherwise you may spill oil all over the engine. Empty the contents away and thoroughly flush out the sludge deposits with paraffin. Check the condition of the gasket between the upper and

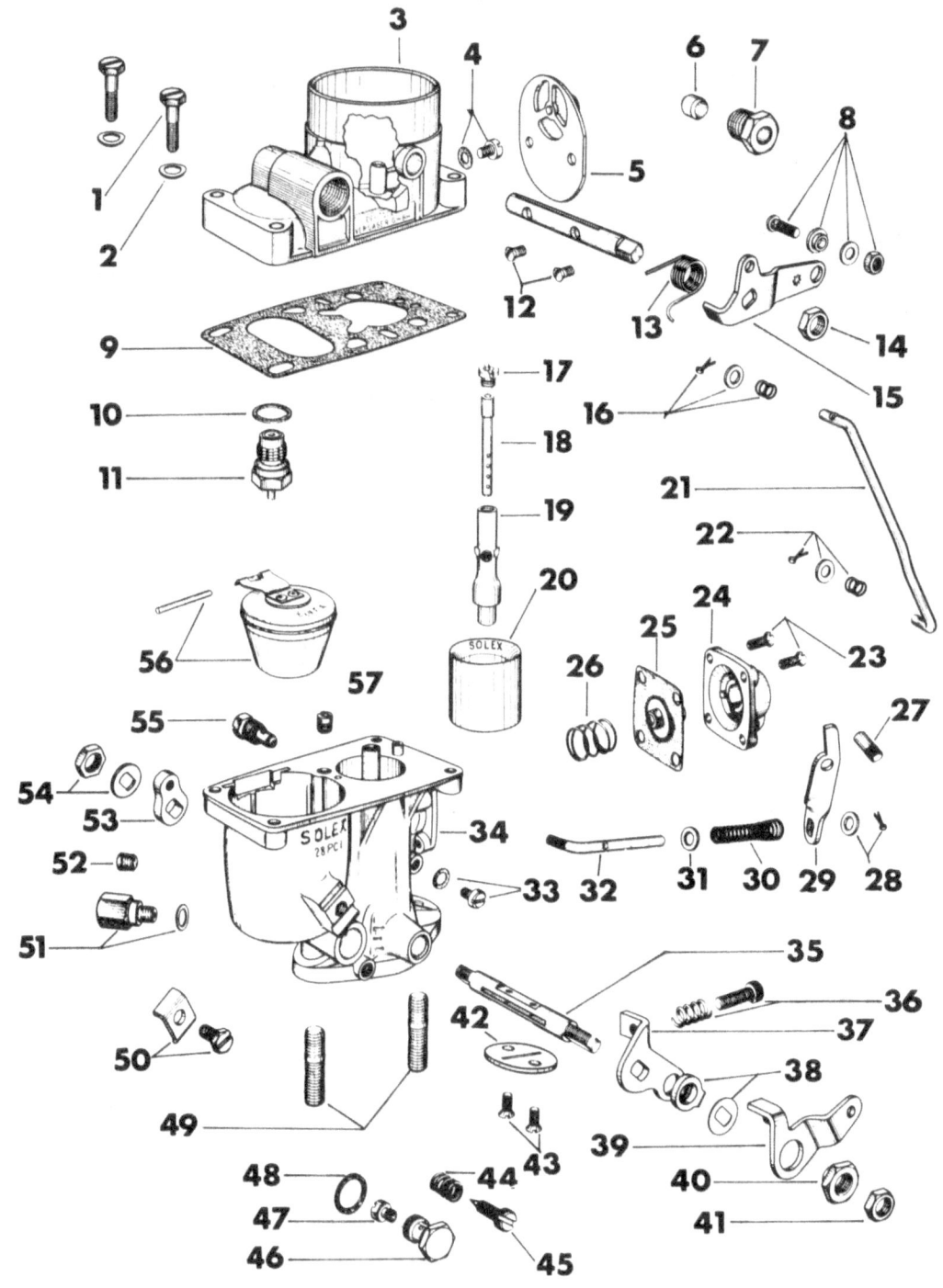

Fig.3.1. SOLEX 28 PCI CARBURETTOR — EXPLODED VIEW

1 Cover screw
2 Washer
3 Cover
4 Securing screw and washer
5 Choke butterfly
6 Petrol pipe olive
7 Petrol pipe union
8 Choke cable connection
9 Gasket
10 Needle valve washer
11 Needle valve
12 Choke butterfly screws
13 Choke spindle return spring
14 Spindle nut
15 Choke lever

16 Connecting rod washer and
   retaining pin
17 Air correction jet
18 Emulsion tube
19 Emulsion tube support
20 Choke tube
21 Connecting rod
22 Connecting rod washer and
   retaining pin
23 Cover screws
24 Accelerator pump cover
25 Accelerator pump diaphragm
26 Spring
27 Pump lever pivot pin
28 Washer and split pin

29 Pump lever
30 Return spring
31 Washer
32 Operating rod
33 Securing screw and washer
34 Main body
35 Throttle spindle
36 Throttle stop screw and spring
37 Throttle lever
38 Spindle washer
39 Intermediate lever
40 Spindle nut
41 Lock nut
42 Throttle flap
43 Throttle flap screws

44 Spring
45 Volume control screw
46 Main jet holder
47 Main jet
48 Washer
49 Mounting studs
50 Cable clamp and screw
51 Vacuum pipe/distributor
   union
52 Vacuum pipe union olive
53 Intermediate lever
54 Spindle washer and nut
55 Pilot jet
56 Float and pivot
57 Pilot air bleed

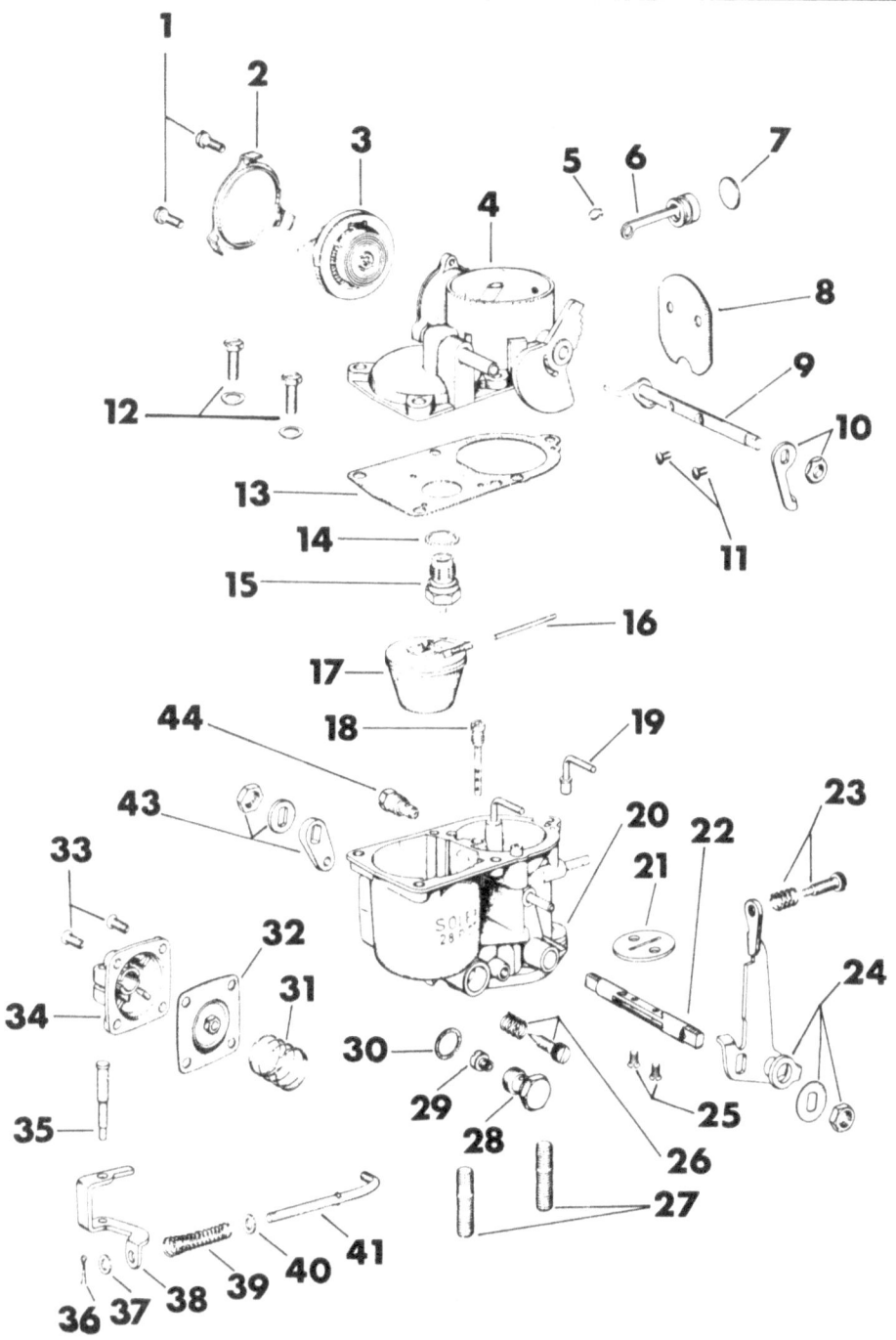

Fig.3.2. SOLEX 28 PICT CARBURETTOR – EXPLODED VIEW

1 Retaining screws	12 Cover screws	23 Throttle stop screw	34 Pump cover
2 Cover retaining ring	13 Gasket	24 Throttle lever washer and nut	35 Pivot pin
3 Automatic choke element	14 Washer	25 Throttle flap screws	36 Split pin
4 Upper body	15 Needle valve	26 Volume control screw	37 Washer
5 Clip	16 Float pivot	27 Mounting studs	38 Pump lever
6 Vacuum piston link	17 Float	28 Main jet carrier	39 Spring
7 Plug	18 Emulsion tube	29 Main jet	40 Washer
8 Choke butterfly	19 Accelerator pump discharge	30 Washer	41 Pump rod
9 Choke spindle	20 Lower body	31 Pump spring	43 Intermediate lever, washer
10 Lever and nut	21 Throttle flap	32 Pump diaphragm	and nut
11 Choke butterfly screws	22 Throttle spindle	33 Pump cover screws	44 Pilot jet

lower halves and renew it if necessary.

4. Replace the lower bowl on the carburettor. This can be done either before or after the new oil is put into it. Fit the top cover in place and reconnect the hoses and clips. It is a good idea to check also that the counter weighted flap on the air cleaner inlet tube is free to move. This flap only opens when the movement of air into the carburettor (at high speed) is sufficient to swing it back thus letting cold air pass in. Otherwise the air is drawn from the pre-heater hose. It is important that the air cleaner assembly should be removed and replaced with care. Any excessive strain can cause it to crack at the bottom where the collar joins the carburettor. You will soon find out about this because the outside of the carburettor will get covered in oil and the level in the cleaner will eventually drop to zero.

5. Remember that in exceptionally dusty conditions the sludge build-up will be much more rapid.

4. Solex Carburettor - Description

The carburettor is basically a tube through which air is drawn into the engine by the action of the pistons and en route fuel is introduced into the air stream in the tube due to the fact that the air pressure is lowered when drawn through the 'tube'. A scent spray works on the same principle.

The main fuel discharge point is situated in the 'tube' - choke is the proper name for the tube to be used from now on - between two flaps which can block off the tube. One of these is the throttle flap - operated by the accelerator pedal and positioned at the engine end of the choke tube. The other is the strangler - which is operated by a manual knob or an automatic device.

When the engine is warm and running normally the strangler is wide open and the throttle open partially or fully - the amount of fuel/air mixture being controlled according to the required speed.

When cold the strangler is closed - partially or fully and the suction therefore draws more fuel or less air, i.e. a richer mixture to aid starting a cold engine.

At idling speeds the throttle flap is shut so that no air and fuel can get to the engine in the regular way. For this there are separate routes leading to small holes in the side of the choke tube, on the engine side of the throttle flap. These 'bleed' the requisite amounts of fuel and air to the engine for slow speeds only.

The fuel is held in a separate chamber alongside the choke tube and its level is governed by a float so that it is not too high or low. If too high it would pass into the choke tube without suction. If too low it would only be drawn in at a higher suction than required for proper operation.

The main jet, which is simply an orifice of a particular size through which the fuel passes, is designed to let so much fuel flow at particular conditions of suction (properly called depression) in the choke tube. At idling speed the depression draws fuel from orifices below the throttle which has passed through the main jet and after that a pilot jet to reduce the quantity further.

Both main and pilot jets have air bleed jets also which let in air to assist emulsification of the eventual fuel/air mixture.

On later 1200 engines a power fuel system is an additional source of fuel which improves performance at high engine speeds when the main jet cannot pass enough. It is in effect a supplementary main jet.

The strangler flap is controlled by either a manually operated wire on early models or an electrically operated bi-metal strip. This latter consists of a coiled bi-metal strip connected to the choke flap spindle. When the ignition is switched off the coiled metal strip is cold and the flap is shut. When the ignition is switched on current flows through the strip which heats up and uncoils - opening the choke flap after two to three minutes. If anything should go wrong with this electrical arrangement the flap will return to the closed position.

With the flap closed there are two features which partially open it immediately the engine starts. The flap spindle is offset so one side tends to turn around the spindle under the depression in the choke tube. Also there is a diaphragm valve connected to another rod attached to the flap spindle. Depression in the choke tube also operates this. If these devices did not exist no air at all would get through with the fuel. This would then flood the engine.

Finally there is another device - an accelerator pump. This is another diaphragm operated pump which is directly linked to the accelerator controls. When sudden acceleration is required the pump is operated and delivers neat fuel into the choke tube. This overcomes the time lag that would otherwise occur in waiting for the fuel to be drawn from the main jet. The fuel in the float chamber is regulated at the correct height by a float which operates a needle valve. When the level drops the needle is lowered away from the entry orifice and fuel under pressure from the fuel pump enters. When the level rises the flow is shut off. The pump delivery potential is always greater than the maximum requirement from the carburettor.

Another device fitted to later models was an electro-magnetic cut-off jet. This is a somewhat unhappy feature which is designed to positively stop the fuel flow when the engine is stopped. Otherwise the engine tends to run on - even with the ignition switched off!

5. Solex Carburettor - Removal, Dismantling and Replacement

1. The carburettor should not be dismantled without reason. Such reasons would be for cleaning or renewal of the float and needle valve assembly and, in rare circumstances, the jets. Partial dismantling would also be necessary for checking and setting the float chamber fuel level.

2. Remove the air cleaner and then detach the accelerator cable from the throttle control lever. Undo the screw which holds the cable end to the link, withdraw the cable and remove the link so that it does not fall out and get lost. Do not disturb the spring and washer further back on the cable. Pull off the wire connection clips from the automatic choke and electro-magnetic cut-off as necessary. On early models unclamp the strangler control wire from the operating arm.

3. Undo the two nuts which hold the carburettor to the inlet manifold and lift the carburettor off. The exterior of the carburettor should be clinically clean before dismantling proceeds.

4. The first stage of dismantling should be to remove the screws holding the top to the base. Separate the two halves carefully and remove the paper gasket taking care to keep it from being damaged. It can be re-used.

5. To clean out the float chamber, invert the carburettor body; the float complete with pivot pin will fall out. If it needs a little help to get it out do not under any circumstances strain it in such a way that the pin or bracket are bent. When the float is removed the bowl may be flushed out and sediment removed with a small brush.

6. The needle valve is screwed into the top cover and when taking it out note the washer mounted underneath it. The simplest way to check this for leaks is to try blowing through it. It should not be possible to do so when the plunger is lightly pushed in. If in doubt, then renew the assembly, as a leaking valve will result in an over-rich mixture with consequent loss of performance and increased fuel consumption.

7. The accelerator pump diaphragm may be examined when the four cover securing screws and cover have been removed. Be careful not to damage the diaphragm. Renew it if there are signs of holes or cracks which may reduce its efficiency.

8. The electric automatic strangler may be removed for cleaning but do not use petrol on the cover. If any part is suspected of malfunction the whole unit must be renewed. When refitting the bimetal spring the looped end must be positioned so that it hooks over the end of the lever. Then the cover should be turned so that the notch lines up with the notch on the carburettor. Do not overtighten the securing screws.

9. The main jet is situated behind a hexagonal headed plug in the base of the float chamber. This can of course be removed without taking the carburettor off the car. Remove the plug and then unscrew

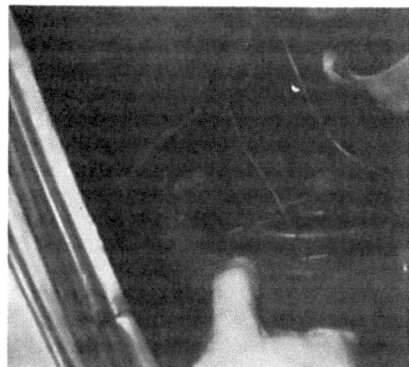
Remove the air pre-heater pipe (Section 3.3)

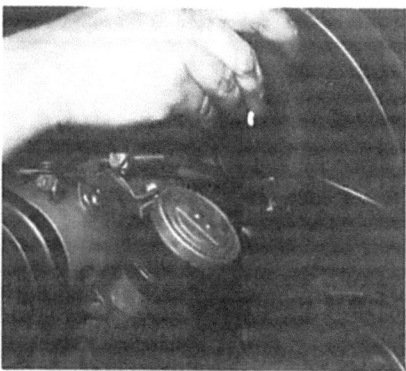
Remove the crankcase breather pipe (Section 3.3)

Slacken the clamp screw at the base of the air cleaner (Section 3.3)

Removing the filter element from the air cleaner (Section 3)

Refill the bowl with oil (Section 3)

Slacken the clamp screw of the throttle cable (Section 5.2)

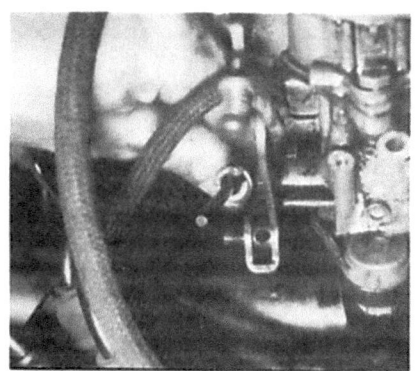
Remove the cable end from the lever (Section 5.2)

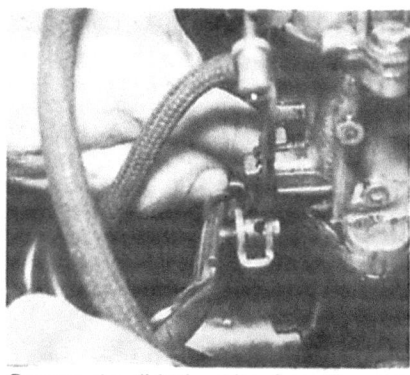
Remove the dished washer from the cable (Section 5.2)

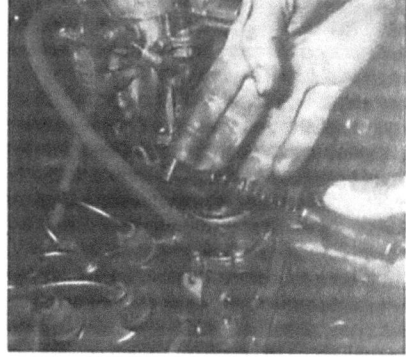
All components may now be removed (Section 5.2)

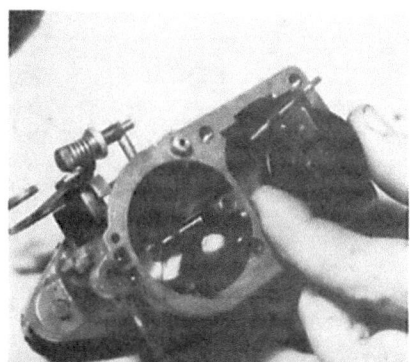
Carburettor float chamber (Section 5.5)

Carburettor float chamber gasket (Section 5.5)

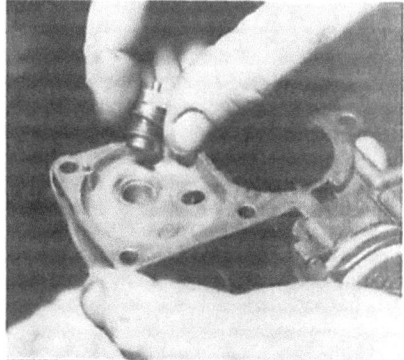
Removing the needle valve (Section 5.6)

the jet from behind it with a screwdriver. The pilot jet is fixed similarly in the body alongside the accelerator pump housing. When cleaning these jets do not use anything other than air pressure. Any poking with wire could damage the fine tolerance bores and upset the fuel mixtures.

10 The air correction jet and emulsion tube is mounted vertically in the body of the carburettor by the side of the choke tube. This too may be unscrewed for cleaning. Blow through the passageway in the carburettor also when it is removed.

11 Before reassembly check that the float is undamaged and unpunctured. It can be checked by immersion in hot water.

12 The volume control screw which adjusts the amount of mixture metered for idle speeds should be removed and the tapered end examined. If it is scored, bent, or grooved it will be virtually impossible to set a smooth tickover.

13 The accelerator pump inspection tube may be inadvertently moved so check that the outlet points down in such a way that the jet of fuel cannot impinge on any part of the carburettor or open throttle on its k ay down to the inlet manifold.

14 If the throttle flap spindle should be very loose in its bearings in the main body of the carburettor then air may leak past and affect the air to fuel ratio of the mixture. In such cases the easiest remedy is a new carburettor. An alternative is to drill and fit bushes to suit but this needs some expertise and time.

15 Reassembly is a reversal of the dismantling procedure but the following points should be watched carefully. Do not forget the washer when replacing the needle valve. Make sure that the gasket between body and cover is correctly positioned. When refitting the accelerator pump cover, the screws should be tightened with the diaphragm centre pushed in. This means holding the operating lever out whilst the screws are tightened. Do not bend or distort the float arm when replacing it into the float chamber. When reconnecting the accelerator cable take heed of the procedure given at the end of the next section.

6. Solex Carburettor · Adjustments

1. It must be emphasised that if the engine is running smoothly and that performance and fuel consumption are satisfactory there are no adjustments that will materially improve any of these conditions beyond the manufacturers' specifications. If the engine is not performing as it should be sure to check the ignition system before assuming that the carburettor is the cause of the trouble.

2. Assuming all components are clean and in good condition there are only two adjustments that can be made - these being the fuel level in the float chamber and the slow running speed.

3. To check the fuel level the carburettor must be fitted to the engine. The car should be standing on a level surface. Run the engine and then switch it off and remove the fuel line from the carburettor.

4. Remove the air cleaner assembly and then take out the five screws securing the upper half of the carburettor to the lower. Put a finger over the fuel inlet pipe (to prevent the little fuel in the top cover coming out when the top is lifted) and take off the top cover and gasket.

5. The level of the fuel - with the float in position - should be 12 - 14 mm below the top edge of the float chamber. This can be measured by using a depth gauge or by placing a straight edge across the top of the float chamber and measuring down with a suitable rule. Do not measure too near the edge as capilliary action up the side of the chamber could cause a false reading. If the level is incorrect it may be altered by fitting a washer of a different thickness under the needle valve which is screwed into the top cover. Washers are available in a range of thicknesses from ½ to 1½ mm. (it can be seen that the fuel level measurement has to be taken fairly accurately to be of any use in deciding whether alteration is necessary). If the level in the chamber needs raising a thinner washer should be fitted and vice versa. If you are tempted to try and alter the level by bending the bracket on the float - forget it. It cannot be done accurately

enough to be of any use and more often than not the result of such attempts is either breakage or distortion. In the latter case the net result is a sticking float which gives you more problems than you had to start with.

6. Whilst the cover is removed it would be as well to check the condition of the needle valve as described in the previous section.

7. Reassemble the top cover with the gasket the correct way round, reconnect and clip the fuel line and replace the air cleaner. If wished the level may be checked again once any adjustment has been made but it should not be necessary provided the needle valve is in good order and the measurements were accurately taken.

8. Slow running adjustment is only carried out when the engine is warm and the strangler flap fully open.

9. With the engine adjusted on the throttle stop screw to a speed of 700 - 800 r.p.m. (fast tickover) turn the volume control screw clockwise until the speed decreases. Then turn it back until even running occurs. Then continue to turn it another ¼ revolution. Note that if this adjustment is carried out before the engine is warm (and the automatic choke fully open) the throttle stop screw may still be resting on one of the steps of the cam attached to the strangler flap spindle. These steps are intended only to keep up the engine speed during the warm up period by restricting the throttle from closing fully even when the accelerator pedal may be released completely. When the volume control screw has been set the throttle stop screw may be re-adjusted to give a suitable idling speed. Do not try to set the idling speed too low - particularly if the engine is not in the first flush of youth. You will waste hours trying to achieve the impossible.

10 The setting of the accelerator cable into the throttle operating arm is important if full throttle opening is to be possible and also if excessive strain is to be avoided. Obviously one wants to have the throttle flap fully open when the accelerator pedal is fully depressed. At the same time one does not want to have the throttle fully open and up to the stop **before** the pedal has been fully depressed, otherwise the pedal pressure will stretch the cable and put considerable strain on the bracket and spindle. With the accelerator cable end in position but unclamped, move the throttle lever round to the fully open position, up to the stop. Then let it come back so that there is a gap of 1 mm between the stop and the lever. At the same time someone else should depress the accelerator pedal right to the floor. In this position the cable end may be tightened into position. Check the accelerator pedal movement to see that the gap is maintained when the pedal is pressed to the floor.

7. Fuel Pump · Removal and Replacement

1. The fuel pump is mounted on the crankcase to the left of the distributor on early models and below the carburettor on later ones. The principle of all the pumps is the same but changes did occur. Early models had a filter screen housed under a hexagonal plug in the top of the pump and the latest have a similar device mounted in the side. The pump which was fitted to the car used for this book had a disc filter mounted under the top cover.

2. To remove the pump first disconnect both fuel pipes, undoing the unions or pulling off the flexible pipes as fitted. If the fuel tank is very full petrol may come out of the pipe leading from the tank, in which case it must be blocked. Chewing gum or Plasticene have been used but do not leave any behind. A better way is to find a length of flexible pipe which can be connected so that the effective end of the pipe can be raised higher in the air. Then slacken and remove the two nuts holding the pump to the crankcase and lift the pump off. Pull out the pushrod and remove the gasket from between the pump and the plastic intermediate flange. It is not necessary to disturb the intermediate flange but stuff a piece of rag into it as if anything drops down it could be extremely difficult, if not impossible, to extract.

3. If you are suffering from persistent fuel pump trouble of one sort or another (starvation of fuel or regularly punctured diaphragms) it is possible that the push rod is not functioning correctly. Turn the

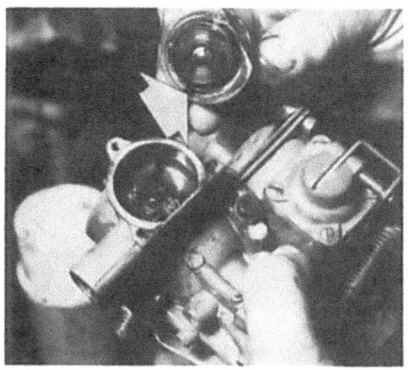

Replacing the auto strangler element (Section 5.)

Screwing down the top cover. Note hook on flap (Section 5)

The stepped plate on the choke spindle which regulates the throttle stop position (Section 5)

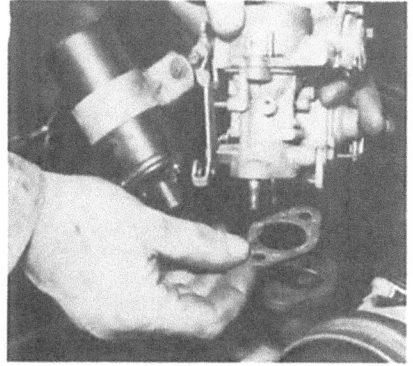

Replacing the carburettor and gasket to the manifold (Section 5)

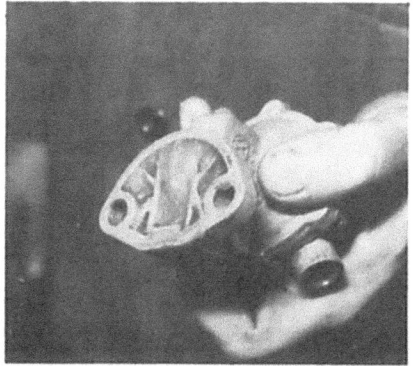

Fuel pump showing base packed with grease (Section 7.4)

Replacing the gasket on the fuel pump base and inserting the push rod (Section 7.3)

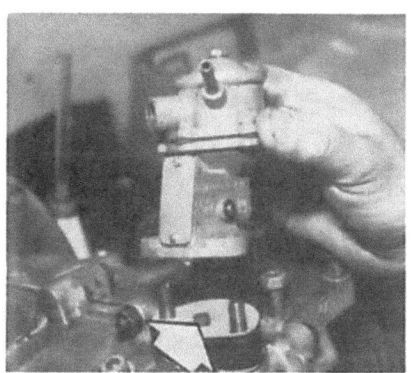

Note the protrusion of the pushrod (Section 7.3)

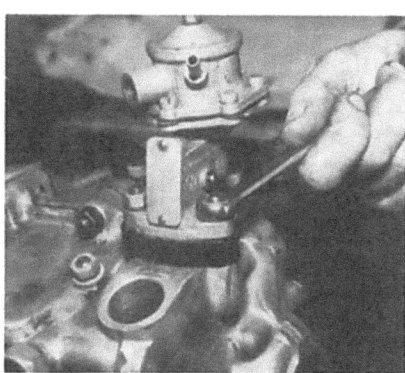

Securing the pump (Section 7.4)

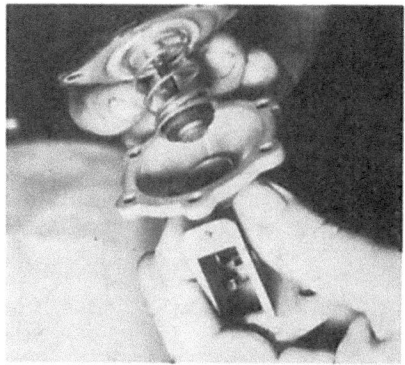

Fuel pump. Fitting the diaphragm (Section 8.9)

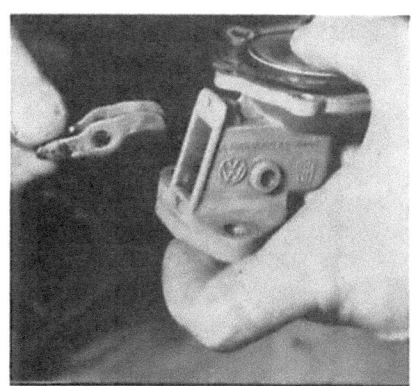

Refitting the diaphragm operating lever (Section 8.9)

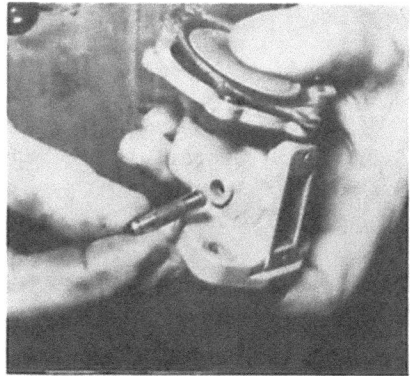

Replacing the pivot pin (Section 8.9)

Refitting the circlip to the pivot pin (Section 8.9)

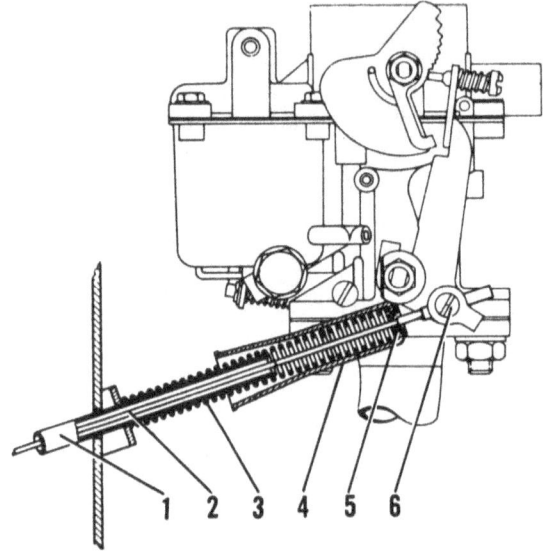

Fig. 3.3. THROTTLE CABLE CARBURETTOR ATTACHMENT
SECTIONAL DRAWING

1 Guide tube (through fan   2 Throttle wire   4 Outer sleeve   6 Cable end clamp screw
  housing)   3 Return spring   5 Convex slotted retaining washer

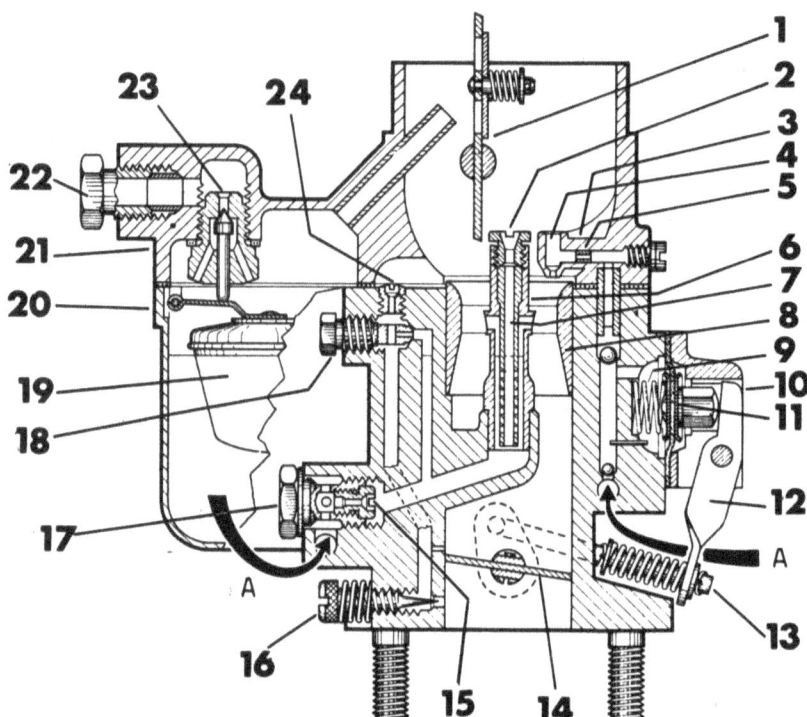

Fig. 3.4. SOLEX 28 PCI CARBURETTOR – CROSS SECTION DRAWING

1 Strangfer flap	8 Choke tube	15 Main jet	21 Top cover
2 Correction jet	9 Pump diaphragm spring	16 Slow running mixture	22 Fuel inlet union
3 Accelerator pump injector	10 Accelerator pump	adjusting screw	23 Needle valve assembly
4 Air bleed	11 Pump diaphragm	17 Main jet carrier plug	24 Pilot jet air bleed
5 Pump jet	12 Pump lever	18 Pilot jet	A Fuel inlet points
6 Main jet bridge	13 Pump operating rod	19 Float	
7 Emulsion tube	14 Throttle flap	20 Carburettor body	

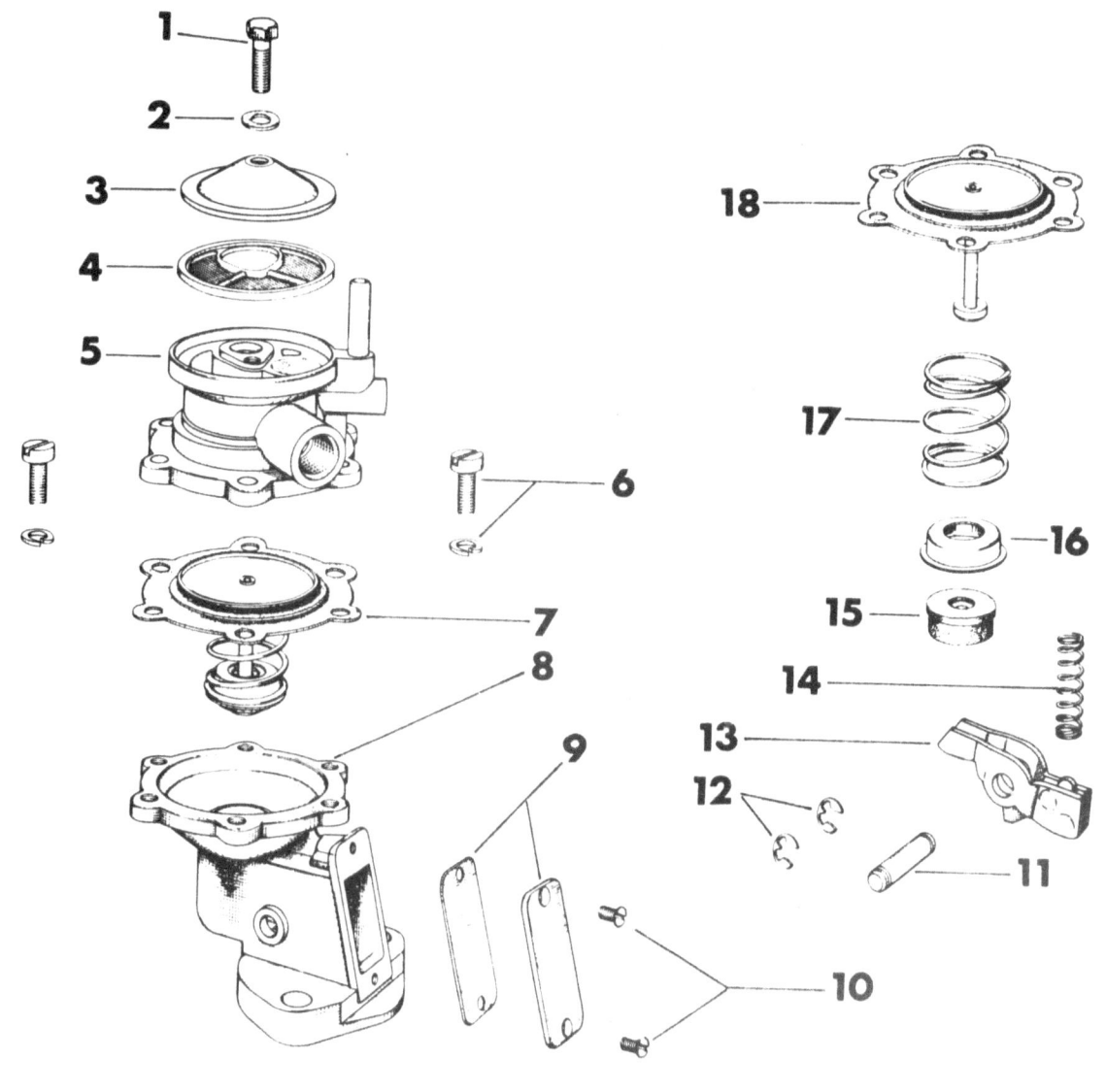

Fig. 3.5. FUEL PUMP - EXPLODED VIEW

1 Top cover screw
2 Washer
3 Top cover
4 Filter screen
5 Upper pump body

6 Pump body screw and washer
7 Diaphragm assembly (Items 15—18)
8 Lower pump body
9 Cover plate and gasket

10 Cover plate screws
11 Operating lever pivot pin
12 Pivot pin 'E' clips
13 Operating lever
14 Lever return spring

15 Oil seal
16 Oil seal retainer
17 Diaphragm spring
18 Diaphragm and pull rod

engine until the rod protrudes the maximum amount above the intermediate flange. The normal gaskets should be fitted under the intermediate flange. The rod should project 34 mm on early models, or 13 mm on later versions, above the flange. It is possible to vary this by putting more or less gaskets under the intermediate flange. If the rod projects too much the diaphragm will be strained and may be punctured.

4. Before replacement the base of the pump should be packed with grease and a gasket, preferably new, fitted between pump and flange. Refit and tighten the nuts. After connecting the fuel lines run the engine to confirm that there are no fuel leaks.

8. Fuel Pump - Dismantling, Examination and Reassembly

1. Before dismantling a fuel pump with a view to repairing it make sure you can obtain a repair kit - that is a new diaphragm and filters and washers. If not then you are wasting your time and will be better off buying another pump. It may be possible to use a repair kit from another make of pump to cut out another diaphragm but this will be a somewhat expensive repair of a temporary nature.

2. Undo the top cover bolt and remove the cover and filter. On early models there is no top cover. On later models what looks like a top cover (and is held by four screws) is in fact another diaphragm chamber operating a fuel cut-off valve when the engine is stationary. Do not disturb this if you are only concerned with the operation of the main pump diaphragm.

3. After scratching lining up marks unscrew the six screws which hold the two halves of the pump together. The top half can then be lifted off.

4. In order to remove the diaphragm it is first of all necessary to take out the operating lever pivot pin. This is held by a circlip at each end. First remove the small cover plate and gasket which is held to the lower body by two small screws. Then remove one circlip from the end of the pivot pin and force the pin out.

5. Press the centre of the diaphragm down and the lever can be pulled out. Do not lose the spring.

6. Draw out the diaphragm and spring assembly.

7. Inspect the diaphragm for holes or cracks in the flexible material. The material should be supple and if it is getting brittle and stiff renew the diaphragm assembly.

8. The condition of the two valves should also be checked. One is a petrol valve of shim steel and this should lie quite flat. The other is a conventional disc valve which is an assembly staked into position in the top cover. Should either of these be malfunctioning it is easy to renew the petrol valve but the other is slightly more difficult. It may be difficult to get the necessary parts also. If you have plenty of time to spare it might be worth waiting for spares.

9. When refitting the diaphragm make sure that the sealing ring fits snugly into its recess in the lower body. Then press the diaphragm down in the centre so that the forks of the operating lever may engage over the toggle at the bottom of the diaphragm pull rod. Still holding the diaphragm replace the pivot pin and refit the circlip.

10 The operating lever return spring can be lifted now. Engage one end on the inner lug in the pump body and snap the other end into position on the lever.

11 When refitting the top half of the pump make sure the inlet and outlet pipes are correctly positioned in relation to the lower half. If you have marked both parts prior to dismantling, this will present no difficulty. Replace all six screws loosely and then press the operating lever to a position which is halfway through its full stroke. Then tighten the six screws alternately and evenly.

12 Replace the filter screen in the top half of the body ensuring that the projections are intact. These act as spacers and prevent the screen from fluttering up and down inside the cover. Some models may have a spacer collar round the cover screw instead. Fit a new cover sealing ring and replace the cover and screw. Do not overtighten the screw or there is danger of stripping the thread on the body of the pump.

13 Repack the base of the pump with a suitable grease - Castrol LM

being ideal.

9. Fuel Tank, Fuel Taps and Fuel Gauge Sender Unit

1. The fuel tank is mounted in the front luggage compartment and on early models there was no fuel gauge (except as an extra) but a tap operated by a control on the bulkhead could switch over to a reserve supply when necessary, indicating that you had better fill up again fairly soon. Later models had a gauge which is operated mechanically rather than electrically.

2. For models fitted with a gauge, access is from the luggage compartment having first removed the lining material from behind the dashboard and on top of the tank. The fuel gauge sender unit is mounted in the top of the tank and has a snap fit cover. The back of the gauge has an adjusting screw so that if necessary it may be re-calibrated. To do this move the lever at the sender unit with the cable still connected so that the gauge reads more or less empty. The lever must be kept pushed back as far as it will go. If the screw on the back of the gauge is now turned in the direction of the arrow the needle of the gauge can be set to zero. When this is done there will be about 1 gallon left on the reserve mark on the gauge. Assistance will, of course, be required to do this adjustment as someone will be needed to watch the gauge inside the car.

3. In the rare circumstances of having to remove the sender unit - a leaking float can be about the only reason - first unhook the cable from the lever. Do **not** undo all five securing screws. Take out four only. If one of these four is larger than the others put it back and screw it in a few turns and remove the other four. If you do not keep one screw in position you will drop the clamp ring into the fuel tank. With the clamp ring slack one end can be hooked over the hole in the tank itself and the whole unit lifted out. Examine the float for punctures. Replacement is a reversal of the removal procedure. If you want to fit a new cork gasket it will be necessary to remove the float arm from the body because the float is too big to pass the gasket over. Refit the long screw into a hole at one end of the clamp ring and put the whole unit back. Pick up the other screw holes in the clamp ring and tighten the unit down firmly. If you suffer from petrol smells after filling up with fuel the fuel gauge sender unit is often the culprit. The only answer is not to overfill.

4. On those models fitted with a tap the control lever inside is at normal when pointing vertically upwards and on reserve when pointing to three o'clock. The off position is either halfway between main and reserve or over at nine o'clock. If the lever does not move to nine o'clock then you know it must be the former. Once again the tap rarely needs attention but if it becomes excessively stiff or loose then it will be necessary to examine the valve itself. The valve is situated in an awkward position centrally over the tunnel and behind the front suspension torsion bar tubes. To get at it remove either one of the front wheels. If you wish to remove it completely you must first drain the fuel tank so gather together containers sufficient to collect all the fuel in the tank and a piece of flexible pipe with a bore of about 1/8 inch. It should be at least three feet long unless you wish to grovel around under the car.

5. Turn the top to 'off' and pull off the flexible pipe. Connect your drain pipe and open the valve (to reserve position) and drain out the fuel.

6. Remove the pin connecting the operating lever to the valve and unscrew the valve from the base of the tank.

7. The valve may be dismantled by removing the lock screws or circlips (according to type) which hold the cylinder into the barrel. Renew the seal and thoroughly clean the interior and filter. Blow out with compressed air if possible. If the interior shows signs of scoring or serious wear, buy a new tap.

8. Reassemble in the reverse order and check that the operation is firm yet free and smooth before replacement. Before reconnecting the operating rod make sure it moves freely in the grommet through the bodywork.

9. From time to time it may become necessary to take the fuel tank from the car, if only to clean it out thoroughly.

The components of the fuel pump laid out ready for assembly - Section 8.

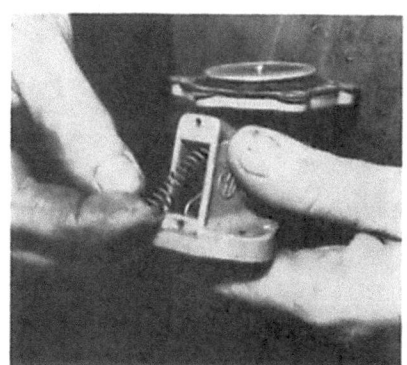

Refitting the return spring (Section 8.10)

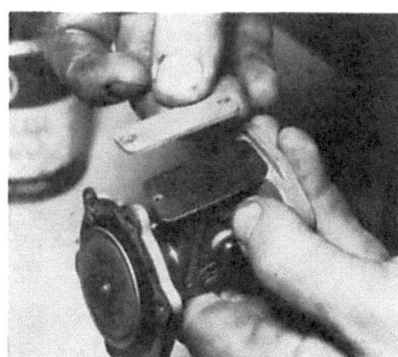

Replacing the cover (Section 8.10)

Reassembling the pump halves. Note the position of the petal (inlet) valve and disc (outlet) valve (Section 8.11)

Tightening down the two halves of the pump (Section 8.11)

Replacing the filter to the fuel pump (Section 8.12)

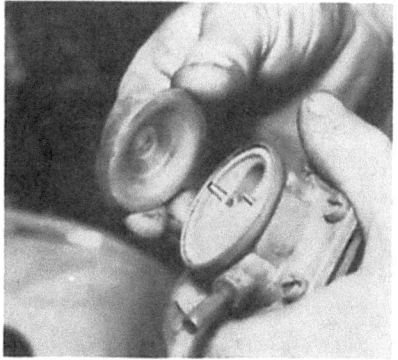

Refit the top over the gasket (Section 8.12)

10 First disconnect the fuel gauge cable from the sender unit or disconnect the tap as described (or both if a fuel gauge has been added). Pull off the vent pipe from the filler neck. Then undo the clamp screws and lift the tank out.

10. Induction Manifold - Removal, Inspection and Replacement

1. The inlet manifold will be removed during the course of an overhaul or if there are reasons to suspect that it is damaged or incorrectly seated thus giving rise to air entering the system and affecting performance. It comprises two pipes jacketed together. One pipe carries out the normal function of conveying the fuel/air mixture to the cylinders via each cylinder head and the other acts as a heater. This second pipe uses heat from the exhaust manifolds to which it is clamped.

2. With the engine installed the fan generator assembly must first be removed followed by the generator pedestal. On early models with an integral pedestal the fan housing must be taken off. Both these items are dealt with in Chapter 2.

3. Remove the carburettor as described in Section 5.

4. The manifold is secured to the cylinder head by two nuts on each side; and to the exhaust pipes by two small bolts on each side. Before removing any of these you must make sure that you have the neces-

sary new gaskets. Re-use of the old ones is impracticable. Once the nuts and bolts have been removed, the manifold can be lifted off.

5. Inspect the manifold and the mounting flanges for any signs of holes, cracks or distortion. It is possible to repair holes and cracks by welding or - if not very significant - with a resin filler. All the flanges should be flat on their mating faces and free from pitting. To check distortion the best way is to put the manifold in position, without gaskets, and see that all the mating faces and bolt holes match up. No stress should be necessary in order to achieve this. If necessary the pipe(s) may be heated so that they can be set correctly. Make sure any loose scale is removed from inside the pipes if this is done.

6. The pre-heater pipe ends may be carboned up and this should be cleaned away. (The reason for the small hole at one end is so that the gases flow in one direction. If both holes were the same there would be no differential, no flow and therefore no heat).

7. Remove the old gaskets from the cylinder heads and manifold connections. Those in the cylinder heads will be compressed into place and will probably need digging out.

8. Take great care at all times to avoid dropping any foreign bodies into the inlet ports of the cylinder heads. It is strongly advised that a piece of cloth be stuffed in to prevent accidents of this sort.

9. Replacement of the manifold is a straight forward reversal of the removal procedure. Always use new gaskets and be careful not to overtighten the mounting nuts and bolts. A stripped thread or broken stud can cause a lot of trouble unnecessarily.

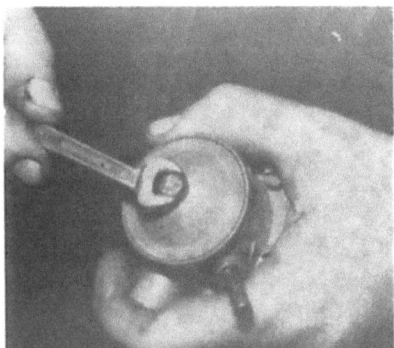
Tightening down the fuel pump cover (Section 8.12)

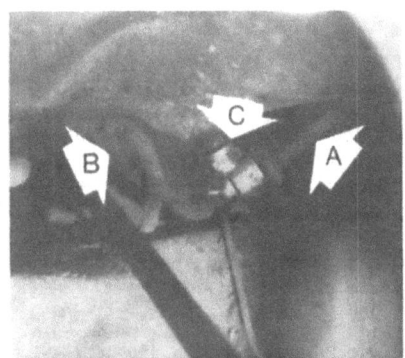
Fuel tap. (a) control rod (b) outlet pipe (c) valve (Section 9)

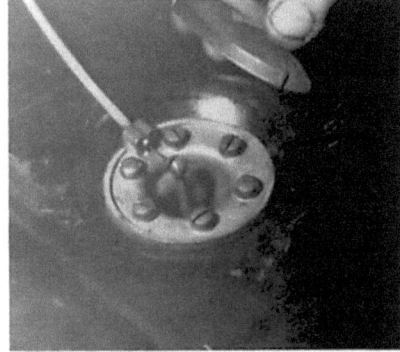
Fuel gauge sender unit showing cable connections (Section 9)

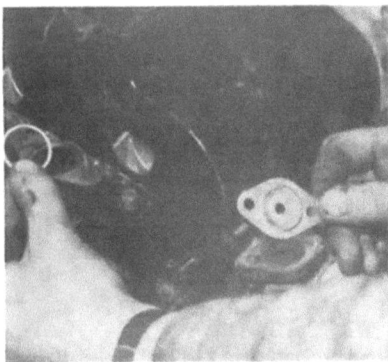
Induction manifold; positioning gaskets (Section 10.9)

Positioning the manifold for assembly (Section 10.9)

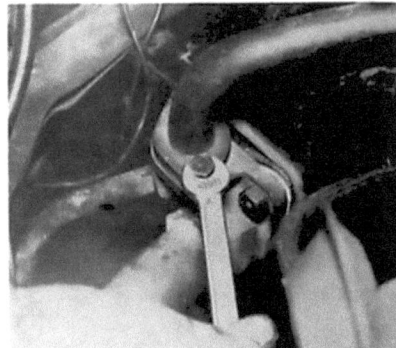
Tightening down the inlet manifold (Section 10.9)

Fault Finding Chart - Fuel System & Carburation

Unsatisfactory engine performance and excessive fuel consumption are not necessarily the fault of the fuel system or carburettor. In fact they more commonly occur as a result of ignition and timing faults. Before acting on the following it is necessary to check the ignition system first. Even though a fault may lie in the fuel system it will be difficult to trace unless the ignition is correct. The faults below, therefore, assume that this has been attended to first (where appropriate).

Symptom	Reason/s	Remedy
Smell of petrol when engine is stopped	Leaking fuel lines or unions	Repair or renew as necessary.
	Leaking fuel tank	Fill fuel tank to capacity and examine carefully at seams, unions and filler pipe connections. Repair as necessary.
Smell of petrol when engine is idling	Leaking fuel line unions between pump and carburettor	Check line and unions and tighten or repair.
	Overflow of fuel from float chamber due to wrong level setting or ineffective needle valve or punctured float	Check fuel level setting and condition of float and needle valve and renew if necessary.
Excessive fuel consumption for reasons not covered by leaks or float chamber faults	Worn jets	Renew jets.
	Sticking strangler flap	Check correct movement of strangler flap.
Difficult starting, uneven running, lack of power, cutting out	One or more jets blocked or restricted	Dismantle and clean out float chamber and jets.
	Float chamber fuel level too low or needle valve sticking	Dismantle and check fuel level and needle valve.
	Fuel pump not delivering sufficient fuel	Check pump delivery and clean or repair as required.
	Intake manifold gaskets leaking, or manifold fractured	Check tightness of mounting nuts and inspect manifold.

Chapter 4 Ignition system

Contents

Specifications

Note: The type number references given are only general. It is outside the scope of this book to give the full range of detailed changes which have occurred to component specifications and references over the years. We can only emphasise that although a certain distributor off a 1960 engine will fit a 1966 engine its characteristics will differ and although the engine will run it will not be performing properly. When obtaining replacements the engine number reference is all important. It must be appreciated that ignition timing design changes.

Spark Plugs

Type - 14 mm	Bosch W175 TI - (later W145 TI)
	Champion L10, L85, L87y
	KLG, F70
Electrode gap	0.6 - 0.7 mm (.024 - .027 inch)

Distributor and Ignition Timing

6 volt - early models	VJU 4BR8 - Bosch
6 volt - later models	ZV PAU 4R Series
	111 905 205 Series
Static ignition timing - 30 b.h.p.	7½º BTDC
- 34 b.h.p. to 1966	10º BTDC
- 34 b.h.p. 1966 on	7½º BTDC
Timing marks	On crankshaft pulley. To be lined up with crankcase dividing joint.
Pulleys with 1 notch only	mark indicates 7½º BTDC
" " 2 noches	L.H. notch 7½º BTDC
	R.H. notch 10º BTDC
" " 3 notches	L.H. notch 0º
	Centre notch 7½º BTDC
	Right notch 10º BTDC
Firing sequence	1, 4, 3, 2
Contact points gap	0.4 mm (.016 inch)
Automatic advance	Vacuum only
Coil - 6 volt	111 905 105L Series

1. General Description

Ignition of the fuel/air mixture in the Volkswagen 1200 engine is conventional in that one spark plug per cylinder is used and the high voltage required to produce the spark across the plug electrodes is supplied from a coil (transformer) which converts the six volts from the supply battery to the several thousand necessary to produce a spark that will jump a gap under the conditions of heat and pressure that obtain in the cylinder.

In order that the spark will occur at each plug in the correct order and at precisely the correct moment the low voltage current is built up (into the condenser) and abruptly discharged through the coil when the circuit is broken by the interrupter switch (contact points). This break in the low voltage circuit, and the simultaneous high voltage impulse generated from the coil, is directed through the selector switch (rotor arm) to one of four leads which connect to the spark plugs. The condenser contact points and rotor arm are all contained in and operated at the distributor.

Due to different spark timing requirements under certain engine conditions (of varying speed or load) the distributor also has an automatic advance device (advancing the spark means that it comes earlier in relation to the piston position). In the Volkswagen 1200 engine this device is operated by suction only from the induction

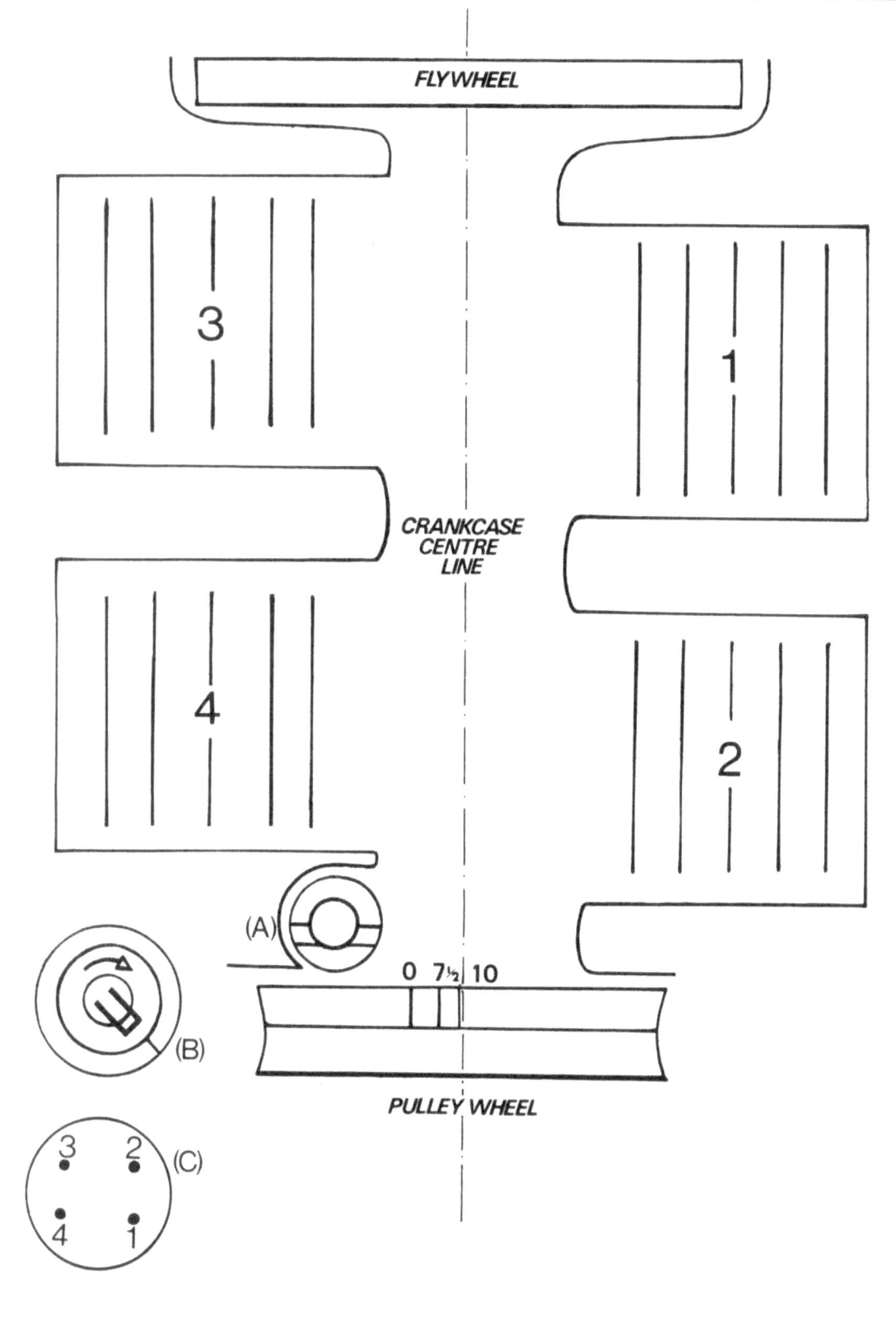

Fig. 4.1. Schematic illustration of static ignition timing details.

manifold. When the suction is high, for example when the throttle is almost closed at low engine speeds, the ignition is retarded. It advances when the throttle opens and reduces the suction. (On some other types of engine an automatic advance device operated by centrifugal force of high speeds is used. This is not used on the Volkswagen 1200 which is a low-reving low stressed engine producing moderate power for a long time as opposed to high power for a short time).

2. Routine Maintenance

1. Every 3,000 miles the spark plugs should be removed, cleaned and the electrode gap reset.
2. Every 3,000 miles the contact breaker points should be examined for signs of deterioration and the gap measured and reset if necessary.
3. Examine the condition of the high tension leads at the same time as the other checks are being carried out and make sure that all connections are secure and clean and that there are no cracks in the insulation of the wire. The low tension connections to the coil should also be secure and clean.
4. When examining the contact breaker points examine also the inside of the distributor cap. The small spring loaded carbon brush in the centre should be unchipped and free moving. The four metal contacts should also be free of oil or corrosion. Scrape them if necessary.
5. Do not interfere with the static ignition timing. Once set right the only thing that can alter it is the changed condition of the breaker points (under normal circumstances).

3. Contact Breaker Points - Removal, Replacement and Adjustment

1. Volkswagen service agencies will insist that the only way to set a Volkswagen ignition timing correctly is by using special equipment. This will permit the points to be set not so much to a specific gap as to the cam dwell characteristics on the distributor shaft. This is doubtless correct but for those who have neither the time nor money available the alternative, which is a perfectly reasonable one, is to set the ignition according to the static timing marks, the breaker points gap and engine performance.
2. First remove the distributor cap.
3. Before starting to set the breaker points they should first be examined. Both surfaces should be smooth and clean. Neglected contacts will probably have a hole or pit in one surface and a corresponding hard peak on the other. It is impossible to set such contacts correctly so they must be renewed or cleaned up. This involves removal. If the contacts are clean continue with the adjustment procedure as described later in this section.
4. Early types of contact breaker points came in two separate parts with separate insulating washers and so forth. Even those earlier types are more often than not renewed nowadays with the one-piece assembly which comprises the fixed contact, moving breaker arm and mounting plate. This type is illustrated but in order that no mistakes occur it is as well to point out the principles to ensure correct reassembly of earlier types encountered. The fixed contact is the earth side so it is mounted and in contact with the distributor body itself via the base plate. The moving contact is the 'live' side and when assembled it must be insulated from earth. The current travels from the L.T. wire on the coil to the end of the spring arm along the spring to the contact or condenser. The end of the spring arm (and the wires connected to it) must be insulated from the distributor. Similarly the pivot point of the moving contact must be insulated. If this is borne in mind there should be no problem. When finally assembled the two contact breaker surfaces should line up.
5. To remove the points assembly first remove the securing screw which clamps the fixed point plate into position. The whole assembly may then be lifted up off the pivot post. A small screw and nut holds the spring end and the L.T. wires to the nylon insulation block and

if this is removed the wire connections can be removed.
6. If the points are being cleaned it is best to separate the two parts. This can be done by pulling the end of the spring out of the insulation block. The pivot insulation will come out of the hole in the fixed point plate.
7. To clean up the faces of the contacts use a very fine oil stone. Stone the two faces flat ensuring particularly that the 'peak' is completely removed. If the pit in the other contact is very deep do not try and grind it right out. The points can be adjusted once the peak is removed. Make a note to get a new set at the earliest opportunity.
8. Reassemble the two halves if separated and connect the L.T. and condenser leads and tighten the securing screw. Replace the assembly over the pivot post and put back the securing screw but do not fully tighten it down.
9. To set the gap it is first necessary to set the cam follower on the moving arm so that it rests on one of the four high points on the cam. To do this turn the engine by engaging a gear and pushing the car a little at a time until the cam follower rests on a high point.
10 Using a screwdriver in the notch, move the fixed contact plate so that a feeler blade of 0.4 mm thickness (.016 inch) just slides lightly between the two points. Tighten the clamping screw and re-check the gap once more. Sometimes the action of tightening the screw moves the plate slightly.

4. Distributor - Removal and Replacement

1. The distributor should be removed only if indications are such that it needs renewal or overhaul.
2. Take off the distributor cap and pull the L.T. wire which runs to the coil off the coil terminal. Detach the pipe which fits to the vacuum advance unit.
3. The distributor is held in position by a clamp which grips the lower circular part of the body. The clamp itself is held to the crankcase by a single bolt. If the bolt is removed the distributor and clamp together may be lifted out of the crankcase.
4. It must be realised that if the bolt which secures the clamp to the distributor is slackened - and the relative positions of distributor and clamp altered - then the static ignition timing is upset.
5. The lower end of the distributor drive shaft has a driving dog with offset engagement lugs. These engage into corresponding slots in the distributor drive shaft. Being offset it ensures that the shaft cannot be inadvertently set 180° out of position when the distributor is replaced.
6. Replacement of the distributor is a reversal of the removal procedure. See that the offset drive shaft dogs are correctly aligned otherwise they will not engage and the body will not go fully home.
7. It is a good idea to renew the rubber 'O' ring in the annular exterior groove of the body if possible. This seal prevents oil from creeping up on the outside of the body.

5. Condenser - Testing, Removal and Replacement

1. The condenser or capacitor as it is sometimes called, functions as a storage unit for the low tension current which flows into it when the points are closed. When the points open it discharges and sends a boost through the L.T. circuit to the coil. If the condenser does not function correctly the current shorts to earth across the contact points. This causes arcing and rapid deterioration of the points and also causes the spark producing properties of the coil to malfunction or cease entirely. If, therefore, persistent misfiring and/or severe burning and pitting of the contact points occurs, the condenser is suspect and should be tested right away.
2. To make a simple check on the condenser remove the distributor cap and turn the engine until the contact points are closed. Then switch on the ignition and push open the points with something non-metallic. If there is a considerable spark then this confirms that the condenser is faulty. Normally there should be a very mild spark -

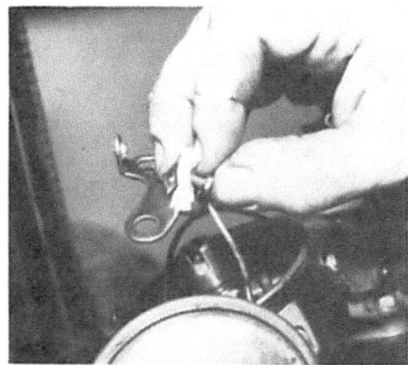

Attaching the condenser lead to the fixed contact insulated terminal block (Section 3.8)

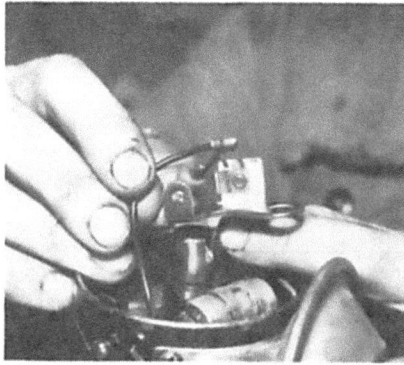

Attaching the coil LT lead to the fixed contact insulated terminal block (Section 3.8)

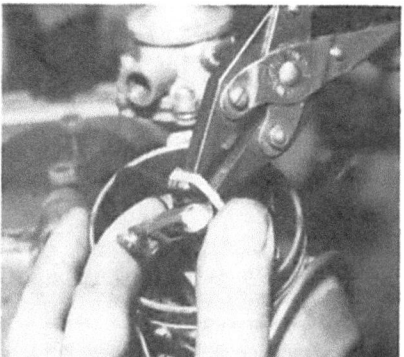

Tightening the terminal block clamp screw after fitting the moving contact spring (Section 3.8)

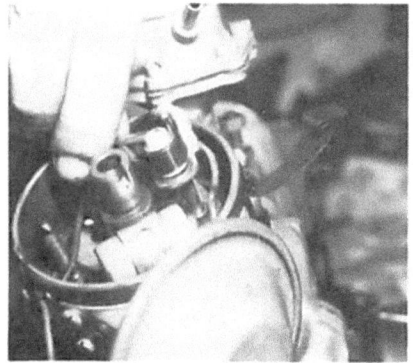

Placing the assembly over the pivot post (Section 3.8)

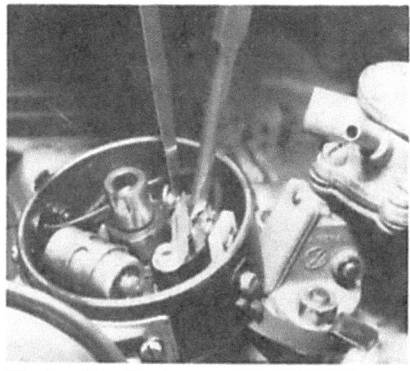

Moving the fixed contact to adjust the gap (Section 3.10)

Tighten the locking screw with the feeler blade still in position (Section 3.10)

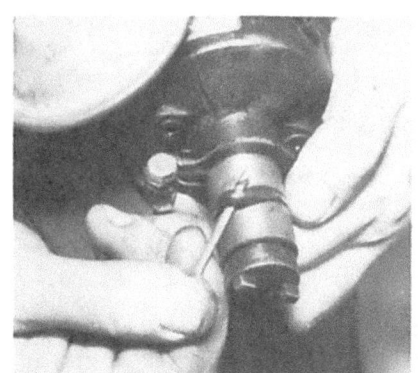

Pulling of the old sealing ring (Section 4.7)

Replacing distributor in block (Section 4.6)

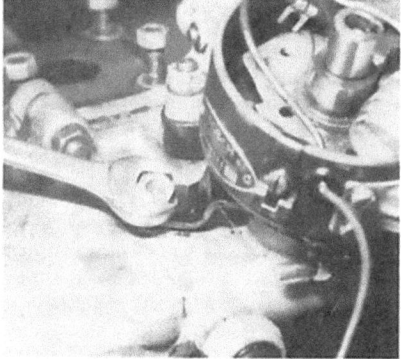

Tightening the mounting bolt (Section 4.6)

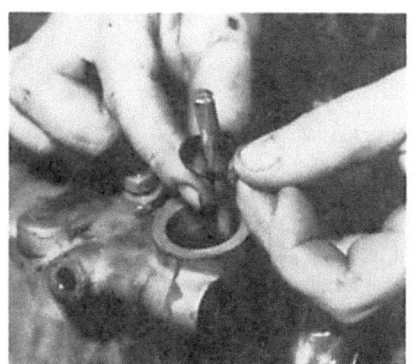

Replacing washer under distributor drive shaft into crankcase (Section 7.6)

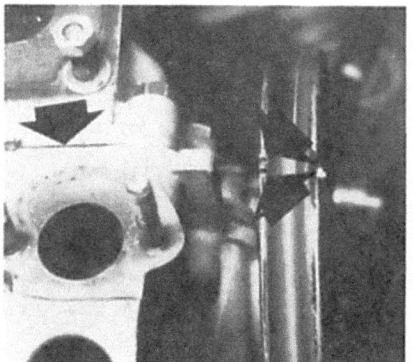

Showing crankcase centre line and notches (arrowed) for setting No 1 piston at timing point 7½º or 10º BTDC (Section 7.8)

Offset in distributor drive shaft in No 1 firing position (also drive shaft removal position (Section 7.8)

almost invisible - across the points.

3. To remove the condenser involves lifting the points out as well because the screw securing the condenser lead to the nylon terminal block is inaccessible otherwise. The condenser clamping screw may then be undone and the condenser removed. (Later types are different in detail making removal more simple).

4. Replacement is a reversal of the removal procedure.

6. Distributor - Inspection, Dismantling, Repair and Reassembly

1. Provided the component parts are kept in good order there should be little need to take the distributor apart except in cases of neglect or very high mileages. One of the indications is when the measured gap of the contact points is difficult or impossible to set accurately and consistently. This is due to wear of the shaft or shaft bushes or, more rarely, wear on the cams. When the shaft or bushes are worn the movement can be felt when sideways rocking pressure is applied to the top of the shaft.

2. In either case the only solution is to remove the distributor and renew the shaft or bushes or both. Alternatively one may find it simpler to renew the whole assembly. This might be necessary as the trend among manufacturers nowadays is generally this way. Check first that you can obtain the parts you may need.

3. Having removed the distributor, take out the contact points and condenser as described earlier.

4. The next job is to remove the driving collar from the bottom of the shaft but before doing this it is important to note which way it is fitted. See which way the driving dogs are offset in relation to the rotor arm notch in the top of the shaft. The notch and the offset of the dogs should face the same way.

5. When the relative position is noted clamp the collar in a vice and punch out the retaining pin. The collar may then be drawn off the shaft followed by the shims which control the end float of the shaft in the body.

6. Carefully unhook the pull rod from the vacuum unit to the contact breaker mounting plate and after removing the screws take off the vacuum unit. Then remove the mounting plate and shaft taking note of the position of the thrust washers.

7. If the shaft is obviously badly worn it must be renewed and it is most likely that the bushes will need renewal also.

8. The old bushes can be removed by driving them out with a long, flat ended punch from the inside. Take care not to damage the bore of the body. New ones can be drawn in with a long bolt and nut with a suitable flat washer at each end. New bushes should not normally need reaming but make sure that the shaft is not too tight a fit.

9. New distributor shafts when in position may need a variation in the thickness of the shims fitted between the driving dog and the body.

10 Reassembly is a reversal of the dismantling procedure. Make sure the driving dog is fitted the correct way round and when the pin is fitted peen the ends so that it cannot drop out.

7. Static Ignition Timing and Distributor Drive Shaft

1. As stated in the introduction there should be little need to alter the timing except in cases of engine overhaul or distributor overhaul.

2. If the timing has to be reset from scratch the distributor should be removed first so that the distributor drive shaft position may be verified and set as required.

3. The distributor drive shaft may be removed and installed with the engine assembled and in the car provided that the distributor, fuel pump and fuel pump intermediate flange have first been removed. (The distributor drive shaft also drives the fuel pump push rod from a face cam incorporated on the shaft). If the engine is being reassembled after overhaul the drive shaft should be refitted after the oil pump, lower cover plate and crankshaft pulley have been refitted.

4. To withdraw the drive shaft from the crankcase first set No. 1 cylinder to firing position. This is done by setting the correct mark on the pulley wheel (7½° or 10° BTDC) to the crankcase joint. The offset slot in the top of the shaft should then be parallel with and towards the pulley wheel. (This, of course, assumes that the shaft is correctly engaged. If the shaft is incorrectly engaged turn the engine so that the slot is positioned the same but ignore the timing marks on the pulley wheel). This positioning is necessary so that a cut-out specially machined in the shaft lines up with the worm gear on the crankshaft. If it is not lined up the shaft will jam on the worm gear. Remove the central spring if fitted. The shaft may now be lifted up and out, rotating anti-clockwise as it is lifted. The main problem is getting hold of it. If you do not have the special tool there are a variety of ways namely: joining a piece of suitably sized wooden dowel into the centre hole, gripping the sides of the hole with a pair of long nosed expanding circlip pliers, jamming a piece of thin wooden batten into the slot.

5. When the shaft is successfully removed take out the thrust washers (one or two) from the bottom of the bore in the crankcase. This must be done carefully because if they are tipped into the timing gear chamber alongside, it may be impossible to get them out without stripping the engine.

6. To replace the distributor drive shaft, first put the thrust washers in position in the base by dropping them down over a suitable piece of rod. This will guide them where you want them to go.

7. Next turn the engine so that No. 1 piston is in the correct firing position - that is 7½° or 10° BTDC on the compression stroke. To find the compression stroke with the distributor drive shaft removed is not easy because there are no reference points. The only sure way is to remove No. 1 sparking plug and turn the engine until compression is felt when the timing marks come into line. It is easy to feel the compression by placing a finger over the plug hole. If the right hand rocker cover is removed the compression stroke can also be pinpointed when both valves are closed.

8. The distributor drive shaft should now be lowered into the crankcase with the offset slot positioned slightly anti-clockwise from its final correct position as detailed in paragraph 4. When it is lowered into mesh with the crankshaft worm gear it will turn slightly clockwise to the final correct position. Should you position the shaft too far anti-clockwise, or not far enough, it will not go into position for the reasons given in paragraph 4. Provided, therefore, that the timing marks on the pulley are correct, and No. 1 piston is on compression, it is practically impossible to fit the drive shaft incorrectly meshed.

9. With the engine and distributor drive shaft set and not moved from the position as described in the preceding paragraph the distributor may be placed in position with the shaft lined up so that the eccentric dogs engage the eccentric slots. Provided the clamp has been undisturbed no further adjustment is necessary after the clamp securing bolt has been replaced and tightened.

10 If the clamp ring has been slackened the body of the distributor should be turned so that the centre line of the rotor arm electrode matches up with the notch in the edge of the distributor body. This gives the near correct position. Final adjustment is made after the contact points have been checked and the gap set. With the crankshaft at the No. 1 firing position the contact points should just be opening. To do this with precision the distributor body should be turned clockwise a fraction from the setting mark until the points are shut. The body is then turned anti-clockwise until they are just open. This point is best determined electrically. Using a 6 volt bulb or voltmeter make a connection from the moving contact to earth via the bulb or voltmeter. Switch on the ignition. There will be a light or reading when the points open. At this position tighten the distributor clamp bolt.

11 No two engines are exactly the same and when the car is road tested the performance may indicate that the ignition timing needs minor adjustment still. Sluggish acceleration through the gears indicates that the timing may need advancing a little more (turn the distributor body anti-clockwise). Conversely, 'pinking' and inflexibility at low engine revolutions would indicate that the timing is too far advanced and needs retarding a little (turn the distributor body clockwise). One word of warning - do not over-advance the timing - it can cause damage if allowed to persist. Remember the 1200 Beetle

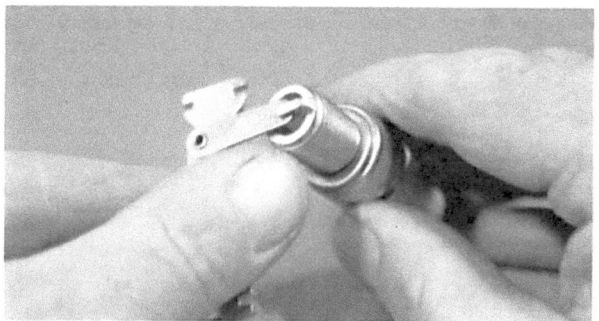

Measuring plug gap. A feeler gauge of the correct size (see ignition system specifications) should have a slight 'drag' when slid between the electrodes. Adjust gap if necessary

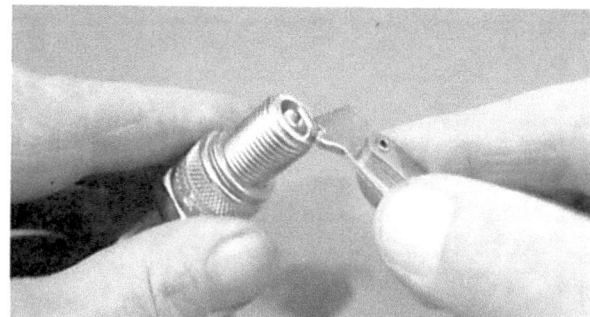

Adjusting plug gap. The plug gap is adjusted by bending the earth electrode inwards, or outwards, as necessary until the correct clearance is obtained. Note the use of the correct tool

Normal. Grey-brown deposits, lightly coated core nose. Gap increasing by around 0.001 in (0.025 mm) per 1000 miles (1600 km). Plugs ideally suited to engine, and engine in good condition

Carbon fouling. Dry, black, sooty deposits. Will cause weak spark and eventually misfire. Fault: over-rich fuel mixture. Check: carburettor mixture settings, float level and jet sizes; choke operation and cleanliness of air filter. Plugs can be re-used after cleaning

Oil fouling. Wet, oily deposits. Will cause weak spark and eventually misfire. Fault: worn bores/piston rings or valve guides; sometimes occurs (temporarily) during running-in period. Plugs can be re-used after thorough cleaning

Overheating. Electrodes have glazed appearance, core nose very white – few deposits. Fault: plug overheating. Check: plug value, ignition timing, fuel octane rating (too low) and fuel mixture (too weak). Discard plugs and cure fault immediately

Electrode damage. Electrodes burned away; core nose has burned, glazed appearance. Fault: pre-ignition. Check: as for 'Overheating' but may be more severe. Discard plugs and remedy fault before piston or valve damage occurs

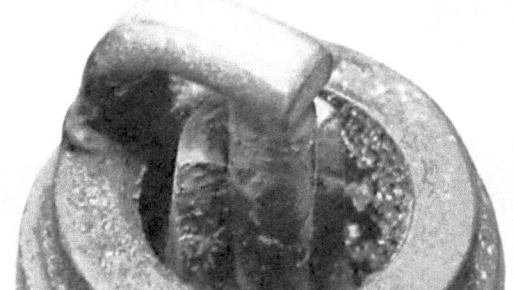

Split core nose (may appear initially as a crack). Damage is self-evident, but cracks will only show after cleaning. Fault: pre-ignition or wrong gap-setting technique. Check: ignition timing, cooling system, fuel octane rating (too low) and fuel mixture (too weak). Discard plugs, rectify fault immediately

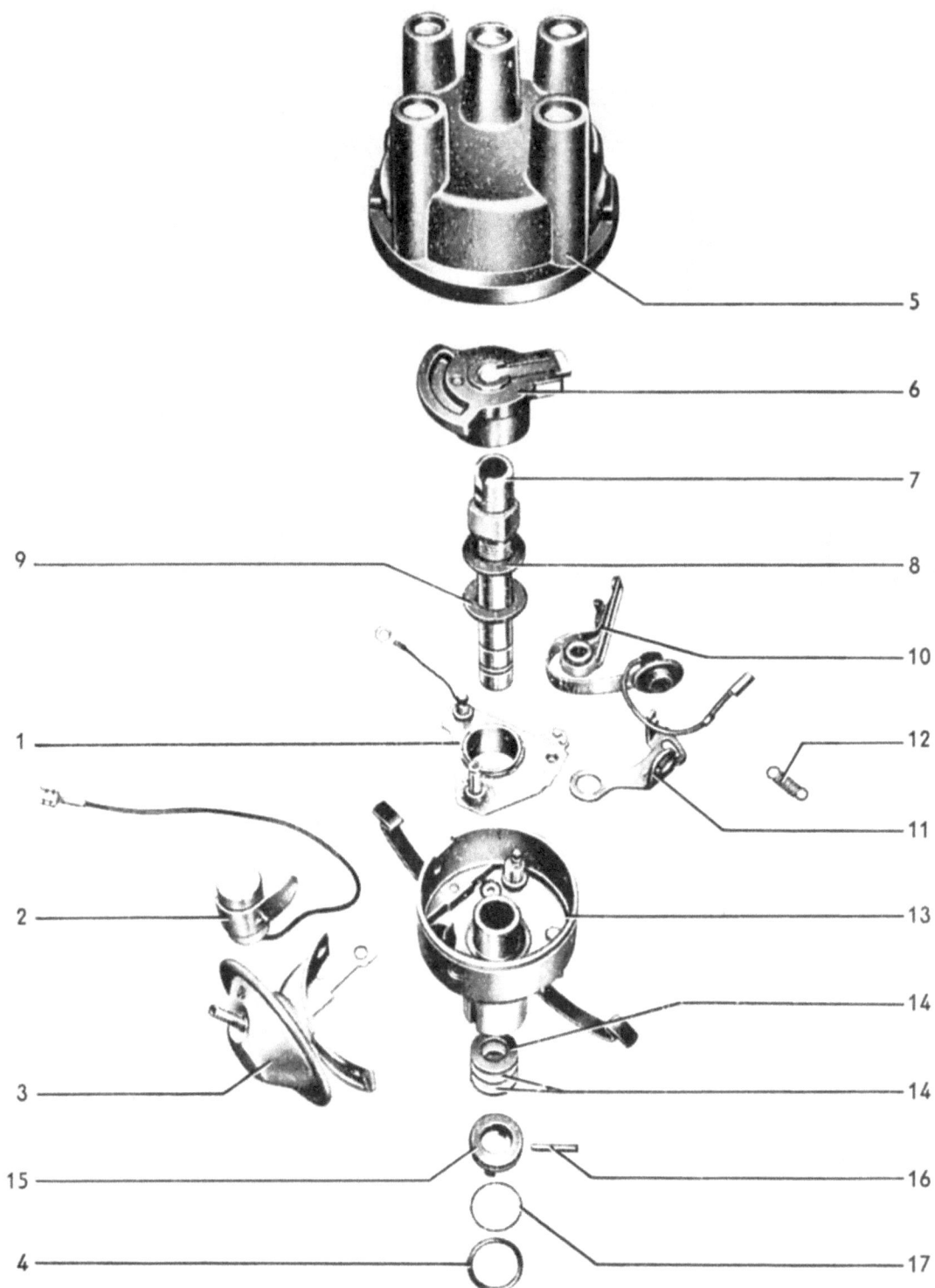

Fig. 4.2. DISTRIBUTOR WITH VACUUM ADVANCE (LATER TYPE)
(EXPLODED VIEW)

1 Contact breaker mounting
  plate
2 Condenser
3 Vacuum unit
4 'O' ring
5 Distributor cap

6 Rotor arm
7 Drive shaft (incorporating
  breaker cams)
8 Shim
9 Fibre washer
10 Moving breaker contact and

spring
11 Fixed contact
12 Mounting plate return
  spring
13 Distributor housing
14 Steel washers

15 Driving dog
16 Dog securing pin
17 Circlip

engine is not designed, in standard form, for rocket-like acceleration. It will however cruise all day flat out in top gear. Its cruising speed is maximum speed (which makes it so good for motorway work).

8. Sparking Plugs and H.T. Leads

1. The proper operation of the spark plugs is essential to good engine performance and economy. They are also useful indications of engine condition and settings.

2. Make sure you use the correct plugs as listed in the specifications. Every engine has its own characteristics calling for a certain type of spark plug. A different type may be too 'cold' causing deposits to form on the electrodes which would normally burn off. This would result in poor sparking and eventual misfiring. Other plugs may be too 'hot'. These are much more dangerous as the electrodes would overheat and burn away and localised overheating could burn a hole in the piston.

3. Sparking plugs today are generally very reliable and give no trouble in an engine which is in normally good condition. Every 3,000 miles however it is beneficial to remove, examine, clean and reset them. To remove the Volkswagen plugs it is best to use the special plug spanner supplied with the vehicle. This is quite conventional except that a rubber insert is fitted which grips the plug and enables you to lift it out through the top cover plate attached to the spanner. If the plug drops loose under the cover plate you can waste an awful lot of time fiddling about in order to get it out; and may even be obliged to remove one or more of the cover plates.

4. The colour of a normally operating plug is a dirty greyish brown and any deposits on it are usually light. Whitish deposits indicate weak fuel mixtures or overheating, whereas blackish deposits indicate over-rich fuel mixtures.

5. If you are unable to have the plugs sand blasted and tested at a garage on a proper machine (you could if you carried a spare set) first clean off the deposits with a wire brush or by scraping. Considerable deposits may accumulate round the porcelain insulator of the central electrode. This can be scraped out with a fine pointed article (such as an old hacksaw blade ground to a point) but care must be taken not to damage the porcelain. If the porcelain is chipped or cracked anyway the plug must be discarded.

6. The actual electrodes must also be in good condition which means unburnt and comparable to the original length. The centre electrode must project above the end of the threaded body of the plug and the side electrode project across the full diameter of the centre one. The easiest way to assess deterioration is by comparison with a new plug. For cleaning the electrodes, the side one may be bent up a little to permit a fine file or emery to be used to face off the opposing surfaces of both electrodes. The surfaces should be flat. Then tap the side electrode down carefully with a feeler blade between the two. The correct gap is 0.6 - 0.7 mm (.024 - .027 inch). Do not try and bend the centre electrode. The insulation will crack.

7. Do not soak plugs in petrol or paraffin. Even after the spirit is burnt off the residual deposits do more harm than good. If you get persistent problems with plugs oiling up you may have to wash them in spirit but when you get the engine put right buy a new set of plugs.

8. If the exterior insulation is damaged or loose the plug must be renewed. Streaky marks running up the insulation indicate a gas leak between body and insulation. Renew the plug under such circumstances.

9. When replacing the plugs use a new washer if possible - although most plugs nowadays are fitted with captive washers which makes it somewhat difficult. You are being persuaded to buy new plugs all the time. In any case try to make sure that the seating in the cylinder head where the plug fits is clear of grit or other things that could cause a poor seal. When cleaning the seats it is important to prevent bits dropping into the cylinder. As the Volkswagen plugs are less accessible than most the simplest way is to screw in the plugs a few threads and then direct as strong an air blast as you can find around the plug before tightening it down.

10 The leads for the plugs must be examined carefully along their length and at each end. The insulation should be clean, uncracked and undamaged in any other way. The metal ends should be free of corrosion. Everything should be dry. Renew any doubtful items and do not try to make do with repairs using insulating tape or such. It is not worth it.

9. Coil - Testing

1. The coil serves to convert the 6 volt battery current to the high voltage required to generate a spark at the sparking plugs. It consists of a primary winding (low tension) and a secondary winding (high tension) which delivers the high voltage to the distributor rotor and thence to the plugs.

2. It is not normally tested separately, but during the tests applied to the whole ignition system in the course of diagnosing some fault. The testing involves checking that current flows through the primary windings and that the secondary winding delivers a high voltage. As this is most easily done with the coil in circuit normally no separate procedure is given for a coil which is taken out of circuit.

10. Ignition Troubles - Diagnosis and Fault Finding Table

1. Failure of the engine to start, or start easily, misfiring and poor acceleration and fuel consumption can usually be attributed to faults in the ignition system assuming, of course, that the engine is otherwise in reasonable condition. Volkswagen engines (those fitted with automatic chokes in particular) have a tendency to be fussy when starting hot. Do not attribute this to ignition until you have tried the hot start method of first pressing the accelerator pedal slowly right to the floor before operating the starter motor. This overcomes the tendency to flood the warm engine with excess fuel.

2. The table shows the logical progression to be followed in any circumstance where the ignition is being checked for correct operation. Do not by-pass any part of this procedure unless the fault is particularly obvious and rectification solves the problem. Such obvious faults would be broken or detached wires. It is assumed that the battery is in good condition and fully charged. It is impracticable to test the circuit otherwise. It also assumes that the battery is connected properly and that the starter motor turns the engine over normally.

FAULT	CHECK
No start or starts with fuss and difficulty.	1. Remove H.T. lead from centre of distributor cap and verify that spark jumps to earth when engine is turned. If it does, fault lies in rotor arm, distributor cap, plug leads or plugs which should be checked in that order.
	2. If no spark from coil H.T. lead check L.T. circuit in order:
	a) Disconnect L.T. lead from terminal 15 of coil and with 6 v bulb or voltmeter check that current is coming to the end of the lead when the ignition is switched on. If not check wiring from ignition switch.
	b) Remove the distributor cap. Turn the engine until the points are closed. Switch on the ignition. Hold the H.T. lead from the coil near a metal earth and open the points with a non-metallic article. If a spark now jumps from the end of the H.T. lead clean and reset the points to cure the trouble.
	c) If there is no spark from the H.T. lead but a large spark from the points when opened as in para (b) the con-

denser is faulty. It should be renewed.
d) If there is no spark from the H.T. lead, and no spark large or small at the points when opened as in para (b) the winding of coil has probably failed. Repeat test with a voltmeter on terminal 1 of coil. If there is no reading then renew the coil.

Engine starts readily but the performance is sluggish, no misfiring.

1. Check the contact breaker points gap.
2. Check the plugs.
3. Check the static ignition timing.

Engine misfires, runs unevenly, cuts out at low revolutions only.

Engine misfires at high revolutions.

4. Check the fuel octane rating.

1. Check the contact breaker gap (too large).
2. Check the plugs.
3. Check the fuel system (carburettor).
4. Check wear in distributor shaft.

1. Check the plugs.
2. Check the contact breaker gap (too small).
3. Check the fuel system (carburettor).
4. Check the distributor shaft wear.

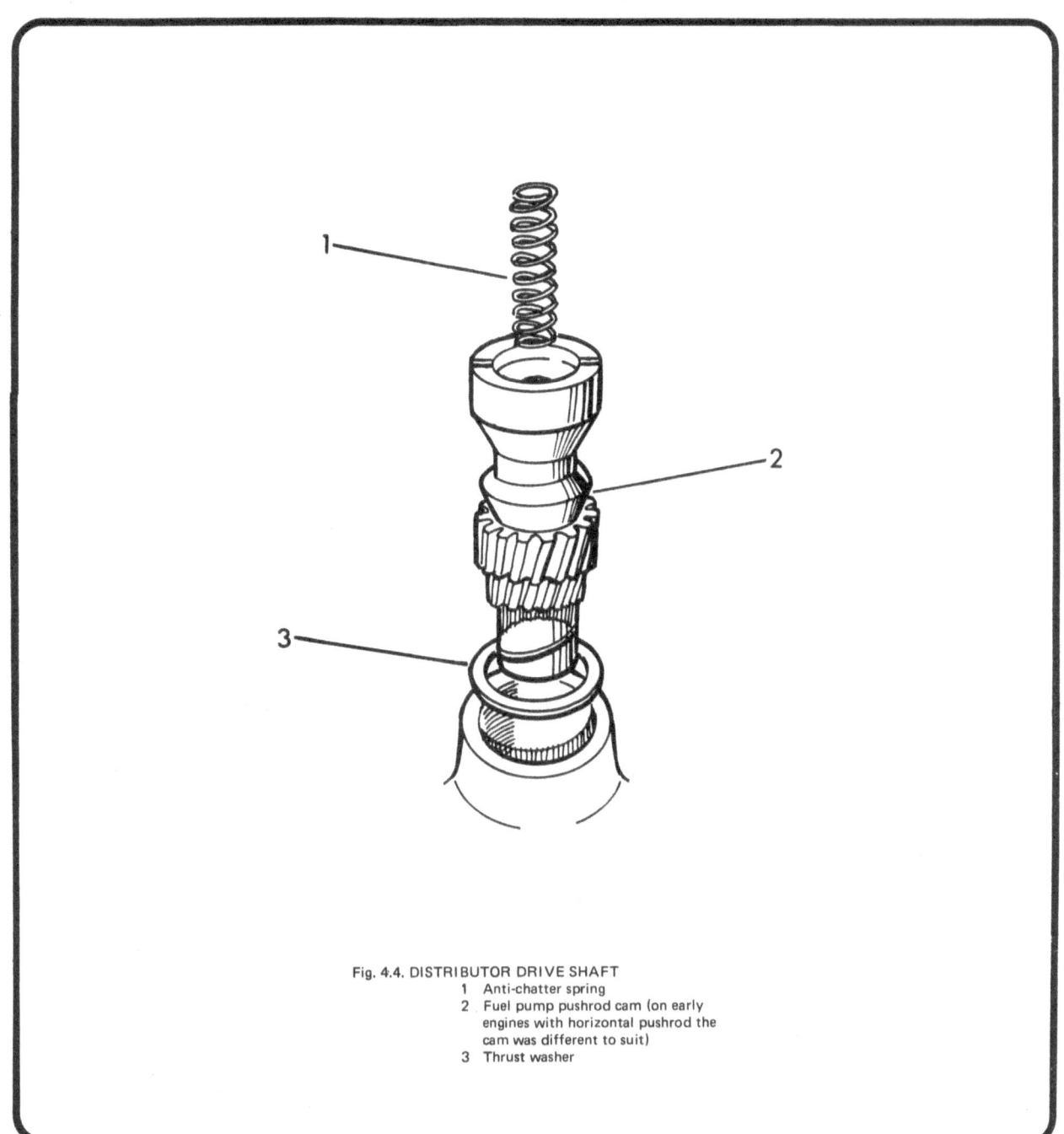

Fig. 4.4. DISTRIBUTOR DRIVE SHAFT
  1 Anti-chatter spring
  2 Fuel pump pushrod cam (on early engines with horizontal pushrod the cam was different to suit)
  3 Thrust washer

Castrol GRADES

Castrol Engine Oils

Castrol GTX

An ultra high performance SAE 20W/50 motor oil which exceeds the latest API MS requirements and manufacturers' specifications. Castrol GTX with liquid tungsten† generously protects engines at the extreme limits of performance, and combines both good cold starting with oil consumption control. Approved by leading car makers.

Castrol XL 20/50

Contains liquid tungsten†; well suited to the majority of conditions giving good oil consumption control in both new and old cars.

Castrolite (Multi-grade)

This is the lightest multi-grade oil of the Castrol motor oil family containing liquid tungsten†. It is best suited to ensure easy winter starting and for those car models whose manufacturers specify lighter weight oils.

Castrol Grand Prix

An SAE 50 engine oil for use where a heavy, full-bodied lubricant is required.

Castrol Two-Stroke-Four

A premium SAE 30 motor oil possessing good detergency characteristics and corrosion inhibitors, coupled with low ash forming tendency and excellent anti-scuff properties. It is suitable for all two-stroke motor-cycles, and for two-stroke and small four-stroke horticultural machines.

Castrol CR (Multi-grade)

A high quality engine oil of the SAE-20W/30 multi-grade type, suited to mixed fleet operations.

Castrol CRI 10, 20, 30

Primarily for diesel engines, a range of heavily fortified, fully detergent oils, covering the requirements of DEF 2101-D and Supplement 1 specifications.

Castrol CRB 20, 30

Primarily for diesel engines, heavily fortified, fully detergent oils, covering the requirements of MIL-L-2104B.

Castrol R 40

Primarily designed and developed for highly stressed racing engines. Castrol 'R' should not be mixed with any other oil nor with any grade of Castrol.
†Liquid Tungsten is an oil soluble long chain tertiary alkyl primary amine tungstate covered by British Patent No. 882,295.

Castrol Gear Oils

Castrol Hypoy (90 EP)

A light-bodied powerful extreme pressure gear oil for use in hypoid rear axles and in some gearboxes.

Castrol Gear Oils (continued)

Castrol Hypoy Light (80 EP)

A very light-bodied powerful extreme pressure gear oil for use in hypoid rear axles in cold climates and in some gearboxes.

Castrol Hypoy B (90 EP)

A light-bodied powerful extreme pressure gear oil that complies with the requirements of the MIL-L-2105B specification, for use in certain gearboxes and rear axles.

Castrol Hi-Press (140 EP)

A heavy-bodied extreme pressure gear oil for use in spiral bevel rear axles and some gearboxes.

Castrol ST (90)

A light-bodied gear oil with fortifying additives

Castrol D (140)

A heavy full-bodied gear oil with fortifying additives.

Castrol Thio-Hypoy FD (90 EP)

A light-bodied powerful extreme pressure gear oil. This is a special oil for running-in certain hypoid gears.

Automatic Transmission Fluids

Castrol TQF

(Automatic Transmission Fluid)

Approved for use in all Borg-Warner Automatic Transmission Units. Castrol TQF also meets Ford specification M2C 33F.

Castrol TQ Dexron®

(Automatic Transmission Fluid)

Complies with the requirements of Dexron® Automatic Transmission Fluids as laid down by General Motors Corporation.

Castrol Greases

Castrol LM

A multi-purpose high melting point lithium based grease approved for most automotive applications including chassis and wheel bearing lubrication.

Castrol MS3

A high melting point lithium based grease containing molybdenum disulphide.

Castrol BNS

A high melting point grease for use where recommended by certain manufacturers in front wheel bearings when disc brakes are fitted.

Castrol Greases (continued)

Castrol CL

A semi-fluid calcium based grease, which is both waterproof and adhesive, intended for chassis lubrication.

Castrol Medium

A medium consistency calcium based grease.

Castrol Heavy

A heavy consistency calcium based grease.

Castrol PH

A white grease for plunger housings and other moving parts on brake mechanisms. *It must NOT be allowed to come into contact with brake fluid when applied to the moving parts of hydraulic brakes.*

Castrol Graphited Grease

A graphited grease for the lubrication of transmission chains.

Castrol Under-Water Grease

A grease for the under-water gears of outboard motors.

Anti-Freeze

Castrol Anti-Freeze

Contains anti-corrosion additives with ethylene glycol. Recommended for the cooling systems of all petrol and diesel engines.

Speciality Products

Castrol Girling Damper Oil Thin

The oil for Girling piston type hydraulic dampers.

Castrol Shockol

A light viscosity oil for use in some piston type shock absorbers and in some hydraulic systems employing synthetic rubber seals. It must not be used in braking systems.

Castrol Penetrating Oil

A leaf spring lubricant possessing a high degree of penetration and providing protection against rust.

Castrol Solvent Flushing Oil

A light-bodied solvent oil, designed for flushing engines, rear axles, gearboxes and gearcasings.

Castrollo

An upper cylinder lubricant for use in the proportion of 1 fluid ounce to two gallons of fuel.

Everyman Oil

A light-bodied machine oil containing anti-corrosion additives for both general use and cycle lubrication.

Chapter 5 Clutch and actuating mechanism

Contents

Specifications

Clutch

Type	Single plate disc - Fichtel & Sachs
Operation	Mechanical - cable
Diameter	180 mm (5.1 inch)
Total lining area	236 cms^2 (36 sq.ins.)
Pedal free play travel	10 - 20 mm (.4 to .8 inch)

Torque Wrench Setting

Clutch cover to flywheel bolts	18 lbs.ft. (2.5 mkg)

1. General Description

The clutch is a single disc design and incorporates a driven plate (which carries the friction material on each side) and a pressure plate and cover assembly. The pressure plate is tensioned by five coil springs and the pressure is taken off by a central release ring linked to three release levers which pivot on the cover.

The clutch operating lever pivots in the forward end of the gearbox casing and a thrust bearing on the inner end bears on to the release ring when the arm is operated. The operating arm is moved by a cable from the clutch pedal.

As the friction surfaces of the driven plate wear so the clearance between the thrust ring and release ring decreases. This clearance is reflected in the free play movement of the clutch pedal. This movement can be adjusted by altering the length of the cable. This is effected by turning the adjuster nut fitted to the clutch end of the cable.

2. Routine Maintenance

Routine maintenance is confined to checking the clutch thrust bearing clearance by measuring the pedal free play.

If the adjustment is nearing its limit this is an indication that the friction lining material is nearing the limit of its useful life.

3. Clutch Cable - Removal, Replacement and Adjustment

1. Clutch cables rarely break and do not stretch significantly so if you find that the clutch is slipping and further adjustment is not possible the cause is the clutch friction plate. Do not think that the cable is at fault.

2. To remove the cable jack up the rear of the car and remove the left hand wheel. Unscrew the cable adjusting nut from the threaded end and then disengage the cable from the clutch lever.

3. Inside the car it is necessary to detach the foot pedal cluster assembly. On right hand drive cars this is a task which takes care and patience. For details refer to Chapter 9.

4. Having unhooked the front end of the cable it can be drawn out of the guide tube. A new cable can be fed into the tube in the same manner although it may be a bit of a fiddle to get it started as you are working partly blind. Make sure the cable is well greased and try and keep the grease off the interior trim and seats. The real difficulty comes when hooking the end on to the lever and reassembling the pedal cluster. This is covered in Chapter 9.

5. Once the cable has been connected properly at the front, and after the pedal cluster has been reassembled, replace it through the operating lever at the other end and refit the adjusting nut.

6. When adjusting the clutch, the pedal is the indicating factor. The top of the pedal should move forward ½ inch (12 mm) before firmer resistance is felt. If it moves more than this the adjuster needs screwing up to shorten the cable. If it moves less then slacken the adjuster. When the adjustment is taken up all the way and the free play is excessive then the driven plate is in need of replacement. Sometimes after replacing a cable it is found that the threaded rear end is too short to reach the operating lever easily. This is because the other end is not properly engaged in the hook recess. With luck a bit of waggling back and forth on the clutch pedal will settle it in position.

7. Stiff or uneven operation of the clutch could be due to several factors. One check worth making before doing anything too drastic is on the cable outer cover between the rear end of the terminal and the lug on the transmission casing. The outer sleeve should have a bend in it and the lowest point of this bend should be between 1 - 1¾ inches (25 - 45 mm) from an imaginary straight line between the ends of the sleeve. The latitude is generous so the measurement is easy enough. Should there be a variation outside these limits (a most unusual occurrence unless the sleeve has been disconnected and wrongly refitted) adjustments can be made. Disconnect the inner cable from the clutch operating lever, draw the sleeve out of the lug

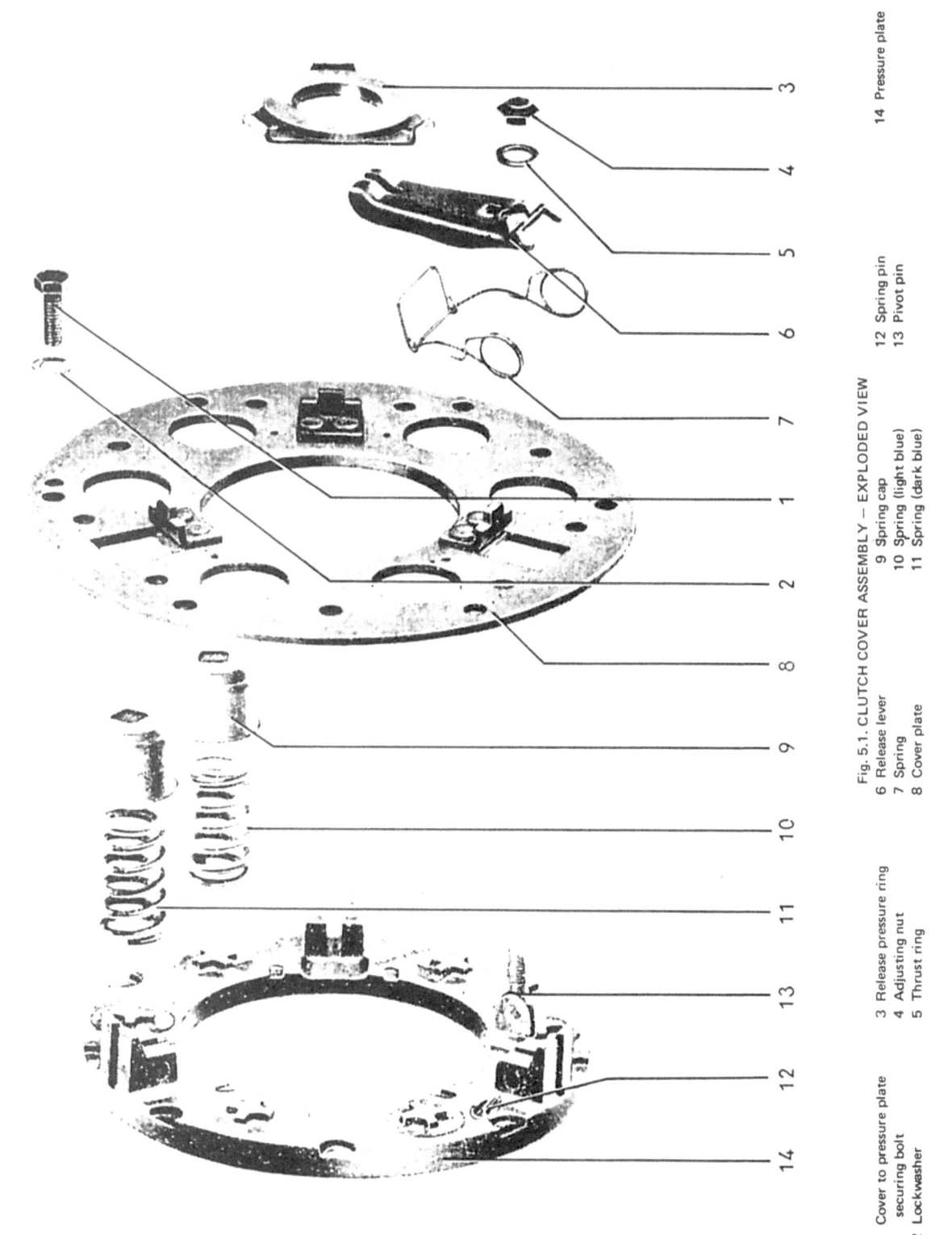

Fig. 5.1. CLUTCH COVER ASSEMBLY – EXPLODED VIEW

1 Cover to pressure plate
  securing bolt
2 Lockwasher

3 Release pressure ring
4 Adjusting nut
5 Thrust ring

6 Release lever
7 Spring
8 Cover plate

9 Spring cap
10 Spring (light blue)
11 Spring (dark blue)

12 Spring pin
13 Pivot pin

14 Pressure plate

on the transmission casing and add or remove washers to the shoulder of the sleeve as required.

4. Clutch Assembly - Removal, Inspection and Replacement

1. Remove the engine as described in Chapter 1.
2. Mark the flywheel and clutch cover with a punch so that they may be lined up on replacement if the old cover is being fitted again.
3. Working with a diagonal rotation slacken the six mounting bolts which hold the clutch cover to the flywheel - slackening each one a little at a time until the tension on the pressure springs is completely relieved. Lift off the cover and clutch driven plate.
4. The clutch driven plate should be inspected for wear and for contamination by oil. Wear is gauged by the depth of the rivet heads below the surface of the friction material. If this is less than .025 inch (0.6 mm) the linings are worn enough to justify renewal.
5. Examine the friction faces of the flywheel and clutch pressure plate. These should be bright and smooth. If the linings have worn too much it is possible that the metal surfaces may have been scored by the rivet heads. Dust and grit can have the same effect. If the scoring is very severe it could mean that even with a new clutch driven plate, slip and juddering and other malfunctions will recur. Deep scoring on the flywheel face is serious because the flywheel will have to be removed and machined by a specialist, or renewed. This can be costly. The same applies to the pressure plate in the cover although this is a less costly affair. If the friction linings seem unworn yet are blackened and shiny then the cause is almost certainly due to oil. Such a condition also requires renewal of the plate. The source of oil must be traced also. It will be due to a leaking seal on the transmission input shaft (Chapter 6 gives details of renewal) or on the front of the engine crankshaft (see Chapter 1 for details of renewal).
6. If the reason for removal of the clutch has been because of slip and the slip has been allowed to go on for any length of time it is possible that the heat generated will have adversely affected the pressure springs in the cover. Some or all may have been affected with the result that the pressure is now uneven and/or insufficient to prevent slip, even with a new friction plate. It is recommended that under such circumstances a new assembly is fitted.
7. Although it is possible to dismantle the clutch cover assembly and, in theory, renew the various springs and levers the economics do not justify it. Clutch cover assemblies are available on an exchange basis. The component parts for their overhaul are held at the Central Reconditioning Depots and are not readily available at the Store Depots. It will probably be necessary to order an assembly in advance as most agencies other than the large Central Depots carry stocks only sufficient to meet their own requirements. However it is possible to get assemblies from reputable manufacturers other than Volkswagen; Borg & Beck for instance.
8. When replacing the clutch, hold the cover and support the friction disc on one finger through the centre. Be sure that the facing with radial lines goes towards the flywheel. Position the cover so that the locating marks line up. If a new cover is being fitted it will be necessary to check whether there are any imbalance marks on either the flywheel or cover. On the flywheel this can be indicated by a 5 mm diameter countersunk hole or a white paint mark on the outer edge. On the clutch cover it would be indicated by a white paint mark on the outer edge. If only one (flywheel or cover) has an imbalance mark it does not matter how the cover is fitted. If both have marks make sure that they are 180° apart (i.e. on opposite sides of the circle).
9. Replace the six securing bolts and screw them up evenly just

enough to grip the friction plate but not enough to prevent it being moved. It is important to line up the central splined hub with the roller bearing in the counterbore of the flywheel locking bolt. If this is not done it will be impossible to refit the engine to the transmission. It is possible to centralise them by eye but a simple surer way is to select a suitable piece of bar or wooden dowel which will fit reasonably into the flywheel nut and round which some adhesive tape can be wound to equal the diameter inside the friction plate boss. By inserting this the friction plate can be moved and centralised with sufficient accuracy.
10 Finally tighten up the six cover securing bolts evenly and diagonally a little each at a time to a final torque of 18 lb/ft.
11 Before refitting the engine after a clutch overhaul check the transmission input shaft oil seal (Chapter 6) and the clutch release operating mechanism (see Section 5).
12 Before finally offering up the engine dust the splines of the gearbox input shaft (which should, of course, be clean and in good condition) with a little graphite or molybdenum powder. Also put a little molybdenum paste (not oil or grease) on the face of the release bearing and clutch release ring.

5. Clutch Release Operating Mechanism - Inspection and Repair

1. Clutch operation can be adversely affected if the release thrust ring and retaining springs are worn or damaged. Squeals, juddering, slipping or snatching could be caused partly or even wholly by this mechanism.
2. Full examination is possible only when the engine has been removed and normally it is carried out when the clutch is in need of repair. The mechanism is contained in and attached to the transmission casing. Check first that the operating lever return spring mounted on the exterior of the shaft on the left hand side is not broken. If it is it can be renewed without removing the engine; once the lever has been disconnected from the cable and taken off the cross shaft. However, the damage which failure of this spring may have caused has probably occurred already. If you are going to examine the clutch anyway it will be easier to renew the spring after the engine is removed.
3. With the engine removed examine the release bearing and the plastic face. It should spin silently and show no signs of wear or other damage. The retaining 'U' clips at each side must be a tight fit so that the bearing does not rattle about on the mounting forks.
4. Do not wash the bearing in any cleaning fluid. It is sealed and although fluid may wash some grease out you cannot get any more in. If it needs renewal pull off the clips and lift it out.
5. When replacing the thrust release bearing fit the straight ends of the 'U' clips into the holes in each end of the pivot pins on the bearing and hook the curved ends into position round the back of the operating forks.
6. Check that the cross shaft moves freely in the transmission casing. When fitting a new operating lever return spring (on the outside of the casing) it is necessary to disconnect the clutch cable and pull off the arm from the cross shaft.
7. To remove the cross shaft the clamp bolt must be completely removed as it engages in a cut-out in the cross shaft. Place the new spring over the cross shaft so that the straight end is innermost and resting on the lug. The hooked end goes in front of the lever.
8. Apply a little molybdenum paste to the face of the thrust bearing before refitting the engine.
9. Re-adjust the pedal free play once the engine is re-installed.

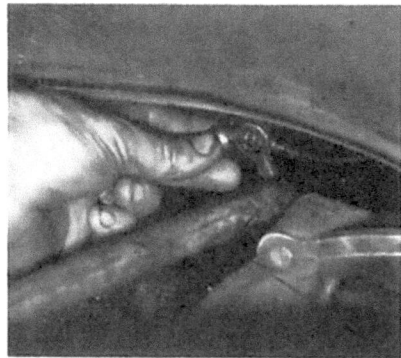

Replacing clutch cable adjustment nut. Engine removed, access otherwise from under the car (Section 5.5)

Offering up cover and driven plate to flywheel (Section 5.8)

Matching up cover plate to flywheel alignment marks (Section 5.9)

Centre the driven plate with a suitable bar (Section 5.9)

Tighten securing bolts to a torque of 18 lb ft (Section 5.10)

Positioning return spring of clutch operating lever (Section 5.7)

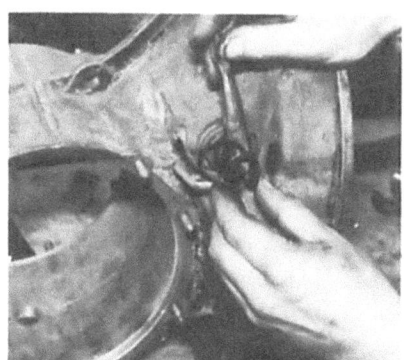

Refitting operating lever (Section 5.7)

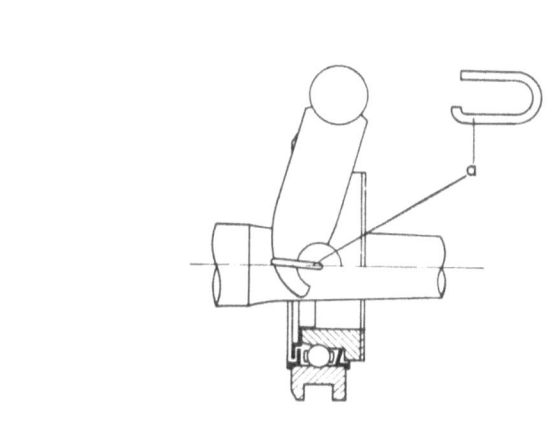

Fig. 5.2. Clutch release bearing - Cross section showing shape and location of retaining clip (a)

Thrust release bearing with one U clip hooked into pivot pin prior to clipping behind fork arm (Section 5.5)

Fault Finding Chart - Clutch & Actuating Mechanism

Symptom	Reason/s	Remedy
Judder when taking up drive	Loose engine gearbox mountings or over flexible mountings	Check and tighten all mounting bolts and replace any 'soft' or broken mountings.
	Badly worn friction surfaces or friction plate contaminated with oil carbon deposit.	Remove engine and replace clutch parts as required. Rectify any oil leakage points which may have caused contamination.
	Worn splines in the friction plate hub or on the gearbox input shaft	Renew friction plate and/or input shaft.
	Badly worn bush in flywheel centre for input shaft spigot	Renew bush in flywheel.
Clutch spin (or failure to disengage) so that gears cannot be engaged	Clutch actuating cable clearance too great	Adjust clearance.
	Clutch friction disc sticking to pressure surface because of oil contamination (usually apparent after standing idle for some length of time)	As temporary remedy engage top gear, apply handbrakes, depress clutch and start engine. (If very badly stuck engine will not turn). When running rev up engine and slip clutch until disengagement is normally possible. Renew friction plate at earliest opportunity.
	Damaged or misaligned pressure plate assembly	Replace pressure plate assembly
Clutch slip - (increase in engine speed does not result in increase in car speed - especially on hills)	Clutch actuating cable clearance from fork too little resulting in partially disengaged clutch at all times	Adjust clearance.
	Clutch friction surfaces worn out (beyond further adjustment of operating cable) or clutch surfaces oil soaked	Replace friction plate and remedy source of oil leakage.

Fig. 5.3. CLUTCH DRIVEN PLATE — FLYWHEEL FACE AND
CROSS SECTION
A   Driven plate
B   Lining springs
C   Linings

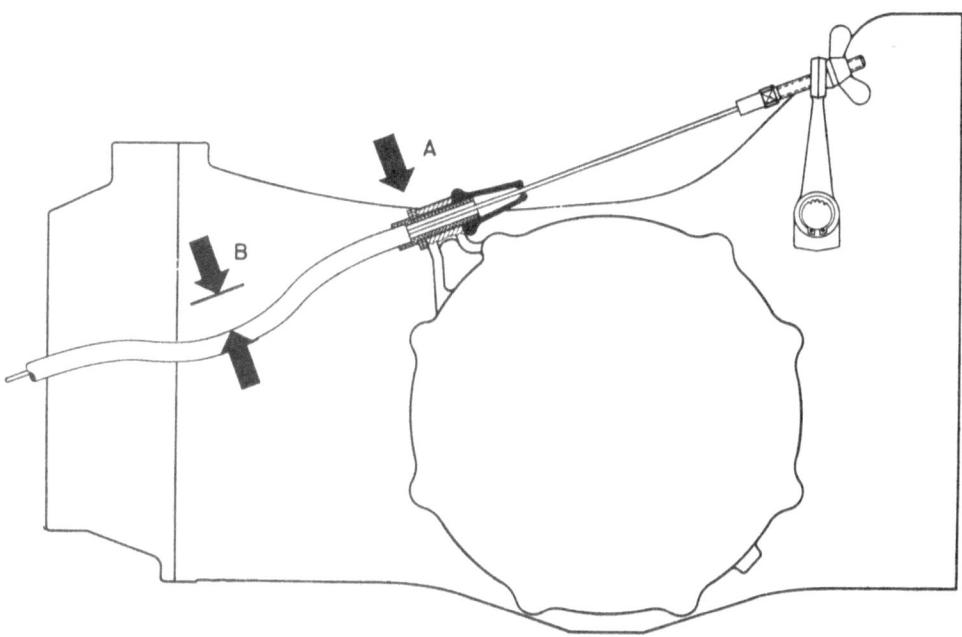

Fig. 5.4. Clutch operating cable outer sleeve. Drawing showing bend measurement (B) and adjustment washer location (A)

Chapter 6 Transmission. One piece casing

Contents

Specifications

General

Final drive and gearbox main casing - 1960 on	Alloy casting - one piece tunnel type
Number of gears	4 forward, 1 reverse
Synchromesh	Baulk ring
Oil capacity of casing	3.0 litres (5.3 pints)
Refill quantity required	2.5 litres (4.4 pints)

Gearbox Ratios
4 speed synchro

1st	3.80 : 1
2nd	2.06 : 1
3rd	1.26 : 1
4th	0.82 or 0.89 : 1
Reverse	3.88 : 1 (3.62 : 1 from August 1967)
Final drive ratio	4.375 : 1
Gearchange	Manual floor mounted lever through remote control mechanical linkage.

Torque Wrench Settings

Oil drain plugs	22-29 lb/ft (3.0-4.0 mkg)
Oil filler plug	14 lb/ft (2.0 mkg)
Transmission carrier to frame bolts	166 lb/ft (23.0 mkg)
Spring plate bolts/nuts	72 lb/ft (10.0 mkg)
Final drive cover nuts	22 lb/ft (3.0 mkg)
Gear shift cover to carrier nuts	11 lb/ft (1.5 mkg)
Gear carrier to housing nuts	14 lb/ft (2.0 mkg)
Pinion bearing retainer screws	36 lb/ft (5.0 mkg)
Pinion shaft nut	43 lb/ft (6.0 mkg)
Input shaft nut	43 lb/ft (6.0 mkg)
Reverse lever guide screw	14 lb/ft (2.0 mkg)
Selector fork screws	18 lb/ft (2.5 mkg)
Pinion shaft round nut (ball bearings)	87 lb/ft (12.0 mkg)
(taper roller bearing)	144 lb/ft (20.0 mkg)

1. Transmission - General Description

The gearbox and final drive is a single composite assembly housed in a die cast magnesium casing which, prior to 1961, was split vertically into two halves but thereafter was cast in one piece. The input or main shaft carries the 3rd and 4th gear hub and is mounted above the output or pinion shaft which carries 1st and 2nd gear hub. The pinion shaft meshes directly with the crown wheel of the differential assembly. On early models which had the split casing,

87

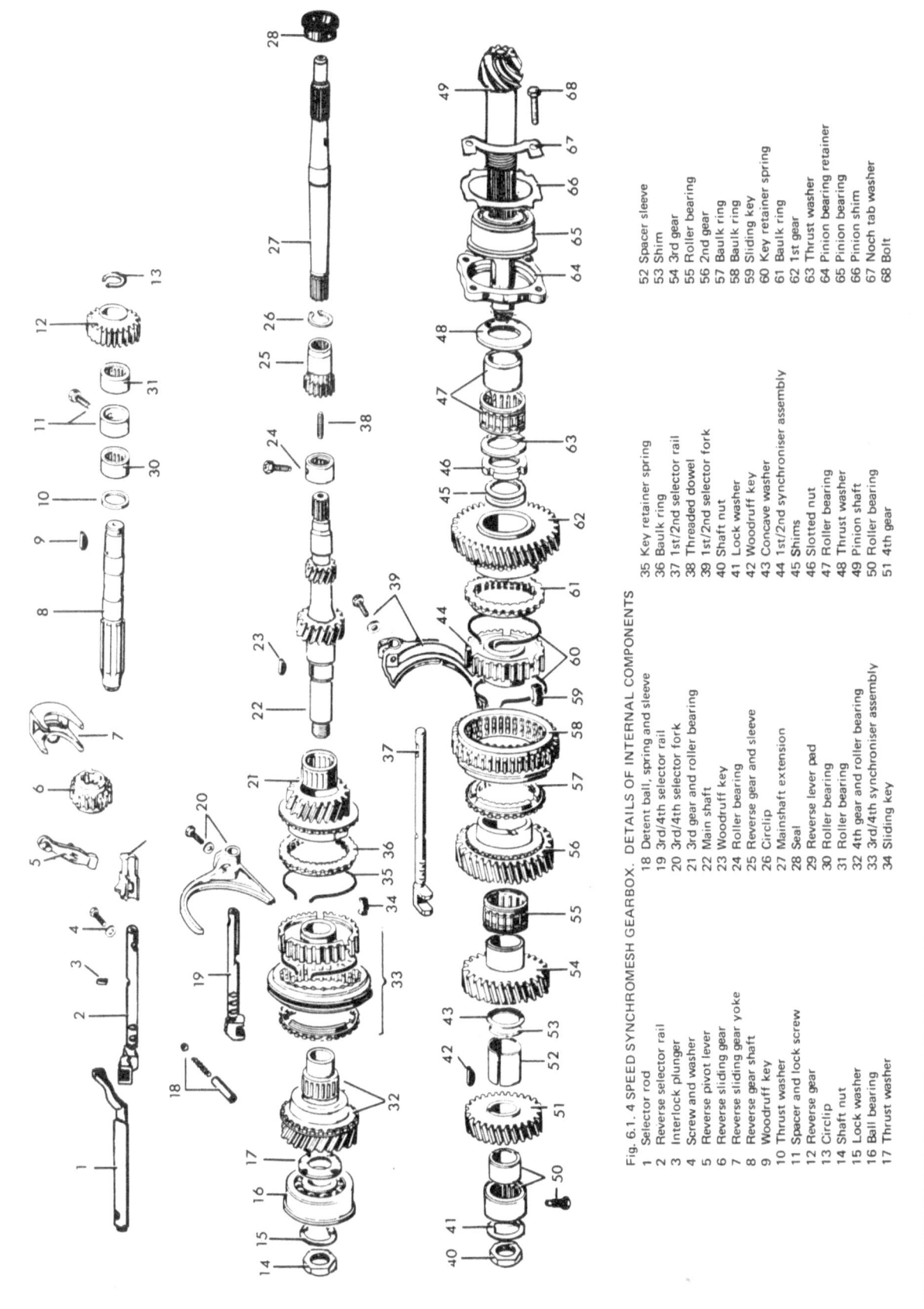

Fig. 6.1. 4 SPEED SYNCHROMESH GEARBOX. DETAILS OF INTERNAL COMPONENTS

1 Selector rod
2 Reverse selector rail
3 Interlock plunger
4 Screw and washer
5 Reverse pivot lever
6 Reverse sliding gear
7 Reverse sliding gear yoke
8 Reverse gear shaft
9 Woodruff key
10 Thrust washer
11 Spacer and lock screw
12 Reverse gear
13 Circlip
14 Shaft nut
15 Lock washer
16 Ball bearing
17 Thrust washer

18 Detent ball, spring and sleeve
19 3rd/4th selector rail
20 3rd/4th selector fork
21 3rd gear and roller bearing
22 Main shaft
23 Woodruff key
24 Roller bearing
25 Reverse gear and sleeve
26 Circlip
27 Mainshaft extension
28 Seal
29 Reverse lever pad
30 Roller bearing
31 Roller bearing
32 4th gear and roller bearing
33 3rd/4th synchroniser assembly
34 Sliding key

35 Key retainer spring
36 Baulk ring
37 1st/2nd selector rail
38 Threaded dowel
39 1st/2nd selector fork
40 Shaft nut
41 Lock washer
42 Woodruff key
43 Concave washer
44 1st/2nd synchroniser assembly
45 Shims
46 Slotted nut
47 Roller bearing
48 Thrust washer
49 Pinion shaft
50 Roller bearing
51 4th gear

52 Spacer sleeve
53 Shim
54 3rd gear
55 Roller bearing
56 2nd gear
57 Baulk ring
58 Baulk ring
59 Sliding key
60 Key retainer spring
61 Baulk ring
62 1st gear
63 Thrust washer
64 Pinion bearing retainer
65 Pinion bearing
66 Pinion shim
67 Noch tab washer
68 Bolt

only three speeds were synchromesh (1st being non-synchro) and on those models the input shaft was in effect the layshaft because the synchro hubs for 2nd gear and 3rd/4th gears were all mounted on the pinion (output) shaft.

On later models with the one piece casing the input shaft is divided into two parts for dismantling and assembly reasons. The joint is located by a screwed stud and the joining ends are splined. The drive power is taken by a collar which also incorporates the reverse drive gear. In order to dismantle the gearbox the axle shaft tubes and differential assembly have to be first of all removed.

In view of the relative complexity of this complete unit, it is felt that a few words of warning should be given in order to let potential dismantlers fully realise what they may be letting themselves in for. First of all decide whether the fault you wish to repair is worth all the time and effort involved. Secondly, if the gearbox is in a very bad state then the cost of the component parts may well exceed the cost of a new replacement unit. Thirdly, remember that a basic knowledge of gearbox construction and function is a bare necessity before tackling this one. If you are doing one for the first time do not start on a Volkswagen!

Finally, two technical musts. You must be able to have access to the use of a press. So check this before you start. Make sure that you have made contact with an agent who is likely to be able to supply all the new gaskets and parts that may be required. It is not possible to work out exactly what may be required before you start but the minimum will be a gasket set, baulk rings and bearings so check that you can at least get these. The press is essential for dismantling the two shaft assemblies which is necessary if you want to replace the baulk rings. On later models (1967 on) some minor changes in assembly make things more difficult for the do-it-yourself men. Where shims and nuts were once used circlips of selective thicknesses combined with dished 'pressure' washers have replaced them. In such instances a selection of circlips must be available and a press and suitable assembly tool are essential. If, therefore, you have no Volkswagen agent within reasonable range you could get into difficulties on reassembly.

For those with the need to dismantle and overhaul the pre-1960 type gearbox it can be said that it is generally less difficult. However it is most important to verify spares availability before venturing too far.

2. Transmission - Removal and Replacement

1. Remove the engine as described in Chapter 1.
2. Detach the starter motor from the transmission casing if not already done.
3. It will be necessary to undo the axle shaft outer nuts if the tube and shaft need to be separated for any reason. In any case it is a good idea to loosen these nuts in case of unforeseen circumstances so do it now while the wheels are still on and the vehicle is on the ground. You will not be able to do it when the assembly is removed from the car. The requirements for setting about slackening these very large and very tight nuts is given in Chapter 9 in connection with removal of the rear brake drums.
4. Having slackened the axle shaft nuts and wheel bolts jack up the car and remove the road wheels. Note that the road wheel bolts are much tighter on a Volkswagen than other cars - 65 - 79 ft/lbs of torque. Support the car on stands underneath the two rear jacking points.
5. Remove one of the front seats and the rear seat and move the other front seat fully forward.
6. Take up the floor covering and the shroud over the handbrake lever.
7. Undo the locknuts and adjusting nuts on each of the handbrake cable ends and take them off.
8. Take off the circlip in the groove at one end of the handbrake lever pivot pin and drive out the pin. Move the handbrake lever rearwards a little and it may then be lifted out. Do not press the ratchet

release button whilst doing this or the ratchet mechanism will fall out.
9. The two handbrake cables may now be drawn out from the transmission casing tubes.
10 From inside the car once more, remove the cover over the frame tunnel under the back seat. It is located by a single screw. Underneath, the gear shift rod coupling will be seen and the rear square headed screw should be removed after cutting off the locking wire. If the gear lever is then moved the coupling will separate.
11 Next disconnect the rear hydraulic flexible brake hoses, one on each side where they connect at the bracket mounting on top of each axle tube. For details of this procedure refer to Chapter 9
12 Next, if you have not already done so, clean off the area where the suspension plates are bolted to the outer ends of the axle tubes. Apply some penetrating oil now to the three nuts and bolts on each side to assist removal later (see Chapter 8 for details).
13 On the flange nearest the top nut and bolt which holds the axle to the spring plate will be seen a 'V' notch in the casting. Another notch, exactly in line with it, should be made with a chisel in the edge of the spring plate alongside. The bolt holes in the plate are slotted and it is most important that the axle tube is correctly positioned on replacement.
14 Now undo and remove the bolts which secure the lower ends of the shock absorbers.
15 The clutch cable locknut and adjusting nut should next be removed from the end of the cable and the inner cable drawn out from the clutch operating lever.
16 Undo the nuts and bolts securing the axle tubes to the spring suspension plates. The axle tubes may then be moved out and down on each side (see Chapter 8).
17 All that now remains is to remove the two nuts and two bolts mounting the unit to the frame. First remove the two nuts at the front end which hold the casing onto the flexible mounting. Take off the washers also.
18 Next support the whole unit on a jack. A trolley jack and piece of stout board is the best way of doing this. The unit can then be lowered easily. If you do not have a trolley jack then the stout board may be supported on static jacks or bricks, whichever is most convenient and stable.
19 Having prepared the necessary support the two large bolts, one into each end of the rear frame tubes, should be removed with a socket spanner. They are not excessively tight.
20 The whole assembly can then be moved rearwards. Depending on how you have arranged and positioned your support will depend how the whole lot is balanced. Most likely it will try and drop at the front so be prepared for this. Lower it down carefully until it can be drawn out from under the rear of the car.
21 Replacement of the assembly is an exact reversal of the removal procedure. Note the following points. When the unit is in position the mounting bolts at the rear should not be tightened until the nuts securing the flexible mountings have been slackened. Then tighten the two large bolts; next the two front mounting nuts and finally the four rear mounting nuts once more. This prevents distortion stresses being set up in the flexible rubber mountings.
22 Do not forget that the line up of the notches in the axle bearing housings and spring plates is important. The hydraulic system will need bleeding after connecting the brake hoses and the handbrake cables reconnected to the lever.
23 The correct coupling of the gear shift to the shift operating rod is essential. Make sure that the point of the locking screw engages the dimple in the shaft exactly and re-lock the screw with wire. If it is found that gear selection is not quite satisfactory on completion it is in order to make minor adjustments to the position of the gear lever mounting. Details and explanations can be found at the end of Section 8 in Chapter 7.
24 Do not forget to refill the transmission with the correct quantity and grade of oil. 5¼ pints are needed. This is more easily done from above before the engine is replaced. Make sure the two drain plugs are tight and that the filler/level plug is slackened before putting the transmission back.

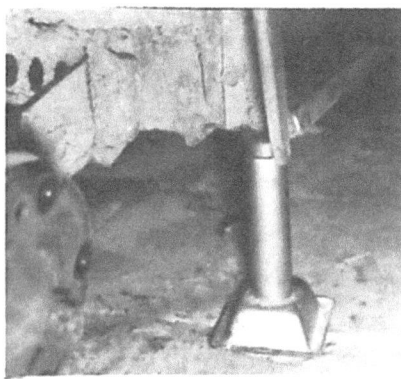

Body supported at rear jacking point (Section 2.4)

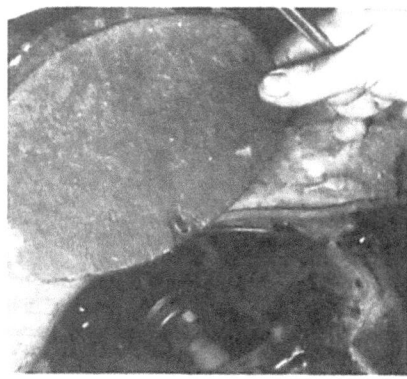

Gearchange rod connection under rear seat (Section 2.10)

Dismantling gearchange rod (Section 2.10)

Gearchange rod disconnected (Section 2.10)

Transmission supported on a trolley jack and packing (Section 2.18)

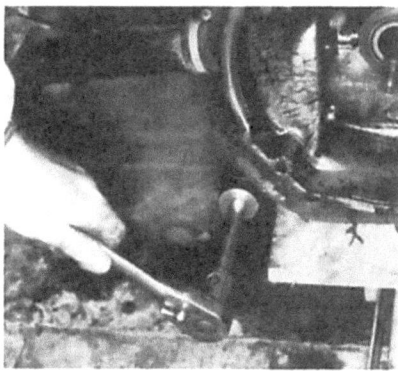

Removing rear mounting bolts (Section 2.19)

Work the whole assembly backwards (Section 2.20)

Transmission removed (Section 2.20)

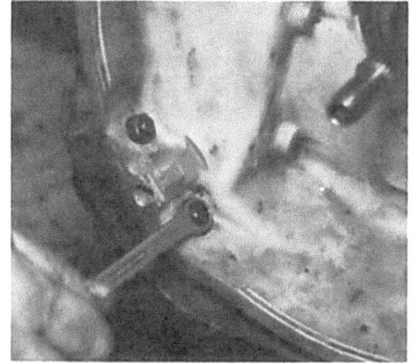

Tightening the transmission rear flexible mounting bolts (Section 2.21)

Refilling with oil (Section 2.24)

Drifting the gearbox assembly from the casing (Section 3.10)

Drifting the side bearing off the differential casing (Section 3.14)

3. Transmission - Dismantling

1. Before proceeding according to the directions given in this Chapter read the 'General Description' section first. It is assumed that the unit has been removed from the car and the axle shafts and axle tubes removed as described in Chapter 8. Do not throw away gaskets when dismantling. They act as a guide when working out what new ones to use from the gasket set bought (see Reassembly section). Clean the casing exterior thoroughly.

2. Remove the nuts holding the gear selector lever housing and remove the housing together with the lever.

3. The main nuts on the ends of the input and output (pinion) shafts are now revealed. On later models these nuts are dispensed with and circlips are used instead. One of these circlips, on the input shaft end, must be removed before the two shafts can be drawn out of the bearings in the gear carrier. This circlip is under tension from a dished thrust washer underneath and is liable to 'fly' when released from its groove. So take care and cover the end with a cloth when releasing it. Tap back the tabs of the lockwashers which lie along a flat of each of the nuts. To prevent the shafts from rotating pull and/or push the two outer selector fork rails which protrude from the end of the casing. This will lock the two shafts by engaging two gears at once. Using a suitable socket or ring spanner the nuts can then be undone.

3. Next remove the nuts from the studs which secure the end casing (called the gear carrier) to the main casing and take off the braided electrical earth strap at the same time.

4. Turn the whole unit on its side so that the left side final drive cover is upwards. (Remember, the narrow end of the casing is the front.) Then undo the nuts securing the cover to the casing.

5. With a soft-faced mallet the cover plate can now be gently tapped off from the casing. The main advice here is 'easy does it'. Do not use any force. The side bearing may or may not come off with the cover and between the bearing inner race and the differential there is a shim. If the bearing comes away with the side cover this shim(s) will be freed so collect it and tape it to the bearing to ensure it is not lost, damaged or mixed up with the shim or shims which come off in due course from the opposite side. If the bearing remains on the differential, leave it for the time being. Note the paper gasket between cover and casing.

6. Turn the casing over. With a suitable drift positioned against the inner race of the right hand bearing the whole of the differential assembly may now be tapped out. Take care to support the weight and prevent the assembly from dropping under its own weight. If it is found that it is easier to drift out the differential with the bearing left in the side cover this is in order but remember to collect up the shims which will be released between bearing and differential and tape them to the differential straight away.

7. Going back to the other side again, release the circlip which locates the splined collar/reverse gear to the input shaft. Slide it back along the shaft and slide the collar along behind it. The rear end of the shaft may now be unscrewed from the other half. Then take off the collar/gear and remove the circlip from the shaft also. The shaft may then be drawn out from the rear through the oil seal. It will be as well to replace this oil seal but if not take care not to damage it. (Note that this oil seal can be renewed with the transmission unit installed in the car. Access can be gained once the engine is removed).

8. Remove the nuts holding the right hand final drive cover and with a suitable drift gently tap it free from the inside. Note the paper gasket between cover and casing.

9. Four bolts will be seen securing the pinion shaft bearing retainer plate. Pry up the lock tabs on each bolt taking care that the tool used does not slip and come in contact with the pinion gear. Remove the bolts, still guarding against possible pinion damage.

10 The whole gearbox assembly is now ready to come out of the casing. This can be achieved by using a heavy copper faced mallet and striking the end of the pinion. Another way is to insert a scissor jack shallow enough to fit between the pinion and the casing opposite. Pad the head of the jack against the pinion and press it

out. Be sure to support the gear carrier when the gear shafts come away. As soon as it is clear, be sure to collect the shim(s) from the pinion flange.

11 The main casing has two needle roller bearings still left in it. One has the reverse gear and shaft running in it. To remove the gear first remove the circlip. The gear is a slide fit on a key and can be pulled off - levering a little with a screwdriver if necessary. The key must then be removed from the shaft and the shaft can be taken out from the front.

12 To remove the needle roller bearings of the reverse shaft, first unscrew the locating screw from the casing. This secures the spacer sleeve between the two bearings. A drift of suitable diameter can then be used to drive the two needle rollers and spacer out towards the rear of the casing.

13 Similarly, the other needle bearing outer race (no spacer) is secured by a screw in the casing. Once this is removed the needle roller bearing race may be drifted out. (This bearing is the one that supports the rear end of the forward half of the input shaft).

14 The large side bearings, which will be located in either the covers or on the differential, may remain where they are unless inspection indicates that they are worn and need renewal. They can be drifted off the differential or out of the covers. If being taken out of the covers make sure that the covers are firmly and evenly supported and drift the bearings. Do not attempt to do it the other way round or you may damage the cover and that it not the part you intend to renew.

15 So far, the dismantling process has been relatively straightforward. Now is the time to stop and reassemble if you are getting cold feet! The next step is to separate the two shafts with their clusters of gears from the gear carrier. To renew the baulk rings - which is one of the usual remedies for a less than perfect synchromesh action - this further dismantling is necessary.

16 First remove the small sliding gear and fork (reverse) from the pivot on the reverse lever.

17 Next loosen the clamping bolts which hold the two other selector forks to their respective rails. The fork for 1st and 2nd gear selection on the output (pinion) shaft can be lifted away after the rail has been drawn back sufficiently far. The other fork is shrouded by the gear carrier and is not lifted out at this stage. The rail for this one should be driven back far enough to free it from the fork. Do NOT drive the rails out of the gear carrier. If you do a lot of extra work will be caused, probably unnecessarily, because the detent balls and springs will be released.

18 The two shafts with their clusters of gears may now be removed from the carrier. It is a good plan to hold both together with a strong elastic band or a few turns of self-adhesive tape. Then, when the ends of the shaft are released, they will not fall about the place. Two pairs of hands are needed. One pair should hold the carrier - with the shafts hanging down whilst another person strikes the end of the input shaft with a soft faced mallet and supports the weight of the gear shafts as they are driven out. Do not let them drop down.

19 Once the shafts are clear of the carrier the two bearings in the carrier may be removed. The needle roller bearing is located by a screw similar to the needle roller bearings withdrawn previously. The main (input) shaft front bearing is driven out from the inside of the carrier. This particular ball bearing is flanged on the outer race and will only come out in one direction.

20 To dismantle the input shaft first take off the spacer ring, then 4th gear together with the needle bearing cage on which it runs. Remove the baulk ring. This leaves the inner race on the shaft. To get this off a press is needed and the 'V' blocks should be suitably positioned to provide support behind the 3rd gear wheel. In this way there will be no danger of damage to the shaft or gears and the synchro hub assembly will be kept together. Make sure that all parts are supported and held whilst being pressed. 3rd gear may then be taken off together with its needle roller bearing. The 3rd gear bearing inner race need not be removed nor the key which locates the synchro hub. Keep the baulk rings with their respective gears for future reference - fix them with adhesive tape to prevent muddling.

21 The output (pinion) shaft should only be dismantled to a limited

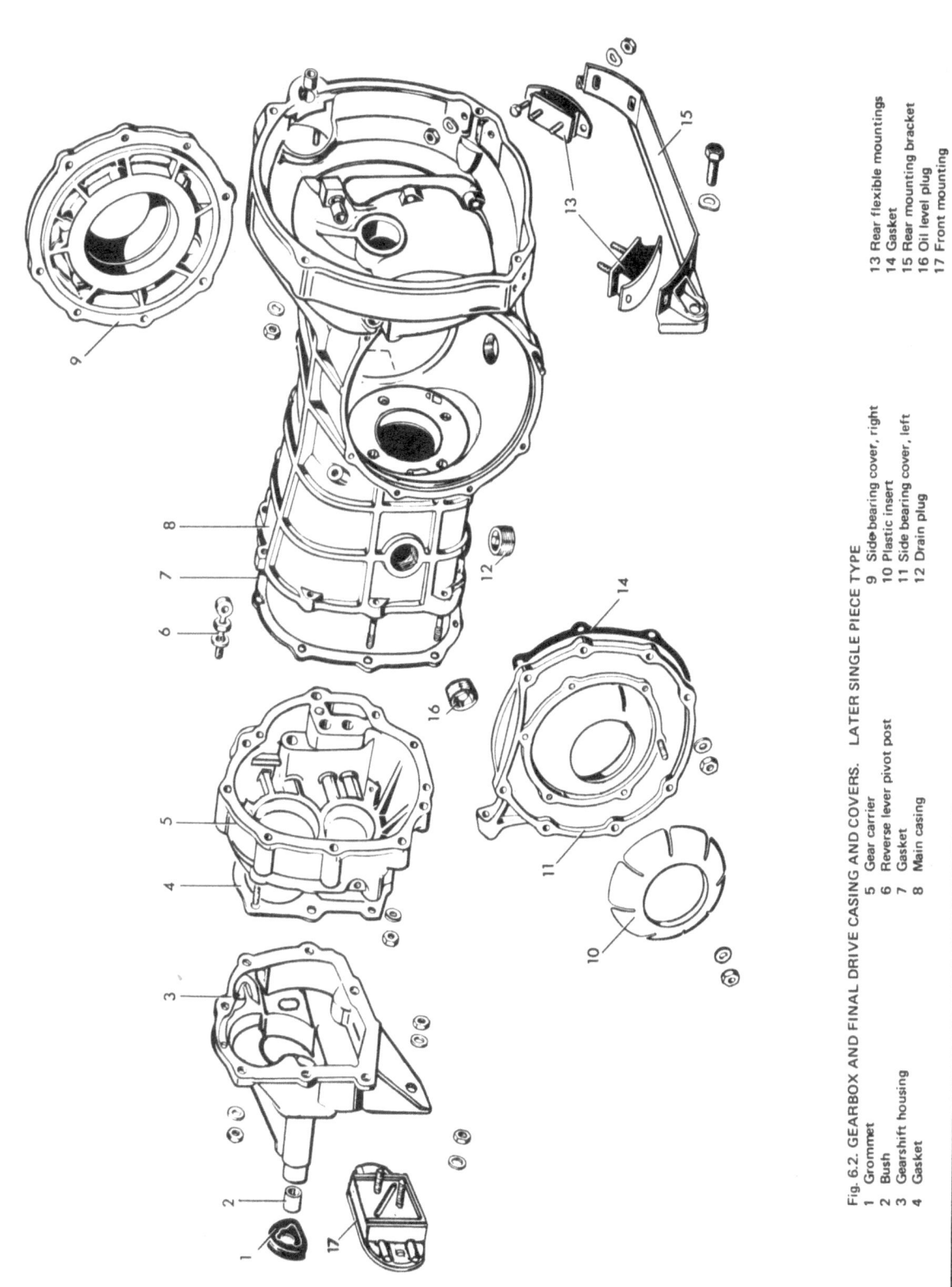

Fig. 6.2. GEARBOX AND FINAL DRIVE CASING AND COVERS.   LATER SINGLE PIECE TYPE

1 Grommet
2 Bush
3 Gearshift housing
4 Gasket

5 Gear carrier
6 Reverse lever pivot post
7 Gasket
8 Main casing

9 Side bearing cover, right
10 Plastic insert
11 Side bearing cover, left
12 Drain plug

13 Rear flexible mountings
14 Gasket
15 Rear mounting bracket
16 Oil level plug
17 Front mounting

extent - which is sufficient to remove the gears, synchro hub and baulk rings. The pinion double taper roller bearing which is held by the notched locking nut should be left intact as this requires the use of more special tools to which we do not feel most owners will have ready access. The services of a press will be required in order to carry out the partial dismantling necessary to remove the baulk rings. Repeated striking on the threaded end of the shaft - even with a soft headed mallet - can distort the threads and if this were severe the shaft could be ruined. Any conventional press with V-blocks will suit. 4th gear together with the inner race of the needle bearing which is still on the shaft, can be pressed off. Behind 4th gear is a spacer and then, in order follows a shim, concave washer, 3rd gear, needle roller bearing and 2nd gear and the 1st and 2nd gear synchro hub. The baulk rings are then able to be renewed if required. On later models which have no nuts on the ends of the two shafts there is a circlip which must first be removed. Then the 4th gear wheel and the inner race may be pressed off. Behind the gear there is a spring spacer and another circlip which must be removed before 3rd gear can be drawn off.

22 The synchro hub assemblies should be handled with care so as to prevent them coming apart inadvertently. It is important that if the centre hub and outer sleeve are separated that they be refitted in the same relative position. Some hubs have marks etched on each part to aid reassembly so before anything else examine them on both sides for such marks. If none can be found make some of your own with a small dab of paint to ensure reassembly in the same position. To dismantle the hubs first lift out the spring retaining clip on each side. Then carefully slide the sleeve from the hub taking care not to drop and lose the three sliding keys.

23 Do not remove the selector fork rails from the gear carrier casing unless inspection indicates that there is something wrong with the detent balls and springs.

---

4. Inspection for Wear in Transmission Components

1. As mentioned in the introduction to this Chapter the degree of wear in the components will to a large extent dictate the economics of repair or replacement with a new unit. If the crown wheel and pinion is obviously badly worn, resulting in noise and significant backlash, then it is possible that this may be repaired alone for approximately half the cost of a new unit provided that is the only major complaint. Such work is not within the competence of the average owner and this manual does not cover it as the author did not do the job. The gearbox used for the illustrations in this Chapter was fitted with new ball bearings, baulk rings and synchro hub keys and retaining clips. Apart from the press all dismantling and reassembly was carried out with normal hand tools.

2. Having been able to obtain the use of a simple mechanical press it is possible to remove all baulk rings for examination. The grooved taper face of the ring provides the braking action on the mating face of the gear wheel cone and if the ridges are worn the braking or synchro action will be less effective. The only way to determine the condition effectively is by comparison with new parts. As the parts are relatively cheap it is considered foolish not to renew them all anyway once the gearbox is dismantled. As a guide, when a baulk ring is fitted over its cone on the gear wheel there should be a minimum gap of .6 mm (.024 inch) between the baulk ring and the gear teeth. The normal gap is 1.1 mm (.043 inch) so it is obvious that if the gap is near the lowest limit new rings should be fitted. When obtaining new baulk rings make sure that you get the parts store to identify and mark each one according to its appropriate gear. Modifications have taken place over the years and although the new ones will still fit and work they are not necessarily identical to the ones you take out. So if you muddle them up you could get problems. They are also not all the same in the set - some have wider cut-outs for example. So mark the new ones you get carefully.

3. Two types of bearings are fitted - ball and needle roller. As a rule needle roller bearings wear very little, not being subject to end thrust of any sort. Check them in position and if there are signs of

rock of roughness then they should be renewed. The ball bearings are the two large side bearings and the special flanged bearing which carries the forward end of the input shaft. If any of these bearings should feel the slightest bit rough or show any sign of drag or slackness when revolved then it should be renewed. The double taper roller bearing should be similarly checked. If there is any sign of roughness or end float then this is a task for a specialist. If this bearing is needing renewal the condition of the pinion gear and crownwheel must be very carefully examined. Once these need renewal then the setting of the whole box is altered and clearances and shims have to be re-calculated and changed.

4. The teeth of all gears should be examined for signs of pitted mating surfaces, chips or scoring. It must be appreciated that if one gear is damaged then its mate on the other shaft will probably be as bad and that one way or another a new shaft could be required.

5. The synchro hubs should be assembled for checking. It is important that there is no rock or backlash on the splines between the inner hub and outer sleeve. When the baulk rings are being renewed it is good policy to renew the three sliding keys and their locating spring rings as well. The keys fit into the cut-outs in the baulk rings and are subject to wear and the springs weaken with time.

6. One of the most critical parts of the Volkswagen gearbox is the operation of the selector forks. The two forks run in grooves in the outer sleeves of the synchro hubs and if the clearance of the forks in the grooves is excessive then there is a likelihood of certain gears jumping out. The clearance of the fork in the groove should not exceed 0.3 mm (.012 inch). Clearance in excess of the maximum could be due to wear on the fork or in the groove or both. It is best therefore first of all to take the forks along to the spares supplier and ask him to compare their thickness with new ones. If the difference in thickness is not enough to compensate for the excess gap between fork and hub groove then the hub assembly will need replacement as well. This is an expensive item but as the gap is somewhat critical there is no alternative. Much depends on the total degree of wear.

7. The selector rails on which the forks are mounted need not be removed from the casing. A certain force is needed in order that they overcome the pressure of the spring loaded ball in the groove. This can be measured with a spring balance hooked on to the end of each selector fork. If the required pull is significantly outside the range of 15 - 20 kgs (33 - 44 lbs) then it is advisable to check the detent springs and balls. To do this push the selector rods right out of the casing. This will release the ball and spring but to get the springs out it is necessary to prise out the plastic plugs from the drillings opposite. Before doing this make sure you obtain some new plugs to drive in when reassembling. Check the spring free length which should be 25 mm (1 inch). If less than 23 mm they should be changed. The balls should be free from pitting and grooves and the selector rods themselves should not be a sloppy fit in the bores. The detent grooves in the rails should not be worn. When the rails are removed do not lose the interlock plungers which fit between the selector rod grooves.

9. Examine all parts of the casing for signs of cracks or damage, particularly near the bearing housings and on the mating surfaces where the gear carrier and side bearing plates join.

10 It should not normally be necessary to completely wash all the gearbox components in fluid - wipe components on clean cloth for examination. In this way the likelihood of dry spots during the first moments of use after reassembly are minimised. The casing itself should be thoroughly washed out with paraffin and flushed afterwards with water. Do not leave the needle roller bearings in position when doing this.

---

5. Transmission Reassembly - General

Spend time in preparing plenty of clean, clear space and if your work bench is rough cover it with hardboard or paper for a good non-gritty surface. Do not start until you have all the necessary parts and gaskets assembled and make sure that all the ones you have

Pressing the inner bearing race, synchro hub and third gear from the input shaft (Section 3.20)

Close up of picture on the left

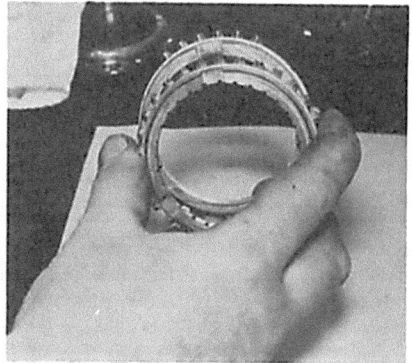

Showing the difference in cut-out width in a set of synchro rings (Section 4.2)

Using a feeler gauge to check the fit of the 3/4th selector fork in the sleeve groove (Section 4.6)

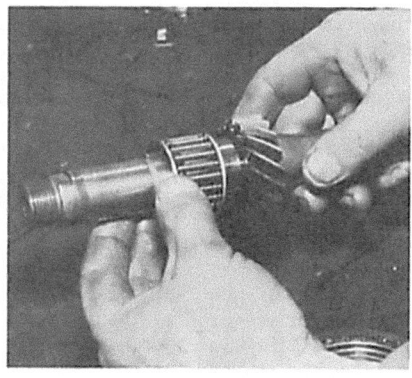

Input shaft. Fitting 3rd gear and roller bearing (Section 5a 1)

Input shaft - fitting synchro ring (Section 5a 1)

Input shaft - fitting 3rd/4th speed synchro hub (Section 5a 2)

Line up the keyway (Section 5a 2)

Drive the hub home using a tube and heavy hammer (Section 5a 2)

Driving the inner sleeve for the 4th gear needle race onto the shaft (Section 5a 3)

Replace the needle cage (Section 5a 3)

Replace the synchro ring and 4th gear (Section 5a 3)

obtained are going to fit. Gasket sets often contain items covering a variety of models so you will not need them all - this is why it helps to keep the old gaskets you take off until the job is eventually finished.

5(a) Input Shaft - Reassembly

1. First reassemble the input shaft, beginning by putting the needle roller cage for 3rd gear in position on the shaft. Then put third gear with its matching synchro ring onto the roller bearings with the cone towards the threaded end of the shaft.

2. The 3rd/4th gear synchro hub assembly goes on next. This has to line up with the key in the shaft. Once the key way in the centre part of the hub is lined up with the key in the shaft the hub can be driven on using a suitable piece of tube and heavy hammer. There are three very important points to note when doing this. Make sure that the hub is on the right way round - some later models have a groove in the outer sleeve 1 mm deep and this must be towards the threaded end of the shaft. If there is no indication then you may put the hub on either way round. Secondly, make sure that you only drive the centre part of the hub. Otherwise it will come apart and have to be reassembled. Thirdly, the slots in the baulk ring must be lined up with the keys in the hub. This is best done by someone holding the baulk ring in position with the keys whilst the hub is driven on the final amount. Be careful not to trap any fingers!

3. Next the inner race for the 4th gear needle roller bearing has to be driven on to the shaft in the same manner that the hub was driven on before it. Drive it right down to the hub. Then replace the needle roller cage followed by the baulk ring and 4th gear. The baulk ring also has three cut-outs which engage with the sliding keys in the hub.

4. Finally, place the thrust washer on the end of the shaft with the V cuts (if any) facing the threaded end of the shaft. Temporarily replace the shaft nut and put the whole assembly on one side for the time being. If you have one of the later gearboxes with circlip fixing put the new dished washer and circlip with the shaft for future assembly.

5(b) Pinion Shaft - Reassembly

1. As pointed out earlier, the pinion shaft has been dismantled only as far as the pinion bearing which has been left in position. If this bearing has been renewed then the gearbox and final drive will need resetting and this is a skilled job requiring special equipment and a selection of special shims to hand from which the necessary requirements are available.

2. The first 'loose' item therefore which goes behind the pinion bearing locking ring is the shim or shims which control 1st gear end float. This end float is measured after the 1st gear and hub are installed. The gap is that between the thrust washer (already locked in position behind the 1st gear needle bearing) and the face of the gear. If the gap should be outside the limits of .10 - .25 mm (.004 - .010 inch) then different shims will be required to correct this. The shims in effect determine the position of the inner sleeve of the 1st/2nd gear synchro hub in relation to the captive thrust washer. 1st gear end float is controlled between the thrust and centre hub face.

3. Next put the bearing retainer over the shaft and up to the pinion bearing with the smooth, machined face towards the pinion gear at the end of the shaft.

4. Now put 1st gear (the largest one with helically cut teeth) in position on the needle roller bearings with the cone face of the synchro pointing away from the pinion gear.

5. Select the 1st gear baulk ring and place it over 1st gear and then replace the 1st and 2nd gear hub over the splines on the shaft with the selector fork groove of the outer sleeve facing towards the threaded end of the shaft. Make sure that the three cut-outs in the synchro ring engage with the sliding keys in the hub before pushing the hub fully home. Remember that the baulk rings for 1st and 2nd gears are slightly different. That for 1st gear has narrower cut-outs

than those in the 2nd gear ring.

6. Now check the 1st gear end float as mentioned in paragraph 2.

7. Put the 2nd gear baulk ring in position in the hub so that the slots engage with the sliding keys.

8. Replace 2nd gear with the cone towards the hub.

9. Third gear, which has a large bearing boss integral with it, should now be replaced with the needle roller bearing which fits together with 3rd gear, inside 2nd gear.

10 The dished washer is now put over the shaft with the raised inner circumference towards the end of the shaft. After this goes the shim. If the only renovations to the pinion shaft have been new baulk rings, then one may assume that the existing washer and shim can be fitted as before. If, however, the synchro hub or any gears have been renewed then it is most likely that the shim thickness will need alteration. The dished washer is designed to exert a pressure of approximately 100 kg (220 lbs) on to 3rd gear and the hub to eliminate sloppiness along the shaft. The critical distance is that between the face of 3rd gear and the shoulder on the shaft up to which 4th gear will be fitted. This length of shaft has a spacer collar which bears on the concave washer (and shim) when 4th gear is finally installed. Obviously a thicker shim will increase the pressure and vice versa. If, therefore, it is necessary to recalculate the shim requirement an accurate measuring device is necessary. The dished washer is given a spring travel of .17 mm in order to exert its pressure and is also a constant thickness of 1.04 mm. Thus the length of the distance collar plus the total concave washer dimensions (1.23 mm) should equal the shaft distance from 3rd gear face to 4th gear shoulder. The appropriate shims are selected to make this distance up.

11 On later gearboxes a selective circlip is fitted where the concave washer would go and the end play of 3rd gear measured with a blade between the gear and circlip. This should be .10 and .25 mm (.004 - .010 inch).

12 Install the shim after the dished washer and then put the spacer sleeve on top of that (later models have a spring spacer after the circlip).

13 4th gear is now ready to go on. Although it could be pressed off it cannot be pressed on as it is virtually impossible to line it up to the keyway as once started it cannot be re-aligned. It must therefore be heated to at least 90ºC (194ºF) in order that it may expand enough to slide easily down the shaft and over the key. This heating is best done in a bath of oil. A blow torch can be used provided a careful watch is kept to prevent overheating. 4th gear must only go on one way and that is with the wider protruding face of its hub towards the spacer collar. Put the hot gear on to the shaft and make sure it is fully home to the shoulder on the shaft.

14 Last of all, the inner race for the needle roller bearing is pressed or driven on to the shaft. On later models the gear is pressed on against the spring spacer and a circlip is installed afterwards. Then the inner race for the needle bearing is pressed on. The pinion shaft is now assembled and should be put on one side.

5(c) Main Casing - Installing Needle Bearings and Reverse Gearshaft

1. Two sets of needle roller bearings are fitted at the rear end of the main casing. One set comprises two roller cages and a spacer between and in this the reverse drive shaft runs. Drive one cage into the casing with a socket on an extension or suitable drift so that it is flush with one end of the bore. The metal face of the needle cage end should face inwards. The spacer should then be inserted with its slot so lined up that it will engage with the locking bolt which is screwed in through the side of the casing. Put the locking bolt in position and then drive the other needle roller bearing into the other end of the bore.

2. The other bearing supports the rear end of the input shaft front half. Fit the single needle roller cage into the larger bore so that the circular recess in the outer race will line up with the lock screw hole in the casing. Tap it into position and replace and tighten the lock screw.

Reassemble the thrust washer (Section 5a 4)

Completed input shaft assembly (Section 5a)

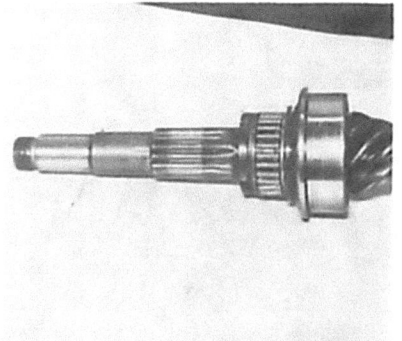

Pinion shaft, pinion bearing, first gear needle ring and thrust ring already assembled (Section 5b)

Shim for 1st gear (Section 5b 2)

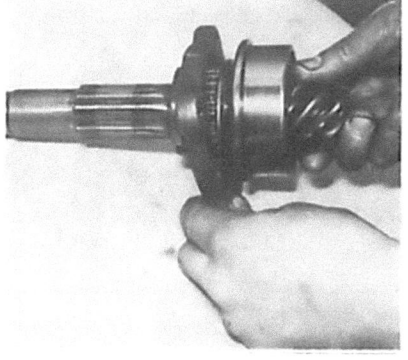

Pinion shaft bearing retainer being assembled (Section 5b 3)

Bearing retainer in position (Section 5b 3)

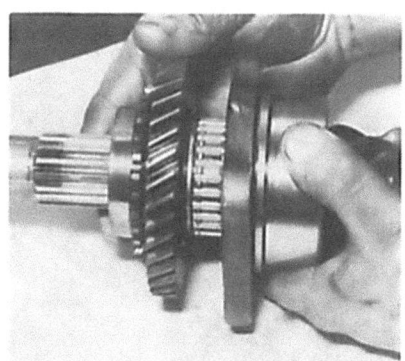

Pinion shaft - fitting 1st gear (Section 5b 4)

Pinion Shaft. Placing 1st/2nd gear synchro hub in position (note baulk ring resting on 1st gear; arrowed) (Section 5b 5)

Checking 1st gear end float with a feeler (Section 5b 6)

Pinion shaft - replacing 2nd gear synchro ring (Section 5b 7)

Replacing 2nd gear (Section 5b 8)

Replacing 3rd gear together with the idler bearing (Section 5b 9)

Pinion shaft - replacing the concave washer (Section 5b 10)

Pinion shaft - replacing the shim (Section 5b 10)

Pinion shaft - replacing the spacer sleeve (Section 5b 12)

Replacing the (hot) 4th gear (Section 5b 13)

Replacing the inner race for the needle roller (Section 5b 14)

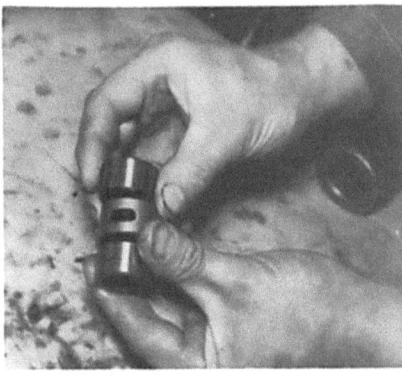

Fitting reverse gear roller bearings (Section 5c 1)

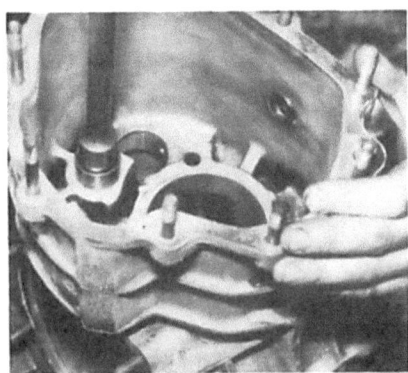

Fitting the shaft into the casing (Section 5c 1)

Fitting the locating screw for the reverse gear shaft (Section 5c 1)

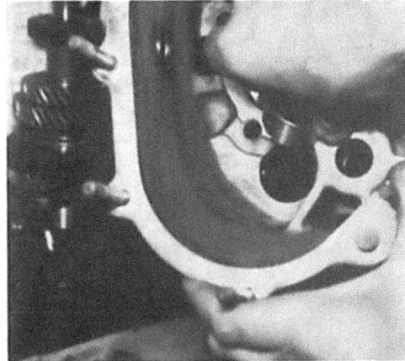

Fitting the roller bearing for the input shaft (Section 5c 2)

Tap the bearing into position (Section 5c 2)

Fit the locating screw for the input shaft roller bearing (Section 5c 2)

Reverse gear shaft (Section 5c 3)

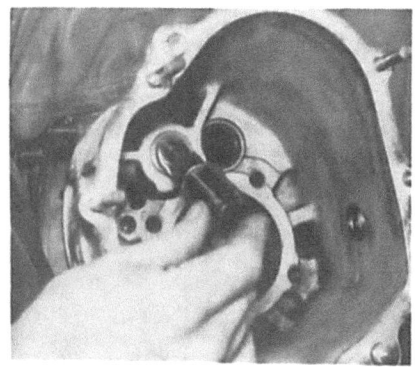

Reverse gear shaft being fitted into the casing (Section 5c 3)

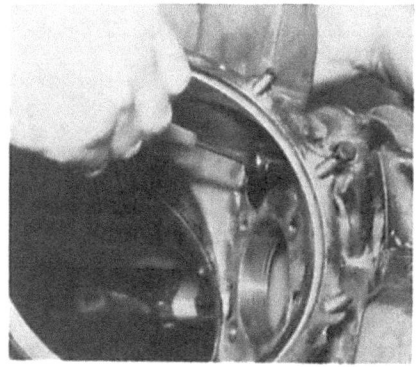

Reverse gear shaft - fitting the key (Section 5a 3)

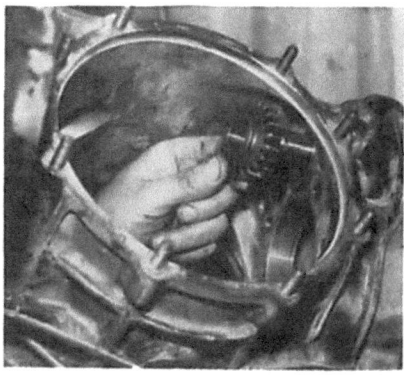

Reverse gear shaft - replacing the reverse gear (Section 5c 3)

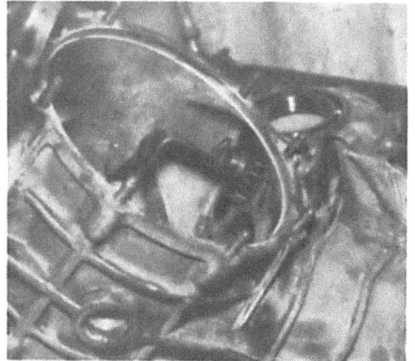

Reverse gear shaft - fitting the circlip (Section 5c 3)

Reverse gear shaft - circlip in place (Section 5c 3)

Gear carrier - placing the needle roller bearing in position (Section 5d 1)

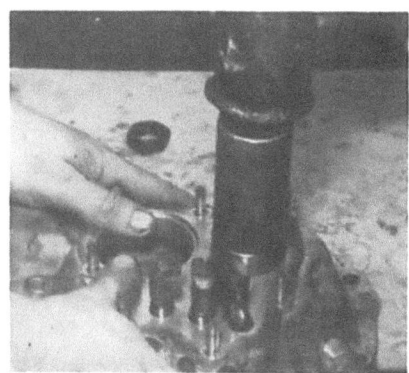

Gear carrier - tapping the roller bearing home (Section 5d 1)

Fitting the securing screw to the roller bearing (Section 5d 1)

Fitting the flanged race to the gear carrier (Section 5d 2)

Driving the flanged race into the casing (Section 5d 2)

Gear carrier assembly - taping the two shafts together (Section 5e 2)

Gear carrier assembly - positioning 3rd/4th gear selector fork (Section 5e 3)

3. The reverse gear shaft may now be fitted. First slide the spacer key over the shaft so that it abuts the splined section. Then pass it through in the needle bearings from the front of the casing. Fit the key into the keyway, tilting the outer end down a fraction to aid fitting the gear. Support the front end of the shaft and push the gear on engaging the key. The projecting side of the gear hub should face outwards. Finally, fit the circlip into the groove making quite sure that it is fully seated all round.

5(d) Gear Carrier - Fitting Bearings

1. The needle roller bearing for the forward end of the pinion shaft should be lined up so that the hole for the locking screw corresponds with the recess in the bearing. Tap it into position and fit the locking screw.

2. The special ball bearing with the flange outer race should then be driven into position from the outside of the carrier casing.

5(e) Gear Carrier - Refitting Shafts and Selector Forks

1. It is assumed that the selector rails are in order (see Section 4, paragraph 7) and the forks are a correct fit in the hub sleeve grooves (Section 4. paragraph 6).

2. The first task is to fit the two shafts into the gear carrier. First of all place the two assemblies together and hold them with strong elastic bands or adhesive tape as available.

3. When the two shafts are finally in position in the carrier the selector fork for 3rd/4th gear is shrouded so this must be put in position on the synchro hub and kept there whilst both shafts are being pushed home. For the same reason the fork rail must be pulled back so that as the fork is carried in with the shaft it can be fitted on to the rail. It will be appreciated that there are several things to keep in line therefore and more than one pair of hands is almost essential.

4. With the selector fork for 3rd/4th speeds in position in its groove - with the clamp lug facing outwards from the casing - offer up the two shafts together into their bearing locations. The main resistance will be from the ball bearing and this will tend to come out of the carrier as the shaft is tapped in. Put something behind the bearing therefore to support it.

5. As the two shafts progressively go into the casing line up the selector fork with its appropriate rail so that eventually that is being pushed on as well. It is important to ensure that the fork does not jam. Also once the fork is on the rail the rail may be moved back in line with the others.

6. Once both shafts are fully home in the carrier bearings, the shaft nuts have to be replaced and tightened. Fit new lock washers (from the gasket set) and make sure that the tags engage in the grooves in the shaft. Put the nuts on finger tight. In order to hold the whole assembly whilst the nuts are tightened it is simplest to replace it temporarily over the studs of the main casing.

7. Stand the main casing on end and carefully place the gear carrier assembly in it so that the studs are engaged sufficiently for the unit to be held firm. Then tighten both of the nuts to a torque of 87 ft.lb. (12 mkg) and slacken them off. Retighten to 43 ft.lbs. (6 mkg). Do not bend up the lock washers on to the nuts just yet in case some disaster necessitates them being undone again. On later models that have circlip fixings instead of nuts a dished washer and circlip are fitted to the input shaft. As the washer has to be compressed in order to fit the circlip into its groove a press and suitable tubular tool are needed in order to do this successfully.

8. Once the nuts have been tightened the gear carrier should be removed from the casing in preparation for setting the selector forks.

9. The selector forks setting is critical. If the wear between the fork and groove is outside the limit the possibility of a gear not being fully engaged and jumping out is increased. If you can get the unit set up in a Volkswagen agent's jig you would be well advised to do so. Otherwise, lay the assembly on the bench and fit the selector fork for

1st/2nd gears into its groove and mount it on the selector rail.

10 Set all three selector rails in the neutral position, which is when the cut-outs in their ends all line up, and set the synchro hub outer sleeves also in neutral with the forks in position. Then tighten the fork clamp bolts sufficiently to prevent them slipping. Now push each selector in turn so that each gear is fully engaged. The outer sleeve of the appropriate synchro hub must move fully over the dogs of the baulk ring and gear in question. In each gear selected the fork must not bind in the groove. If difficulty is experienced in engaging a gear slacken the fork clamp nut and get the synchro hub sleeve fully into mesh and then retighten the fork clamp in position. Then move the selector back to neutral and into the opposite gear position. In all three positions there must be no semblance of pressure in either direction from the fork on to the groove in which it runs. Do not forget also that the synchro hub and 2nd and 3rd gears on the pinion shaft are pre-loaded with the dished washer and will be stiff to rotate. This may cause something of a struggle in order to line up the dogs when engaging 2nd gear. Once both forks have been correctly set the clamp bolts may be tightened to a torque of 18 ft.lbs. (2.5 mkg).

11 No mention has been made yet of the reverse selector rod and relay lever. This would not have been dismantled from the gear carrier except in rare circumstances because it is the least likely to suffer from wear. The small sliding gear and yoke (which will have come off the lug from the relay lever during dismantling of the unit) may now be repositioned on it. To check that the setting is correct first engage second gear. The reverse sliding gear should be held square and in this position should be midway between the straight cut teeth on the synchro hub sleeve and the helical teeth of 2nd gear on the input shaft. Then move out of 2nd gear and shift into reverse and check that the reverse gears mesh completely. Adjustment can be made if necessary on the block which is clamped to the selector rail. It is most unlikely that the relay lever pivot post is incorrect but as a check the distance from the centre of the eye to the face of the gear carrier should be 38.6 mm (give or take .4 mm).

5(f) Gear Carrier - Assembly to Main Casing

1. The main casing should be ready with bearings and reverse gear shaft installed.

2. In order to assist lining up the bolt holes in the pinion bearing flange (which is impossible to move when fully in position) two studs about three inches long are fitted into the flange. These will act as leaders in to the holes in the casing and automatically line up the flange. If you have no metal studs with suitable threads (or bolts with the heads cut off) find two pieces of wooden dowel rod a suitable size which can be screwed into the flange. Make sure they will not splinter or break.

3. Fit the pinion setting shims in position on the face of the flange. The two guide studs will help to locate them. If the flange has small 'pips' cast into the edge line up the shim accordingly and note that they should line up with the corresponding points in the casing. Put a dab of grease on the shim to prevent it falling off later.

4. Place a new gasket over the studs on the casing, having made sure that no traces of old gasket are left and that the two mating surfaces are quite clean and smooth.

5. Make sure that the reverse sliding gear is not forgotten. It can be prevented from dropping out if reverse gear is engaged.

6. It is best to fit the gear carrier to the casing with the casing standing upright. There are three points to watch.

a) See that the pinion shim stays put.

b) Guide the temporary studs into the bolt holes in the casing so that the flange lines up properly.

c) See that the splined reverse gear shaft lines up with and goes into the sliding reverse gear.

Provided the foregoing points are watched carefully the whole unit will drop into place quite easily and a few final taps with a soft

Gear carrier assembly - retracting the fork rail (Section 5e 3)

Gear carrier assembly - tapping the input shaft into the flanged bearing (Section 5e 4)

Gear carrier assembly - checking that the selector fork engages on the rail (Section 5e 5)

Gear carrier assembly - engaging lockwasher tab in the shaft groove (Section 5e 6)

Follow on with the second washer (Section 5e 6)

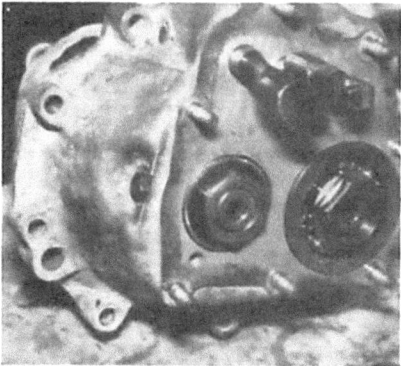

Gear carrier assembly - fit the shaft nuts hand tight (Section 5e 7)

Tightening the nuts correctly (Section 5e 7)

Gear carrier assembly - positioning 1st/2nd gear selector fork to the selector rail (Section 5e 9)

Gear carrier assembly - clamp the 1st/2nd gear selector fork to the rail (Section 5e 9)

Gear carrier assembly - positioning reverse gear sliding pinion (Section 5e 11)

Gear carrier assembly - clamping the selector block to the reverse selector rail (Section 5e 11)

Locating studs fitted to pinion bearing flange (Section 5f 2)

mallet will butt the mating faces together. If for any reason something 'solid' is encountered while replacing the assembly stop and look. Do not force anything. Remember the three points mentioned that have to line up.

7. As soon as the gear carrier is in position turn the casing on its side and remove the two guide studs from the pinion bearing flange. Using the new lock plates (included in the gasket set) replace the four pinion flange bolts and tighten them diagonally and evenly to 36 ft.lbs. (5 mkg). The bolt head nearest the splined end of the pinion shaft should be arranged so that a flat on the head faces the shaft. This prevents any possibility of the reverse gear sleeve fouling the bolt head. Do not exceed the specified torque to do this. Back the bolt off if necessary and retighten to a slightly lower torque. Take care to avoid slipping and damaging the pinion in any way when tightening up. Bend up the lock plate tabs.

8. Replace the carrier nuts, noting that one carries the earth strap, and tighten them all evenly to a torque of 14 ft.lbs. (2 mkg).

9. Provided all is well and the shafts revolve freely the lock washers for the two shaft nuts may now be turned up against a flat on the nuts.

10 The front section of the input shaft is now ready for installation. Oil the land in the centre which will run in the oil seal and see that the small link stud is screwed into the end of the shaft. Then carefully insert the shaft through the oil seal link stud end leading from the rear of the main casing.

11 Once through, fit the circlip - preferably a new one - over the splines and past the groove onto the smooth part of the shaft.

12 Put the reverse gear/splined sleeve onto the shaft, plain end first. Then screw the shaft stud into the end of the protruding input shaft. Screw it in as far as it will go and then come back one spline in order to let the splined collar engage both halves of the shaft. Do not under any circumstances engage the sleeve with the ends of the shafts butted tight together. Move the sleeve forward so that the gears engage and then move the circlip back along the shaft so that it engages fully into the groove.

5(g) Gear Shift Housing - Reassembly

1. Clean up the mating surfaces on the end of the gear carrier and shift housing and place a new gasket in position over the studs in the gear carrier.

2. See that the gearbox is in neutral by checking that the cut-outs in the ends of the three selector rods are lined up.

3. The gear change lever in the housing should be an easy slide fit in the housing. If it is sloppy in any way it could cause jamming or other problems of changing gear.

4. Fit the housing over the studs, at the same time fiddling the lever so that the end locates in the cut-outs of the ends of the three selector rails.

5. Replace the nuts and tighten to 11 ft.lbs. (1.5 mkg).

5(h) Differential and Side Bearings - Replacement

1. Ensure that all parts are scrupulously clean and that the shims and spacers are correct for each side of the differential casing. Remember that the shims fitted serve two functions - one is to put a pre-load on the side bearings and the other is to position the crownwheel correctly in relation to the pinion.

2. It may be argued that if new bearings are fitted then the shim requirements should be recalculated. In practice this is not necessary provided that the same crownwheel and pinion are being refitted and that no previous shim alteration has taken place in an abortive attempt to improve some earlier malfunction.

3. When fitting new bearings, support the side cover evenly and securely and arrange the bearing so that the closed side of the ball race faces the outside of the casing on assembly. The bore in the side cover must be scrupulously clean and free of any snags or burrs.

4. The new bearing can be tapped into place using a heavy mallet and a suitable article to apply the load evenly across it. Make sure

that it does not tilt, particularly at the start. If it does, bring it out and start again.

5. The right hand side bearing and cover is installed first. Make sure both mating faces are perfectly clean and fit a new gasket over the studs of the casing. No sealing compound is necessary. Place the cover in position (it will only fit one way) and tighten the nuts evenly to 22 ft.lbs. of torque (3 mkg).

6. The differential assembly goes in next. With everything perfectly clean the shims may be held in position with a dab of grease. If for some reason there has been a mix up with the shims and you do not know which should go on each side, you are in trouble because you will be unable to set the pinion/crownwheel backlash correctly. In such cases you should take the whole assembly to a Volkswagen specialist and ask him to reset it. With the proper gear it will not take too long. Do not guess!

7. If you know exactly what shims came off each side make sure they are arranged so that the thicker spacer ring is fitted first, with the chamfered side inwards and the shims after that (so that they go between the ring and the bearing).

8. With the spacer and shims in place put the differential into the casing carefully and tap it in so that the shoulder abuts fully against the inner race of the bearing in the cover already fitted.

9. Make sure the remaining shims are properly located on the crownwheel end of the differential and then fit the left hand final drive cover into position using a new gasket as for the other one. As this cover has to fit over the differential it will be necessary to tap it down into position fully before the nuts can be replaced. It is important to note that the cover retaining nuts must not be used to pull the cover and bearing down. This could easily crack or break it. Tighten the nuts finally to the same torque as the other cover.

10 The transmission case is now completely reassembled and ready to receive the axle shafts and tubes.

6. Synchromesh Hub Assemblies - Dismantling, Inspection and Reassembly (All Types)

1. Unless the transmission is the victim of neglect or misuse, or has covered very high mileages, the synchro hub assemblies do not normally need replacement. If they do they must be renewed as a complete assembly. It is not practical to fit an inner hub or outer sleeve alone - even if you could buy one.

2. When synchro baulk rings are being renewed it is advisable to fit new blocker bars (sliding keys) and retaining springs in the hubs as this will ensure that full advantage is taken of the new, unworn cut-outs in the rings.

3. Whether or not a synchro hub is dismantled intentionally or accidentally there are some basic essentials to remember:

a) The splines of the inner hub and outer sleeve are matched - either by selection on assembly or by wear patterns during use. Those matched on assembly have etched lines on the inner hub and outer sleeve so that they can be easily realigned. For those with no marks, a paint dab should be made to ensure correct reassembly. If the hub falls apart unintentionally and there are no marks made then you will have to accept the fact that it may wear more quickly (relatively speaking) in the future. But do not have a heart attack if this happens - it will still work for a long time to come.

b) Fit the retaining spring clips so that the ends fit behind but not into the keys; and that the clips overlap on each side, i.e. do not have more than two clip ends over one key (see sketch   6.3.)

c) On early three speed synchro units make sure that the three dimples in the splines of the outer sleeve line up with the three keys on assembly.

4. When examining for wear there are two important features to look at:

a) The fit of the splines. With the keys removed, the inner and outer sections of the hub should slide easily with minimum backlash or

Casing assembly - fitting shim to pinion bearing (Section 5f 3)

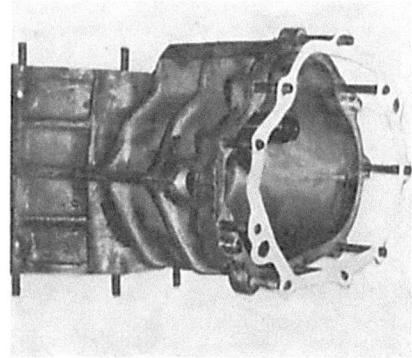

Casing assembly - fitting gasket (Section 5f 4)

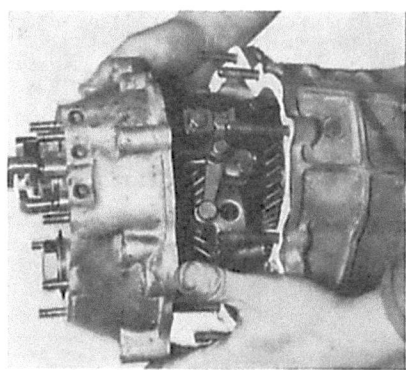

Casing assembly - gear carrier being lowered into casing (Section 5f 6)

Tightening the pinion flange bolts (Section 5f 7)

Setting bolt head flats (Section 5f 7)

Bend the lock plate tabs (Section 5f 7)

Tighten carrier securing nuts (Section 5f 8)

Bend up the shaft nut lock washer tabs (Section 5f 8)

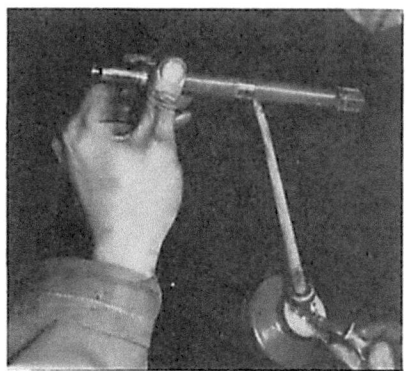

Front section of input shaft (Section 5f 10)

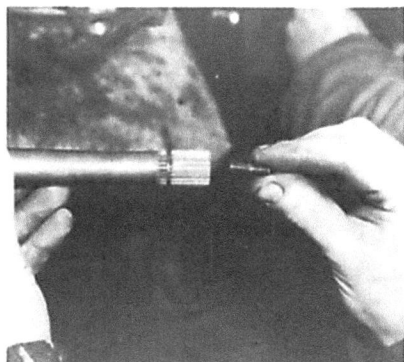

Screw the small link stud into the end of the shaft (Section 5f 10)

Input shaft front section - assembling circlip (Section 5f 11)

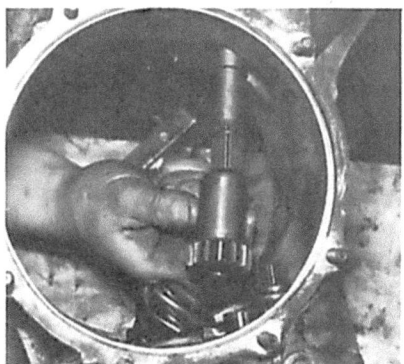

Replacing the reverse gear splined sleeve over the input shaft front half (Section 5f 11)

Front input shaft link screw joining the two halves of the input shaft (Section 5f 12)

Slide the sleeve into mesh before assembling the circlip (Section 5f 12)

Gear shift housing - new gasket fitted (Section 5g 1)

Fitting the gear shift housing over the studs (Section 5g 4)

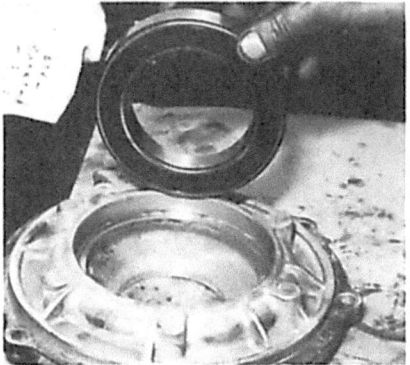

Side bearing replacement - everything must be clean (Section 5h 3)

Tapping the side bearing into the casing (Section 5h 4)

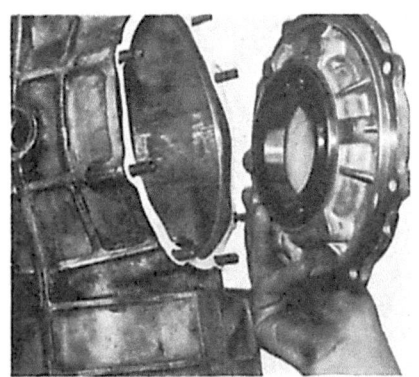

Fitting the right hand cover to the casing (Section 5h 5)

Fitting right hand differential shims (Section 5h 6)

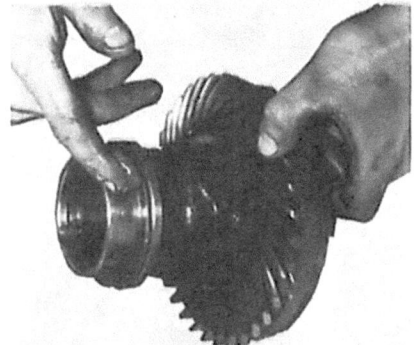

Keep the shims in place with a dab of grease (Section 5h 6)

Placing the differential into the casing (Section 5h 6)

Differential in the casing (Section 5h 6)

Refitting left hand cover plate (Section 5h 9)

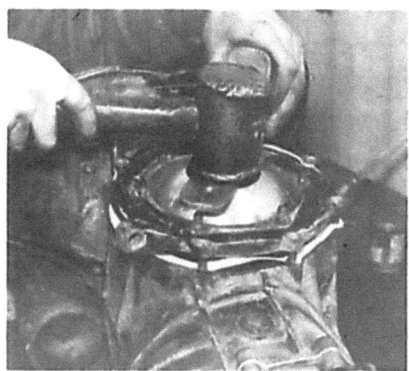

Fitting left hand final drive cover (Section 5h 9)

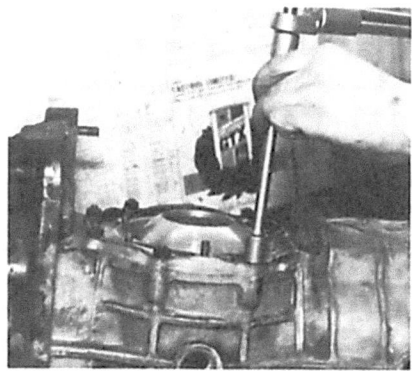

Tightening down left hand final drive cover (22 lb ft) (Section 5h 9)

Synchro hubs - fitting retaining spring clips (Section 6.3b)

Another view of the sliding key retaining clips (Section 6.3b)

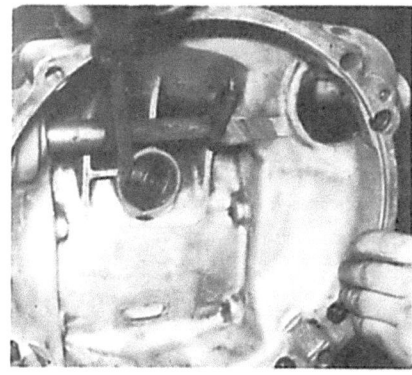

Removing the old input shaft oil seal (Section 7.3)

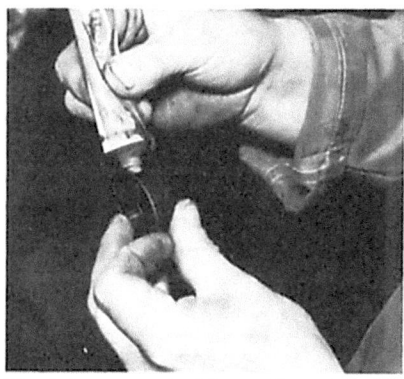

Treat the new seal with a sealing compound before assembly (Section 7.4)

Tap the new seal home (Section 7.4)

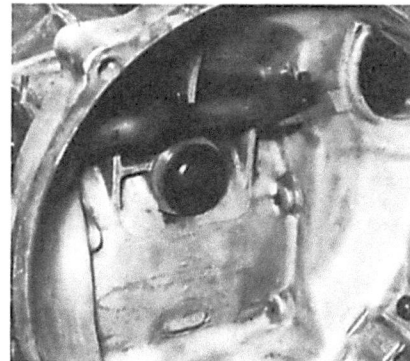

Seal correctly in position (Section 7.6)

axial rock. The degree of permissible wear is difficult to describe in absolute terms. No movement at all is exceptional yet excessive 'slop' would affect operation and cause jumping out of gear. Ask someone with experience for advice.

b) Selector fork grooves and selector forks should not exceed the maximum permissible clearance of 0.3 mm (.012 inch). The wear can be on either the fork or groove so it is best to try a new fork in the existing hub first to see if the gap is reduced adequately. If not, then a new hub assembly is needed. Too much slack between fork and groove induces jumping out of gear. Where a hub also carries gear teeth on the outer sleeve these should, of course, be in good condition - that is unbroken and not pitted or scored.

7. Input Shaft Oil Seal - Removal and Replacement

1. It is possible that clutch contamination may be caused by failure of the oil seal that goes round the input shaft in the transmission casing. During the course of transmission overhaul it would be automatically renewed but it is possible to fit a new one with the

transmission installed. The engine must be removed first.

2. With the engine removed detach the clutch release bearing from the operating forks.

3. The seal surrounds the input shaft where it goes through the casing. It can be dug out with a sharp pointed instrument provided care is taken to avoid damaging the surrounding part of the transmission casing.

4. A new seal should be treated with sealing compound on the outside rim (taking care to prevent the compound getting anywhere else on the seal) and then placed in position with the inner lip of the seal facing into the transmission. Be careful not to damage the lip when passing it over the splines of the shaft and make sure it does not turn back when it reaches the part of the shaft on which it bears.

5. It should be driven into position squarely and a piece of tube is ideal for this put round the shaft. If the seal should tip in the early stages of being driven in take it out and start again. Otherwise it may be badly distorted and its life will be shortened considerably.

6. The seal should be driven in until the outer shoulder abuts the casing.

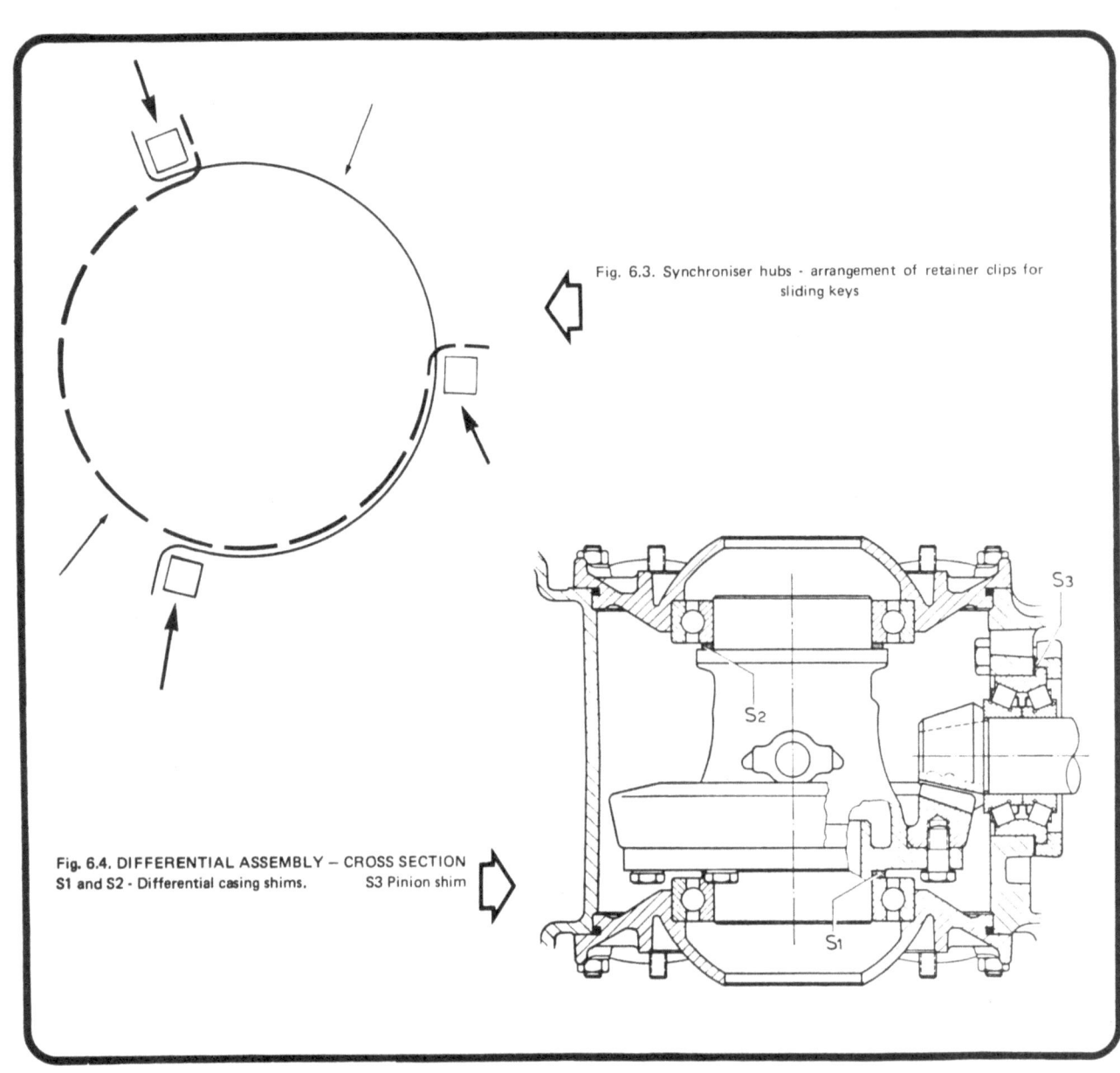

Fig. 6.3. Synchroniser hubs - arrangement of retainer clips for sliding keys

Fig. 6.4. DIFFERENTIAL ASSEMBLY – CROSS SECTION
S1 and S2 - Differential casing shims.   S3 Pinion shim

Chapter 7 Transmission. Split casing type

Contents

Specifications

General

Gearbox and final drive main casing	Alloy casting split vertically into two halves.
Number of gears	4 forward, 1 reverse
Synchromesh (where fitted)	Baulk ring
Oil capacity of casing	3.0 litres (5.3 Imp. pints)
Refill quantity required	2.5 litres (4.4 Imp. pints)

Gear Ratios

	Non-synchro	3 speed synchro
1st	3.6 : 1	3.6 : 1
2nd	2.07 : 1	1.94 or 1.88 : 1
3rd	1.25 : 1	1.23 or 1.22 : 1
4th	0.80 : 1	0.82 : 1
Reverse	6.60 : 1	4.63 : 1

Final drive ratio	4.375 : 1
Gear change	Manual , floor mounted lever through remote control mechanical linkage.

Torque Wrench Settings

Transmission casing nuts and bolts	14 lb/ft (2.0 mkg) (See text for sequence)
Oil drain plugs	22 - 29 lb/ft (3.0 - 4.0 mkg)
Oil Filler plug	14 lb/ft (2.0 mkg)
Transmission carrier to frame bolts	166 lb/ft (23.0 mkg)
Spring plate bolts/nuts	72 lb/ft (10.0 mkg)
Gear shift cover to carrier nuts...	11 lb/ft (1.5 mkg)
Gear carrier to casing nuts	14 lb/ft (2.0 mkg)
Pinion shaft nut (early)	80 - 87 lb/ft (11.0 - 12.0 mkg)
(later - new lock washer)	58 - 65 lb/ft (8.0 - 9.0 mkg)
Input shaft nut	30 - 36 lb/ft (4.0 - 5.0 mkg)
Reverse selector fork screw	14 lb/ft (2.0 mkg)
Selector fork clamp screws	18 lb/ft (2.5 mkg)
Pinion shaft slotted nut (non synchro)	36 lb/ft (5.0 mkg)

1. Transmission - General Description

The basic detail differences between this type of gearbox and the later model are all given in the General Description details of Chapter 6, Section 1.

2. Transmission - Removal and Replacement

The removal and replacement procedures are the same as those described in Chapter 6, Section 2.

3. Transmission - Dismantling

1. The procedures as described for the removal of the whole assembly from the car having been carried out the outer bearings and axle tubes should also have been removed in just the same way as described in Chapter 8. There, however, the similarity stops. It is not possible to remove the axle shafts until after the gear casing has been split.

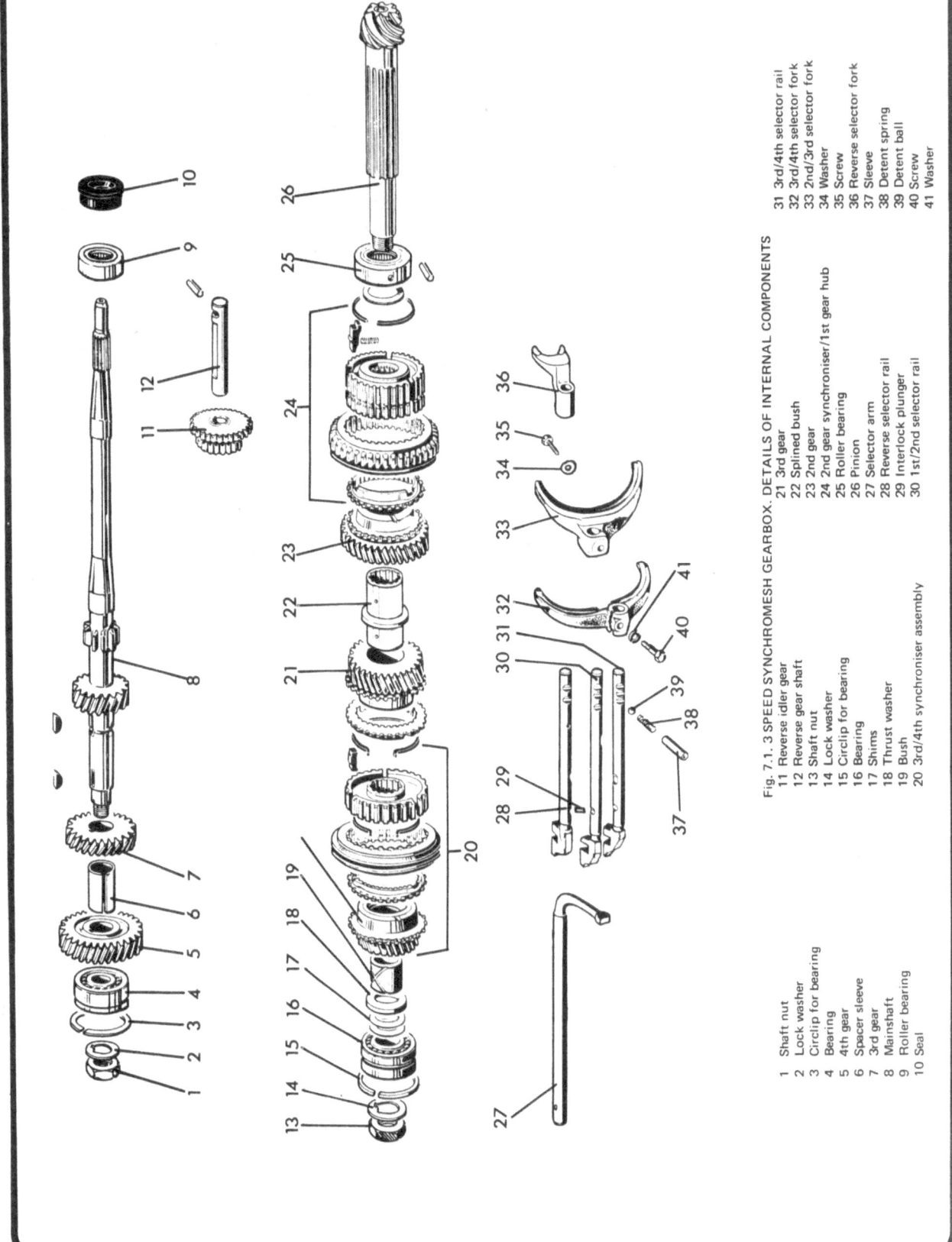

Fig. 7.1. 3 SPEED SYNCHROMESH GEARBOX. DETAILS OF INTERNAL COMPONENTS

1 Shaft nut
2 Lock washer
3 Circlip for bearing
4 Bearing
5 4th gear
6 Spacer sleeve
7 3rd gear
8 Mainshaft
9 Roller bearing
10 Seal

11 Reverse idler gear
12 Reverse gear shaft
13 Shaft nut
14 Lock washer
15 Circlip for bearing
16 Bearing
17 Shims
18 Thrust washer
19 Bush
20 3rd/4th synchroniser assembly

21 3rd gear
22 Splined bush
23 2nd gear
24 2nd gear synchroniser/1st gear hub
25 Roller bearing
26 Pinion
27 Selector arm
28 Reverse selector rail
29 Interlock plunger
30 1st/2nd selector rail

31 3rd/4th selector rail
32 3rd/4th selector fork
33 2nd/3rd selector fork
34 Washer
35 Screw
36 Reverse selector fork
37 Sleeve
38 Detent spring
39 Detent ball
40 Screw
41 Washer

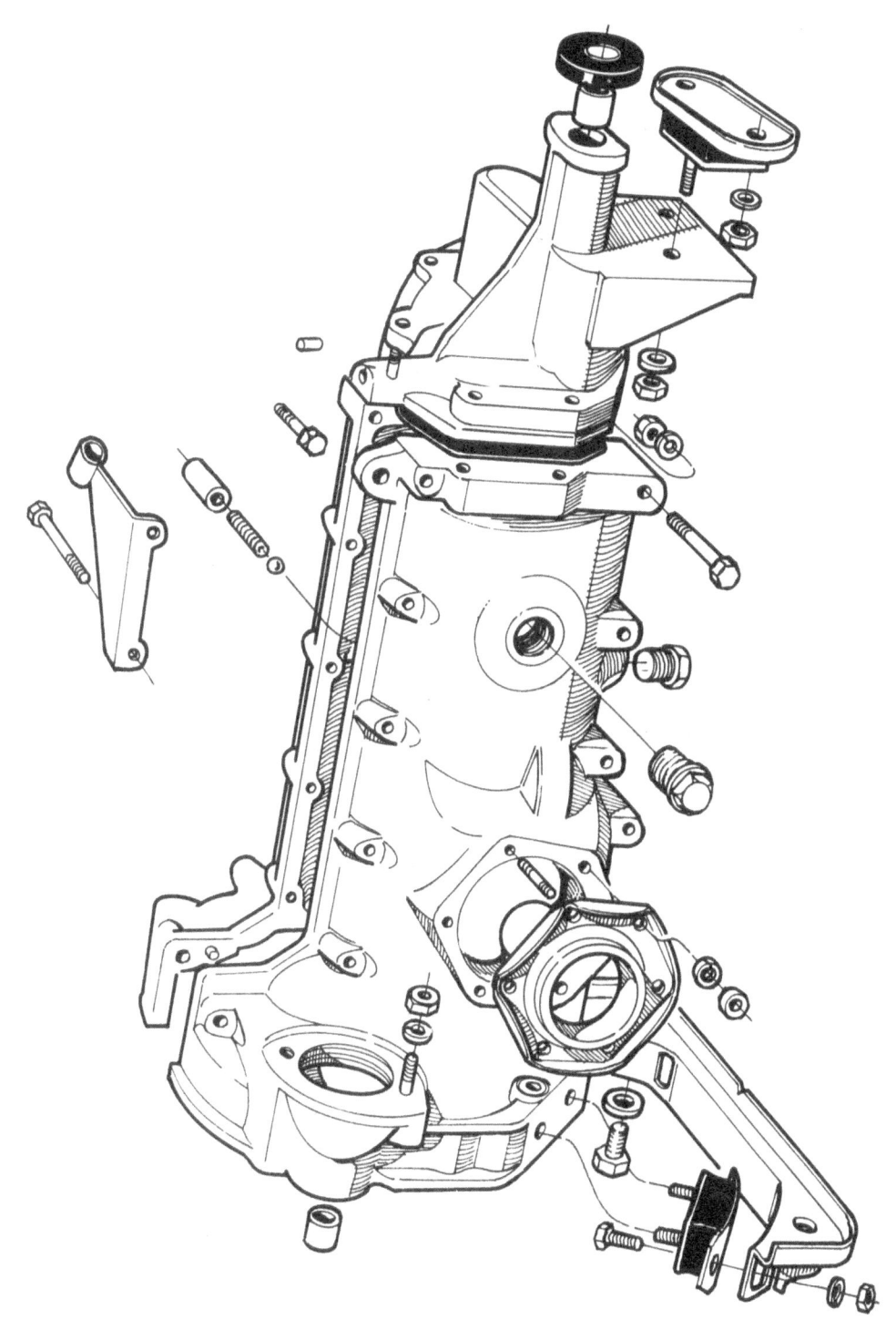

Fig. 7.2. GEARBOX AND FINAL DRIVE CASING AND COVERS.
EARLY SPLIT TYPE

2. Remove the clutch thrust ring from the fork by detaching the clips (see Chapter 5 for details) and remove the rear mounting bracket.

3. Remove the nuts holding the gear change rod housing at the front of the casing and take off the housing. If you have forgotten to drain out the oil do it now before it pours all over your work bench.

4. Unlock the two tab washers from the large nuts on the ends of the input and pinion shafts which are now exposed.

5. In order to slacken these two nuts (do it now while it is easy) engage two gears simultaneously. This can be done by pulling out the outer two selector fork rails. This locks the two shafts and the nuts can be slackened.

6. Now remove all the through bolts and nuts that clamp the two halves of the casing together. Do not overlook the bolts inside the bellhousing part of the casing, nor the long thin through bolt that goes right through the centre of the casing.

7. Once all the bolts are removed the only thing preventing the two halves from falling apart is the fit of the two side bearings. A few gentle taps with a mallet or block of wood will soon ease the two halves apart. Do not under any circumstances use force or leverage between the two mating faces or serious damage could result, making the fit round the bearings inaccurate - apart, of course, from the likelihood of causing the oil leaks.

8. Draw one half of the casing off over the axle shaft and the two gearbox shafts can simply be lifted out of the casing. The axle shafts and differential assembly may then be detached from the other half of the casing. Except in rare circumstances the differential side bearings will remain in each half of the casing. This will mean that the spacer rings and shims fitted on the differential housing will be free to come off. It is essential that these are not mixed up - side for side. As each casing half is removed therefore see that the shims on each side are carefully kept together and marked for the appropriate side. Tape them in position on the differential if you wish. The gearbox is now dismantled into the main sub-assemblies.

9. To dismantle the pinion shaft first remove the nut which has been slackened already and take off the washer behind it.

10 The ball bearing (with the retaining ring fitted in its outer groove) can be removed by holding the bearing so that the shaft hangs down and then striking the end of the shaft with a soft faced hammer. If you have no one to support the shaft hold it just above the bench surface over a small pile of rags.

11 Next remove the shims, spacer ring and 4th gear together with its separate bearing bush.

12 4th gear synchro ring followed by the 3rd/4th synchro hub may now be removed, taking care not to let the hub come apart if it should be a little tight on the splines.

13 Then in sequence comes 3rd gear synchro ring followed by 3rd gear bearing bush, 2nd gear and synchro ring.

14 When drawing off the 2nd gear/1st gear hub care must be taken to watch for the three springs which will be released on the inside of the centre sleeve when the shaft comes out.

15 Finally remove any shims (noting how many) and the outer race of the pinion roller bearing. The inner race of this bearing is a tight press fit on the shaft. It is very difficult to get off without a proper gripping tool and press, the main danger being damage to the pinion.

16 There is little need for dismantling the input shaft unless the two removable gears are badly worn or damaged. The other two gears are part of the shaft so if they are damaged a new shaft is required.

17 Having removed the shaft nut and lock washer the front bearing and gears may be pressed off or drawn off with a conventional puller. The other bearing may be driven off after removing the retaining circlip.

18 The reverse gear pinion runs on a spindle which is locked in position in the casing by a pin, the protruding end of which also serves to locate the rear ball bearing of the input shaft. Remove the pin and the shaft can be pulled out. Note that the gear runs on a bushing and if this is worn it should be renewed. Any slack between the gear and shaft, which would cause the gear to rock, contributes to the fault of reverse gear jumping out of engagement under load.

19 In order to remove the selector forks it is first of all necessary to take the two screwed plugs out of the casing so that the heads of the clamping screws can be slackened off. Do not remove the rails from the casing unless necessary (see under 'Inspection for Wear'). The selector forks need not be removed unless inspection indicates that they are too slack a fit in the sleeve grooves.

4. Inspection for Wear in Transmission Components

1. The principles as described in Section 4 of Chapter 6 all apply. The only differences to note are in the selector fork rails. Because the construction is different the detent balls and springs are released inside the casing when the rails are pulled out. Therefore keep a hand over the hole to prevent them flying out.

2. Some gears run on separate bushes on the shaft so check that there is no wear or slackness between the gear, bush and shaft. If there is a new bush will probably cure the trouble. Do not forget to check the reverse gear bush as well.

3. The gearbox used in the illustration was old and had done a high mileage. Also it came out of a transporter which meant that it had worked much harder than in a saloon, due to the reduction gearing which is incorporated on the outer ends of the axle shafts. Apart from the serious pinion damage the rest of the unit - bearings and synchro hubs in particular - were all well worn and needed renewal if the transmission was to be overhauled. There would have been little point in renewing the crownwheel and pinion alone. It was estimated that to bring the gearbox back to scratch would cost about 65 - 70% of the cost of a complete new unit, including reassembly by experienced specialists with the special setting equipment facilities.

5. Transmission Reassembly - General

1. The same remarks as given for the later models (Chapter 6) apply. Although assembly is generally much simpler for the do-it-yourself man this only applies in circumstances where small renovations have been carried out. Where the crownwheel and pinion have to be re-set the side bearing adjustment involves assembling the complete box and then taking it apart again at least once more because if the side bearing shims need altering the casing has to be split. As all bolts have to be tightened to the correct torque each time this is a lengthy assembly procedure. No doubt it was one of the contributing factors towards the later design change.

2. It is important to see that the faces of both halves of the casing are perfectly clean and unmarked by dents or burrs. Use a solvent (carbon tetrachloride or methylated spirits) to remove traces of old sealing compound. Obtain good quality sealing compound which is known to be suitable for alloy for re-preparing the surfaces.

3. Ensure that new gaskets are available. This is particularly important for the refitting of the gearchange end cover because the thickness of the gaskets is responsible for the pressure on the shaft bearings to ensure they have no axial movement.

5(a) Pinion Shaft - Reassembly

1. Reassembly of the pinion shaft is in the reverse order of dismantling and if only new synchro rings have been fitted no problems with shim settings need arise - provided they were carefully removed and their number and position noted.

2. It is possible for the owner to assemble a new pinion shaft if he is renewing the crownwheel and pinion provided he has access to an assortment of shims and is able to get the inner race of the pinion bearing heated and pressed properly on to the shaft. He is advised however that the setting of the crownwheel and side bearing pre-load is more complex and requires a setting gauge. This is best done by a specialist with the facilities needed.

3. When reassembling the 1st/2nd gear hub it is important to get things the proper way round. First fit the single, square section key retaining ring into the groove in the centre section of the hub and

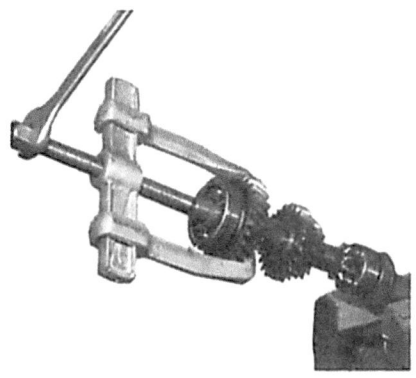

Input shaft - drawing off bearing and 4th gear (Section 3.11)

Badly damaged pinion shaft (Section 4)

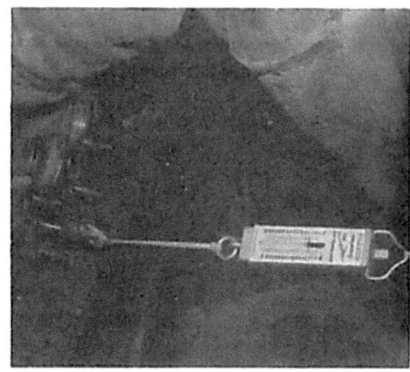

Testing pull required to move selector rails (Section 4)

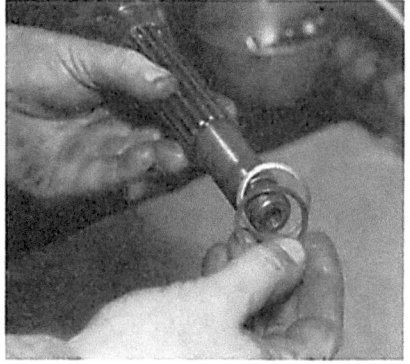

Pinion shaft reassembly. Fitting shims (Section 5a 1)

Pinion shaft assembly - fitting pinion bearing (Section 5a)

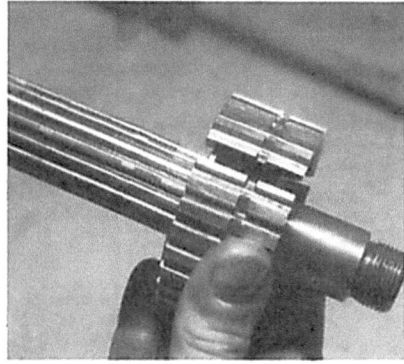

Pinion shaft assembly 1st/2nd gear hub (Section 5a)

Pinion shaft assembly sliding key springs (Section 5a 3)

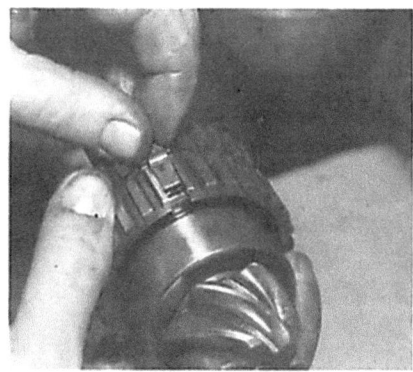

Pinion shaft assembly - fitting sliding keys (Section 5a 3)

Depression in spline (Section 5a 3)

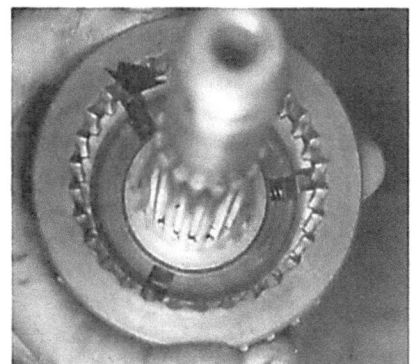

Lining up depression in spline with cut-out 2 keys omitted in photo (Section 5a 3)

Replacing 2nd gear synchro ring (Section 5a)

Replacing 2nd gear (Section 5a)

then slide the hub onto the shaft with the retaining ring nearest the pinion gear. Then place the three key springs into the holes. After this hook the flat, stepped end of each sliding key under the retaining ring so that the raised 'pimple' faces outwards. It should be possible to do this and hold all the keys in position with one hand. Finally the outer sleeve has to be put over the hub so that the keys are trapped and held in position. If marks exist or have been made on the inner and outer hubs there is no problem in lining up the splines. If otherwise, look inside the outer sleeve and make sure that the three depressions in three of the splines line up with the centres of the three sliding keys.

4. As a check that correct assembly has been made, when the 3rd/4th synchroniser hub has been fitted to the shaft the inner sleeve should line up with the end face of the splined part of the shaft. This line up should not vary by more than .05 mm (.002 inch) and if it does then the assembly is wrong or the shim thickness next to the roller bearing is incorrect.

5. Replace the 4th gear and bushing, thrust washer and shims and refit the ball bearing, driving it fully home to the shims. Note that the grooves in the washer face the gear. The lockwasher and shaft nut should be replaced but not tightened fully at this stage.

5(b) Input Shaft - Reassembly

1. The tricky part with this shaft is lining up the keyways to tight fitting gears and the only satisfactory way is to heat the gears to about 90ºC (in an oil bath preferably). They can then be put on and positioned over the keys without difficulty. Make sure that the Woodruff keys are a good fit and fully engaged in their slots otherwise they may move and jam before the gear is fully in position. The smaller (3rd) gear goes on first and should butt right up to 2nd gear on the shaft. This is followed by the spacer and then 4th gear which should butt up tight to the spacer.

2. The two bearings can be drifted on using a tube of suitable diameter but if you have a hot oil bath already prepared the same method can be used. Do not heat the ball bearings in any other manner.

3. Note that the bearing which has a retaining circlip in its outer race goes on the threaded end of the shaft with the circlip nearest to the threaded end in most cases. However there may be exceptions so examine the place in the casing where the bearing fits. Normally the circlip fits in a recess in the front face but it may fit a groove instead. In either case the bearing should not protrude more than a fraction of a millimetre in front of the casing.

4. Replace, but do not fully tighten, the lockwasher and nut.

5(c) Reverse Gear and Spindle - Reassembly

1. The reverse gear must be fitted to the casing before the input shaft is replaced. First fit the sleeve into the gear and then hold the gear in position in the casing with the smaller of the two rows of gear teeth towards the front.

2. Put the spindle through the casing from the rear, plain end first and line up the cut-out with the hole in the bearing housing. Then replace the locking pin.

5(d) Casing - Reassembly

1. So many things have to be put together simultaneously that it is almost essential to have two people to assemble the casing. Before beginning assembly proper put the assembled pinion shaft into position in the left hand half of the casing so that the setting of the selector forks can be verified. This is particularly necessary if the forks have been disturbed (or their rails) as would be the case if new ones have been fitted. Put the rails in the neutral position and with the forks engaged correctly in their hub grooves, see that both synchro hub outer sleeves are in the central neutral position on their hubs.

Then engage all gears in turn to ensure that the sleeves mesh correctly. There is no fine adjustment at this stage. If trouble is experienced later, then further adjustment can be made with the gearbox installed. Reverse gear selector fork cannot be adjusted later so the input shaft should also be installed temporarily so that when reverse gear is engaged the correct line up of the gears can be seen. If necessary move the selector fork along the rail until the sliding pinion small gear is in full mesh with the gear teeth of the 1st/2nd hub on the pinion shaft. The larger gear of the sliding pinion should be in mesh with the gear teeth on the input shaft at the same time. Then select neutral and first gear, in turn, to ensure that the sliding reverse gear pinion is well clear of engagement with anything else.

2. Work out first which way round the crownwheel goes so that you get the axle shaft assembly in the right way round. The car version has the crownwheel in the left hand half of the casing. This half also carries the selector mechanism. So the axle/differential assembly must go in first.

3. Make sure the correct shims are in position on the crownwheel side of the differential casing.

4. Position the left hand half of the casing in a suitable position, bearing in mind that from now on the two axle shafts have to be conveniently positioned and supported so that their weight does not keep upsetting the balance of the casing. If new side bearings need to be fitted these should have been dealt with following the same principles as described for the later type gearbox in Chapter 6. Smear the mating face of the casing with a thin even film of the approved jointing compound.

5. Put the axle shaft through the bearing and guide the differential into the casing with the crownwheel side going in first - that is with the teeth visible. It will most likely be necessary to tap the casing so that the bearing goes fully onto the shoulder of the differential.

6. Next put the pinion shaft assembly into position. The selector forks should be in the neutral position and they must engage in the grooves of the hub sleeves. At the same time the rear bearing outer race should be turned so that the peg in the casing engages the hole.

7. Next place the input shaft in position, once again ensuring that the hole in the rear bearing engages on the protruding end of the reverse shaft locking pin.

8. The right half of the case is now ready to go on. First check that the differential side bearing shims are in position on the differential. Then put the casing over the shaft and up to the differential so that the bearing locates on the shoulder. This is usually the point where all the shafts fall out of position (and the bad language starts!) whilst you try and support the weight of the axles, hold the case and try and re-align the bearings onto the dowel pegs all at the same time. It helps if the left hand shaft can be arranged into as near vertical a position as possible by hanging it over the edge of the bench. If this is difficult or the whole assembly is in imminent danger of crashing to the floor maybe two wooden boxes on end, side by side, stood on the floor, could be arranged with the shaft hanging down between them. The casing will need tapping into position, for the last inch or so, onto the shoulder of the differential. If difficulty is experienced in getting the two halves to finally butt together it will probably be because of one or other of the bearing dowel pegs not being located properly. Do not force anything. Take it off and have a look.

9. Once the two halves are properly together replace all the nuts and bolts with the washers under the nuts. Note that one or two are longer than the others. Do not forget the long centre bolt. Before tightening up it is a good idea to fit the oil seal over the rear end of the input shaft and into position in the casing between the two halves. This will be easier than when the halves are bolted up tight. Ensure that the lip of the seal faces into the casing. Smear the outer edge with jointing compound before putting it into position.

10 The casing bolts must be tightened finally in a certain order but first take them all to a torque of 7 - 10 ft/lbs. Make sure that both shafts revolve freely and that you are able to engage each of the gears. If for some reason either of these functions is impossible, something must be wrong so open up and have a look. If all is in order tighten down the casing bolts in the sequence shown in Fig. 7.4 to a torque of 14 lb/ft. (2 mkg). Do not be tempted to overtighten.

Pinion shaft assembly - fitting shouldered bush (Section 5a)

Pinion shaft assembly - **replacing** 3rd gear (Section 5a)

Pinion shaft assembly - replacing 3rd gear synchro ring (Section 5a)

Pinion shaft assembly - replacing 3rd/4th synchro hub assembly (Section 5a 4)

Pinion shaft assembly - replacing 4th gear bush (Section 5a 5)

Pinion shaft assembly - replacing 4th gear synchro ring (Section 5a 5)

Pinion shaft assembly - replacing 4th gear (Section 5a 5)

Replacing thrust washer (Section 5a 5)

Replacing shims (Section 5a 5)

Replacing double ball bearing (Section 5a 5)

Driving home the bearing onto the shaft (Section 5a 5)

Reverse gear and spindle - fitting the bush (Section 5c 1)

11 Next the two shaft nuts can be fully tightened up. The procedure here is to engage two gears by pulling out the two outer selector rods. Tighten the larger, pinion shaft nut to between 58 - 65 lb/ft (8.0 - 9.0 mkg). On earlier transmissions fitted in Chassis numbers up to 1,454,550 (or 238,499 on transporters) this nut should be tightened to 80 - 87 lb/ft (11.0 - 12.0 mkg). If in doubt use the lesser torque figure. The input shaft nut should be tightened to 30 - 36 lb/ft (4.0 - 5.0 mkg). Bend up the block tabs against a flat on the nuts.

12 The fitting of the gear change rod housing on the end of the casing is quite important because the gasket thickness determines the pressure applied to the outer races of both ball bearings to prevent any movement when end thrust is applied. The gaskets should pre-load .02 - 0.1 mm (.001 - .004 inch). The dimensions which are relevant to this are calculated on the basis of the depth of recession of the input shaft bearing and, on the pinion shaft, the difference between the protrusion of the bearing and the depth of the recess in the cover. Referring to figure 7.3 the thickness of the single large gasket (which affects the pinion bearing) should be 'a'– 'b' minus (say) .002 inch. For the input shaft the thickness of the second gasket should be dimension 'c' plus (say) .002 inch.

13 When placing the end cover in position the selector rails should be in neutral and care taken to see that the change rod fits in the cut-out slots in the ends of the rails. Replace the nuts and tighten them evenly to 11 lb/ft (1.5 mkg) of torque.

14 Refit the mounting bracket and flexible mounting blocks, clutch release thrust ring and the unit is ready for replacement in the car.

6.   Synchromesh Hub Assemblies - Dismantling, Inspection and Reassembly

1. The principles are exactly the same as those described in Chapter 6, Section 6 with a few exceptions.

2. The clearance between selector fork and hub groove is not quite so critical because there is provision for further adjustment of the forks after the gearbox is assembled. The maximum groove clearance is 0.4 mm (.016 inch).

3. Due to the fact that bottom gear is not synchromesh the 1st/2nd gear hub is a direct straight tooth gear engagement in one direction. It is most important therefore that it is assembled the correct way round. The hub can only be assembled as part of the overall assembly of the pinion shaft and the details are therefore included in Section 5(a) of this Chapter. The reason is that the sliding keys are spring loaded by radial coil springs rather than circumferential wire clips.

7. Input Shaft Oil Seal - Removal and Replacement

1. The seal can be replaced without dismantling the gearbox and the procedure is the same as described in Chapter 6, Section 7.

2. If the seal is being renewed as part of a general overhaul then it is simpler to fit it when reassembling the two halves of the split casing. This is covered in this Chapter in Section 5(d).

8. Selector Forks - Adjustment

1. It is possible to make adjustments to the forward speed selector forks (not reverse) with the transmission installed in the car. Such adjustments may be necessary and could cure the fault of any gear which jumps out of mesh when the car is being driven. It must be emphasised however that such adjustments are normally only necessary just after the transmission has been overhauled. Under any other circumstances adjustment can only compensate for wear in one direction and if, say, it is made to cure a 3rd gear jump out one could well find next that top gear jumps out instead. The same applies to first and second so before you start adjusting decide which gear is going to bother you least if it jumps out!

2. On the lower forward end of the left hand side transmission casing there are two large plugs which cover holes through which access to the clamp screws of the selector forks can be made. The front one is for the 3rd and 4th selector fork and the other for 1st/2nd.

3. To make an adjustment select neutral and remove the plug in order to get the appropriate fork clamp bolt slackened off. If only 1st gear jumps out it is best left alone as the fault is unlikely to be the selector fork setting. If 2nd gear jumps out move the rear selector fork forwards a fraction on the rail, reclamp the screw, replace the plug and road test.

4. For 3rd gear jump out move the front selector fork backwards a fraction, retighten and road test. For top gear jump out move the front selector fork forwards.

5. If the gearbox is badly worn anyhow you may find that any adjustments result in all gears jumping out. So as we said earlier you will have to decide which ones cause least inconvenience and take up the 'slack' in the appropriate direction. It must also be pointed out that jumping out of gear, particularly with the power on, can be dangerous - for example when overtaking - so do not be too casual in your approach to rectifying this fault. If you get into the habit of holding a gear in mesh you can expect accelerated wear of everything connected with the synchromesh mechanism.

6. It is possible also that there is wear in the gearchange lever mechanism itself. The gear lever is easily removed by undoing the two securing bolts in the floor tunnel. A certain amount of adjustment is also possible. By slackening the two securing bolts the whole assembly can be moved a little in either a forward or backwards direction. This is due to the mounting plate holes being elongated. If the assembly is moved forward, engagement of 2nd and 4th gears will be more positive and if moved rearward, 1st and 3rd. It must be remembered once again that such adjustment is normally used only to seek the exact central position. Adjustment could have exactly the same results as adjustments of the selector forks.

Reverse gear and spindle shaft - fitting the shaft (Section 5c 2)

Reverse gear and spindle shaft - fitting the lockpin (Section 5c 2)

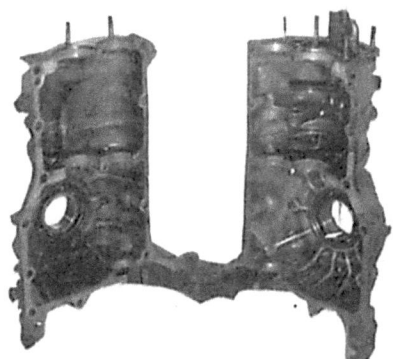

Casing halves ready for assembly (Section 5d 1)

Further view of casing ready for assembly (Section 5d 1)

Pinion shaft assembly being placed in position in LH casing. Crownwheel and pinion omitted. (Note locating peg) (Section 5d 6)

Pinion shaft in position (Section 5d 6)

Input shaft ready for replacement. Crownwheel and pinion omitted. (Note dowel) (Section 5d 7)

Input shaft in position (Section 5d 7)

Positioning oil seal on input shaft (Section 5d 9)

Replacing the long centre through bolt (Section 5d 9)

Removing the front cover plug (Section 8) ...

... to give access to the 3rd/4th gear selector fork clamp bolt

Fault Finding Chart - Gearbox

Symptom	Reason/s	Remedy
Ineffective synchromesh	Worn baulk rings or synchro hubs	Dismantle and renew .
Jumps out of one or more gears (on drive or over-run)	Weak detent springs or worn selector forks or worn gears	Dismantle and renew.
Noisy, rough, whining and vibration	Worn bearings and/or laygear thrust washers (initially) resulting in extended wear generally due to play and backlash	Dismantle and renew.
Noisy and difficult engagement of gears	Clutch fault	Examine clutch operation.

NOTE: It is sometimes difficult to decide whether it is worthwhile removing and dismantling the gearbox for a fault which may be nothing more than a minor irritant. Gearboxes which howl, or where the synchromesh can be 'beaten' by a quick gear change, may continue to perform for a long time in this state. A worn gearbox usually needs a complete rebuilt to eliminate noise because the various gears, if re-aligned on new bearings, will continue to howl when different wearing surfaces are presented to each other.

The decision to overhaul therefore, must be considered with regard to time and money available, relative to the degree of noise or malfunction that the driver has to suffer.

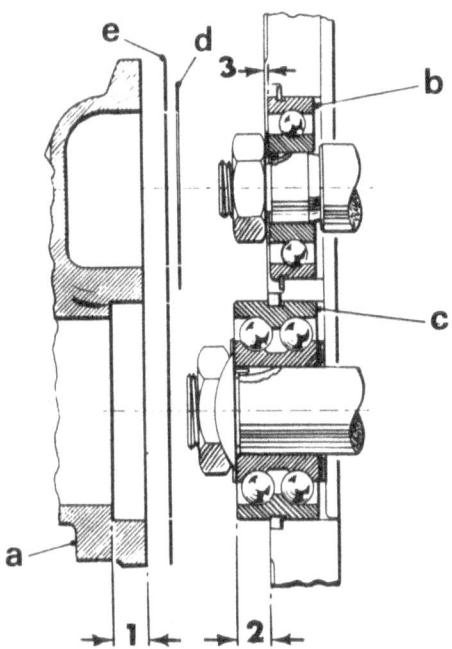

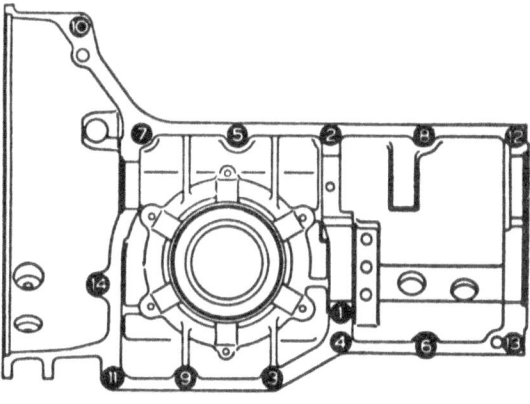

Fig. 7.4. Diagram illustrating sequence of tightening transmission casing bolts

Fig. 7.3. DRAWING SHOWING LAYOUT OF
GASKETS TO LOAD FRONT
BEARING

(a) Gearshift lever housing   (d) Circular gasket
(b) Input shaft bearing   (e) Main cover gasket
(c) Pinion shaft bearing

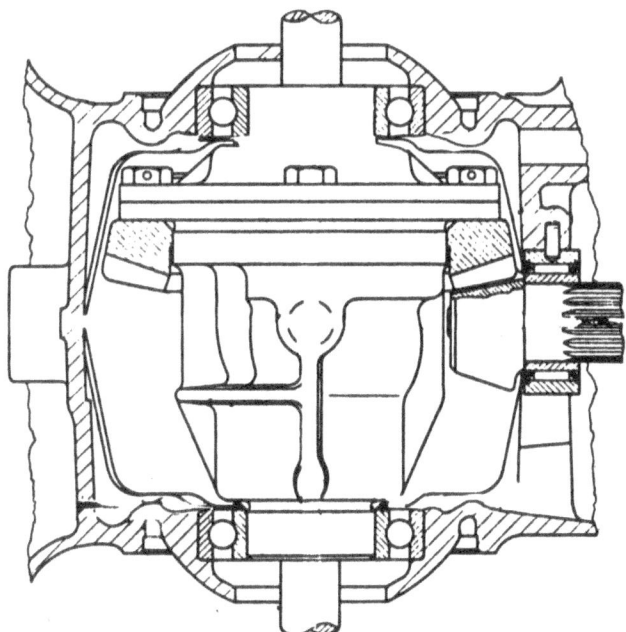

Fig. 7.5. Differential assembly - cross section

Chapter 8 Axle shafts and tubes

Contents

Specifications

Axle shaft max. run out (between centres)		0.5 mm (.020 inch)
Axle shaft/differential side gear clearances and groups:		
End clearance (across spade end) in side gear		.03 - 0,1 mm (.001 - .004 inch)
Side clearance (spade to fulcrum plates)		.035 - .244 mm (.001 - .010 inch)

	Side gear inner diameter	Axle shaft spade end dimension
Yellow	59.93 - 59.97 mm (2.32 - 2.361 ins.)	59.87 - 59.90 mm (2.357 - 2.3582 ins.)
Blue	59.98 - 60.0 mm (2.361 - 2.3622 ins.)	59.91 - 59.94 mm (2.3582 - 2.3598 ins.)
Pink	60.01 - 60.04 mm (2.3625 - 2.3638 ins.)	59.95 - 59.97 mm (2.3602 - 2.361 ins.)

Torque Wrench Settings

Axle tube retainer nuts	14 lb/ft (2.0 mkg)
Bearing retainer screws	43 lb/ft (6.0 mkg)
Axle shaft nut	217 lb/ft (30.0 mkg)
Axle tube/spring plate bolts and nuts	72 lb/ft (10.0 mkg)

---

1. General Description

The axle shafts to the Volkswagen rear wheels are independently suspended. The inner ends are located in the transmission casing in a spade type universal joint. Each axle shaft runs in a tube, the outer end of which is attached to the rear suspension plate. The outer end of the tube also carries the bearing. It can be seen therefore that the shaft and wheel form a rigid unit, pivoted at the inner end. This is called the swinging axle type of drive.

The axle tubes are oil filled from the transmission casing and this provides lubrication for the outer wheel bearing. Oil is retained at the outer end by a conventional seal on the shaft and at the inner end by a heavy duty flexible boot which shrouds the axle tube retainer plate. The lateral location of each axle is all carried at the inner end by the axle tube retainer plate. It can be seen that the shaft outer bearing and tube are all locked together so that the side thrust is therefore carried by the inner pivoting end of the tube. The spade end of the axle shaft in fact floats in the side gear. The side gear lateral location is by a thrust ring and circlip.

On the earlier models with split gear casings the principle of axle shaft and tube is exactly the same. However the side gears are located by the differential casing itself in these models. As the spade ends of the shafts cannot pass through these side gears they have to be taken out from the inside after dismantling the gearbox.

The outer bearing and oil seal are secured by a bearing cover plate on the tube and the drum and wheel secured to the axle by a single nut.

2. Routine Maintenance

The lubrication of rear axle bearings is covered by the lubrication of the transmission casing as a whole. Regular inspection should be made for signs of oil leaks at the inner and outer ends of the axle tube. A slight 'weep' of oil at the outer seal is normal and a collection disc is fitted inside the brake drum to prevent this oil from reaching the braking surfaces. At the inner end of the axle tube the oil retaining boot should show no traces whatsoever of any oil leakage. If necessary a special split type replacement can be fitted without requiring the dismantling of the axle shafts and tubes.

3. Oil Seals and Bearings - Removal and Replacement

1. To renew an oil seal or bearing requires the rear axle shaft nut to

Oil seal - punching out old oil seal (Section 3.11)

Fitting the new oil seal (Section 3.11)

Use a block of wood to tap in the new seal (Section 3.11)

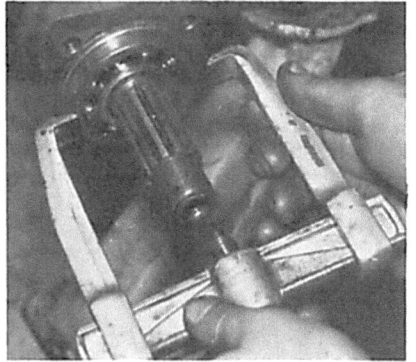
Using a puller to remove the bearing (Section 3.6)

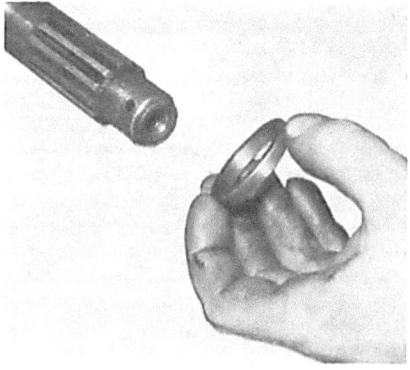
Replacing the inner spacer (Section 3.7)

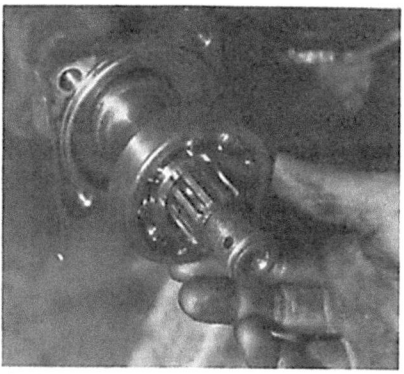
Replacing the bearing (Section 3.8)

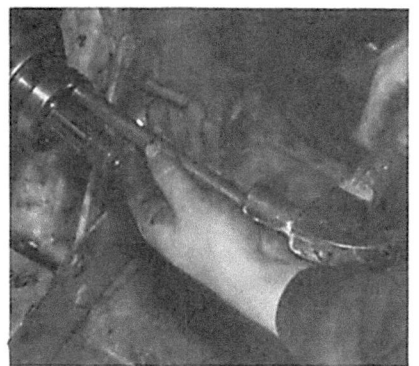
Drifting the bearing home (Section 3.8)

Replacing the large 'O' ring (Section 3.9)

Replacing the bearing washer (shim) (Section 3.10)

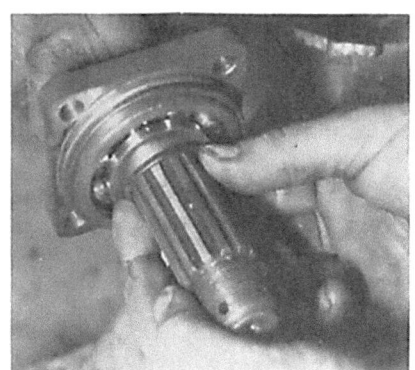
Replacing the small 'O' ring (Section 3.10)

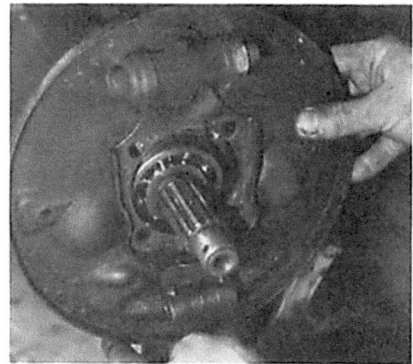
Replacing the brake backplate (Section 3.12)

Replacing the bearing retainer (Section 3.13)

be undone so before jacking the car up remove the hub caps and take out the split pin from the castellated nut on the shaft. Using a 36 mm socket spanner and a proper long handle attachment slacken the nut. It is advisable to have the handbrake on also. If the wheel still turns then some additional weight will be needed in the back of the car to prevent the wheels slipping on the ground. Slacken the road wheel bolts at the same time as these are much tighter than on many other cars.

2. Jack up the car, remove the road wheel and take off the hub nut.

3. Slacken off the brake shoe adjusters as far as they will go (see Chapter 9 for details).

4. It should now be possible to draw the brake drum off the splined end of the drive shaft. If any difficulty is experienced it should be tapped with a soft mallet progressively round the edges. If this does not seem to work bolt the wheel back onto the drum again and see whether the additional grip provided enables you to pull the drum off with it. If the drum should be really tight and unmovable then it will be necessary to obtain a puller which will hook into the holes in the drum and bear on to the outer end of the axle shaft. Do not strike the drum hard around the edges or you will probably crack it.

5. Once the drum is removed the heads of four bolts which hold the bearing cover to the axle tube are revealed. This cover houses the oil seal. The brake backplate is also held by the four bolts and although the illustrations show the brake shoes removed the whole plate assembly may be moved off the axle and hung on one side without disconnecting either the hydraulic fluid pipes or handbrake cable. The bearing cover is removed so that the 'O' ring round the bearing may be renewed at the same time as the main seal. This 'O' ring should be taken off now and if only the seal renewal is being done then the procedure as described later in this section should now be adopted.

6. To remove the bearing take off the shim next. The easiest way to remove the bearing is with a fine pronged puller which engages in between the steel balls of the bearing itself; but this is a special tool which may be difficult to obtain. It is possible to drive the shaft inwards just far enough to enable the bearing and shaft together to be pulled out of the housing just enough to get levers behind the bearing; and so remove it with a more conventional puller. There is sufficient clearance at the inner end of the shaft to permit this, but great care must be taken not to overdo it or damage will be caused to the differential pinion gears. Make sure to protect the splined and threaded end of the shaft by replacing the nut and using a block of wood as further protection. Use a heavy hammer and after each blow check by pulling the shaft outwards how far the bearing has moved in relation to it. Once there is a gap sufficient to get a lever in, stop striking the shaft. A third alternative is to lock a self-grip wrench on to the lip of the outer bearing race and then use the nose of the wrench jaws to lever against to ease the bearing out. Two wrenches - one at each side - are best for this method and the jaw teeth must be in good condition. Once the bearing is clear of the housing it is a reasonably straightforward operation to get it right off.

7. Behind the bearing is another spacer but this need not be disturbed. If it comes out make sure it goes back the same way - with the bevelled edge inwards.

8. To replace the bearing put it over the shaft with the covered side of the ball race if any, facing outwards. It can then be 'drifted' right into the housing.

9. Next fit the large 'O' ring from the seal kit round the outside of the bearing and up to the axle tube flange.

10 Fit the shim over the shaft followed by the smaller rubber 'O' ring.

11 Next drive out the old seal from inside the bearing cover using a suitable punch. Take care not to damage the inner surface of the flange. The new seal may then be driven into the cover with the lip of the seal facing inwards. If, when you drove out the old seal a washer came out from behind it make sure that the hole which is in one edge of the bearing cover is clear and that the washer goes into the cover before the seal - which can only be fitted from the inside. Tap the seal in with a soft faced mallet or block of wood until the

outer face is flush with the cover.

12 Next replace the brake backplate onto the axle tube flange (with the hydraulic cylinder uppermost).

13 Place the bearing cover in position. The cover has either a raised lug or a hole in one edge. In either case the lug or the oil drain hole goes on the bottom edge but the cover with the oil hole has a paper washer between it and the backplate. If you obtained the correct seal kit for your chassis number the paper washer will be included.

14 Replace the four cover bolts and tighten them evenly to a torque of 43 ft/lbs (6 mkg).

15 The outer spacer collar should be lubricated on its outer face and put on the shaft with the bevelled inner edge inwards. Push it into the oil seal.

16 Replace the brake drum (fitted with the oil flinger on those earlier models that do not have an oil drain in the bearing cover) and refit the nut. Replace the road wheel and tighten the axle shaft nut as described in Chapter 6, Section 5(e).

4. Axle Shafts and Tubes - Removal and Replacement (1 Piece Casing Type Transmission)

1. The need to renew an axle shaft is rare and can only be caused by breakage or damage to the splined and threaded outer end. If it is suspected of being badly worn on the inner spade end a check can be made but it is most unusual for such wear to take place separately from any other general wear in the transmission or final drive. Volkswagen do not recommend the removal of axle shafts unless the whole of the transmission assembly has just been removed from the vehicle. This is because in order to assess the correct clearance of the axle tube at the inner end it is considered necessary to be able to swing the tube around freely - without the restriction which results from it being in position on the car. Nevertheless it can be done; although the placing of the necessary gaskets and the constant guard against dirt contaminating the differential make it something of a struggle. It is reasonable to say that if you have no other reason to remove engine and transmission it would be a lot of effort just to remove an axle shaft. Note that for split case transmission units that the axle shafts can only be taken out after the transmission has been taken out. Details are given in Chapter 6.

2. To remove an axle shaft first remove the wheel, brake drum, brake backplate assembly and bearing as described in the previous section. Do not forget to drain out the oil first.

3. Thoroughly clean the whole area surrounding the axle tube retainer plate on the transmission casing. Clean also the axle tube itself for a distance of about six inches back from the end of the large oil retainer boot. Then slacken both boot retainer clips and draw the boot off the retainer plate and leave it a little way down the tube. This is done so that it does not get abnormally stretched and possibly ruptured during subsequent operations.

4. The next task is to detach the outer end of the axle tube which is secured to the suspension arm plate by three nuts and bolts. Clean up the bolts thoroughly and apply penetrating oil.

5. The position of the outer end of the axle tube in relation to the suspension plate can vary and it is most important that a mark is made to ensure correct re-alignment. A notch exists in the top edge of the axle tube flange so with a cold chisel make another notch exactly in line with it in the edge of the suspension plate. Be accurate.

6. Remove the bolt securing the lower end of the telescopic damper and then put a suitable support under the end of the axle and remove the three nuts and bolts. They are big, tight and probably rusty so make sure you have two spanners of the correct size available - socket or ring. It is quite likely that the spring washers for the nuts will break when the nut is undone so make a note to get some more. They are important. Note also that the front bolt of the three also secures the bump stop buffer bracket. As a result it is slightly larger then the other two.

7. With the bolts removed the axle tube outer end may be moved to the rear, clear of the suspension plate. If you have been reading this in connection with the removal of the transmission unit (Chapter 6)

Tightening up the bolts to a torque of 43 lb ft (Section 3.14)

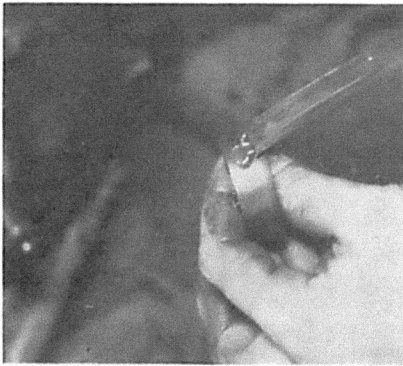
Oiling the outer spacer prior to refitting inside the oil seal in the bearing housing (Section 3.15)

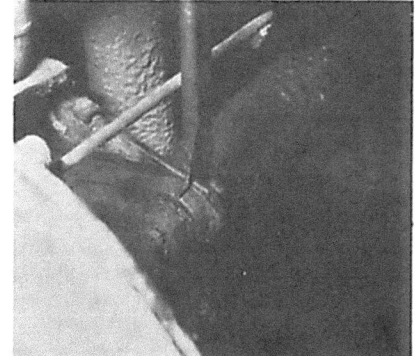
Axle tube removal - marking the suspension plate (Section 3.5)

Removing the side gear retaining clip with circlip pliers (Section 4.11)

LH tube end showing notch and damper mounting lug facing forward (Section 4.14)

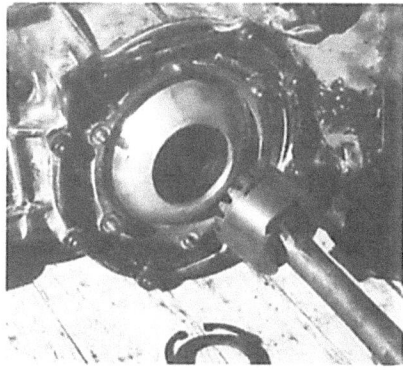
Inserting the shaft with the side gear into the transmission case (Section 4.12)

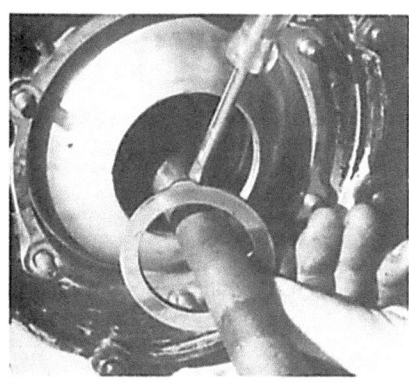
Refitting the thrust ring (Section 4.13)

Refitting the retaining circlip (Section 4.13)

Replacing the plastic packing (Section 4.15)

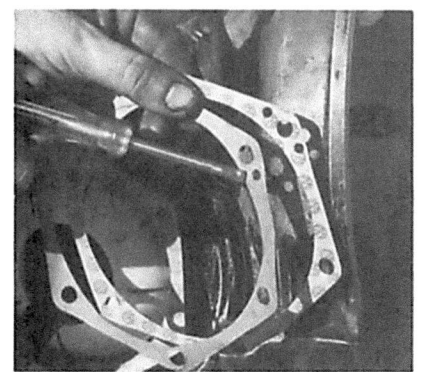
Selecting gaskets (Section 4.15)

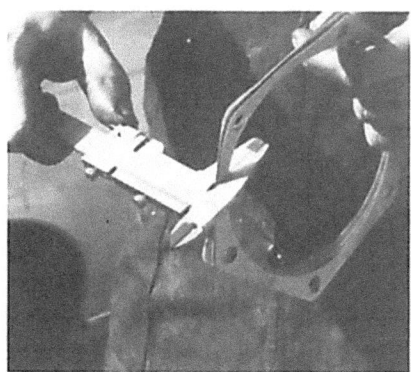
Measuring the thickness of the gaskets (Section 4.16)

Positioning gaskets (Section 4.16)

this is as far as you need go here now. Go back to Chapter 6 until you have removed the transmission from the car. Then come back here!

8. Moving to the inner end of the axle tube, next remove the six nuts securing the axle tube retainer plate (do not confuse these with the eight nuts surrounding them).

9. The retainer plate may now be pulled off the studs and the axle tube, together with the plate, taken right off the axle shaft. Carefully remove, intact if possible, the gaskets between the retainer plate and the transmission housing.

10 Fitted over the convex face of the axle tube location on the transmission casing is a plastic hemispherical packing piece. Carefully take this off.

11 Inside the transmission housing it will be possible to see the two eyes of a large circlip which needs contracting in order to be released. Do this with a pair of circlip pliers. The circlip and thrust ring behind it will now come out. The axle shaft, fulcrum plates and side gear can all be withdrawn also.

12 Replacement of the axle shaft and axle tube is a reversal of the removal procedure but there are one or two points which must be carefully considered.

13 When refitting the thrust ring for the side bearing note the protrusion in the outer edge which engages a groove in the casing to prevent it rotating.

14 If the transmission has been completely dismantled and both axle tubes have been removed you must make sure you get them back on the correct side as they are handed. With the notch in the bearing housing upwards the shock absorber mounting lug faces forward and down.

15 It will be appreciated that the domed end of the axle tube pivots on the mating face of the transmission. The plastic packing piece in between acts as a bearing surface. The two are held together by the retainer plate. The thickness of the gaskets behind the retainer plate determines the amount of pressure it applies. Too few gaskets and it will be so tight it will move only with difficulty. Too many and it will be slack and result in end float of the whole axle assembly. Provided there was no evidence of excessive end float on dismantling and that the plastic packing piece is in good condition there is no reason why the same gaskets should not be refitted. The theoretical clearance is between 0.00 - 0.2 mm (0.00 - .008 inch) but as there is no satisfactory way of measuring this the only practical way is by moving the axle tube in all directions as far as possible. Friction should be felt but there should be no jamming or sticking at any point.

16 If the gaskets have been damaged carefully separate them to see how many there are. Each is identified by having one or two holes punched in it indicating that it is either 0.1 or 0.2 mm (.004 or .008 inch) thick. Make up a pack the same thickness and then add or subtract as required.

17 On later models there is an additional rubber 'O' ring which fits in the recess in the bearing cover inside the gaskets. This should always be renewed on reassembly. Do not fit it until the gasket thicknesses have been worked out. Then fit it after the gaskets so that their edges do not get caught up on it causing possible distortion.

18 If you have some molybdenum disulphide paste available (or the moly additive will be better than nothing) smear the mating faces of the axle tube and packing to aid lubrication particularly in the early stages of re-use. In any case lubricate them well with transmission oil. Tighten the retainer plate securing nuts evenly to 14 lb/ft (2.0 mkg).

19 When reconnecting the outer end of the axle tube to the suspension plate make sure that the two marks made before removal line up exactly. Do not forget to re-fix the bump stop bracket to the front bolt. Incidentally, the bolts should be fitted with their heads inwards (to the centre of the car).

20 Do not try and replace the rubber boot until the axle tube has been re-installed. It is much easier (and less likely to cause strain) to fit when the axle is as near horizontal as possible. Make sure that the parts are perfectly clean and that the clips are serviceable and not overtightened.

21 Refill the transmission with oil.

5. Axle Shafts - Removal and Replacement (Split Casing Transmission)

1. In rare circumstances of breakage or damage it may be found necessary to renew a half shaft. In order to do this it is necessary to dismantle the gearbox as described in Chapter 7.

2. With the gearbox dismantled the two axle shafts are seen to be part of the differential assembly. The differential casing is in two parts - these being joined together by six bolts which also secure the crown wheel (ring gear) to the differential casing. It is necessary to remove these bolts so that the cover may be removed. The axle shaft whose inner end is located in the cover can then be taken out together with the fulcrum plates and side gear pinion. To remove the other shaft from the differential casing it is necessary first to remove the differential pinion shaft. This can be done by driving out the lock pin with a punch and tapping out the shaft. The pinions and side gear can then be removed and the shaft drawn out.

3. The correct tolerances of fit for the inner end of the axle shaft should be checked as described in Section 6.

4. Reassembly is a reversal of this procedure. Great care must be taken to ensure that when the crown wheel is refitted that the mating surfaces are perfectly clean and unmarked. If the crown wheel does not fit perfectly flush on the differential casing it will run out of true causing excessive noise and early failure.

5. The six lock bolts must be tightened evenly to a torque of 43 lb/ft (6.0 mkg) and locked together with iron securing wire.

6. Axle Shafts and Tubes - Examination for Wear

1. Under normal circumstances the wear on the inner spade ends of the axle shaft will be negligible and in any case should not be greater or less than the wear that will occur in the transmission unit generally.

2. To check the wear place the end of the shaft in the side gear. First measure the gap across the end with a feeler. If it exceeds 0.20 mm (.008 inch) then a new shaft, new gear or both will be needed to reduce it.

3. Next fit the fulcrum plates into the side gear and refit the shaft. Then measure the clearance between shaft and fulcrum plate. On split case transmissions this clearance should not exceed 0.30 mm (.012 inch). On later 1-piece casing models it should not exceed 0.25 mm (.010 inch). It is possible to obtain oversize fulcrum plates in order to rectify any excessive clearance here. Renewal plates have grooves cut in their flat faces so you will be able to tell if this has already been done.

4. If examination shows that the gear/shaft clearances warrant buying new parts it should be remembered that the gear and shaft are grouped by size tolerance. These tolerances are colour coded and the shaft has a paint band round it. The gear has a matching colour in a recess. The specifications section gives the details.

5. Axle shafts should, of course, be straight and with the shaft held between centres the run-out at the bearing seat should not exceed .05 mm (.002 inch). As this is not the sort of measurement that can be made accurately without precision holding and measuring equipment you should not need to worry about checking it unless you have specific reason for thinking the shaft is bent. Shafts can be straightened - cold only - so it is best to get this done at a Volkswagen agency.

6. The splines and thread on the end of the shaft should not deteriorate unless you have had the misfortune to have the shaft nut come loose for some rare reason. The best way to test the thread is with the full torque of 217 lb/ft when the nut is retightened. If nothing gives then you can assume that it will serve. If the thread strips - on either nut or shaft - then you will probably need a new shaft as well as nut.

7. Axle tubes should not deteriorate. Examine the concave bearing

Assembling axle tube (Section 4)

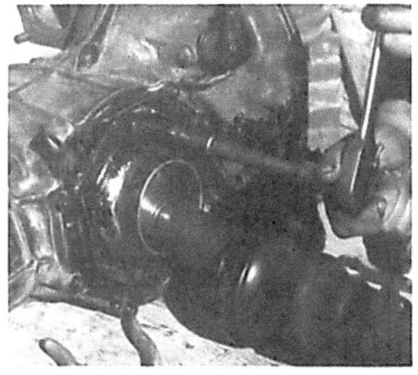

Securing axle tube retainer plate nuts (14 lb ft) (Section 4.18)

Positioning the axle tube to the suspension plate (Section 4.19)

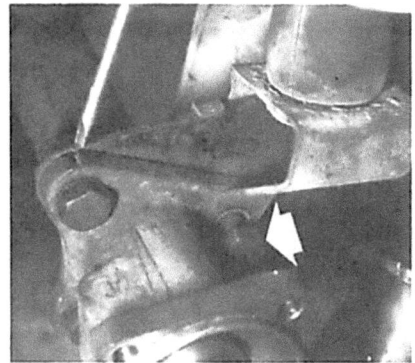

Lining up the notches. Note bump stop bracket fixing (Section 4.19)

Differential casing with axle shafts fitted (Section 5)

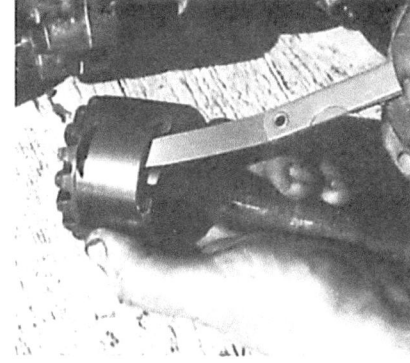

Checking shaft to side gear clearance across the spade end (Section 6.2)

Replacing fulcrum plates (Section 6.3)

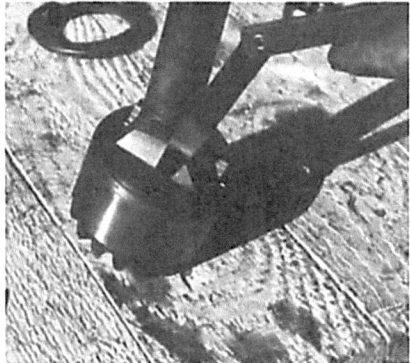

Check clearance along the flat surface (Section 6.3)

Preparing gaiter joint faces with sealing compound (Section 7.4)

Positioning round the axle tube (Section 7.4)

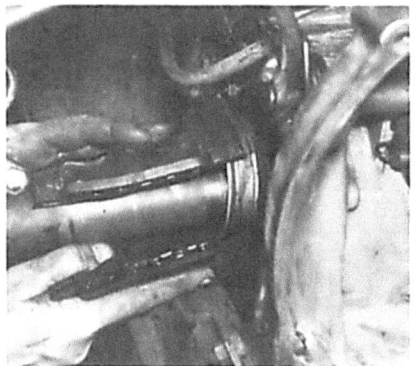

Fit the gaiter carefully (Section 7.4)

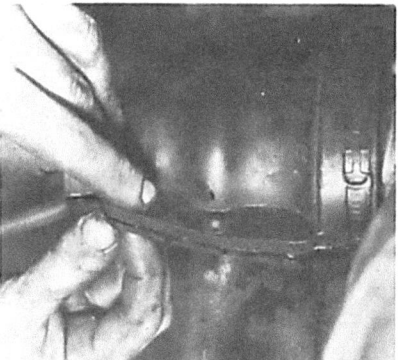

Put in the gaiter screws (Section 7.5)

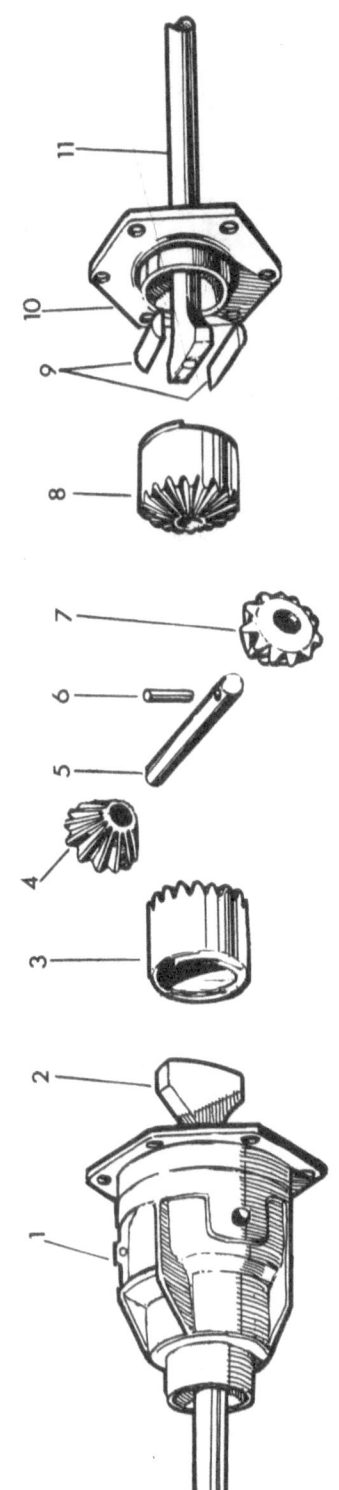

Fig. 8.1. DIFFERENTIAL CASING AND DRIVE SHAFT ASSEMBLY. EARLY TYPE - SPLIT TYPE

1 Differential casing
2 Drive shaft
3 Side gear

4 Differential pinion
5 Pinion shaft
6 Shaft locking pin

7 Differential pinion
8 Side gear
9 Fulcrum plates

10 Differential casing cover
11 Drive shaft

NOTE: Crownwheel and securing bolts omitted.

123

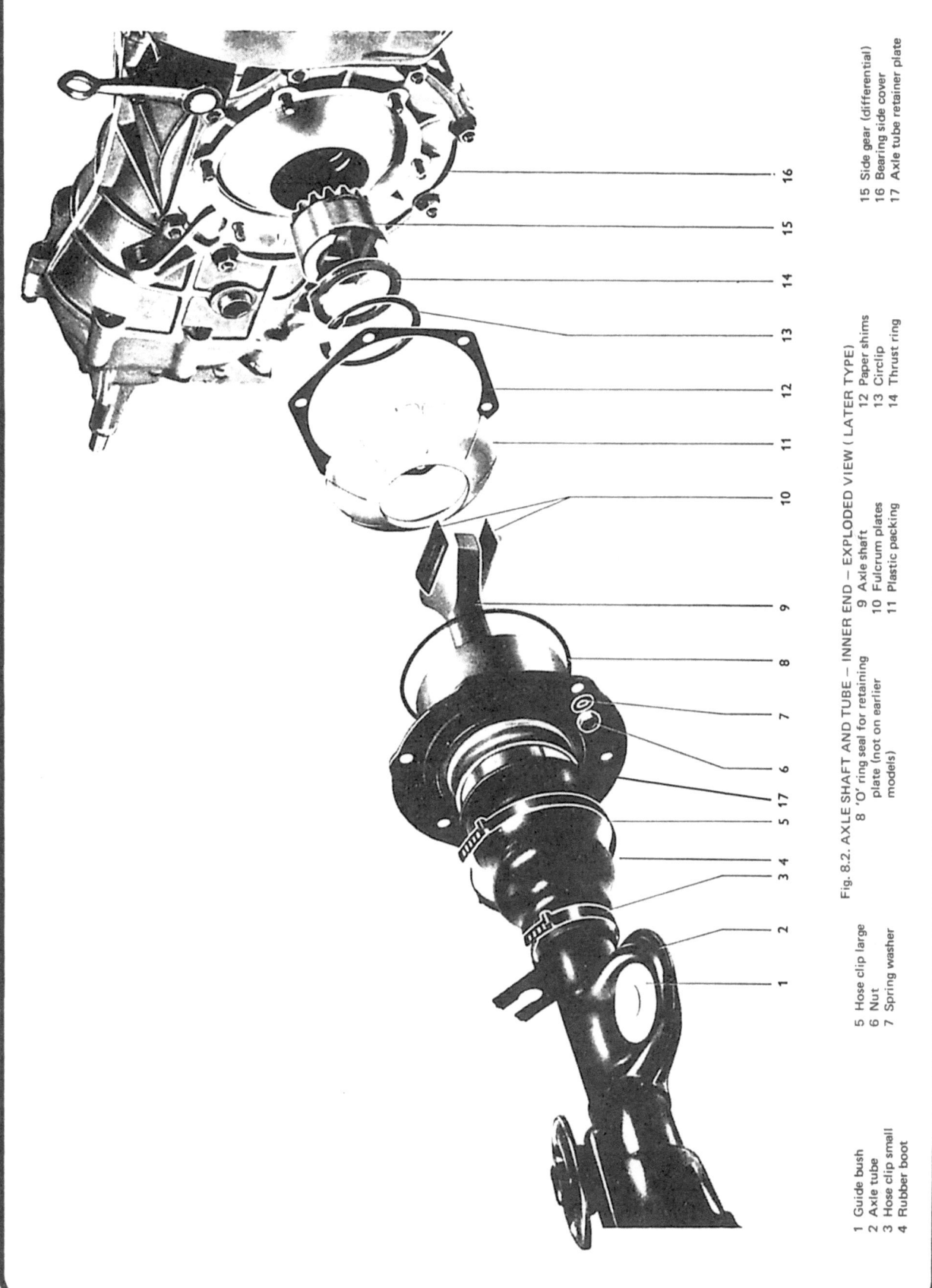

Fig. 8.2. AXLE SHAFT AND TUBE — INNER END — EXPLODED VIEW (LATER TYPE)

1 Guide bush
2 Axle tube
3 Hose clip small
4 Rubber boot

5 Hose clip large
6 Nut
7 Spring washer

8 'O' ring seal for retaining plate (not on earlier models)
9 Axle shaft
10 Fulcrum plates
11 Plastic packing

12 Paper shims
13 Circlip
14 Thrust ring

15 Side gear (differential)
16 Bearing side cover
17 Axle tube retainer plate

surface at the inner end and check that the plastic packing is not breaking up. The bearing housings have been known to get damaged in cases of extreme bearing wear or seizure with the result that a new bearing does not fit tightly. In such cases a new housing can be fitted to the tube but once again you are advised to have this done by a Volkswagen agent.

7. Axle Tubes - Oil Seal Gaiter Renewal

1. If an axle tube oil seal gaiter leaks oil action must be taken without delay. Replacements are split so that they can be fitted without having to dismantle everything.
2. Drain off at least 2 - 3 pints of the transmission oil unless you have lost so much that it will not run out when the gaiter is removed.
3. Undo the clips and cut the old gaiter off. The new split gaiter will be supplied complete with screws and clips.
4. Thoroughly clean the retainer plate and axle tube where the gaiter fits. Then coat the joining edges of the new gaiter with sealing compound and place it in position round the tube so that the joint faces towards the rear of the car. Do not put sealing compound on the ends where the circular clips go.
5. Put the small screws into position with a washer under the head and fit the nuts with a washer also. Tighten them all up evenly but do not overtighten. If the washers appear to be squeezing into the rubber the bolts are too tight.
6. Put the two clips in position and tighten them but not so much that they squeeze and distort the gaiter.

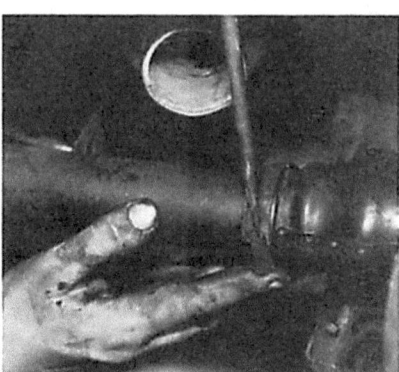

Fitting the inner gaiter clip (Section 7.6)

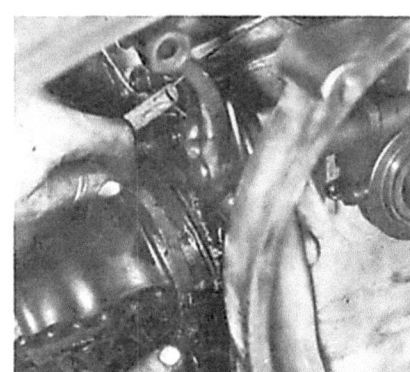

Fitting the outer gaiter clip (Section 7.6)

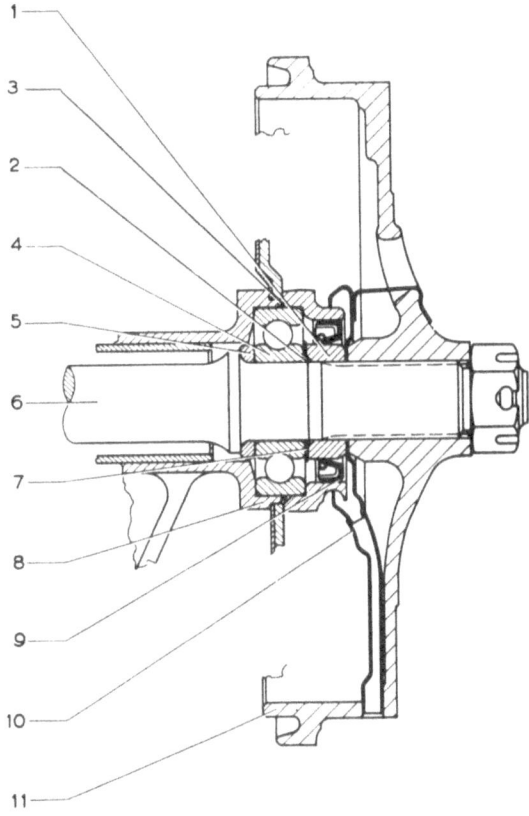

Fig. 8.3. CROSS SECTION DRAWING OF REAR
BEARING AND HUB ASSEMBLY
(EARLY TYPE)
1 Outer spacer
2 Large 'O' ring seal
3 Small 'O' ring seal
4 Bearing
5 Inner spacer
6 Axle shaft
7 Thrust washer
8 Bearing housing
9 Oil seal
10 Oil slinger and tube
11 Brake drum

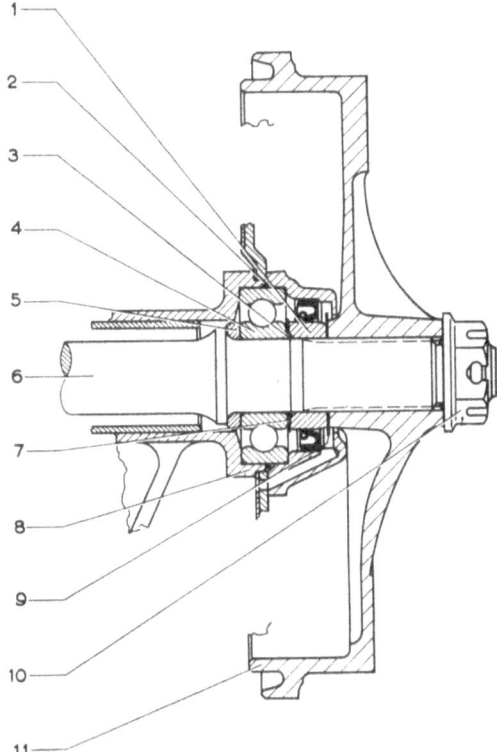

Fig. 8.4. CROSS SECTION DRAWING OF REAR
BEARING AND HUB ASSEMBLY
(LATER TYPE)
1 Outer spacer
2 Large 'O' ring seal
3 Small 'O' ring seal
4 Bearing
5 Inner spacer
6 Axle shaft
7 Thrust washer
8 Bearing housing
9 Oil deflector disc
10 Shaft nut
11 Brake drum

Chapter 9 Braking system

Contents

Specifications

Type	Hydraulically operated shoes to drums front and rear. Handbrake operates a flexible cable to each rear wheel, independently.
Hydraulic Fluid	Volkswagen or Lockheed

Brake Drums

Internal diameter	230.1 mm (max. 231.5)
Maximum run-out - radial	0.15 mm (.006 inch)
- lateral	0.25 mm (.016 inch)

Brake Linings

Width	30 or 40 mm, depending on year and model
Thickness (new)	3.8 - 4.0 mm

Master Cylinder

Bore	17.46 or 19.05 mm

Wheel Cylinders

Bore (front)	19.05 or 22.20 mm
Bore (rear)	17.44 or 19.05 mm

Torque Wrench Settings

Master Cylinder to frame bolts	14 - 22 lb/ft (2.0 - 3.0 mkg)
Backplate to steering knuckle screws	36 - 47 lb/ft (5.0 mkg)
Brake hose (flexible) unions	11 - 14 lb/ft (1.5 - 2.0 mkg)
Brake pipe (rigid) unions	11 - 14 lb/ft (1.5 - 2.0 mkg)
Stop light switch	11 - 14 lb/ft (1.5 - 2.0 mkg)

1. General Description

The braking system considered in this book is the hydraulic version. Although the 1200 Standard version of the Beetle was equipped with cable operated brakes as late as 1962 very few of these models ever found their way out of Germany so they are not dealt with here. Hydraulic brakes were fitted on the De Luxe model from 1950 on.

Drum brakes are fitted front and rear and there is a single hydraulic wheel cylinder with two pistons in each drum. This means that there is one leading shoe in each wheel. Each shoe in each drum can be adjusted nearer to the drum by means of a screw type adjuster within the drum.

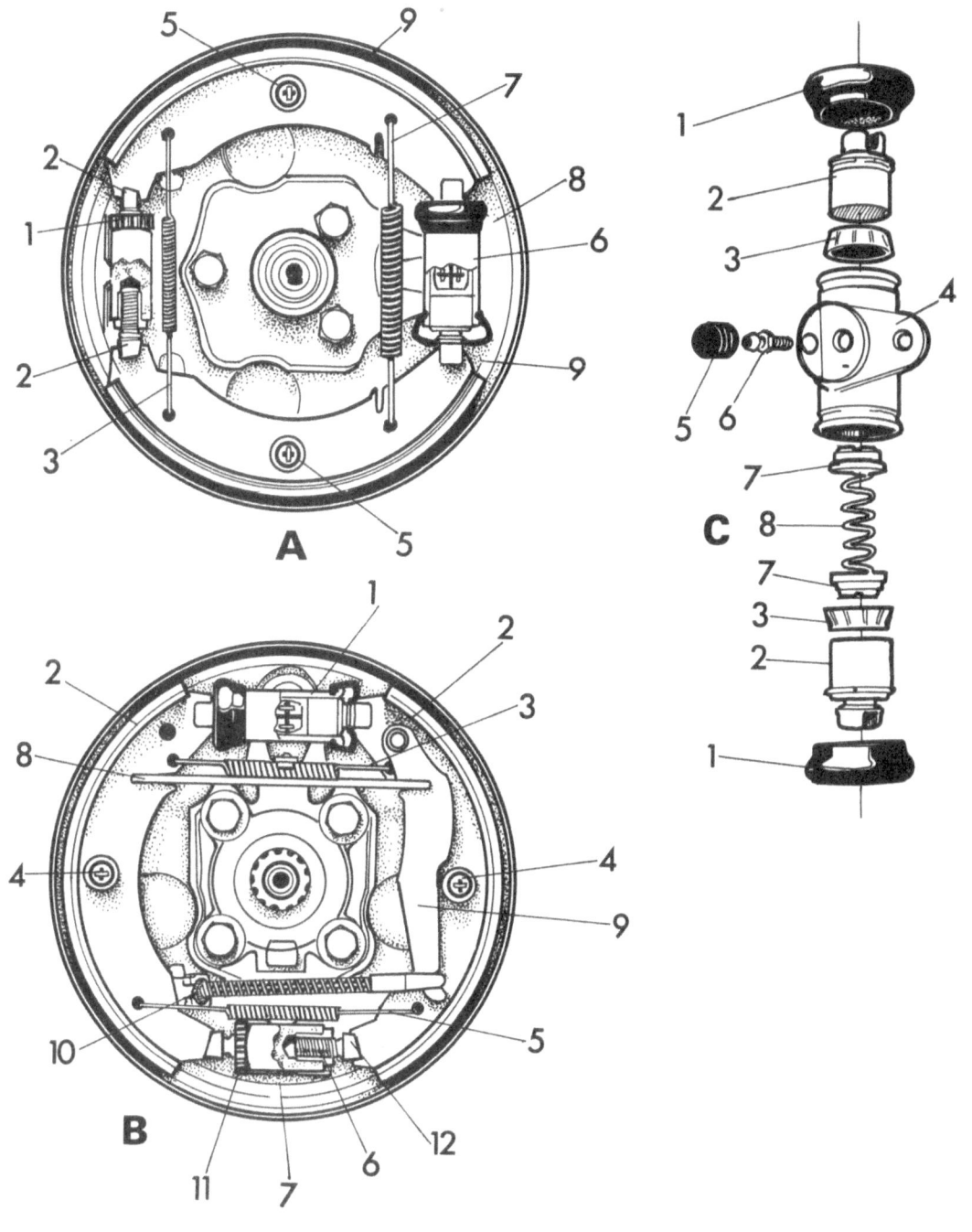

A

B

C

Fig. 9.1A FRONT BRAKE ASSEMBLY - COMPONENTS

1 Adjusting wheel	3 Front retractor spring	5 Steady pin spring and cup retainer	7 Rear retractor spring
2 Anchor piece	4 Adjusting screw		8 Back plate
		6 Hydraulic cylinder	9 Brake shoe and lining

Fig. 9.1B REAR BRAKE ASSEMBLY - COMPONENTS

1 Hydraulic cylinder	4 Steady pin, spring and cup retainer	7 Back plate	10 Handbrake cable
2 Brake shoe and lining	5 Lower retractor spring	8 Connecting plate	11 Adjusting wheel
3 Upper retractor spring	6 Adjusting screw	9 Handbrake connecting lever	12 Anchor piece

Fig. 9.1C HYDRAULIC WHEEL CYLINDER

1 Dust boot	3 Seal	5 Dust cap	7 Seal expander
2 Piston	4 Cylinder	6 Bleed nipple	8 Expander spring

A single master cylinder generates the hydraulic pressure fed to the four wheel cylinders. The pipe lines are rigid metal except where they link from rigid to moving assemblies, viz, from the front axle tube to the wheel cylinder direct, and from the body to each of the swinging rear axle tubes.

The handbrake operates on the rear wheels only and the leverage from the handle is transmitted by two cables running in tubes in the floor tube.

The level of the hydraulic fluid in the system is maintained by a fluid reservoir located behind the spare wheel in the front luggage compartment.

The operation of the system is orthodox. Pressure applied to the foot pedal operates a piston in the master cylinder (in effect a pump) and pressure built up travels along the fluid lines to the four wheel cylinders. The pressure forces the pistons out of the cylinders and these in turn press the shoes against the interior flanges of the drums. When the pressure is relieved the shoes are drawn away from the drums by retractor springs.

A special check valve is installed in the master cylinder ahead of the piston. This permits full flow when pressure is applied and full relief when the piston pressure is taken off. However, it is spring loaded sufficiently to maintain a slight residual pressure in the fluid lines. This reduces the reaction time for pressure build up in the system. Note that master cylinders from cars with disc brakes are not inter-changeable.

2. Routine Maintenance

1. It is difficult to state intervals for brake checks in terms of either times or mileage because conditions can vary so much. Basically the requirement is to be aware of the moment when the brakes need attention. Fractional deterioration in efficiency can pass unnoticed and it is only when an emergency occurs that the stopping power is found to be wanting.

2. The first indications of adjustment requirement is in the distance of travel required by the foot pedal before the brakes start to operate. If it moves more than 25 mm (approximately 1 inch) at the tip of the pedal before any pressure can be felt then adjustment of the brake shoes should be carried out.

3. Other important brake checks have no indications to signify deterioration. Consequently they must be carried out diligently and thoroughly at regular intervals otherwise total failure or at least sudden severe deterioration could take place. These checks must be carried out at minimum intervals of 3,000 miles or 3 months, whichever comes first. If road conditions are regularly rough or corrosive these intervals may need reduction. The items to be checked are listed below.

a) Hydraulic fluid reservoir level
    Clean area round the cap, remove and see that the level is no more than 15 - 20 mm below the level of the bottom of the filler neck. If the level is significantly low check it again after topping up, within a few days. If it has dropped again then something is wrong and for safety's sake further inspection is necessary.

b) Hydraulic pipe lines
    Inspect all hydraulic fluid lines, both rigid and flexible, for signs of damage or corrosion which could lead to leaks. If in doubt renew the part. Your life is at stake.

c) Wheel cylinders
    Examine behind all the brake backplates for signs of fluid which could indicate leakage from the wheel cylinders.

d) Handbrake cable
    Adjust the handbrake cables as necessary but not before adjusting the rear brake shoes first.

e) Brake linings
    Remove the brake drums and examine the shoes to see how much lining material is left before the heads of the rivets will be reached. If the amount is .5 mm (.020 inch) or less then renew the linings.

3. Brake Adjustment (Including Handbrake)

1. All four wheels may have their brakes adjusted without having to remove the wheels although the wheel hub caps should first be removed and each wheel jacked up in turn.

2. For the front wheels the two adjuster wheels are positioned at centre front as you face the wheel so if the wheel is revolved they can be seen through the hole in the drum. For the rear wheels the two adjusters are at the bottom of the drum.

3. Each adjuster should be moved in the appropriate direction (see diagram) with a screwdriver engaged in the notch until it can be moved no further and the wheel is locked. Then back off the adjuster one or two notches until the wheel revolves freely.

4. If any shoe(s) needs considerable adjustment (because they have been allowed to go unadjusted too long) then they will have to 'bed in' again to a different radius and this will call for further adjustment after a shorter interval. This is why regular brake adjustment is necessary to ensure top braking efficiency at all times. The linings will also last longer as it will ensure that the whole surface area is used evenly all the time.

5. When adjusting the rear brakes remember that when turning the wheels the drag of the transmission will be felt. Do not confuse this with binding brake shoes.

6. Having completed adjusting one wheel it is good practice to operate the brake pedal once or twice and then adjust again. Sometimes the shoes can move fractionally off-centre during adjustment. The extra time required is well worth the trouble.

7. If a shoe still rubs against the drum a little even after being backed off more than 3 notches, leave it (provided it is only superficial). However, if the binding is quite severe then it is possible that the lining is very unevenly worn. In such instances remove the drum and have a look.

8. Once the rear brake shoes have been adjusted to the drums the handbrake may be checked. If both back wheels can be jacked off the ground together it will save some time. Pump the footbrake two or three times (to centralise the shoes) and apply the handbrake two notches. Pull back the rubber shroud at the base of the lever and slacken the locknut on the threaded end of each cable. Then tighten each cable with the adjusting nut (holding the cable with a screwdriver in the slotted end) until an equal amount of drag can be felt on each rear wheel when it is turned. Pull the handbrake on four notches. At this it should not be possible to turn the wheels. Make sure any further adjustment is kept even between the two rear wheels.

4. Front Drums and Shoes - Removal, Inspection and Replacement

1. The front brake drums form part of the wheel hub casting so they have to be taken off the stub axle. This involves releasing the front wheel bearings, details of which are given in Chapter 11. Before pulling the drum off it is a good idea to back the shoe adjusters off as far as they will go.

2. In the centre of each shoe a retaining pin, held in position by a spring loaded, slotted cup washer, must first be removed. This can be done with a pair of pliers, turning the washer so that the slot aligns with the head of the pin. Washer, spring and pin can then be removed.

3. Unhook the retractor spring which connects the two shoes nearest to the notched adjusters. The end of one shoe can then be lifted out of the adjuster. Both shoes can then be disengaged quite easily from

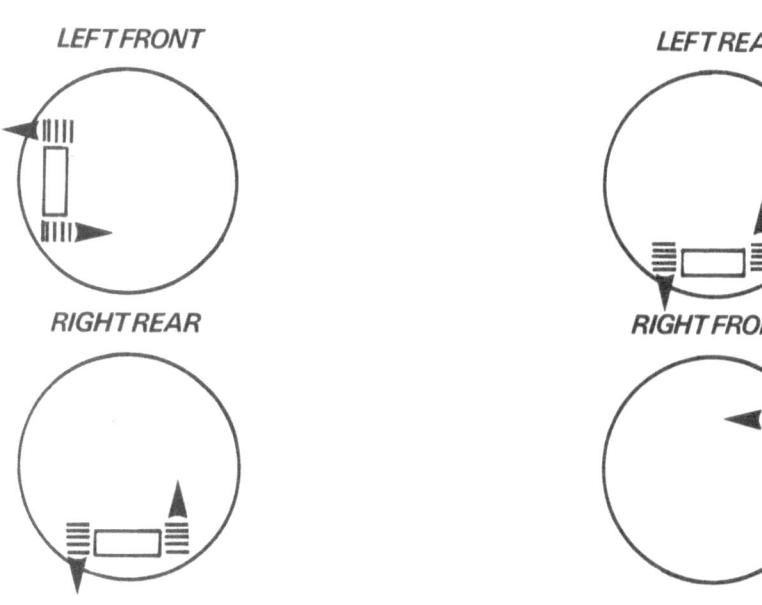

LEFT FRONT

LEFT REAR

RIGHT REAR

RIGHT FRONT

Arrows indicate direction of turning to move shoes to drums

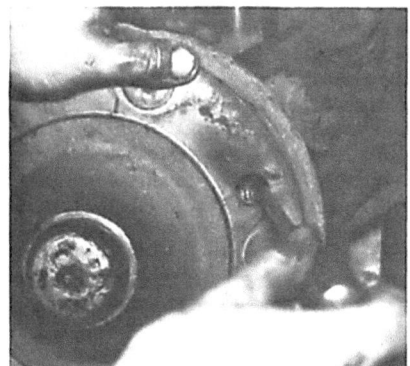

Adjusting a brake shoe. The wheel adjuster can be seen through the hole in the drum. (Section 3.3)

Releasing the small retractor spring (Section 4.3)

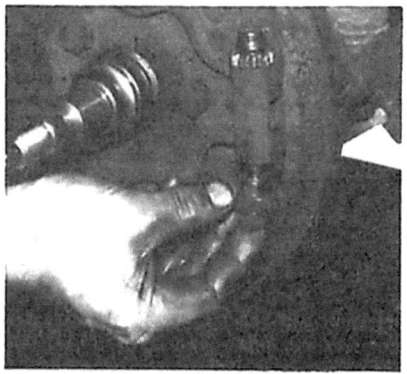

Replacing the adjuster (Section 4.6)

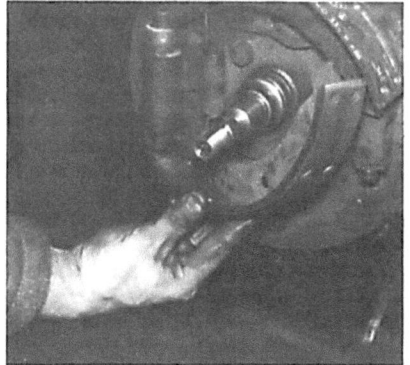

Hooking the shoes into the wheel cylinder notches (Section 4.8)

Hooking the shoes into the adjuster notches (Section 4.8)

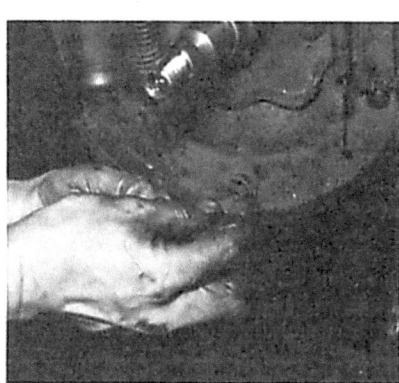

Replacing the steady pins (Section 4.9)

the hydraulic wheel cylinder. Immediately tie a piece of string around the wheel cylinder to prevent the pistons popping out. Do not apply pressure to the brake pedal either. If the pistons come out it will be necessary to bleed the hydraulic system.

4. The shoe lining surface should be not less than 0.5 mm (.020 inch) above the rivet heads. Anything less and new linings should be fitted. If the linings have been contaminated with oil they will not work efficiently again and should be renewed. Great care should be exercised when handling brake shoes as oily or greasy hands can contaminate them significantly. The material is extremely absorbent. It is important to isolate the cause of contamination. If not the wheel cylinder, the only other source can be from grease flung out from the wheel bearing. Make sure the bearing grease seal is intact and renew it if necessary (see Chapter 11, Section 3, which deals with front wheel bearings). Volkswagen supply linings and rivets to fit the original shoes. If you should contemplate renewing the linings yourself it is essential to have the proper punch tools for fixing the rivets. If you do not have these the simplest thing is to ask the supplier to fix them. Provided you have cut off the old linings and rivets it takes about two minutes per lining to fix the new ones, provided you have the correct tools. One of the punches is clamped in the vice and the new lining, shoe and rivet head held over it whilst the end is belled over with the other special punch. Rivetting should start from the centre and work outwards diagonally. Alternatively, other sources of supply may provide exchange shoes complete with linings fitted. Whatever you do it is important that the linings are all of the same make and type. It is best to fit a complete new set and make a proper job of it, or you will have uneven braking and trouble on wet surfaces. Never try to renew the lining on one wheel only, always in pairs, and best in complete sets. Note also that the front brakes shoes may be wider than the rear ones and are not interchangeable.

5. Examine the friction surfaces of the brake drums. If they are in good condition they should be bright, shiny and perfectly smooth. If they show signs of deep scoring (due to over-worn brake linings) then they will need renewal. It may be possible to have them machined out on a lathe but if this is done it will be essential to fit oversize brake linings accordingly. This work should be carried out by a Volkswagen agent or an acknowledged brake specialist. It is a waste of time fitting new linings to work in scored drums (except when the scoring is only very light).

6. Before replacing the shoes the backplate should be thoroughly brushed off and the two adjusters removed and cleaned so that they can be freely turned. The threads may be treated with a very light touch of high melting point grease. Replace the adjusters; if the bottom one tends to fall out leave it until the shoes are refitted. Both adjusters should be screwed right in to the notched wheels.

7. Examine the hydraulic cylinder. The rubber boots should be intact and there should be no sign of fluid leakage. If there is then the cylinders must be overhauled (see Section 8).

8. Assemble the two shoes together with the heavier of the two retractor springs engaged in the two holes nearest the cut-out slots on the inner radius of the shoe. These ends should then be put into place in the slots in the ends of the pistons. Next fit the other ends of the shoes into the adjusters (replace the bottom one now) so that they fit properly in the adjuster slots. Then hook the other retractor spring into the holes in the shoes.

9. Reassemble the steady pins, springs and washers, turning the washers 90° across the pin heads to secure them. If you have dismantled all the brakes together note that the steady pins may be different lengths (front wheels 40 mm) so do not get them mixed up. This is when the front linings are wider than the rear - wider linings - wider pins.

10 Centralise the shoes (otherwise you may have difficulty replacing the drum) and then refit the drum and wheel bearing, adjusting the bearings as described in Chapter 11. If the wheel cylinders have been overhauled bleed the hydraulic system (Section 12).

11 Adjust the shoes to the drums as described in the previous section. If new linings have been fitted further adjustment may be needed after a few hundred miles.

5. Rear Brake Drums - Removal and Replacement

1. Removal of the rear brake drums is a considerable task which necessitates having a suitable socket (36 mm) and handle available to undo the axle shaft nut which is tightened to a torque of 30 mkg (217 lb/ft). The drum is splined to the shaft and if these are a very tight fit a special puller may be required to get the drum off the axle shaft. Fit new split pins of the correct size when replacing the axle shaft nut. Under no circumstances should any attempt be made to remove the nuts with anything other than a proper socket spanner otherwise damage will be done. The car must be standing firm on the ground when the nuts are being loosened initially.

2. Remove the hub cap and extract the split pin from the end of the axle shaft. Put the handbrake on and place the socket and handle on the nut. You will almost certainly need a piece of pipe to give you 4 - 5 feet of leverage (single handed).

3. If the handbrake does not hold the wheels then adjust it until it does. Alternatively, chock the wheels and put some people or weight in the back seat to hold the wheels from turning. Once the nut is slackened enough to move normally do the same for the other brake drum.

4. Slacken off the wheel bolts and then jack the car up and remove the wheel.

5. Remove the nut from the axle shaft.

6. Release the handbrake and back off the brake shoe adjusters as far as they will go. If you are fortunate, careful tapping around the edge of the drum with a soft faced mallet (a heavy one) or block of wood and hammer, will move the drum off the splines of the shaft. If the drum does not come off by this method then you will have to use a wheel puller, taking care not to distort the drum. Once removed, examine the drum for signs of scoring on the friction surfaces (see details as for front drums). On early models an oil collector and thrower disc is fitted to the centre of the drum and held in position with a malleable clip. A pipe leads to the periphery of the drum through which oil seeping past the seal is flung by centrifugal force. (Later models have an oilway in the bottom of the bearing housing). Make sure this item is intact and that the pipe is not blocked or damaged.

7. Before replacing the brake drum it is as well to check the efficiency of the axle shaft oil seals. If these are leaking and causing contamination of the brake linings then replacement is relatively simple now that the drum has been removed. For details see Chapter 8.

8. Centralise the brake shoes and see that the adjusters are fully backed off. Thoroughly clean the splines of both shaft and drum and smear them with a little grease or one of the proprietry anti-seize compounds if you have some.

9. Fit the drum on the splines and push it fully home and then refit the axle shaft nut as far as possible.

10 Replace the wheels and bolts and lower the car to the ground.

11 It is possible that you do not have a torque wrench so to tighten the nut first fit the socket with a standard handle, say 12 - 18 inches long, and tighten as far as you possibly can. It is unlikely that you will be capable of overtightening the nut with a regular handle. Then look carefully at the shaft and the split pin hole that you are going to need to use will almost certainly be showing - albeit not yet quite lined up. If no hole shows yet, put a piece of pipe extension onto your handle and move the nut a fraction more at a time until one does appear. Then continue turning the nut carefully until the pin hole lines up with a slot in the nut. This should be the correct tightness. Appreciate that the amount of turn needed to increase the torque from say, 150 lb/ft to the required 217 lb/ft may be less than 3° (or a twelfth of a revolution). If you are using a torque wrench the same principle applies. Look for the hole once you have reached somewhere between 150 - 200 ft/lbs. You do not want to go past it. Provided the nut was correctly tightened and pinned before you took it off it must go back to the same position. If it does not then the threads must have been damaged. Take it off, sort out the thread damage, and try again.

12 The importance of correct tightening of the axle shaft nut cannot

Complete assembly. Left wheel. The other photos are right wheel. (Section 4.10)

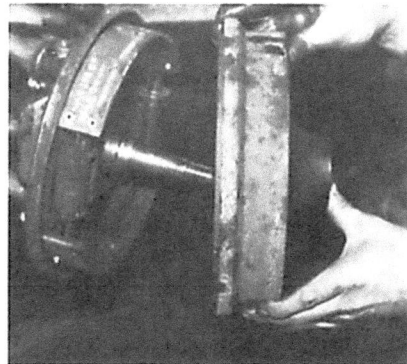

Replacing the left wheel drum (Section 4.10)

Brake relining. Cutting off the old lining (Section 4.4)

Lining ready to fit to shoe. (Section 4.4)

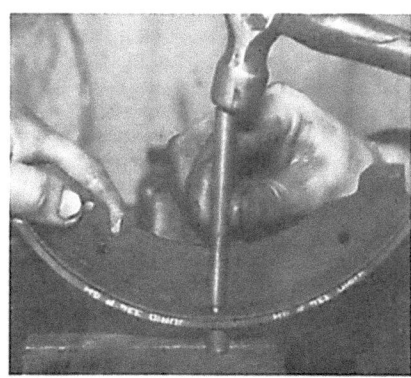

Rivetting the new lining (Section 4.4)

Start from the centre and work outwards (Section 4.4)

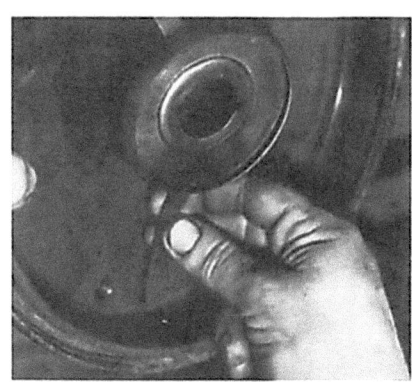

Rear brake drum, positioning the oil slinger (Section 5.6)

Fitting the drum to the shaft (Section 5.9)

Note the oil slinger clip through the drum (Section 5.9)

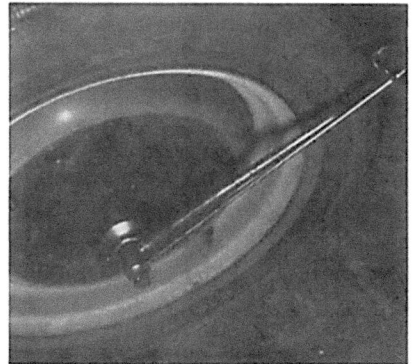

Tighten the wheel nut with the torque wrench (Section 5.11)

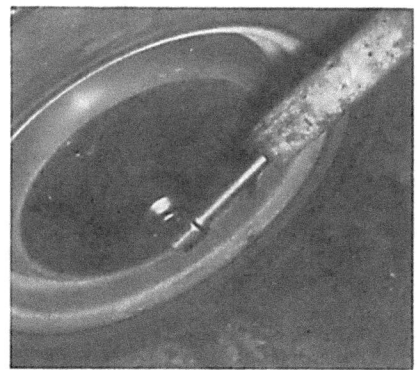

Tighten further until the split pin can be inserted (Section 5.11)

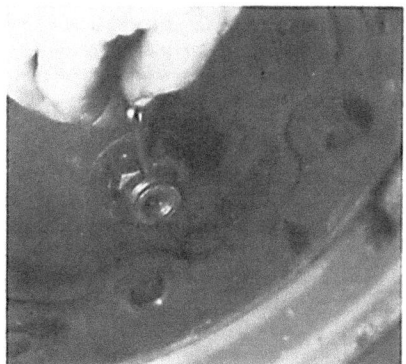

Fit the split pin and bend it over (Section 5.11)

be over-emphasised. It locates the axle shaft and bearing as well as the brake drum and any mistake could result in serious (and expensive) faults developing.

6. Rear Brake Shoes - Removal, Examination and Replacement

1. Remove the car brake drum.
2. Remove the steady pins, springs and washers in the same fashion as for the front brake drums.
3. Unhook the lower of the two retractor springs and then unhook the handbrake cable from the operating lever.
4. Disengage the ends of the two shoes from the adjusters and the two shoes together with the handbrake lever and plate may be lifted out.
5. Linings should be renewed if the surface is worn to within .5 mm (.020 inch) or less of the rivet heads at any point. Also, if there is any indication of oil contamination the linings must be renewed. Details for relining may be found in the section dealing with front brakes.
6. If the shoes are to be changed remember to remove the handbrake operating lever by pulling off the clip which fixes it to the shoe.
7. When reassembling the two shoes prior to refitting, the spreader plate should engage in the two slots and the shoe with the lever attached goes to the rear with the lever notch facing the rear.
8. Make sure that the adjuster wheels are free-moving and fully backed off before locating the ends of the shoes in the slots.
9. It must be emphasised that any leaks, either from the bearing or the hydraulic cylinder, should be dealt with to prevent both further contamination or failure of the hydraulic system.

7. Handbrake Cables and Lever - Removal and Replacement

1. Slacken off the locknuts at the lever end of both handbrake cables and remove them together with the adjusting nuts.
2. Remove the rear brake drums and unhook the cable from the operating lever on the shoe.
3. Undo the bolt which holds the outer sleeve clip to the brake backplate where the cable passes through. Disengage the clip from behind the washer and spring on the cable and draw the cable out from the backplate. Then pull the cables out of the tube from the other direction.
4. Before fitting a new cable make sure that at the brake end the spring and washer are properly fitted between the eye of the cable and the outer sleeve.
5. It is necessary to remove the handbrake lever before the threaded ends of the cable can be reconnected to it. Remove one of the circlips from the end of the lever pivot pin and withdraw the pin. Keep the hands well clear of the ratchet button and then move the whole lever assembly forward so that it disengages from the floor plate. If the ratchet button is inadvertently pressed the ratchet will fall down. It must be put back before replacing the lever.
6. Put the cable through the backplate and then work the sleeve clamp through the hole in the backplate so that the spring and washer are on the inside of the slotted bracket of the clamp. Replace the bolt into the back of the backplate and tighten it. Then hook the cable onto the lever.
7. Feed the threaded end of the cable into the tubes in the frame fork and finally see that the outer sleeve fits into position in the end of the tube. The threaded ends should appear inside the car under the handbrake lever mounting position. It may be necessary to hook them up with a piece of wire.
8. Making sure that they are not crossed, insert the cables into the two eyes in the base of the lever and then put the lever in position checking that the rear section engages properly in the floor section. Once again be careful not to press the ratchet release button. Replace the pivot pin and circlip and screw on the adjuster and locknuts.
9. Adjust the handbrake as described in Section 3.

8. Hydraulic Wheel Cylinders - Renewal of Seals and Cylinders

1. If the wheel cylinders show signs of leakage, or of pistons being seized up, then it will be necessary to dismantle them and fit new seals. The procedures for front and rear cylinders are the same although the bores of the cylinders are different requiring different diameter seals.
2. Remove the brake drum and the brake shoes and seal the cap of the fluid reservoir with a piece of plastic film to minimise loss of fluid from the system when the cylinder is dismantled.
3. Pull off the rubber boots from the ends of the cylinder, bringing the pistons and slotted ends with them. Behind the pistons are the seal cups and in the centre there is a spring with two 'cup expanders' which fit inside each seal and as their name implies force the seals outward into the cylinder bore under the pressure of the spring.
4. With the cylinder clear examine the bore surfaces for signs of ridging or scoring. Any residue stuck in the bore should be cleaned out with brake fluid or meths - if very stubborn a delicate rub with some No. 400 wet and dry paper will clean it up. Any noticeable scores or ridges indicate that a new cylinder should be fitted. No attempt should be made to smooth them out as this will be unsuccessful.
5. To remove the cylinder undo the brake pipe union from behind the backplate. Cover the end of the pipe with the dust cap from the bleed nipple pro tem. Undo the two securing screws from the backplate and the cylinder may be lifted out. If a new cylinder is fitted the diameter of the bore must be exactly the same as the plan diameter of the one being replaced, otherwise the balance of the brakes will be upset.
6. With the cylinder perfectly clean lubricate the bore with brake fluid and insert the spring complete with seal cup expanders at each end.
7. Lubricate the new seals with fluid and put one in at each end of the cylinder with the lip facing inwards. Take great care not to turn the lip back whilst doing this.
8. Put a piston in behind each seal with the hollow end of the piston facing outwards. Assemble the rubber boot to the slotted end pieces and fit the boots over the ends of the cylinder with the slotted part (for the brake shoe) pointing outwards.
9. Absolute cleanliness of hands and parts is essential during reassembly.
10 If a new wheel cylinder is being fitted reconnect the brake pipe union taking care not to cross the thread, kink the pipe or overtighten the union.

9. Hydraulic Master Cylinder - Removal, Replacement and Pushrod Setting

1. Provided the slave cylinders and fluid lines are all in good condition and there is no air in the system then any softness or sponginess in the system will probably be due to worn seals in the master cylinder. As these are internal there will be no visible leak to indicate this.
2. To remove the cylinder assembly first jack up the car and remove the right hand front wheel (R.H. drive) or left as the case may be. The cylinder is bolted to the bulkhead alongside the floor tunnel.
3. Have a suitable receptacle handy to collect the contents of the fluid reservoir - if possible siphon the contents out of the reservoir itself. Otherwise pull the pipe and plug from the top of the cylinder body and drain it into the receptacle there. Keep fluid away from paintwork.
4. Unscrew the three rigid pipe unions from the body of the pump. It is not necessary to undo the brake light switch. Just disconnect the wires.
5. The two screws in the bulkhead behind the brake pedal should now be removed to release the assembly. Take care not to drop the washers or spacers off the screws into the space below or you may have a difficult job retrieving them.
6. Replacement is a reversal of the removal procedure. Make sure

Working the brake shoe assembly into the slave cylinder piston ends (Section 6)

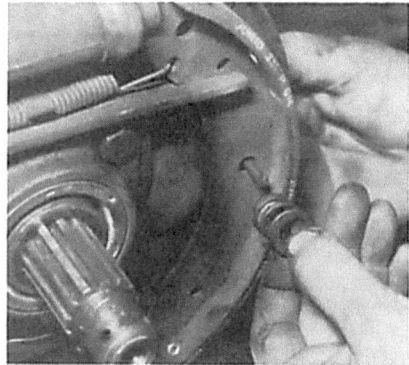

Place the steady pins in position (Section 6)

Twist the steady pins home securely (Section 6)

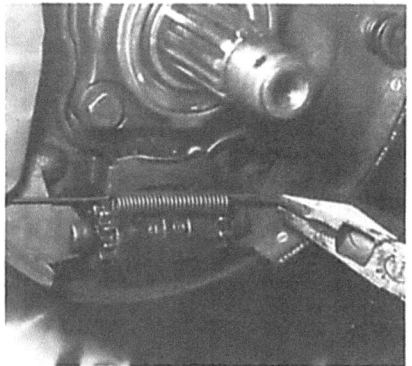

Fit the bottom retractor spring (Section 6)

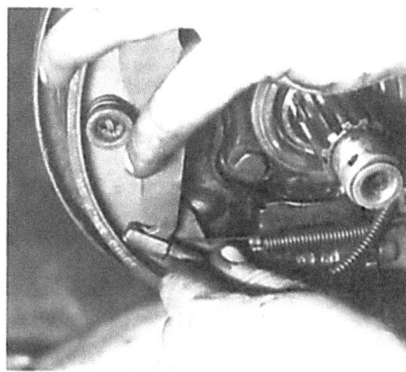

Hook in the handbrake cable (Section 6)

Fitting the handbrake cable clamps to the backplate (Section 7.6)

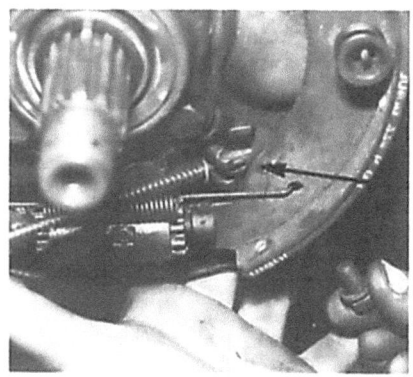

Note the position of the spring and washer in relation to the slotted fork on the clamp (arrowed) (Section 7.6)

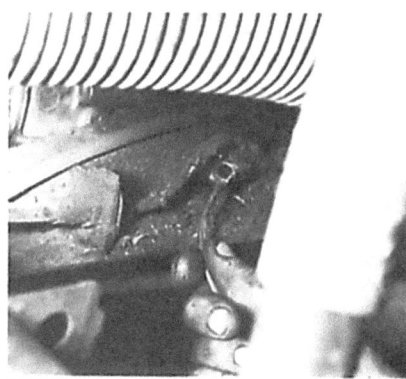

Feeding the cable into the tube on the frame (Section 7.7)

Both cables engaged, lever ready for fitting. Note lug (arrowed) which must fit under the tunnel plate (Section 7.8)

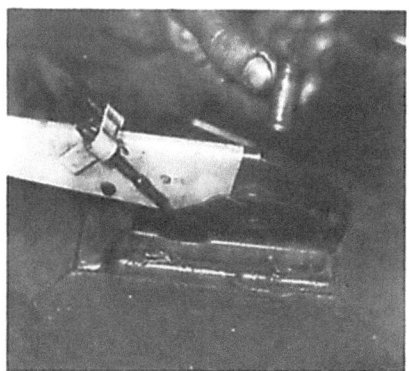

Lever positioned for the hinge pin (Section 7.8)

Adjust the handbrake (Section 7.9)

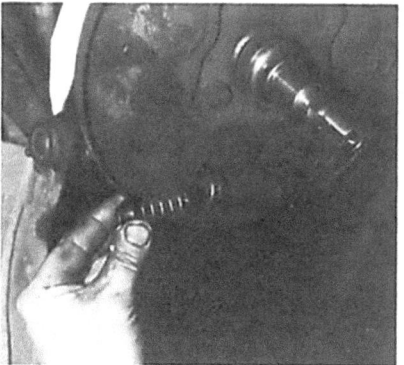

Hydraulic wheel cylinders - inserting spring and spreader (Section 8.6)

that the spacers are correctly refitted. As soon as the unions have all been reconnected and the system replenished with fluid and bled, see that the unions are all perfectly leakproof.

7. It is important that the pushrod which operates the plunger from the brake pedal is correctly set. In the rest position, the ball end of the pushrod should have a 1 mm clearance before it contacts the bottom of the recess in the piston. If this clearance is absent (and the piston cannot return fully) the operation of the system is seriously affected. To adjust the length of the rod slacken the locknut and screw the rod in or out as required. This adjustment will also be affected if the pedal cluster mounting plate is moved.

10. Hydraulic Master Cylinder - Dismantling, Overhaul and Re-assembly

1. Obtain a complete repair kit which contains all the necessary seals which must all be used.
2. Thoroughly clean the exterior before beginning dismantling.
3. Unclip the circlip from inside the cylinder bore and remove the various parts in order. Pull out the reservoir pipe sealing plug.
4. Examine the inside of the cylinder bore for any sign of scoring or pitting. Unless it is perfectly smooth the body should be renewed.
5. Thoroughly clean all parts. Pull off the seal from the groove in the piston.
6. Before reassembly lubricate all parts with clean brake fluid.
7. Assemble the wide end of the spring to the boss on the check valve and place both in position in the cylinder.
8. Place the new primary cup seal into the cylinder, concave side inwards and take great care to ensure that the lips of the seal edges do not turn back in the process. Put the piston washer in immediately behind it.
9. Take the piston and fit the new secondary seal into the groove at the rear end. This seal must be fitted so that the tapered lip faces into the cylinder when the piston is replaced. Make sure it is squarely seated in position.
10 Put the piston into the cylinder (the recessed end faces outwards) and when the seal goes in once again make quite sure that the lip does not turn back.
11 Fit the stop plate followed by the circlip which must snap securely into the annular groove in the cylinder.
12 Make sure that the rubber plug washer and elbow are intact and ready for connection to the reservoir feed pipe on installation. The rubber boot is fitted over the cylinder (or pushrod) before the cylinder is replaced.

11. Hydraulic Fluid Lines and Hoses - Examination, Removal and Replacement

1. Regular examination of the pipes which convey the pressurised fluid from the master cylinder to the four wheel cylinders is very important. Any sudden leak due to fracture or corrosion will result in total loss of pressure and the brakes will be inoperative except on the handbrake which is inadequate for driving purposes.
2. Trace the routes of all the rigid pipes and wash or brush away accumulated dirt. If the pipes are obviously covered with some sort of underseal compound do not disturb it. Examine for signs of kinks of dents which could have been caused by flying stones. Any instances of this mean that the pipe section should be renewed but before actually taking it out read the rest of this section. Any unprotected sections of pipe which show signs of corrosion or pitting on the outer surfaces must also be considered for renewal.
3. Flexible hoses, running to each of the front wheels and from the underbody to each rear axle tube, should show no signs of external signs of chafing or cracking. Move them about and see if surface cracks appear. Also if they feel stiff and inflexible or are twisted they are nearing the end of their useful life. If in any doubt renew the hoses.
4. Before attempting to remove any pipe for renewal it is important

to be sure that you have a replacement source of supply within reach if you do not wish to be kept off the road for too long. Pipes are often damaged on removal. If a Volkswagen agency is near, you may be reasonably sure that the correct pipes and unions are available. If not, check first that your local garage has the necessary equipment for making up the pipes and has the correct metric thread pipe unions available. The same goes for flexible hoses.
5. Where the couplings from rigid to flexible pipes are made there are support brackets and the flexible pipe is held in place by a 'U' clip which engages in a groove in the union. The male union screws into it. Before getting the spanners on, soak the unions in penetrating fluid as there is always some rust or corrosion binding the threads. Whilst this is soaking in, place a piece of plastic film under the fluid reservoir cap to minimise loss of fluid from the disconnected pipes. Hold the hexagon on the flexible pipe coupling whilst the union on the rigid pipe is undone. Then pull out the clip to release both pipes from the bracket. For flexible hose removal this procedure will be needed at both ends. For a rigid pipe the other end will only involve unscrewing the union from a cylinder or connector. When you are renewing a flexible hose, take care not to damage the unions of the pipes that connect into it. If a union is particularly stubborn be prepared to renew the rigid pipe as well. This is quite often the case if you are forced to use open ended spanners. It may be worth spending a little money on a special pipe union spanner which is like a ring spanner with a piece cut out to enable it to go round the tube.
6. If you are having the new pipe made up take the old one along to check that the unions and pipe flaring at the ends are identical.
7. Replacement of the hoses or pipes is a reversal of the removal procedure. Precautions and care are needed to make sure that the unions are correctly lined up to prevent cross threading. This may mean bending the pipe a little where a rigid pipe goes into a fixture. Such bending must not, under any circumstances, be too acute, otherwise the pipe will kink and weaken.
8. When fitting flexible hoses take care not to twist them. This can happen when the unions are finally tightened unless a spanner is used to hold the end of the flexible hose and prevent twisting.
9. After removal or slackening of a brake pipe union the hydraulic system must be bled.

12. Hydraulic Brake System - Bleeding

1. The purpose of the process known as bleeding the brakes is to remove air bubbles from the hydraulic system. Air is compressible - hydraulic fluid is not. Bleeding should be necessary only after work on the hydraulic system has allowed air into the system. If it is found necessary to bleed brakes frequently then there is something wrong and the whole system should be checked through to find where the air is getting into the system. Cars left unused for a long time may also require brake bleeding before full efficiency is restored.
2. Normally, if work has been carried out at the extremities of the system - e.g. at wheel cylinders or adjacent pipes, then it should only be necessary to bleed that particular section. Work on the master cylinder however would call for all four wheels to be bled.
3. Before starting, make sure you have an adequate supply of the proper fluid, a clean receptacle and a tube which will fit over the bleed nipple securely and which is conveniently long enough. A useful device is the tube which is fitted with a non-return valve. This avoids the necessity of keeping the other end of the tube submerged in liquid whilst bleeding is in progress.
4. Clean off the bleed nipple (or pull off the protective cap). Put about 1 inch depth of fluid in the receptacle (a salad cream jar is ideal and needs less fluid!). Connect the pipe to the nipple and put the other end in the jar and undo the nipple about half a turn - no more is necessary.
5. A second person is needed to operate the brake pedal at your instruction. The pedal should be depressed smartly one full stroke to the floor and allowed to return slowly. This should be repeated until no more bubbles emerge from the tube in the jar. Smart operation of the pedal ensures that the air is forced along the pipe

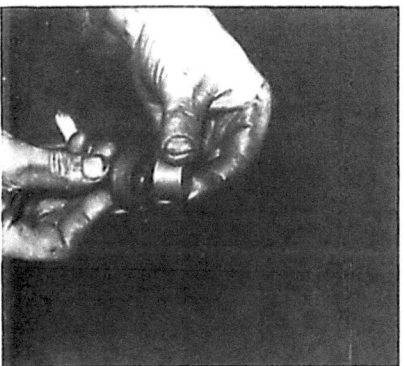
Fitting the boot (Section 8.8)

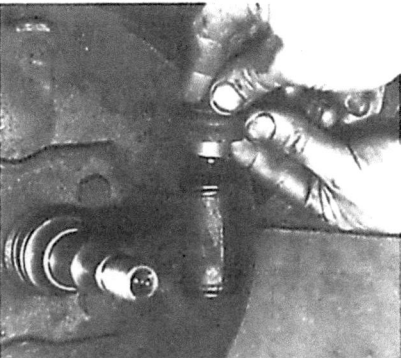
Assembling the boot and piston to the cylinder (Section 8.8)

Location of the hydraulic master cylinder (Section 9.2)

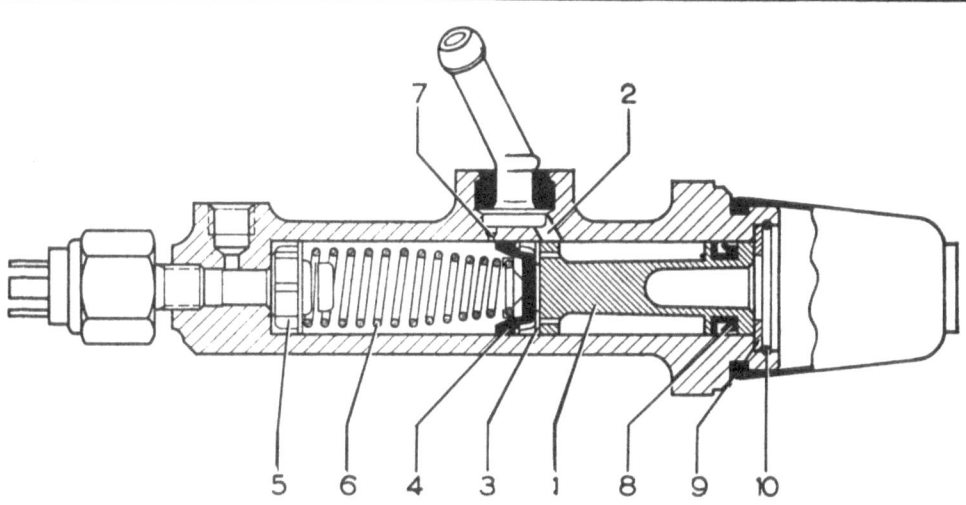

Fig. 9.3. HYDRAULIC MASTER CYLINDER — CROSS SECTION DRAWING

1 Piston	3 Piston washer	6 Check valve spring	8 Secondary cup seal
2 Intake port (fluid from reservoir)	4 Primary cup seal	7 Compensating port (excess fluid back to reservoir)	9 Stop plate
	5 Check valve		10 Circlip

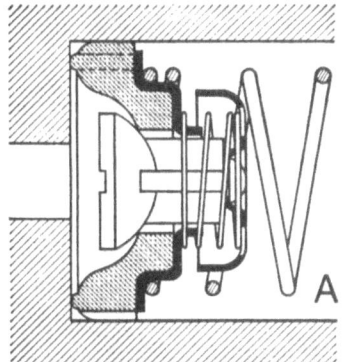
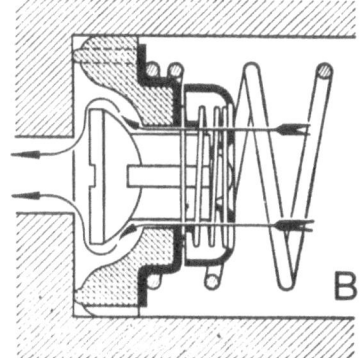
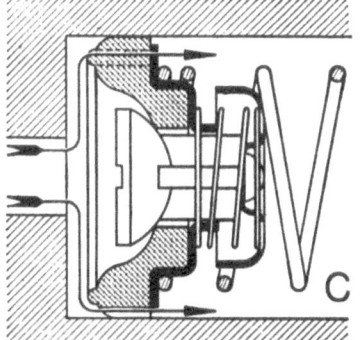

Fig. 9.4. DIAGRAM TO SHOW THE FUNCTION OF THE MASTER CYLINDER CHECK VALVE

A At rest. Main valve seated on end of cylinder under main spring pressure and inner valve seated in centre of main seal under secondary spring pressure

B Braking. Secondary valve opens under pressure of fluid which passes into system.

C Brakes released. Main valve opens under fluid back pressure until main spring overcomes pressure - keeping some pressure in system. Secondary valve stays seated.

rather than by-passed. Keep a watch on the level of fluid in the reservoir. If it gets too low it will let air into the master cylinder and then you will have to bleed all four wheels.

6. Once all the air is expelled, the best moment to tighten the bleed nipple is during the return stroke of the pedal.

7. Repeat the procedure for each wheel as necessary. Do not put fluid bled out of the system back in. Always use fresh.

8. It is considered by many a good idea to completely replenish the brake fluid, by bleeding, at regular intervals. Such intervals would be two years or 30,000 miles, whichever came first. Renewal of the slave cylinder seals (at least) at the same time would be well worth the small cost and time involved.

13. Brake Backplates - Removal and Replacement

1. If it is necessary to remove the brake backplates for any reason, which would be rare, then the brake drums and shoes must first be taken off. This procedure is described in Sections 4 and 5 of this Chapter. To remove the front brake backplates all that is then required is to remove the four securing screws.

2. The rear brake backplate is clamped behind the bearing housing cover. Care must be taken when removing the cover to avoid any damage to the seals and gasket.

3. Check first which kind of rear bearing and seal arrangement you have and arrange to renew the 'O' rings and gaskets if possible. Details of these can be ascertained from the relevant section in Chapter 8.

14. Brake and Clutch Pedal Cluster - Dismantling and Reassembly

1. The brake and clutch pedals are mounted on a common shaft which in turn is supported by two brackets. One of these brackets (on R.H. drive cars) is fitted to the right of the brake pedal and is held to the floor by two bolts. The other is bolted to the left hand side of the floor tunnel. In addition, the shaft is hollow and the accelerator operating rod passes through it. At the left hand end of the pivot shaft a bracket links to the accelerator cable. The clutch cable hooks onto a lug which is part of the pedal inside the tunnel. This section explains how to deal with matters connected with all three items on the cluster.

2. Remove the carpet from the left hand toe panel and pull out the panel.

3. Remove the two bolts holding the cover on the side of the tunnel. These two screws hold the bracket supporting the left end of the cross shaft as well so some movement will be noticed.

4. If only the accelerator cable is being renewed the split pin can be removed from the clevis pin, the cable eye released and the cable

drawn out. If the cross shaft is being taken out then remove the lever from the accelerator rod by taking off the circlip.

5. At the other end of the shaft remove the clevis pin securing the brake master cylinder pushrod to the pedal. It is held in position by a circlip.

6. Then remove the large circlip on the end of the main cross shaft next to the mounting bracket. The two mounting bracket bolts can then be undone. When these bolts are being undone take precautions to ensure that the clutch pedal remains in an upright position - it does not matter about the brake pedal which can fall back to the floor. This will ensure that the clutch cable does not get unhooked inside the tunnel. Note that these bolts on earlier models also clamp another plate underneath. This plate has two upturned lugs on the front edge which act as pedal return stops. On later models where the pedal shafts are spaced much further apart on the cross shaft, there is a separate plate.

7. Unclip the accelerator rod from the back of the accelerator pedal, remove the link and draw the brake pedal and accelerator rod out of the tube together with the brake pedal return spring. Note the position of the intermediate washers.

8. If you wish to draw out the clutch pedal and cable detach the other end of the cable from the clutch operating lever on the transmission casing.

9. Now draw out the clutch pedal and shaft together, keeping the pedal as upright as possible so that the cable may be drawn out with it.

10 A new clutch cable must be fed into the tube through the aperture in the tunnel. All that is needed is patience to guide the end into the tube.

11 Reassembly is a reversal of the dismantling procedure. The resetting of the pedal stop plate requires some care, bearing in mind that the clutch pedal free play adjustment is affected and also the setting of the master cylinder pushrod. When replacing the clutch pedal the end of the cable has to be hooked on first and then the pedal manoeuvred into position without letting the end of the cable come loose or get snagged on the hook in the wrong position. It is best to get a second person to hold the other end of the cable and keep tension on it whilst the pedal is being positioned. If the cable appears to be too short after positioning, it is probably because the hook has slewed round. Waggle the pedal back and forth a few times - still with the other end of the cable being held, and it will probably straighten out. If it does not go back to square one.

12 Before finally tightening the mounting bracket bolts check that at the end of the return movement the rubber faces of both pedals are vertical. If they are not the stop plate has slotted holes to allow their adjustment to the vertical.

13 Finally check the master cylinder pushrod clearance (as described in Section 9 of this Chapter) and then check and if necessary, adjust the free play of the clutch pedal (as described in Chapter 5).

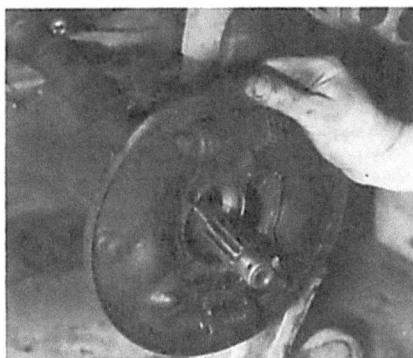

Removing rear brake backplate (Section 13)
In this photo the axle shaft bearing has also been removed.

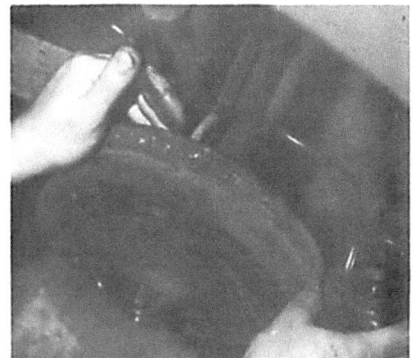

Bleeding a rear brake (Section 12)

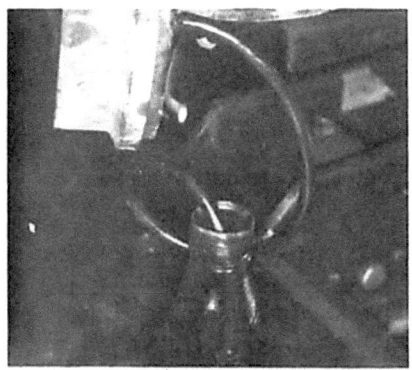

Bleeding a front brake (Section 12)

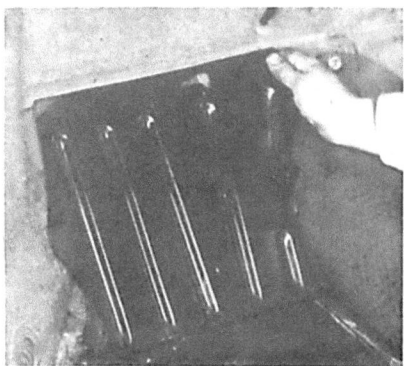

Removing left side toe plate (Section 14.2)

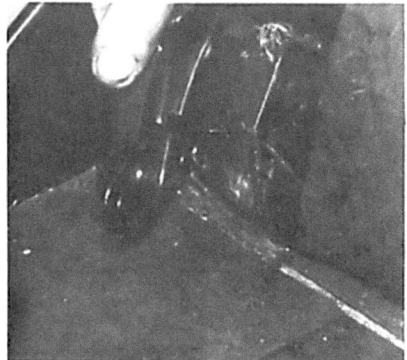

Removing left mounting cover (Section 14.3)

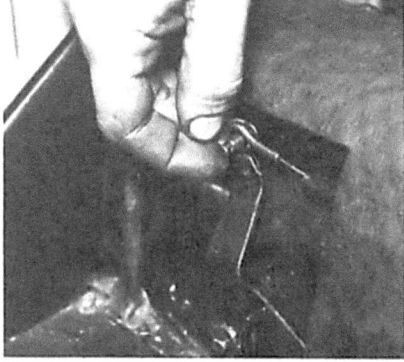

Disconnecting the accelerator cable (Section 14.4)

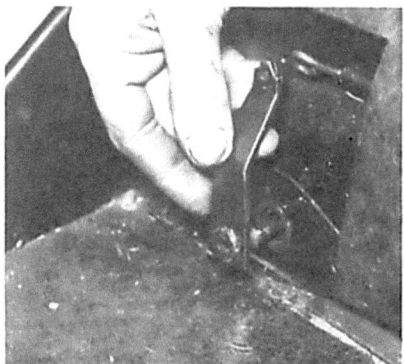

Removing the accelerator lever (Section 14.4)

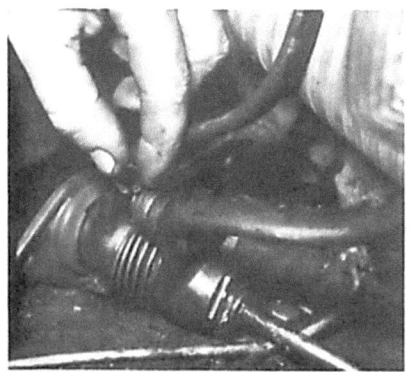

Removing the circlip from the master cylinder pushrod pivot pin (Section 14.5)

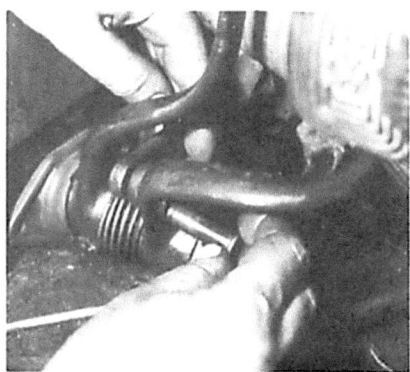

Removing the pivot pin (Section 14.6)

Disconnecting the mounting bracket (Section 14.6)

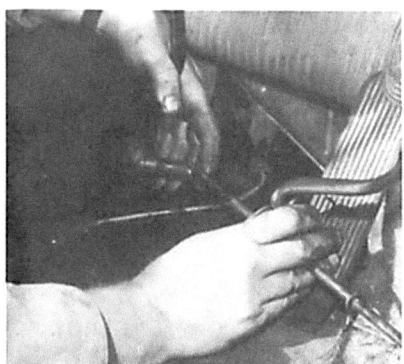

Removing the brake pedal and accelerator rod (Section 14.7)

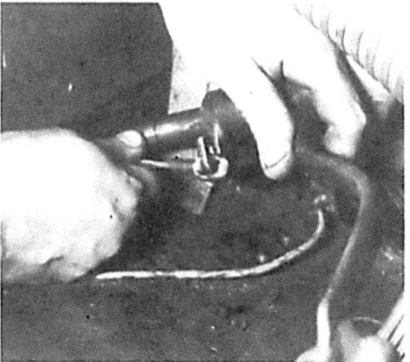

Clutch cable attachment (Section 14.8)

Accelerator pedal link (Section 14.7)

Fault Finding Chart - Braking System

Before diagnosing faults from the following chart, check that any braking irregularities are not caused by:

1 Uneven and incorrect tyre pressures
2 Incorrect 'mix' of radial and cross-ply tyres
3 Wear in the steering mechanism
4 Defects in the suspension and dampers
5 Misalignment of the bodyframe

Symptom	Reason/s	Remedy
Pedal travels a long way before the brakes operate	Brake shoes set too far from the drums	Adjust the brake shoes to the drums.
Stopping ability poor, even though pedal pressure is firm	Linings and/or drums badly worn or scored	Dismantle, inspect and renew as required.
	One or more wheel hydraulic cylinders seized, resulting in some brake shoes not pressing against the drums (or pads against discs)	Dismantle and inspect wheel cylinders. Renew as necessary.
	Brake linings contaminated with oil	Renew linings and repair source of oil contamination.
	Wrong type of linings fitted	Verify type of material which is correct for the car and fit it.
	Brake shoes wrongly assembled	Check for correct assembly.
Car veers to one side when the brakes are applied	Brake linings on one side are contaminated with oil	Renew linings and stop oil leak.
	Hydraulic wheel cylinder(s) on one side partially or fully seized	Inspect wheel cylinders for correct operation and renew as necessary.
	A mixture of lining materials fitted between sides	Standardize on types of linings fitted.
	Unequal wear between sides caused by partially seized wheel cylinders	Check wheel cylinders and renew linings and drums as required.
Pedal feels spongy when the brakes are applied	Air is present in the hydraulic system	Bleed the hydraulic system and check for any signs of leakage.
Pedal feels springy when the brakes are applied	Brake linings not bedded into the drums (after fitting new ones)	Allow time for new linings to bed in after which it will certainly be necessary to adjust the shoes to the drums as pedal travel will have increased.
	Master cylinder or brake backplate mounting bolts loose	Retighten mounting bolts.
	Severe wear in brake drums causing distortion when brakes are applied	Renew drums and linings.
Pedal travels right down with little or no resistance and brakes are virtually non-operative	Leak in hydraulic system resulting in lack of pressure for operating wheel cylinders	Examine the whole of the hydraulic system and locate and repair source of leaks. Test after repairing each and every leak source.
	If no signs of leakage are apparent the master cylinder internal seals are failing to sustain pressure	Overhaul master cylinder. If indications are that seals have failed for reasons other than wear all the wheel cylinder seals should be checked also and the system completely replenished with the correct fluid.
Binding, juddering, overheating	One or a combination of causes given in the foregoing sections	Complete and systematic inspection of the whole braking system.

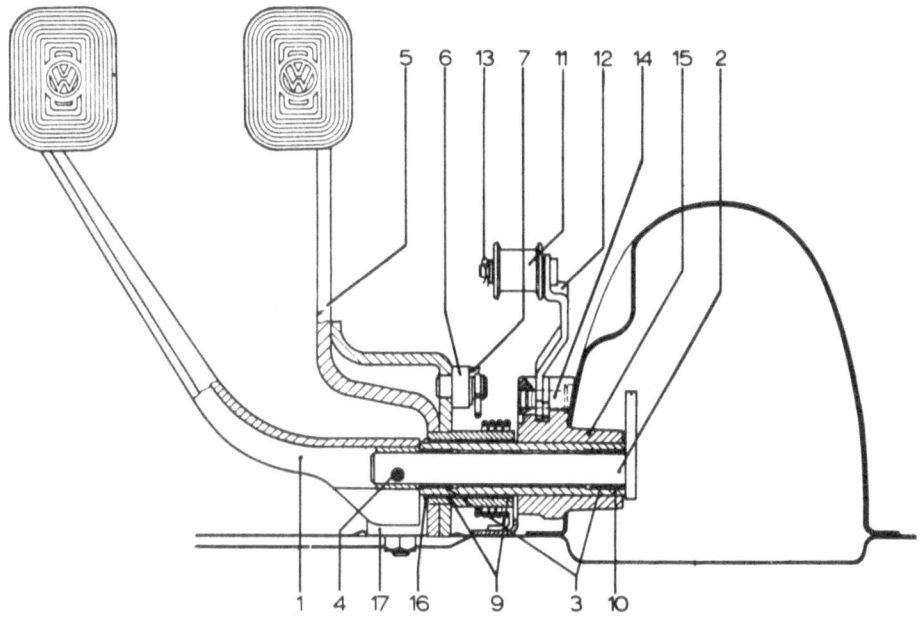

Fig. 9.5. BRAKE AND CLUTCH PEDAL CLUSTER — CROSS SECTION VIEW
LHD (LATER TYPE)

1 Clutch pedal	5 Brake pedal	10 Mounting tube	14 Accelerator pedal lever pin
2 Pedal shaft	6 Master cylinder pushrod	11 Accelerator pedal roller	15 Mounting bracket
3 Bush	7 Pushrod lock plate	12 Accelerator connecting lever	16 Circlip
4 Locating pin	9 Bush	13 Clip	17 Stop plate

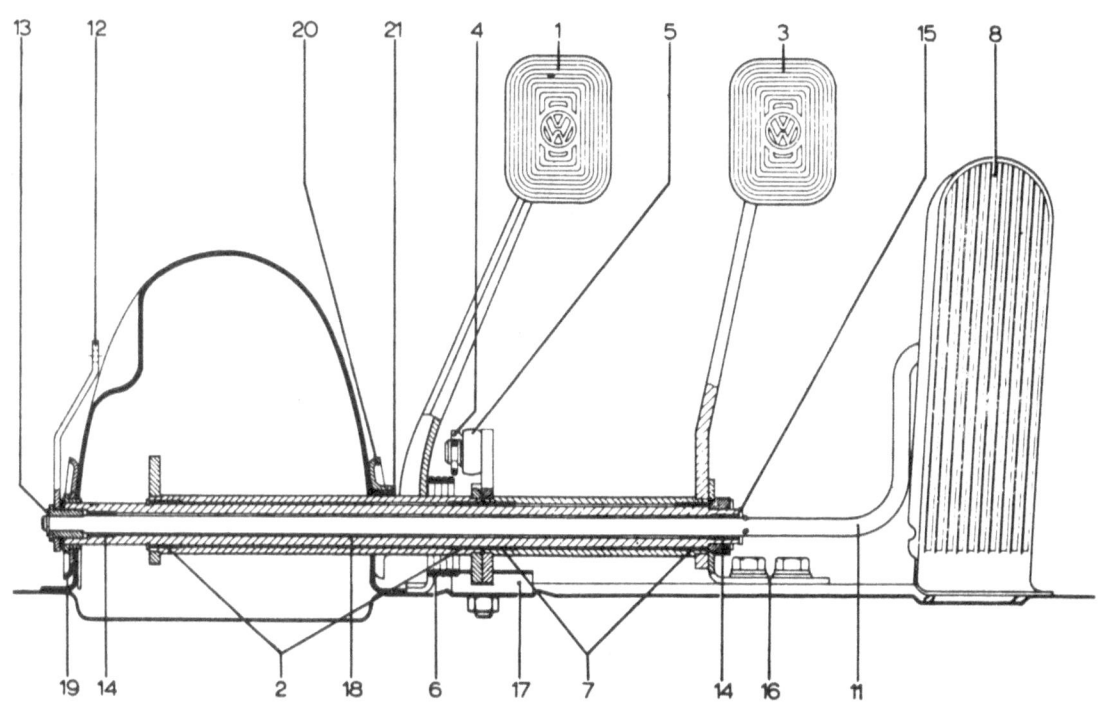

Fig. 9.6. BRAKE AND CLUTCH PEDAL CLUSTER — CROSS SECTION VIEW
RHD (LATER TYPE)

1 Clutch pedal	6 Brake pedal return spring	13 Circlip	18 Cross shaft
2 Bush	7 Bush	14 Bush	19 Mounting bracket
3 Brake pedal	8 Accelerator pedal	15 Washer	20 Cover plate
4 Pushrod lock plate	11 Accelerator pedal shaft	16 Mounting bracket	21 Cover plate guide
5 Master cylinder pushrod	12 Accelerator connecting lever	17 Stop plate	

Chapter 10 Electrical system

Contents

Specifications

Battery

Type	6 volt
Capacity	70 or 66 amp/hours
Earth	Negative

Generator

Type	Bosch or Volkswagen D.C.
Max. current	45 amps
Mean regulating voltage	7
Nominal output speed	2500 rpm
Commutator minimum diameter	32.8 mm
Segment insulation undercut	0.5 mm
Brush length	End flush with holder (minimum)
Pulley ratio, crankshaft/generator	1 : 1.8

* Regulator

Type	Bosch or Volkswagen

* Starter Motor

Type	Bosch or Volkswagen pre-engaged 6 volt
Power	0.5 h.p. nominal

There have been many changes and varieties of starter motors and generators fitted over the years and all types cannot usefully be listed completely here. It could therefore be misleading to quote a few numbers here under the vague definition of 'early' or 'late'. Many are interchangeable - i.e. later types can be fitted to earlier model cars. The main thing to bear in mind is that the generator and regulator are matched. If either of these is faulty it is essential that the replacement is identical with the original. All are marked with serial numbers.

Lights

Headlamps	Asymmetrical low beam with built in parking light
Headlamp bulb	45/40 w
Parking lamp bulb	4 w
Stop/tail lamp bulb	18/5 w or 21/5 w
Turn indicator lamp bulbs	18 w or 21 w
Rear number plate bulb	10 w festoon
Interior light bulb	10 w festoon
Warning lamp bulbs	2 w or 1.2 w

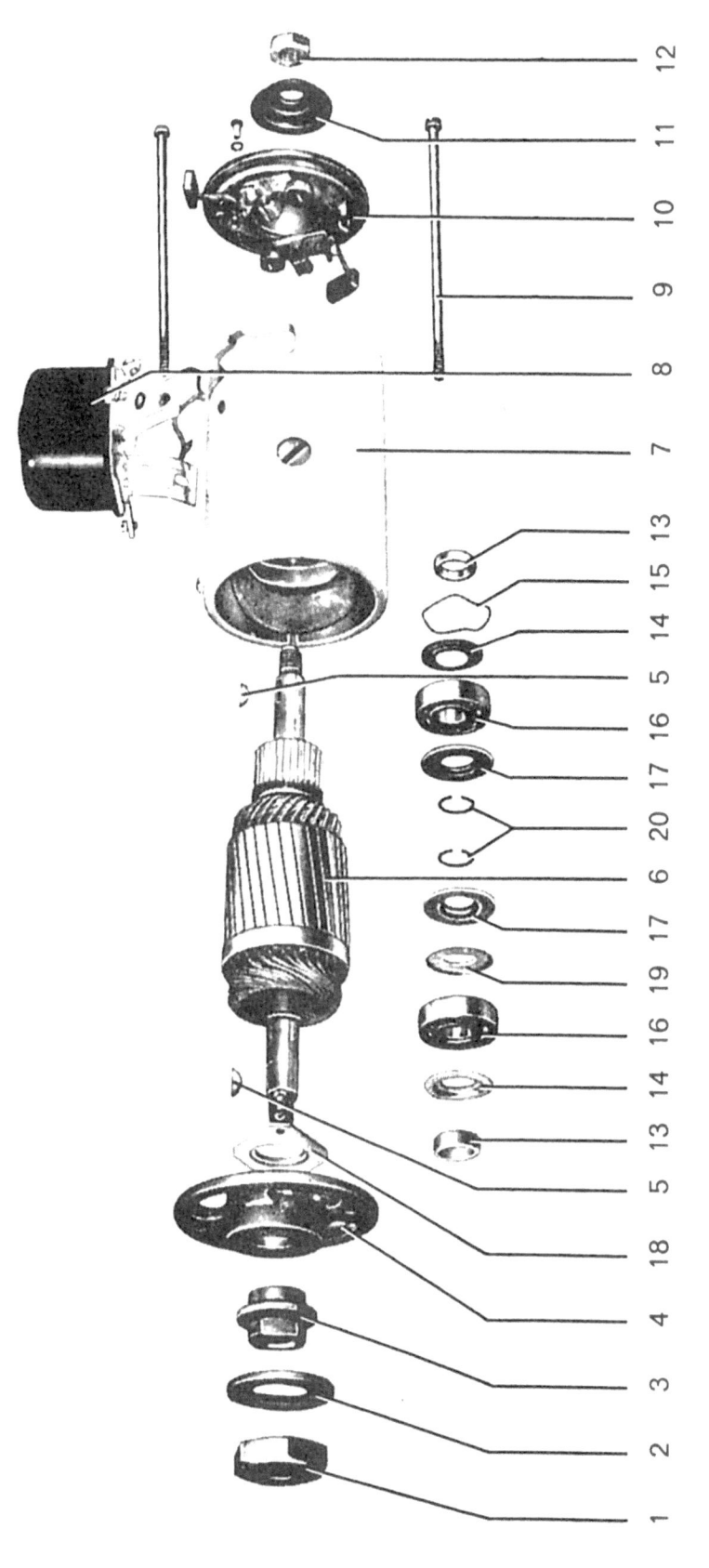

Fig. 10.1. BOSCH GENERATOR – EXPLODED VIEW

1 Fan nut
2 Carrier plate
3 Fan hub
4 End cover
5 Woodruff key

6 Armature
7 Yoke and field coils
8 Regulator unit

9 Through bolts
10 Commutator end plate
11 Spacer washer

12 Drive pulley nut
13 Spacer collar
14 Oil slinger disc

15 Wave washer
16 Ball bearing
17 Oil slinger

18 Bearing retainer
19 Bearing cover washer
20 Circlips

Fuses (Numberings are from left to right)

Very early models	... ...	6 fuses, 2 near fuel tank for headlamp main beams plus block of 4 under dashboard (as for block 2 below)
Early models	... ...	8 fuses in two blocks of four

Block 1 (near fuel tank)
  1 Main beam R
  2 Main beam L and warning light
  3 Low beam R
  4 Low beam L
Block 2 (instrument panel)
  1 Interior light and horn
  2 Screen wiper,stop lights and indicator lights
  3 Parking lights and tail light right
  4 Tail light left and number plate light

Later models   ... ...   Single 8 fuse block (instrument panel)
  1 Windscreen wiper, turn signals, horn and stop lights
  2 Headlamp main beam left and indicator light
  3 Headlamp main beam right
  4 Headlamp low beam left
  5 Headlamp low beam right
  6 Parking lamps left
  7 Parking lamps and number plate lamp right
  8 Interior light and radio

Torque Wrench Settings

Generator pulley nut	... ...	40 - 47 lb/ft (5.5 - 6.5 mkg)
Fan nut	... ...	40 - 47 lb/ft (5.5 - 6.5 mkg)

1. General Description

The system is 6 volt comprising:

A 6 volt battery with negative earth mounted in a carrier under the rear seat.

A.D.C. generator mounted on a pedestal above the engine driven by a belt from the crankshaft pulley. The generator armature shaft also carries the cooling fan at the opposite end.

A voltage regulator and cut-out unit mounted on the generator (or under the back seat in later versions).

A starter motor of the pre-engaged type (that is one which meshes with the flywheel ring gear before the power is switched to the motor).

The battery provides the necessary power storage source for operating the starter and providing the current to operate the lights, accessories and ignition circuit. It is kept in a state of full charge by the generator and the regulator controls the generator output. This control automatically adjusts according to the state of charge of the battery, the electrical load demanded and engine revolutions in such a way that the generator is never overloaded and the battery never over or undercharged. It must be appreciated that indiscriminate additions of electrical accessories can upset this automatic balance.

The starter motor is mounted on the transmission casing. Drive pinion engagement and switching is effected by a solenoid. The pinion is engaged by the solenoid before the same solenoid switches current to the starter motor itself. The pinion is driven through a one-way roller clutch to obviate any damage from over-run.

Due to the 6 volt system the current loadings are double those of 12 volt systems and the cables are consequently heavier.

2. Battery - Removal and Replacement

1. The battery is fixed under the rear seat which must first be lifted up and out. A metal strap and clip hold a cover over the battery and to release the clip the panel on the front edge of the seat needs removing.
2. Take care when removing both strap and cover as it is easy to cause an accidental short circuit with them.
3. Unclamp the battery terminals (earth (or negative) terminal first) and lift the battery out vertically to prevent electrolyte spillage.
4. When replacing the battery see that both terminals and terminal clamps are clean and free from corrosion or deposits of any sort. Smear them with petroleum jelly (not grease) before connection. See also that the insulation on the inside of the cover is intact before replacing it. Never replace the rear seat without the battery cover in position. The springs of the seat can short circuit the terminals and start a fire.

3. Battery - Maintenance and Inspection

1. Normally weekly battery maintenance consists of checking the electrolyte level of each cell to ensure that the separators are covered by ¼ inch of electrolyte. If the level has fallen, top up the battery using distilled water only. Do not overfill. If a battery is overfilled or any electrolyte spilled, immediately wipe away the excess as electrolyte attacks and corrodes any metal it comes into contact with very rapidly.
2. As well as keeping the terminals clean and covered with petroleum jelly, the top of the battery, and especially the top of the cells, should be kept clean and dry. This helps prevent corrosion and ensures that the battery does not become partially discharged by leakage through dampness and dirt.
3. Once every three months, remove the battery and inspect the battery tray and battery leads for corrosion (white fluffy deposits on the metal which are brittle to touch). If any corrosion is found, clean off the deposits with ammonia and paint over the clean metal with an anti-rust/anti-acid paint.
4. At the same time inspect the battery case for cracks. If a crack is found, clean and plug it with one of the proprietary compounds marketed by firms, such as Holts, for this purpose. If leakage through the crack has been excessive then it will be necessary to refill the appropriate cell with fresh electrolyte as detailed later. Cracks are

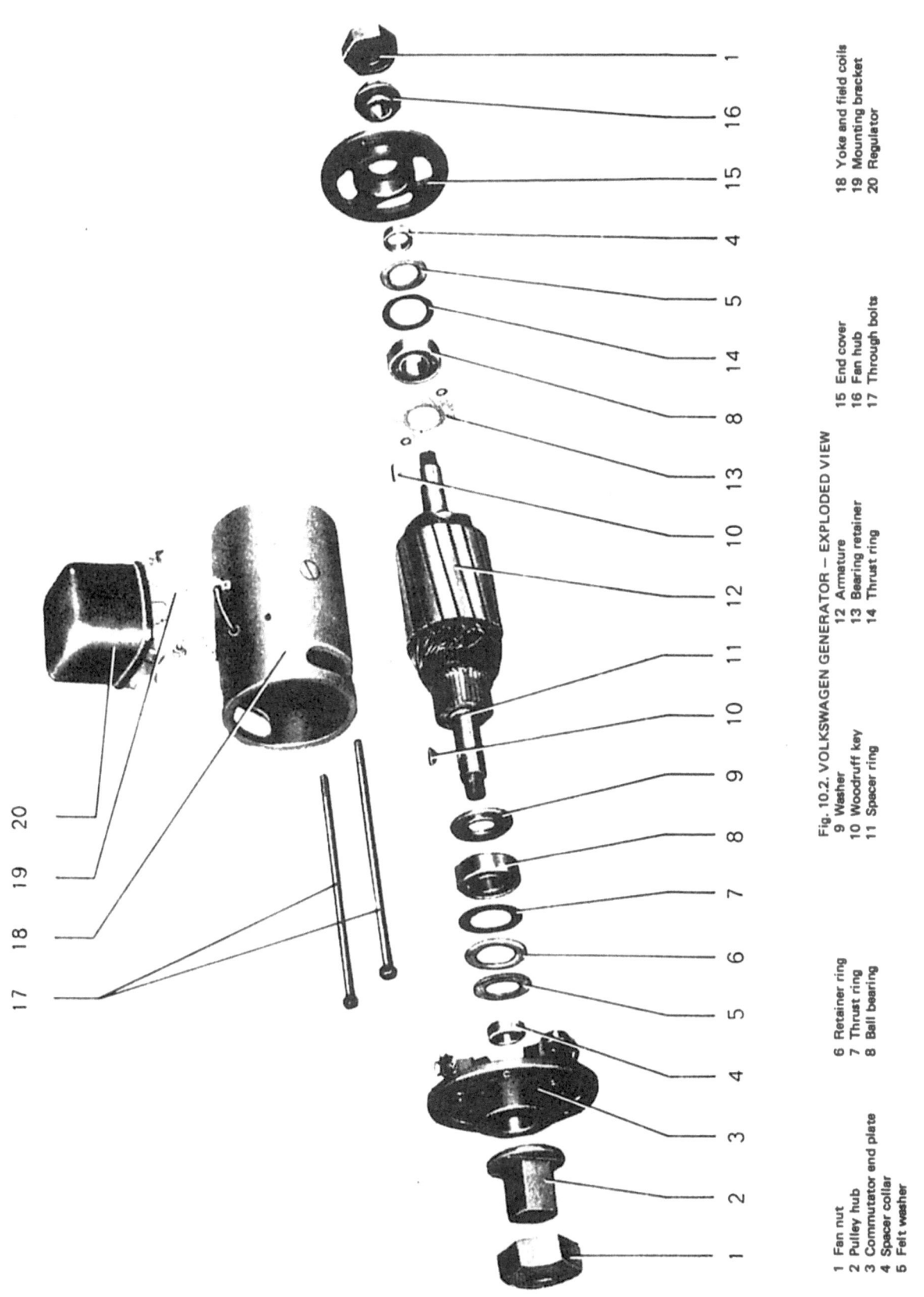

Fig. 10.2. VOLKSWAGEN GENERATOR – EXPLODED VIEW

1 Fan nut
2 Pulley hub
3 Commutator end plate
4 Spacer collar
5 Felt washer

6 Retainer ring
7 Thrust ring
8 Ball bearing

9 Washer
10 Woodruff key
11 Spacer ring

12 Armature
13 Bearing retainer
14 Thrust ring

15 End cover
16 Fan hub
17 Through bolts

18 Yoke and field coils
19 Mounting bracket
20 Regulator

frequently caused in the top of the battery cases by pouring in distilled water in the middle of winter after instead of BEFORE a run. This gives the water no chance to mix with the electrolyte and so the former freezes and splits the battery case.

5. If topping up the battery becomes excessive and the case has been inspected for cracks that could cause leakage, but none are found, the battery is being over-charged and the voltage will have to be checked and reset.

6. With the battery on the bench at the three monthly interval check, measure its specific gravity with a hydrometer to determine the state of charge and condition of the electrolyte. There should be very little variation between the different cells and if a variation in excess of 0.025 is present it will be due to either:

a) Loss of electrolyte from the battery at some time caused by spillage or a leak, resulting in a drop in the specific gravity of the electrolyte when the deficiency was replaced with distilled water instead of fresh electrolyte.

b) An internal short circuit caused by buckling of the plates or a similar malady pointing to the likelihood of total battery failure in the near future.

7. The correct readings for the electrolyte specific gravity at various states of charge and conditions are:

	Temperate	Tropical
Fully charged	1.285	1.23
Half charged	1.20	1.14
Discharged	1.12	1.08

4. Electrolyte Replenishment

1. If the battery is in a fully charged state and one of the cells maintains a specific gravity reading which is 0.025 or more lower than the others, and a check of each cell has been made with a voltage meter to check for short circuits (a four to seven second test should give a steady reading of between 1.2 to 1.8 volts), then it is likely that electrolyte has been lost from the cell with the low reading at some time.

2. Top the cell up with a solution of 1 part sulphuric acid to 2.5 parts of water. If the cell is already fully topped up draw some electrolyte out of it with a pipette.

3. When mixing the sulphuric acid and water NEVER ADD WATER TO SULPHURIC ACID - always pour the acid slowly onto the water in a glass container. IF WATER IS ADDED TO SULPHURIC ACID IT WILL EXPLODE.

4. Continue to top up the cell with the freshly made electrolyte and then recharge the battery and check the hydrometer readings.

5. Battery - Charging

1. In winter time when heavy demand is placed upon the battery, such as when starting from cold, and much electrical equipment is continually in use, it is a good idea occasionally to have the battery fully charged from an external source at the rate of 3.5 to 4 amps.

2. Continue to charge the battery at this rate until no further rise in specific gravity is noted over a four hour period.

3. Alternatively, a trickle charger, charging at the rate of 1.5 amps, can be safely used overnight.

4. Specially rapid 'boost' charges which are claimed to restore the power of the battery in 1 to 2 hours are most dangerous as they can cause serious damage to the battery plates through over-heating.

5. While charging the battery note that the temperature of the electrolyte should never exceed 100°F.

6. Check that your charging set is capable of dealing with 6 volt batteries and set it accordingly.

6. Generator - Routine Maintenance

1. The main requirement is maintaining the fan belt at the proper tension as described in Chapter 2.

2. Both armature shaft bearings are sealed and additional lubrication is not possible as a frequent routine.

3. Keep an eye on the condition of the commutator and carbon brushes. These can be seen through the aperture in the casing. (On early models there is a cover to be moved first). The brushes should protrude from the upper ends of their holders. If they do not then they are getting short and need renewal. The commutator should not show serious signs of discoloration and there should be no indication of a channel worn where the brushes track.

7. Generator - Testing in Position - General

1. If the ignition warning light does not go out when the engine is running at a fast tickover or only goes out at high revolutions it is usually due to a fault in either the generator or regulator. If checked and dealt with quickly is often possible to avoid expensive repairs.

2. First examine the generator brushes and the surface of the commutator. If the brushes are worn or commutator dirty it is possible to deal with them without removing the generator from the car. Section 8 explains how to remove the brushes and clean the commutator.

3. In order to carry out even the simplest check a voltmeter is required.

8. Generator - No Load Voltage Check

1. Disconnect the wires from terminal 51 (B+) on the regulator and make sure the ends cannot touch any nearby part and short to earth.

2. Connect the positive lead from the voltmeter to terminal 51 (B+) on the regulator and the negative lead to earth.

3. Start the engine and increase speed slowly to a fast tickover. The voltmeter should rise to a reading of 7 - 8 volts and stay there. If there is no reading the fault is most likely in the generator. If the reading is incorrect then the regulator is most probably at fault. Nevertheless, both could be faulty in either case.

9. Generator - Voltage Check without Regulator Connected

1. This check will tell you if the generator is at fault and must be done quickly or you could damage an otherwise sound generator.

2. Disconnect both cables from terminals 51 and 61 on the regulator and then connect terminal DF (F) on the generator to earth with a piece of wire. It will be necessary to undo the two regulator mounting screws in order to get to this terminal and the D+ terminal.

3. Connect the voltmeter + terminal to the D+ terminal on the generator and the voltmeter negative terminal to earth.

4. Start the engine and at a fast tickover the voltage should be approximately 6 volts. At twice that speed (3,000 rpm) it should be 18 volts. Check quickly and switch off within a few seconds. If the voltage is nil or low then the generator is at fault.

10. Generator - Current Output Check

1. The two previous tests have confirmed the presence or lack of voltage. This does not confirm the presence or lack of amps which are needed to charge the battery (even though the warning light may go out). For the current output check you will need an ammeter - with a range of 50 amps negative and positive. (If you have fitted an ammeter as an extra into the charging circuit already, this, of course, performs the function of this test and in fact tells you at all times whether the generator is doing its job properly.)

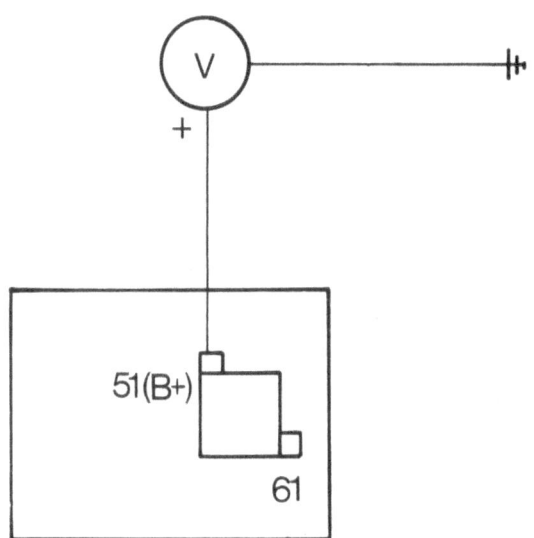

Fig. 10.3. Connection of voltmeter for no load voltage check (Section 8)

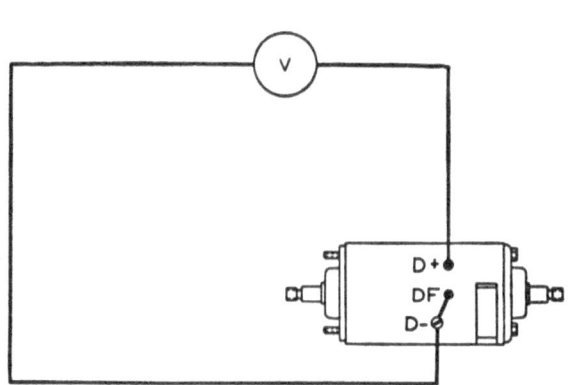

Fig. 10.4. Connection of voltmeter for generator voltage check (Section 9)

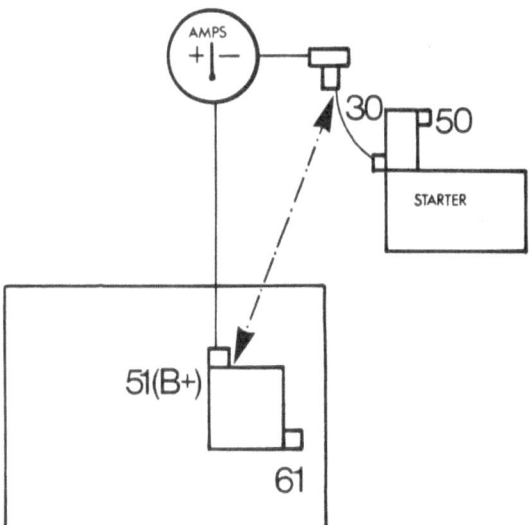

Fig. 10.5. Connection of ammeter for current output check (Section 10)

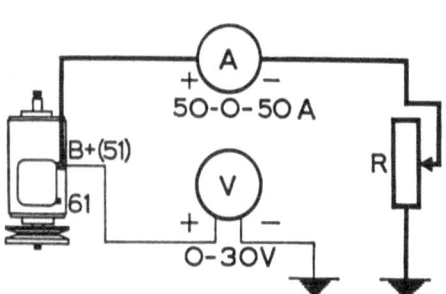

Fig. 10.6. Connection of instruments for full current regulator output check (Section 10)

2. Disconnect the battery negative (earth) terminal. There are two cables on terminal 51 (B+) on the regulator. Detach the one that comes from the starter motor terminal (leaving the other in position which leads on to the fuse block). Then connect the ammeter between the end of this disconnected cable and terminal 51 (B+) on the regulator in such a way that none of the connections touch earth.

3. Reconnect the battery and start the engine. Switch on all the lights. At low speed the ammeter should show a discharge although at very low idling speed it should move to zero when the regulator cut-out functions. At high engine speed the ammeter should show a positive reading. If the lights are switched off this reading should increase for a short time and then settle back to a 1 - 3 amp positive reading. The actual charge rate depends on the state of the battery.

4. If no positive ammeter reading can be obtained then the regulator is defective.

5. To check the current regulator independently, a voltmeter, a 50 amp ammeter and a variable resistance are required. However, if you have already established that the regulator is faulty there is no point in going any further. Regulators cannot be repaired - they must be renewed as a unit. The connections necessary for regulator checking are shown in the diagram for academic interest.

11. Regulator - Removal and Replacement

1. Disconnect the cables from terminal 51 (B+) and 61 taking care not to short those from 51 to earth. (It is a wise precaution to disconnect the battery). Undo the two screws which hold the regulator to the generator, lift it up and then disconnect the two wires from terminals + (D+) and F (DF) on the regulator.

2. Replacement is a reversal of this procedure. Note that the thicker of the two wires from the generator is the one that connects to terminal + (D+).

12. Generator - Removal, Dismantling and Replacement

1. The generator is removed in the manner described for the fan in Chapter 2. Before deciding to take it out completely make sure that the renewal of the brushes and cleaning the commutator are not the sole things to be done because these can be dealt with without removing the generator.

2. If the brushes need renewing, hook up the ends of the springs which press them into the holders and then pull the brushes out. Then undo the screw which connects the leads.

3. Whilst the brushes are removed the commutator can be cleaned with a piece of clean cloth soaked in petrol. If the commutator is very scored, changing the carbon brushes may improve things temporarily but the generator output is likely to be low and short lived.

4. When fitting new brushes make sure that they are of the correct type and fit snugly in the holders and slide freely. Brushes which are too loose will clatter about and soon wear out. Those which are tight will probably stick and eventually lose contact with the commutator as they wear away.

5. If any of the brush retaining springs are broken or the commutator is scored the generator must be removed for the repairs to be made.

6. To dismantle the generator is not a procedure we recommend, principally because there is very little the normal do-it-yourself man can do to repair it anyway. If the bearings have failed (a very rare occurrence) then the armature will need reconditioning. Skimming the commutator must be done in a lathe. Should the insulation of the armature or field coils have broken down then they will need renewal.

7. Having removed the generator and taken off the fan, therefore, we recommend it be replaced with an exchange unit or overhauled by a specialist firm dealing with auto electrics. Make sure when taking it to the repair firm that the regulator goes with it as their tests after rebuild will cover the complete unit.

8. Replacement of the generator is also described in Chapter 2.

Check that the spacer collar behind the fan hub is in position, otherwise the shaft will bind solid when the fan nut is tightened.

13. Starter Motor - Testing, Removal and Replacement

1. On the Volkswagen the starter is an inaccessible article and short of checking that the mounting bolts are tight and the electrical connections (2) properly made to the solenoid, there is nothing else to be done except take it out if it malfunctions. If the starter fails to kick at all ascertain that current is being fed from the starter switch to the solenoid. This can be done by connecting a suitably long lead to the two terminals on the solenoid in turn, and connecting the other end via a voltmeter or 6 volt bulb to earth. When connected to the smaller terminal (the lead from the ignition switch) there should be an indication on the bulb or voltmeter when the starter switch is operated. If there is not then check the other end of the wire at the starter switch terminal (50) in the same way. If there is no voltage then the fault is not with the starter. Then connect the lead to the larger terminal on the solenoid. If there is no voltage when the starter switch is operated the solenoid is defective. If there is voltage and the starter does not turn the starter is defective.

2. Disconnect the battery and pull off the right heater hose. The starter motor is secured by two bolts, the top one also being the upper right engine mounting bolt. To get this undone a spanner has to be put on the nut in front of the fan housing in the space between it and the bodywork. With luck the nut will turn without the bolt moving. If the bolt turns then another spanner (a socket with long extension) will have to be put on the bolt head from underneath the car.

3. From underneath the car, pull off the small lead at the connection and then undo the nut securing the large cable. All this must be done mainly by feel. Do not confuse the two large terminal nuts on the solenoid. The lower one connects the strap between solenoid and starter.

4. Remove the lower bolt and the starter can be lifted out.

5. Replacement is a reversal of the removal procedure. Before fitting, grease the end of the pinion shaft. It runs in a plain bush in the engine crankcase casting.

14. Starter Motor - Dismantling and Reassembly

1. The first stage of dismantling is to remove the end cover plate to get access to the brushes. If these do not protrude above the tops of their holders renewal is necessary, which calls for further dismantling.

2. Undo the nut connecting the strap between the solenoid and the starter and undo the two screws holding the solenoid casing to the end frame.

3. The solenoid plunger can now be unhooked from the operating lever inside the end frame.

4. If the solenoid only is faulty this is as far as it is necessary to go. A new solenoid unit can be fitted now.

5. Undo the two hook studs or bolts which clamp the end frame to the main casing of the starter.

6. Hook up the springs holding the carbon brushes in the holders and push them to one side so that the pressure is relieved.

7. Undo the nut on the end of the shaft and take off the three washers behind it noting their order of assembly. The end frame and armature shaft can now be pulled out. Do not lose the washers on the end of the shaft next to the commutator. If the commutator is badly scored it will need renovation in the same manner as for the generator.

8. To remove the end frame from the drive end of the shaft first push back the stop ring with a suitable tube so that the jump ring underneath can be released from its groove. The end cover assembly complete with pinion may then be drawn off.

9. To renew the brushes, two may be detached by simply removing the screws whilst the other two need to be cut off and new ones soldered to the braided leads. Leave sufficient length to solder the

Removing the end cover of the starter motor (Section 14.1)

Removing the solenoid bracket bolts (Section 14.2)

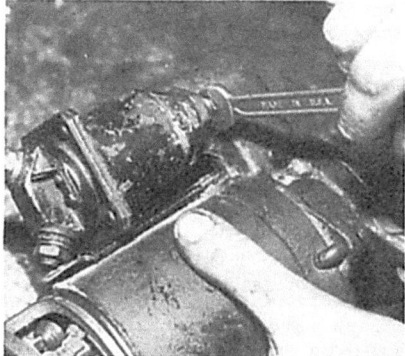

Removing the solenoid bolts from the end frame (Section 14.2)

Solenoid removed from starter motor casing (Section 14.3)

Removing the jump ring and pinion stop ring (Section 14.8)

Disconnecting the end frame (Section 14.8)

Removing the end frame (Section 14.8)

View of operating lever inside the end frame (Section 14.8)

Fitting the washers under the shaft nut, commutator end (Section 14.18)

The plain steel washer thickness regulates the end float (Section 14.18)

Staking the stop ring over the jump ring (Section 14.14)

Hooking the brush springs back over the bushes. Spring (arrowed) holds bush in raised position (Section 14.6)

new ones onto easily.

10 The pinion drive should turn one-way only inside the clutch easily. If it does not the whole unit needs renewing. The pinion teeth should not be badly worn or chipped. The yoke of the pinion operating lever should be a good fit in the groove of the pinion sleeve.

11 Reassembly is a reversal of the dismantling procedure. Thoroughly grease the moving parts of the pinion operating lever first.

12 The carbon brushes should all be held up in their holders and this can be achieved if the springs are jammed against the sides of the brushes. The armature has three washers on the end and these must be fitted so that the curved spring washer goes on first, the steel washer next with the lug towards the spring washer, followed by the fibre bearing washer.

13 If either of the bearing bushes for each end of the shaft are a very slack fit then they should be driven out and new ones fitted. Use a shouldered mandrel and soak them in oil well in advance.

14 When the pinion stop ring is refitted stake it into position over the jump ring after the latter has been fitted in its groove.

15 Fit the fibre washer, steel washer and nut on the end of the shaft.

16 Lift up the brush springs and reposition them over their respective brushes.

17 When refitting the solenoid ensure the plunger hooked end is securely placed over the operating lever.

18 The screw heads and joint faces of the commutator end cover, the solenoid and end frame should all be treated with sealing compound to keep water out. Use the Volkswagen product specially prepared for this if possible. It is important that it is not applied too thickly, otherwise clearance distances may be upset. If, after reassembly, the endfloat of the shaft exceeds .012 inch it should be reduced by adding shim washers behind the lockwasher on the commutator end of the armature shaft.

19 Because the pinion end bearing (bush) is located in the crankcase casting, it is not possible to rotate the starter under load or at speed when not fitted to the engine. The customary bench tests are therefore not applicable to this starter.

15. Fuses

1. The fuses are located under the dash panel. The wire connections to the fuse block however are to be found in the other side by removing the fibre cover panel inside the front luggage compartment. Their function is as detailed in the specification. If any fuse should blow it is normally due to a short circuit in the circuit concerned. With the aid of the wiring diagram, therefore, first check visually at all the points in the circuit where such a fault is most likely to occur. The most likely places are where wires pass through individual holes into lamp units or through holes in the bodywork where grommets have been disturbed. In the ignition circuit check the connections at the coil and choke. Remove the fibre cover from behind the dash panel in the front luggage compartment and see if there are any broken or loose wires. Feel switches to see if they are hot, which they should not be.

2. If no obvious solutions occur disconnect all items on the particular circuit (e.g. the parking light bulbs on the left if that is the circuit concerned). Fit another fuse of the proper rating. Then reconnect one item at a time, switching on each time until the fuse blows again. This will isolate the faulty part of the circuit and a closer examination can be made in that area. If you choose to fit a fuse of a much higher rating to try and overcome persistent blowing, the least that can happen is that the wiring will burn out somewhere. The worst result could be a fire.

16. Direction Indicators - Fault Tracing and Rectification

1. Whether the type of indicators fitted be the old semaphore type

or the modern flasher, one of the most usual causes of failure is due simply to bad connections to earth. This can occur at the bulb holders (usual) or the terminal connections. If, therefore, the flashers can be heard but do not light - or only operate slowly - check all the bulbs, holders and screws for signs of whitish corrosion deposits (which may have been caused by seepage of water past the lamp housing seals). Check also the appropriate fuse.

2. On vehicles fitted with semaphore arms the subsequent procedure is to remove the trim inside the car so as to get access to the unit itself. Before removing it, rig up an independent 6 volt supply so that you can check that the fault is not in the switching. The most regular fault with semaphores is a sticking solenoid plunger or rusty pivot pin.

3. With flasher units first check that the relay itself is not faulty. The simplest way to do this is by substitution with a new one. The relay is located behind the dash panel and access is from inside the luggage compartment.

4. Finally, the fault may be in the indicator switch. Before going to the trouble of taking this off, which involves removal of the steering wheel (see Chapter 11), a check can be made at the flasher relay terminals. (This of course assumes that the flasher relay is in working order). The feed wire to the switch from the flasher relay is that leading from terminal 'S'. If this is disconnected and another temporary feed wire connected then it can be used to bridge out the switch. It merely needs connection to the feed wire to one of the flasher bulbs. When the ignition is switched on the flasher should operate both the bulbs of the side linked in. If they still do not work then there is more than just the switch at fault.

17. Windscreen Wipers - Fault Finding

1. If the wipers do not work when they are switched on first check the fuse. If this is sound then there is either an open circuit in the wiring or switch, the wiper motor is faulty, or the pivot spindles or linkages may be binding.

2. If the wipers work intermittently then suspect a short circuit in the motor or a poor contact to earth. The earth is connected at the main mounting screw. Alternatively, the armature shaft end float adjustment may be too tight or the wiper linkage may be binding.

3. Should the wipers not stop when they are turned off there must be a short circuit in the switch or wiring.

18. Windscreen Wiper Motor - Removal and Replacement

1. Disconnect the battery earth lead.

2. Slacken the clamping screw on the wiper arm brackets and pull the arms off the spindles.

3. Remove the hexagon nut, washers and seals from around the spindles.

4. Remove the glove box if necessary and the fresh air vent (if fitted).

5. Disconnect the cables from the motor.

6. Undo the screw which holds the motor and frame to the strip steel mounting bracket. The motor and the linkage can then be removed together.

7. To detach the motor from the linkage first remove the lockwasher and spring washer from the motor shaft and detach the connecting rod. Then undo the motor shaft clamp nut and the single screw holding the motor to the frame and take the motor away from the frame.

8. Replacement of the motor and wiper mechanism is a reversal of the removal procedure. Ensure the replacement of the spring washer between the motor shaft and frame and the coil spring between the connecting rod and frame. When refitting the unit to the car make

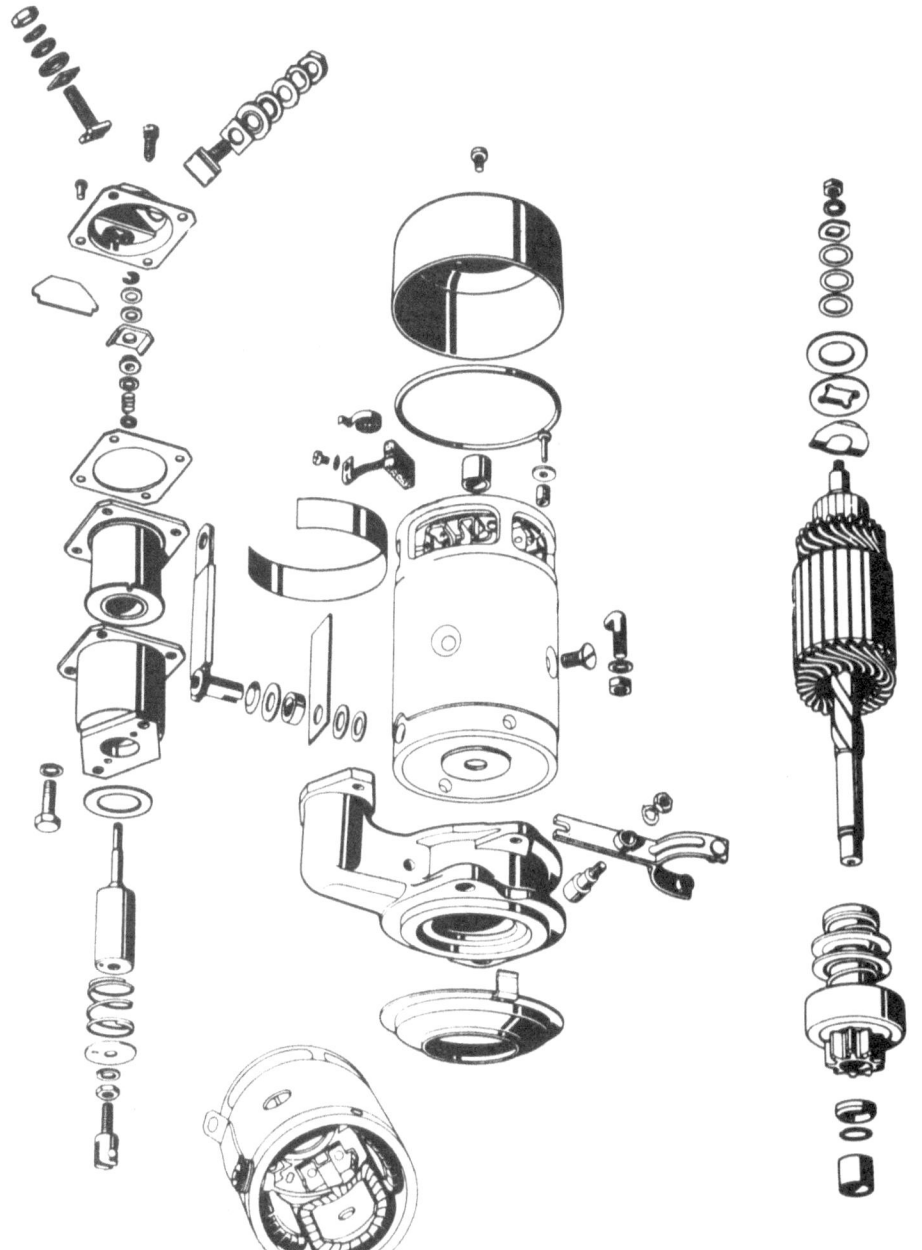

Fig. 10.7. BOSCH STARTER MOTOR — EXPLODED VIEW

sure the spindles are at right angles to the windscreen. The mounting hole in the frame is slotted to permit adjustment. The earthing strip contact at the mounting screw should be clean.

9. The sealing washers around the spindles must be correctly positioned and care taken not to overtighten the clamping screw - the correct torque being 2 - 3 lb/ft (30-40 cmkg).

19. Windscreen Wiper Motor - Dismantling and Reassembly

1. Other than for renewal of the carbon brushes, dismantling for further repair is not economical.
2. To renew the carbon brushes the wiper motor and frame assembly must be removed from the car as described in the previous sections and the motor separated from the frame.
3. Remove the armature end cover by undoing the screw or clip.
4. The brush holders are held in tension against the commutator by a common spring. Unhook this and swing the holders outwards. The old brushes can be removed with a pair of fine nosed pliers. The new ones should be a tight fit in the holders and should seat squarely onto the commutator when the holder is moved back into position.
5. On motors fitted with a self-parking device check that the points gap is 0.8 mm (.031 inch) and that the points are clean.

20. Windscreen Wiper Spindle Bearings - Renewal

1. One of the causes of jamming could be due to wear in the spindle bearings and these can be renewed after the assembly has been removed from the car.
2. Having disconnected the driving link and connecting rod by means of removing the spring clips and washer, take off the seal and washer and undo the locknut securing the bearings to the frame.
3. Replace any of the smaller nylon bushes that may be worn also.
4. When reassembling see that the hollow sides of the pressed steel links face towards the frame.

21. Windscreen Wiper Switch and Washer Pump - Removal and Replacement

1. The combined wiper switch and washer pump can be easily removed after first disconnecting the battery earth cable and unscrewing the knob from the switch.
2. Then, from behind the panel (in the front luggage compartment), pull off the wires and washer pipes. Unscrew the retaining ring and take off the switch.

22. Windscreen Washer - Fault Finding

1. Early models had a single mechanical pump which was incorporated in the wiper switch body. When pulled out and released water is drawn from the reservoir (behind the spare wheel) and sprayed onto the screen through two fine jets mounted on the front compartment lid. Later models have a valve incorporated in the switch and the water reservoir tank is pressurised so that water is automatically forced along the pipes when the valve is opened.
2. If no water issues from the jets first check that all pipes are connected and intact and that the reservoir is pressurised where applicable.
3. Then check that the nozzles of the jets are clear. Use a piece of fine wire to poke them out if necessary.
4. If it becomes obvious that the pump/valve is not working, then it must be renewed.

23. Instrument Panel, Speedometer and Warning Lights

1. Access to all instruments on the panel is from behind, after the front luggage compartment lid has been raised, and the fibre backing panel taken off.
2. The ignition, main beam and oil warning lamp bulbs are contained in snap fit holders in the speedometer head and can be renewed and changed simply by pulling out the holders.
3. The speedometer cable can be detached from the head by unscrewing the knurled retaining collar. The other end is driven by the bearing dust cover on the front left wheel and this can be released after removing the hub cap and taking the clip off the end of the cable. The cable may then be drawn out.
4. The speedometer head is released once the two retaining screws are slackened. If turned anti-clockwise the mounting lugs will disengage and the whole head can be lifted out. Make sure that the warning lamps, panel lamp and earth lead have been disconnected also.

24. Stop Lamps - Fault Finding

1. The stop lamps are operated by a hydraulic switch mounted on the end of the brake master cylinder (see Chapter 9).
2. If, after checking that the bulbs, fuse and connections are in order, the brake lights still do not work (with the ignition switched on) pull off the two leads from the hydraulic switch and touch them together. If the stop lamps now light the switch is at fault and should be renewed. The brakes must be bled afterwards (see Chapter 9).
3. If the stop lights still do not work when bridging the terminals of the switch then the fault lies in the wiring circuit. First check that voltage is coming to the switch terminal and carry on from there, tracing back to the connections with the aid of the wiring diagram.

25. Horn

1. The single horn is mounted behind the left front wing (behind a small oval grille. It has a 16 amp fuse).
2. If the horn should fail to work after checking the fuse check that the horn ring is operating the contact in the centre of the steering wheel. This can be seen after the steering wheel hub has been levered out. The three screws will release the ring.
2. On early models there is a ring halfway down the steering column with the horn wire attached to a carbon brush which bears on the ring. Check that the ring and carbon brush are in good order. On later models there is a connection at the steering column coupling. It must be remembered that when the ignition is switched on the current flows first to the horn and the circuit is made when the horn ring switch is earthed.
3. The terminals on the horn itself should be perfectly clean and the insulation in good condition.
4. If the horn has to be removed check it once again with an independent 6 volt supply before condemning it. There is a central adjusting nut in the back of the horn which may possibly give advantageous results if rotated in one direction or the other. It is not normally adjustable and if wrongly set can damage an otherwise good horn. It is important to emphasise therefore that any 'fiddling' with this is a positively last resort, having checked the complete circuit first.
5. The horn is removed by undoing the mounting bolt which secures it to the bracket.
6. When refitting the horn it is important to make sure that it does not contact the surrounding bodywork in any way. If it does it will not function properly.

26. Headlamps, Side Lamps and Stop Lamps - Bulbs and Alignment

1. Arrangement and fixings have varied somewhat over the years but the principles are much the same. Rear lamp bulbs are accessible after removing the lenses. These are held by two screws on the out-

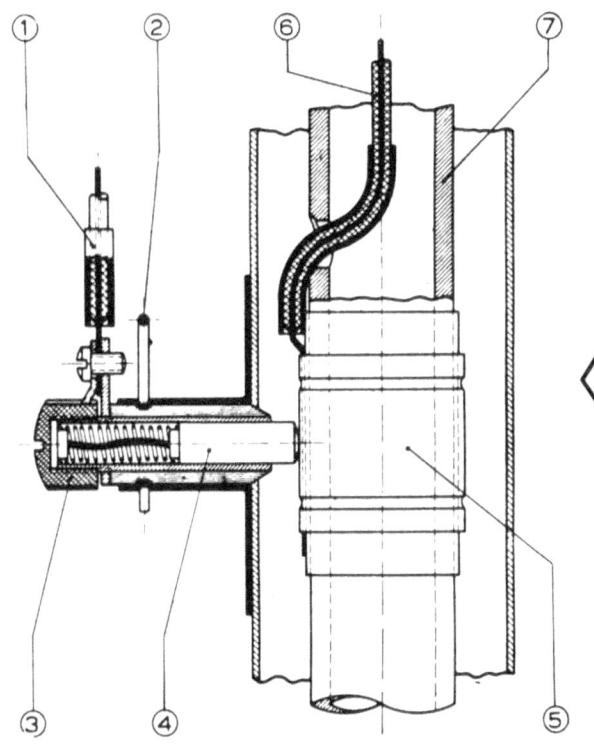

Fig. 10.8. HORN — STEERING COLUMN CONNECTIONS
EARLY MODELS

1 Cable from horn (live -
  insulated from earth)
2 Spring clip
3 Brush retainer cap
4 Brush and spring
5 Contact ring
6 Cable to steering wheel horn
  push
7 Steering column

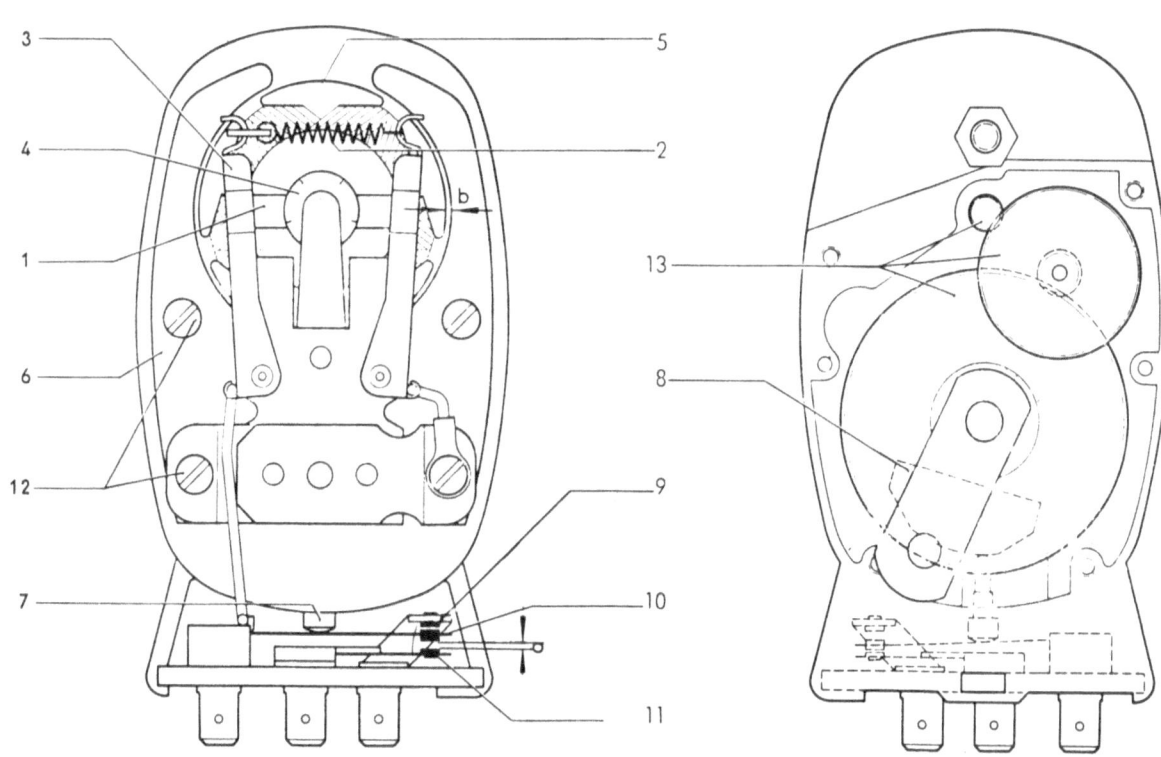

Fig. 10.9. WINDSCREEN WIPER MOTOR — VIEW OF EACH END

1 Brush
2 Brush holder spring
3 Brush holder
4 Commutator
5 Armature
6 Pole shoe
7 Cylinder plunger
8 Cam
9 Contact points
10 Spring
11 Contact point
12 Clamp screw
13 Drive gears

(a) Contact gap 0.8 mm
    (.031 inch)
(b) Gap between armature and
    pole shoes

side. The same goes for the front direction indicator lamps mounted on the wings. With the lenses removed the bulbs can be extracted by pressing them in firmly and turning them anti-clockwise and releasing. The twin filament stop/tail light bulb only fits one way and for this reason the bayonet pins are offset. Check the offset when replacing them.

2. Headlamp units also incorporate the front parking light which is a separate bulb set into the reflector casing. On some models fitted with sealed beam units the parking light bulb holder is mounted in the lower part of the main casing instead.

3. To remove the headlamp unit from the car, unscrew the lowest screw which secures the rim. Lift up the lower edge of the rim to unhook the top edge and then pull the whole lot out.

4. To remove the bulb undo the bulb holder from the back of the reflector by turning it anti-clockwise and then pull the bulb and connection apart.

5. When fitting the new bulb avoid handling the glass with the fingers which will leave a deposit which can eventually cause discoloration. Fit the bulb and connector together and then fit the holder into the reflector so that the lugs and notches line up.

6. Should the headlamp lens need renewal proceed as described in paragraphs 3 and 4 and pull out the parking lamp bulb holder as well.

7. It will then be necessary to remove the adjusting screws; so if these are very rusty, clean them properly first.

8. The reflector is held into the rim with long curved wire springs and these must be held at one end whilst the other is carefully released. They are strong and could 'fly'; prevent accidents by taking precautions.

9. When fitting a new glass the same type must be used and the sealing ring should be in perfect condition. Make sure the glass is fitted the correct way up.

10 Replace the spring clips and put the adjusting screws back.

11 On sealed beam lamps the bulb and reflector are a single unit and can be identified by the absence of a bulb holder. The wire connection fits straight onto the three terminals at the back of the unit. This item is removed and replaced in the same way that would be used for releasing the reflector and glass on a conventional model.

12 Headlamp alignment is a task which can only be done properly with optical alignment equipment. However, a rough setting can be made until the time when the beams can be properly set. Regulations vary between countries and dimensions given here apply to right hand drive vehicles in the United Kingdom.

13 The car should be standing on level ground with the tyre pressures correct and the equivalent of a 70 kg (154 lbs) passenger in the back seat. For headlamps fitted with replaceable headlamp bulbs the car should face a vertical wall 5 metres (16½ feet) away. It is important that the centre line of the car be exactly at right angles to the wall. Measure the height of the lamp centres above the ground and make a horizontal line on the wall at a height 5 cms (2 inches) less. Then mark the centre line of the car on the wall. This is best done by reference to an adjacent wall or building but can be done by careful sighting. Measure the distance between the headlamps and mark two points on the horizontal line equal to this distance. The points should be equidistant from the car centre line. These are the reference points and with the headlamps dipped the angle point between the dark/light zones should coincide for each lamp. Cover the lamp not being adjusted. The adjusting screws are in the lamp rim and the upper one does the vertical adjustment. For sealed beam lamps follow the same procedure with the car 25 feet from the wall. Aim the light intensive areas to that the top edge coincides with the lamp centre line height and the right hand edge is 5 cms (2 inches) to the left of the vertical centres. The two sketches indicate the requirements.

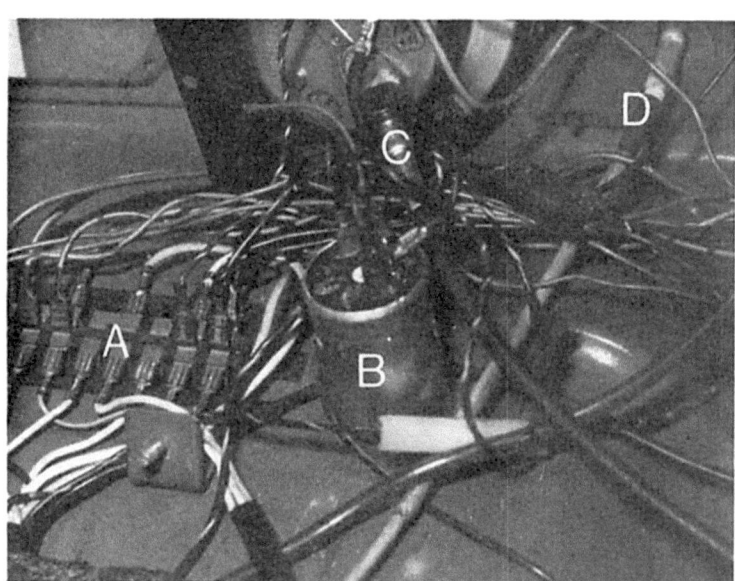

Fig. 10.12. REAR VIEW OF INSTRUMENT PANEL

A Fuse block connections　　　C Speedometer cable retaining
B Flasher relay　　　　　　　　　　collar
　　　　　　　　D Fuel gauge line

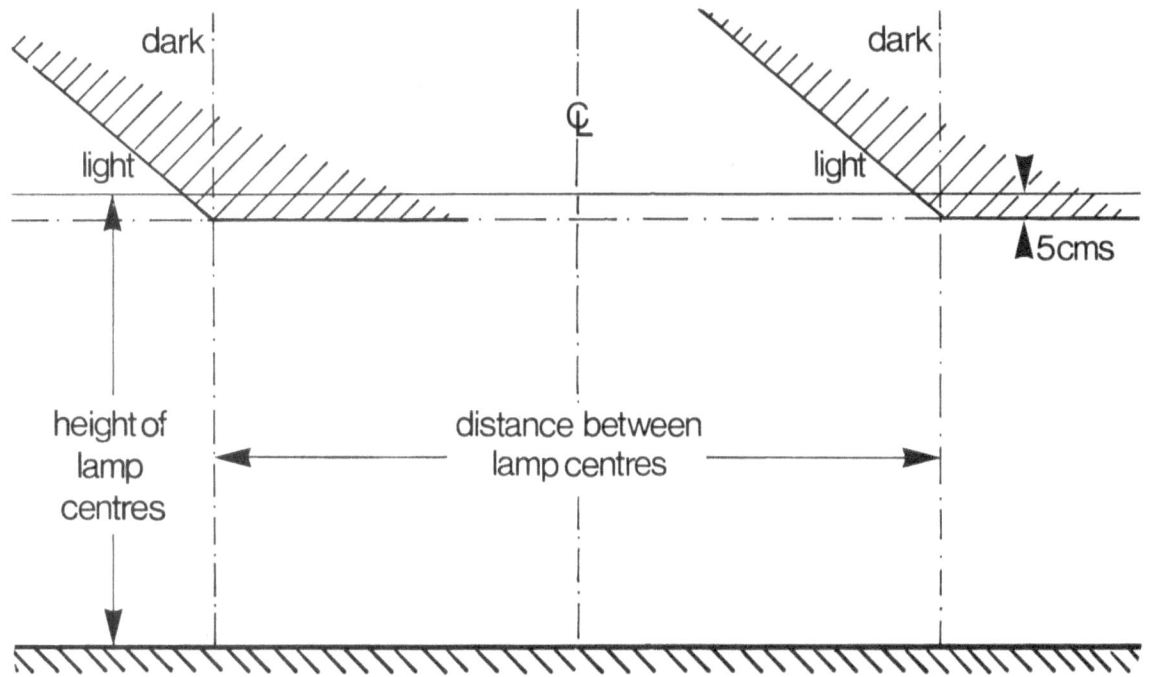

Fig. 10.10. Diagram showing alignment requirements of headlamp main beams (replaceable headlamp bulbs)

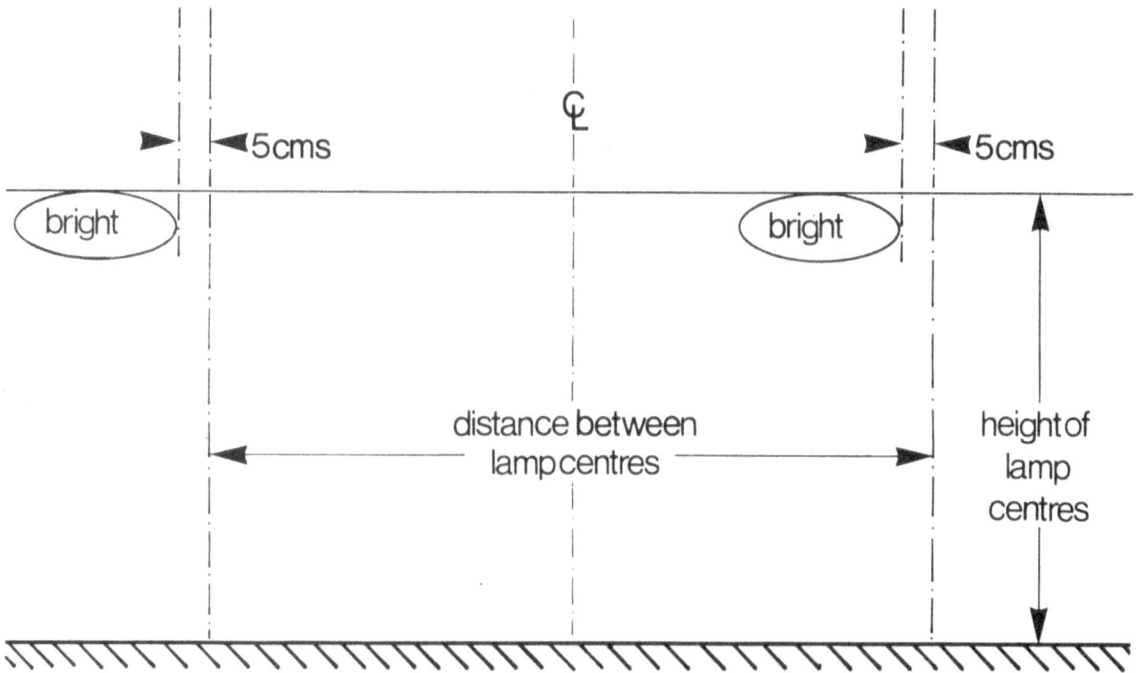

Fig. 10.11. Diagram showing alignment requirements of headlamp main beams (sealed beam headlamps)

Wiring Diagram - Early models (LHD shown)

1 Battery
2 Starter
3 Generator
4 Ignition switch
5 Windscreen wiper switch
6 Light switch
7 Direction indicator switch
8 Horn button
9 Horn
10 Horn contact brush
11 Wiper motor
12 Dip switch
13 Stop light switch
14 Oil pressure switch
15 High beam warning light
16 Instrument lights
17 Oil pressure warning light
18 Generator/fan warning light
19 Indicator warning light
20 Headlamp bulb
21 Sidelight bulb
22 Distributor
23 Coil
24 Spark plug connectors
25 Spark plugs
26 Radio
27 Radio aerial
28 Fuse block (near tank)
29 Fuse block (instrument panel)
30 Connectors
31 Direction indicators
32 Door switch courtesy light
33 Courtesy light
34 Stop lights
35 Tail lights
36 Number plate lamp

Special Note
Small figures alongside cables refer to cross-section area (and therefore current carrying capability) measured in square millimetres.

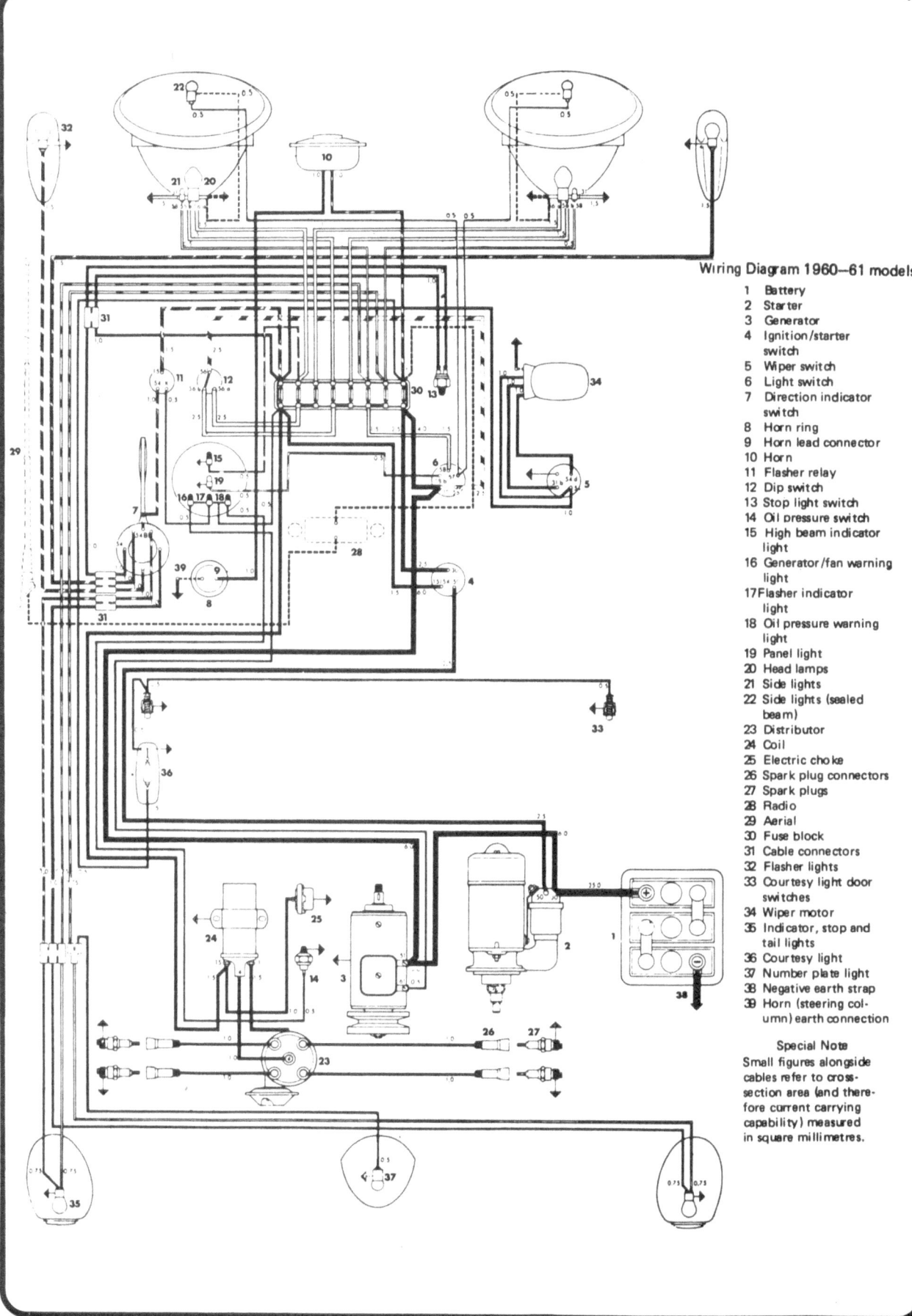

Wiring Diagram 1960—61 models

1 Battery
2 Starter
3 Generator
4 Ignition/starter switch
5 Wiper switch
6 Light switch
7 Direction indicator switch
8 Horn ring
9 Horn lead connector
10 Horn
11 Flasher relay
12 Dip switch
13 Stop light switch
14 Oil pressure switch
15 High beam indicator light
16 Generator/fan warning light
17 Flasher indicator light
18 Oil pressure warning light
19 Panel light
20 Head lamps
21 Side lights
22 Side lights (sealed beam)
23 Distributor
24 Coil
25 Electric choke
26 Spark plug connectors
27 Spark plugs
28 Radio
29 Aerial
30 Fuse block
31 Cable connectors
32 Flasher lights
33 Courtesy light door switches
34 Wiper motor
35 Indicator, stop and tail lights
36 Courtesy light
37 Number plate light
38 Negative earth strap
39 Horn (steering column) earth connection

Special Note
Small figures alongside cables refer to cross-section area (and therefore current carrying capability) measured in square millimetres.

Wiring Diagram 1962 on

1 Battery
2 Starter
3 Generator
4 Ignition/starter switch
5 Windscreen wiper switch
6 Light switch
7 Direction indicator dip switch
8 Emergency light switch
9 Horn ring
10 Steering column connector
11 Horn
12 Flasher relay
13 Dip relay
14 Stop light switch
15 Oil pressure switch
16 Main beam indicator light
17 Generator/fan warning light
18 Flasher indicator light
19 Oil pressure warning light
20 Panel light
21 Fuel gauge light
22 Headlamps
23 Side lights
24 Distributor
25 Coil
26 Electric choke
27 Spark plug connections
28 Spark plugs
29 Radio
30 Aerial
31 Fuse box
32 Cable adaptor
33 Cable connections
34 Flasher lights
35 Courtesy light switches
36 Windscreen wiper motor
37 Stop, turn and tail lights
38 Interior light
39 Number plate light
40 Battery earth connection
41 Steering column to earth connection

Special Note
Small figures alongside cables refer to cross-section area (and therefore current carrying capability) measured in square millimetres.

Chapter 11 Suspension, dampers and steering

Contents

Specifications

Front Suspension

Type   ... ...   Independent, twin transverse laminated leaf torsion bars each with a trailing arm to the steering knuckle.

Torsion bars		No. of leaves	Length	Fitting angle
(a)	(Top	8	941.5 mm	$49^{o} \pm 1^{o}$
	(Bottom	8		59° 30' $\pm 1^{o}$
(b)	(Top	10	954 mm	$44^{o} \pm 30'$
	(Bottom	10		35° 30' $\pm 30'$

(a) Up to 1965 inclusive
(b) From 1966 on (Chassis No. 116,000,0001)
Ball joints for steering knuckle (max. wear)
  Upper joint vertical play   ... ...   2.00 mm
  Lower ball joint   ... ...   1.00 mm

Rear Suspension

Type   ... ...   Independent, single divided transverse solid - torsion bar with trailing spring plate to outer end of each swing axle tube.

Torsion bar	Length (each side) mm	Diameter mm	Spring plate angle
Up to Chassis No. 929,745 (end 1955)	626	24	$13^{o} \pm 30'$
" " " " 2,232,161 (mid 1959)	626	24	$12^{o} \pm 30'$
" " " " 2,528,667 (end 1959)	626	24	$11^{o} \pm 30'$
" " " " 116,1021297 (end 1966)	552	22	17° 30' $\pm 50'$
1967 on	552	22	18° 30' $\pm 50'$

Steering

Type (a)   ... ...   Worm and sector
    (b)   ... ...   Worm and roller

(a) Discontinued on standard models as late as 1962 - on others in 1958
(b) Grease packed as opposed to oil filled.

Steering Geometry

Toe-in   ... ...   30'
Toe-in with 10 kg pressure on wheels   ... ...   5'
Front wheel camber - straight ahead ... ...   30' — 40'

Toe-out on 20° lock (unpressed):

LHD	left	... ...	1° 20'
	right	... ...	2° 10'
RHD	left	... ...	2° 15'
	right	... ...	1° 35'
Rear wheel camber (minimum)	(a)	... ...	2° positive
	(b)	... ...	0°
	(c)	... ...	1° negative

(a) Up to Chassis No. 2,528,667 (1959)

(b) 1959 to 116,1021297 (1966)

(c) 1967 on

Rear wheel toe-out ... ...   5'

Dampers ... ...   Telescopic, double acting, front and rear

Wheels and Tyres

Type ... ...   Steel disc, bolt fixing

Rim ... ...   4J x 15 (standard)

Tyres and Pressures (p.s.c.)

	5,60 — 154 PR		155 SR 15	
	Front	Rear	Front	Rear
Up to two people	16	24	18	27
Fully loaded	17	26	18	27

Torque Wrench Settings

Front Axle

Front damper bolt on side plate	24 lb/ft (3.4 mkg)
Front damper nut on side plate	14 lb/ft (2.0 mkg)
Front damper nut on lower torsion arm	24 lb/ft (3.4 mkg)
Steering ball joint nuts M12	38 lb/ft (6.0 mkg)
" " " M10	33 lb/ft (4.5 mkg)
" " " " with split pin	22 lb/ft (3.0 mkg) *
Wheel bearing inner nut	29 lb/ft (4.0 mkg)
Wheel bearing lock nut	50 lb/ft (7.0 mkg) *
Wheel bearing clamp nut socket screw	9 lb/ft (1.3 mkg) (max.)
Steering damper nut on tie rod	18 lb/ft (2.5 mkg)
Steering damper screw on axle tube	31 lb/ft (4.4 mkg)
Torsion bar setscrew & locknut	33 lb/ft (4.5 mkg)
Link pin clamping screw to torsion arm	32 lb/ft (4.5 mkg)

Rear Axle

Spring plate nuts and bolts ... ...   72 lb/ft (10.0 mkg)

* See text for procedure.

1. General Description

The Volkswagen Beetle suspension has always been noted for its strength which is due largely to the use of torsion bars as the method of springing. At the front, two torsion bars - made of leaves clamped together - are mounted across the car, one directly above the other. Each runs in a tube and in the centre it is clamped to the tube. The outer ends fit into the tubular ends of the torsion arms (which support the wheels). These tubular ends of the torsion arms themselves fit inside the axle tubes and pivot on needle roller bearings and plain bushes. The rearward facing torsion arms, two on each side support the king pin carrier (or link) and stub axle. Up till 1965 the torsion bars supported the link on pins running in plain bushes and the steering pivot was a king pin running in plain bushes. After that the function of link pins and king pins was taken over by ball joints, two each side.

A single telescopic hydraulic damper is attached to the lower torsion arm on each side and to a body bracket. An anti-roll bar connects the lower torsion arms on each side also.

The rear axle is in effect incorporated with the gearbox. The axle shafts and their tubes pivot at their inner ends. Two separate torsion bars are used for the rear suspension, so although they are in effect like a single bar clamped in the centre running across the car each half can be removed separately. A centrally mounted splined boss supports the inner ends of each torsion bar and the outer end is splined to the front end of the spring plate. The spring plate trails rearward and the rear end is attached to the outer end of the axle tube. A single double acting hydraulic damper is attached to a bracket which is part of the end of the axle tube.

Steering is by a worm and sector operated drop arm on early models. Later versions use a worm and roller type steering gear.

From the drop arm a single track rod runs directly to the steering knuckle of each front wheel. A hydraulic piston type damper mounted transversely is fitted to absorb transmitted road shock on all but the very early models.

2. Routine Maintenance

1. The front suspension and steering linkage have grease points. The outer ends of the two torsion bars run in needle bearings and there

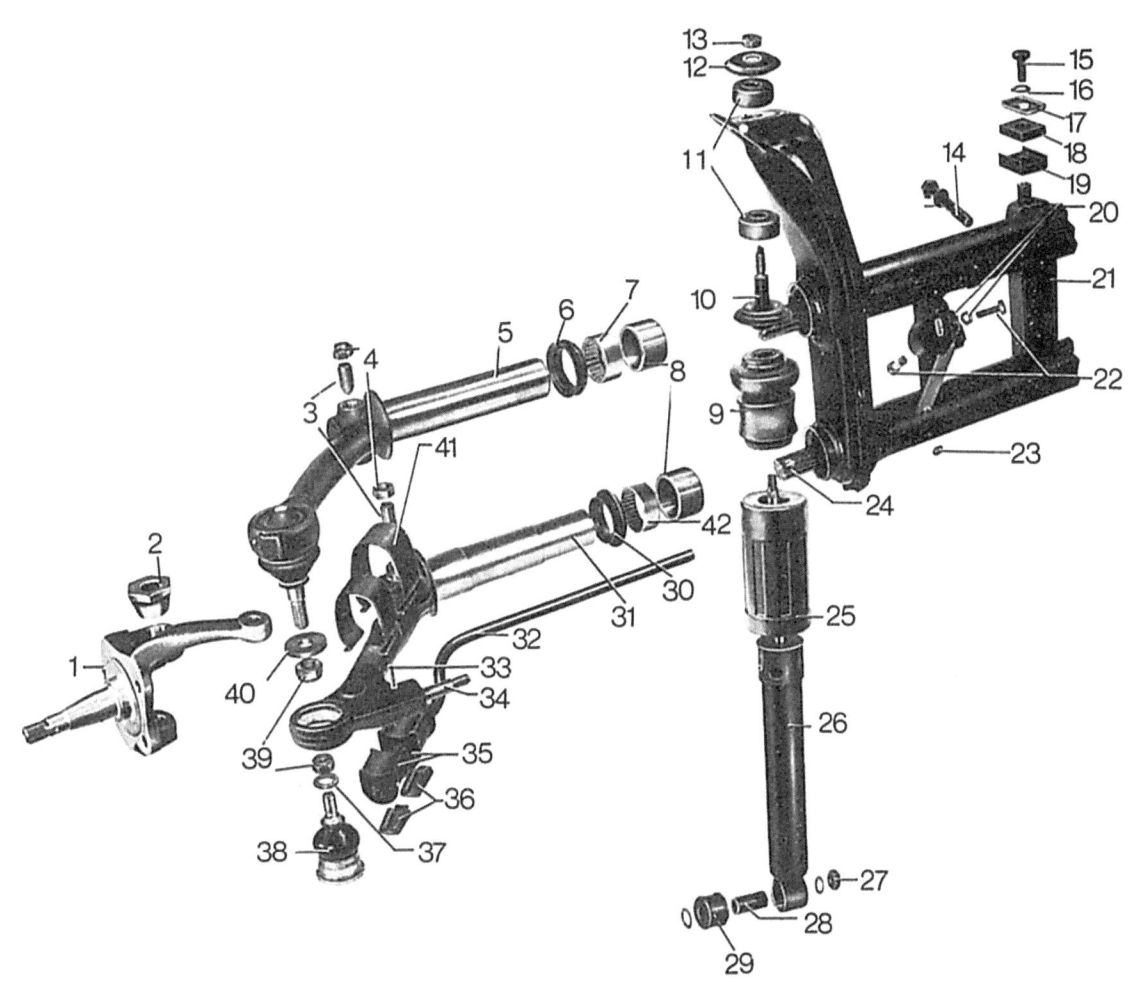

Fig.11.1. FRONT AXLE ASSEMBLY – BALL JOINT TYPE – EXPLODED VIEW

1 Steering knuckle	12 Plate	23 Grease nipple	34 Damper pin
2 Camber adjuster	13 Nut	24 Torsion bar	35 Rubber block
3 Grub screw	14 Bolt	25 Outer tube	36 Clip
4 Nut	15 Bolt	26 Damper	37 Washer
5 Upper arm	16 Spring washer	27 Nut	38 Ball joint
6 Seal	17 Plate	28 Sleeve	39 Self-locking nut
7 Bearing	18 Rubber packing	29 Bush	40 Washer
8 Bush	19 Rubber packing	30 Seal	41 Clamp
9 Buffer	20 Locknut	31 Lower arm	42 Needle bearing
10 Pin	21 Axle beam	32 Stabilizer	
11 Damper ring	22 Steering stop screw	33 Pin	

is a grease nipple for each one - four in all. Every 6,000 miles grease these nipples with Castrol LM Grease.

2. On early models the track rod end ball joints also had grease nipples and these should be greased at 6,000 mile intervals or more often in severe conditions.

3. These same models also had grease nipples for the upper and lower king pin bushes, two on each side. Grease these every 6,000 miles.

4. Later models gradually replaced the ball joints and king pins with sealed ball joints which required no further lubrication. The four torsion bar grease points still remain.

5. When the greasing is done the torsion arm link pins should be checked for play. Adjustment should be made as necessary as described in Section 4.

6. Front wheel bearings should be dismantled, flushed and repacked with Castrol LM grease at intervals of 30,000 miles. If they are removed and dismantled for any reason they should be repacked in the same way.

7. The steering box on earlier models was filled with oil. The filler plug can be seen if the spare wheel is taken out and the cover plate removed from the recess. Oil should be added until the level is up to the edge of the plug threads. On later models the box is filled with a transmission grease and needs no attention.

3. Front Wheel Bearings - Removal, Replacement and Adjustment

1. There are two types of front wheel hub bearings. Prior to 1965 two ball races were fitted and adjustment was made by two nuts on the end of the stub axle. Later models have taper roller bearings and the two nuts have been replaced by a special nut which incorporates a clamp bolt to lock it in position when the correct adjustment has been made.

2. The left hand front hub has a left hand thread for the nuts. The axle is hollow to permit the speedometer drive cable to go through it. This cable is driven by a square hole in the bearing dust cover. Jack up the wheel and remove the securing bolts and wheel.

3. To remove the bearing dust cover, first take out the split pin or circlip securing the speedometer cable and tap the dust cover from side to side until it comes free.

4. Bend back the lock tab and undo the outer nut, remembering to turn it clockwise on the left hand threaded left side stub axle. Pull off the tab washer and undo the inner locknut.

5. If the thrust washer is now taken off, the complete drum may be removed. There will be the outer races of each bearing left in the hub and the inner race of the inner bearing left on the axle. These should be drifted out of the hub from the inside, if the bearings are to be renewed. If the same bearings are being replaced, they may be left in position and merely flushed out. The race on the shaft should be drifted off also. Note that if the ball races are renewed then the oil seal on the inner part of the hub will be driven out at the same time as the ball race. This must be renewed as well.

6. On the axle behind the bearing race is a spacer on which the oil seal runs. If this is grooved on its outer face it should be renewed also.

7. It is possible that the bearing race is a loose fit on the shaft. If this is so, which would tend to let it turn, a few centre punch marks around the axle where it fits will give it some grip once again when fitted.

8. Refitting of new bearings means that the outer races will first have to be driven into the hub and the new oil seal fitted on the inside. Coat the bearings and the space between them in the hub with liberal quantities of Castrol LM Grease and place the hub back on the shaft. Fit the outer bearing followed by the thrust washer and screw on the inner locknut. Replace the double tab washer (a new one) and the other nut.

9. To adjust the bearing and float correctly the inner nut should be tightened up firmly to make sure the bearings are properly located, spinning the wheel at the same time to ensure the bearings are not overtightened. Then the nut should be backed off until the thrust washer can just be moved by pushing it with the edge of a screwdriver blade. A thin section spanner will then be required to hold the nut whilst the outer one is locked up until it is tight. Check that the thrust washer still moves a little and bend the lock tabs, one against a flat on the inner nut and the other against the outer nut. On those later models fitted with a single nut with clamp bolt the adjustment is correct when the axial play is between .03 - .12 mm (.001 - .005 inch) at the spindle. This seems quite a lot and can result in some quite noticeable rock at the outer rim of the wheel. It is nevertheless correct although the axial play should be kept to the lower limit where possible.

10 Replace the hub cover and re-secure the speedometer drive cable where appropriate. Replace the wheel and lower to the ground.

4. Torsion Arm Link Pins - Removal, Replacement and Adjustment

1. The stub axle assembly is held to the two torsion arm eyes by link pins which run in steel bushes in the king pin carrier. The outer end of the pin is flanged and the inner end is clamped into the split eye of the torsion arm by a pinch bolt. The bolt locks into a groove in the pin. However, this groove spirals part way round the pin so that if the pin is rotated axial tension can be applied to take up any play which may develop between the torsion arm and the king pin carrier. The inner end of the pin has two flats machined on to it to enable it to be turned with a spanner.

2. To remove the link pins first jack up the car and remove the road wheel. Then remove the front wheel bearings and brake drum as described earlier. The brake backplate complete with shoes still attached should then be unbolted from the stub axle mounting flange. It is not necessary to disconnect the hydraulic brake flexible hose. Hook up the assembly to one side with a piece of wire.

3. Slacken the nut on the pinch bolt in the end of the torsion arm. When it is free tap the end of the pinch bolt to make sure it is free and then remove the nut and take out the bolt. The link pin may then be drifted out of the torsion arm and king pin carrier. If the link pins and/or bushes are badly worn then they should be renewed. Wear can also occur on the shim washers preventing full adjustment from taking place. At the same time, assess whether the king pins and bushes are worn. If the link pin bushes are worn it will probably be necessary to renew the king pin bushes. Check them for wear.

4. Whether or not the original or new pins and bushes are being fitted the procedure for ensuring the correct shimming should be followed. This involves measuring the offset of the torsion arms. A steel straight edge and rule (or caliper gauge) are required and measurement has to be accurate to 0.5 mm (.020 inch) which is possible with a good steel rule.

5. Place the straight edge across the eye of the lower torsion arm in such a way that you are able to measure the distance from the straight edge to the face of the upper torsion arm eye. This measurement should not be more than 9 mm or less than 5 mm on any model and if it is, one or both of the torsion arms must be distorted and need renewal.

6. Having determined the offset difference the correct shim selection can be made. Note that in 1960 the number of shims changed from ten to eight (with a dust washer as well as the eight shims). The tables below, read in conjunction with Figure 11.5 will indicate the number of shims to be fitted to the upper and lower link pins and on which side of the link they go. It is important to get this right.

For ten shim models up to 1960

Transmission offset in mm	A	Upper B		C	Lower D
5	3	7	7	3
5.5	3	6	7	3
6	4	6	6	4
6.5	5	5	6	4
7	5	5	5	5
7.5	6	4	5	5

Centre punching the stub axle to remedy loose inner bearing race (Section 3.7)

Greasing the ball race in the hub (Section 3.8)

Fitting the thrust washer (Section 3.8)

Fitting the inner locknut (Section 3.8)

Fitting the tab washer (Section 3.8)

Fitting the outer locknut (Section 3.8)

Checking the thrust washer movement (Section 3.9)

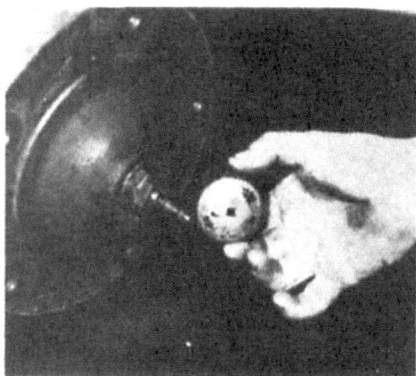

Replacing the bearing cover (Section 3.10)

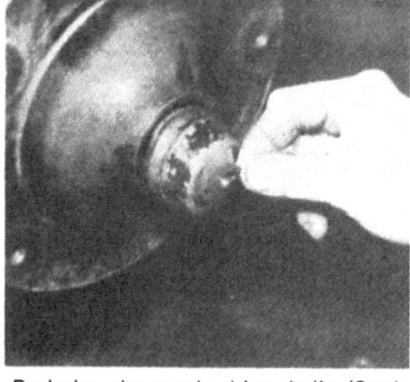

Replacing the speedo drive circlip (Section 3.10)

Stub axle assembly (Section 4.1)

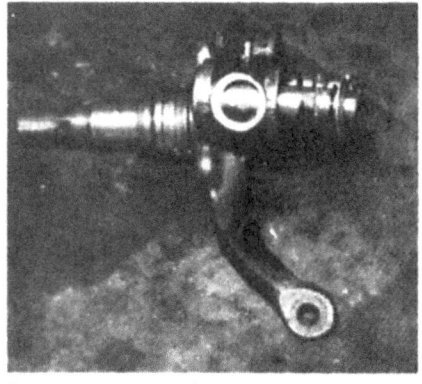

Stub axle assembly (Section 4.1)

Measuring the offset of the torsion arms (Section 4.5)

Offering up the assembly to the torsion arms (Section 4.7)

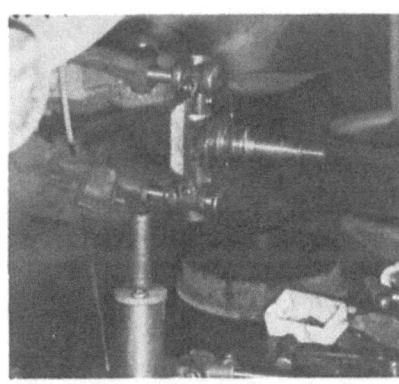

Jacking up the lower torsion arm (Section 4.7)

Lining up the shim cover washer dimple in the slot. Arrow to speedo cable hole (Section 5.6.)

Installing pinch bolt (Section 4.8)

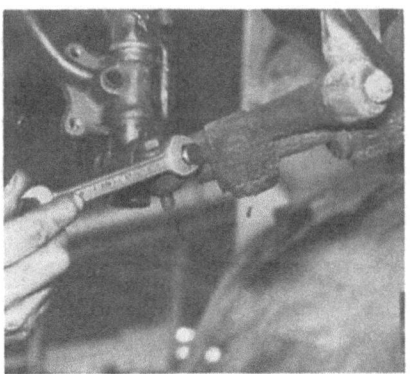

Rotating link pin to take up play (Section 4.9)

King pin carrier (upside down) showing bushes fitted with top bush notched (arrow) (Section 5.6)

Fig. 11.2. Withdrawing front torsion bar with arm (Section 7)

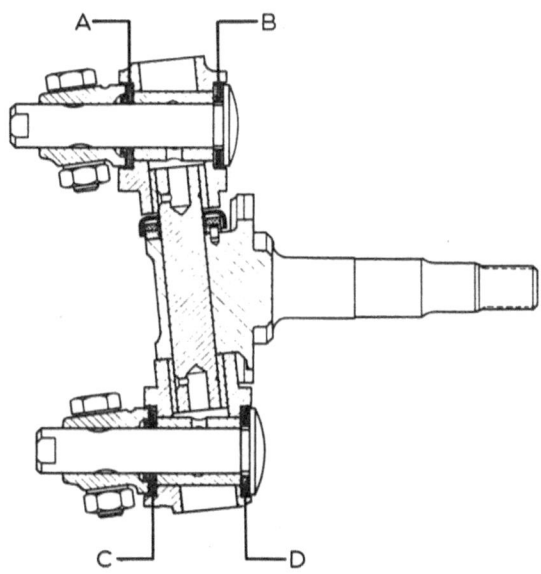

Fig. 11.3. King pin carrier and steering knuckle - link pin type A—D indicate shim locations (Section 4)

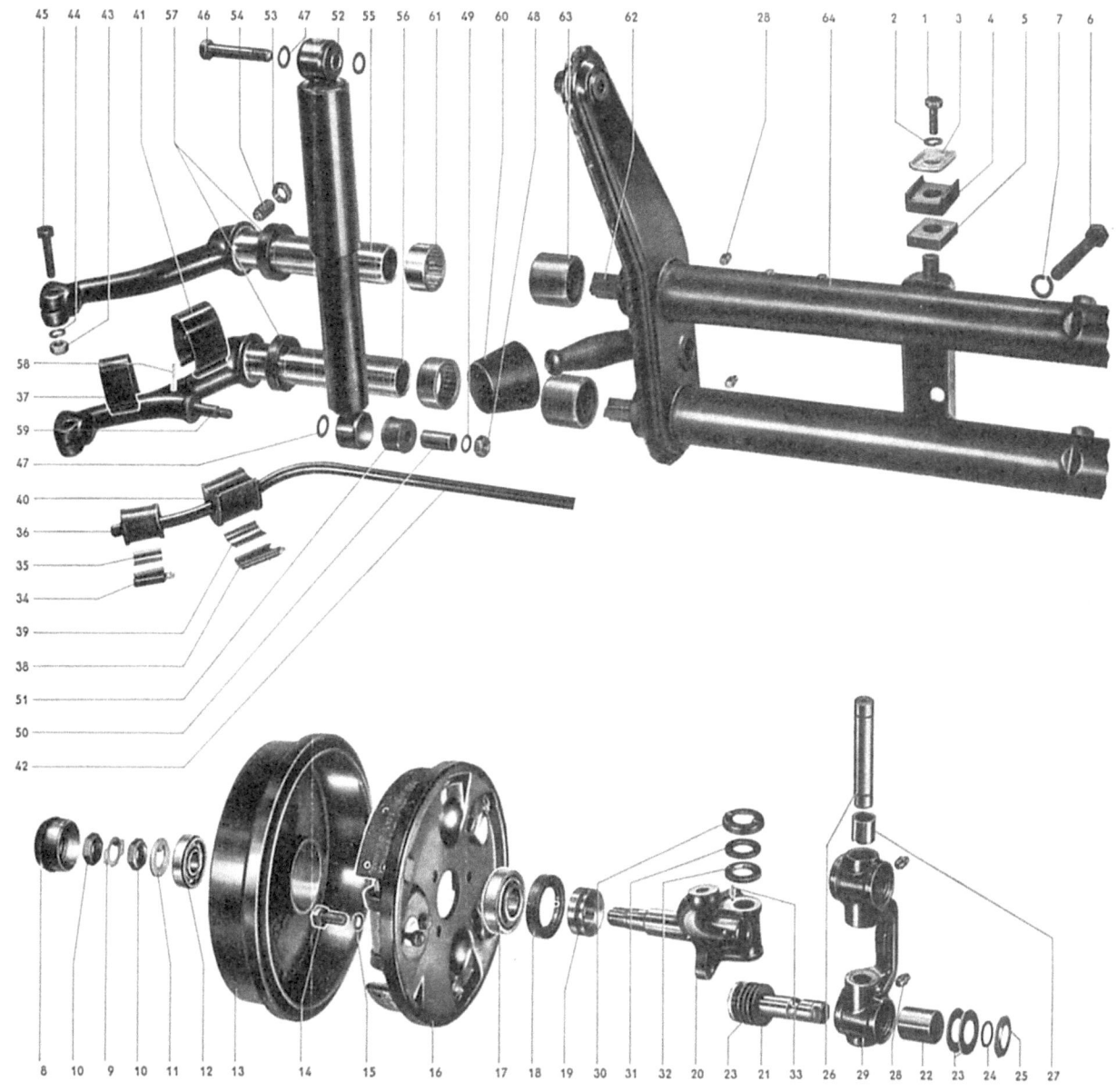

Fig. 11.4. FRONT AXLE ASSEMBLY — LINK PIN TYPE — EXPLODED VIEW

1 Body mounting bolt	17 Bearing	33 Dowel pin	49 Lockwasher
2 Washer	18 Oil seal	34 Clip	50 Sleeve
3 Plate	19 Spacer	35 Plate	51 Rubber bush
4 Rubber packing	20 Steering knuckle	36 Rubber mounting	52 Damper
5 Rubber packing	21 Link pin	37 Clamp	53 Locknut
6 Axle assembly mounting bolt	22 Bush	38 Clip	54 Setscrew torsion arm
7 Spring washer	23 Shims	39 Plate	55 Upper torsion arm
8 Bearing dust cover	24 Seal	40 Rubber mounting	56 Lower torsion arm
9 Tab washer	25 Seal retainer	41 Clamp	57 Seals
10 Adjustment nut	26 King pin	42 Stabiliser bar	58 Dowel pin
11 Thrust washer	27 Bush	43 Link pin pinch bolt nut	59 Damper mounting pin
12 Bearing	28 Grease nipple	44 Washer	60 Bump stop
13 Brake drum	29 King pin carrier (link)	45 Link pin pinch bolt	61 Needle bearing
14 Backplate bolt	30 Cover for thrust washer	46 Damper mounting bolt	62 Torsion bar (8 leaves)
15 Washer	31 Thrust washer (plastic)	47 Lockwasher	63 Bush
16 Backplate	32 Thrust washer (steel)	48 Nut	64 Axle beam (tube)

8	6	4	4	6
8.5	7	3	4	6
9	7	3	3	7

For eight shim models 1960 on

5.5	2	6	5	3
6	2	6	4	4
6.5	3	5	4	4
7	3	5	3	5
7.5	4	4	3	5
8	4	4	2	6
8.5	5	3	2	6

7. Assemble the correct number of shims under the head of the upper link pin, put it through the link and put the remainder on the other side together with the protective washer on the eight shim type. Do the same with the lower pin and then offer the pins up to the torsion arm eyes. Make sure you have the thing the right way up! It will be necessary to put a jack under the lower arm to raise it in relation to the other so the pins can go in. Make sure that everything is perfectly clean and suitably greased.

8. The protective washers should be lined up so that the projection fits into the gap of the eye of the torsion arm. Then rotate the pins until it is possible to put the pinch bolts back.

9. The correct setting of the link pins is important. If they are over-tightened the up and down movement of the road wheels will be affected and rapid wear will develop where the shims are fitted. If too slack movement will result. First tighten the link pin (by rotating it with a spanner) as far as possible. Then back it off $1/8$ revolution. Tighten again until resistance can just be felt. If the pin is rotated as far as it will go and play still exists between the link and torsion arm then the shims or their bearing surfaces are worn. A new set of shims may cure the problem but do not just add shims. You may cure the play but the steering geometry will be thrown out of alignment. If the adjustment is being made as part of routine maintenance and lubrication has been neglected it may be necessary to dismantle the assembly to clean it up and lubricate the pins and bushes properly.

10 When the pin setting is correct tighten the pinch bolt nut to the specified torque of 32 lb/ft.

11 If the pins were removed rather than just simply adjusted, replace the brake backplate assembly, hub and road wheel.

5. Link Pin and King Pin Bushes - Renewal

1. If wear between pins and bushes is such that the wheels may be moved sufficiently to affect steering properties they must be renewed. If the king pins and bushes need replacement the link pin bushes have to be taken out first. The king pin bushes need reaming to size after fitting. The link pin bushes do not. Pins and bushes must be renewed in sets. You must not renew the pins only or bushes only. When you buy the pin and bush sets the new washers and shims are all included.

2. First remove the link pins so that the assembly can be removed from the car as described in the previous section. It will be necessary to detach it from the track rod outer ball joint also. If this proves stubborn use a claw clamp or strike each side of the eye with hammers simultaneously to 'spring' the taper pin.

3. To remove the link pin bushes a big vice or press is needed. If one tries to beat them out the link is liable to become distorted. Obtain a piece of steel tube or a suitably sized socket and press the old bush out between the vice jaws.

4. The link should then be clamped in the vice and the king pin drifted out. The steering knuckle can then be tapped out of the link.

5. The king pin bushes can be driven out with a suitable drift. They are not a very tight fit. Take care not to damage the bores into which they fit.

6. The fitting and reaming of the bushes to fit the new pin is a job that calls for a special tool and some skill. If you do not have an expanding parallel reamer we strongly recommend that you take the whole lot to a specialist and have it done by him. If you possess an expanding reamer of the correct size range (an expensive tool) then you should know how to use it so it is sufficient to say that the pin should be a push fit with no play. Note that the bushes should be fitted with a stepped drift to avoid the possibility of spreading or breakage during the initial positioning. The upper bush must also be notched with a file to match the notch in the housing after fitting. Do this before reaming to avoid burrs.

6. To reassemble the king pin, link and knuckle first fit the thrust washer on the knuckle so that it locates on the dowel pin, followed by the friction washer and cover. Note that the cover has two raised pips to line up with the notches in the link mentioned earlier. Put the knuckle into position so that the king pin holes line up. The knuckle will need to be tapped into position in the link because there is an interference fit of .02 mm (.0008 inch). If it can be positioned easily then it indicates that the thrust washer (the one with the dowel hole) should be increased in thickness. Variations up to a maximum of 4.30 mm (.172 inch) are available. If end float is allowed to exist in the knuckle the king pin bushes will deteriorate more rapidly. Next drive the king pin into position. It will be a much tighter fit in the stub axle than in the bushes. It should be driven home so that the ends are flush with the ends of the bushes. The knuckle should swivel freely in the link and no slackness or localised tight spots should occur. If they do then the bushes have been insufficiently reamed or reamed out of alignment.

7. When fitting the link pin bushes (made of steel) it is very important that they are lined up so that the grease ways will enable grease pumped into the nipple to reach both the link pin bushes and the king pin bushes. When this line up is correct the steel bushes may be pressed in, between the jaws of a vice. Use a suitably sized socket to ensure that the ends are flush with the ends of the bore. If they are not flush the king pin inclination can be seriously affected on installation and upset all the steering geometry. If you find that the bushes project beyond the shoulders of their locations then this means that the links are seriously worn and must be renewed. (Otherwise they will be able to move in relation to the bushes when shock loads are applied).

6. Steering Knuckle Ball Joints - Removal, Inspection and Replacement

1. From 1965 on the steering knuckle assembly was modified and the link pins and king pins were replaced by ball joint swivels. With the exception of the correct setting of the camber adjusting bush on the upper joint pin there are no adjustments or lubrication requirements. When the joints are worn beyond specification limits they must be renewed.

2. To check the vertical play first turn the front wheels to one side and find a jack that will fit under the lower torsion arm at the ball joint end. If ground clearance is too little jack the car up and rest the wheel on a block. If the jack under the torsion arm is now raised any play in the joint should be apparent. It is difficult to measure accurately unless you have a caliper gauge which can be placed across the head of the joint pin and the bottom of the torsion arm.

3. The upper joint is a little more difficult but in general practice if the lower joint is within tolerance limits the upper one will be also. If the lower one is not then it is easier to check the top one when the steering knuckle has been removed. In any case the joints should normally be renewed in pairs on each side.

4. In order to renew the ball joints they have first to be removed from the knuckle by unscrewing the taper pin nuts and pressing them out of the knuckle eyes with a claw clamp. To do this, first remove the hub and brake backplate assemblies as described earlier and disconnect the upper damper mounting. It must be emphasised here that these ball joint pins are usually a very tight taper fit. If you do not have a proper clamp you might succeed by striking the side of the eye with a hammer to spring it loose. If this does not succeed do not risk bending anything by excessive use of striking force. Also the

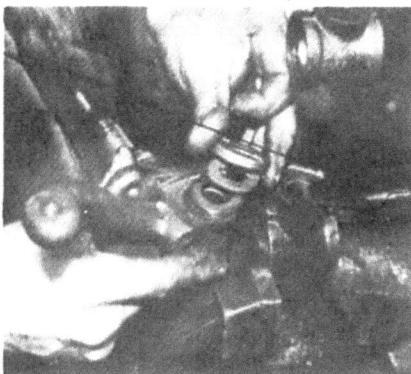

Positioning the dowelled thrust washer, friction washer and cover to the steering knuckle (Section 5.6)

Lining up washer and cover to slot in king pin carrier (Section 5.6)

Commencement of fitting of king pin (Section 5.6)

Driving the king pin home (Section 5.6)

King pin fully home through steering knuckle (Section 5.6)

Lining up link pin bush (Section 5.7)

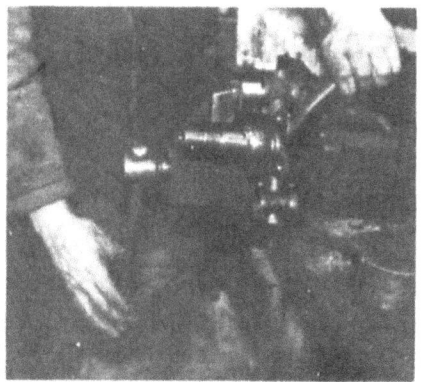

Pressing home the link pin bush. 1st stage (Section 5.7)

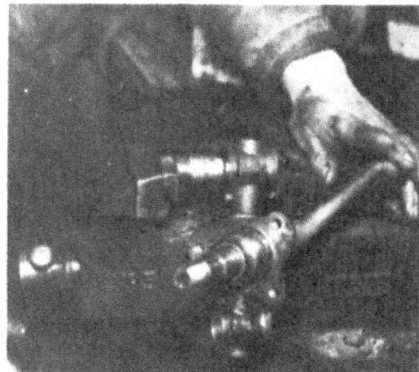

Pressing home the link pin bush. 2nd stage (Section 5.7)

Link pin bush correctly lined up with shoulder (Section 5.7)

Inner track rod arms fitted to drop arm (Section 6)

Outer track rod end being fitted to steering arm (Section 6)

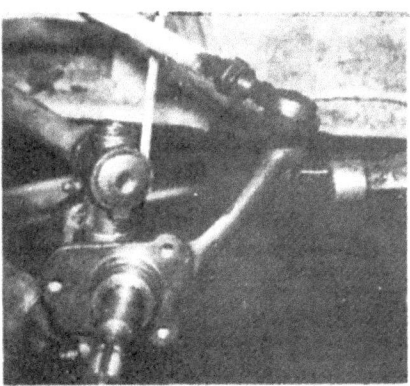

Fit the split pin to the nut (Section 6)

two torsion arms will have a tendency to force the two joints towards each other so before they can be taken out of the knuckle the two torsion arms must be spread apart. One way to do this is by using a scissor jack between them.

5. Finally the ball joints have to be pressed out of the torsion arms and to do this the torsion arms must be removed from the torsion bars. The renewal of the torsion bars is explained in the next section.

6. With the torsion bars removed we strongly recommend that you take them to the Volkswagen agent when the new parts are to be ordered and get him to fit them. Without the proper press tools it is easy to make a real nonsense of this job. If they are not properly fitted the whole safety and steering properties of the car are in jeopardy.

7. With new ball joints fitted the torsion arms are replaced and the knuckle refitted in the reverse order of removal. The top ball joint is fitted with an eccentric bush which controls the camber angle setting. This bush has a positioning notch in the edge which should be set to face directly forward. The nuts (new ones always) should be tightened to the specified torque.

7. Torsion Arms - Removal and Replacement

1. If indications show that a torsion arm is distorted or worn then it must be renewed.

2. First remove the wheel hub assembly and on earlier models take out the link pins and link nut. If a lower torsion arm is being removed the stabiliser bar must also be taken off (see Section 9).

3. Loosen the lock nuts on the ends of the torsion arm securing pins and then screw the pins right out. The torsion arm can then be pulled out of the axle tube. The torsion arm tube is positioned in two bearings - an inner bush and outer needle roller. If either of these is seriously worn causing radial movement of the torsion arm they should be renewed by a specialist with the correct tools. If you have already carried the dismantling of the front axle a considerable way it may be simplest to disconnect the brakes and steering gear as well and detach the whole assembly from the car. This can be done by removing the four securing screws from the centre section (see Section 12 for complete procedure).

4. Replacement is a reversal of the removal procedure.

8. Torsion Bars (Front) - Removal and Replacement

1. One would normally only need to remove a torsion bar if it broke and this is a rare occurrence.

2. First remove the hub and steering knuckle and torsion arm from one end of the torsion bar concerned. Then detach the steering knuckle from the torsion arm on the opposite side but do not remove the other arm from the torsion bar.

3. In the centre of the torsion bar tube slacken the locating pin locknut and remove the pin. The bar and the attached torsion arm may then be drawn out.

4. The torsion bar is composed of a number of leaves and this number varies between models and over the years. Make sure that any replacement is of the correct type.

5. When refitting a torsion bar make sure first it is liberally coated with grease and position it so that the recesses for the locating pins will line up. Fix the centre pin and locknut and then reassemble the torsion arm and steering assemblies in the reverse order of dismantling.

9. Stabiliser Bar - Removal and Replacement

1. The stabiliser bar is fixed to the lower torsion arms on each side of the car and is clamped in position. The bar is held by special clamps secured by sliding clips. Lift up the lug on the end of the clip and slide it off the ends of the clamp which goes round metal securing plates.

2. When refitting the clamps and clips note that the tapered slot end goes towards the wheel and that the lugs which bend down on the clips point towards the centre of the car when being installed.

10. Dampers - Removal and Replacement

1. Rear dampers are simply removed by undoing the nut and bolt which secures them at top and bottom.

2. Front dampers can be a little more difficult due to the upper mounting which is through a horizontal plate. The buffer stud at the top is also detachable from the main piston rod of the damper.

3. Jack up the car and remove the wheel.

4. The steering tie rod on the same side should also be detached from the steering knuckle or it will be severely strained by the downward force exerted by the torsion bars when the damper is released.

5. The top hexagon nut of the damper should now be undone. If the whole rod turns, the hexagon on the buffer stud must be held with a 42 mm, thin open ended spanner. If difficulty is experienced the alternative is to unscrew the piston rod from the buffer stud now. This will make it easier to detach the damper from the bracket.

6. Remove the nut securing the lower end to the torsion arm and take the damper off.

7. If the upper mounting buffers and damper rings are damaged they should be renewed. The stud can be unscrewed from the piston rod to release the buffer.

8. The lower bush is a tight press fit. If this needs renewal use the new one and a piece of tube to press out the old one between the jaws of a vice.

9. When refitting the damper make sure that the buffer stud is screwed back tightly on to the piston rod and that the damper rings are fitted one each side of the mounting plate with the shoulders against the plate.

11. Torsion Bars (Rear) and Spring Plates - Removal, Replacement and Setting

1. Before any work can be carried out on the rear torsion bars and spring plates it is necessary to detach the rear axle tubes from the ends of the spring plates. To do this it will be first necessary to support the car firmly on axle stands under the rear jacking points and remove the wheels. The handbrake cables should be slackened off at the hand lever and the spring plate marked so that it can be lined up with the axle tube on replacement. Details of the foregoing are given in the sections dealing with transmission removal and axle shaft and tube removal. The damper should be disconnected at the lower mounting. The three large mounting bolts securing the axle tube flange to the plate must then be undone and the axle tube drawn back.

2. The spring plate butts up against a lug in the frame casting along its lower edge and to relieve residual tension in the torsion bar it must be sprung out so that it rides over the lug. This can be done quite easily with a tyre lever.

3. At this stage the setting of the suspension can be checked. The angle of the plate in this unstressed position should be somewhere between 11° and 18½° (see Specifications for model differences) from the horizontal line of the car. For this measurement therefore a spirit level and protractor are needed. The horizontal line of the car is taken from the bottom of the door opening in the body shell. Using a level and protractor work out how far this now deviates from the true horizontal.

4. Measure the angle of the spring plate from the true horizontal in the same way, eliminating any play there may be by lifting the plate while the measurement is taken.

5. Depending on which way the body deviates, the angle is added or subtracted to the plate angle to give the difference between the two. Reference to the sketch will illustrate the examples given below.

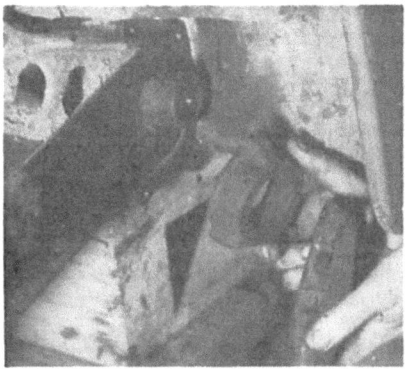

Rear suspension spring plate with rubber mounting and cover removed (Section 11)

Another view of the spring plate (Section 11)

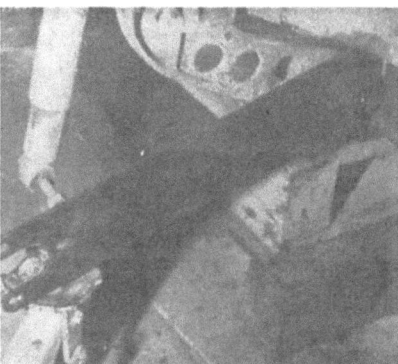

Close up view of the spring plate end (Section 11)

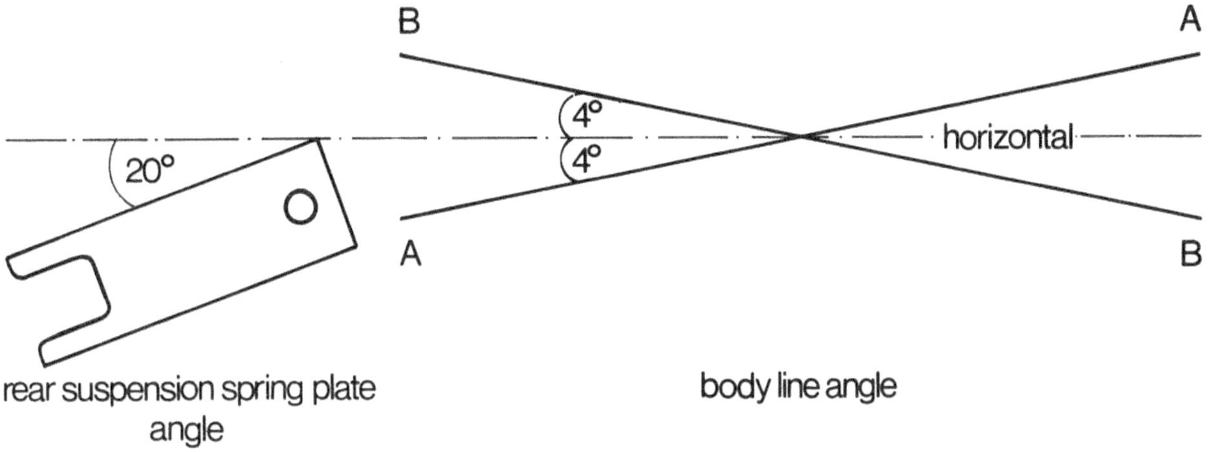

B   A

4°

4°

horizontal

20°

O

A   B

rear suspension spring plate
angle

body line angle

Fig. 11.5. Diagram to explain the calculation of the spring plate setting angle on the rear torsion bars (Section 11)

Body deviation angle 4°
Plate deviation angle 20°
Plate/body angle (AA) 16°
Plate body angle (BB) 24°

If the correct plate/body angle is 17° 30' then in situation AA the plate angle needs increasing by 1° 30'. In BB it needs decreasing by 6° 30'.

6. The torsion bars are splined at each end. The inner end anchors to a splined bracket fixed in the centre of the cross tube. The outer end is splined to the spring plate. The inner end has forty splines (9° per spline) and the outer has forty-four splines (8° 10' per spline) affording an alteration possibility in graduations of 50' (9° - 8° 10'). In example AA, if the inner end of the torsion bar is rotated anticlockwise two splines (18°) and the spring plate rotated clockwise on the outer end by two splines (16° 20') the net increase in the angle will be 18° - 16° 20' = 1° 40' which is as near as one can get. In example BB the inner end is rotated clockwise eight splines (72°) and the plate on the outer end rotated anti-clockwise eight splines (65° 20'). The net decrease in the angle is thus 6° 40'.

7. To withdraw the torsion bar sufficiently to rotate the splines for adjustment first remove the four screws which secure the cover clamping the rubber cushion mounting. The spring plate can now be pulled off the torsion bar and at the same time the inner end of the bar may be drawn out of the centre splined location. (Note that if one wishes to take the torsion bar right out then about five or six of the screws which hold the forward edge of the rear mudguard to the body must be removed. The mudguard can then be pulled out of the way. Torsion bars are not interchangeable side for side).

8. Having reset the torsion bar so that the plate angle is correct make sure that the rubber outer mounting bush is in good condition. Renew it if in doubt. Cover it with flake graphite (to prevent squeaking) and make sure it is installed the proper way up. (The top edge is marked 'Oben'). Before the cover is re-installed over the rubber bush it will be necessary to raise the plate above the stop lug on the frame casting. If this is not done now the pre-loading of the rubber bushing will be all wrong when the cover is put back. It will also be very nearly impossible to move the plate. To lift the plate put a jack under the end. If it looks as though the car is going to lift before the plate is up in position get some people to sit in the back seat for a minute or two. With the plate held in position replace the cover plate and setscrews.

9. It may be difficult to get the four plate securing screws to pick up their threads on replacement - particularly with a new bush. In such instances two larger screws will have to be obtained and used diagonally so that the plate may be drawn down enough to refit the shorter screws. (The short screws must be used finally otherwise the cover plate will not pull down far enough to stress the rubber bush properly).

10 With the cover tightened down the rear axle tube may be re-assembled to the spring plate.

11 The angle adjustment of the spring plates must be the same on both sides of the car.

12 If the spring plates have been renewed or any other work has been carried out on the rear suspension which could affect the alignment then it is important that the camber and toe-out settings (yes - toe-out on the rear wheels!) be checked with optical alignment equipment. It would also be timely to mention here that if the rear suspension spring plate settings are purposely altered to give an increased or reduced ground clearance then the effects on handling under certain circumstances are, to say the least, unusual. Tyre wear is also greatly increased if the rear wheel alignment is incorrect.

12. Front Axle Assembly - Removal Complete

1. In certain circumstances, such as damage, which has caused the axle tubes to be bent or where the complete assembly is in need of thorough overhaul and checking, it may be advantageous to remove it as an assembly and dismantle it afterwards. The sequence of operations to be followed and details of the procedure for each stage can be found in the appropriate sections.

1. Detach the flexible fuel hose under the fuel tank and plug or clip it.
2. Remove the fuel tank.
3. Detach the horn cable from the steering column and uncouple the flange of the steering column where it joins the steering box.
4. Unclip the split pin or circlip from the end of the speedometer cable in the left front wheel bearing dust cap. Pull the cable out.
5. Undo the hydraulic brake fluid lines at the unions where the brackets on the axle tube are fitted.
6. Undo the steering damper mounting bolt at the axle end and then undo the two track rod ends on the long track rod. Take off the track rod and damper together.
7. Remove the two body securing screws on the upper side of the top axle tube.
8. Support the axle securely and remove the four setscrews holding the assembly to the frame head.
9. The complete unit can now be lowered and taken out.

13. Steering Gear - Removal and Replacement

1. The steering gear is mounted on the upper axle tube and held by a clamp. It is connected to the steering column by a flanged coupling.
2. The simplest way to disconnect the gear from the track rods is to pull the drop arm off the shaft with the tie-rods still attached. This can be done after undoing the drop arm clamping screw and turning the wheels to a position where the arm can be drawn away.
3. Moving to the coupling flange undo the clip holding the horn wire and then remove the two nuts and bolts from the flange.
4. Before undoing the two bolts which clamp the steering box to the upper axle tube it is important to make sure that you know the correct position to refit it. Later models have a cut-out in the clamp plate which locates over a welded stud on the tube. Earlier models did not have this positive location reference so it is advisable to make clear marks on the casing and axle tube to aid positioning later. On these early models the distance from the steering gear filler plug centre line to the axle tube centre is 10¼ inches.
5. Once the correct repositioning of the steering box is assured undo the clamp bolts and take it off.
6. When replacing the later versions of the clamps with positive location make sure that the clamp is fitted the correct way round. There will be two numbers on it, 13 and 14, next to the two cut-outs. No. 13 is the one for Beetles and the arrow should point forward with the cut-out on the left.
7. Always use new lock plates on the clamp bolts and bend the tabs down over the hexagon flats. It is also recommended that new self locking nuts are used for the column coupling flange.
8. The steering geometry should be checked for alignment after replacing the steering gear.

14. Steering Gear - Adjustments

1. If play in the steering can be positively traced to the steering gear rather than wear in the track rod ends or suspension linkage it is possible to make certain adjustments (with the steering gear fitted in the car) to improve the situation. Play occurs at two main points - in the worm shaft bearings and between the worm and sector (early models) or worm and roller (later models).
2. Dealing with the early models first (identifiable by the presence of an oil filler plug in the top cover) the adjustment for the worm shaft bearings is by a bronze sleeve clamped into the shaft housing. This sleeve has a spiral groove located under the housing pinch bolt and if revolved it moves up or down. (The principle is identical to the front suspension link pins). This adjustment is the one to make first although the other adjuster screw for the sector shaft should be

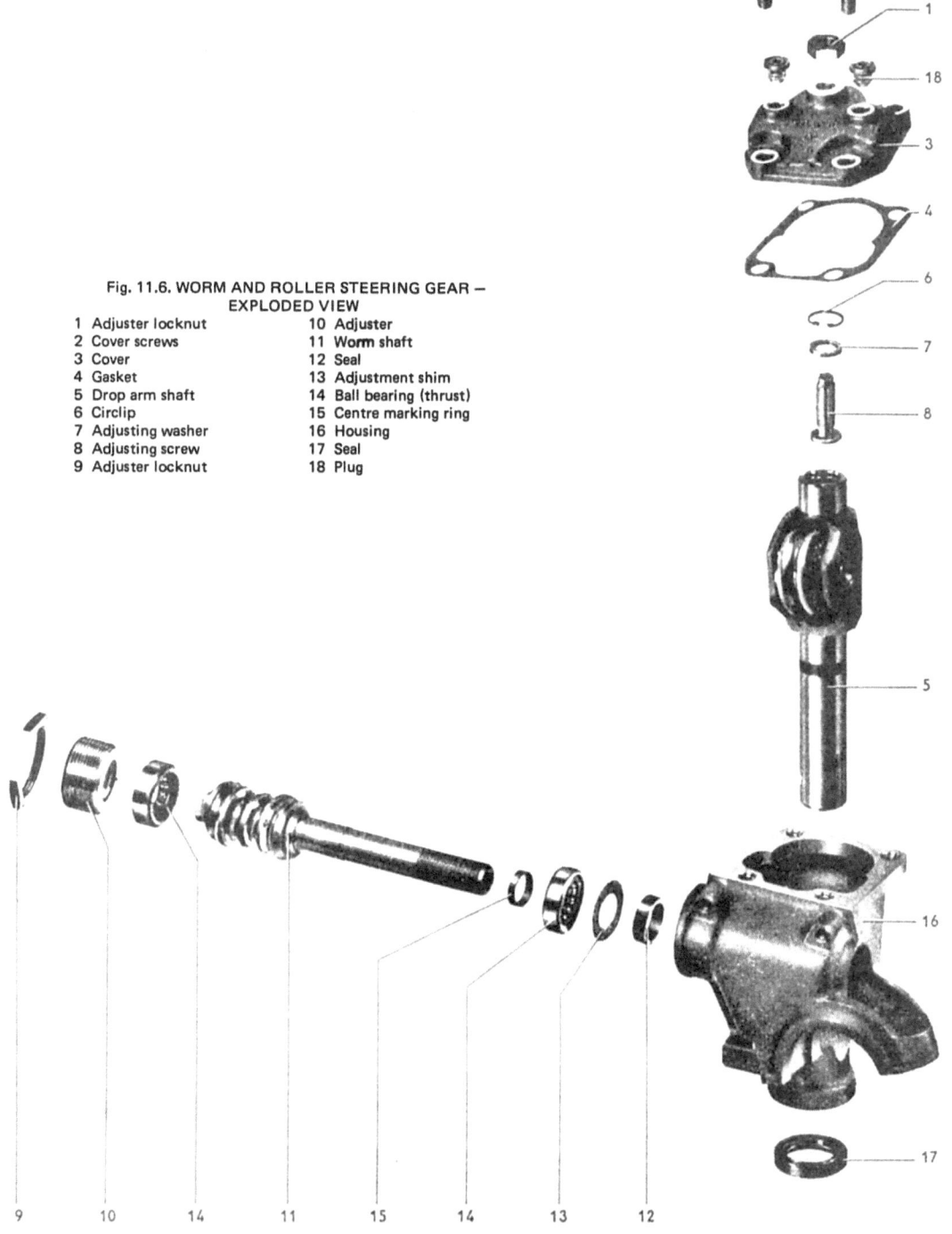

Fig. 11.6. WORM AND ROLLER STEERING GEAR —
EXPLODED VIEW

1 Adjuster locknut	10 Adjuster
2 Cover screws	11 Worm shaft
3 Cover	12 Seal
4 Gasket	13 Adjustment shim
5 Drop arm shaft	14 Ball bearing (thrust)
6 Circlip	15 Centre marking ring
7 Adjusting washer	16 Housing
8 Adjusting screw	17 Seal
9 Adjuster locknut	18 Plug

slackened off before making the adjustment.

3. First raise the wheels off the ground. Slacken the sector shaft adjuster locknut and screw and then slacken the pinch bolt round the worm bearing adjuster sleeve. The sleeve should then be rotated to take up any slack that exists. Do not overdo it and keep turning the steering wheel to ensure that the shaft turns smoothly from lock to lock. Any roughness or 'lumpiness' persisting indicates wear that is beyond adjustment.

4. When the sleeve has been adjusted retighten the pinch bolt.

5. The second adjustment - that of the sector shaft - is made by the screw on top of the steering box which can be reached through a small cover in the rear side of the spare wheel well. With the wheels in the straight ahead position screw in the adjuster until it will go no further and then back it off 1/8 of a revolution. Tighten the locknut and check the steering from lock to lock. Any binding which occurs must be relieved by backing off the sector shaft adjuster nut. If this results in play developing again it means that the parts are too worn for rectification by simple adjustment.

6. After adjustment make sure the oil level is correct by topping up with Hypoy 90 to the lower edge of the filler plug hole.

7. On the later versions (identified by two plastic plugs in the top - grease filled) the principles are the same but the adjustment of the worm shaft bearings can be made at the lower end by means of a plug screw held by a large (41 mm) locknut.

8. To adjust the steering installed in the car first note that there are three main causes of play, viz:

    a) axial play of the worm spindle
    b) play between roller and worm
    c) axial play of roller

Should the first two adjustments not solve the problem the third requires dismantling of the box.

9. To check the worm axial play (i.e. in the bearings) first set the wheels straight ahead and move the steering wheel from side to side until resistance is felt. The circumferential movement of the wheel should not exceed 25 mm total across this central position. If it does, begin the adjustment check by getting hold of the steering column at the coupling (with the wheels now lifted from the ground) and turning it from side to side. Any end float in the shaft will be visible.

10 To adjust the play turn the steering to either side on full lock. Then loosen the large locknut on the adjuster plug at the lower end of the steering box and with a suitable box spanner turn the adjuster until no more end play can be discerned in the worm shaft. Hold the adjuster and tighten the locknut. Turn the steering from lock to lock. There should be no tight spots whatsoever.

11 If the original overall steering play (as measured at the steering wheel) is still not eliminated, go to the next step which is adjustment of the play between the worm and roller. With the front wheels still off the ground set the steering to the straight ahead position.

12 Turn the steering wheel 90° only to left or right.

13 Loosen the drop arm shaft adjuster locknut which can be reached through the hole in the floor pan. Turn the adjuster anti-clockwise about one turn. Then turn it clockwise until the roller can be felt just to make contact with the worm. Do not overtighten.

14 Hold the screw and tighten the locknut.

15 Lower the vehicle to the ground and with the steering wheel set in turn at the 90° position both left and right, check that the circumference backlash does not exceed 25 mm at each position. If it does repeat the adjustment on the affected side only.

16 Before a conclusive road test can be made the toe-in adjustment must be checked. Then go on the road and check that the steering still has its self centring action. If it does not then the drop arm shaft adjustment must be slackened off. Otherwise damage can occur to either the worm or roller.

17 If neither of the foregoing adjustments rectifies the play in the steering gear then the third involves dismantling the assembly to check the axial play on the roller itself. If this is excessive the whole unit needs renewal or reconditioning.

15. Steering Gear - Dismantling and Overhaul

1. The decision to dismantle and rebuild a steering gear assembly will depend to a large extent on the availability of parts. It is inevitable that if adjustments fail to rectify play adequately then most of the interior components will need renewal. The later type of steering gear with the hour glass worm and roller is subject to some very critical settings and requires shims and setting jigs which only a Volkswagen agency is likely to have. We do not therefore recommend that the do-it-yourself owner attempts this job. The time and cost expended to do the job properly cannot justify any saving over the purchase of a replacement unit.

2. Early models - with the parallel worm and sector are easier to dismantle and reset but parts availability must first be checked as this type was discontinued in 1961. However, for those who have been able to obtain the spares the basic procedure is given.

3. Having removed the unit from the car, find a piece of tube the same size as an axle tube and clamp the steering gear to it. Then clamp the tube in a vice. This will give a firm working support.

4. Undo the coupling flange pinch bolt and pull the pinch bolt off the end of the worm shaft.

5. Remove the drop arm and the shims behind it.

6. Undo the four screws holding the top cover in place and lift out the thrust pin and spring from the end of the sector shaft.

7. Lift out the sector shaft and the bronze worm nut.

8. Undo the pinch bolt clamping the adjusting sleeve and the adjusting sleeve and worm shaft can be lifted out together. With the adjusting sleeve taken off the worm shaft the thrust bearing can be lifted off. The lower bearing can be removed inwards if the seal plug is first driven out from the inside.

9. It is best to renew all worn parts as a set, i.e. new worm shaft, sector shaft and worm nut. Check also the fit of the new sector shaft in the bushing in the casing. Any wear at this point will nullify most of the improvement contemplated from renewing the other parts. Great care must also be taken not to damage the oil seals - one inside the adjusting sleeve and the other in the sector shaft bush. Fit new ones anyway if possible.

10 Reassembly is a reversal of the dismantling procedure. Take care not to damage the seals and use sealing compound for the lower worm shaft bearing plug.

16. Steering Wheel and Column - Removal and Replacement

1. The steering wheel is fixed to the column on a splined boss. Before starting to take it off detach the battery earth lead to prevent accidental short circuits. Carefully prise away the cover in the centre of the wheel and then disconnect the wire from the horn switch underneath. Remove the nut and spring washer in the centre of the wheel and pull off the wheel together with the horn ring.

2. If it is wished to remove the column (shaft) it is not necessary to take the wheel off at this stage although it is easier to slacken the nut now. If the car is fitted with a steering lock, however, the wheel must be taken off. Then the indicator switch must be taken off as well.

3. Next go to the coupling at the bottom end of the shaft and disconnect the horn cable connection there. On some early models this will consist of a carbon brush running on a brass slip ring mounted higher up the column. Release the brush spring and lift out the carbon brush.

4. Still at the coupling remove the single screw which clamps the shaft into the upper coupling half.

5. The column may now be drawn out of the tube with or without the steering wheel as appropriate. Where there is a steering lock fitted take care not to damage the bearing in the process.

6. The bearing is now accessible in the tube and can be renewed if necessary. On models with a steering lock it will come out with the column. The bearing inner support ring and thrust spring are held to

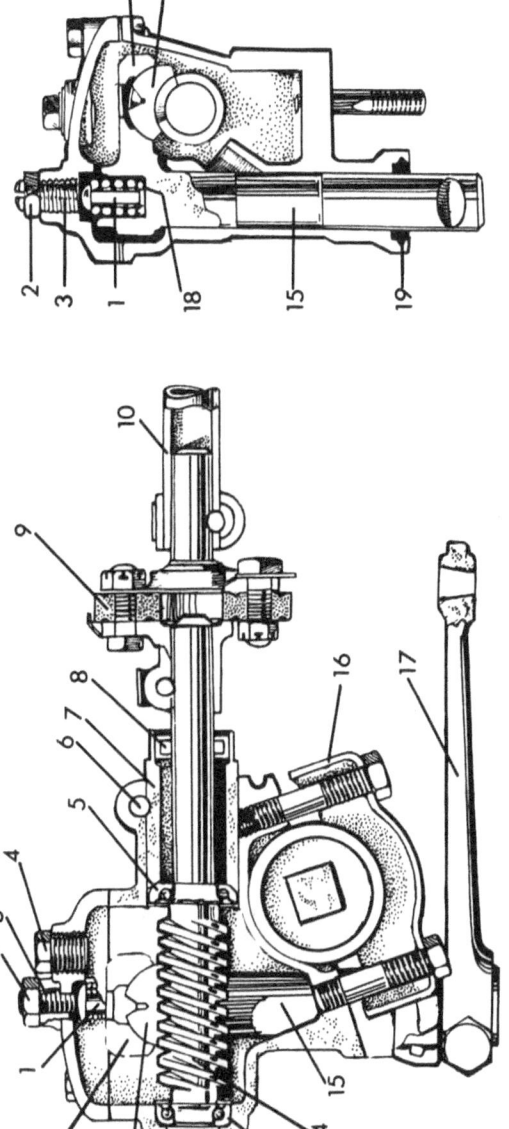

Fig. 11.7. STEERING GEAR. EARLY TYPE WORM AND SELECTOR. CROSS SECTIONS.

1 Pin
2 Locknut
3 Adjuster screw
4 Oil filler plug
5 Bearing
6 Pinch bolt
7 Sleeve
8 Oil seal
9 Flexible coupling
10 Steering shaft
11 Sector
12 Sector nut
13 Bearing
14 Worm shaft
15 Sector shaft
16 Mounting clamp
17 Pitman arm
18 Spring
19 Shaft seal

the top of the column by a circlip. The brass washer with the cut-out for the indicator cancellation is also held there. Renew the support ring if badly worn.

7. On models with steering locks fit the ball bearing to the column first.

8. Fit the bearing support ring, spring, brass washer and circlip.

9. Put the bearing in position in the tube for non-lock columns then replace the column shaft. The bearing on the column will have to be driven into the tube on the locked steering models.

10 Turn the brass washer on the column so that the cut-out portion faces exactly to the right with the wheels in the straight ahead position.

11 Replace the steering wheel with the spokes horizontal and with the tongue of the cancelling ring in the centre of the washer cut-out. Replace the spring washer and nut and secure the wheel by tightening the nut (36 lb/ft.).

12 Move the steering wheel and column in or out so that the gap between the lower edge of the wheel hub and the indicator switch sleeve is between 1 and 2 mm (.040 - .080 inch).

13 Using a new lock plate the screw clamping the bottom end of the column into the upper part of the mounting flange may now be tightened. Check finally that the wheels, steering wheel and indicator cancellation are all centred correctly.

17. Steering Track Rods and Joints - Removal and Replacement

1. From the drop arm (or steering arm) on the steering gear the movement is transmitted to each wheel by a track rod. The inner and outer ends each have a swivel ball joint which allows the variety of angles to be adopted by the wheels during movement of steering and suspension. If the track rods are bent, or of the incorrect length, or if the swivel joints are worn, the wheels will take up an incorrect position of alignment or, in the case of worn joints, be able to move independently of the steering gear. Both these conditions result in inaccurate steering and control.

2. Each ball joint is attached to the steering knuckle at the outer end, or drop arm at the inner end by a tapered pin through a tapered hole and secured by a hexagon nut. The joints are screwed on to the tie-rods with a left and right hand thread on each rod.

3. Jack up the car and remove the wheel(s). Remove the split pin from the hexagon nut and take off the nut. The joint pin may be a very tight fit. If you have no proper extractor hold a hammer to one side of the eye and strike opposite with another. This normally succeeds.

4. One track rod has the steering damper fitted into it so this must be detached from it if the whole rod is to be removed. If only the outer ball joints are being renewed it is, of course, unnecessary to detach the joints from the drop arm.

5. The ball joints are screwed into the rod and held by one of two methods - both of which may be used on the same vehicle. The ends of the tie-rods are split and these are clamped to the threaded end of the ball joint. The difference is in the method of clamping. One uses a simple U clamp and pinch bolt. The other method uses a sleeve with a tapered inner face and a hexagon outer face. This taper is forced up to the matching tapered end of the tie rod by a second hexagon nut. Between the two there is a double tab washer. Whichever type is used slacken it off but before screwing out the joint take careful note of its position (by counting the number of visible threads). This will help to ensure that the toe-in setting is disturbed as little as possible when it is replaced.

6. When obtaining a new joint make quite sure that the correct handed thread is obtained.

7. Screw the new track rod end on to the rod but do not lock it tight yet.

8. If the steering damper has been detached at one end take the opportunity to check it as described in the next section.

9. If a track rod is bent it must be replaced with a new one.

Attempts to straighten it can only weaken the metal and may result in fracture with disastrous results on the road. If the rubber bush for the steering damper in the long rod is in poor condition take the opportunity to renew it.

10 It is most important that the rubber seals on the track rod joints are intact and capable of retaining grease. On early models fitted with grease nipples this problem is not so critical because grease may be added easily. On later, sealed joints any grease which escapes or which is contaminated needs special attention. It is possible to fit new seals and have them repacked but more often than not it is too late by the time the fault is seen in which case the joint must be renewed.

11 When the track rods are fitted with the ends replace the taper pins into their respective eyes and refit and tighten the hexagon nuts to the correct torque (see specifications - depending on type of thread fitted). Replace the split pins for earlier types after lining up the holes.

12 It is important to see that both ball joints are correctly aligned on the rod so push both of them either fully forward or backwards. Then tighten the nut or pinch bolt and bend over the lock tabs.

13 It is important to have the wheel alignment checked properly at the earliest opportunity.

18. Steering Damper - Removal, Checking and Replacement

1. The steering damper is a double acting piston which serves to smooth out vibration and shocks through the steering. One end is attached to a bracket on the top axle tube in a rubber bush. The other is fitted similarly to the longer of the two track rods.

2. If the bushes are worn allowing play the damper and tie rod should be removed and new bushes fitted. New bushes comprise a rubber buffer with a steel central sleeve. They can be cut or driven out and new ones pressed in between the jaws of a vice.

3. Remove the two securing bolts which will necessitate jacking up the car and removing the front wheels.

4. To test the action of the damper push and pull the piston throughout its full travel. There should be no roughness or variations in resistance anywhere along the travel of the piston. If there is it should be renewed. Note that the damper is different between vehicles with right and left hand drive.

5. Replace the damper (with the piston end inwards) by fitting the securing bolts and nuts and tightening them to the specified torques.

19. Steering Geometry and Wheel Alignment

1. The correct alignment of the front wheels does not normally alter and the need for checking and re-aligning only normally occurs after certain conditions, namely:

   a) renewal of track rod joints
   b) damage to front suspension or steering linkage

Theoretically, if worn ball joints, wheel bearings and so on, are all renewed the steering geometry will automatically be correct. This, of course, presumes that no adjustment has been made in a misguided attempt to compensate for wear. If adjustments have been made then, of course, when the various parts are renewed the steering will have to be re-aligned.

2. The only adjustments which can be made to the geometry (except of course outside the standard specifications) are on the track rods or the king pin carrier - the latter by link pin shims or the eccentric bush on the upper ball joint of later models. Alteration of the king pin inclination automatically alters the camber angle because the relationship between these two is fixed in the design of the king pin carrier/steering knuckle assembly.

3. Adjustments to steering geometry should never be made in a

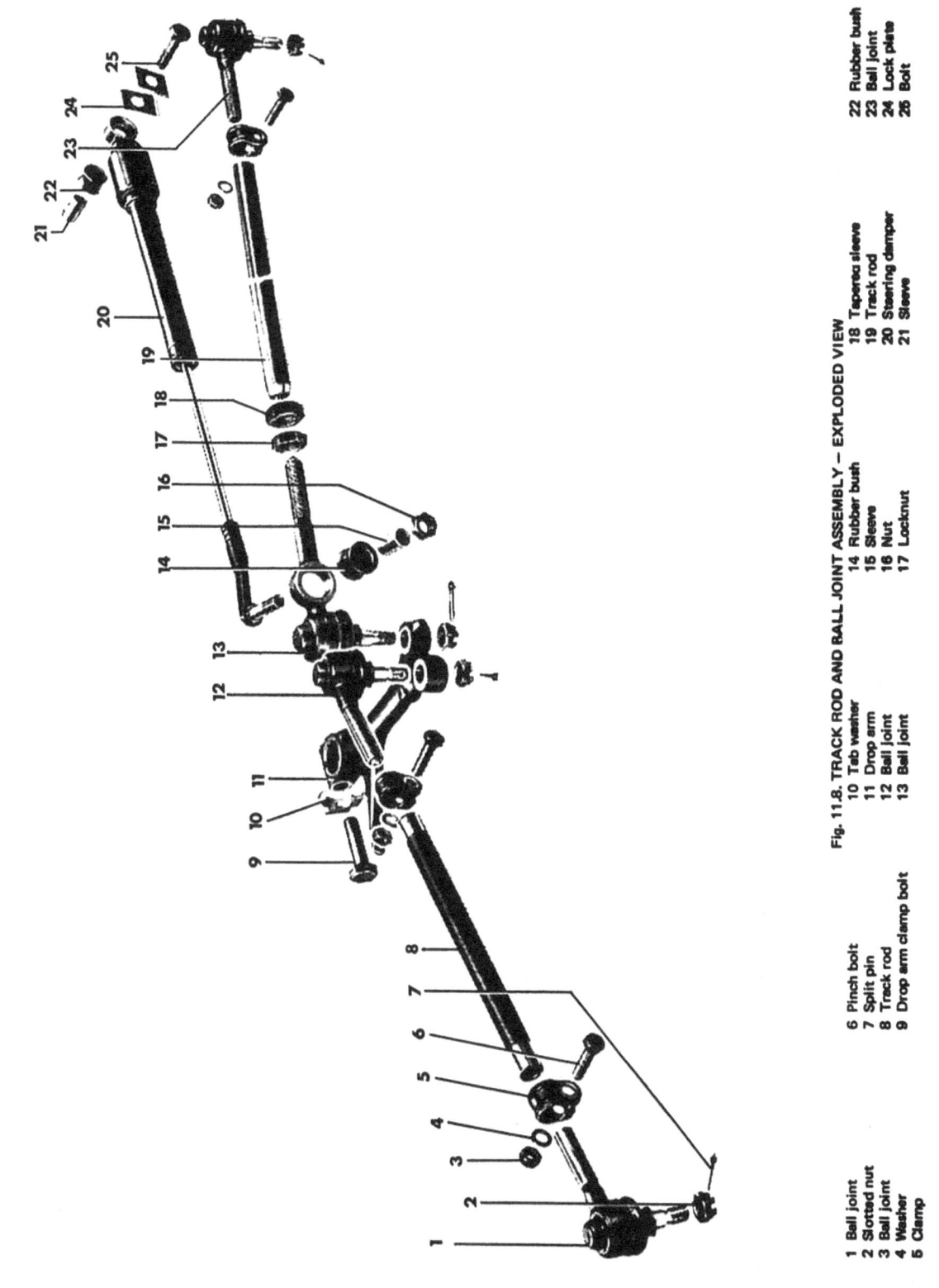

Fig. 11.8. TRACK ROD AND BALL JOINT ASSEMBLY – EXPLODED VIEW

1 Ball joint	6 Pinch bolt	10 Tab washer	14 Rubber bush	18 Tapered sleeve	22 Rubber bush
2 Slotted nut	7 Split pin	11 Drop arm	15 Sleeve	19 Track rod	23 Ball joint
3 Ball joint	8 Track rod	12 Ball joint	16 Nut	20 Steering damper	24 Lock plate
4 Washer	9 Drop arm clamp bolt	13 Ball joint	17 Locknut	21 Sleeve	25 Bolt
5 Clamp					

haphazard manner. In order to check all the angles correctly proper equipment is needed. Furthermore it is quite pointless trying to re-align the steering if one or more of the components is worn. A reputable garage would not normally undertake to re-adjust steering which had significant wear - although they may be prepared to inform you of the state of the alignment.

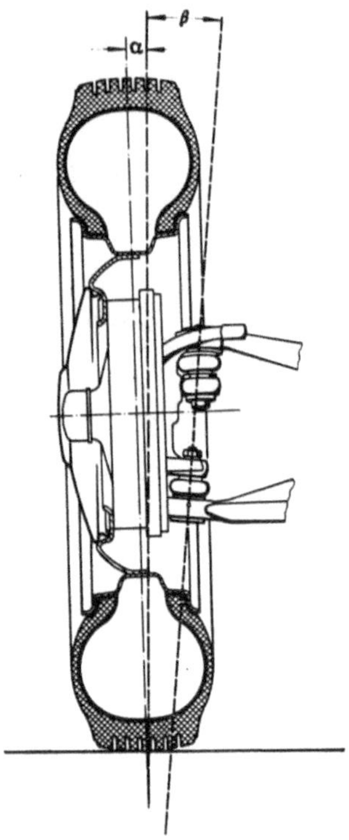

Fig. 11.9. Diagram illustrating camber and king pin inclination
Angle 'A' = camber, Angle 'B' = king pin inclination

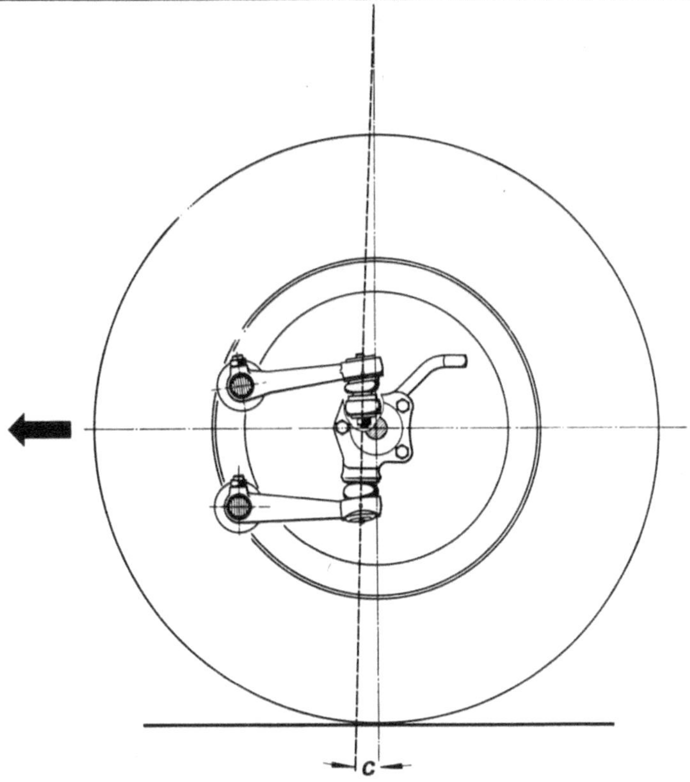

Fig. 11.10. Diagram illustrating caster angle. Angle 'C' = caster angle

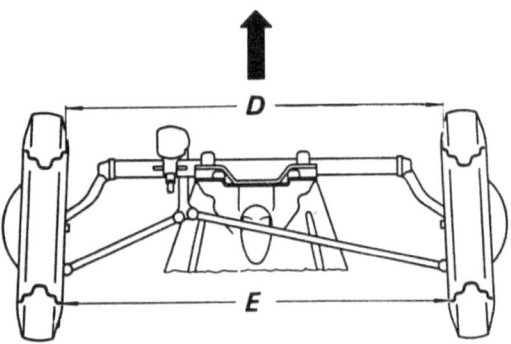

Fig. 11.11. Diagram illustrating toe in. 'D' is smaller than 'E' = toe in

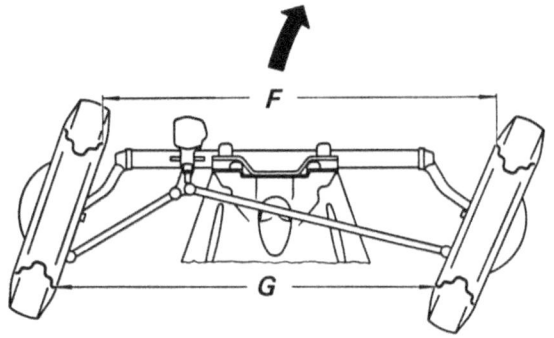

Fig. 11.12. Diagram illustrating toe out. 'F' is greater than 'G' = toe out

Fault Finding Chart - Suspension - Dampers - Steering

Before diagnosing faults from the following chart, check that any irregularities are not caused by:

1 Binding brakes
2 Incorrect 'mix' of radial and cross-ply tyres
3 Incorrect tyre pressures
4 Misalignment of the bodyframe or rear axle tubes

Symptom	Reason/s	Remedy
Steering wheel can be moved considerably before any sign of movement of the wheels is apparent	Wear in the steering linkage, gear and column coupling	Check movement in all joints and steering gear and overhaul and renew as required.
Vehicle difficult to steer in a consistent straight line - wandering	As above	As above.
	Wheel alignment incorrect (indicated by excessive or uneven tyre wear)	Check wheel alignment
	Front wheel hub bearings loose or worn	Adjust or renew as necessary
	Worn king pins, link pins or ball joints	Renew as necessary
Steering stiff and heavy	Incorrect wheel alignment (indicated by excessive or uneven tyre wear)	Check wheel alignment
	Excessive wear or seizure in one or more of the joints in the steering linkage	Repair as necessary
	Excessive wear in the steering gear unit	Adjust if possible or renew
Wheel wobble and vibration	Road wheels out of balance	Balance wheels.
	Road wheels buckled	Check for damage.
	Wheel alignment incorrect	Check wheel alignment.
	Wear in the steering linkage or suspension	Check and renew as necessary
Excessive pitching and rolling on corners and during braking	Defective dampers and/or broken torsion bar	Check and renew as necessary

Chapter 12 Bodywork and underframe

Contents

1. General Description

The bodywork of the Volkswagen is noted for its simplicity, rigidity and corrosion free properties.

It consists basically of a flat floor pan stiffened down the centre with a fabricated sheet steel tube. At the front is a 'frame head' to which the front axle assembly is bolted and at the rear a 'frame fork' into which the engine/transmission assembly is bolted. Just forward of the frame fork a lateral tube is welded to which the rear suspension spring plate supports are fitted at the outer ends. The frame tunnel is closed in underneath and carries inside it the necessary guide tubes for brake cables, heater cables, clutch cable, accelerator cable and gear change connecting rods.

The bodywork is a unit fabricated from steel panels welded together with the exception of sill panels, wings, doors and engine and luggage compartment lids. The unit is bolted to the floor frame. The doors, wings, lids and sill panels are bolted to the body and are readily detachable.

The whole frame body assembly is remarkable for its lack of 'nooks and crannies' where water/dirt can collect and is notable for being almost airtight (it is virtually impossible to slam the doors shut with the windows closed due to the air pressure build up inside).

2. Maintenance - Bodywork and Underframe

1. The Volkswagen is a particularly easy car to keep clean due to its aerodynamic shape. The general condition of a car's bodywork is the one thing that significantly affects its value. Maintenance is easy but needs to be regular and particular. Neglect, particularly after minor damage, can lead quickly to further deterioration and costly repair bills. It is important also to keep watch on those parts of the car not immediately visible, for instance, the underside, inside all the wheel arches and the engine compartment.
2. The basic maintenance routine for the bodywork is washing - preferably with a lot of water, from a hose. This will remove all the solids which may have stuck to the car. It is important to flush these off in such a way as to prevent grit from scratching the finish. The wheel arches and underbody need washing in the same way to remove any accumulated mud which will retain moisture and tend to encourage rust. Paradoxically enough, the best time to clean the underbody and wheel arches is in wet weather when the mud is thoroughly wet and soft. In very wet weather the underbody is usually cleaned of large accumulations automatically and this is a good time for inspection.
3. Periodically it is a good idea to have the whole of the underside of the car steam cleaned, engine compartment included, so that a thorough inspection can be carried out to see what minor repairs and renovations are necessary. Steam cleaning is available at many garages and is necessary for removal of accumulations of oily grime which sometimes cakes thick in certain areas near the engine and transmission. If steam facilities are not available, there are one or two excellent grease solvents available which can be brush applied. The dirt can then be hosed off.
4. After washing paintwork, wipe it off with a chamois leather to give an unspotted clear finish. A coat of clear protective wax polish will give added protection against chemical pollutants in the air. If the paintwork sheen has dulled or oxidised, use a cleaner/polisher combination to restore the brilliance of the shine. This requires a little more effort, but is usually caused because regular washing has been neglected. Always check that door and ventilator opening drain holes and pipes are completely clear so that water can drain out. Bright work should be treated the same way as paintwork. Windscreens and windows can be kept clear of the smeary film which often appears if a little ammonia is added to the water. If they are scratched, a good rub with a proprietary metal polish will often clear them. Never use any form of wax or chromium polish on glass.

3. Maintenance - Upholstery and Floor Coverings

1. Mats and carpets should be brushed or vacuum cleaned regularly to keep them free of grit. If they are badly stained remove them from the car for scrubbing or sponging and make quite sure they are dry before replacement. Seats and interior trim panels can be kept clean

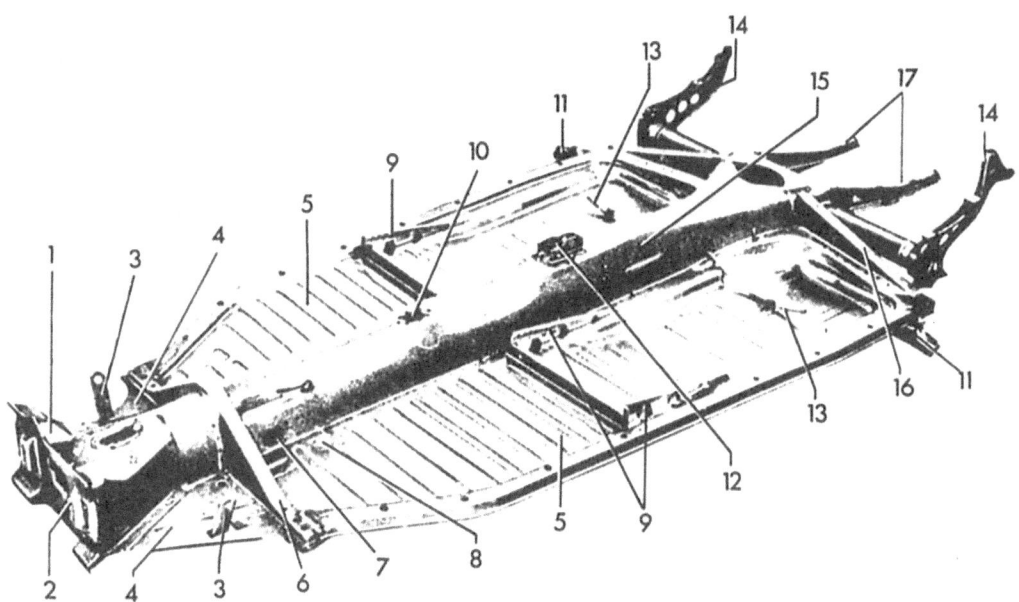

Fig. 12.1. MAIN FRAME

1 Frame head
2 Frame head front plate
3 Brake hose bracket
4 Frame head plate
5 Floor pan

6 Front cross bracing
7 Pedal cluster shaft aperture
8 Accelerator pedal mounting
  (LHD)
9 Seat runners

10 Gear lever hole
11 Jacking points
12 Handbrake lever mounting
13 Heater control cable tube
   (later models)

14 Spring plate brackets
15 Safety belt anchorages
16 Rear cross bracing
17 Frame fork

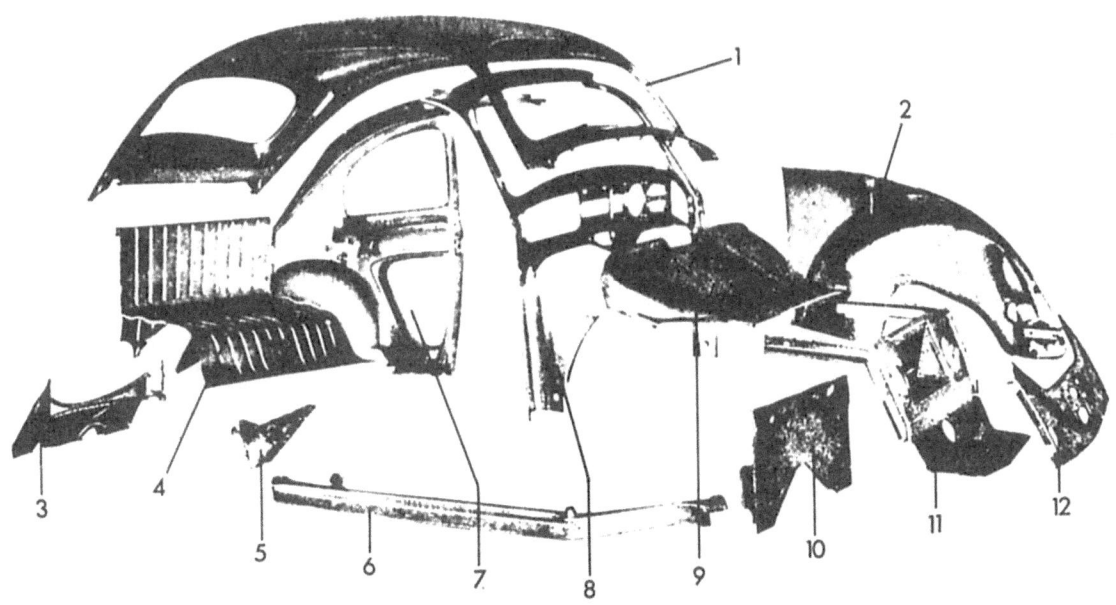

Fig. 12.2. BODY — EXPLODED VIEW OF WELDED SECTIONS

1 Roof
2 Side panel
3 Rear apron

4 Front compartment floor plate
5 Rear cross member
6 Side member

7 Quarter panel
8 Instrument panel
9 Luggage compartment panel

10 Cross panel
11 Reinforcement panel
12 Front apron

by a wipe over with a damp cloth. If they do become stained (which can be more apparent on light coloured upholstery) use a little liquid detergent and a soft nailbrush to scour the grime out of the grain of the material. Do not forget to keep the head lining clean in the same way as the upholstery. When using liquid cleaners inside the car do not over-wet the surfaces being cleaned. Excessive damp could get into the seams and padded interior causing stains, offensive odours or even rot. If the inside of the car gets wet accidentally, it is worthwhile taking some trouble to dry it out properly, particularly where carpets are involved. Do NOT leave oil or electric heaters inside the car for this purpose.

4. Minor Body Repairs

1. A car which does not suffer some minor damage to the bodywork from time to time is the exception rather than the rule. Even presuming the gatepost is never scraped or the door opened against a wall or high kerb, there is always the likelihood of gravel and grit being thrown up and chipping the surface, particularly at the lower edges of the doors and sills.
2. If the damage is merely a paint scrape which has not reached the metal base, delay is not critical, but where bare metal is exposed action must be taken immediately before rust sets in.
3. The average owner will normally keep the following 'first aid' materials available which can give a professional finish for minor jobs:

    a) A resin based filler paste.
    b) Matched paint either for spraying in a gun or in an aerosol can.
    c) Fine cutting paste.
    d) Medium and fine grade wet and dry abrasive paper.

4. Where the damage is superficial (i.e. not down to the bare metal and not dented) fill the scratch or chip with sufficient filler to smooth the area, rub down with paper and apply the matching paint.
5. Where the bodywork is scratched down to the metal, but not dented, clean the metal surface thoroughly and apply a suitable metal primer first. Fill up the scratch as necessary with filler and rub down with wet and dry paper. Apply the matching colour paint.
6. If more than one coat of colour is required rub down each coat with cutting paste before applying the next.
7. If the bodywork is dented, first beat out the dent as near as possible to conform with the original contour. Avoid using steel hammers - use hardwood mallets or similar and always support the back of the panel being beaten with a hardwood or metal 'dolly'. In areas where severe creasing and buckling has occurred it will be virtually impossible to reform the metal to the original shape. In such instances a decision should be made whether or not to cut out the damaged piece or attempt to re-contour over it with filler paste. In large areas where the metal panel is seriously damaged or rusted, the repair is to be considered major and it is often better to replace a panel or sill section with the appropriate part supplied as a spare. When using filler paste in largish quantities, make sure the directions are carefully followed. It is false economy to try and rush the job as the correct hardening time must be allowed between stages or before finishing. With thick application the filler usually has to be applied in layers - allowing time for each layer to harden. Sometimes the original paint colour will have faded and it will be difficult to obtain an exact colour match. In such instances it is a good shceme to select a complete panel - such as a door, or boot lid, and spray the whole panel. Differences will be less apparent where there are obvious divisions between the original and re-sprayed areas.

5. Major Body Repairs

1. Volkswagen owners are fortunate in that what would be relatively severe damage in some cars is not so for them. This is where wings or sills are badly damaged beyond economical repair. Being bolted on they can be removed and a new unit fitted by the owner (see subsequent sections).
2. Where serious damage has occurred or large areas need renewal due to neglect, it means certainly that completely new sections or panels will need welding in and this is best left to professionals. If the damage is due to impact it will also be necessary to completely check the alignment of the body structure. In such instances the services of a Volkswagen agent with specialist checking jigs are essential. If a body is left mis-aligned it is first of all dangerous as the car will not handle properly - and secondly, uneven stresses will be imposed on the steering, engine and transmission, causing abnormal wear or complete failure. Tyre wear will also be excessive.

6. Front Wings - Removal and Replacement

1. Jack up the car and remove the headlamp and direction indicator lamp housing.
2. Pull the wires and grommets out of the holes where they pass through the wing.
3. Remove the nut and bolt holding the wing to the sill panel and subsequently the nine bolts holding the wing to the bodywork. It is more than likely that these bolts are difficult to move. If this is so clean the heads and surround thoroughly and use plenty of penetrating fluid to ease the threads. If resort to cutting is necessary - with either saw or chisel - take care not to damage or bend the bodywork. One of the safest ways if you have a power drill and stone is to grind the heads off stubborn bolts first and then drill out the shank. On such occasions the holes will need retapping - probably for an oversize bolt.
4. When clear lift off the wing and beading strip.
5. It is a good idea to fit a new beading strip when putting the wing back. If the wing is a new one do any necessary paint spraying before fitting.
6. Use new bolts and treat them with grease or some anti-seize compound before fitting. There should be a new rubber washer on the bolt between wing and sill panel.
7. The headlamp must be realigned after replacement. Make sure all the wires and grommets are properly replaced to avoid chafing or strain which could lead to failure.

7. Rear Wings - Removal and Replacement

1. The principle of removing and replacing the rear wing is exactly the same as that for the front wing as described in the previous section except that the rear bumper and bumper brackets should be removed first. Do not forget to remove the bolt securing the wing to the sill panel.
2. On replacement fit new beading and rubber washer between wing and sill as required.

8. Sill Panels - Removal and Replacement

1. The sill panel is bolted to the body and to the wings at the front and rear. Once all the bolts have been removed - bearing in mind the precautions for stubborn bolts as mentioned in the section on front wing removal - the sill can be lifted off.
2. When fitting a new sill panel make sure the washers fit correctly over the slots and when tightening the bolts tighten up the ones to the bodywork before the ones to the wings.

9. Front Bumper - Removal and Replacement

1. The bumper can be removed together with the brackets or otherwise as wished. The bumper can be detached from the brackets by undoing the two screws holding it to each bracket. To remove the brackets unship the spare wheel from its well and undo the two screws holding the brackets in place.

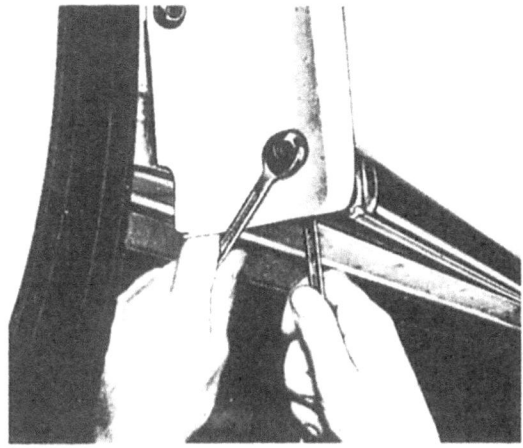

Fig. 12.3. Removing front wing to sill panel bolt

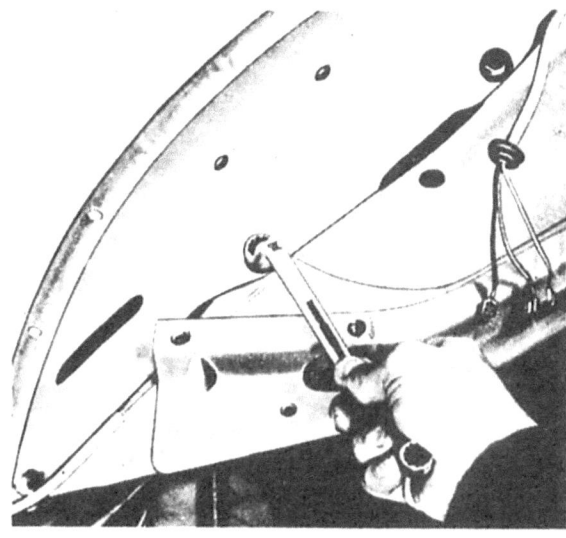

Fig. 12.4. Removing rear wing bolts

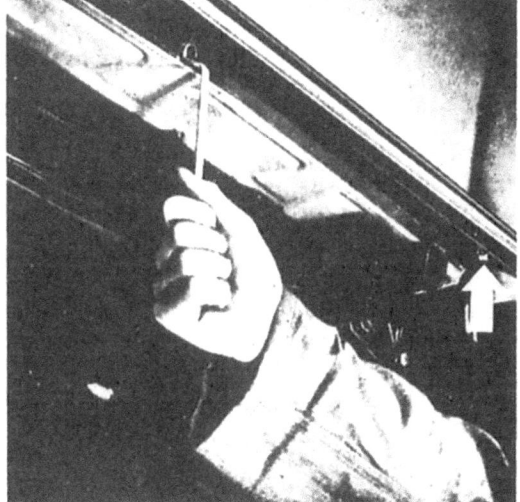

Fig. 12.5. Removing sill panel - Note bolt arrowed joining seal to rear wing

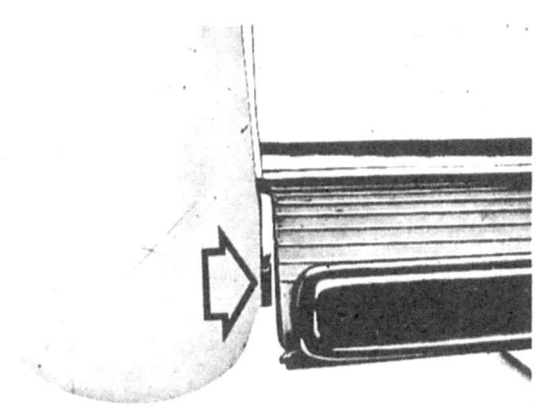

Fig. 12.6. Rubber washer (arrowed) between wing and sill panel

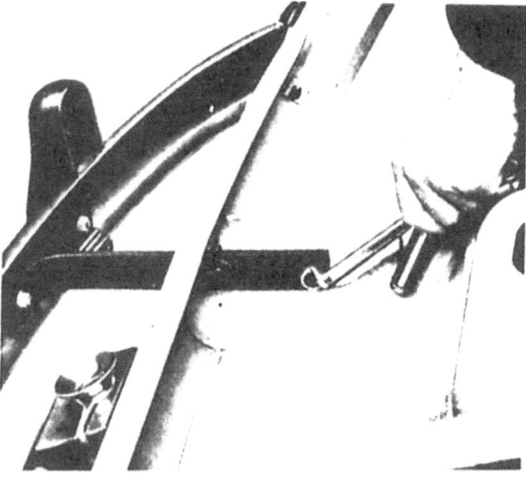

Fig. 12.7. Undoing front bumper bracket mounting bolts

2. When replacing a bumper assemble the bumper to the brackets (loosely at first) and then bolt the brackets in position. If the bumper is not level or the gaps at each end between the bumper and wing are uneven then the brackets must be bent (if the bumper is new).

3. Make sure the bracket rubber seals are in good condition if you wish to prevent the spare wheel and well getting wet and rusty.

10. Rear Bumper - Removal and Replacement

The rear bumper is mounted in exactly the same way as the front one and should be removed and refitted in the same manner.

11. Windscreen and Fixed Glass - Removal and Replacement

1. Make sure you know what kind of glass is fitted. Toughened safety glass will stand a certain amount of impact blows without breaking but any other kind will crack at least and only carefully applied sustained pressure may be used with safety.

2. After taking off the windscreen wiper arms, loosen the rubber sealing strip on the inside of the car where it fits over the edge of the window frame. Use a piece of wood for this. Anything sharp may rip the rubber weatherstrip. The screen can be pushed out, weatherstrip attached, if pressure is applied at the top corners. Two people are needed on this to prevent the glass falling out. Push evenly and protect your hands to avoid accidents. Remove the finisher strip from the weatherstrip.

3. When fitting a screen first make sure that the window frame edges are even and smooth. Examine the edges of the screen to see that it is ground smooth and no chips or cracks are visible. Any such cracks could be the source of a much bigger one. The rubber weatherstrip should be perfectly clean. No traces of sealing compound should remain on rubber, glass or metal. If the sealing strip is old, brittle or hard, it is advisable to fit a new one even though they are not cheap.

4. Fit the weatherstrip to the screen first so that the joint comes midway along the top edge.

5. Next fit the decorative moulding into the weatherstrip. This is done by first feeding fine cord into the slot (use a piece of thin tubing as a guide and time saver) and leave the ends overlapping sufficiently to grip later. The two halves of the moulding are then put in place and the cord drawn out so that the edge of the strip locks them into place.

6. Apply suitable sealing compound to the weatherstrip where it will seat onto the metal window frame and also onto the outside faces of the frame at the lower corners.

7. Fit a piece of really strong thin cord into the frame channel of the weatherstrip as already described and then offer up the screen to the aperture. A second person is essential for this.

8. When you are sure that the screen is centrally positioned, pull the cord out so that the lip of the weatherstrip is drawn over the inner edge of the frame flange. One of the most frequent difficulties in this job is that the cord breaks. This is often because of sharp or uneven edges on the frame flange so a little extra time in preparation will pay off.

12. Doors - Removal and Replacement

1. The door hinges are welded to the door and fixed to the car by four countersunk crosshead screws. Two of the screws are concealed under rubber plugs in the body.

2. If the same door is being put back the simplest way to take it off is to drive out the hinge pins with a punch but you will have to remove the sill panel to get at the bottom one. If this is done no re-alignment problems will occur.

3. To slacken the hinge screws an impact screwdriver is essential. Similarly for tightening them properly on replacement.

4. When hanging a new door (or re-aligning one which is out of position) insert all hinge screws loosely and then tighten just one in

each hinge sufficiently to hold the door whilst it is set centrally and flush in the opening. It makes things easier if you remove the latch striker plate whilst this is being done.

13. Door Rattles - Tracing and Rectification

Door rattles are due either to loose hinges, worn or maladjusted catches, or loose components inside the door. Loose hinges can be detected by opening the door and trying to lift it. Any play will be felt. Worn or badly adjusted catches can be found by pushing and pulling on the outside handle when the door is closed. Once again any play will be felt. To check the window mechanism open the door and shake it with the window first open and then closed. Rattles will normally be heard.

14. Door Latch Striker Plates - Adjustment and Renewal

1. Rattles in doors are usually due to an incorrect striker plate position or the wedge being out of adjustment.

2. First check that the door fits the aperture properly by seeing that the gaps are more or less equal all round and that it fits flush with the side panel of the bodywork. There should be no rubbing and all the weatherstrip should show signs of equal compression.

3. Then make sure that the latch on the door is working properly. The top and bottom surfaces of the latch housing must be flat and the openings in it should not be worn. When the latch button is operated the bolt should retract fully.

4. If there are signs of wear on the lower surface and notches of the striker plate then it should be renewed. Similarly the plastic wedge should be renewed if worn.

5. Slacken all the striker plate mounting screws and tighten them just enough to prevent the plate from moving easily.

6. Loosen the locknut on the wedge adjusting rod and turn the screw until the stop comes against the housing. This gives the wedge maximum free movement.

7. To adjust the plate laterally first close the door gently and push or pull it until the door lines up with the body. To adjust the striker plate vertically it is best to pull back the weatherstrip so that the latch housing can be seen when the door is nearly shut. The bottom of the latch should ride on the plate and rise about 2 mm when the door is fully closed. To judge this, see that the gap between the latch and striker plate is less at the bottom than at the top. These adjustments, if done properly, take quite a time so a certain amount of patience is necessary.

8. Finally the wedge must be set. Its job is to keep the door held tight when shut. When the door closes the wedge is pushed in and its inward movement is stopped by the shoulder on the screwed pin. If this shoulder is too far out the wedge will butt against it before the door is fully closed and it will require excessive force or be impossible to close the door. If the shoulder is too far the other way the door will rattle. Consequently the adjusting screw should be turned until a little drag is felt when operating the latch and opening the door. When the wedge is set satisfactorily, tighten the locknut on the screw.

9. The fitting of a new striker plate assembly merely requires that the mounting screws are completely removed. They lock into a movable keep plate in the body pillar.

15. Door Trim Panels - Removal and Replacement

1. First remove the window winder and door handles by pressing the escutcheons against the panel so that the locating pins can be punched out. Then use a piece of flat metal strip to put round the edge of the panel and pull out the retaining clips. Take care not to tear the clips off the trim panel itself. On the passenger side it will be necessary to lift the panel a little to disengage the arm rest inner support from the door panel.

2. Replacement is a reversal of the removal procedure.

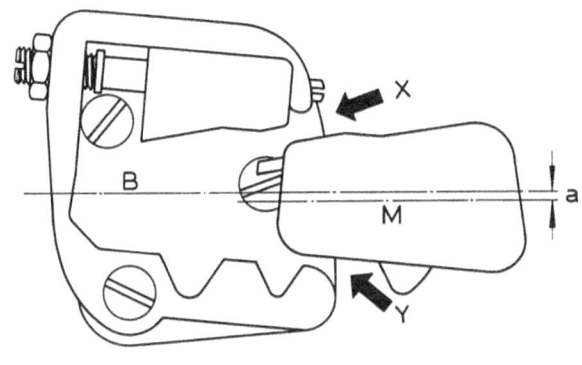

Fig. 12.8. Diagram showing striker plate and catch gap differential (x greater than y) and rise of catch on engagement. a = 2mm

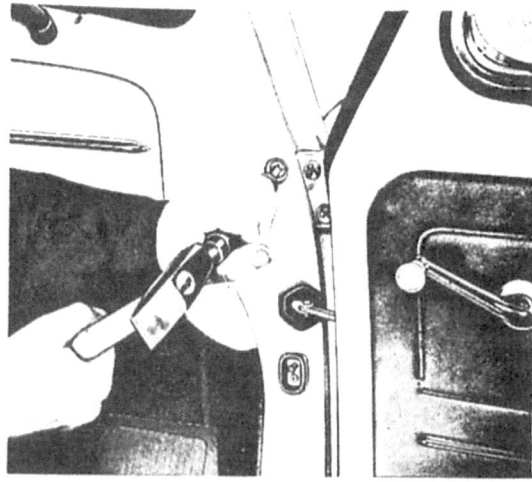

Fig. 12.9. Using impact screwdriver to loosen the door hinge screws

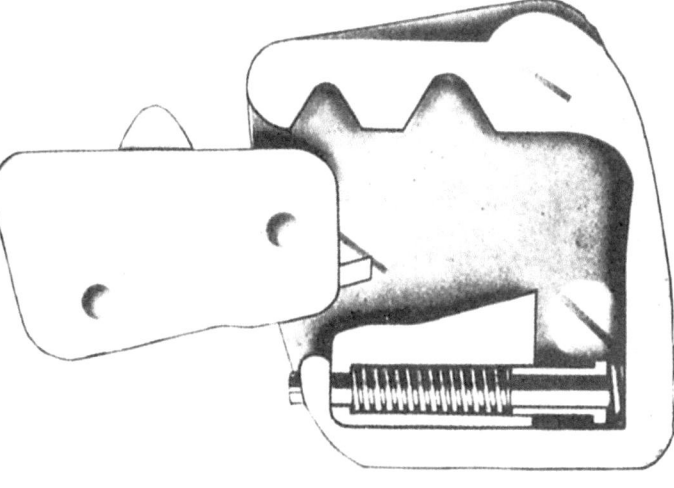

Fig. 12.10. Striker latch plate entering

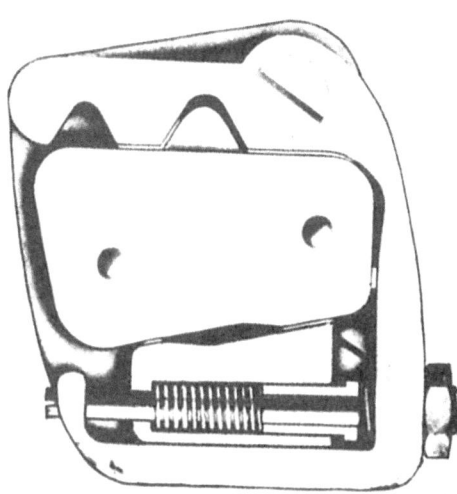

Fig. 12.11. Striker latch plate fully engaged

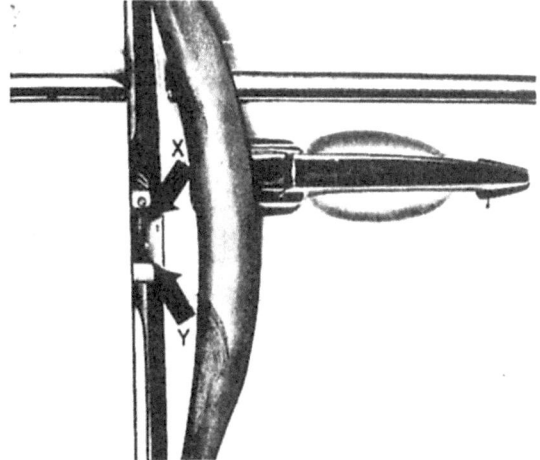

Fig. 12.12. Weatherstrip pulled back in order to see the position of the latch relative to the striker plate

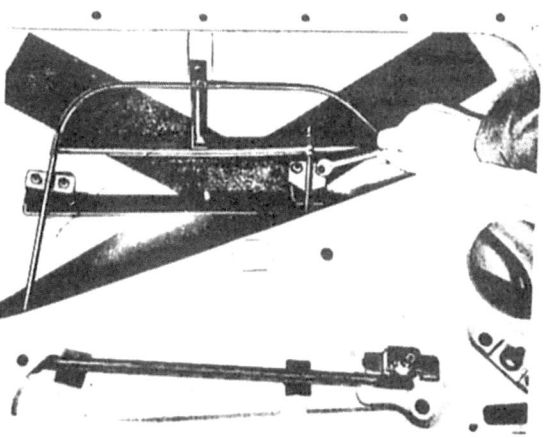

Fig. 12.13. Slackening the window lifter channel screws and drawing out the lifter

16. Door Window Lifter Mechanism - Removal and Replacement

1. Remove the door trim panel.
2. Disconnect the door check strap by taking out the link pin.
3. Take out the four screws holding the window lifter channel and push the window up and jam it. On earlier models the lifter is an arm running in a groove in the channel support. This arm can be disengaged from the channel once the winding mechanism has been unbolted from the door panel. There is also a vertical stay on the panel which must be removed.
4. Remove the five screws holding the window lifter to the door panel and another screw which holds the dividing strip between quarterlight and window. Pull the lifter mechanism out from the bottom of the door.
5. Replacement is a reversal of this procedure. Check the operation of the mechanism before replacing the trim panel.

17. Door Window Glass - Removal and Replacement

1. Remove the door trim and lifter mechanism.
2. Take out the wedges used to jam the glass in position when the lifter was taken out and then lower and tilt the glass so that it comes out of the bottom of the door. Replacement is a reversal of the procedure.
3. If new glass is being fitted into the existing channel the rear end of the channel must be positioned 80 mm from the rear corner of the glass.

18. Quarterlight - Removal and Replacement

1. Remove the door trim, lifter mechanism and main window glass.
2. Undo the crosshead screw securing the top of the quarterlight frame to the door frame and the whole assembly can be lifted out.
3. Replacement is a reversal of this procedure.

19. Door Catch Mechanism - Removal and Replacement

1. Remove the door trim.
2. Take out the two bolts holding the remote control handle shaft to the door frame and disconnect the link arm.
3. Remove the three crosshead screws holding the latch to the door and then push it inside the door and down - manoeuvring the link arm sufficiently to enable it to come clear so that it can be disconnected.
4. Replacement is a reversal of the removal procedure.

20. Engine Compartment Cover - Removal and Replacement

1. The lid is held by two conventional hinges and is kept open by a strong spring.
2. Mark the position of the hinge and brackets as clearly as possible and slacken off all the hinge and bracket bolts. Remove the spring by squeezing the two 'L' shaped ends out of their holes. If you have doubts about the spring flying off and causing an accident leave it where it is and undo the bolts, using the cover to hold and eventually ease the spring tension.
3. If the cover is being removed in order to remove the engine fan housing the hinge brackets will need taking off as well.
4. When replacing the cover the spring can be fitted after the lid has been attached provided you are able to get sufficient leverage on to it. If not, replace the brackets and then hook the spring into position and use the cover once again to take up the tension whilst the hinge bolts are replaced.
5. Do not first attach the hinge brackets to the cover. It is much easier to fit the brackets to the body and then fit the cover to the brackets.
6. It is important to position the lid so that when closed it is central in the aperture. For this reason the bracket holes are slotted to allow adjustment.

21. Luggage Compartment Cover - Removal and Replacement

1. Mark the position of the hinge plates on the cover and then slacken all the upper hinge mounting bolts and remove one from each side.
2. Support the cover and remove the bolt securing the top end of the telescopic prop.
3. Remove the other hinge bolts with assistance from another person and lift the cover off.
4. Replacement is a reversal of the removal procedure. Fit all the hinge bolts loosely to start with so that the cover can be positioned correctly in the slotted holes.

22. Engine Compartment Cover Latch - Adjustment

1. Before adjusting the latch the cover must be correctly set on its hinges so that it fits centrally in the aperture. If the cover is distorted or out of position no adjustment of the latch can rectify it.
2. The adjustment is confined to the striker plate fitted to the body. The hook on the latch should centralise in the notch and the plate should be raised or lowered to ensure adequate engagement. Slacken the two striker plate mounting screws and move the plate as required.

23. Luggage Compartment Cover Latch - Adjustment and Release Cable

1. Before any adjustment is made see that the cover fits centrally over the aperture. If it has been buckled the latch can be adjusted only a limited amount to compensate for it.
2. To centralise the lock bolt (on the cover) to the aperture in the latch, the latch must be removed after first slackening the latch securing screws. To adjust the engagement of the lock bolt into the latch plate the lock bolt can be lengthened or shortened in its mounting. The bolt should engage when firm pressure is applied to the bottom of the cover. If the cover needs slamming the bolt should be screwed out a little. If the cover rattles, move the bolt in.
3. The latch has a fail safe arrangement in the design so that if the cable breaks the latch will release rather than lock the cover.
4. To gain access to the cable end the latch mounting screws should be removed and the cover plate cased down from the lower half. The clamping screw is undone and the cable drawn out of the bracket. It can then be drawn out from inside the car.
5. When fitting a new cable into the bracket push the bracket back against the spring tension before tightening the screw.

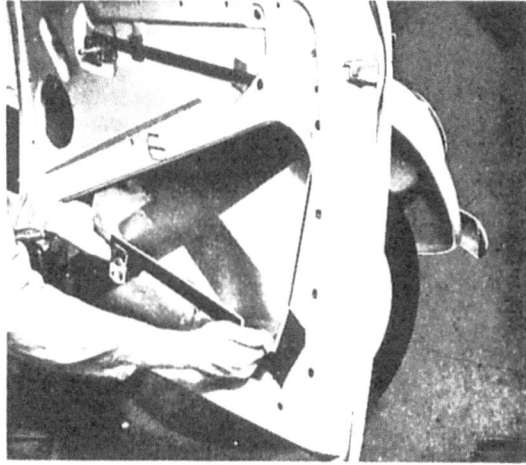

Fig. 12.14. Lowering the window glass from the door

Fig. 12.15. Slackening the clamp screw securing the latch release cable

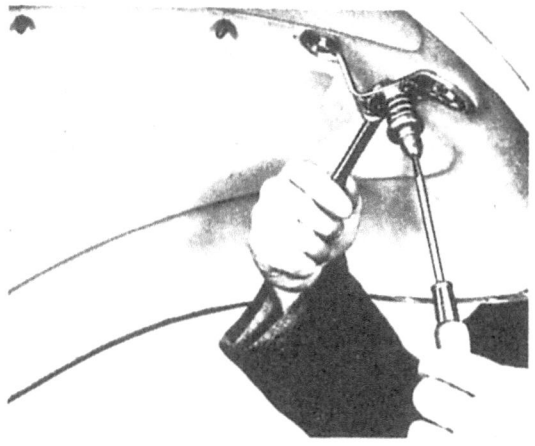

Fig. 12.16. Adjusting the front compartment locking bolt

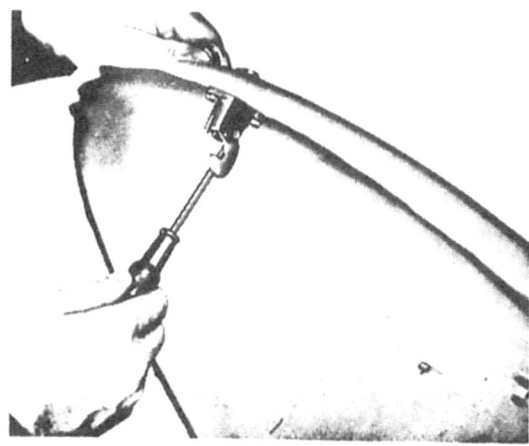

Fig. 12.17. Adjusting the rear engine compartment catch striker plate

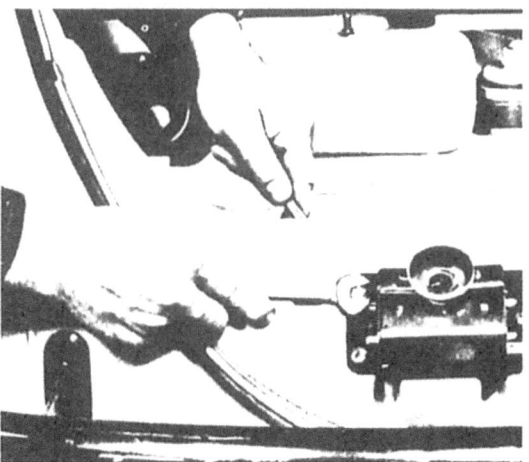

Fig. 12.18. Slackening the luggage compartment latch screws

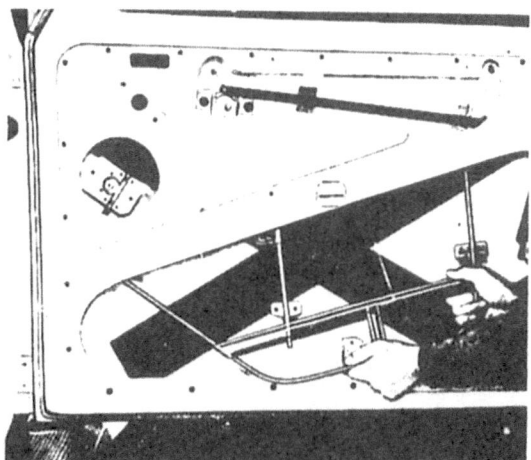

Fig. 12.19. Drawing out window lifter

Chapter 13 Supplement

Contents

Specifications

Engine

Valve clearances (November 1964 onwards)
Inlet and exhaust (cold engine)... ... ...   0.006 in (0.15 mm)

Crankshaft regrind sizes

	Main bearings 1, 2, 3 and crankpins	Main bearing 4
1st undersize diameter in (mm)	2.1556 (54.75)	1.5650 (39.75)
2nd undersize diameter in (mm)	2.1457 (54.50)	1.5552 (39.50)
3rd undersize diameter in (mm)	2.1358 (54.25)	1.5457 (39.25)
4th undersize diameter in (mm)	2.1260 (54.00)	1.5355 (39.00)

Compression ratio (February 1973 onwards) ... ...   7.3 : 1

Flywheel
Flange minimum re-machined thickness ... ...   0.244 in (6.2 mm)

Torque wrench setting

	lbf ft	kgf m
Flywheel securing bolt (D type engines)	253	35

Fuel system and carburation

Air cleaner
Type:
  Up to August 1975 ... ...   Oil bath, pre-heated
  August 1975 onwards ... ...   Dry paper element, thermostatically controlled air intake

Fuel pump
Type ... ...   Mechanically operated diaphragm; drive by pushrod from cam on distributor driveshaft. Four types fitted - see text
Output (minimum) ... ...   400 cc/min
Pressure (maximum)... ... ...   4.5 lbf/in^2 (0.32 kgf/cm^2)

Fuel tank
Capacity ... ...   8.8 Imp gal (40.0 litres) (10.6 US gal)

Carburettors
Type ... ...   Solex downdraught with accelerator pump, automatic electrically operated choke, and solenoid operated cut-off valve

Solex carburettor type designation	28 PICT	28 PICT-1	28 PICT-28
Engine code application...	—	—	D
Date introduced	1.8.60	12.11.63	1.8.66
Engine number introduced	5000002	8154031	D095050
Venturi diameter in (mm)	0.89 (22.5)	0.89 (22.5)	0.89 (22.5)
Main jet	112.5	122.5	122.5
Air correction jet	130y	130y	130y
Pilot jet	g55	g55	g55
Pilot air jet	200	200	200
Enrichment with ball	85	85	85
Injection capacity cc per stroke	1.1 to 1.4	1.1 to 1.4	1.1 to 1.4
Float needle diameter in (mm)...	0.059 (1.5)	0.059 (1.5)	0.059 (1.5)
Float needle washer thickness in (mm)	0.039 (1.0)	0.039 (1.0)	0.039 (1.0)
Octane requirement RON	87	87	87
Idling speed rpm	750 to 900	750 to 900	750 to 900
CO content %...	3 ± 1	3 ± 1	3 ± 1

Solex carburettor type designation	28 PICT-2 (6 volt system)	28 PICT-2 (6 volt and 12 volt systems)
Engine code application...	D	D
Date introduced	1.8.67	1.8.69
Engine number introduced	D0234015	D0525050
Venturi diameter in (mm)	0.89 (22.5)	0.89 (22.5)
Main jet	122.5	122.5
Air correction jet	140z	135z
Pilot jet	g55	55
Pilot air jet	200	200

Enrichment without ball	75	75
Injection capacity cc per stroke	1.1 to 1.4	1.1 to 1.4
Float needle diameter in (mm)	0.059 (1.5)	0.059 (1.5)
Float needle washer thickness in (mm)	0.039 (1.0)	0.039 (1.0)
Octane requirement RON	87	87
Idling speed rpm	750 to 900	750 to 900
CO content %	3 ± 1	3 ± 1

Note: *The 6v and 12v carburettors are identical except for the electrical component*

	30 PICT–3 ‡	30 PICT–3 *	30 PICT–3
Solex carburettor type designation			
Engine code application...	D	D	D
Date introduced	1.8.70	1.6.74	1.8.75
Engine number introduced	D0675001	D1268063	†
Venturi diameter in (mm)	0.94 (24)	0.94 (24)	0.94 (24)
Main jet	112.5	112.5	112.5
Air correction jet	170w	170w	170w
Pilot jet	55	50	47.5
Pilot air jet	150	150	150
Auxiliary fuel jet...	40 **	40	40
Auxiliary air jet	130	130	130
Enrichment without ball	2 x 85	2 x 85	2 x 85
Injection capacity cc per stroke	1.05 to 1.35	1.05 to 1.35	1.05 to 1.35
Float needle diameter in (mm)...	0.059 (1.5)	0.059 (1.5)	0.059 (1.5)
Float needle washer thickness in (mm)	0.059 (1.5)	0.059 (1.5)	0.059 (1.5)
Octane requirement RON	87	87	87
Idling speed rpm	750 to 900	750 to 900	800 to 950
CO content %	2 to 4	2 to 4	1 to 3

†   *Fitted to engines with air cleaners with plastic case and paper element*
‡   *Issued with 6v and 12v circuits. Change electrical parts where necessary. Mechanically identical*
 * *12 volt only*
** *Quoted as 50 in December 1970*

Ignition system

Distributor

Automatic advance:
    Up to June 1974... ... ...   Vacuum only
    June 1974 onwards ... ...   Vacuum and centrifugal

	1. 8. 66	1. 8. 70	1. 6. 74	1. 8. 75
Modification dates				
Engine number	D0095050	D065001	D1268063	—
Ignition timing (vacuum advance hose disconnected)	7½° BTDC at 800 to 900 rpm	TDC at 800 to 900 rpm	7½° BTDC at 750 to 900 rpm	7½° BTDC at 750 to 900 rpm
Dwell angle	44° to 50°	44° to 50°	44° to 50°	44° to 50°
Dwell angle wear limit	42° to 58°	42° to 58°	42° to 58°	42° to 58°

Spark plugs

Electrode gap:
    Up to 1974 ... ...   0.028 in (0.7 mm)
    1974 onwards ... ...   0.024 in (0.6 mm)
Type ... ...   Bosch W145 T1, Beru 145/14 or Champion L88 A

Transmission

Gear ratios

	Up to Nov '72	Nov '72 on
1st	3.8 : 1	3.78 : 1
2nd	2.06 : 1	2.06 : 1
3rd...	1.26 : 1	1.26 : 1
4th...	0.88 : 1	0.93 : 1
Reverse	3.8 : 1	3.79 : 1
Final drive	4.375 : 1	4.375 : 1

Torque wrench settings

	lbf ft	kgf m
Gearbox to final drive cover	24	3.5
Gearbox to bearing carrier	15	2
Bearing carrier to shift housing...	10	1.5
Gear shift lever bracket	15	2

Axle shafts and tubes

Torque wrench settings

	lbf ft	kgf m
Axle shaft nut	253	35

Braking system

Tandem master cylinder
Bore diameter	0.750 in (19.05 mm)
Piston to pushrod clearance	0.04 in (1.0 mm)

Piston stroke:
Primary	0.492 in (12.5 mm)
Secondary...	0.610 in (15.5 mm)

Pedal (tandem master cylinder)
Minimum movement of pedal to stop	7.5 in (190 mm)
Pedal free travel	0.25 $\pm$ 0.04 in (6 $\pm$ 1 mm)

Front disc brakes
Caliper piston diameter	1.575 in (40.4 mm)
Disc diameter...	8.937 in (277.0 mm)

Disc thickness:
New	0.378 in (9.5 mm)
Minimum	0.335 in (8.5 mm)
Maximum run-out of disc	0.008 in (0.2 mm)

Pad thickness:
New	0.433 in (11.5 mm)
Minimum	0.079 in (2.0 mm)
Maximum clearance between pad and disc	0.008 in (0.2 mm)

Torque wrench settings

	lbf ft	kgf m
Master cylinder stop bolt	7	1.0
Residual pressure valve/housing	14	2.0
Brake light switch/housing	14	2.0
Master cylinder to body...	18	2.5
Brake pipe to master cylinder	11	1.5
Splash plate/steering knuckle	7	1.0
Caliper housing (Teves) screws - initial torque	7	1.0
Caliper housing (Teves) screws - final torque...	14	2.0
Caliper to steering knuckle	30	4.0
Bleed valve/caliper (max)	3.5	0.5
Brake hose/caliper	11	1.5

Electrical system - charging and starting systems

Battery
Capacity (12 volt system)	36 amp hours

12 volt dynamo
Maximum current	30 amp
Mean regulating voltage	14 volts
Nominal output speed	2000 rpm
Cut-in speed	1450 rpm
Commutator minimum diameter	1.29 in (32.8 mm)
Segment insulation undercut	0.02 in (0.5 mm)
Brush length	Longer than holder (minimum)
Pulley ratio, crankshaft/dynamo	1 : 1.8

12 volt alternator
Output current (max)	50 amp
Regulating voltage	14 volts
Test output voltage at 3000 rpm with 30 amp load	12.5 to 14.5 volts
Stator resistance between phases	0.11 to 0.14 ohms
Rotor resistance between slip rings	4.4 to 4.9 ohms
Slip rings minimum diameter	1.075 in (27.3 mm)

Length of protrusion of brush from holder:
New	0.4 in (10 mm)
Minimum	0.2 in (5 mm)

Electrical system - lights, instrument and electrical accessories

Bulb chart (12 volt system)

	Wattage
Headlight (normal)	45/40
Headlight (halogen)	60/55
Parking light	4
Turn signal light	21
Brake/tail light	21/5
Rear number plate light...	10
Interior light	10
Reversing light	21

Fuses (12 volt system)

The fuse box contains 12 fuses numbered 1 to 12 from left to right. Numbers 9 and 10 are rated at 16 amps, the remainder at 8 amps. Two typical circuits are given although there may be variations on these.

Fuse no.	Circuit protected	
	1972 models	**1975 models**
1	Right tail light Right parking light Left parking light Rear number plate light	Left tail light
2	Left tail light	Right tail light Left parking light Right parking light Rear number plate light
3	Right headlight low beam	Left headlight low beam
4	Left headlight low beam	Right headlight low beam
5	Left headlight high beam and high beam warning light	Left headlight high beam and high beam warning light
6	Right headlight high beam	Right headlight high beam
7	Spare	Spare
8	Hazard warning system	Hazard warning system
9	Interior lights Headlight dip and flasher relay	Interior lights Headlight dip and flasher relay
10	Windscreen wiper Heated rear screen switch current	Windscreen wiper Heated rear screen switch current
11	Horn Brake lights	Horn Brake lights
12	Dual brake circuit warning light Turn signal and hazard lights relay warning light	Dual brake circuit warning light Handbrake warning light Turn signal and hazard lights relay warning light
21 (in engine compartment)	Reversing lights	Reversing lights
22 (in engine compartment)	Heated rear screen relay	Heated rear screen relay

Relays

The number of relays used depends on the year of the vehicle, type of generator and number of accessories

Designation	Description	Location
J1	Headlight dip and flash relay	Behind dash (rectangular)
J2	Turn signal and hazard lights relay	Behind dash (cylindrical)
J6	Voltage stabilizer or vibrator unit	Rear of speedometer head
J9	Heated rear screen relay	Under rear seat

J5 ... ...   Fog lamp relay   *
J39 ... ...   Headlight washer   *
J11 ... ...   Intermittent wash/wipe   *

* optional extra (later models only) — no standard location

Torque wrench setting	lbf ft	kgf m
Steering wheel nut	36	5.0

Steering and suspension

Tyre pressures (cross ply)	Front	Rear
Normal use (lbf/in^2)	16	27
Fully loaded (lbf/in^2)	18	27

Steering
Castor ... ... 3° 20'
Circumference backlash at steering wheel (max)... ... ...   0.6 in (15 mm)

Torque wrench settings	lbf ft	kgf m
Steering column tube clamp screws	7	1.0
Steering wheel nut	36	5.0
Column holding bolts	7	1.0

1 Introduction

The purpose of this Supplement is mainly to provide additional information concerning later models of the Beetle 1200. In particular it includes details of the later type Solex carburettors, major modifications to the braking system, and the later 12 volt electrical system. As such, it should be used in conjunction with the relevant information contained in Chapters 1 to 12.

3 Engine

1 The lubrication system described in Chapter 1 has been modified on three separate occasions since 1970.
2 In 1970 a pressure control valve was added to the system. This serves to maintain oil pressure at the crankshaft bearings when the oil is hot and thin. This pressure should be in the region of 42 lbf/in^2 (3 kgf/cm^2) at normal running temperature (80°C) at 2000 rpm. On a worn engine this may drop to around 28 lbf/in^2 (2 kgf/cm^2), after which an engine overhaul will be necessary.
3 The pressure relief valve does not now have a return drilling. This means that oil flows direct to the bearings when the valve is open, and via the oil cooler when closed.
4 The diameters of the oil passages in the crankcase, oil pump housing and oil cooler have been increased on later models. Therefore, when renewing any of these items, your local VW dealer should be consulted for advice on matching of parts.
5 In August 1970, the pressure control valve spring was modified to increase its loading.
6 In September 1972 the engine drain plug was deleted, making it necessary to remove the oil strainer cover to drain the oil. It is best to remove all but one of the cover retaining nuts and then prise the cover away at one side, so allowing the oil to run out. The remaining nut is now removed to release the cover, and the strainer can then be carefully cleaned. Refitting is a straightforward reversal of this procedure.

Cylinder modifications
7 In 1969 the recesses in the crankcase to accommodate the cylinders were increased in size. Old and new crankcases, cylinders and piston assemblies may therefore not be compatible. For an overhaul that requires renewal of any of these parts, you should consult your VW dealer.

Valve tappet clearance - modification
8 In October 1971 a revised valve clearance was specified for all engines manufactured since November 1964 (engine code D). This clearance is given in the Specifications.

Exchange engines
9 The specifications given in Chapter 1 do not always apply to factory reconditioned exchange engines.
10 An identification letter will be stamped on the joint flange of the right-hand half of the crankcase, at the end just below the generator pedestal. A 'P' indicates that the engine is built to original (or planned) specifications and an 'O' indicates that certain components of the engine have been reworked oversize or under-size.
11 Oversize crankshaft pulleys may be fitted to engines stamped 'O'. The crankcase cylinder seats may have been machined deeper, and spacer rings fitted; the crankcase and/or crankshaft may be machined/reground; the camshaft bores and/or camshaft journals may be machined/reground; the oil pressure relief valve and pressure control valve bores may have been machined oversize and oversize plungers fitted; the crankshaft seating of the flywheel may have been reworked.
12 As can be seen from this list of reworked parts, there are quite a number of possible combinations present in a factory recondi-tioned engine. Therefore, when renewing parts during the overhaul of such an engine, it is wise to consult your VW dealer for advice, otherwise there is a distinct possibility of fitting unsuitable parts. If any part of the engine needs re-machining, the engineering works that carries out the work will normally supply correct replacement parts to match the reworked components.

Flywheel - fitting replacement or reworked components
13 A revised torque wrench setting has been specified for the flywheel securing bolt. This applies to all engines with the code D. The setting is given in the Specifications.
14 Reworked flywheels may have been machined on the face of the flange through which the crankshaft flange location dowels fit. It is therefore, important to obtain the correct length bolt and dowels or it will not be possible to retighten the flywheel correctly. Your VW dealer should be consulted to ascertain the correct components required.

Pistons - later type
15 In February 1973 a modified piston was introduced for the 1200 cc engine. The flat crown type was replaced by the raised crown type. Although this raises the compression ratio, it does not

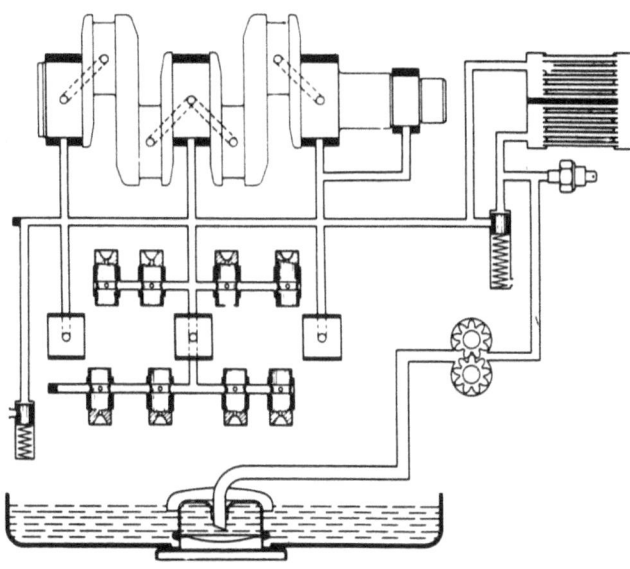

Fig. 13.1. Lubrication system – 1970 onwards

affect the performance of the engine. If raised crown type pistons are being fitted to an older engine, they must be fitted as a complete set of four – flat crown type and raised crown type should never be mixed.

Rocker arms - later type
16 In February 1973 the rocker arms were modified. If one of the old type rockers needs to be renewed by a later type, all the rockers must be renewed as a set – never mix rocker arm types.

Crankcase - cleaning of oilways
17 When overhauling engines, particularly if a new crankcase is fitted, it is essential to check that the drillings for the oil passages are clear. This is most important in the case of the passage to No 4 crankshaft journal bearing. The best way to check this is to clean the drillings carefully and then to fit the two oil valves, ie the regulating valve and the pressure relief valve, and close up the oil cooler holes. Now force oil into No 3 journal hole with a force feed oil can and check that it comes out of the drillings for Numbers 1, 2 and 4 bearings.

Cylinder head - rocker shaft seal
18 From August 1976 the small seal on the stud for the rocker shaft has been deleted.

Telescopic tubes for pushrods - fitting without removing engine
19 The pushrod tubes fitted until May 1976 can only be renewed with the engine dismantled. From this date a new type telescopic tube was fitted which enables removal and refitting with the engine in the car. The method of fitting is given below.
20 Take off the rear wheel and clean round the cylinder head cover. Remove the clip and take off the cover. Undo the nuts and remove the rocker shaft. Pull the pushrods out from the old pushrod tubes.
21 Now clean round the tubes as far as possible and lever them out with a screwdriver.
22 Fit the seals to each new telescopic tube, squeeze it together, and, with the thin end to the cylinder head, fit it into place.
23 Install the pushrods and the rocker shaft, adjust the valve clearance and refit the cylinder head cover and clip.
24 Refit the rear wheel.

4 Cooling, heating and exhaust systems

General description of modifications
1   The arrangements for heating and cooling are identical to those described as the 'clean air' version in Chapter 2. Fig.13.2 gives an exploded view of the fan layout.
2   With the increased load on the generator it has become necessary to adjust the fan belt more exactly. This is explained later in this Section.
3   The fitting of tail pipes must be done very carefully. If the pipe is not correctly fitted, back pressure may cause trouble in the exhaust system. Correct fitting is detailed later in this Section. Apart from this the exhaust system remains as described in Chapter 2.
4   Some more information about the fitting of heater controls is also given in this Section.
5   From September 1975 the 1200L is fitted with a two-speed fresh air blower. This is described later in this Section.

Fan belt - adjustment
6   The old type of belt was tested by pressing, midway between the pulleys, inwards firmly. The deflection should be as given in Chapter 2.
7   A new type of belt, called the XDA, with low stretch characteristics is fitted to all later models.
8   The XDA belt is checked for tension with a special gauge. This is shown at Fig.13.3. The gauge should be obtainable from VW spares specialists.
9   The XDA belts come in two different sizes, one for use with a dynamo, the other with an alternator.
10 Assuming you have access to a gauge, turn back the sleeve to about 20 divisions on the scale. Refer to Fig.13.3 and hook the gauge to the fan belt midway between the pulleys. Turn the sleeve forward so that the front edge of the sleeve is level with the mark on the plunger. Remove the gauge from the belt and check the reading, whole divisions on the white scale and the vernier reading on the leading edge of the plunger, level with the top edge of the white scale. Add the readings together. (The vernier reading shown in the illustration is 0.5).
11 Compare the reading with the figures below.

> Dynamo belt:
>   new   16 to 17
>   used 15.5 to 16.5
> Alternator belt:
>   new   17 to 18
>   used 16.5 to 17.5

12 Adjust the belt tension by adding or removing spacers as in Chapter 2, Section 4.
13 If you do not have a gauge the 'thumb' method of testing should give a reading of between 0.4 in (10 mm) for a new belt, and 0.5 in (12 mm) for a used belt, but have it checked properly and avoid belt trouble.

Silencer tail pipes - fitting precautions
14 The pre-heater pipe extends into the silencer, and if the tail pipe is not inserted carefully to the correct depth there is a risk that back pressure will build up in the silencer with probable damage to the engine.
15 Using a suitable rule push it down the tail pipe when fitting the pipe to the silencer, until the rule butts up against the pre-heater pipe. Move the tail pipe in or out to correspond with the table below. Repeat for the second pipe.

Length of tail pipe	Measurement at open end (installed)
10.86 in (276 mm)	10.63 in (270 mm)
9.80 in (249 mm)	9.57 in (243 mm)
8.90 in (226 mm)	8.66 in (220 mm)

The 8.90 in (226 mm) pipe is the one usually fitted to the 1200 cc engine.

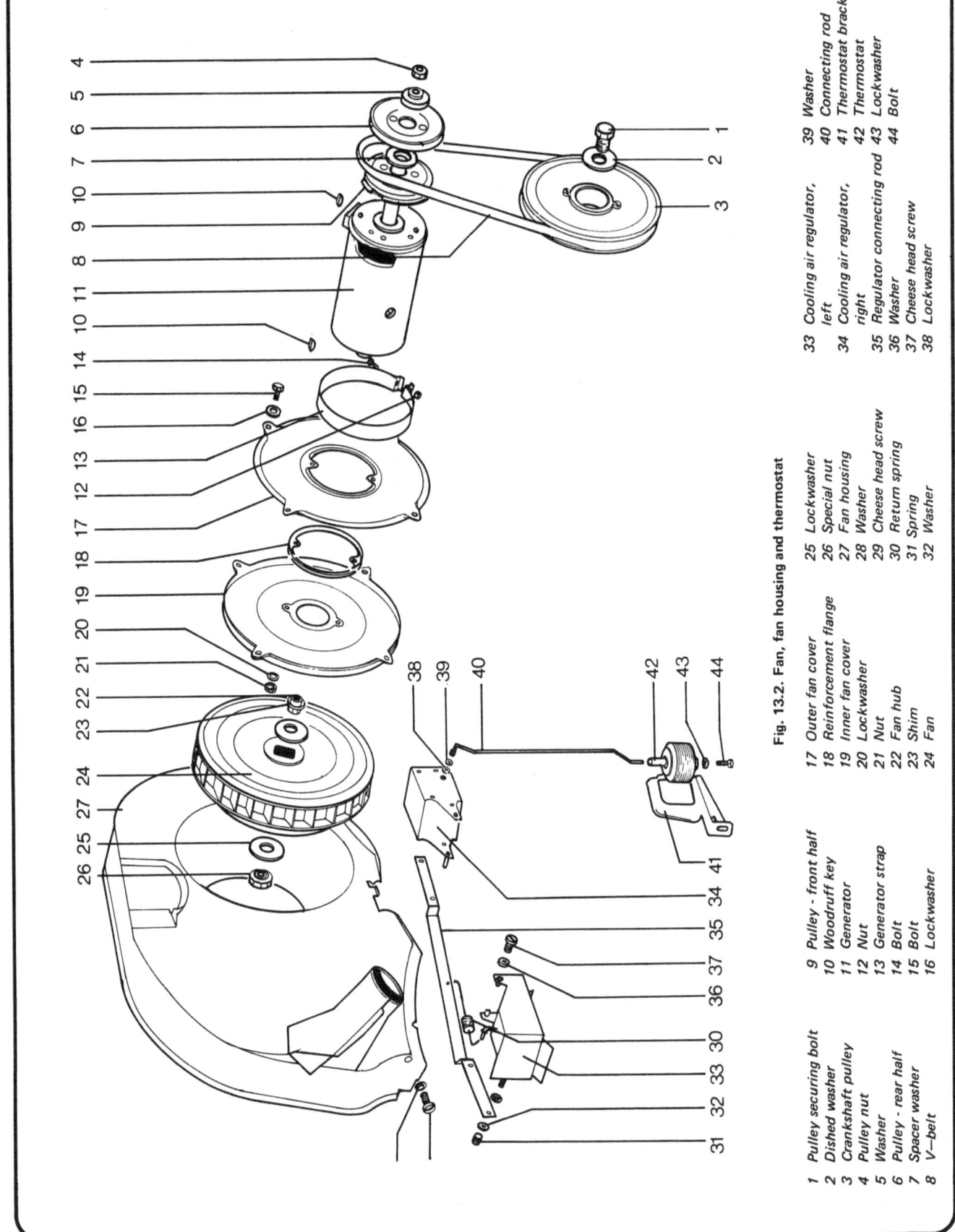

Fig. 13.2. Fan, fan housing and thermostat

1 Pulley securing bolt
2 Dished washer
3 Crankshaft pulley
4 Pulley nut
5 Washer
6 Pulley - rear half
7 Spacer washer
8 V–belt

9 Pulley - front half
10 Woodruff key
11 Generator
12 Nut
13 Generator strap
14 Bolt
15 Bolt
16 Lockwasher

17 Outer fan cover
18 Reinforcement flange
19 Inner fan cover
20 Lockwasher
21 Nut
22 Fan hub
23 Shim
24 Fan

25 Lockwasher
26 Special nut
27 Fan housing
28 Washer
29 Cheese head screw
30 Return spring
31 Spring
32 Washer

33 Cooling air regulator,
   left
34 Cooling air regulator,
   right
35 Regulator connecting rod
36 Washer
37 Cheese head screw
38 Lockwasher

39 Washer
40 Connecting rod
41 Thermostat bracket
42 Thermostat
43 Lockwasher
44 Bolt

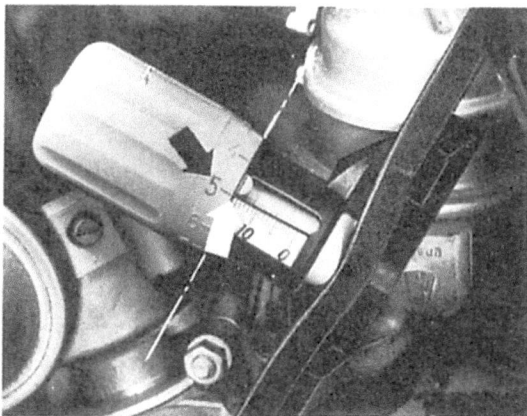

Fig. 13.3. Fan belt tester
White arrow shows leading edge in line with the mark on the plunger
Black arrow shows vernier scale

Heater controls - fitting

16 The method given for the 'clean air' type in Chapter 2, Section 9 is generally correct for all later models, but there are some small changes.

17 Once the flap control wires are disconnected from the clevis pull the wires out of the clevis pins. Remove the plugs from the guide tubes. Inside the car remove the nut securing the right-hand operating lever, remove the friction washers and pull the lever away. Then disconnect the hooked ends of the control wires and pull them out.

18 When fitting new cables, grease them first and refit them in the reverse order of removal. Note that the longer one goes in the lower guide tube.

19 Refit the sealing plugs securely in the guide tubes and make sure that they exclude water.

20 Clamp the outer end of the cable to the flap operating levers and make sure the flaps operate through their full range.

21 The control wires and flaps for the heater outlets to the rear footwell operate on the same principle except that the cables are joined together where they are connected to the left-hand lever and may not be renewed separately. Access to the ends of these cables is by removing the rear seat and the vertical kick board in front of it. The cable clamps may then be disconnected.

Fresh air blower - description and servicing

22 A fresh air blower is fitted to the 1976 model 1200L and later versions of this Beetle.

23 A fresh air box at the rear of the dashboard takes in air from the luggage compartment or from the heater according to the setting of the levers. The flow of air is directed by the control knobs on the dash which alter the positions of the flaps in the fresh air box.

24 In the centre of the fresh air box a two-speed motor is used to accelerate the air flow as required.

25 Stale or used air escapes through the slots behind the rear side windows.

26 The control wires are accessible from behind the radio aperture. The fresh air box is an integral part of the body framework. The air ducts containing the fan motor are held together with clips.

27 If the fuse blows the circuit may be found on the current flow diagram. The switch is removable as detailed later in this Supplement.

28 If the fan motor is defective it may be renewed only as a complete unit after the ducting has been removed.

29 We do not recommend that the owner dismantles the fresh air ducting; it is fragile and unless great care is taken when dismantling it the ducting will break. This job is best entrusted to the dealer, who has the tools required to do it properly, unless the owner is confident that he can carry out the job with the extreme care necessary.

5 Fuel system and carburation

General description of changes

1 The 1200 cc engine has been fitted with a Solex downdraught carburettor since its introduction in August 1960. From that date until August 1970 various models of the 28 PICT carburettor were fitted. The electrically operated automatic choke was introduced during this period.

2 In August 1970 a major change was made. The Solex 30 PICT carburettor with bypass air drillings was fitted, the pilot jet cut-off valve was discontinued and an electromagnetic cut-off valve was fitted to cut off the fuel supply when the ignition is turned off.

3 The jet sizes in the various carburettors are given in the Specifications.

4 From the early stages until the 1976 model a metal-bodied oil bath air cleaner was fitted. Two types existed; they are described later in this Section. In August 1976 the system was changed to a paper element type with a plastic body. The oil bath type and paper element type are not interchangeable.

5 The fuel pump is operated by a pushrod in contact with a cam on the distributor driveshaft. Three types are described, the latest one incorporating a built in cut-off valve. Later models of this type have an inclined pump body to make room for the increased bulk of the generator.

Air cleaners - description and servicing

6 Three types of air cleaner have been fitted. The earliest type used until August 1969 is described in Chapter 3.

7 In August 1969 a change was made; the flap controlling the air intake is controlled by the same thermostat that controls the air intake to the fan. The flap is operated by a bowden cable from the right regulating flap of the fan housing.

8 In August 1975 the air cleaner changed again. This latest type has a rectangular plastic body and a dry paper element. The air intake system is controlled by a thermostat built in to the air cleaner.

9 Refer to Fig.13.4 which is a sketch of the original type of air cleaner. The top may be removed by undoing the snap type retaining clips and the oil level checked. There must be 0.2 in (5 mm) depth of oil above the sludge. If the sludge is to be cleaned out then the lower half must be removed from the carburettor. Remove the crankcase ventilation hose and the pre-heater hose. Slacken the clip which clamps the air cleaner body to the carburettor and lift off the lower half. Be careful not to spill the oil. Take the cleaner away and remove the old oil and the sludge. Refitting is the reverse of removal. Fit the lower half back to the carburettor before filling it with oil. Check that the flap valve works freely. Fig.13.5 gives an exploded view of the cleaner. The cleaner shown with two inlets may be encountered on some models. This type has two air intake hoses and two flap valves. Maintenance is the same, but there is a little more work to remove the second hose. In both types check that the lever with the weight does not foul the casing. There should be an 0.2 in (5 mm) gap between it and the casing when the flap is shut.

10 Removal and refitting of the type fitted in August 1969 is as for the earlier type, but the bowden cable must also be removed before the body can be taken off the carburettor. Unclip the cable from the warm air flap lever, then undo the screw clamping the end of the outer cable into the clip mounted on the air cleaner and pull the outer cable away from the clip.

11 When installing the cable, check that the warm air flap is closed at the same point as the right-hand cooling air flap. This can be done by connecting the inner cable to the warm air flap operating arm, installing the outer cable in the clip and moving the outer cable until both flaps close at the same time, or more exactly, that the warm air flap is adjusted to close at the same moment as the fresh air control flap.

12 The plastic-bodied, paper element type cleaner has the air intake flap controlled by a built-in thermostat. Fig.13.6 shows the cleaner in position. To clean the element it is necessary to remove the entire unit from the engine compartment. To do this remove the

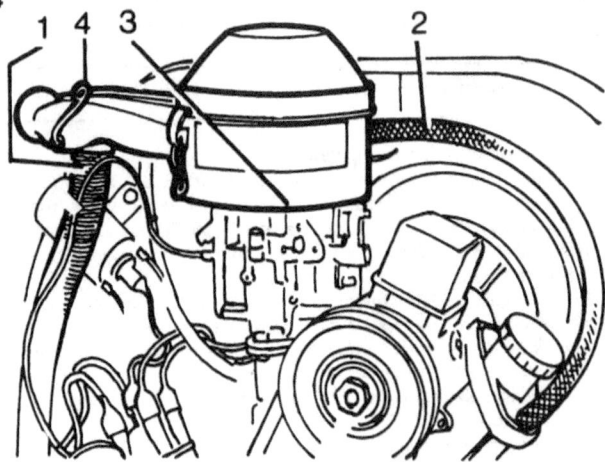

Fig. 13.4. Air cleaner — oil bath type

1 Pre-heater air hose   3 Retaining strap
2 Crankcase ventilator hose   4 Lever with balance weight

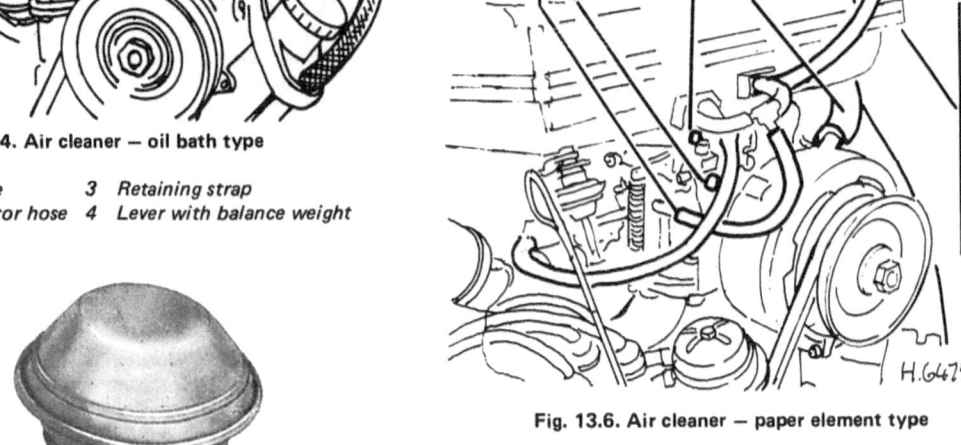

Fig. 13.6. Air cleaner — paper element type

1 Hose to carburettor   5 Retaining clips, top to base
2 Screws in support plate   6 Vacuum hose
3 Carburettor clamp screw   7 Warm air hose from pre-
4 Crankcase ventilation hose   heater

Fig. 13.7. Air cleaner — paper element type — exploded view

Fig. 13.5. Air cleaner — oil bath type — exploded view

Above — early type   Below — later type

hose from the vacuum unit on the air cleaner. Now detach the large warm air intake hose for the air cleaner from the pre-heater pipe. Remove the crankcase breather hose from the engine oil filler, undo the screws in the support plate and on the carburettor, and lift the complete assembly away.

13 Take the air cleaner cover off the body by releasing the four snap clips and prising the cover away. Lift the element out of the body and place it on a sheet of newspaper (Fig.13.7). Tap it gently until no more dust comes out of it. Do **not** blow it clean with compressed air or wash it in solvent. If it is torn or frayed then fit a new one. Assembly is the reverse of removal.

14 Opinions differ about the servicing interval. The element should be renewed every 18 000 miles (30 000 km) if the vehicle is used in 'clean' operating conditions. If you are operating in dusty or sandy country, we recommend looking at it at weekly intervals until you find out just what the necessary period between servicing should be. A choked filter will let dust through only if it is torn, but it will seriously affect the running of the engine. If you run in dusty conditions with a torn element you will soon require a new engine as well as a new filter element!

Fuel pumps - description of changes

15 The fuel pump described in Chapter 3 was later replaced by a pump of the same design but having the filter in the inlet pipe. An exploded view of the pump is given in Fig.13.8. It will be seen that this pump has two diaphragms, the lower one forcing the petrol through the pump and the upper one acting as a cut-off valve. This stops the supply of fuel to the pump by gravity from the tank when the engine is stationary. More details of this pump are given later in this Section. It may be dismantled and repaired if spares are available.

16 In September 1970 a different type of pump was introduced. Externally it looks much the same, and is operated in the same manner by a pushrod, but the filter has now been changed to the original disc type in the upper body. This pump is not repairable, other than to change the filter. The cut-off valve is a separate item fitted externally in the fuel line. Fig.13.9 shows an exploded view and details are given later. Fig.13.10 shows the cut-off valve.

17 In March 1972 a third type was introduced, this time with a built in cut-off valve, details are given in Fig.13.9 and the relevant text.

18 The pump was again modified when the alternator was fitted. To make room for the greater bulk of the alternator, the top portion of the pump is set at an angle of 15º to the body. This is shown in Fig.13.11 and described in the relevant text.

Fuel pump - removal, refitting and checking of pushrod

19 The first problem is to cut off the flow of fuel from the tank to the pump. Some vehicles are fitted with a tap (and no fuel gauge). In this case turn the tap to 'off'. With the others, the pipes are fitted with a clip at each joint. Make a wooden plug for the pump inlet pipe, detach the pipe and plug it quickly. Next remove the pump outlet hose, undo the two nuts holding the pump to the housing and lift the pump away.

20 The pump used from September 1970 to March 1972 has an external cut-off valve (photo). Refer to Fig.13.10. In this case disconnect the hose from the tank at the cut-off valve and plug it. Remove the hose from the cut-off valve to the carburettor and plug it as well. Remove the cut-off valve with the fuel pump (photo).

21 The amount that the pushrod protrudes from the gasket is critical. It should be 0.5 in (13 mm). If it differs from this (at the top of its cam) then the thickness of the gasket must be adjusted. The pushrod for the older type pumps is 3.9 in (100 mm) long. For the pump set at an angle the length is 4.25 in (108 mm). If the rod protrudes too much it may tear the diaphragm. Too little protrusion can result in poor acceleration due to fuel starvation.

Fuel pump (up to September 1970) - servicing and testing

22 This type may be dismantled completely and serviced. However, before taking it to pieces, check that a spares kit is available. If not, a new pump must be fitted.

23 Before removing the pump check the filter. To do this remove

and block the inlet hose from the tank. At the side of the top section of the pump there is a hexagonal plug just above the inlet hose connector. (Refer to Fig.13.8). Remove this plug and the filter may be removed (photo). If this is clogged, wash it carefully in fuel and then refit it and refit the plug. Connect the input hose and disconnect the hose from the pump to the carburettor at the carburettor. Put the end of this hose in a glass jar and then spin the engine. If the petrol squirts out in regular pulses the pump is working. It should deliver approximately ¾ pint (400 cc) per minute. There is no need to run it for a minute; ten seconds should give approximately 70 ccs. Disconnect the HT lead from the coil first and tie it away safely, or the engine may start on the fuel in the carburettor. Be careful **not** to have any sparks, do **not** smoke, and don't spill the fuel. If the pump delivers the right amount then you have cleared the fault by cleaning the filter. If it does not then remove the pump as detailed in this Section.

24 Scratch a mark across the flanges so that you can reassemble the pump correctly, remove the six securing screws (photo) and take the top from the bottom (photo). You can now see the diaphragm. If this is hard, stiff or torn it must be renewed. To do this the pivot pin of the pump lever must be removed and the lever with return spring taken out (Fig.13.8). Take the circlip off one end of the pin. Remove the cover plate (two screws), push the pin out of the housing, removing the lever and the spring by pressing down the diaphragm.

25 The diaphragm may now be lifted out, inspected carefully, and a new one fitted if necessary. Clean the lower pump body and refit the diaphragm (photo), pressing it down gently so that the forks of the operating lever can be fitted over the toggle at the end of the diaphragm pull rod (photo). Still holding the diaphragm down, refit the pivot pin and circlip (photo). Refit the spring by fitting one end over the lug inside the pump body and snapping the other end into position on the lever (photo). Work the lever up and down a few times and check that the diaphragm fits snugly into the body.

26 Now look at the inlet and outlet valves (photo 5.24b). Before removing them check that spares are available. One is a petal type flap valve of shim steel which may be removed quite easily. It should lie quite flat. The other is staked into the housing and may be prised out gently. It is a disc type valve. Neither is repairable and if they are damaged then new ones must be fitted.

27 Finally the fuel cut-off valve must be checked. Take the four screws out holding the cover to the body and lift off the cover. The condition of the cut-off diaphragm may now be checked (photo).

28 Reassemble the cover and the two halves of the body, taking care to line up the halves of the body with the scratch marks made before dismantling. If possible fit new gaskets. Refit the operating lever cover, also with a new gasket.

29 Refit the pump on the engine and check the output as in paragraph 23. Do not forget to refit the filter and plug.

30 When refitting the pump, fit a new gasket onto the intermediate flange and make sure the pushrod is the correct way round (photo).

Fuel pump (September 1970 to March 1972) - servicing and testing

31 Refer to Fig.13.9 and photo 5.20b. See also Fig.13.10 for details of the cut-off valve connections.

32 If the pump is not delivering fuel, the only practicable servicing procedure is to clean the filter. This is done by removing the screw from the top and lifting the cover off. There is no need to disconnect the hose, and if fuel flows in quantity when the cover is removed then the cut-off valve is faulty.

33 Lift the cover off and remove the filter (photo). Clean it carefully and refit it. Test the pump output as in paragraph 23.

34 If the filter is clean, then there is no further repair possible to the pump and it must be renewed if faulty. It may be worth checking that the cut-off valve is not faulty. Move the inlet hose from the cut-off valve to the pump inlet and check the pump operation. The pump operation is distinguished by the pulsation of flow, as opposed to the gravity feed with steady flow. Do not try to check the pump output with this makeshift set-up.

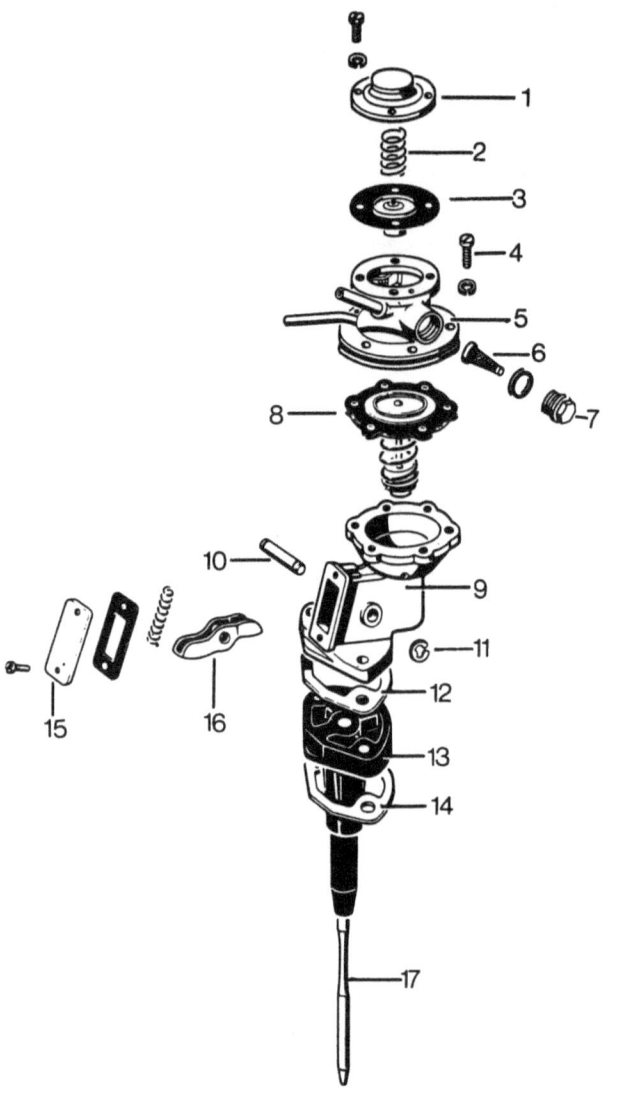

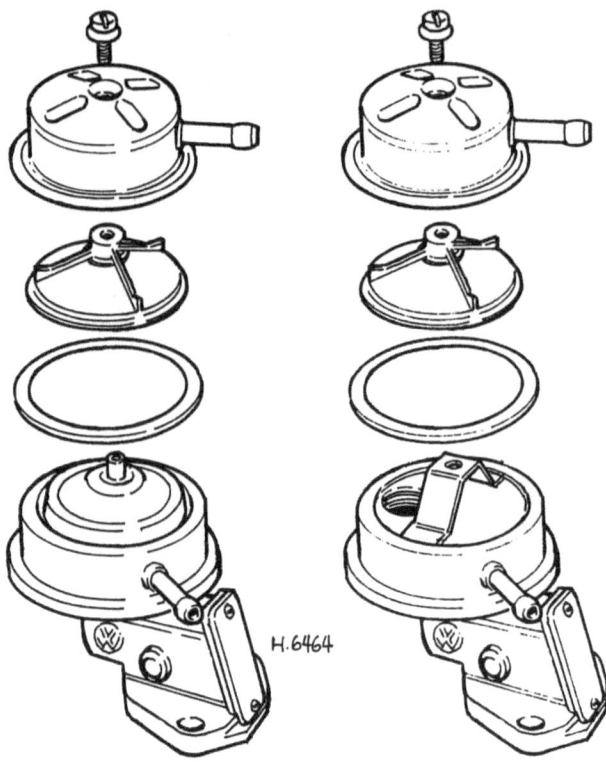

Fig. 13.9. Fuel pump — exploded view

Right: Type fitted with external cut-off valve, used from September 1970 to March 1972

Left: Type fitted with built-in cut-off valve, used from March 1972 onwards

Fig. 13.8. Fuel pump — up to September 1970 — exploded view

1 Fuel cut-off diaphragm cover	9 Pump— lower body
2 Cut-off diaphragm spring	10 Operating lever spindle
3 Cut-off diaphragm	11 Circlip
4 Retaining screw	12 Gasket
5 Pump—upper body	13 Intermediate flange
6 Filter	14 Gasket
7 Filter recess plug	15 Cover plate
8 Pump diaphragm	16 Operating lever
	17 Pushrod

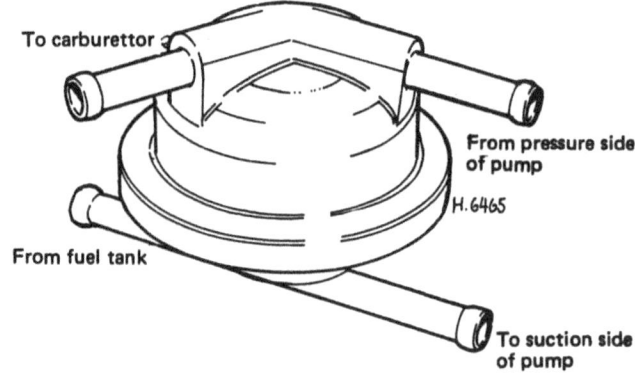

Fig. 13.10. Fuel pump cut-off valve — used from September 1970 to March 1972

Fuel pump (March 1972 onwards) - servicing and testing
35 Refer to Fig.13.9. This type of pump has a built-in cut-off valve. Removal of the filter is as in paragraphs 31 to 33. Remove the top screw and lift off the cap. If petrol starts to flood out as the screw is loosened either turn the tank tap to 'off', or retighten the cap, remove the inlet hose and plug it. If this has happened then the cut-off valve is not working. The pump is not repairable, other than to clean or renew the filter and cover gasket.
36 The angled pump for the alternator type engine is serviced in the same way.

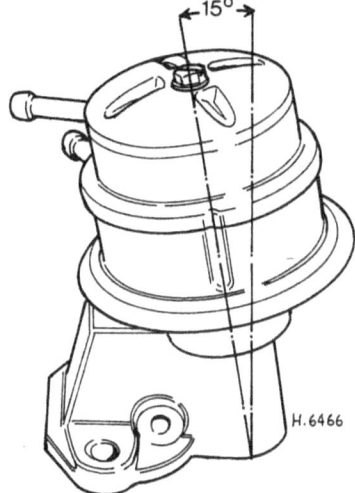

Fig. 13.11. Fuel pump as fitted to engines with alternators

5.20a Early type fuel pump with external cut-off valve; A-inlet, B-outlet

5.20b Removing early type fuel pump

5.23 Removing fuel pump filter screen

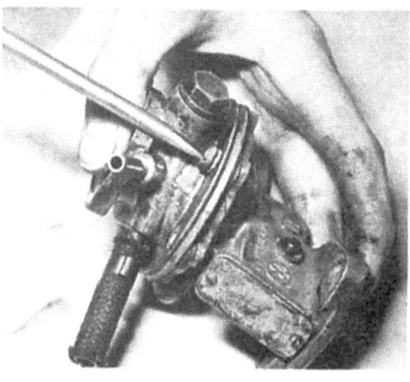

5.24a Loosening the main body securing screws

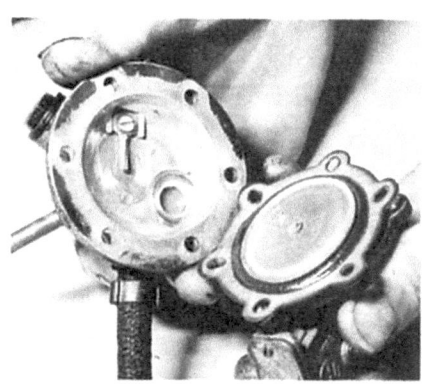

5.24b Separating the two halves of the pump

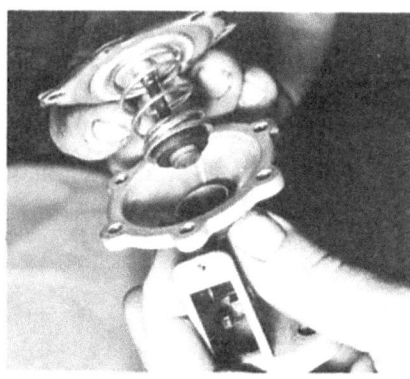

5.25a Fitting diaphragm to lower pump body

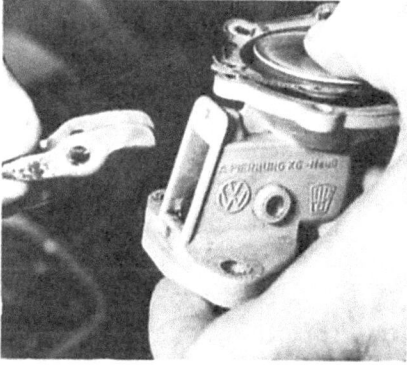

5.25b Fitting pump lever . . .

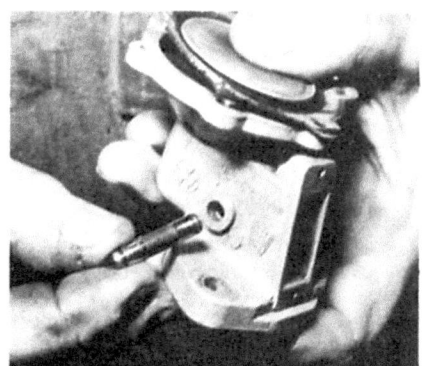

5.25c . . . and pivot pin

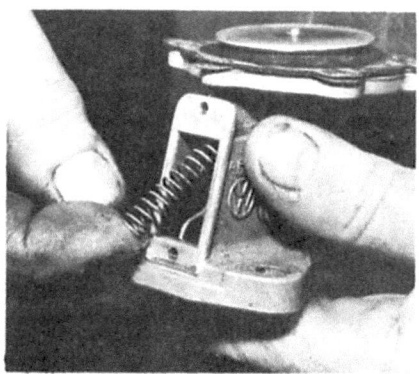

5.25d Fitting pump lever return spring

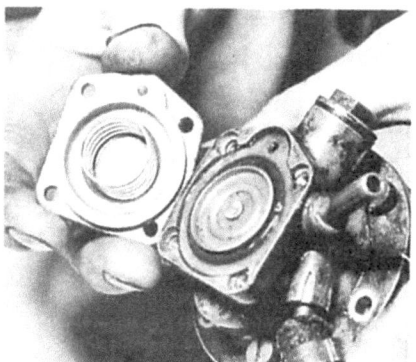

5.27 Checking cut-off valve

5.30 Fitting a new gasket, and then the pushrod

5.33 Removing the filter (early type pump)

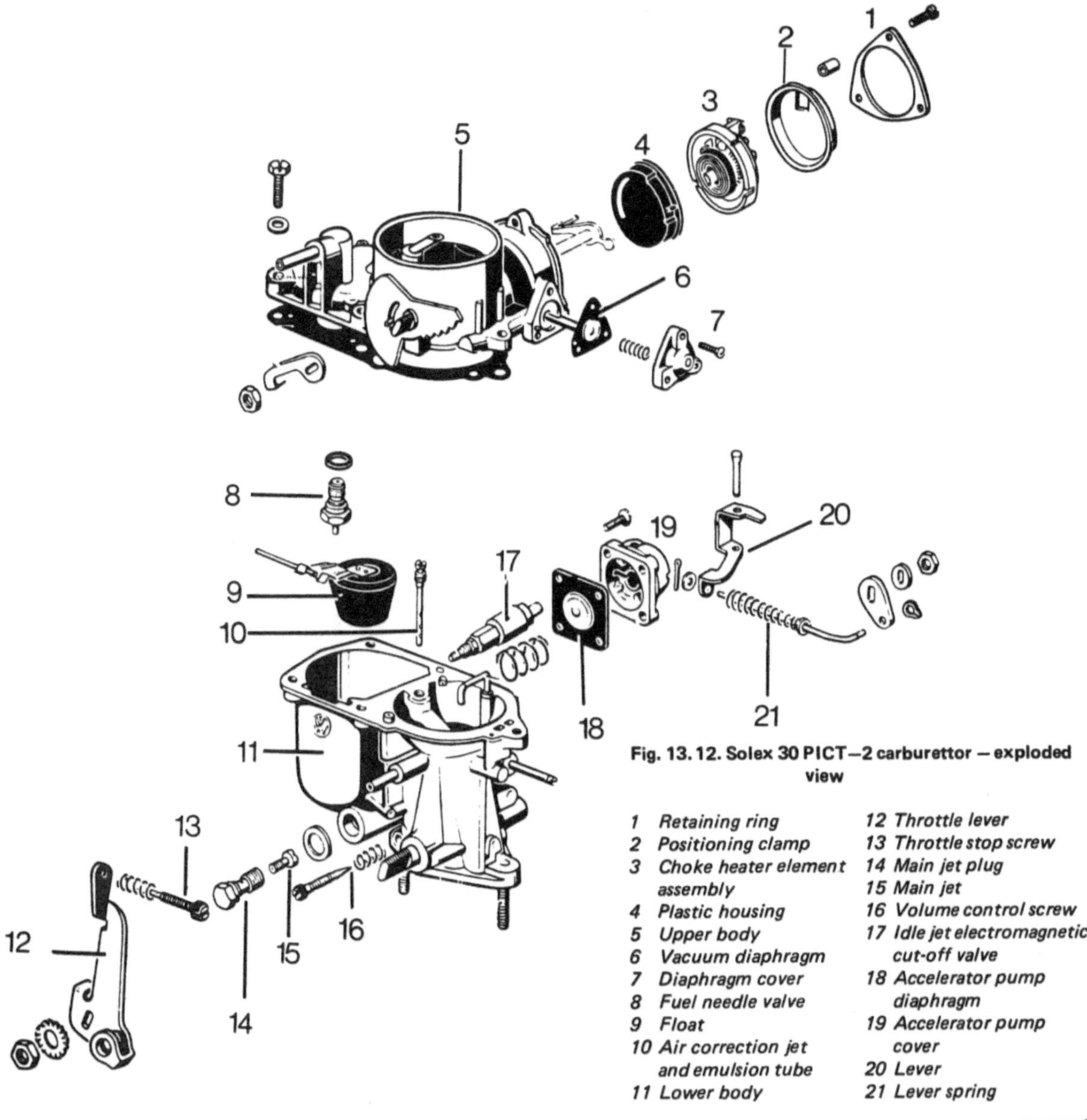

Fig. 13. 12. Solex 30 PICT—2 carburettor — exploded view

1 Retaining ring	12 Throttle lever
2 Positioning clamp	13 Throttle stop screw
3 Choke heater element assembly	14 Main jet plug
	15 Main jet
4 Plastic housing	16 Volume control screw
5 Upper body	17 Idle jet electromagnetic cut-off valve
6 Vacuum diaphragm	
7 Diaphragm cover	18 Accelerator pump diaphragm
8 Fuel needle valve	
9 Float	19 Accelerator pump cover
10 Air correction jet and emulsion tube	
	20 Lever
11 Lower body	21 Lever spring

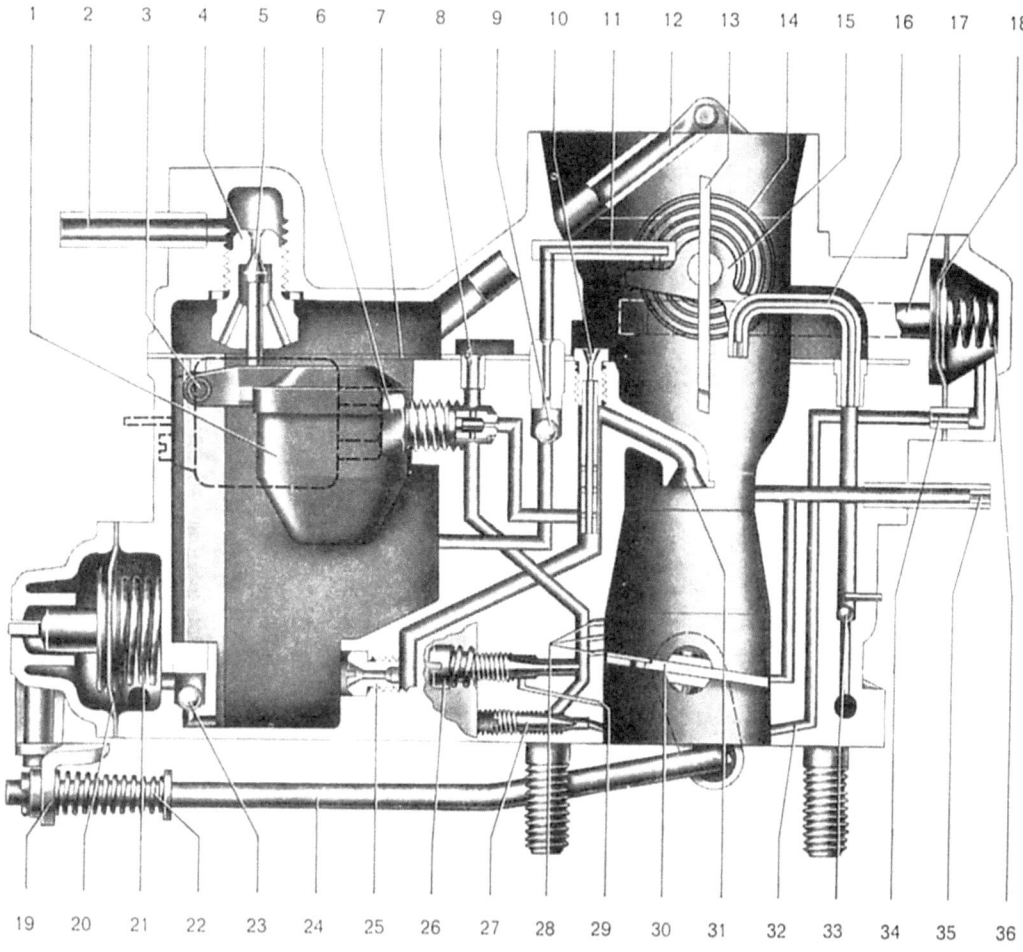

Fig. 13.13. Solex 30 PICT—2 carburettor — cross-section view

1 Float	10 Air correction jet and	19 Pump lever	28 Bypass ports
2 Fuel line	emulsion tube	20 Pump diaphragm	29 Idle port
3 Float lever	11 Power fuel tube	21 Pump spring	30 Throttle valve
4 Needle valve	12 Vent tube	22 Spring	31 Main discharge beak
5 Needle	13 Choke flap	23 Non-return ball,	32 Vacuum drilling
6 Pilot jet (electromagnetic	14 Bi-metal choke spring	pump, inlet	33 Non-return ball, pump
cut-off shown in dotted	15 Choke lever	24 Pull rod for pump	outlet
line)	16 Accelerator pump dis-	diaphragm	34 Jet orifice
7 Gasket	charge tube	25 Main jet	35 Vacuum connection
8 Pilot air drilling	17 Vacuum diaphragm rod	26 Volume control screw	36 Vacuum diaphragm spring
9 Non-return ball	18 Vacuum diaphragm	27 Idle bleed screw	

Solex 28 PICT—2 and 30 PICT—2 carburettors - general description and adjustments

37 It is difficult to be specific as to how the Solex 28 PICT—1 became 28 PICT—2 and then 30 PICT—2. All the time the pressure to reduce the carbon monoxide (CO) content of exhaust emissions was increasing and several modifications appeared to meet this demand. An exploded view is given at Fig.13.12 of the 30 PICT—2. Its construction and testing is as described for the 28 PICT in Chapter 3.

38 The first modification, announced as the Solex 28 PICT—2 had a smaller taper on the volume control screw and a finer thread for adjusting the screw, which was factory sealed with a plastic cap to stop amateurs altering its setting. At the same time the 30 PICT—2 was fitted with two volume control screws, one to adjust for CO content and the other for idle speed adjustment (See Fig.13.13). At this stage also, stricter instructions for adjusting the carburettor were issued. A summary is below.

39 Check ignition timing, valve clearances, dwell angle and engine oil temperature. The engine should be run to normal operating temperature. Connect a tachometer to the engine and start the engine. Screw in the volume control screw until the engine speed drops, so that the engine runs unevenly, then turn the screw back until the engine runs smoothly. Now adjust the throttle control screw until the engine speed is between 850 and 900 rpm. If necessary turn the volume control screw to achieve even running again.

40 At this point screw in the volume control screw until the engine speed drops 50 rpm. If the engine now runs roughly turn the screw out slightly until the engine runs smoothly again.

41 Later versions of this carburettor have a magnetic cut-off valve fitted to the pilot jet. If it is necessary to remove the pilot jet for cleaning, remove the solenoid with it and use two spanners to separate them. Do **not** grip the solenoid by its case, either with pliers or in the vice; the case is thin and the wiring will be damaged.

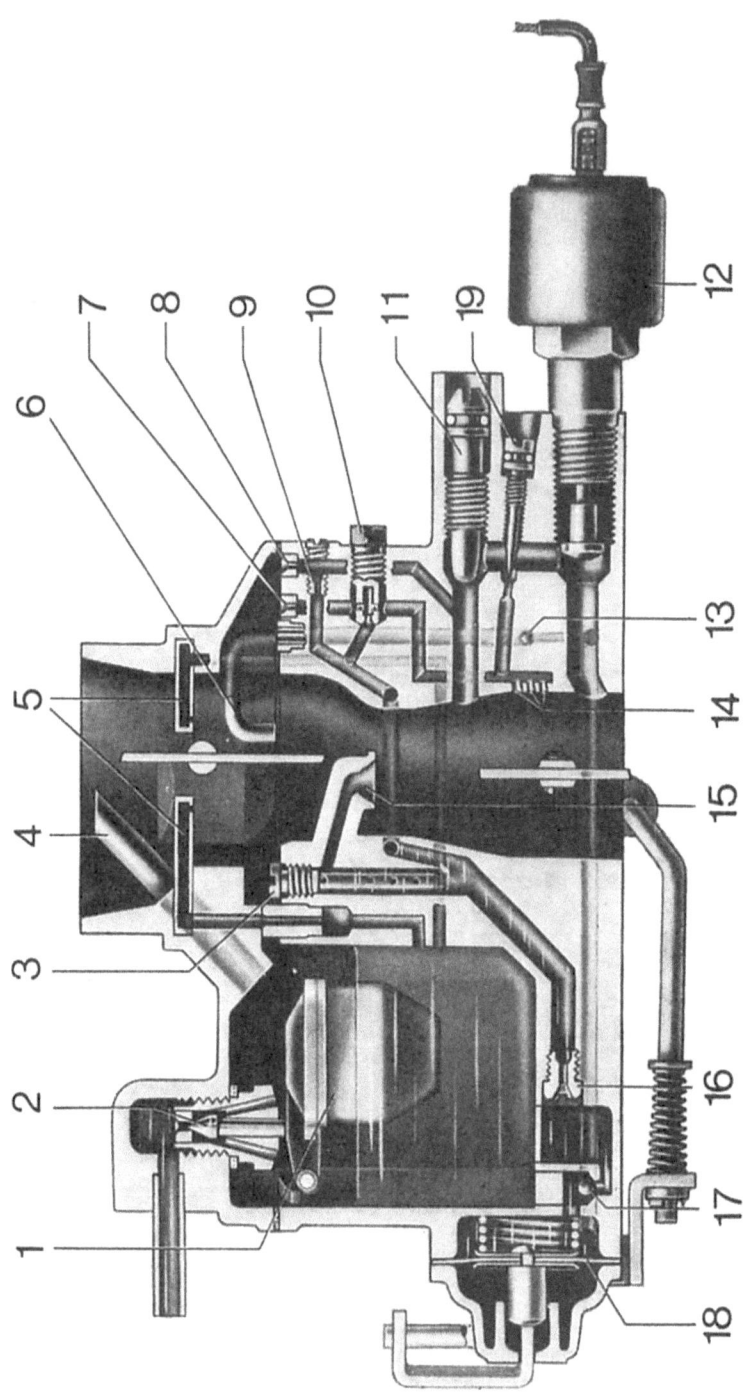

Fig. 13.14. Solex 30 PICT–3 carburettor – cross-section view

1 Float
2 Float needle valve
3 Air correction jet and emulsion tube
4 Air inlet to float chamber
5 Power fuel tubes

6 Injector pipe from accelerator pump
7 Pilot air jet
8 Auxiliary air jet
9 Auxiliary fuel jet
10 Pilot jet

11 Bypass air control screw
12 Magnetic cut-off valve
13 Ball valve
14 Bypass drilling
15 Discharge tube

16 Main jet
17 Ball valve
18 Accelerator pump diaphragm
19 Volume control screw

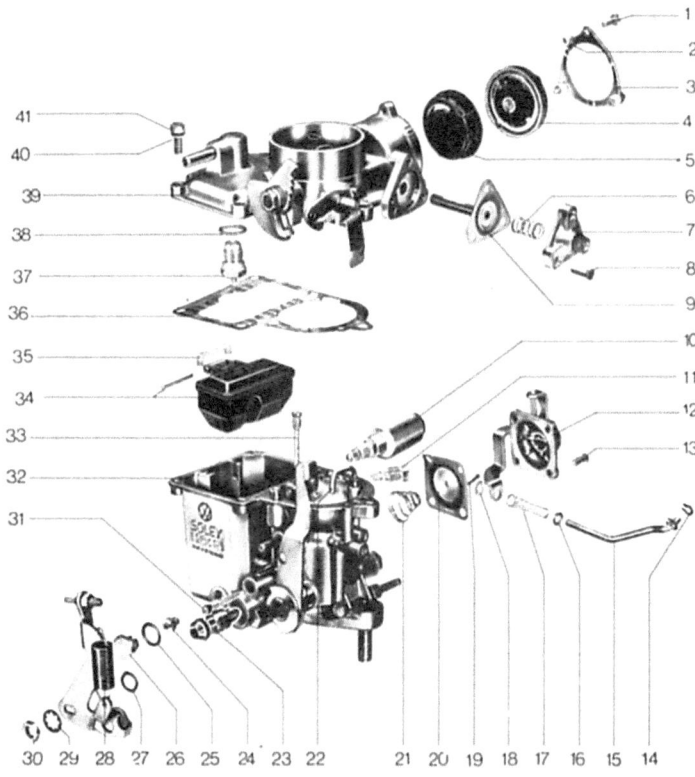

Fig. 13.15. Solex 30 PICT—3 carburettor (earlier type) — exploded view

1 Screw	11 Pilot jet	21 Accelerator pump	31 Volume control
2 Spacer	12 Accelerator pump	diaphragm spring	screw
3 Cover retaining ring	cover	22 Injector tube	32 Float chamber
4 Cover with heater	13 Screw	23 Bypass air screw	33 Air correction jet
element and spring	14 Circlip	24 Main jet	34 Float and hinge pin
5 Plastic cap	15 Connecting rod	25 Sealing washer	35 Pin retainer
6 Spring	16 Washer	26 Plug	36 Gasket
7 Cover	17 Spring	27 Spring, flat coiled	37 Needle valve
8 Screw	18 Washer	28 Accelerator cable	38 Washer
9 Vacuum diaphragm	19 Split pin	spring	39 Upper body
10 Magnetic cut-off and	20 Accelerator pump	29 Lockwasher	40 Spring washer
auxiliary fuel jet	diaphragm	30 Nut	41 Screw

Solex 30 PICT—3 carburettor - description

42 This carburettor, introduced in December 1970, incorporated extra air drillings, and the electromagnetic cut-off valve was moved from the pilot jet to the auxiliary fuel drillings as shown in Fig.13.14.

43 Three versions of the 30 PICT—3 have appeared. The Specifications are given at the start of this Section. Exploded views of the carburettor are given at Fig.13.15 and Fig.13.16. It will be seen that on one type the magnetic cut-off valve closes the auxiliary fuel drilling, on the other the pilot valve. Two adjusting screws, one for bypass air and one for idle mixture, are fitted to both types.

Solex 30 PICT—3 carburettor - removal, overhaul and refitting

44 Removal of the carburettor is generally the same as the method laid down in Chapter 3 for the 28 PICT model. The method of removing and refitting the air cleaner is described earlier in this Section. The carburettor was slightly modified to accept the paper element type air cleaner, and the oil bath type air cleaner will not fit on this later type.

45 Dismantling is also generally the same as laid down in Chapter 3, but there are some small points to note for the new type. The

carburettor is carefully set at the factory and the bypass air screw and the idle mixture screw should not be disturbed unless it is possible to carry out the tests described in the next sub-Section. To do these requires an exhaust gas analyser and a tachometer. If you do have to remove the screws, count the exact number of turns (including fractions of a turn) required to screw them out and use that number to refit them.

46 Before dismantling the carburettor clean the outside thoroughly and then lay out a clean sheet of paper and a notebook and pencil. Make sure your tools are clean and wash your hands before taking the carburettor to pieces. Use non-fluffy rag for any cleansing. Remember also that there is still petrol in the float chamber. Note the angle at which controls are set and the location of each screw. Be careful not to tear gaskets, and renew any seals which seem even slightly faulty. This applies also to the accelerator pump diaphragm.

47 Do not grip the magnetic cut-off valve solenoid case with a vice or pliers. Remove the assembly using a spanner (photo). If you grip the case the solenoid windings may be damaged.

48 The carburettor should be dismantled and cleaned as described in Chapter 3. The jets and drilling should only be cleaned by using compressed air, and not by poking with wire. Any jets should be renewed as necessary. Check that no foreign matter has lodged

Fig. 13.16. Solex 30 PICT—3 carburettor (later type) — exploded view

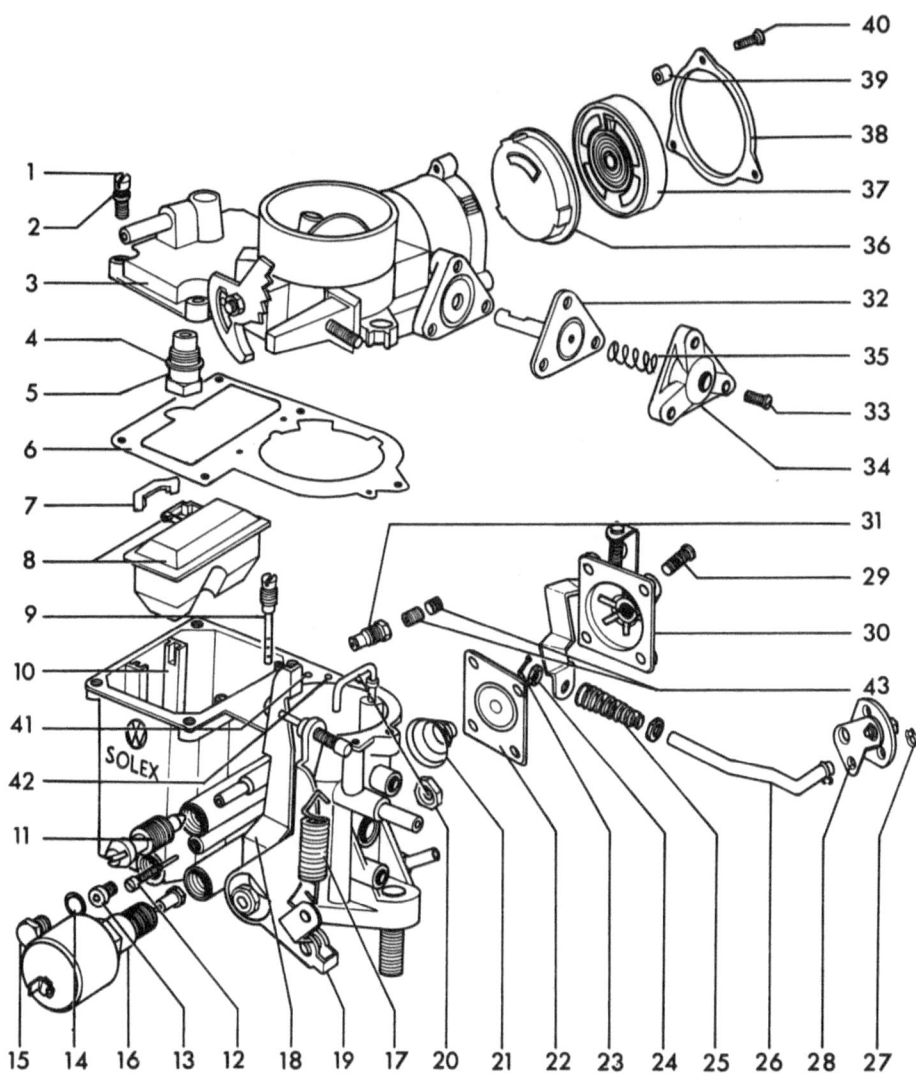

1 Cover screw
2 Spring washer
3 Top cover
4 Needle valve washer
5 Needle valve
6 Gasket
7 Float pin bracket
8 Float and pin
9 Air correction jet and emulsion tube
10 Carburettor lower housing
11 Bypass air screw
12 Idle mixture control screw
13 Main jet
14 Washer
15 Plug
16 Electromagnetic cut-off valve
17 Return spring
18 Fast idle lever
19 Throttle lever
20 Injection pipe from accelerator pump
21 Diaphragm spring
22 Accelerator pump diaphragm
23 Split pin
24 Washer
25 Spring
26 Connecting link
27 Circlip
28 Bellcrank lever (adjustable)
29 Countersunk screw
30 Pump cover
31 Pilot jet
32 Vacuum diaphragm
33 Countersunk screw
34 Diaphragm cover
35 Spring
36 Protection cap
37 Heater coil and insert
38 Retaining ring
39 Spacer
40 Screw
41 Pilot air jet
42 Auxiliary air jet
43 Auxiliary fuel jet and plug

5.47 The electromagnetic cut-off valve on the pilot jet

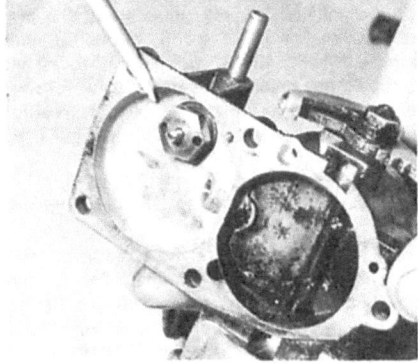

5.48 Needle valve in top cover

behind the needle valve (photo). If there is some then look very carefully at the petrol hose between the pump and the carburettor. Once you are sure the carburettor is clean, reassemble it and then go through the routine tests detailed in paragraph 50 onwards.

49 From October 1975 a modified fast idle cam is fitted witl. one less notch. The automatic choke must be adjusted so that the notch lines up with the lower marking. (The new type can be fitted to previous carburettors). It is identified on new carburettors by a blue paint spot on the automatic choke. The idea is to give the automatic choke a further 0.12 in (3 mm) preload in order to cut out stalling in the warm-up period.

Solex 30 PICT—3 carburettor - tests and adjustments
50 These tests and adjustments can only be carried out with the use of a tachometer and exhaust gas analyser. If you do not have access to such equipment, the work should be entrusted to your local dealer. Before doing the running tests the carburettor must be checked for basic adjustments. These comprise checking the following items:

    a) *Level of fuel in the float chamber*
    b) *operation of the choke valve*
    c) *basic adjustment of the throttle valve*
    d) *correct adjustment of the throttle cable/pedal*
    e) *measuring, and adjusting if necessary, the quantity of fuel injected by the acceleration pump*

51 It is essential also that the valve clearances are correctly set and the ignition correctly timed, spark plug and contact breaker points correctly gapped, dwell angle correct, and that the bores and cylinder heads are in good condition, if the CO content adjustment is to be achieved satisfactorily.

52 *Level of fuel in the float chamber:* Do this test as soon as the carburettor is removed from the vehicle before any fuel is spilled from the float chamber. It is described in detail in Chapter 3, Section 6, paragraph 5.

53 *Operation of the choke valve:* The only way to check this item is to dismantle it and check that the heater unit is intact and correctly installed as described in (photos) Chapter 3. Reassemble the carburettor and check that the choke is closed when the engine is cold and fully open when the engine reaches normal operating temperature. There is no way of repairing the choke other than renewing faulty parts, and if the bearings of the valve spindle are worn the whole carburettor must be renewed.

54 *Basic adjustment of the throttle valve:* Refer to Fig.13.17 which shows the adjustment points. This operation should not be done unless the adjustment has been accidentally altered, as the screw is correctly set at the factory. Locate the throttle adjusting screw bearing on the strangler (fast idle) cam. Turn the screw out until there is a gap between the end of the screw and the cam. Put a piece of thin paper between the screw and the cam and turn the screw in until it just grips the paper. Remove the paper and turn the screw in one further quarter of a turn. Seal the screw in position with a dab of paint or adhesive.

55 *Checking the correct adjustment of the accelerator cable/pedal* is described in Chapter 3, Section 6, paragraph 10.

56 *Checking the accelerator pump:* This may be done with the carburettor in the car or removed from the car. It is essential that the float chamber is full of fuel before starting the test. Open the choke and fix it fully open. It is now possible to see the injection nozzle from the accelerator pump just above the venturi. Use plastic tube to extend the nozzle into a measuring cylinder. Work the throttle until petrol comes out of the pipe into the measuring cylinder. Check that there is no leakage at the joint of your pipe and the nozzle. If all is in order empty the measuring cylinder, check that the float chamber is full, and operate the throttle for five strokes. Make them full strokes and work the lever rapidly. Read the level of fuel in the measuring glass and divide by five. Check the quantity per stroke with the amount given in the Specifications.

57 There are two types of adjustment, early models have a screw as shown in Fig.13.18. Turning this screw adjusts the quantity injected. Later models have a slotted link as shown in Fig.13.19.

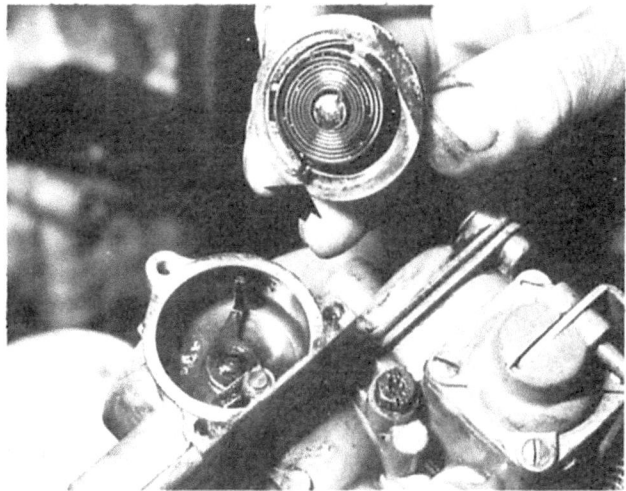

5.53a Automatic choke element with hook (arrowed) to engage the lever

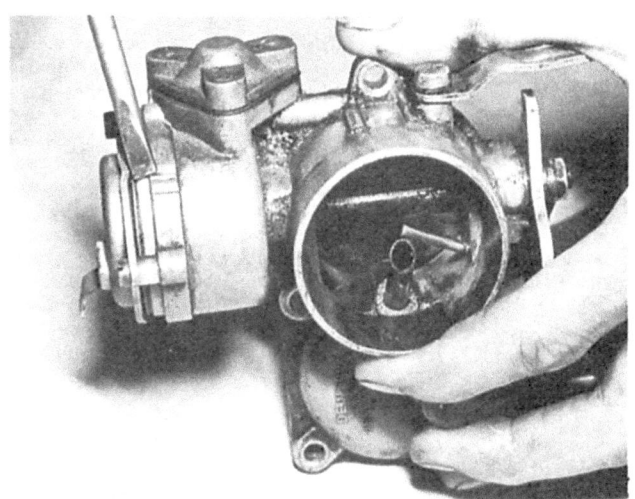

5.53b Automatic choke cover alignment marks

Fig. 13.17. Solex 30 PICT—3 carburettor — adjustment points

    (a) Throttle stop screw on choke cam in open position
    (b) Bypass air screw
    (c) Idle mixture adjustment
Note: from October 1975 the cam has one less step

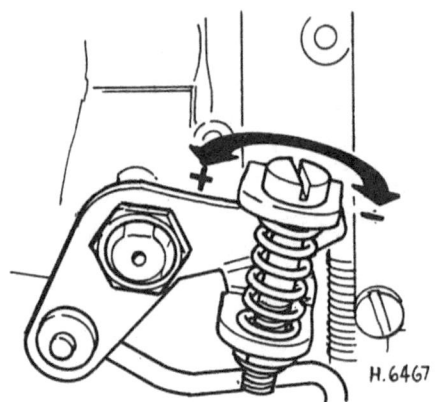

Fig. 13.18. Solex 30 PICT—3 carburettor — adjustment screw
for accelerator pump — early type

(—) amount reduced
(+) amount increased

Slacken the screw and move the quadrant to alter the length of the
rod as required.
58 Once the carburettor is adjusted the carburettor may be finally
set for idle speed and CO content as follows. Check that the
engine is at normal operating temperature and that the choke is
fully open. Fit the tachometer according to maker's instructions
and adjust the idle speed by turning the idle adjusting screw (see
Fig.13.17) until the idle speed is between 750 and 900 rpm. At no
time try to adjust the idle speed with the throttle adjusting screw.
59 The CO content must now be checked. Again with the engine
at normal running temperature and choke fully open run the engine
at the correct idle speed and, using an exhaust gas analyser, check
the CO content at the tail pipe. Turn the idle mixture screw one
way or the other until the CO content comes within the limits

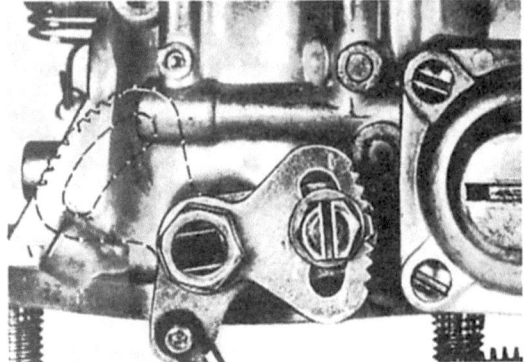

Fig. 13.19. Solex 30 PICT—3 carburettor — accelerator pump
connecting rod adjustment — later types

specified. Now look at the tachometer; the idle speed will probably
have altered a little. Correct it as in paragraph 58 and recheck the
CO content. In this way you can compromise until both values
come within the limits.

Carburettor terminology

60 The following list may be of some use in avoiding the confusion
caused by the use of different names for the same item.

Compensating air jet or air corrector jet	=	air correction jet
Idle air jet	=	pilot air jet
Idle jet	=	pilot jet
Mixture fuel jet	=	auxiliary fuel jet
Float valve seal	=	needle valve washer
Throttle gap	=	throttle valve gap
Choke gap	=	choke valve gap
Idle air control screw	=	bypass air screw
Idle mixture control screw	=	volume control screw

Fault diagnosis — fuel system and carburation

Symptom	Reason/s
No fuel at carburettor	Tank empty. Fuel pump filter clogged. Faulty fuel pump.
Engine will not start	Choke valve stuck. Auto choke not working. Throttle valve stuck. Carburettor flooded by faulty needle valve or punctured float.
Engine hunts or stalls	Air leaks round inlet manifold. Carburettor jets blocked. Idle speed adjustment incorrect.
Engine will not stop when the ignition is switched off	Electromagnetic cut-off valve not working.
Flat spots in acceleration	Accelerator pump faulty. Partial or full load enrichment systems choked. Fuel pump faulty.
Black smoke from exhaust, engine rough at low speeds, plugs fouled	Too much fuel or mixture too rich.
Engine accelerates but lacks power at speed	Enrichment system not working. Air and/or fuel filters blocked.

High fuel consumption

Flat spots with high fuel consumption

Engine cuts out after short distance

---

6 Ignition system

General description

1 The system for later models is changed to 12 volts. The parts for the 6 volt system are not interchangeable with those for the 12 volt system.

2 There have been four different types of distributor (see Specifications) with corresponding changes to the ignition timing; these have coincided with carburettor changes. Up to June 1974 the ignition advance was by vacuum control only. After that date the distributor was fitted with a centrifugal advance mechanism as well. Spark plugs have remained the same throughout, although the gap was decreased slightly in 1974.

3 Overhaul procedures are similar to those described in Chapter 4. However, the centrifugal advance mechanism cannot be repaired, and if faulty or worn, the whole distributor must be renewed.

4 Fig.13.20 shows this later type distributor with the centrifugal advance mechanism. In effect, the distributor shaft is in two halves, the top half carrying the rotor arm. This is connected to the lower half, for drive purposes, by bob weights and springs. As the engine speeds up, the weights move out, stretching the springs and altering the relative angle of the rotor arm to the lower shaft by a small amount. This means that the rotor arm contacts each segment of the distributor cap slightly earlier than it would normally, so the spark at each cylinder occurs slightly earlier, thus promoting the most efficient burning of the air/fuel mixture in relation to that particular engine speed.

5 It is recommended that for adjustment and setting up of contact breaker points gap and ignition timing, the methods described in this Section are used. They are more accurate than the methods described in Chapter 4, and where possible should be used in preference. However, if suitable equipment is not available, the instructions given in Chapter 4 should be adequate provided extreme care is taken to be as accurate as possible.

Ignition system - tracing of faults

6 If the engine rotates but will not start, the problem could be a mechanical defect in the engine, a fault in the fuel system or a fault in the ignition system. Unless something is obviously wrong, the latter should always be checked first, using the following sequence of checks.

7 Remove a plug lead from the plug, bare the end of the lead by turning back the insulating cover, and hold the plug lead so that the metal end of the lead is 1/8 in (3 mm) from the cylinder block. Get someone to operate the starter and as the engine rotates there should be a strong blue spark between the lead and the block. If there is not there is a fault in the ignition circuit.

8 The most important tool required is a simple voltmeter capable of measuring 12 volts. Such a meter is obtained cheaply, can be used for a very large number of jobs on the car, and will soon save its cost in garage bills.

9 To test the·LT circuit first check the voltage at coil terminal '15' with the ignition switched on. No volts means a break in the wire between the coil and switch, or the switch and battery. If the engine does not turn when the starter is operated then the battery is probably at fault so check the voltage across the terminals. It should be 12 volts. The voltage at terminal '15' should be at least 9 volts. If it is less, then there is a loose connection somewhere.

Wrong jets fitted.
Float punctured.
Leaks in petrol hose on tank.
Auto choke incorrectly adjusted.
Brakes binding.
Ignition timing incorrect.

Spring broken in choke cover.

Automatic choke faulty.
Fuel tank vent blocked.

10 If the voltage at terminal '15' is satisfactory, next check the voltage at terminal '1'. Before measuring this, remove the distributor cap and see whether the points are open or closed. If the points are closed the voltage at terminal '1' should be zero - because the terminal is shorted direct to earth through the points. If there is an appreciable voltage when the points are closed then there is an open circuit between terminal '1' and the contact breaker points which must be found. No voltage between terminal '1' and earth when the points are open means either a faulty coil or a faulty condenser. Disconnect the lead from terminal '1' to the distributor and try again. Zero volts (with at least 9 volts at terminal '15') indicates a faulty coil. If the coil is in order then reconnect the lead and check again. Zero voltage this time indicates a short circuit in the condenser, which must be renewed, or a short circuit in the wiring between the terminal '1' and the contact breaker points which must be cleared.

11 If .the.LT circuit is correct, check the contact breaker points. Check that the gap is as specified, and the points' surfaces should be clean. The method of setting is discussed in this Section later on. Make sure this setting is correct, and then, with the knowledge that the LT circuit is in ́order, proceed to test the HT circuit. First of all, repeat the plug lead test. If there is still no spark then a methodical examination of the HT circuit is indicated.

12 The checking of the HT circuit is a little more difficult. Because of the high voltage (15 - 20 kV) it is not possible to use a voltmeter. Remove the HT lead from the centre of the distributor, hold it near the cylinder block and spin the engine with the starter. There should be a strong spark. No spark means either a faulty HT winding in the coil, a faulty lead, or more probably a faulty connection at terminal '4'. Check the lead and the connection. If they are all right then the coil should be taken to the agent for checking and possible renewal. The agent will test the coil under load on a special appliance which involves measuring 18 kV, which the normal owner cannot do.

13 If there is a strong spark then HT is getting to the distributor and the fault is probably here. Check the seating of the centre lead in the distributor cap. Now check the small carbon brush in the cap. It is spring loaded and should make contact with the top of the rotor arm. The blade of the rotor arm should be clean and free from burns; remove any fouling with a fine file or emery paper. The segments in the cap should be equally clean. Examine the cap for 'tracking' which is usually an accumulation of carbon dust and oil in a hair line crack which will short circuit the HT and prevent functioning. Such cracks, or faulty segments or centre brush mean a new distributor cap.

14 Finally check the plug leads. It is most unlikely that all four of them are at fault, but even one will cause hard starting and uneven running. The resistance of the lead overall should be between 5000 and 10 000 ohms. Damage is nearly always obvious on the exterior.

Contact breaker gap and ignition timing - accurate testing

15 Checking the contact breaker points gap is very simple. Connect a dwell angle meter between coil terminal '1' and earth. Trim the meter according to the maker's instructions. Start the engine and let it run at tick-over speed (approximately 850 rpm). Compare the reading on the meter with the Specification given at the start of this Chapter. Adjust the points as described in Chapter 4. Increase the points gap to reduce the dwell angle, decrease it to increase the dwell angle. When the dwell angle is correct check the points gap with a feeler gauge. If the gap is too small you may need a new

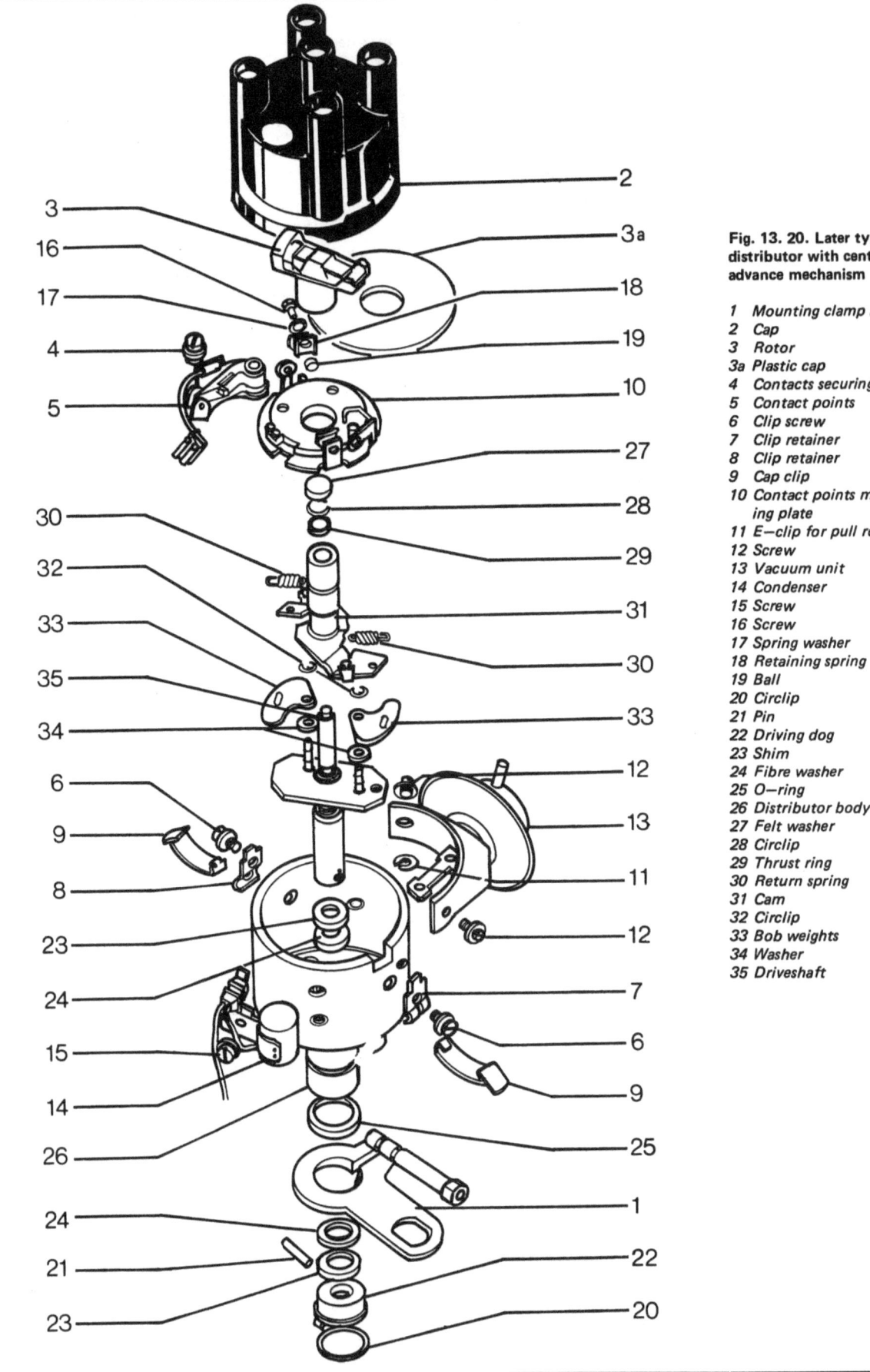

Fig. 13. 20. Later type
distributor with centrifugal
advance mechanism

1   Mounting clamp bracket
2   Cap
3   Rotor
3a Plastic cap
4   Contacts securing screw
5   Contact points
6   Clip screw
7   Clip retainer
8   Clip retainer
9   Cap clip
10 Contact points mount-
    ing plate
11 E—clip for pull rod
12 Screw
13 Vacuum unit
14 Condenser
15 Screw
16 Screw
17 Spring washer
18 Retaining spring
19 Ball
20 Circlip
21 Pin
22 Driving dog
23 Shim
24 Fibre washer
25 O—ring
26 Distributor body
27 Felt washer
28 Circlip
29 Thrust ring
30 Return spring
31 Cam
32 Circlip
33 Bob weights
34 Washer
35 Driveshaft

set of points. Finally, when the gap is correct, or if you cannot get the right dwell angle, run the engine at about 2000 rpm and read the dwell angle again. The reading should not vary from the tick-over reading by more than 1°. If it does, the distributor bearings are worn or the centrifugal advance mechanism is faulty. In either case you need a new distributor.

16 Having checked the points now check the ignition timing. The engine should be run to normal operating temperature. The hose for the vacuum advance should be disconnected at the distributor. A tachometer must be connected to the engine to give an accurate speed setting. Before starting the job clean the 'V' notch on the crankshaft pulley (it is a good idea to put a dab of white paint on it) and clean the pointer. On engines from August 1970 the notch on the pulley represents the correct stroboscopic timing setting (see Specifications). For engines before this date, refer to Chapter 3. Connect the strobe light into No 1 cylinder HT lead as detailed in the maker's instructions. Adjust the engine speed to that given in the Specifications, and shine the strobe light on the 'V' notch in the pulley. The notch should seem stationary opposite the pointer. If it is not then slacken the distributor clamp and move the body slightly until the notch is opposite the pointer. If the distributor clamp is slackened so that you can just move the body, then the adjustment can be done with the engine running, but be careful **not** to get caught up in the fan belt or any other moving part. When the timing is correct tighten the clamp bolt. Now increase the speed of the engine while watching the notch in the beam of the strobe lamp. The notch will move away from the pointer and return when the speed drops. If it does not, the centrifugal mechanism is not working.

17 A simple test to determine whether the vacuum advance is working (*not* whether it is working *correctly*) is to run the engine up to 2000 rpm with the strobe in the circuit and note where the notch moves to, then reconnect the vacuum hose to the distributor. The notch should appear to move still further away from the pointer.

18 If you now suspect a fault in either advance mechanism, further detailed tests should be entrusted to your dealer.

19 If the timing has been altered, the idle speed and exhaust CO content must be checked.

Fault diagnosis — ignition system

Symptom	Reason/s
Engine will not start from cold	Dirty or worn spark plugs. Incorrectly adjusted or worn contact breaker points. Fault in LT or HT circuit.
Engine overheats	Fan belt slipping. Ignition timing and/or contact breaker points incorrectly set. Automatic advance mechanism(s) faulty.
Engine runs roughly and misfires	Dirty or worn spark plugs. Incorrectly adjusted or worn contact breaker points. Distributor shaft and bearings worn.
Engine sluggish and slow to accelerate	Ignition timing and/or contact breaker points incorrectly set. Automatic advance mechanism faulty.

7   Clutch and actuating mechanism

Release mechanism - modifications

1 From July 1970, a modified release mechanism was fitted (starting from assembly number 2867417). This, briefly, incorporates a guide sleeve and modified release bearing, with the transmission case also being suitably modified. Details are shown in Fig.13.21 and the accompanying photo.

2 In September 1971 (starting from assembly number 3957300) a stronger clutch mechanism was fitted, the shaft being increased in size.

3 In October 1971 (starting from chassis number 1122076466) a modified clutch pedal and release lever were fitted.

4 Removal and inspection of the release bearing is as for earlier types. Refer to Chapter 5, Section 5, paragraphs 1 to 4 inclusive.

5 When refitting the thrust release bearing fit the clips so that the ends point upwards (photo).

6 The cross-shaft itself runs through the casing and should move freely without any sign of slackness in the bushes.

7 If it is necessary to renew the bushes the cross-shaft can be taken out after first taking the operating lever and return spring off the end of the shaft. Then remove the screw which locates the bush in the casing and remove all the components. When refitting the shaft lubricate well with molybdenum grease and ensure that the two concertina type grease seals are intact and properly seated inside the casing (photos). If one should come out on the inside of the casing make sure you get it put back. This bush takes considerable forces when the clutch is operated and should not be ignored or treated lightly (photos).

8 When fitting a new return spring first remove the operating lever by undoing the circlip and taking it off the splined shaft. Fit the new spring so that the hooked end will eventually go round the lever and hold it back. Refit the lever and hook the spring end round it (photo).

9 Re-adjust the clutch pedal play after the engine has been refitted.

10 In March 1977 the guide sleeve was modified. It is made of plastic, and has a clamp plate to hold it under the three retaining screws. Fitting is as for the metal sleeve, but it must **not** be greased.

Clutch assembly - later type

11 The basic overhaul procedures for this type of clutch assembly are similar to those described in Chapter 5, the main difference being that the coil springs of the earlier type are replaced by a diaphragm spring (see Fig.13.22).

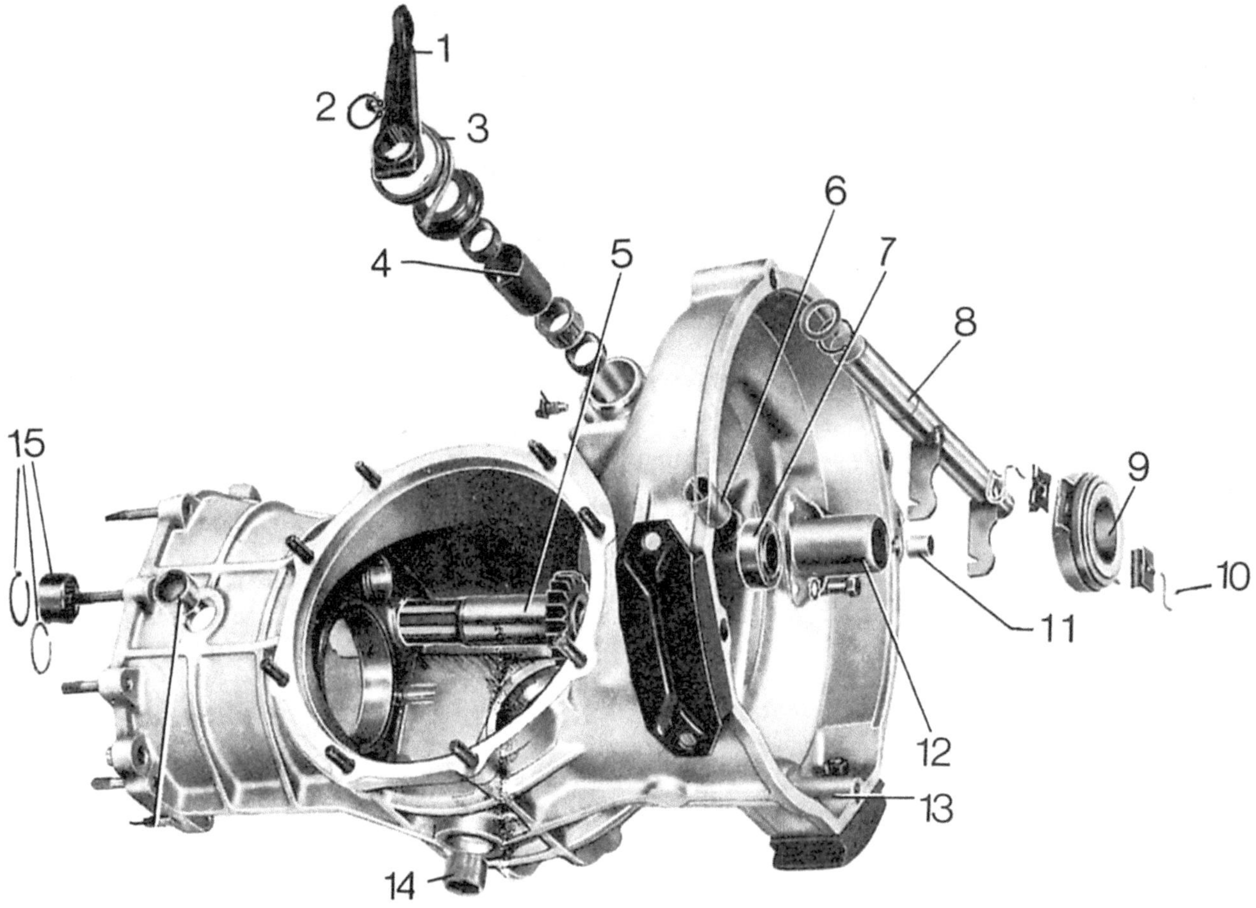

Fig. 13.21. Clutch release mechanism — exploded view

1	Clutch lever	5	Reverse shaft	9	Release bearing	13	Housing
2	Circlip	6	Release shaft bush	10	Clip	14	Oil drain plug
3	Return spring	7	Driveshaft oil seal	11	Starter bush	15	Driveshaft bearing
4	Release shaft bush	8	Release shaft	12	Guide sleeve		

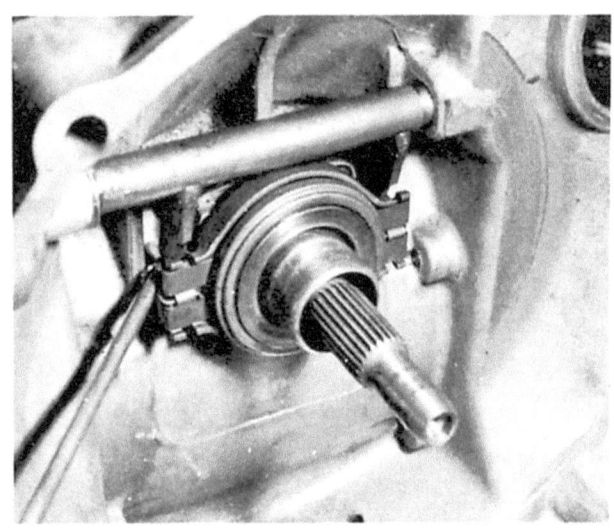

7.1 Clutch thrust release bearing

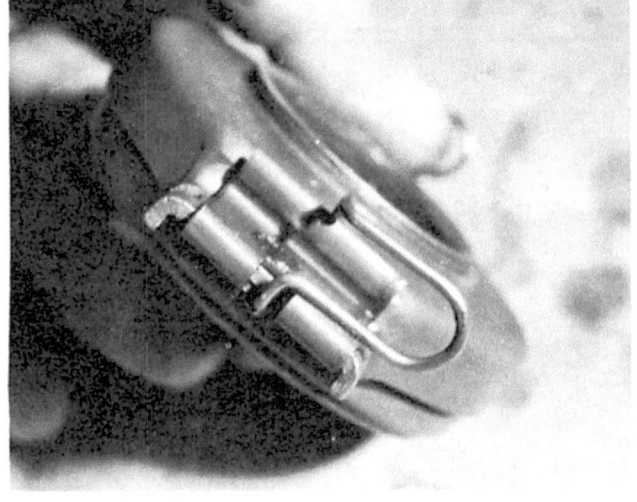

7.5 Thrust bearing clips

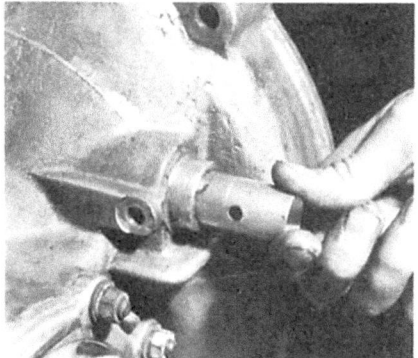

7.7a Fitting the clutch release shaft bush . . .

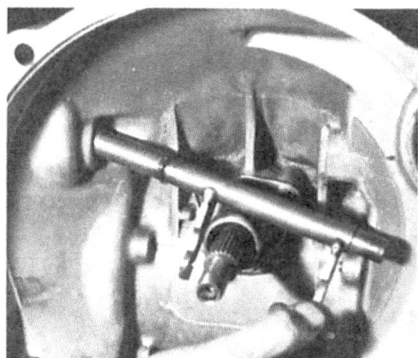

7.7b . . . followed by the shaft . . .

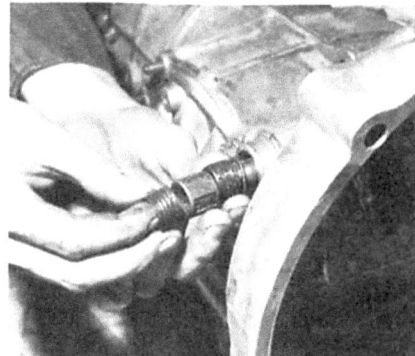

7.7c . . . and the bearing sleeve and seals

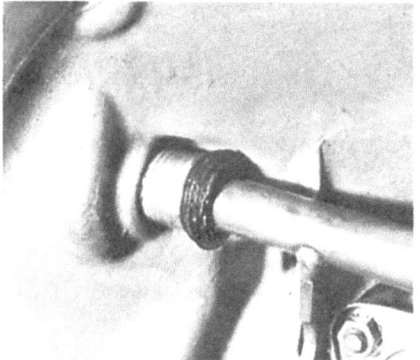

7.7d Make sure that the bush and seal do not come out like this on the inside

7.7e The locating screws for the bush and sleeve

7.8 The release shaft operating lever showing the circlip, splines and return spring

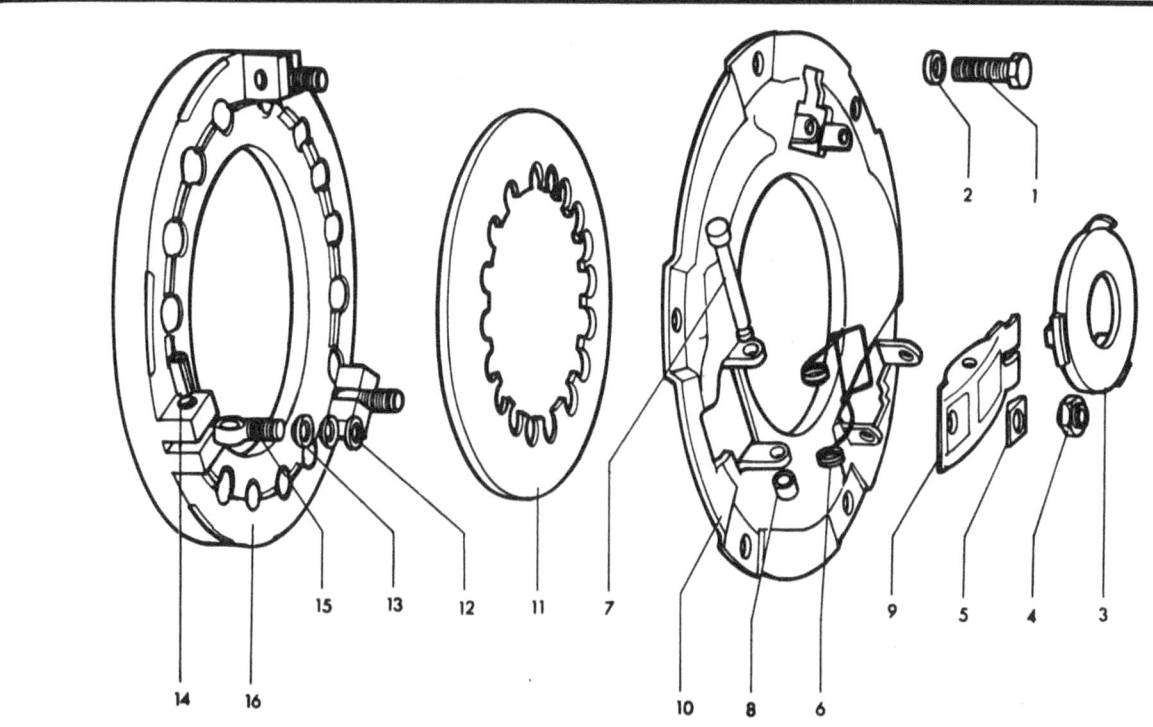

Fig. 13.22. Clutch assembly — later type

1 Bolt	5 Thrust piece	9 Release lever	13 Concave washer
2 Lockwasher	6 Spring	10 Clutch cover	14 Spring pin
3 Release ring	7 Clutch cover pin	11 Diaphragm spring	15 Pivot pin
4 Adjusting nut	8 Locking bush	12 Pivot pin washer	16 Pressure plate

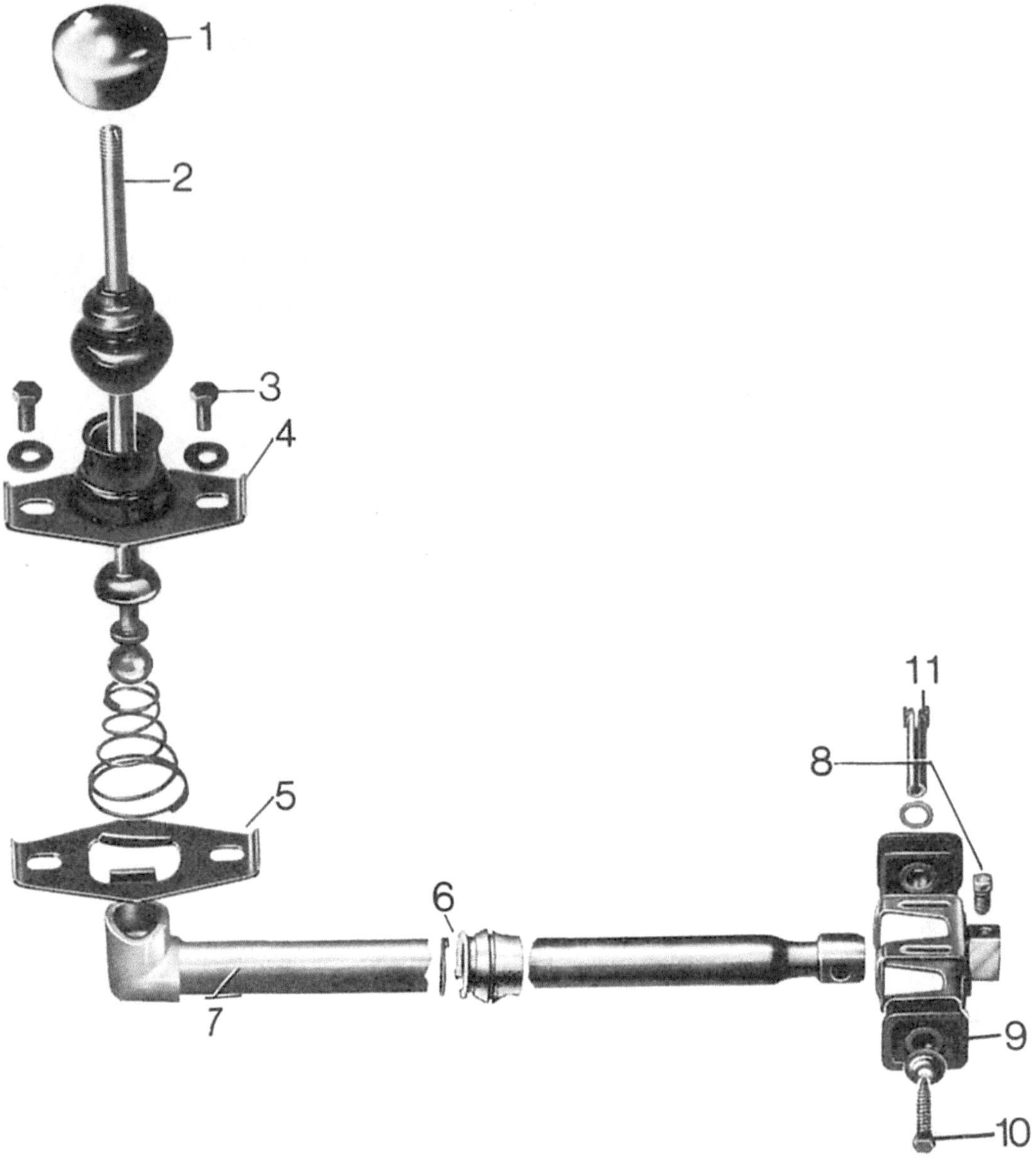

Fig. 13.23. Gear shift mechanism — exploded view

1 Knob
2 Gear lever
3 Bolts
4 Gear lever bracket
5 Stop plate
6 Plastic bush
7 Shift rod
8 Locking screw for coupling
9 Coupling
10 Self tapping screw
11 Spring clip

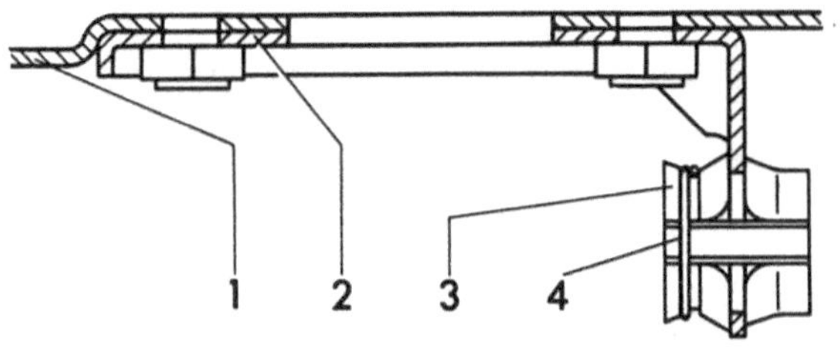

Fig. 13.24. Gear shift mechanism — arrangement of support bush

1 Body panel
2 Reinforcement bracket
3 Bush
4 Retaining ring

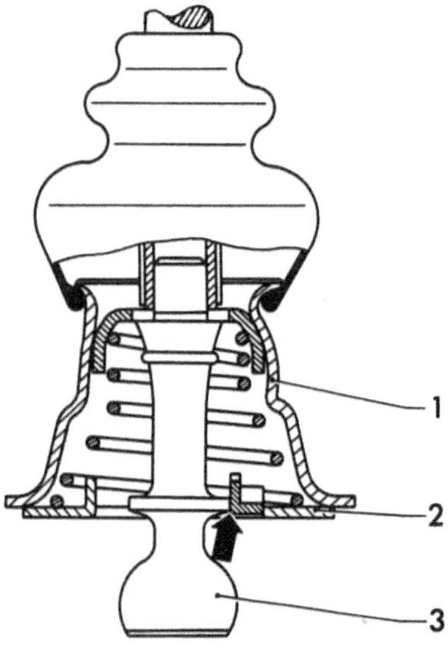

Fig. 13.25. Gear shaft mechanism — cross-section of the gear lever and stop plate

1 Bracket
2 Stop plate
3 Gear lever

The arrow points to the place where the stop plate meets the shoulder on the gear lever

8 Transmission

Modifications to transmission

1 There have been many modifications to the one piece casing transmission over the years. In most cases modified parts will not fit older type transmissions without renewing several other components at the same time; one modified part may cause modification to several other parts directly connected with it in order to allow its fitment.

2 It is suggested that you consult your dealer when obtaining spare parts for the transmission, as he will be able to tell you exactly what components require renewal. You may even then decide it is quicker and/or cheaper to fit a replacement transmission unit.

3 When consulting your dealer, he will require the transmission code. This will be stamped on a rib between the final drive and the shift mechanism on the right-hand side. The transmission type number is 113, code AB. For example, a typical code may be:

AB 24 04 7

where AB is the type code, 24 the day of manufacture, 04 the month and 7 the last digit of the year. This transmission was therefore manufactured on 24th April 1977.

4 It should be noted that overhaul procedures for later models are basically the same as those given in Chapter 6.

Gear shift mechanism - removal and refitting

5 Refer to Fig.13.23 which shows an exploded view of the shift mechanism.

6 To remove the shift mechanism first remove the gear lever. To do this, undo the bolts holding the lever bracket in place and lift out the lever, bracket, spring and stop plate.

7 Lift out the rear seat. Under the seat by the chassis number is a plate over an access hole. Remove this and the shift rod coupling will be seen below. Remove the locking wire and undo the square-headed screw. Remove the tapping screw (Fig.13.23) from the spring pin in the coupling and take the coupling off the shift rod. If you wish to take the shift rod out of the car there is a plate in the front apron secured by two screws which may be removed. If you grip the shift rod with pliers the rod may be extracted through the front of the car.

8 The bush which holds the rod in place may be seen through the apron plate and through the hole in which the gear lever is fitted. Fig.13.24 shows the arrangement. If the bush is worn, push it out and fit a new one. Put the retaining ring on the bush before pressing it into the reinforcement bracket. There is a slot in the bush; this should be at the side when it is installed.

9 Grease the shaft with molybdenum disulphide grease and push it into place through the front apron into the bush until the ball socket appears under the gear lever hole. Install the coupling, fit the spring pin and tighten the square-headed screw. Make sure the coupling fits over both rods firmly. Refit the locking wire. From April 1975 the square-headed bolt is replaced by a bolt with a 10 mm hexagon head. This is much easier to fit. It is held in place by coating the thread with a thread locking compound. The bolt may only be used once so if it is removed a new one must be fitted. Fit the pieces of the gear lever assembly together and insert it in the shift rod socket. One of the slots on the bracket and stop plate has a slight point on it. This must face forwards or it will not be possible to engage reverse gear. Fit the bolts and adjust the lever as detailed in the next sub-Section.

10 Fit the cover plates and refit the rear seat.

11 If the lever rattles in the shift rod socket, fill the socket with grease before installing the lever.

Gear shift mechanism - adjustment

12 Refer to Fig.13.23 and Fig.13.25. Put the lever in second gear. Slacken the bolts holding the lever bracket. Get someone to hold the clutch pedal right down while you adjust the position of the lever.

13 Move the lever, still in second gear, until it is vertical in the lateral plane and sloping about 10° to the rear in the longitudinal plane. Now poke a screwdriver down so that you can move the stop plate under the lever bracket. Move the stop plate to the left until it touches the shoulder on the gear lever and just begins to move the lever. You can't see the shoulder but if the lever just begins to move then the stop plate is in the right place. Tighten the bolts.

14 Check that all four gears engage and that the reverse catch is effective. When checking move from second to first, then to third and fourth. Do not go from second to fourth. Finally retighten the bolts to the specified torque.

9 Axle shafts and tubes

Modifications and overhaul procedures

1 The basic procedures described in Chapter 8 remain unchanged, but there is a revised torque wrench setting given for the axle shaft nut — see Specifications.

2 It is recommended that if the axle shafts are removed for any reason, a new nut is used on reassembly. Undoing the nut poses no real problem provided that a convenient method is found to apply the large torque required. It is most important that the correct size spanner/socket is used or there is danger of damaging the nut, which would then make removal a real problem.

3 Unless a suitable torque wrench is available to tighten the nut, it is best to let your dealer do this properly. If the nut is not tightened the correct amount, damage to bearings may occur.

4 Fig.13.26 shows the arrangement at the outer end of the axle shaft.

5 The boot covering the inner end of the axle is a one piece rubber device held in place with two large jubilee clips. Previously, it was necessary to dismantle the axle assembly in order to renew the boot. However, a special split boot is now available. It is held as before by clips but is split, the joint flanges being held together by six nuts and bolts. If the old boot requires renewal, follow the instructions given here.

6 Clean the exterior of the gearbox and shaft in the vicinity of the boot very carefully. Undo the clips and cut the old boot and remove it. Now clean the axle tube and retainer where the boot has been seated. These surfaces must be completely free of oil or grease. Making sure the clips are in good order, slide them onto the shaft out of the way.

7 Take the new boot and try it in position. Now remove it and coat the flange joint of the boot with sealing compound. VW have a special compound for this purpose. Install the boot so that the joint is horizontal and pointing to the back of the car. Fit the six nuts and bolts and tighten them evenly. Refit the clips carefully. Fit the nuts and bolts and the clips with the car fully loaded. Be careful not to twist the joint or overtighten the screws and clips.

10 Braking system

General description of changes

1 Two significant changes have been made to the braking system; (a) the introduction of the dual braking system and the tandem master cylinder, and (b) the availability as a factory fitted option of front disc brakes.

2 In effect the dual braking system provides separate systems for the front and rear wheels so that if one system fails the other is isolated and continues to provide brake service to two wheels. This is done by the use of a tandem master cylinder.

3 The tandem master cylinder is in effect two master cylinders operated by one pedal. Details are given in this Section. The dual circuit braking system was first fitted in the UK in September 1969 for the 1970 model 1200 Beetle and has remained a standard fitting since then.

4 In 1972 the handbrake was moved closer to the driver's seat to fit the improved type of seat.

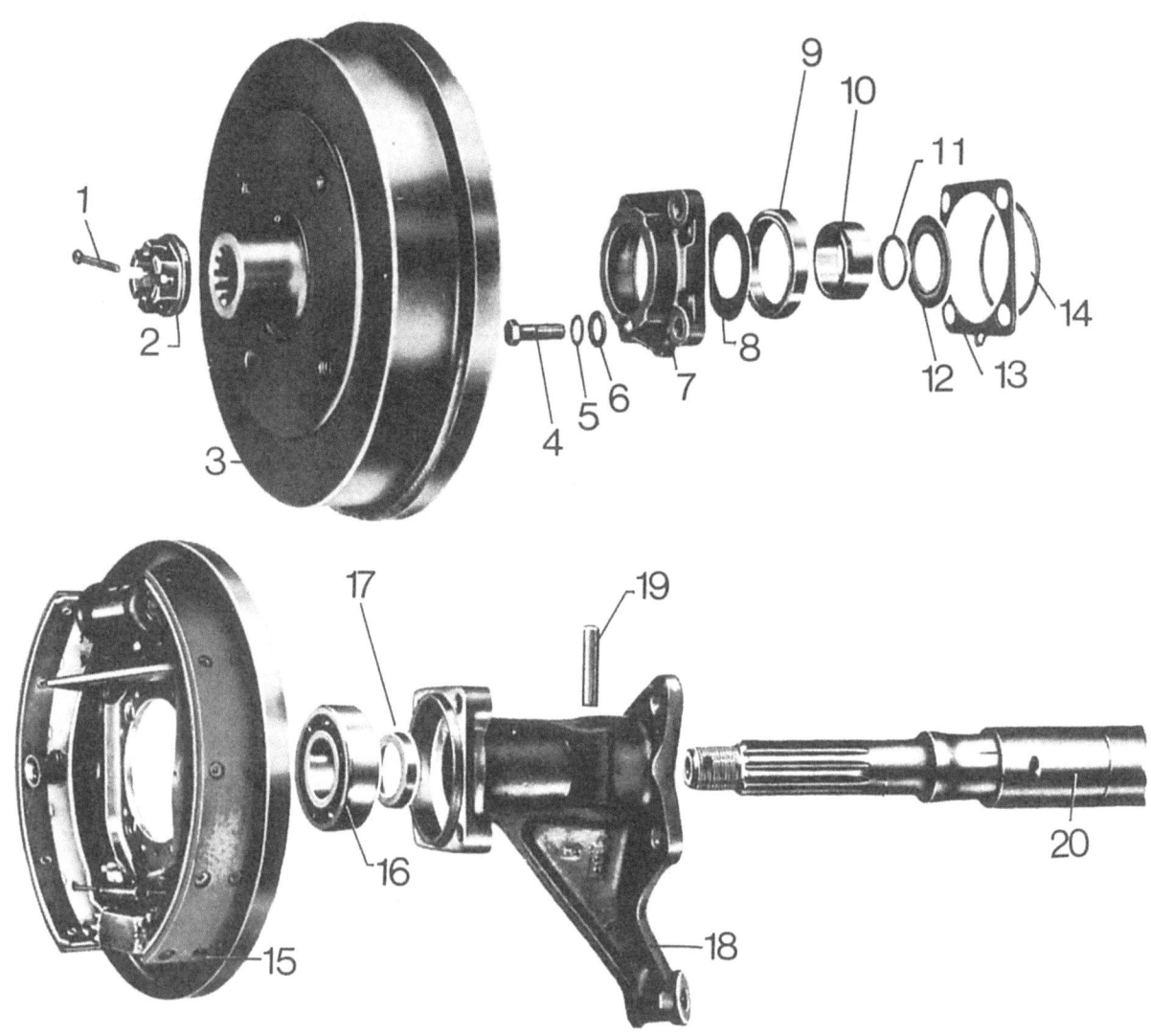

Fig. 13.26. Swing axle — outer end — exploded view

1 Split pin	6 Washer	11 O—ring (small)	16 Ball bearing
2 Axle nut	7 Bearing cover	12 Washer	17 Inner spacer
3 Brake drum	8 Oil deflector	13 Gasket	18 Bearing flange
4 Bolt	9 Oil seal	14 O—ring (large)	19 Dowel pin
5 Spring washer	10 Outer spacer	15 Brake assembly	20 Axle shaft

Tandem master cylinder - description of operation

5   Refer to Fig.13.27. When the brake pedal is in the 'off' position the front and rear pressure chambers are connected to the brake fluid reservoir via the angled pipes, and both chambers are full. The residual pressure valves in the brake line/master cylinder unions are closed, shutting off the cylinder from the brake wheel cylinders.

6   When the pedal is depressed the primary piston (or rear brake circuit piston) is pushed forward by the pushrod. The primary cup moves with the piston and covers the port leading to the reservoir. Pressure now builds up in the primary chamber which moves the secondary piston. This in turn covers the port leading from the reservoir so pressure builds up in the secondary chamber, until the pressures in the two chambers are equal. At the same time the chamber pressures overcome the residual pressure valves in the brake pipe unions sending pressure to the brakes. When the pedal is

released springs return the pistons to the 'off' position and the residual pressure valves close. The ports to the reservoir are un-covered and the pressure in the cylinder reverts to atmospheric pressure.

7   If one circuit fails then the piston of that circuit will move forward against no resistance. In the case of the rear circuit failing the piston will move forward, meeting small resistance, closing the port from the reservoir and driving the fluid out through the non-return valve and out through the leak in the system. It will eventually butt up against the secondary piston, thus moving this forwards and applying the front brakes. The forward movement of the piston is limited by the stop screw. When the leak occurs the first symptom will be a much increased movement of the brake pedal. When the pedal is released the return spring will push the piston back, uncovering the compensating port, and the cylinder

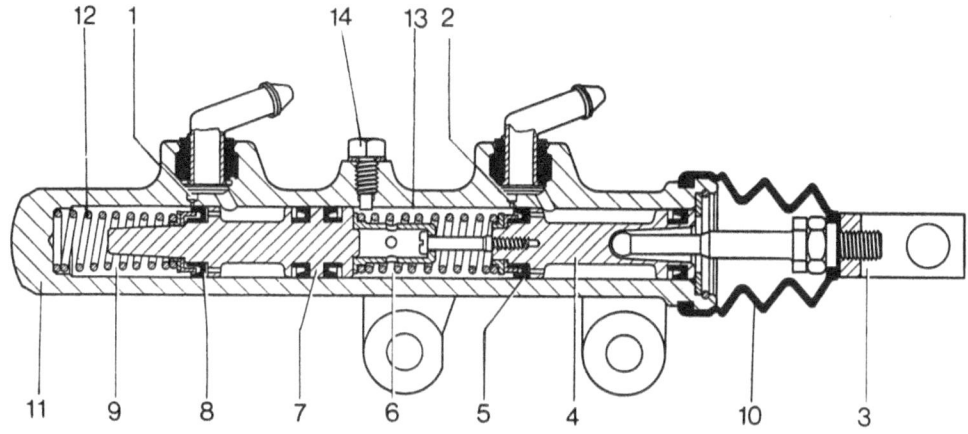

Fig. 13.27. Tandem master cylinder — cross-section

1 Secondary compensating
 port
2 Primary compensating port
3 Pushrod
4 Primary piston (rear brake

 system)
5 Cup seal
6 Primary pressure chamber
7 Secondary piston (front
 brake system)

8 Cup seal
9 Secondary pressure chamber
10 Rubber boot
11 Cylinder body
12 Secondary piston return

 spring
13 Primary piston return
 spring
14 Stop screw

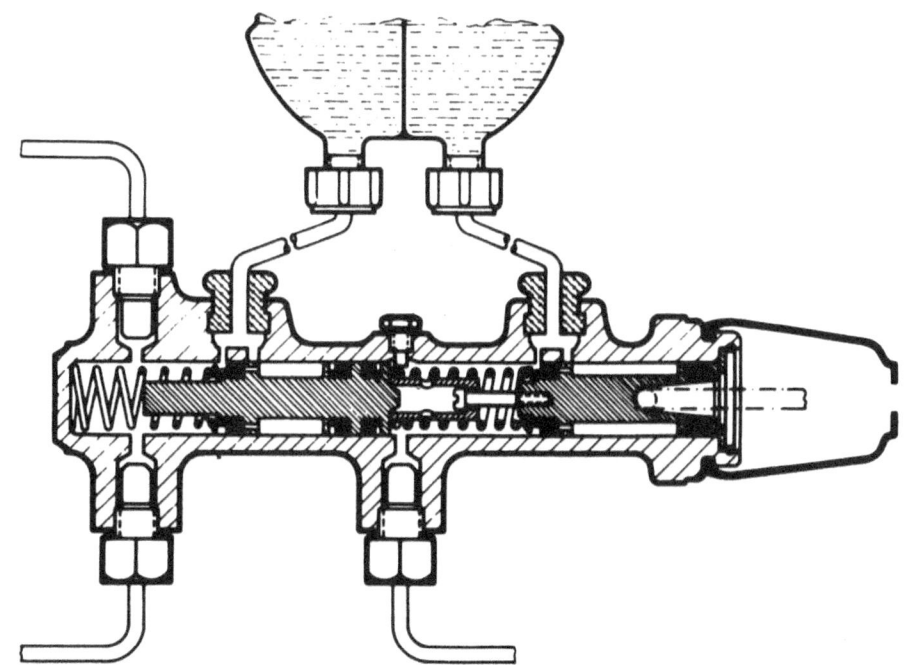

Fig. 13.28. Tandem master cylinder — diagrammatic layout
*The assembly is in the 'brake off' position. The two pipes on the left go to the front brakes, the one in the centre to the
rear brakes*

will fill again with brake fluid which will remain, held by the non-return valve until the pedal is again depressed, when a further amount of fluid will be squirted out of the leak. To prevent the reservoir from emptying by repeated operation of the brakes in this situation, there is a baffle in the reservoir so that the supply to the other system is assured and only half of the reservoir will empty.
8   Failure of the front brake (secondary) system produces much the same result. The primary piston will move forward, building up pressure but the secondary piston will offer little resistance and move down the cylinder until it butts up against the end of the cylinder. The pressure in the primary chamber will then build up, operating the rear brakes. Once again the pedal will go down much further than normal.
9   Fig.13.27 shows a cross-section view of the cylinder, and Fig.13.28 shows the system in more general form. A further illustration, Fig.13.29 gives an exploded view of the cylinder. At

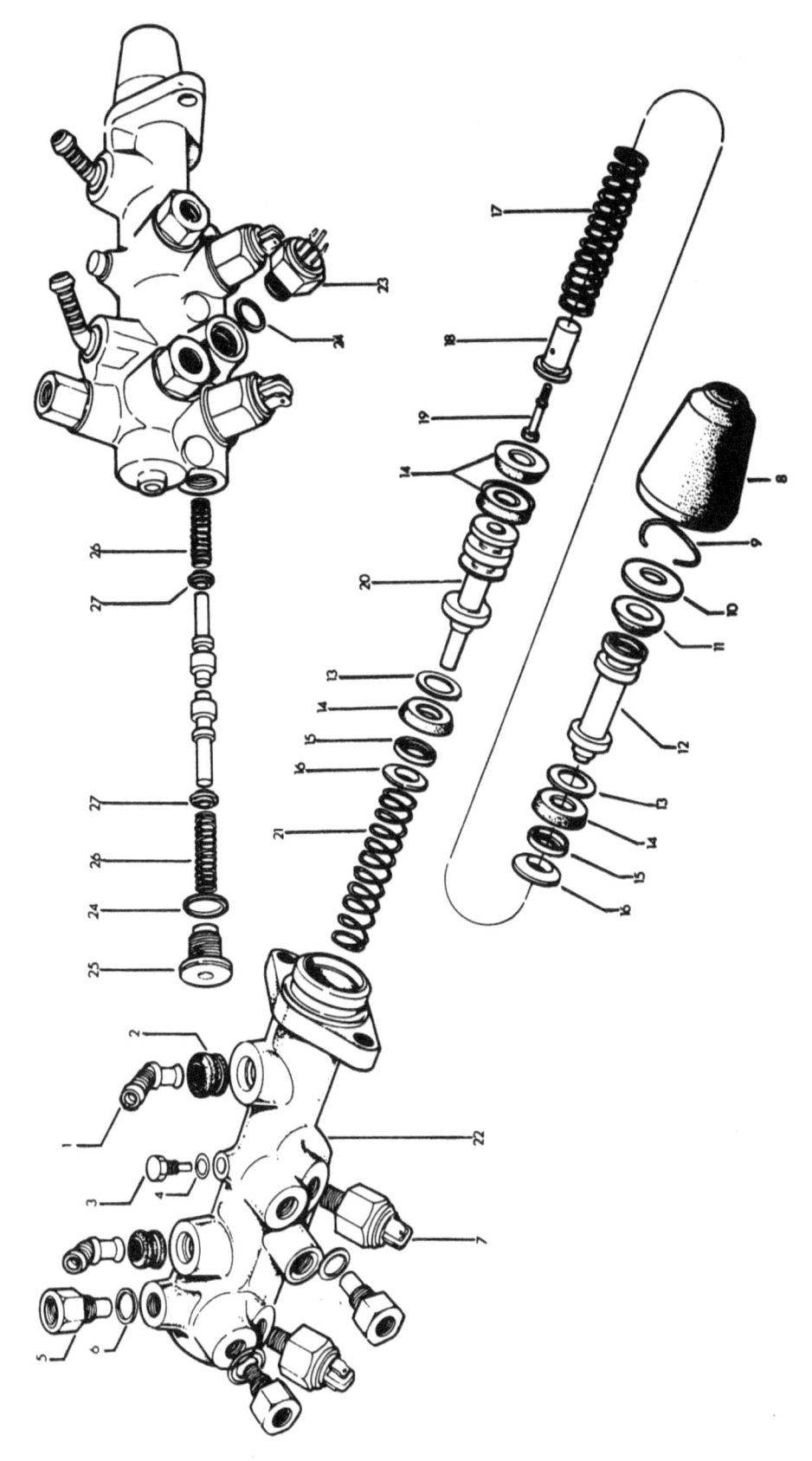

Fig. 13.29. Tandem master cylinder — exploded view

1 Elbow - reservoir inlet pipe	5 Residual pressure valve
2 Sealing plug	6 Sealing ring
3 Stop screw	7 Brake light switch
4 Seal	8 Boot
	9 Circlip

10 Stop ring	15 Support washer
11 Seal	16 Spring plate
12 Primary piston	17 Primary piston spring
13 Cup washer	18 Stop sleeve
14 Cup seal	19 Stroke limiting screw

20 Secondary piston	24 Seal
21 Secondary piston spring	25 Plug
22 Cylinder body	26 Spring
23 Warning lamp switch	27 Cup seal

Note: The cylinder shown at the top has a separate bore for the pressure differential warning system. On vehicles without brake failure warning lights on the dashboard, only one of the switches (7) is used, the other hole being blanked off

the top right of this illustration is a view of a modified cylinder with an additional tapping to accommodate a pressure differential warning switch.

10 Fig.13.30 shows a cross-section of the non-return valve fitted in the brake union. The ball moves to open or close the outlet actuated by one of the two springs according to the pressure in the cylinder. When the brake is applied the ball is forced off its seating and fluid flows into the line. When the pedal is released the pressure in the line closes the valve leaving a small residual pressure in the line which ensures immediate reaction to braking effort. This item is fitted only to lines serving drum brakes. In lines fitted to disc brakes the line is free of pressure when the brake is off. To allow for a small differential pressure for the purpose of bleeding the discs a restriction drilling is made in the outlet to the brake line.

In July 1972, the residual pressure valves were discontinued, and the residual pressure drilling used as on the disc/drum system.

11 It will be seen that at least three types of tandem cylinder have been used. It is essential, therefore, that when buying spares, the exact pattern is quoted. Further, if it is contemplated that fitting discs will upgrade the car then a new upgraded master cylinder must also be used.

Tandem master cylinder - removal and refitting

12 The method of removal and refitting is identical with that of the older single circuit cylinder and is described in Chapter 9, Section 9.

13 If the pedal cluster is disturbed for any reason, it is most important that the brake pedal stop is set back far enough so that if one circuit fails, the brake pedal can move far enough to operate the remaining circuit before it comes up against the panel (see paragraph 92).

Tandem master cylinder - dismantling, overhaul and re-assembly

14 Before commencing overhaul make sure you can get a spares kit. If the system is spongy and there are no external leaks then it is probable that the seals in the master cylinder are at fault. If the seals are at fault, eventually the pedal will go right down with no braking effort resulting.

15 Remove the cylinder as detailed previously and clean it thoroughly. Now clean all the tools, wash your hands and lay out a clean sheet of paper on the bench, a set of clean containers and a notebook and pencil to jot down any important notes.

16 Remove the piston stop screw (see Fig.13.29) and hold the cylinder firmly in the soft jaws of a vice.

17 Remove the boot from the rear of the cylinder and then carefully remove the internal circlip by levering it out with a screwdriver. Hold the pushrod piston in place and remove the cylinder from the vice.

18 The two pistons and all their component parts may then be drawn out. Do this carefully, taking note of the order and position in which they come out.

19 All internal seals are fitted to the grooves in the pistons as indicated in Fig.13.29. They can be pulled off and fitted without special tools but care must be taken not to overstretch them. The secondary piston is fitted with three seals all the same size and shape. The front two face forward and the third to the rear. The primary piston has two seals, both facing forwards.

20 When reassembling the pistons into the cylinder first place the cup washer, cup seal, support washer, spring plate and spring, in that order over the nose of the secondary piston (to which the new secondary cup and rear seal should have been already fitted). Hold the cylinder vertical with the open end downwards and feed the whole assortment back in so that the loose items do not fall off the piston.

21 The primary piston primary cup is held in location by a support washer and spring plate also. These in turn are held firm by the stop sleeve and stroke limiting screw. By undoing the stroke limiting screw inside the stop sleeve all these component parts may be released. The new seal is then easily placed in position.

22 When refitting the primary piston it should be pushed far enough forward to enable the stop screw to be put in so that it

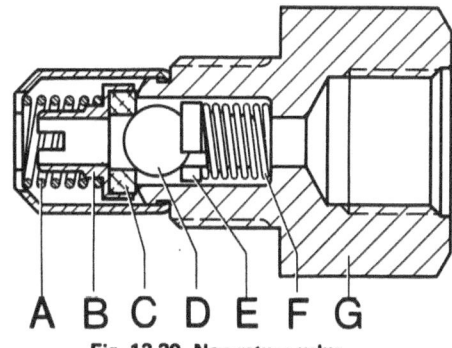

Fig. 13.30. Non-return valve

A Spring	C Seal	E Stop sleeve	G Support
B Sleeve	D Ball	F Spring	

fits behind the rear end of the secondary piston. This is most important. It must not be fitted so that it engages the recessed part in the shank of the secondary piston.

23 Refit the stop ring, circlip and rubber boot over the end of the cylinder.

24 If the brake light switch is faulty, remove it and fit a new one, using the same sealing washer. Tighten it to the specified torque.

25 The tandem master cylinders for disc/drum systems and all-drum systems are not interchangeable. If in doubt, consult your dealer.

Disc brakes - general description

26 The disc brakes are an optional extra for the 1200 Beetle. They are factory fitted on demand. It is not possible to fit front disc brakes to a vehicle fitted originally with drums without fitting a modified steering knuckle. Fig.13.31 shows the detail. The steering knuckle for the disc allows for extra accommodation for the caliper. We do not recommend that owners try this conversion themselves.

27 Two types of disc brake may be encountered. They are generally similar but differ in detail and the manner in which the pads are extracted. Fig.13.32 shows the layout of the type made by Teves (ATE). Fig.13.33 shows the layout of the type made by Girling. Both are fixed caliper types. The disc is identical for both makes of caliper. The illustrations in this Section are of the Teves type but also apply in principle to the Girling caliper. The latter, however, may not be split for overhaul as the joint seal is not a scheduled spare. The Teves type may be split if a new seal is available.

28 The caliper, bolted to the steering knuckle, consists of two frames bolted together, each containing a hydraulic cylinder, piston and seals. Each piston presses against the brake pad when the brake pedal is depressed, forcing it against the disc. A splash plate shields the disc from mud and water thrown up by the wheels.

29 The disc is bolted to the front hub and revolves with the wheel. As the brake pedal is depressed the pads grip the discs on each side of the vehicle and thus slow the vehicle. The system is self adjusting; as the brake pads wear each piston moves further out of its cylinder, thus compensating for this wear.

Disc pads (Teves) - removal, inspection and refitting

30 Remove the front wheel. Refer to Fig.13.32.

31 There are two visual examinations to be made before dismantling anything. These are the thickness of the friction pad and the gap between the pad and disc.

32 Pad friction material thickness must not be less than that given in the Specifications, otherwise the pads should be renewed.

33 The residual clearance should not be more than that given in the Specifications between disc and pad. This can be measured with a feeler gauge.

34 If the gap is greater it is probably due to a sticking piston. A simple remedy is given later on in this Section.

35 If the pads are to be used again mark where they came from

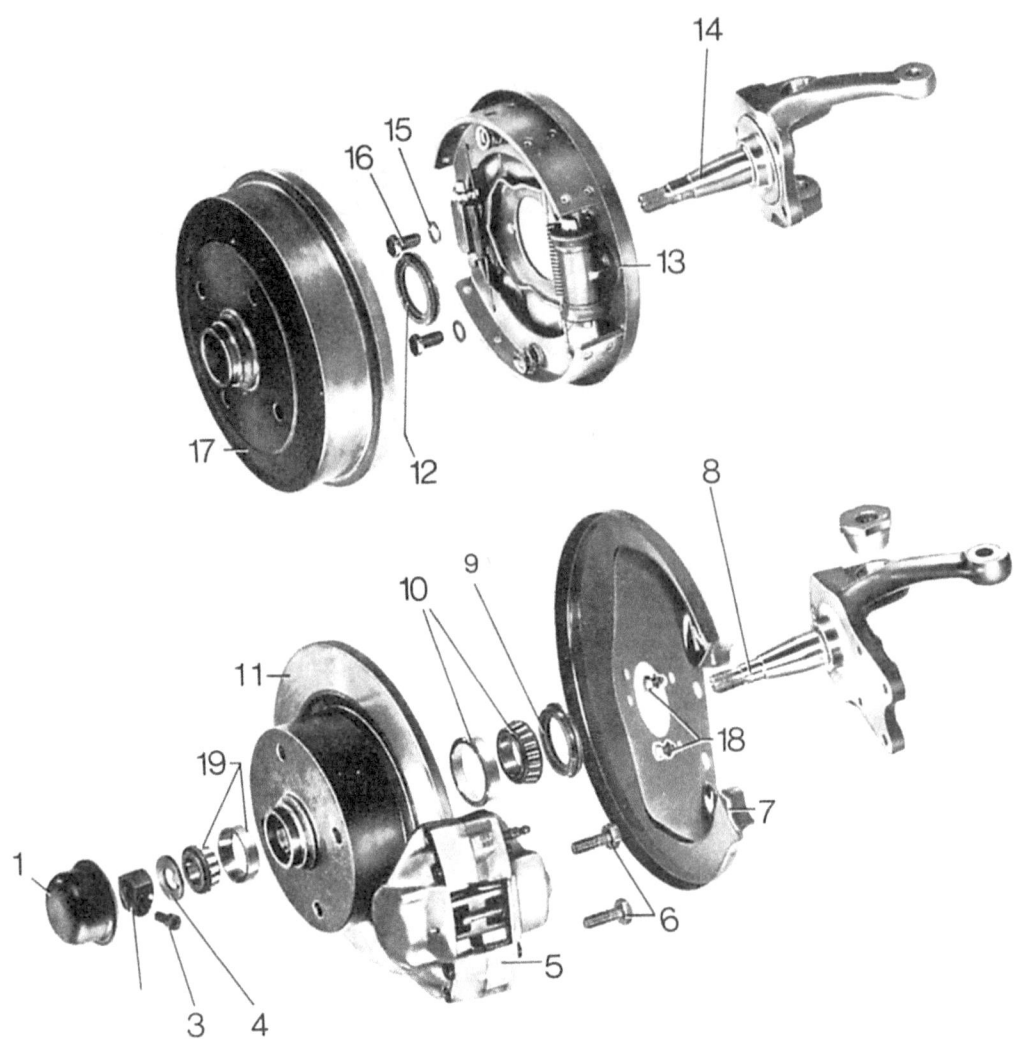

Fig. 13.31. Front brake assemblies — drum (top) and disc (bottom)

1 Cap	6 Caliper bolts	11 Disc	16 Bolt
2 Bearing nut	7 Splash plate	12 Seal	17 Brake drum
3 Lock screw	8 Steering knuckle	13 Backplate assembly	18 Splash plate securing
4 Thrust washer	9 Oil seal	14 Steering knuckle	screws
5 Caliper	10 Inner bearing	15 Lockwasher	19 Outer bearing

beforehand so they may be put back in the same position. Then drive out the retaining pins from the outside with a long nosed punch (photo). Lift off the spring retainer plate (photo).

36 Before removing the old pads it is best to force them away from the disc carefully, with a suitable flat metal lever. This will push the pistons back. Before doing this it will be necessary to remove some hydraulic fluid from the reservoir to prevent it overflowing when the pistons are pushed back. Do this with a suitable suction device such as an empty flexible plastic bottle.

37 Once the pistons are pushed back remove the pads and piston retaining plate (photo). Note that there is a cutaway portion on one side of the piston. Provided the piston is not rotated after the retaining plate is taken out there should be no cause for difficulty on refitting of the plate. For details of the correct position of the piston cut-out refer to the paragraphs on removal and refitting of caliper assembly.

38 Blow out the aperture in the caliper and examine the seal

which should show no signs of cracking or brittleness. If it does it should be renewed.

39 Clean off the piston retaining plate and refit it together with new friction pads. New pad retaining spring plates are normally provided with the pads and these should be used. The spring plates have a wide and narrow side. Put the wide side upwards. When refitting the retaining pins (from the inside) do not use a punch smaller in diameter than the pin. Preferably, use no punch at all, otherwise there is a possibility of shearing the shoulder off against the split clamping bush.

40 Pump the brake pedal to bring the pads up to the disc and check the level of hydraulic fluid in the reservoir.

41 If the clearance between the disc and pad is too great after brake operation then this is an indication that the inner piston rubber seal is sticking somewhat and distorting more than normally. This retracts the piston more than usual when the pressure is taken off. Movement of the piston can usually cure this. Remove a

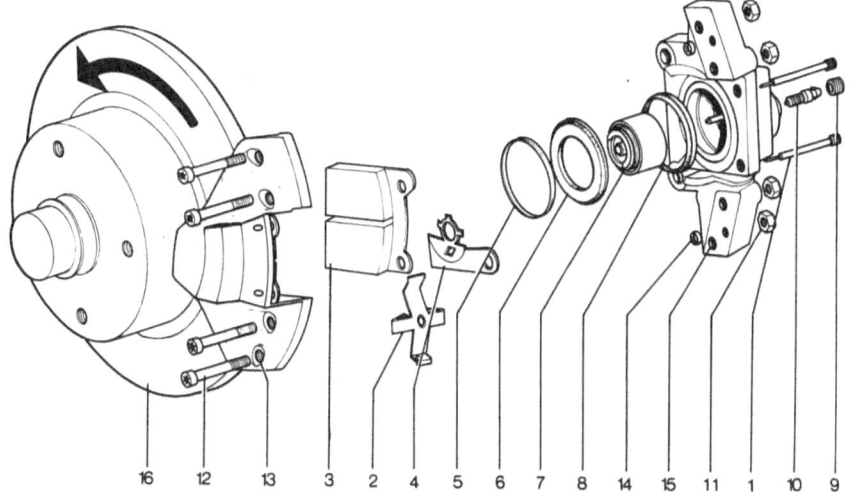

Fig. 13.32. Disc and caliper components (Teves)

1 Pad retaining pin	5 Clamp ring	10 Bleeder valve	14 Seal
2 Spreader spring	6 Seal	11 Hexagon nut	15 Caliper inner
3 Friction pad	7 Piston	12 Cheese head screw	housing
4 Piston retaining	8 Rubber seal	13 Caliper outer housing	16 Brake disc
plate	9 Dust cap	(assembled)	

Note: Arrow shows forward rotation of disc. Later models have modified spreader springs and only 1 retaining pin

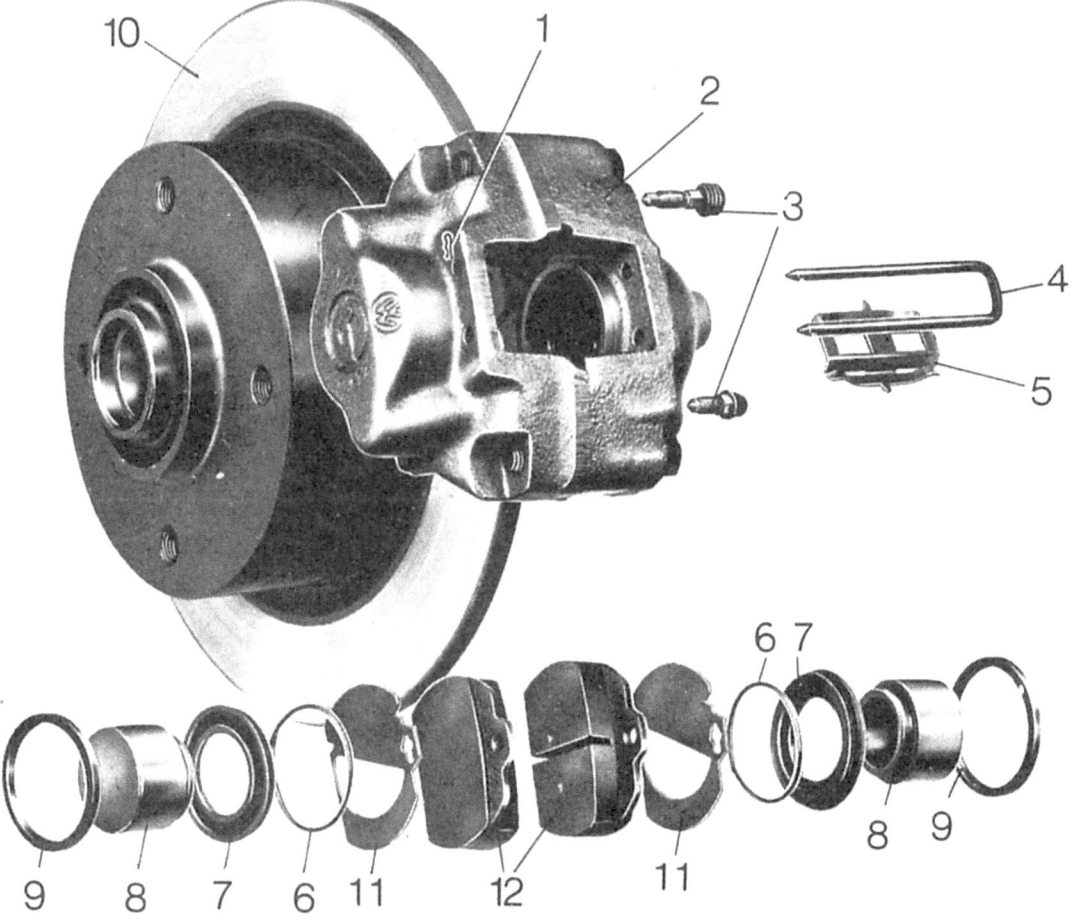

Fig. 13.33. Disc and caliper components (Girling)

1 Locking pin	4 Retaining pin	7 Cap	10 Disc
2 Caliper	5 Spreader spring	8 Piston	11 Noise damping plate
3 Bleed screws	6 Retaining ring	9 Seal	12 Brake pad

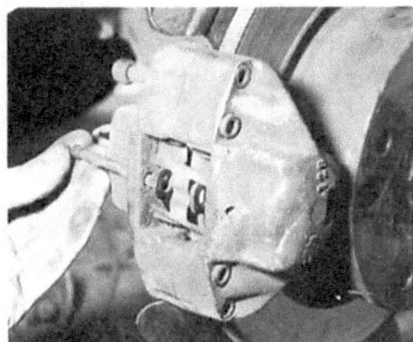

10.35a Removing the retaining pins

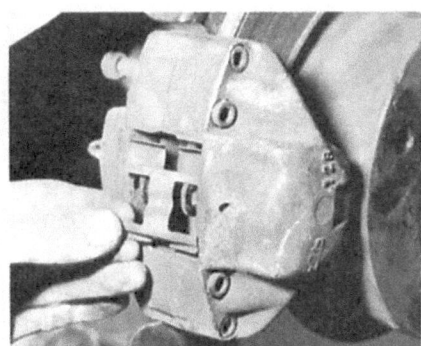

10.35b . . . and removing the spring retainer plate

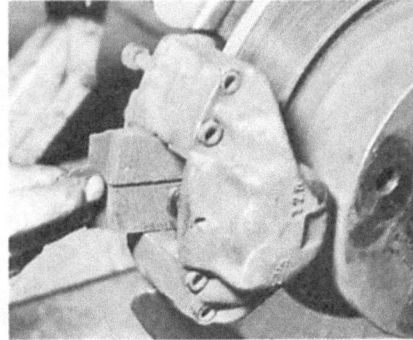

10.37 Removing a disc pad

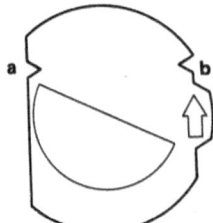

Fig. 13.34. Position of noise damping plate

Note: left-hand plate shown. Notches a and b should be at top. Arrow shows direction of rotation. Right-hand plate is mirror image of left-hand plate

10.56 Removing the caliper securing bolts

10.68 Removing the disc

brake pad and put in a block of wood no less than 0.24 in (6 mm) thick. Pump the brakes to force the piston further out and then force it back again. Do this a few times and the problem should disappear. If not it will be necessary to check the piston seals and caliper cylinders thoroughly as described later in this Section.

Disc pads (Girling) - removal, inspection and refitting
42 Refer to Fig.13.33. Remove the front wheel and support the vehicle firmly. In this operation the caliper must be removed from the steering knuckle.
43 The U-shaped retaining pin is kept in place by a locking clip; remove the clip and lever the pin out. Do not hammer on the ends of it or it will not come out at all. Remove the pad spreader spring.
44 Bend back the locking plates on the caliper mounting bolts and remove the bolts. Support the caliper so that the hydraulic hose is not strained. It is possible to tie the caliper to the upper suspension arm so that it can easily be worked on.
45 If the pads are to be refitted mark them so that they do not get mixed. The pad must go into the same place on reassembly. Ease the pad away from the piston and noise plate, turn it through 90° and draw it carefully out of the caliper. Move the noise damping plates to the centre of the caliper and remove them.
46 If one pad is worn so that the thickness of the friction lining material is less than that specified then all four pads must be replaced by new ones. The pads must always be renewed in sets of four. It is not possible to buy them singly anyway.
47 Clean out the sliding surfaces inside the caliper and blow out all rust and dirt. Inspect the piston seals by pushing the piston in a little. If the seals are swollen or hard and cracked then they must be renewed, as detailed later, while the caliper is away from the disc. Check the disc for run-out and wear as detailed later.
48 The pads must not be damaged in any way, or have cracks or oily patches. Try them in the caliper slides to make sure they move easily. When you are satisfied that all is well, install the pads as follows.
49 Fit the noise damping plates as in Fig.13.34 and then insert

the pads and turn them through 90°. Push them back so that they move the pistons in a little but watch that the brake fluid reservoir does not overflow. Be careful to fit used pads in the position you removed them from.
50 Refit the caliper to the steering knuckle. Be careful how you fit the pads round the disc; the edges of the pad are fragile and chip easily. Fit a new locking plate and tighten the caliper holding bolts to the specified torque. Bend up the tabs of the locking plate.
51 Fit a new pad spreader spring and install the U-shaped pad retaining pin. Fit the locking clip and bend the straight edge of it through 45° to stop it moving. Depress the brake pedal several times to seat the pads and then check the level of the fluid to the reservoir.
52 The calipers are symmetrical, replacement units being supplied without pads, plates and bleeder valves, and may be installed on either side. The long bleeder valve must be at the top when the calipers are fitted to the knuckle.

Discs, calipers, pistons and seals (Teves) - removal, inspection and refitting
53 Before assuming that anything is wrong which requires removal of the caliper pistons make sure that the checks in connection with renewal of the friction pads as described earlier have been carried out.
54 Discs may deteriorate, if left unused, due to corrosion. If this happens it is best to let a VW agency re-surface them. Discs which are badly scored or distorted must be renewed. It is possible to have them re-machined but the economics of this against fitting new parts should be examined.
55 The run-out of the disc can be checked only with a clock gauge micrometer. With the bearing properly adjusted the run-out should not exceed that specified.
56 To renew a disc or repair piston seals, the caliper assembly must first be removed. It is held by two bolts from the back of the steering knuckle (photo). (If the disc only is to be removed it is not necessary to disconnect the hydraulic fluid hose. The whole

assembly should be tied up onto the bodywork to prevent any strain on the hose). If the pistons and seals are to be renewed the hydraulic hose must be removed and plugged with a clean bleeder valve dust cap. If the pistons are to be removed from the caliper thought must first be given as to how pressure can be applied to force them out. Only one piston can be worked on at a time as the other piston must be installed and clamped in position so as to maintain pressure to force the other out. Pressure can be applied from a foot pump if you rig up a spare hydraulic pipe union and short length of pipe to which the pump connector will fit. One piston will have to be clamped in such a way that there will still be room enough for the other to come right out. Some form of clamping device will have to be made up if you are unable to obtain a suitable tool.

57 Mount the caliper assembly in the vice, padding the jaws suitably so that the flange of the caliper will not be scored or marked. The friction pads and retaining plates should be removed.

58 Prise out the spring ring from the outer seal using a screwdriver. Then, with a blunt plastic or wooden tool prise out the seal itself. Do not use sharp tools for fear of scoring the piston or cylinder.

59 Using a clamp to hold one piston force the other out under pressure as described in paragraph 56. To prevent damage in case the piston should come out with force put some cloth in the caliper to prevent it striking the piston and clamp opposite.

60 With the piston out the rubber sealing ring can be taken out of its groove in the cylinder; once again use only a blunt article to get it out.

61 With methylated spirits or hydraulic fluid, clean the piston and cylinder thoroughly. If there are any signs of severe scoring or pitting then renewal will be necessary. With the cylinder this involves renewing the whole caliper unit.

62 When renewing seals the spring ring and piston retaining plate must also be renewed. The VW service kit includes all the items needed. Before reassembly it is advantageous to coat the piston and new rubber seal with VW cylinder paste specially formulated for this job. Otherwise make sure they are thoroughly lubricated with clean hydraulic fluid. On no account use anything else.

63 Fit the rubber seal in the cylinder groove and then fit the piston into the seal. Great care must be taken to avoid misaligning the seal when doing this and the piston must be kept square while it is pushed in. The cut-out portion of the piston should lie at an angle of 20º from a line across the disc diameter facing in to the centre of the disc and against the direction of forward disc rotation. See Fig.13.32.

64 Fit the new outer seal and spring ring.

65 Repeat the process for the other piston.

66 Refit the caliper to the knuckle, tightening the securing bolts to the specified torque. Refit the piston retainer plates and pads as described earlier.

67 The disc itself may be removed after the caliper is taken off.

68 Remove the hub cap - on the left wheel, this involves removing the C-washer securing the speedo cable. Undo the bearing nut clamp screw, remove the nut and pull off the disc which is an integral part of the wheel hub (photo).

69 Refit the disc in the reverse order and re-adjust the wheel bearing as detailed in Chapter 11.

70 Refit the caliper to the knuckle and tighten the two retaining bolts to the specified torque.

71 It is rare that the caliper housing has to be split and this should not be done unless it is obviously leaking. Renewal of the interior O-rings on the fluid channels may then be needed. Undo the four socket head screws to separate the two halves. Remove the two O-rings and fit new ones. Re-align the two halves and refit the screws. Tighten them from the centre outwards in sequence to the specified initial torque, and then again in sequence to the specified final torque.

72 When the caliper is refitted reconnect the hydraulic fluid hose and bleed the system as described.

Discs, calipers, pistons and seals (Girling) - removal, inspection and refitting

73 The procedures for the Girling type brakes are as for the Teves type, except that the caliper must first be removed for removal of the pads.

74 If this caliper leaks, it is not possible to split it and fit new seals as with the Teves type. The unit must be renewed. If this is the case, the bleed valves must be transferred to the new unit from the old one. Make sure that the long one is at the top when the caliper is installed.

75 With the Girling type caliper, the 20º angle of the piston recess does not have to be checked; the noise damping plate may be fitted without this precaution.

76 After reconnecting the hydraulic hose remember to bleed the brakes as described in the following paragraphs.

Hydraulic system - bleeding

77 Bleeding the hydraulic system is as described in Chapter 9, but the following additional information should be noted.

78 The order for bleeding the brakes should be as follows:

   a) Right-hand rear
   b) Left-hand rear
   c) Right-hand front
   d) Left-hand front

79 As from March 1972, the brake fluid reservoir is fitted with a filter to ensure dirt does not get into the brake lines. This filter should be removed while bleeding the system and refitted before adding any more fluid to the reservoir.

80 When all air has been expelled, the bleed valve should be tightened just before the end of the downstroke of the pedal.

81 Fluid which is bled out of the system should never be used again, but should be discarded carefully. It is highly poisonous, a good paint remover and skin irritant.

Hydraulic system - renewal of fluid

82 Brake fluid has the property of being hygroscopic — that is, it absorbs moisture from the atmosphere. Over a period of time, the moisture content of the fluid increases considerably. Continuous use of the brakes will then cause the temperature of the fluid to rise to such an extent that the water in the fluid will boil. This will produce the same effect as air in the system and all the braking effort will be expended in compressing the vapour, with little braking effect on the car. It is therefore important that the fluid should be changed at regular intervals´ — at least once every two years is suggested.

83 To change the fluid, fit four bleed pipes (six if the car has front disc brakes) and open all the bleed valves. The pedal should be pumped to expel all the fluid into suitable containers.

84 The valves should then be closed, the reservoir filled with fresh fluid, and the brakes bled as described previously. Keep an eye on the reservoir to make sure it is kept topped up. Topping up will be required several times before the system is filled with fluid and all air is bled out.

Hydraulic pipes and hoses - inspection and renewal

85 It should be noted that it is possible to purchase nickel copper alloy brake pipes to replace corroded or damaged steel pipes, which are fitted as standard. The cost is more than replacement steel items, but the alloy type are virtually corrosion proof.

86 When inspecting flexible hoses, check that they are not rubbing on the bodywork in any way.

Handbrake - modifications

87 The removal, refitting and adjustment of the handbrake are described in Chapter 3, but there have been two small modifications.

88 The introduction of the three point mounting for the seats in August 1972 made it necessary to move the handbrake lever 2.4 in (60 mm) to the rear. The cable was shortened to suit.

89 Also in August 1972 a modified handbrake lever ratchet was fitted. The old type has a machined hole in the centre. The new one is solid. The new ratchet has three teeth less at the bottom and two more at the top. There is a slot in the back of the handbrake lever for the new type ratchet. The old type and new type levers can be installed only with the correct type of ratchet. The ratchets are not interchangeable.

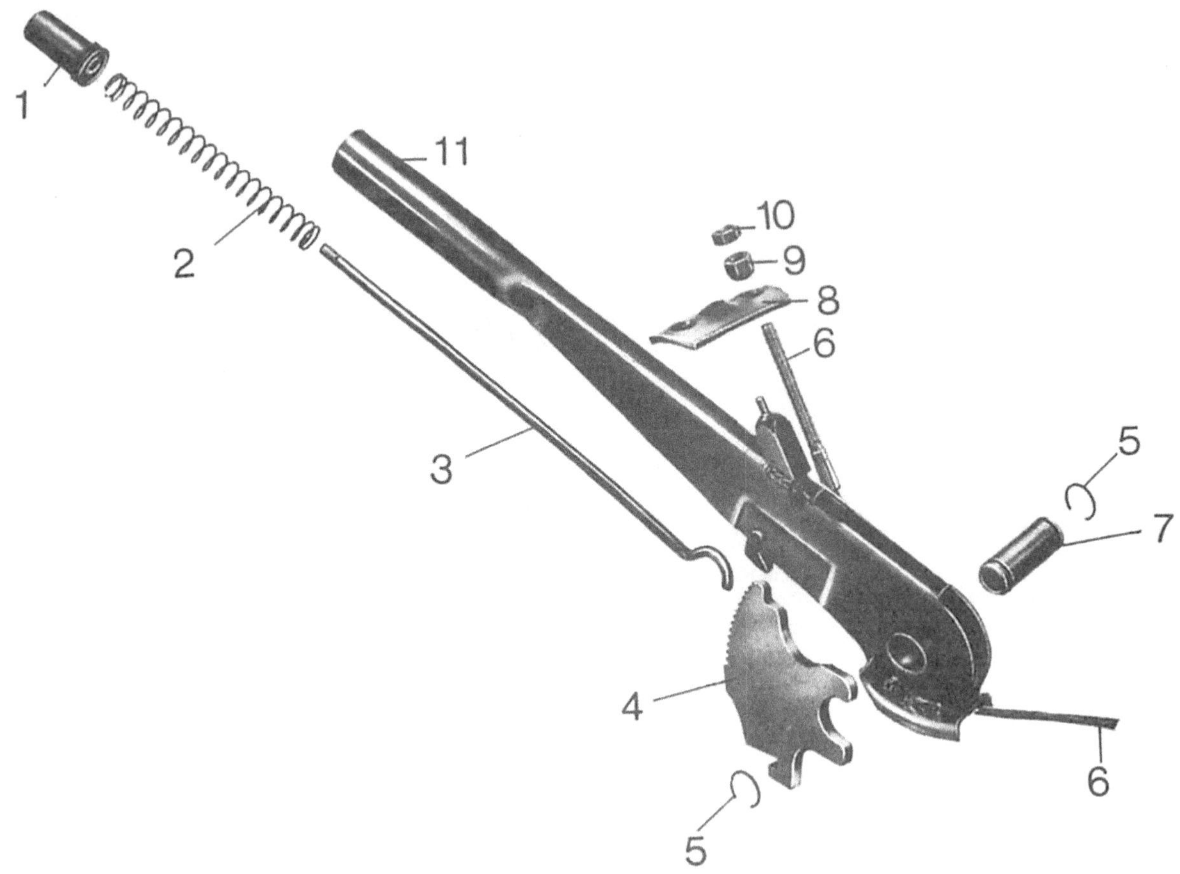

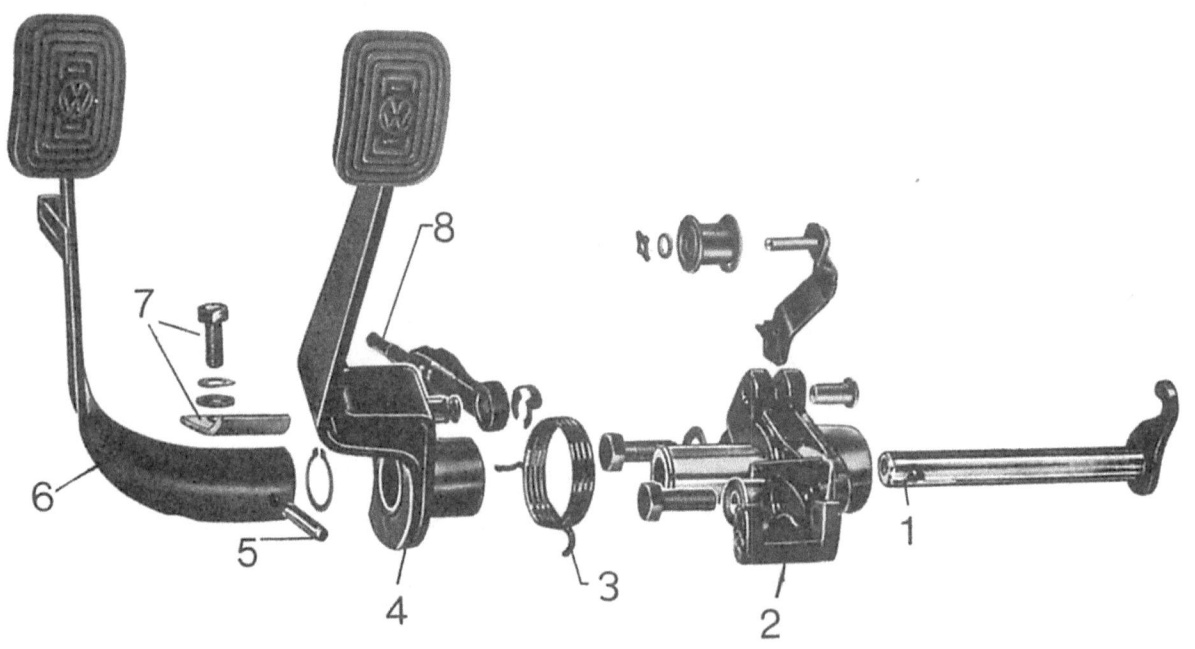

Fig. 13.35. Handbrake lever

1 Cap	3 Release lever	5 Circlip	7 Pivot pin	9 Adjusting	10 Locknut
2 Ratchet spring	4 Ratchet	6 Cable	8 Equalizer plate	nut	11 Lever

Fig. 13.36. Pedal assembly

1 Pedal shaft	3 Return spring	5 Pin	7 Brake pedal stop
2 Bearing bracket	4 Brake pedal	6 Clutch	8 Pushrod

90 An exploded view of the lever with equalizer bar is given in Fig.13.35.

Pedal assembly - adjustment
91 The directions for adjusting the pedal assembly are given in Chapter 3. Fig.13.36 shows the assembly as an exploded view.
92 On models fitted with a tandem master cylinder the pushrod must be adjusted so that there is the specified play at the brake pedal pad. The pedal stop must be adjusted to give the minimum movement of the pedal pad as specified. Test this with the pushrod disconnected. The purpose is to allow the pushrod to be depressed into the cylinder sufficient to take up the extra amount of movement necessary when one braking system fails.

Brake light switch - testing, removal and refitting
93 If the tests in Section 12 of this Chapter indicate that the switch is defective, remove the wires and unscrew the switch from the master cylinder. Plug the hole quickly and check that the fluid level in the reservoir has not sunk; top it up if necessary.
94 Fit the seal to the new switch and then remove the temporary plug in the master cylinder and fit the new switch. Screw it in loosely and then start the engine and depress the brake pedal one or two times to drive out any trapped air. Switch off the engine and tighten the brake light switch to the specified torque.
95 Wipe up any spilled fluid, reconnect the switch wires and test the circuit again.
96 Watch the reservoir while refitting the switch and keep it topped up all the time. If the pedal action is spongy, it will be necessary to bleed the system as described previously.

11 Electrical system - charging and starting systems

General description
1 The precise date of the change from a 6 volt electrical system to 12 volts is difficult to pinpoint owing to conflicting information contained in various Volkswagen publications, but it is thought to have occurred in 1972. All the electrical components required replacement by 12 volt items, and the wiring harness was replaced by a lighter gauge item.
2 The change from a dynamo to alternator type charging system required few modifications, and enabled the fitting of more optional extras without overloading the system. The change is thought to have occurred in 1975.
3 Converting a 6 volt system to a 12 volt one is not impossible, but it is very costly and time consuming. The 12 volt system has certain practical advantages over the 6 volt system, and when fitted during manufacture is cheaper to produce. However, the time and cost involved in a conversion to 12 volts weighed against the advantages gained do not make this a practical proposition.
4 Similarly, a conversion from dynamo to alternator charging system is not impossible, but should be considered impracticable from a time and cost point of view.

Battery - general
5 The general information given in Chapter 10 applies equally to the 12 volt system battery.
6 On some models there is provision to plug the car into a computer diagnostic machine. The battery used on these models has a special centre tapping, and replacements are expensive. A normal 12 volt battery without this tapping may be fitted, but if the car goes for a computer diagnostic service, the operator should be informed of this alteration.
7 In winter the battery is more likely to reach a discharged state owing to the extra loads imposed upon it. Should the battery become fully discharged, there is a possibility of the electrolyte freezing at temperatures below −11ºC (12ºF). This can result in the case cracking and possible electrolyte spillage, with obvious disastrous effects. Precautions should therefore be taken to ensure this does not occur, the battery being removed and stored in a warmer environment if necessary, until charging can be carried out.
8 If the car is to be stored for a period of time, it is important

that the battery is kept charged up. It should be checked every few weeks and charged as necessary, for if the battery is left in a fully discharged condition it will become heavily sulphated and beyond repair.

12 volt dynamo - removal, overhaul and refitting
9 This is as described for the 6 volt unit in Chapters 2 and 10. An exploded view of the unit is shown in Fig.13.37.

12 volt dynamo - testing in car
10 The procedures in Chapter 10 for testing the dynamo apply to the 12 volt unit, but the test values will differ as follows.
11 For the 'no load voltage check' the reading should be 13 to 14 volts.
12 For the 'voltage check without regulator' the value at tickover should be 12 volts, and at 3000 rpm should be 36 volts. This test must last only a few seconds or damage to the windings may result.
13 For the 'current output check' the procedure is as given in Chapter 10, Section 10. The output at 2000 rpm should be 30 amps maximum but the actual output will depend on the state of charge of the battery.

Voltage regulator (12 volt dc circuit) - removal and refitting
14 On early models the procedures are as given in Chapter 10. On later models the regulator is located away from the dynamo, under the rear seat on the left-hand side. Procedures are similar to those given in Chapter 10, the connections being shown in Fig.13.38.

12 volt alternator - precautions
15 The alternator has a negative earth circuit. If the battery is connected the wrong way round the alternator windings will be damaged.
16 Do **not** disconnect the regulator until the engine has stopped and the battery earth strap is disconnected. Unless this precaution is followed the alternator, or the regulator, or both may be damaged.
17 If the battery is to be charged while still in the car from an external source, both battery leads must be disconnected before the external leads are connected to the battery.
18 If electric arc welding is done to the car then both battery leads and the alternator output lead must be disconnected before the welding commences.
19 If electrical tests are being done to the alternator circuit or connected circuits, do **not** use temporary connections which may short circuit accidentally. The fuses may not blow but the diodes may burn out.
20 When replacing a burned out alternator or regulator clear the fault which caused the damage before fitting the new component, or that too may be damaged.

12 volt alternator - servicing
21 The method of removal and refitting of the alternator is identical with that of the dynamo, although the mounting is a different shape to fit the different contour of the alternator casing. The procedure is described in Chapter 2 and Chapter 10.
22 It is most important that the precautions listed previously be observed when dealing with an alternator.
23 The brushes are an integral part of the regulator and may be removed with the regulator (see Fig.13.39). Brushes should protrude from the holder within the limits specified. The brushes and slip rings must be free from grease and there must be no scoring, or sparking will occur with rapid deterioration of the brush and slip ring.
24 The tension of the drivebelt is critical. Refer to Section 4 of this Chapter.

12 volt alternator - testing
25 Testing of the alternator requires both expensive equipment and specialist knowledge. Unless the owner possesses both, it will be necessary to take the alternator to an auto electrical specialist for testing. If a fault is evident, he will advise on any remedial action to be taken.

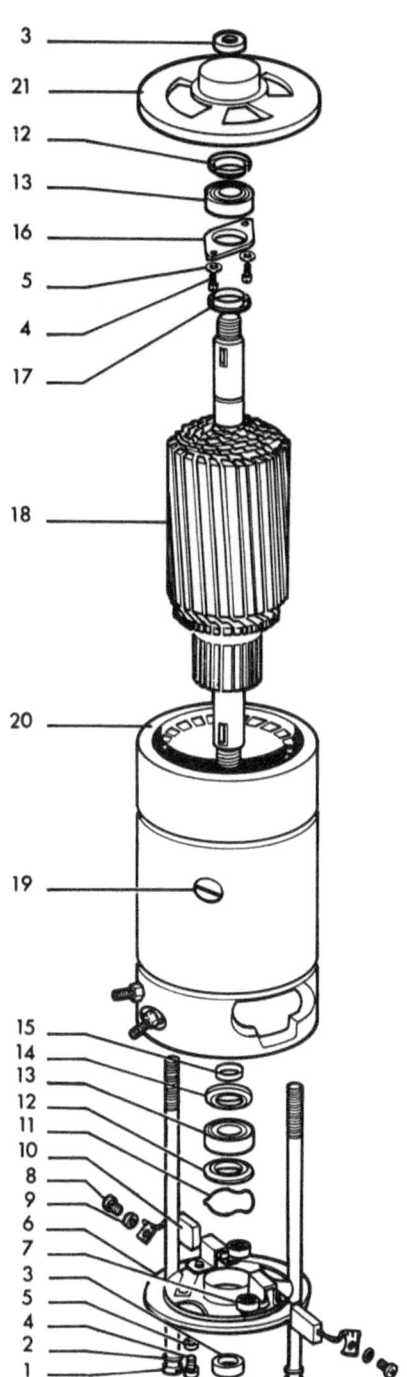

Fig. 13.37. 12 volt dynamo — exploded view

1 Through—bolt	12 Splash shield
2 Lockwasher	13 Ball bearing
3 Spacer ring	14 Splash shield
4 Screw	15 Thrust washer
5 Lockwasher	16 Retaining plate
6 Commutator endplate	17 Splash shield
7 Brush spring	18 Armature
8 Screw	19 Pole shoe screw
9 Lockwasher	20 Field coil
10 Carbon brush	21 Fan endplate
11 Lockwasher	

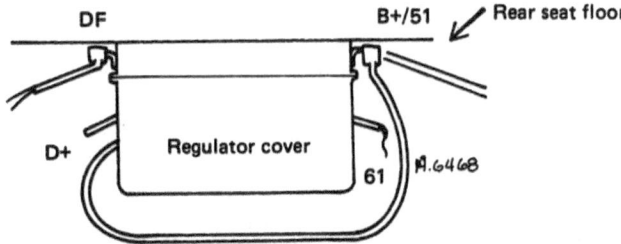

Fig. 13.38. Voltage regulator (12 volt dynamo)

D+   — to battery
DF   — to dynamo DF
B+/51 — to battery + ve and terminal 30
61   — to ignition warning light

Note: this is located under rear seat

12 volt alternator - removal, overhaul and refitting

26 The procedure for removal and refitting of the alternator is similar to that described for the dynamo in Chapters 2 and 10.

27 Overhaul of the alternator is possible provided the owner has confidence that he can carry out the operation satisfactorily. Otherwise it would be better to purchase an exchange unit or entrust the work to an auto electrical specialist.

28 If you have sufficient skill, a soldering iron of less than 300 watts, a pair of long-nosed pliers and an ohmmeter measuring 0 to 20 ohms then you can dismantle and test the alternator, but first check that spares are available. The bearings and rotor may be renewed, and the stator may be unsoldered from the diodes and the diode plate and/or the stator renewed if spares are available.

29 Refer to Fig.13.39, and undo the bolts holding the bearing plate on the drive side. Mark the position of the bearing plate relative to the stator and housing for correct reassembly. If the regulator has not already been removed take off the cover plate and remove the regulator and brush gear. Slacken the screws holding the bearing plate on the fan side.

30 Using a wheel puller, or a bearing extractor, pull the endplate off the drive side. The bearing is held in the endplate. You may be able to prise the plate off, or alternatively, hold the casing and press the shaft steadily from the fan end and drive the rotor bearing out of the bearing plate on the fan side. In the latter case the rotor will come out with the drive side bearing plate in position. Do **not** hammer the shaft out. Watch out for the spacer ring. Check the fit of the bearings and test the rotor windings for open circuit and short circuit. The resistance should be as specified. The minimum diameter of the slip rings should be as specified.

31 Refer to Fig.13.40 which shows the locations of the diodes and heat sinks. Unsolder the stator windings from the diodes. Tag the leads for easy refitting. When carrying out this operation use an iron of less than 300 watts and grip the connector on the diode side of the iron with a pair of long-nosed pliers to act as an extra heat sink. When reconnecting use silver solder and the same precautions to avoid overheating.

32 Having isolated the stator windings test each one to the casing to check for short circuits. If there is a zero reading then a new stator winding is required.

33 Check the resistance between phases; this should be as specified and each pair should be the same.

34 The diode plate may now be checked. Use an ohmmeter and check each diode in turn. Current must flow only one way. Keep the current down to 1 milliamp and do not allow the diode to heat up. High resistance both ways indicates an open circuit, low resistance a short circuit. A single faulty diode means renewal of the complete plate.

35 Assembly is the reverse of dismantling. When fitting the bearing plate on the fan side, the groove in the bearing plate must line up with the lug on the housing. Check that all spacer rings and washers are fitted (see Fig.13.39) and that the bearing plate on the drive side is lined up with the marks made when dismantling the alternator.

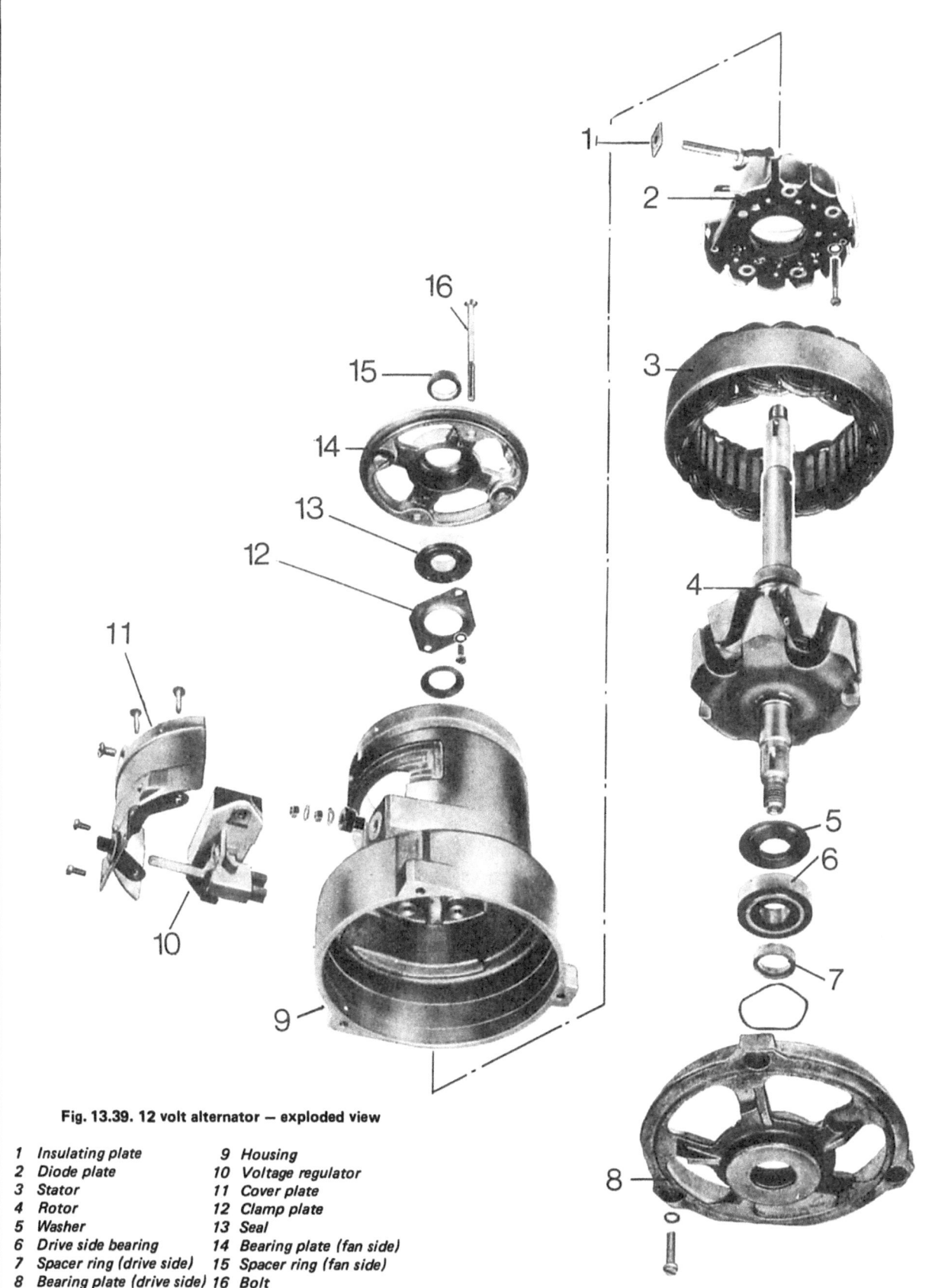

Fig. 13.39. 12 volt alternator — exploded view

1	Insulating plate	9	Housing
2	Diode plate	10	Voltage regulator
3	Stator	11	Cover plate
4	Rotor	12	Clamp plate
5	Washer	13	Seal
6	Drive side bearing	14	Bearing plate (fan side)
7	Spacer ring (drive side)	15	Spacer ring (fan side)
8	Bearing plate (drive side)	16	Bolt

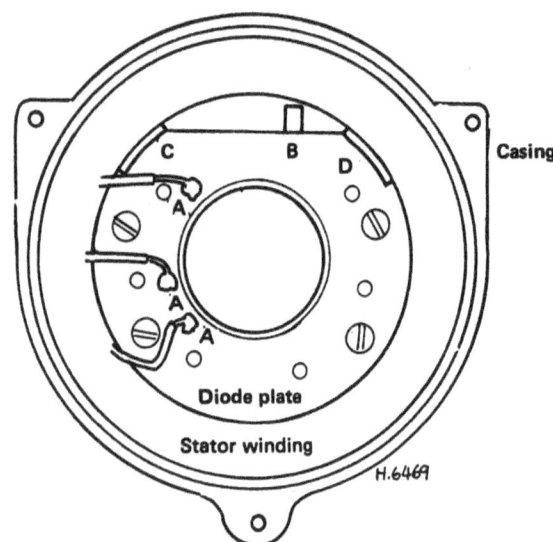

Fig. 13.40. 12 volt alternator – location of stator connections and heat sinks

A Stator winding connections to diodes
B Exciter diode contact strip
C Negative heat sink
D Positive heat sink

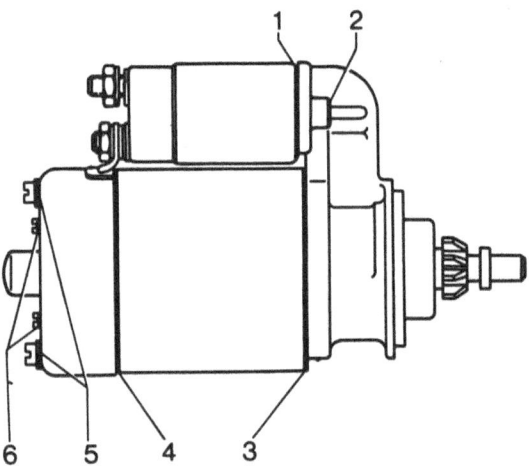

Fig. 13.42. Starter motor sealing points

1 Drive end housing to solenoid switch
2 Solenoid securing screws
3 Housing to bracket
4 Housing to endplate
5 Through–bolts
6 End cap screws

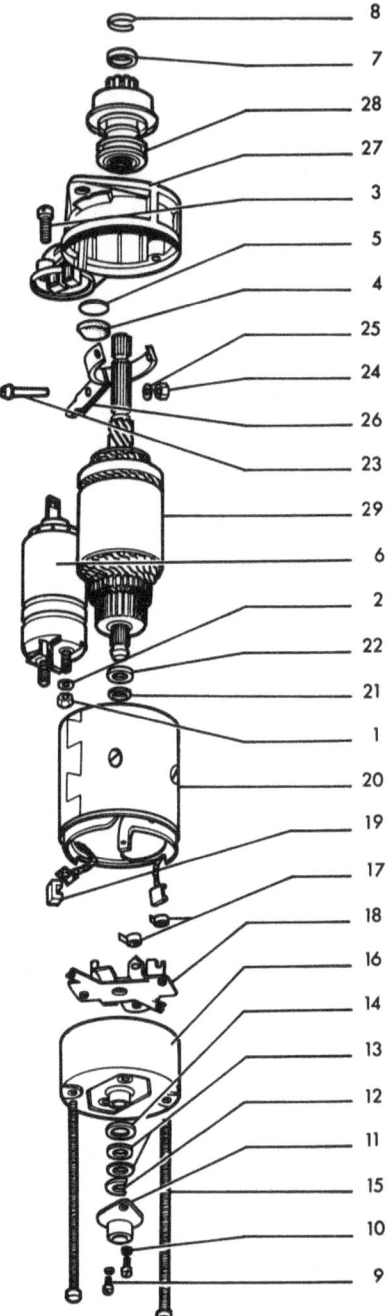

Fig. 13.41. 12 volt starter motor

1	Nut	16	Endplate
2	Lockwasher	17	Spring
3	Screw	18	Brush holder
4	Rubber seal	19	Grommet
5	Disc	20	Housing
6	Solenoid switch	21	Insulating washer
7	Stop ring	22	Thrust washer
8	Circlip	23	Pin
9	Screw	24	Nut
10	Washer	25	Lockwasher
11	End cap	26	Operating lever
12	C–washer	27	Mounting bracket
13	Shim	28	Drive pinion
14	Sealing ring	29	Armature
15	Housing screw		

12 volt starter motor - general

36 Apart from the change to 12 volts the starter circuit remains as described in Chapter 10. The starter has changed a little in construction; an exploded view of the 12 volt starter is given at Fig.13.41. Removal and refitting is as for the 6 volt starter.

12 volt starter motor - overhaul

37 Overhaul is similar to the procedures described in Chapter 10, but the following points should be noted.
38 The minimum commutator diameter is 1.32 in (33.5 mm).

39 If the bush in the endplate is worn, the new bush should be soaked in engine oil for at least six hours prior to fitting. Failure to do this will result in rapid wear of the new bush.
40 To renew the brushes the old ones must be crushed and removed from the leads. Clean the ends of the leads and insert them into the tinned drillings of the new brushes, spreading the ends to fill the drillings. Solder the lead into the brush, ensuring that the joint is not overheated.
41 When reassembling the starter motor it is most important to seal the joint faces, etc, as shown in Fig.13.42. If water enters the starter it will cause it to malfunction.

Fault diagnosis — charging circuit

Symptom	Reason/s
Warning light does not come on when the ignition switch is operated	Battery disconnected, or faulty battery or connections. Bulb burned out. Connections between battery and regulator not properly fitted. Brushes not seating correctly. Open circuit between the warning light, switch and battery. Rota windings (alternator) or field windings (dynamo) damaged.
Warning light does not go out with engine running	Fan belt broken or slipping. Regulator faulty. Field windings diode open circuit (alternator). Alternator/dynamo burned out.
Warning light stays on when ignition is switched off	Positive (main load) diode short circuited (alternator).

Fault diagnosis — starting circuit

Symptom	Reason/s
Starter does not operate when key turned to 'start' position - turn the lights on for this test	Lights go out - loose connections, corroded terminals or flat battery. Lights go dim - battery almost discharged. Ignition switch or connections faulty. Lights stay bright - solenoid faulty.
Drive pinion sticks in mesh with starter ring	Solenoid faulty. Starter motor coarse thread damaged. Flywheel ring gear damaged.
Starter turns slowly and will not start engine	Battery almost discharged. Loose or corroded connections. Brushes not making good contact. Commutator dirty, burnt or damaged. Windings damaged.
Erratic starting, particularly from cold	Faulty battery.
Starter particularly noisy when in operation	Flywheel ring gear damaged. Starter bearing defective.

---

12 Electrical system - lights, instruments and electrical accessories

Current flow diagrams - general description

1 With the advent of the alternator and increasing number of accessories in the electrical system, the old fashioned wiring diagram has become rather more black ink than white paper and requires a magnifying glass to trace a circuit. VW therefore introduced the current flow diagram of which two examples are included here.

2 The symbols used in this system are shown in Fig.13.43. Study this before reading any more. Now refer to Fig.13.44 which shows the circuit for the 1976 model Beetle with an alternator, and Fig.13.45 which shows the 1975 model Beetle with a 12 volt dynamo.
3 At the base of Fig.13.44 is a horizontal line under which there are numbers 1 to 54. The line represents earth and the numbers are the current tracks. Refer to the Key and you will note that B, the starter, is in current tracks 3 and 4. Look at the diagram and there in track 3 is the starter. The thin line to the base line indicates that it is earthed by being bolted to the body frame via the engine

SYMBOL	EXPLANATION	Sample use
	TRANSFORMER, IRON CORE	
	DIODE	Ignition coil
	TRANSISTOR	Alternator
	MECHANICAL CONNECTION / MECHANICAL CONNECTION SPRING LOADED	Voltage regulator
	RELAY, COIL	Double switch / Oil pressure switch
	RELAY, ELECTRO MAGNETIC	(a) Headlamp (b) Cut off valve (carburettor)
	HORN	
	RESISTOR	
	POTENTIOMETER	
	THERMAL RESISTOR AUTOMATIC REGULATING	Temperature sender
	HEATING ELEMENT	Rear window heater
	BATTERY 12 volt	
	MEASURING GAUGE	Fuel gauge / Temperature gauge
	SUPPRESSION WIRE	
	DYNAMO	
	MECHANICAL PRESSURE SWITCH	Door switch for interior light

SYMBOL	EXPLANATION	Sample use
	ALTERNATOR WITH DIODE RECTIFIERS	Alternator
	MOTOR	Radiator fan
	EXTERNAL WIRING / WIRE 10 mm^2 sectional area	
	WIRE JUNCTION FIXED (ISOLDERED)	Relay plate, dash board printed circuit
	WIRE JUNCTION SEPARABLE	Screw on terminals and eyelets
	PLUG, SINGLE OR MULTIPIN	T10 written by the side means a 10 pin plug
	WIRE CROSSING, NOT JOINED	
	GROUND, OR EARTH	
	SWITCH CLOSED	
	SWITCH OPEN	
	MULTI CONTACT SWITCH	
	SWITCH, MANUALLY OPERATED	
	FUSE	
	BULB	
	SPARK GAP	Spark plugs / Distributor points
	CONDENSER	Distributor

Fig. 13.43. Symbols used in current flow diagrams

Fig. 13.44. Current flow diagram — 1200 and 1200L from August 1975 (see pages 228 and 229)

Designation		In current track
A	- Battery	2
B	- Starter	3, 4
C	- Alternator	1
C1	- Regulator	1
D	- Ignition/starter switch	4, 8, 9
E	- Windscreen wiper switch	9, 10, 11
E1	- Lighting switch	17, 19, 20
E2	- Turn signal switch	42
E3	- Hazard light switch	37, 39, 40 44, 45
E4	- Headlight dip and flasher switch	13
E9	- Fresh air fan switch	12
E15	- Heated rear window switch	7
F	- Brake light switch	30, 31
F1	- Oil pressure switch	34
F2	- Left, door contact switch	27
F3	- Right, door contact switch	28
F4	- Switch for reversing lights	46
F9	- Handbrake warning lamp switch	32
G	- Fuel gauge sender unit	36
G1	- Fuel gauge	36
G7	- Sender for TDC marker	54
H	- Horn button	29
H1	- Horn	29
J	- Headlight dip and flasher relay	13, 15, 17
J2	- Turn signal — hazard light relay	38
J6	- Voltage stabilizer	36
J9	- Heated rear window relay	5, 7
K1	- High beam warning lamp	16
K2	- Ignition warning lamp	33
K3	- Oil pressure warning lamp	34
K5	- Turn signal warning lamp	35
K6	- Hazard light warning lamp	45
K7	- Dual circuit brake system and handbrake warning lamp	32
K10	- Heated rear window warning lamp	7
L1	- Left, headlight bulb	14
L2	- Right, headlight bulb	18
L10	- Speedometer light	19, 20
M1	- Left, parking light bulb	24
M2	- Right, tail light bulb	23
M2	- Right, brake light bulb	31
M3	- Right, parking light bulb	25
M4	- Left, tail light bulb	22
M4	- Left, brake light bulb	30
M5	- Left, turn signal front	40
M6	- Left, turn signal rear	41
M7	- Right, turn signal front	44
M8	- Right, turn signal rear	43
M16	- Left, reversing light bulb *	47
M17	- Right, reversing light bulb *	46

Designation		In current track
N	- Ignition coil	49, 50
N1	- Automatic choke	53
N3	- Electromagnetic cut-off valve	52
O	- Distributor	49, 50, 51
P	- Plug connector	49, 50, 51
Q	- Spark plugs	49, 50, 51
S1) to) S12)	Fuses in fuse box	
S21	- Separate fuse for reversing lights (8 amp)	46
S22	- Separate fuse for rear window (8 amp)	5
T	- Cable connector	
b	- behind engine compartment damping	
T1	- Flat connector, single	
	a - behind dashboard	
	b - under rear seat	
	c - behind engine compartment damping	
	d - in front luggage compartment on right	
	e - in front luggage compartment on left	
T2	- Flat connector, 2 pin	
T3	- Flat connector, 3 pin	
	a - in luggage compartment on left	
	b - behind luggage compartment damping on right	
	c - 3 pin connector in engine compartment	
T4a	- Flat connector, 4 pin	
T20	- Central socket	48
V	- Wiper motor— (single speed on 1200)	9, 10
V2	- Fan motor — (1200L only)	12
W	- Interior light	26
X	- Number plate light	22
Z1	- Heated rear window	5

*for 1200L only

1	- Earthing strap from battery to frame	2
2	- Earthing strap from transmission to frame	6
10	- Earthing point (dashboard)	
11	- Earthing point (speedometer)	
15	- Earthing point (front luggage compartment, left)	
16	- Earthing point (front luggage compartment, right)	

Colour code
BK — Black
BU — Blue
BN — Brown
WT — White
YW— Yellow
GN — Green
GY — Grey
RD — Red

Note that where two colours are shown, the upper is
the main colour and the lower the tracer colour

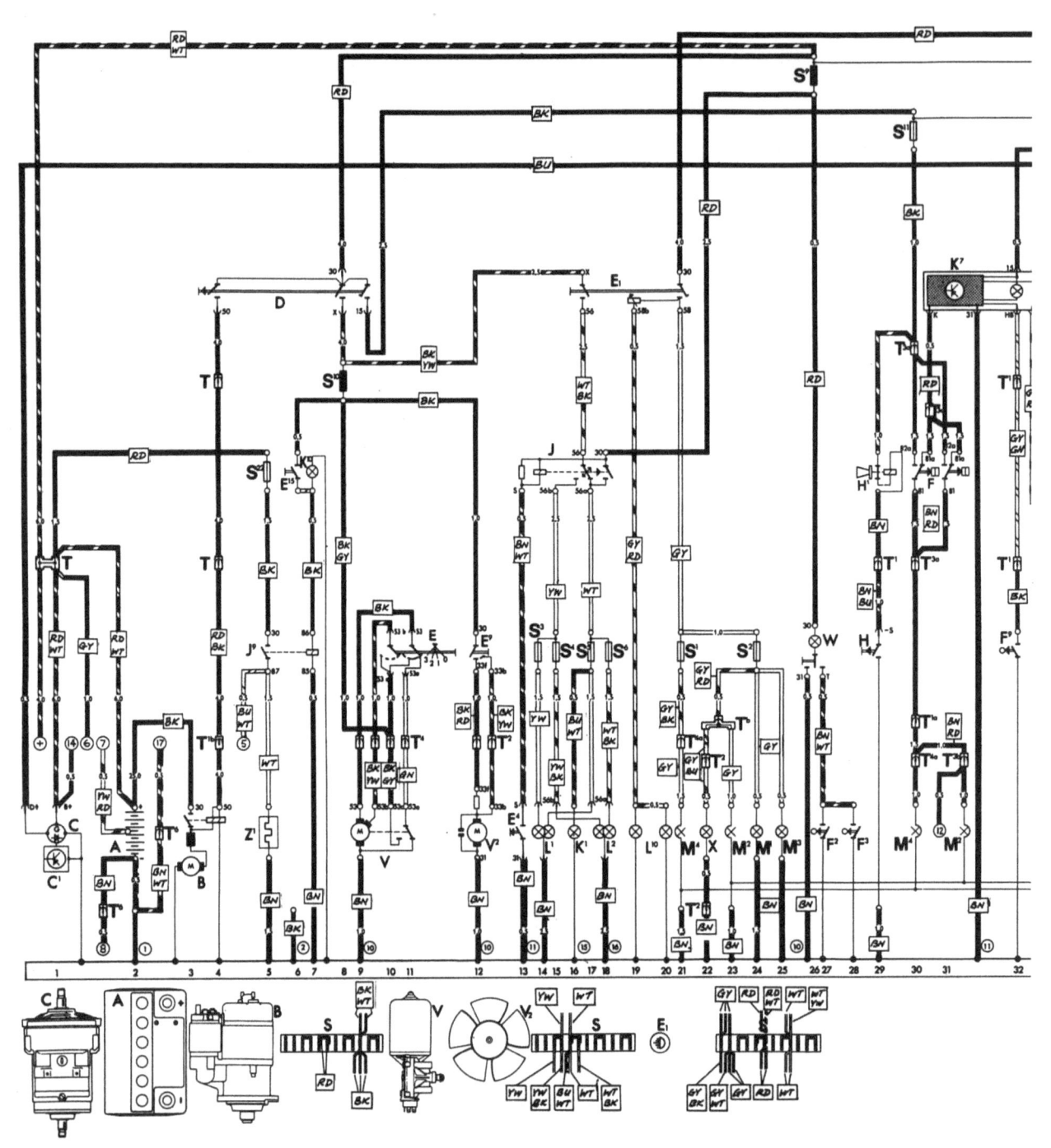

Fig. 13.44. Current flow diagram — 1200 and 1200L from August 1975

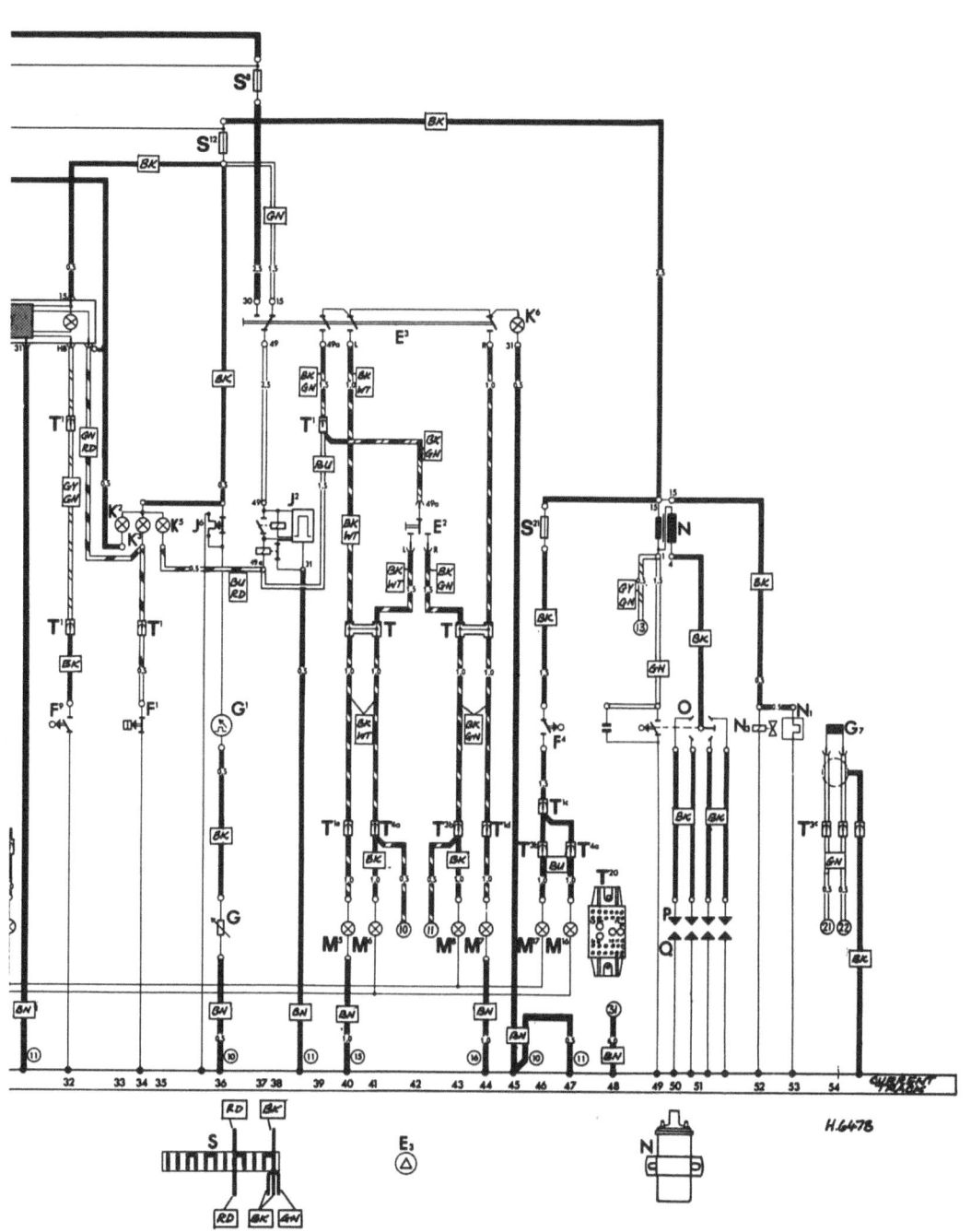

H.6478

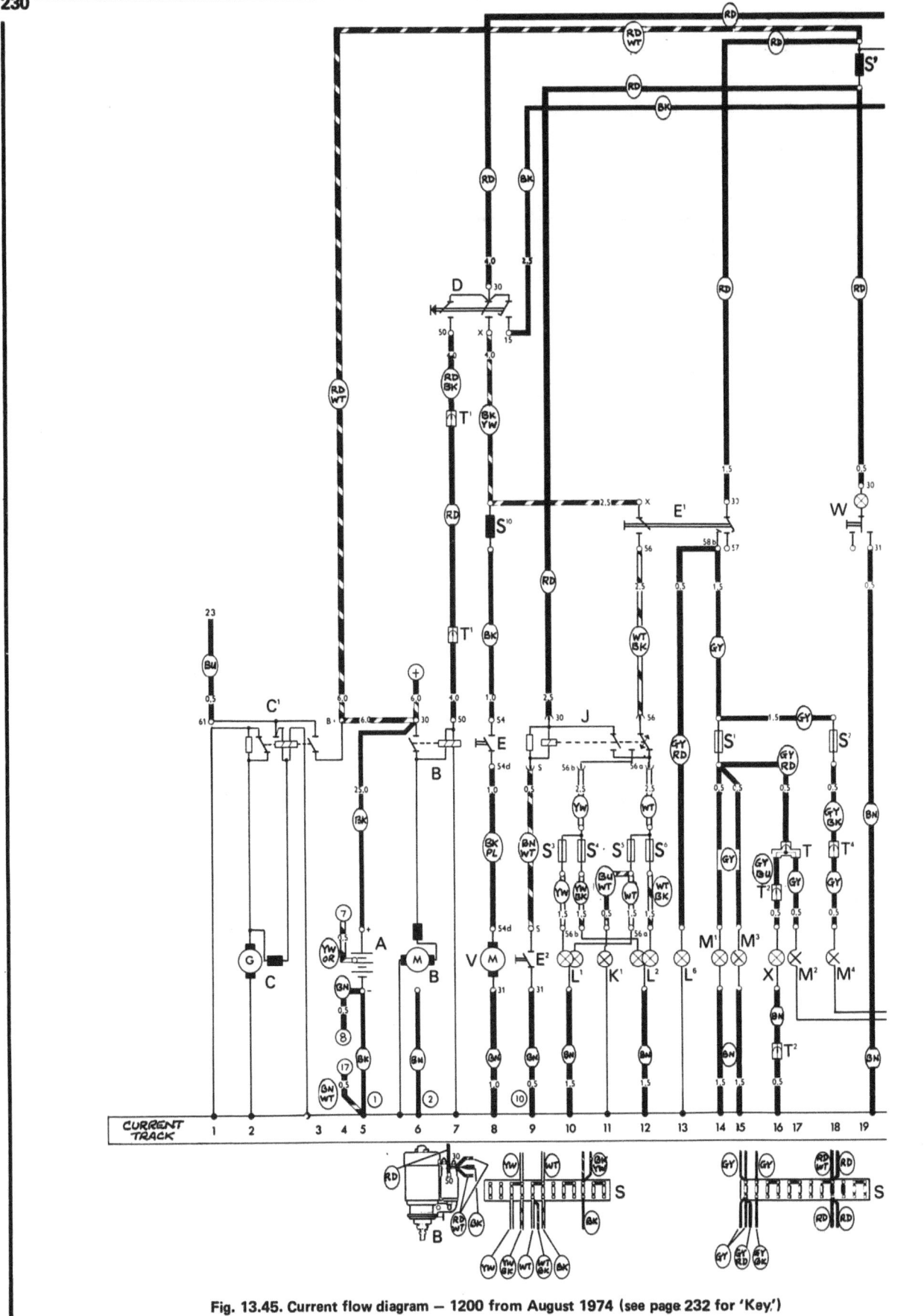

Fig. 13.45. Current flow diagram — 1200 from August 1974 (see page 232 for 'Key.')

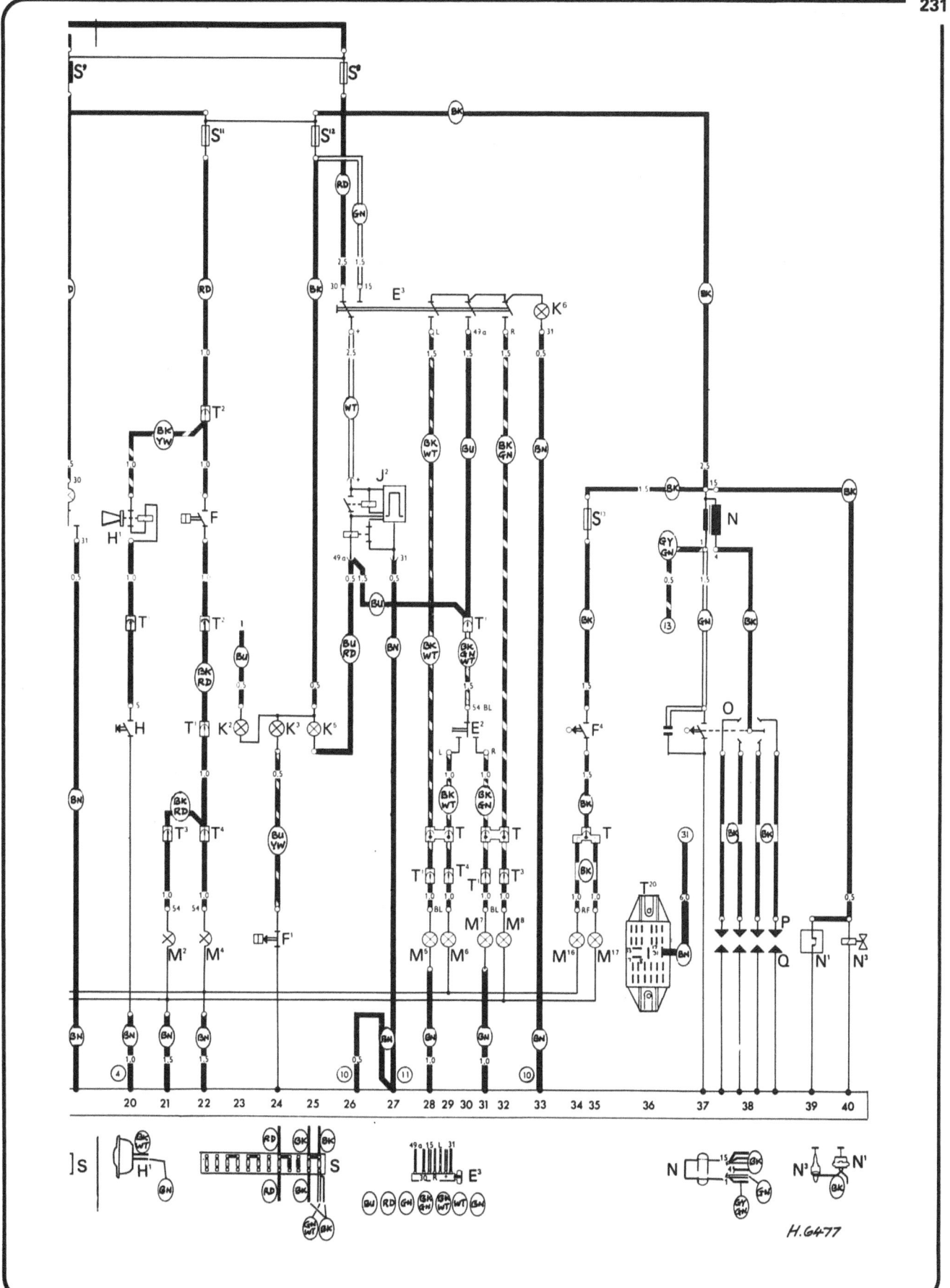

H.G477

Key to current flow diagram — 1200 from August 1974

Designation		In current track	Designation		In current track
A	- Battery	5	M6	- Left turn signal, rear	29
B	- Starter	6, 7	M7	- Right turn signal, front	31
C	- Dynamo	2	M8	- Right turn signal, rear	32
C1	- Regulator	1, 2, 3	M16	- Left reversing light	34
D	- Ignition/starter switch	7, 8	M17	- Right reversing light	35
E	- Windscreen wiper switch	8	N	- Ignition coil	37
E1	- Lighting switch	12, 14	N1	- Automatic choke	39
E2	- Turn signal switch with contact for dip and headlight flasher	9, 29, 30	N3	- Electromagnetic cut-off valve	40
			O	- Distributor	37, 38
E3	- Hazard light switch	26, 28, 30 32, 33	P	- Plug connector	38
			Q	- Spark plugs	38
F	- Brake light switch	22	S1)		8, 10, 12
F1	- Oil pressure switch	24	to) Fuses in fuse box		14, 18, 19
F4	- Switch for reversing light	34	S12)		22, 25, 26
H	- Horn button	20	S13	- Separate fuse for reversing lights (8 amp)	34
H1	- Horn	20	T	- Cable adaptor behind dashboard in engine compartment	
J	- Relay for dip and headlight flasher	9, 10, 12			
J2	- Turn signal — hazard light relay	26, 27	T1	- Cable connector, single under rear seat behind dashboard	
K1	- High beam warning lamp	11			
K2	- Ignition warning lamp	23	T2	- Cable connector, 2 pin in luggage compartment	
K3	- Oil pressure warning lamp	24			
K5	- Turn signal warning lamp	25	T3	- Cable connector, 4 pin behind engine compartment lining, left	
K6	- Hazard light warning lamp	33			
L1	- Left headlight	10	T20	- Central socket	36
L2	- Right headlight	12	V	- Wiper motor	8
L6	- Speedometer light	13	W	- Interior light	19
M1	- Left parking light	14	X	- Number plate light	16
M2	- Right tail light	17			
M2	- Right brake light	21	1	- Earth strap from battery to frame	
M3	- Right parking light	15	2	- Earth strap from gearbox to frame	
M4	- Left tail light	18	4	- Earth wire (steering column coupling)	
M4	- Left brake light	22	10	- Earth point (dashboard)	
M5	- Left turn signal, front	28	11	- Earth point (speedometer)	

Colour code

BK - Black
BU - Blue
BN - Brown
PL - Purple
WT - White
YW - Yellow
OR - Orange
GN - Green
GY - Grey
RD - Red

Note that where two colours are shown together, the upper is the main colour and the lower the tracer colour

and engine earth strap. Certain items have their own earth leads, for example, the wiper motor in track 9.

4 A number of points are marked by a figure inside a circle. These are earth straps. For example, strap I in current track 2; this is the earth strap from the battery to the frame.

5 Fuses are not shown on a fuse board but as they occur in the various circuits. For example, track 27, fuse S9 serves the interior light; it also serves the headlight dip and flasher relay via the relay and terminal 30 of the relay in track 18. The fuse, of course, will be found in the fuse box.

6 There are a number of wires which terminate in a circle with a number, not in a current track. For example, the one connected to the centre of the battery, track 2, which is circle 7. These are the connections to the computer diagnostic plug.

7 A number of items are labelled T with a number by the side. For example T^1 in track 29 is a single wire flat connector. There are a number of T^1 connectors if you look at the key, which gives their location. Likewise T^3 is a three pin flat connector, and T^{20} is the central socket for the computer plug with twenty connections.

8 All the wires disappear into harnesses and only the terminal ends are important. The small figures at terminals indicate the terminal marking on the component.

Headlights and parking lights - removal and refitting

9 Up to 1974 the one-piece headlight described in Chapter 10 was fitted.

10 In 1974 a new pattern light was fitted. In this type the trim ring may be removed leaving the light in place, but the light must still be removed to change the headlight bulb or parking light bulb.

11 Refer to Fig.13.46 which shows a diagram of the front of the light. To remove the trim ring remove screw A, lift the trim ring away at the bottom and disengage it from the lug on the top.

12 Unless it is desired to alter the direction of the beam leave screws F1 and F2 alone. If the object of the exercise is to re-focus the beam then turn screw F1 to alter the direction of the beam in the vertical plane; F2 alters the direction in the horizontal plane. Instructions for setting are given in Chapter 10.

13 If the bulb is to be changed then remove the three screws marked B, (do not touch F1 and F2) and the light will come away from the vehicle body. Refer to Fig.13.47 which gives an exploded view of the light. Pull the three pin connector off and take off the parking light and earth wires. Remove the rubber cap. Push the retaining ring towards the reflector, turn it anti-clockwise and remove it, together with the bulb from the reflector. Use a cloth to hold the bulb and remove it, and still using the cloth fit the new bulb. There are two metal tabs on the bulb flange; these must engage in the recess in the reflector. If you have got this right then the central terminal lug on the bulb is at the top.

14 The parking light bulb holder just pulls out. It is held in by the retaining ring, so when refitting the retaining ring the contact lug must press on the parking light bulb. Models after November 1977 are fitted with a modified parking light holder to improve the water-proofing arrangements. The new light, which cannot be installed in the old pattern headlight, has a coded plug with two wires. The grey wire is positive and the brown one negative. When installing the light the brown wire must be on the side nearest the body, ie furthest from the headlight bulb.

15 Turn the retaining ring in a clockwise direction until it is fully home. Refit the three pin connector and the rubber cap. Make sure the cap fits snugly or water may enter the light.

16 Refit the parking light and earth wires, the grey wire to terminal 58 and the brown wire to terminal 31.

17 Refit the assembly in the car, fitting the three securing screws to the support ring.

18 When refitting the trim ring place it loosely against the wing, fit the retaining screw one or two threads, then lift the ring so that the top lug engages and tighten the screw.

19 Refitting the halogen bulb is slightly different. Continue as for the normal lamp to remove the assembly from the car. Remove the three pin plug and the wires for earth and the parking light. Squeeze the clip which retains the bulb and remove the clip and bulb. Hold the new bulb in a cloth and refit it so that the dimmer shield is at the bottom and the centre tab upwards. Fit the spring

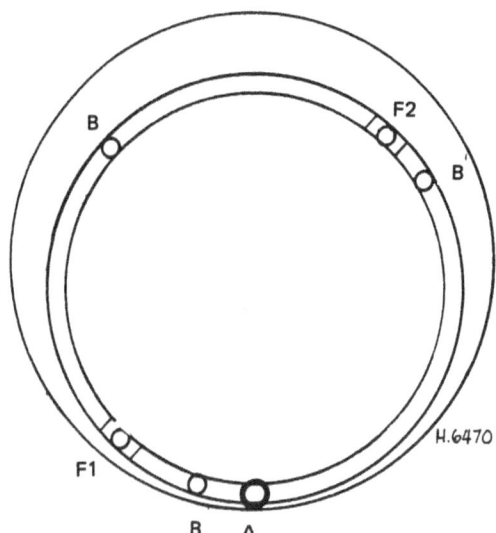

Fig. 13.46. Headlamp securing and focusing screws — 1974 onwards

A   Support ring securing screw
B   Support ring securing screw
F1   Focusing screw — vertical adjustment
F2   Focusing screw — horizontal adjustment

clip over the base of the bulb, press the ends together and fit the clip in the retaining lugs. The procedure is then as for the standard bulb.

20 If you are refitting a parking light bulb, then when removing the old bulb it may be necessary to turn it to the left a little to get it out of the holder. Hold the new bulb in a cloth, insert it into the holder and turn it slightly to the right. Push the holder into the reflector just past the spring contact.

21 The reason for holding the bulb in a cloth is that the bulb temperature is quite high when the light is on and the acid from the natural grease on your fingers will etch your fingerprints on the bulb. This causes the bulb to go slightly dark in that area, with a consequent loss of light output.

Tail light cluster - removal and refitting

22 The details of the tail light cluster differ slightly. The 1972 pattern is held to the rear wing by three screws. Remove these and the lens may be eased away; the screws are captive in the lens. Be careful not to fracture the seal. If you do have this misfortune fit a new one or your rear light will quickly get rusty and need renewal. The bulbs, three in number, may be removed. Use a cloth when handling them. The top bulb is a single filament for the turn signal. The bottom bulb is a single filament for the reversing light. The centre bulb is a twin filament for the brake and tail lights. When refitting this one you will see that the retaining pins are at different distances from the bulb glass. The retaining pin nearest to the bulb glass must be downwards (underneath). This is important for the filaments differ considerably in wattage (21/5 watt) and the bulb will not fit the wrong way round.

23 The later models (1974 onwards) have a wider lens which fits direct onto the wing and is held by four screws. The procedure is as given in paragraph 22 but when refitting the lens, screw the screws in uniformly and do not overtighten them or you will crack the lens.

Front turn signal lights - removal and refitting

24 Two patterns may be encountered. Up to 1975 the turn signal is on top of the wing. It is held in place by a single screw. Remove this and the lens may be lifted upwards. The bulb may then be removed and a new one fitted. If the seal is at all worn or hard, fit a new seal as well.

25 In 1975 the front turn signal was moved to the bumper bar. There is a screw at each end of the lens. Remove these and prise out

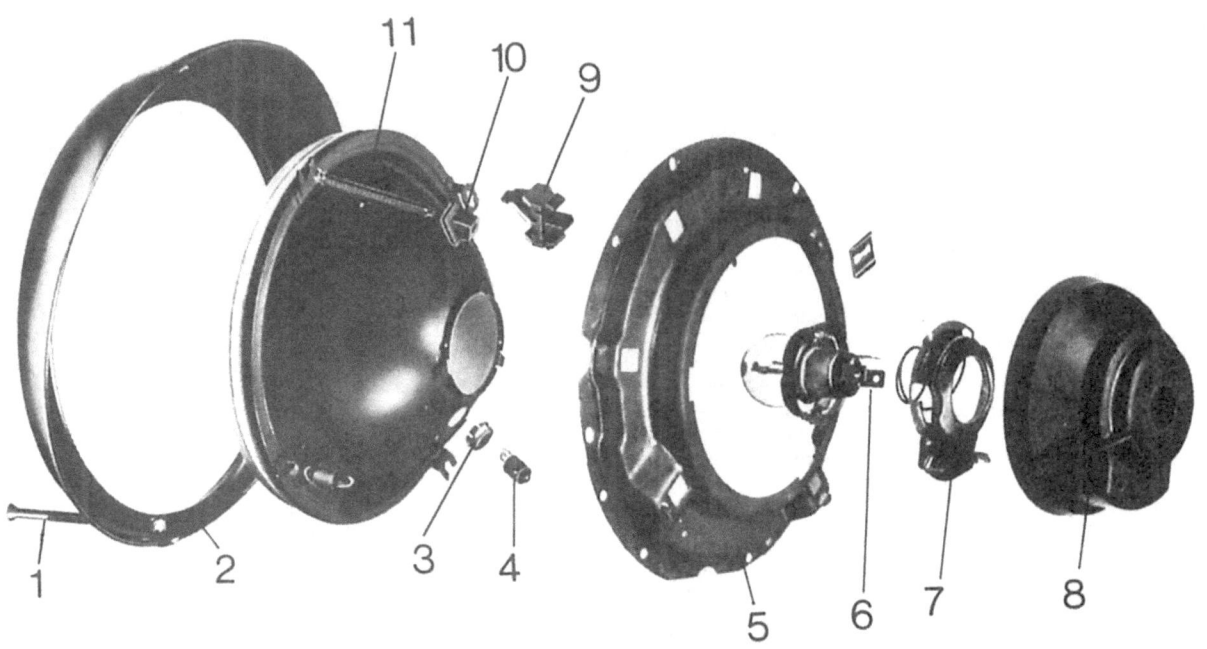

Fig. 13.47. Headlamp — 1974 onwards

1 Trim ring securing screw
2 Trim ring
3 Parking light bulb holder

4 Parking light bulb
5 Support ring
6 Headlight bulb

7 Retaining ring
8 Rubber cap
9 Retainer for insert

10 Focus adjusting nut
11 Headlight insert

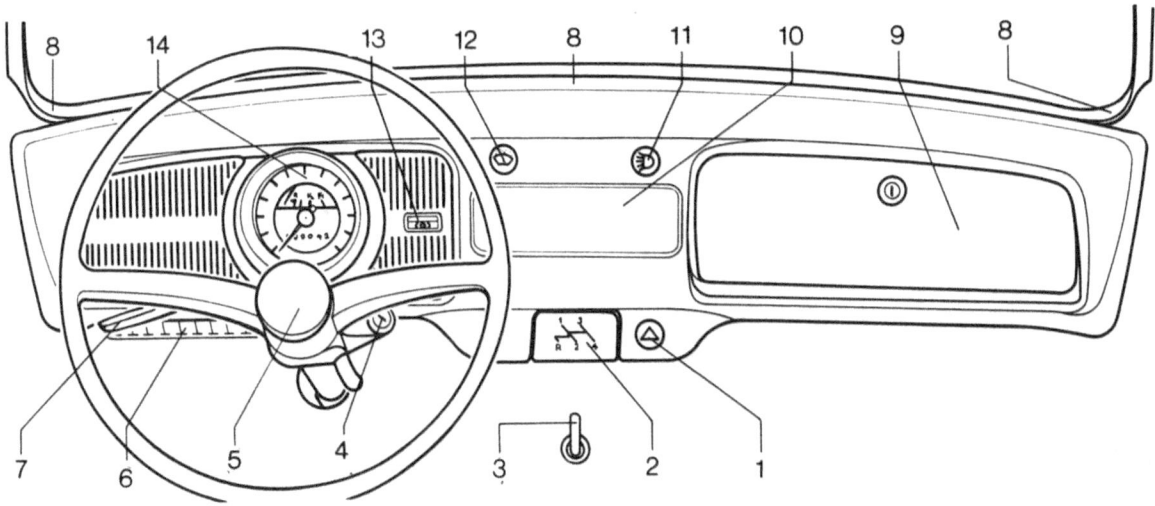

Fig. 13.48. Dashboard layout

1 Hazard lights switch
2 Ashtray
3 Fuel tap*
4 Ignition switch/steering lock
5 Horn button*

6 Fuse box
7 Turn signal/dipswitch
8 Defroster vents
9 Glove box
10 Radio aperture

11 Lights switch
12 Wash/wipe switch*
13 Braking warning light
14 Speedometer and fuel gauge

*These items differ on 1200L models as follows:

3 Fuel tap not fitted
5 Horn pad replaces horn button
12 Steering column stalk switch replaces rotary type on dashboard

the lens. The bulb may now be removed and a new one fitted. When removing the old bulb turn in an anti-clockwise direction. Check that the seal is not worn or damaged, or the lamp will fill with water. Do not overtighten the lens screws, or the lens will crack.

Rear number plate light - removal and refitting
26 Open the engine compartment cover and the light will be seen inside the handle. There are two screws holding the lens in position. Remove these and the lens and bulb holder may be pulled out. Pull the bulb holder out of the lens, push the bulb in a little, turn it, and remove it.
27 Fit a new bulb, push the holder into the lens, check that the cable seal is correctly seated and refit the lens and screws. Do not overtighten the screws or the lens will fracture.

Interior light - removal and refitting
28 The interior light may be removed by inserting a screwdriver blade between the light and the headlining and prising the light out. Go carefully or you will damage the headlining. If the metal is stuck to the lining, insert a thin blade to separate them. The bulb is a festoon type which pulls out of its clips.
29 When refitting the light put the retaining lug in first and then press the light home until the spring clip engages.

Computer diagnosis - general description
30 In 1970 VW introduced the computer diagnosis system. It is a truly immense step forward in preventative maintenance. The system is devised to assess the state of maintenance of all the major and many minor components of the vehicle. Over 80 points are checked, many of them automatically.
31 A multi-pin plug is installed in the engine compartment. The operator at an official agency will check the pressures of your tyres and then plug in a large cable to the diagnosis plug. He selects the correct master card for your vehicle, installs it, and from there on a computer takes over.
32 Items which are checked automatically include steering geometry, ignition and charging systems, cylinder compression, lights and battery. The computer measures the performance of each item and compares it with the required specifications. It then produces a record to show which items require attention.
33 The system has the advantage of accuracy coupled with speed, and can save many hours of work.

Dashboard and instruments - modifications
34 The dashboard and instrument layout has remained almost unchanged since 1971. A typical layout is shown in Fig.13.48.
35 The later 1200L models have a modified horn pad. Details appear later in this Section.
36 Later 1200L models have the wiper switch changed from a dashboard mounted type to a stalk type mounted on the steering column.
37 A hazard warning switch has been fitted to the dashboard on later models. The combined turn signal and headlamp dip switch is mounted on the steering column.
38 On 1200L models a brake failure warning light has been added to the dashboard.
39 Tests for the various instruments and switches are given in the subsequent sub-Sections. A view of the rear of the dashboard is given in Fig.13.49.

Fuses - general
40 The fuse box is located on the left-hand side under the dashboard. It is held to the bulkhead by screws and the lid simply unclips for easy removal.
41 The layout of the fuses varies considerably. Two typical layouts are given in the Specifications but there will be many variations on these.
42 Two fuse ratings are used and it is suggested that at least two spares of each are kept in the car.
43 The driver's handbook supplied with the vehicle does not always give a list of the circuits each fuse protects, so it may be worth making your own list up by removing each fuse in turn and

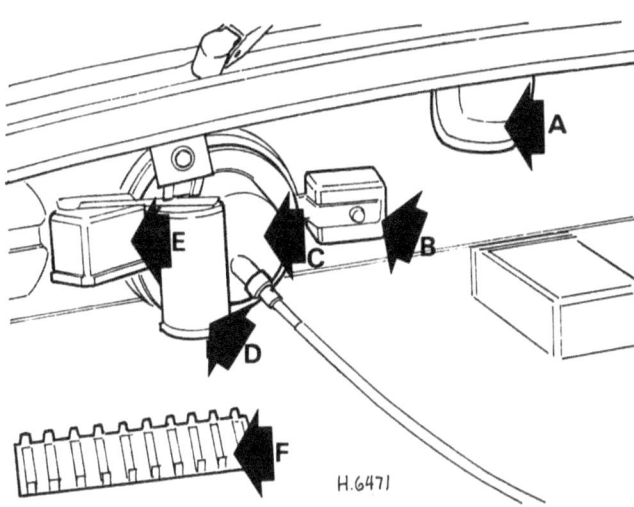

Fig. 13.49. Rear of dashboard viewed from luggage compartment

A	Wiper motor	D	Turn signal relay
B	Fuel gauge	E	Headlight dip/flasher relay
C	Speedometer	F	Fuse terminal block

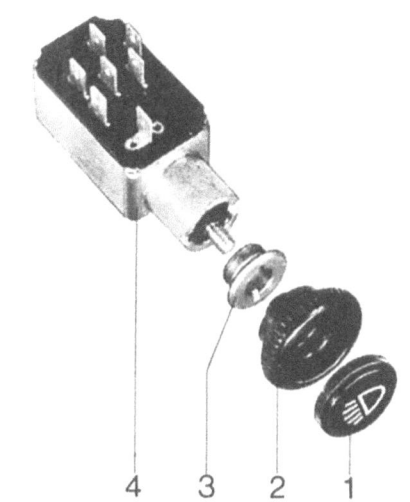

Fig. 13.50. Typical panel switch

| 1 | Cap | 2 | Knob | 3 | Securing nut | 4 | Switch |

noting which items become inoperative. If a fuse blows on the road, at least then you will be able to pinpoint the fuse concerned quickly.
44 Certain circuits are protected by in-line fuses located elsewhere in the vehicle. The locations are not fixed, but typically the heated rear window main current fuse may be under the rear seat, the reversing light fuse in the engine compartment, and the fresh air heater fuse in the front luggage compartment.

Dashboard switches - removal and refitting
45 To remove the push-pull type switch or the rotary type switch, first remove the cover from the back of the dash panel in the luggage compartment.
46 Disconnect the battery for safety reasons.
47 Remove the knob from the switch by unscrewing it. If the stem of the switch revolves with the knob, pull the knob out to the full extent and hold the stem with suitable pliers, (see Fig.13.50).
48 The securing nut really requires a special tool for removal, but

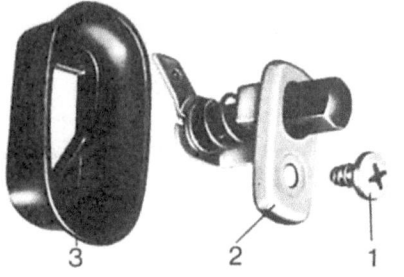

Fig. 13.51. Interior light door pillar switch
1 Screw   2 Switch   3 Seal

Fig. 13.52. Column assembly

1 Steering column
2 Switch housing clamp screw
3 Switch housing
4 Leads from turn signal switch
5 Turn signal/dip switch
6 Steering wheel
7 Horn button
8 Slip ring and cancelling cams
9 Steering wheel nut
10 Lock cylinder
11 Lock
12 Switch
13 Retainer

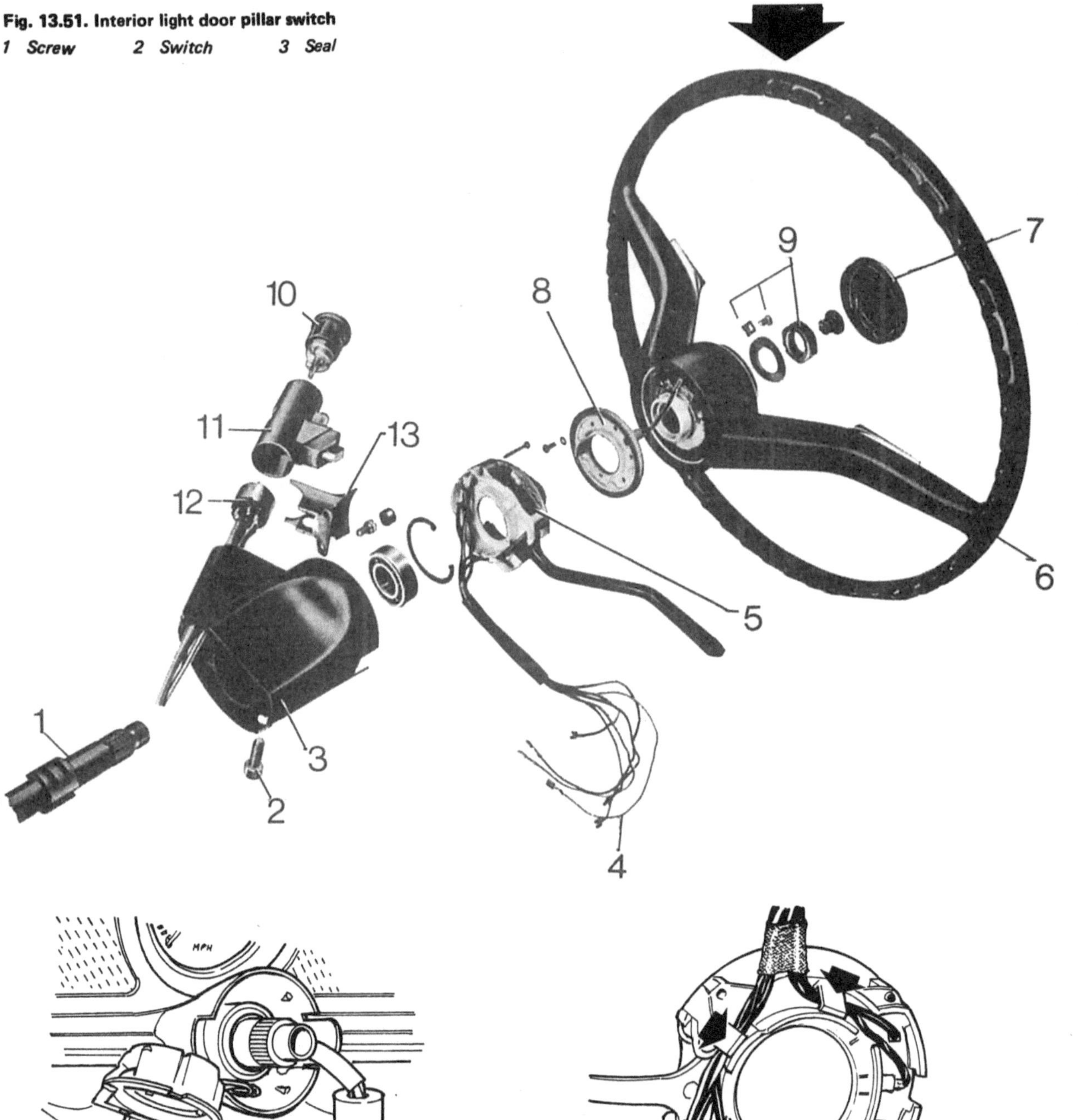

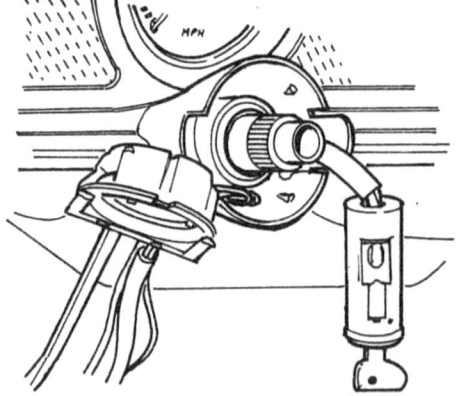

Fig. 13.53. Steering column switches — dismantling

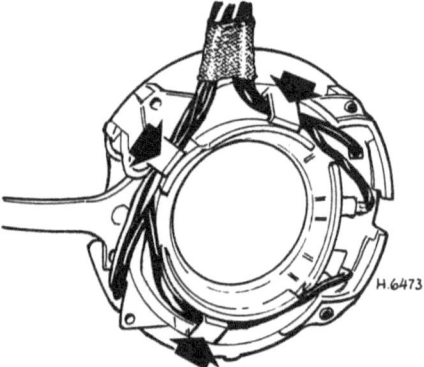

Fig. 13.54. Underside of turn signal switch
Note wires routed under clips (arrowed)

H.6473

it is possible to remove it by placing a small screwdriver in one of the slots and gently tapping it round to unscrew it – do not use great force or damage will occur. Alternatively, a tool may be made up by knocking two panel pins into a piece of wood in such a manner that the protruding pins can be inserted into the two slots at each side of the nut and used to turn the nut.

49 The switch may be removed and the wires disconnected, first noting where each wire goes for correct refitting.

50 Refitting is a reverse of removal.

51 To remove the rocker type switch, squeeze the tabs at each side of the switch hard against the switch body, and pull the switch from the dashboard. Once again, first disconnect the battery for safety reasons.

52 Note all the wire connections and disconnect the wires.

53 Refitting is a reverse of removal.

54 In some of the switches, a small tubular bulb is housed in the spindle and lights when the circuit is switched on. To remove the bulb, either pull the spindle out of the switch and poke the bulb out from the back with a piece of wire, or use a thin plastic tube fitted over the bulb to extract it forwards. The battery should, of course, first be disconnected. Do not handle the bulb with your fingers but hold it in a cloth.

Interior light door pillar switches - removal and refitting

55 Refer to Fig.13.51. Each switch is located in the door pillar and switches the interior light on as the door is opened. The usual problem encountered is that they stick in the 'off' position. Before suspecting the interior light of failure, check that both of the switches work. The plunger should protrude and it should be possible to press it in quite freely.

56 If the switch is not working, remove the battery earth strap and then undo the cross-head screw which holds the switch in the pillar. Pull the switch out of the pillar and disconnect the wire from it. Tie something round the wire to stop it disappearing into the pillar – it takes a lot of finding if it does! The switch can then be repaired or renewed as necessary. The seal will come away with the switch. Be careful to seat it correctly when refitting.

Steering column switches (1200) - removal and refitting

57 There are three switches on the steering column. They are (a) the horn switch actuated by a button on the steering wheel, (b) the direction indicator (turn signal) actuated by a stalk switch under the steering wheel, which also operates the headlight dip mechanism, and (c) the combined ignition switch/steering lock.

58 To service the switches it is necessary to remove the steering wheel. Before starting work disconnect the battery earth strap to avoid accidental short circuits. Then refer to Fig.13.52.

59 Prise off the horn button and remove the spring contact underneath. Undo the nut holding the steering wheel and remove the washer from underneath. Draw the wheel off the splines and turn it over. Note the position of the cancelling cams. Remove the screws holding the slip ring to the wheel and examine the slip ring for burns or pitting. Clean it carefully and check the contact brushes. Check the connector wire. If everything is satisfactory, reassemble the slip ring to the steering wheel.

60 Remove the screws holding the turn signal switch to the column.

61 Lift the switch away and check the wiring underneath and the toggle operation. Six wires in a plastic sleeve are routed to the back of the dashboard. Unless the switch is faulty do not disturb these wires as the switch may be lifted out sufficiently to get at the ignition switch/steering lock without removing the turn signal switch completely.

62 The lock cylinder may be removed without removing the ignition switch. Insert the key and ease the complete assembly out of the casing, feeding the wire gently in from underneath until the retaining spring can be seen through the hole in the steering lock casing. Press the spring down with a small screwdriver and pull out the lock cylinder with the key.

63 If you want to remove the complete assembly take off the retaining clip by removing the screws and then pull the whole assembly out with the key. Fig.13.53 shows the idea.

64 When reassembling there are some points to watch. Refitting

the lock cylinder to the lock must be done carefully. The job must be done with the key out of the cylinder. Press the bottom of the lock cylinder against the key, turn the key to the 'off' position and pull the key out. Now put the cylinder into the lock. Do not force the cylinder in, check that the guide pin at the side moves easily. Fit the lock cylinder, steering lock and starter switch together, ease them into the switch housing and install the retainer with its screws.

65 When refitting the direction indicator switch check that the wires underneath it are safely behind the plastic clips, (see Fig. 13.54).

66 Make sure the cancelling cams on the slip ring are in the right place when refitting the wheel. Torque the wheel nut to the specified torque.

67 It is not necessary to remove the column switch casing when dealing with the switches but the gap between the top of the casing and the bottom of the wheel must be checked after assembling the wheel. It must be between 0.08 and 0.16 inches (2 and 4 mm). The gap should not have altered unless the whole column has been removed, but if it has, slacken the screw clamping the column switch in position (see Fig.13.52) and move the column switch until the correct gap is attained. This gap supersedes the gap given in Chapter 11.

Steering column switches (1200L later models) - removal and refitting

68 The horn push is held to the steering wheel on dowels. It is removed by pulling it upwards – quite a force is required, so take precautions to avoid injury when it does come off suddenly. Refer to Fig.13.55 and Fig.13.56.

69 Remove the steering wheel and disconnect the horn lead. The parts of the horn switch may now be removed. Be careful with the circlip, it may fly off. Remove the contact plate and felt ring.

70 The two stalk switches are interlocked and should be removed together. Press the connection tabs together against the switch housing with a piece of wood. The guide channels may then be removed from the wiper switch. When reassembling be careful not to crush the cables with the wiper switch.

71 The windscreen washer valve may be seen below the column switch. Do not remove the hose unless absolutely necessary. If the hose is removed the clip must not be refitted. A special piece of 'double hose' must be installed (available from VW dealers) and fitted over the washer hose. The washer hose should then be pushed up hard to the enlarged section of the washer valve pipe and the double hose then pushed over the enlarged section. Use a drop of water as a lubricant, but nothing else.

72 The ignition/starter switch is connected to the harness by a multi-pin plug, as are the two stalk switches.

73 The same rules for removing the lock apply as for the 1200 model but there is a lock plate (see Fig.13.56) to be pulled out instead of a retainer. When refitting, this plate should be peened lightly after assembly to keep it in place.

74 The gap between the top of the column switch housing and the underside of the steering wheel must be as for the 1200 model.

Turn signal switch - electrical test

75 Pull the connector off at the column switch on later types or the wire to switch terminal 54B1 (black/white/green) at the flat tag on older types. Check for short circuit between 54B1 on the switch and terminal R or L (see current flow diagram). If there is a short circuit then the switch must be renewed.

Horn circuit - electrical test

76 Check that the gap between the steering wheel and the column switch is correct (see paragraph 67). Adjust it as necessary.

77 Check that the horn fuse has not blown. Turn on the ignition when ready to test in each case.

78 Remove the earth wire from the horn and fit an earth wire from the earth terminal to a good earth point. Turn on the ignition. If the horn blows then the fault is in the column switch because the completion of the horn circuit is through the horn button to earth. Remove the steering wheel and check the horn contacts and wiring.

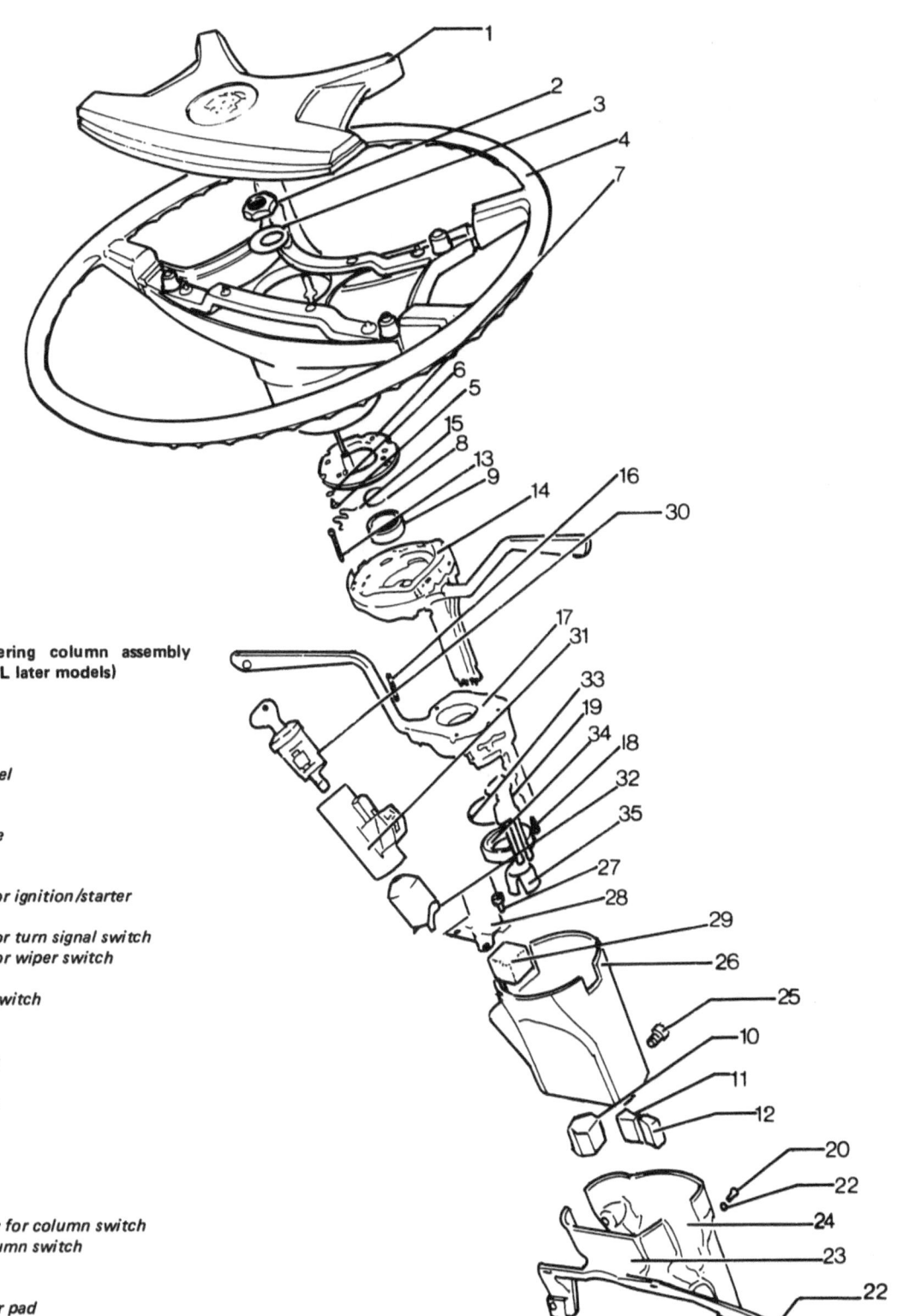

Fig. 13. 55. Steering column assembly (1200L later models)

1 Cap
2 Nut
3 Lockwasher
4 Steering wheel
5 Screw
6 Lockwasher
7 Contact plate
8 Circlip
9 Felt ring
10 Connector for ignition/starter switch
11 Connector for turn signal switch
12 Connector for wiper switch
13 Screw
14 Turn signal switch
15 Spring
16 Spacer
17 Wiper switch
18 Screw
19 Washer valve
20 Screw
21 Screw
22 Washer
23 Cap (upper)
24 Cap (lower)
25 Clamp screw for column switch
26 Steering column switch
27 Screw
28 Retainer
29 Foam rubber pad
30 Lock cylinder and key
31 Steering lock
32 Ignition/starter switch
33 Circlip for ball bearing
34 Ball bearing
35 Contact ring

H.6474

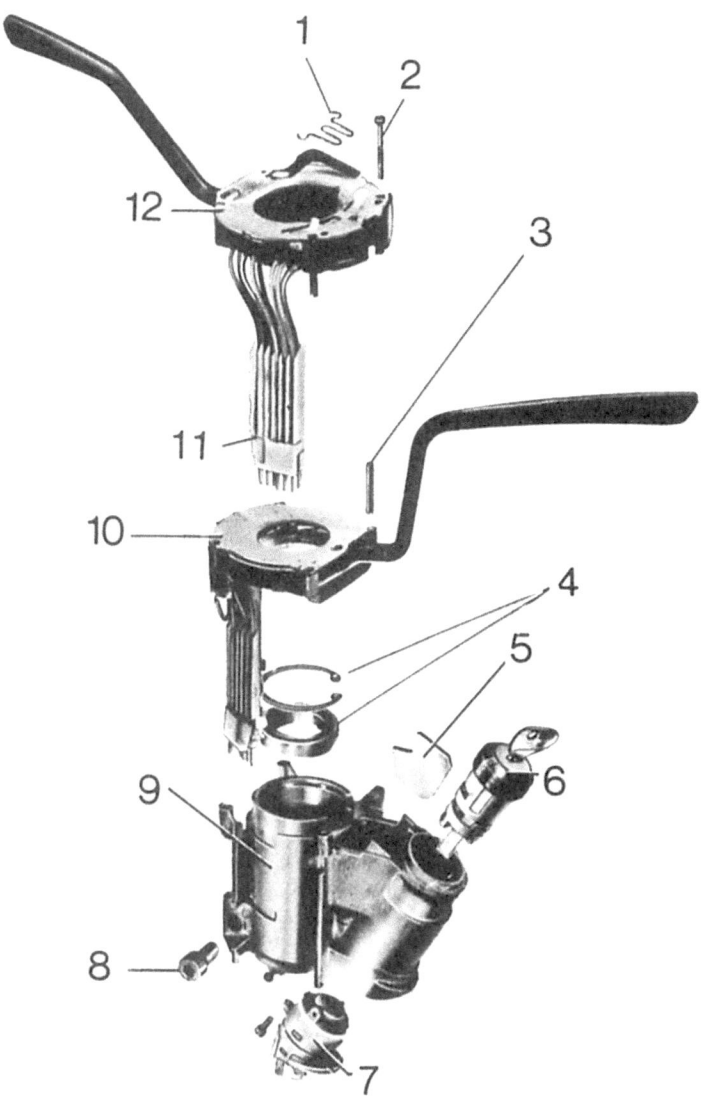

Fig. 13. 56. Steering column switches
(1200L later models)

1 Spring
2 Screw
3 Spacer
4 Circlip and seal
5 Lock plate for steering lock/ignition
  switch
6 Lock cylinder
7 Ignition/starter switch
8 Switch clamp screw
9 Lock housing
10 Wiper switch
11 Leads to plug
12 Turn signal/headlight dip switch

79 If the horn did not blow when the ignition was turned on then either the supply to the horn is defective, or the horn itself is not working. Use a voltmeter or a test bulb to check the supply voltage at the horn terminal. If this is absent then there is a break in the circuit between the fuse box and the horn. Remove the battery earth strap and disconnect the supply wire from the horn and the wire to the horn fuse at the fuse box. Fit a long jumper lead in place of this wire and then reconnect the battery and try again. If the horn now works, this confirms the break in the circuit. If you still cannot get voltage at the horn then check that there is voltage at the fuse box. The supply to the horn fuse comes through the ignition switch so there may be a problem at that point. In the latter case the other components on the horn fuse will not work either.

80 If there is voltage at the horn terminal and the earth connection is in order then the horn itself is at fault, and must be renewed. You can try turning the adjusting screw at the back, which sometimes restores the horn to working order again, but usually only temporarily.

Hazard warning lights switch - testing

81 Remove the battery earth strap, remove the switch and put it in the 'on' position. Referring to the current flow diagram, locate the hazard warning lights switch and check the circuit between terminal 30 on the switch and the battery positive with an ohmmeter. Check terminals L, R, and 49a for continuity. Any open circuit or resistance means the switch must be renewed.

Hazard warning lights/turn signal relay - testing

82 Owing to the comparatively large current needed to operate the hazard warning lights, it is not possible to pass this current through the switch, and a relay must therefore be used. The switch supplies a small current to the relay (located behind the dash), which then operates to close the circuit and supply the operating current to the light bulbs. The same relay is used for both the turn signal and hazard lights.

83 Referring to the current flow diagrams, first check the turn signal switch and the hazard warning switch as detailed previously, then test the relay. There are two patterns used, one with a terminal marked '+', and the other with a terminal marked '+49'.

84 Connect this terminal direct to terminal 30 and work the turn signal switch, and then work the hazard switch. If the lights do not operate on either function, it confirms that the relay is faulty as opposed to either switch, and should be renewed.

Turn signal warning light - checking

85 The only checking that can be carried out is to make sure that the bulb is not blown, that the relevant fuse is not blown and that the relay is operating correctly. The bulb holder and the various connections should also be checked for corrosion.

Headlamp dip and flasher circuit - testing and repair

86 The column switch may be removed for testing and repair or renewal as described previously.

87 The relay is the rectangular one situated adjacent to the turn

signal/hazard relay under the dash. If it is necessary to remove it, first disconnect the battery, then mark each wire for correct refitting and detach it.

88 If the headlights do not work at all, check the supply to the on/off switch, then check the switch. If the lights work but will not dip, then either the column switch or the relay is at fault.

89 To check the switch it is necessary to remove it from the column to identify the leads S and 31. A quick check is to locate terminal S on the relay and check its resistance to earth with the control lever at main beam. At this position the stalk switch is open, so resistance is infinity. Move the stalk switch to low beam and the resistance should be zero, thus indicating that the switch has closed. It will be seen from the wiring diagram that moving the switch connects the relay to earth, completing the activating circuit. This will tell you whether the switch is working, but not what is wrong with it.

90 If the switch is working then a new relay is probably required. Check that the full circuit voltage is present at terminal 30 of the relay. Check also that voltage is present at terminal 56 of the relay when the on/off switch is closed. If voltage is present at both terminals then the relay solenoid is not working and a new relay is required.

Brake lights and warning light for dual circuit brakes - testing and repair

91 The warning light is on the dashboard at the side of the speedometer. The switches to operate this light are on the brake master cylinder.

92 To check the brake light contact (81 and 82a) pull the multi-pin connector off the front brake circuit switch (on the master cylinder). Switch on the ignition and depress the brake pedal, checking that the brake light in each rear light cluster is working. Refit the connector and repeat the test with the other switch.

93 If the light fails to come on when either of these switches are worked then the switch must be renewed. If the light does not operate at all check the fuse and the wiring. Check the bulbs as well, but it is unlikely that both bulbs will fail at the same time.

94 Having ascertained that the brake lights work, now check the warning lamp. For this locate contacts 81 and 81a. These are connected to the black and the black/red wires in each of the switches on the brake cylinder. Put a wire bridge across the 81 and 81a contacts of the rear circuit switch. Pull the other switch connector off and start the engine. The dual circuit warning lamp should light up. Depress the brake pedal, and the warning light should go out. Switch off and repeat the test replacing the front circuit switch connector with a bridge across terminals 81 and 81a and removing the connector from the rear circuit switch. Start the engine and check again.

95 If the light operates for one circuit but not the other then renew the switch on the non-operative circuit (see Section 10). If the light does not operate at all, check the fuse and the bulb, the wiring and all the connections. The light should come on when the ignition is switched on and go out when the engine is started. To remove the bulb pull out the lens with the marking symbol and fit a piece of 5 mm insulation tube over the bulb and withdraw it. If a replacement bulb does not work either, then pull the red connector off terminal K on a brake light switch and connect it to terminal 30 in the fuse box. When voltage is applied to terminal K the warning light should light up. If it does not the holder needs renewal.

Turn signal lights - fault finding and renewal of relay

96 The information in Chapter 10 is still applicable. If the indicator (turn signals) work but the bulb of the warning light does not work read paragraph 85 of this Chapter.

97 If the turn signals do not work at all, then first check that the relevant fuse is in order.

98 If the fuse is blown then the short circuit must be found before fitting a new one. Trace the circuits on the current flow diagram.

99 The turn signal switch may be tested as in paragraph 75 and the hazard warning lights switch as in paragraph 81.

100 If the hazard warning lights work but the turn signals do not, or vice versa then the problem is not in the relay. If neither of them work check the relay as follows.

101 Take off the cover in the luggage compartment to expose the back of the dashboard. Two makes of relay have been used. Locate either terminal '+' or terminal '−49' depending on the make of relay. It is a wise precaution at this point to disconnect the battery earth. Connect either '+' or '−49' to terminal 30 of the fuse box. Refit the earth strap, turn on the ignition and operate the turn signal switch. If the direction indicators work then the relay is in good order. If they do not, then, having checked the switch, it is likely that the relay is faulty. Before purchasing a new one, carry out the following check.

102 Take the lens of each of the indicator lamps in turn and check the bulbs, wiring, and earth of each installation, as detailed previously. Check all the connectors in the system. If one unit is not working properly then it may cause the whole system to fail. If you are satisfied that all four units are in good order proceed as follows.

103 Remove the battery earth strap. Disconnect the relay, putting a tag on each wire for easy and correct refitting. Remove the relay, and replace it with a new unit. The terminal markings may be different on the new relay, so be sure to find out which terminal is which before fitting it and connecting it up. Refit the earth strap and test the circuit again for correct operation.

104 If the system still does not work, there may be a fault in the wiring harness. In this case you should consult your dealer.

Windscreen wipers and washers - general

105 The wipers and washers remain basically unchanged, but certain later models have a steering column mounted switch instead of the dashboard mounted type, as described earlier in this Section.

106 It is possible to have fitted as an optional extra an intermittent wash/wipe system. The fitting of this is quite involved, and advice should be obtained from the local dealer.

Fuel gauge and voltage stabilizer - testing

107 On vehicles fitted with an electrically operated fuel gauge, it is possible to check the gauge and stabilizer accurately without much trouble. The sender unit is in the top of the fuel tank and has two wires going to it; the one going to the larger, shielded terminal is from the gauge; the other one, which is brown, is the earth wire.

108 Remove these from the sender unit and in place of the sender unit connect them successively to resistances 10 ohms, 22 ohms and 47 ohms. With the 10 ohm resistance in the circuit the gauge should have the needle registering around 'full'. For the 22 ohm resistance the needle should register 'half full', and when the 47 ohm resistance is connected the needle should be in the reserve zone. The ignition must, of course, be switched on.

109 If this is not so then either the gauge, the voltage stabilizer or the wiring is faulty. If the wiring is faulty either the gauge will not register at all (open circuit) or it will register more than full all the time (short circuit).

110 Before testing the voltage stabilizer it is necessary to find out which kind is fitted. Vehicles sold without a fitted radio usually have a bi-metallic vibrator type of stabilizer bolted to the back of the speedometer. This type cannot be dismantled for repair. Measure the voltage across it while the circuit is fully connected. This voltage reading should oscillate, ie it is a pulsating voltage. If it is not then a new stabilizer is required.

111 The other type of stabilizer fitted is a Zener diode type, used where a radio is fitted. It is fastened to the back of the speedometer head as with the bi-metallic type. By pressing the two lugs towards the holding clip the lid may be released and lifted off. Inside is a small festoon type bulb at the back of which a small diode is fitted in the case. Fig.13.57 shows a diagram of the lid and Fig.13.58 a diagram of the case with lid removed.

112 To test the circuit refer to Fig.13.59. Remove the wire from terminal J, switch on the ignition and measure the voltage at J. Zero voltage indicates a faulty stabilizer. Remove the lid, take out the bulb and check it, renewing if defective. To check the diode use an ohmmeter. Disconnect the leads from terminal + and terminal J. Connect the ohmmeter between J and the speedometer case on the securing screw. Read the resistance; it will either be a low one or a high one. Change the leads over and measure again. If the same reading is obtained then the diode is faulty, and should be renewed.

Fig. 13. 57. Zener diode voltage stabilizer — layout of cover

Fig. 13.58. Zener diode voltage stabilizer — lid removed

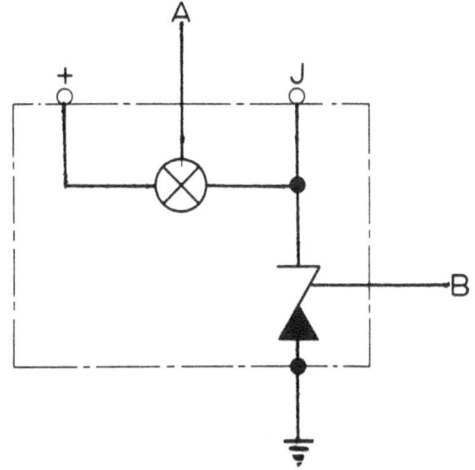

Fig. 13.59. Zener diode voltage stabilizer — circuit diagram

A Bulb   B Diode

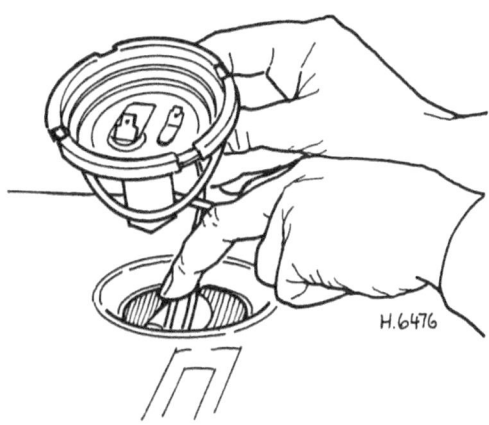

Fig. 13. 60. Removing fuel gauge sender unit

113 If the fuel gauge and stabilizer are in order and the wiring is correct then the sender must be checked, as detailed in the next sub-Section.

Fuel gauge sender unit - removal, refitting and testing

114 Before deciding that the fuel gauge sender unit is to be renewed it is as well to be sure that the gauge and stabilizer are working correctly and that the connecting and earth wires are in good order.
115 The fibre board lining in the luggage compartment should be removed and the tank wiped free from dust. The sender unit is more or less centrally placed in the tank. There are two terminals on it, one with a shield, which is the wire terminal to the gauge, the other, which has a brown wire, being the earth terminal. Check very carefully that when the ignition is switched on there is voltage at the input terminal, and check that the earth lead is properly connected to earth. If these are correct and the gauge and regulator are correct then the sender must be removed.
116 The tank must be drained, disconnected and pulled forward before the sender unit can be extracted, and this is not an easy task.
117 Disconnect the battery earth strap and tie it firmly to one side.
118 The tank should be drained of fuel, although it is possible to do the job by running the car until the petrol is as low in the tank as possible. Then disconnect the inlet hose and ease the tank forwards. Disconnect the wires from the gauge.
119 With the tank about 12 inches (30 cm) forwards the sender unit may be removed. If you look at the sender you will see that a line drawn through the terminals would be parallel to the stiffening

rib in the tank. Note the position of the terminals. Press the sender unit down and turn it in an anti-clockwise direction until it can be lifted away from the tank a small amount. Before lifting any more turn the sender so that the terminals are in the position they were before you started undoing the screw, ie parallel with the rib. There is a baffle plate inside the tank which shrouds the sender unit arm on both sides. Lift the unit clear to the back, pressing down the float arm so that the float does not jam in the baffle. Do not use force or the float may be damaged. (Refer to Fig.13.60).
120 There is little that can be done to repair the electrical circuit of the unit; check it with an ohmmeter to see if there are any obvious breaks. Then check the mechanical operation. If the unit is not working properly do not attempt makeshift repairs, fit a new one.
121 When installing the unit hold it in a vertical position with the float arm parallel to the stiffening rib of the tank. Put a little graphite powder on the seal. Lower the float into the hole and manipulate the float arm so that the float can slide along the bottom of the tank as the rest of the unit fits into place. Once the unit is in place turn it clockwise (to the left) to start the bayonet thread, press the sender down and turn it anti-clockwise (to the right) until the terminals are in the correct position. If you are not used to this sort of job have a practice refit with the old unit to get the feel of the job.
122 Refit the tank carefully, making sure the filler hose is properly seated. Reconnect the leads to the sender unit, refit the battery lead, turn on the ignition, and check the reading on the gauge. Refill the tank, checking the gauge at intervals. Finally, refit the board cover in the luggage compartment.

Heated rear window - general

123 Fitting a heated rear window is one of the jobs which should be left to the local dealer, as it is very easy to break, damage or fit it incorrectly.

124 The relay which supplies the current to the heated rear window is located under the rear seat, as is the fuse for that circuit. The switching current to the relay is routed from the fuse box via a rocker type switch in the dashboard.

125 If the heater does not work, first check that the relay is earthed properly to the car body, and that the switch, wiring and fuse are all working correctly.

126 The only other fault could be a broken element. Provided the break is not too large, it is possible to repair it by bridging the gap with a special repair compound available from your local dealer or auto electrical specialist.

127 Fit masking tape along each side of the break in the element and paint on the repair compound to fill the gap. After allowing it to dry for at least one hour, remove the tape and surplus compound. It may be necessary to trim the edge of the compound with a sharp knife to allow the tape to come away without disturbing the repaired element.

128 Finally, check the operation of the heated rear window.

Fault diagnosis — windscreen wipers

Symptom	Reason/s
Motor does not work, runs slowly or stops	Fuse blown. Loose connections. Linkage stiff or seized. Armature burnt out. Brushes excessively worn. Switch defective.
Wiper arms do not park correctly	Cable to terminal 53 of motor loose or broken. Drive crank not in correct position. Open circuit between terminal 58 and fuse. Faulty switch.
Motor continues to run when switched off	Defective switch.
Motor runs slowly with high pitched noise	Gear housing incorrectly seated. Motor faulty.
Wiper blades judder as they sweep screen, or do not wipe screen satisfactorily	Blade damaged. Wiper arm bent. Incorrectly adjusted wiper arm.

13 Suspension, dampers and steering

General description

1 The system remains almost unchanged for later models, with the exception of the fitting of the safety type steering column.

2 Although the rear suspension is unchanged, Fig.13.61 is included to show its construction.

3 Fitting of heavy duty shock absorbers can prove beneficial for use on rough terrain or for towing. This is discussed in this Section.

4 There are some minor modifications to the Specifications as detailed.

Steering column (safety type) - removal and refitting

5 Refer to Fig.13.62 which shows the detail of the column tube. The purpose of this design is to protect the driver from chest injury in the event of a collision. The column tube is fixed to the underside of the dashboard by a mounting plate. The guide pieces are fastened to the mounting plate with plastic rivets. Heavy pressure on the steering wheel will shear these rivets and the mounting plate will disintegrate, allowing the column to slide forward into the bush in the bulkhead and to crumple the lattice work of the steering column.

6 Removal of this gear entails considerable work. Remove the earth strap from the battery before starting work. Open the luggage compartment and remove the hardboard lining. Remove the connections from the petrol gauge sender unit and then undo the hoses and clamps and remove the fuel tank.

7 Disconnect the earth wire from the coupling (the horn wire) and undo the clamp holding the column to the steering gearbox. There is a support ring which holds the column tube in place on the bulkhead. Bend up the locking tabs, undo the bolts and take the support away. The column is now free at the lower end. The rest of the work is inside the car.

8 Take off the steering wheel and column switch (see Section 12). The switches do not need to be disconnected; hang them to one side. Undo the three screws holding the switch case to the body and remove the switch case. Undo the clamp for the steering column bolts and remove the clamp. If this clamp has sheared it will be easier to remove the steering wheel before disconnecting the lower end of the shaft. Note carefully which way round the clamp is fitted as the new one must go on the same way.

9 Now pull the column tube and column up and out into the car. If the lattice is distorted it may not come through the rubber support on the bulkhead. In this case it may be necessary to saw off the distorted portion. Do not force it through the rubber support or the support will be damaged. Fitting a new one is a difficult, tedious job.

10 If your car is fitted with a steering lock secured by anti-theft shear bolts, the bolts must be drilled out. This must be carried out with extreme care, and if you doubt your capabilities to carry out this operation satisfactorily, entrust the work to a dealer. If the tapped hole threads are damaged then you are in real trouble and the repair will be lengthy and expensive.

11 Refitting is basically the reverse of removal. Fit the clamp for the column tube to the body, taking care to position it the right way up. The closed side must face forward. Tighten the screws to the specified torque.

12 If you are fitting a new steering column then the old one will have been extracted from the tube by undoing the circlip and sliding the column out of the tube. Take the contact ring off the column, noting which way up it goes.

13 Fit the column tube into the rubber support on the bulkhead. Push the steering column into the column tube, fit the clamp bolts

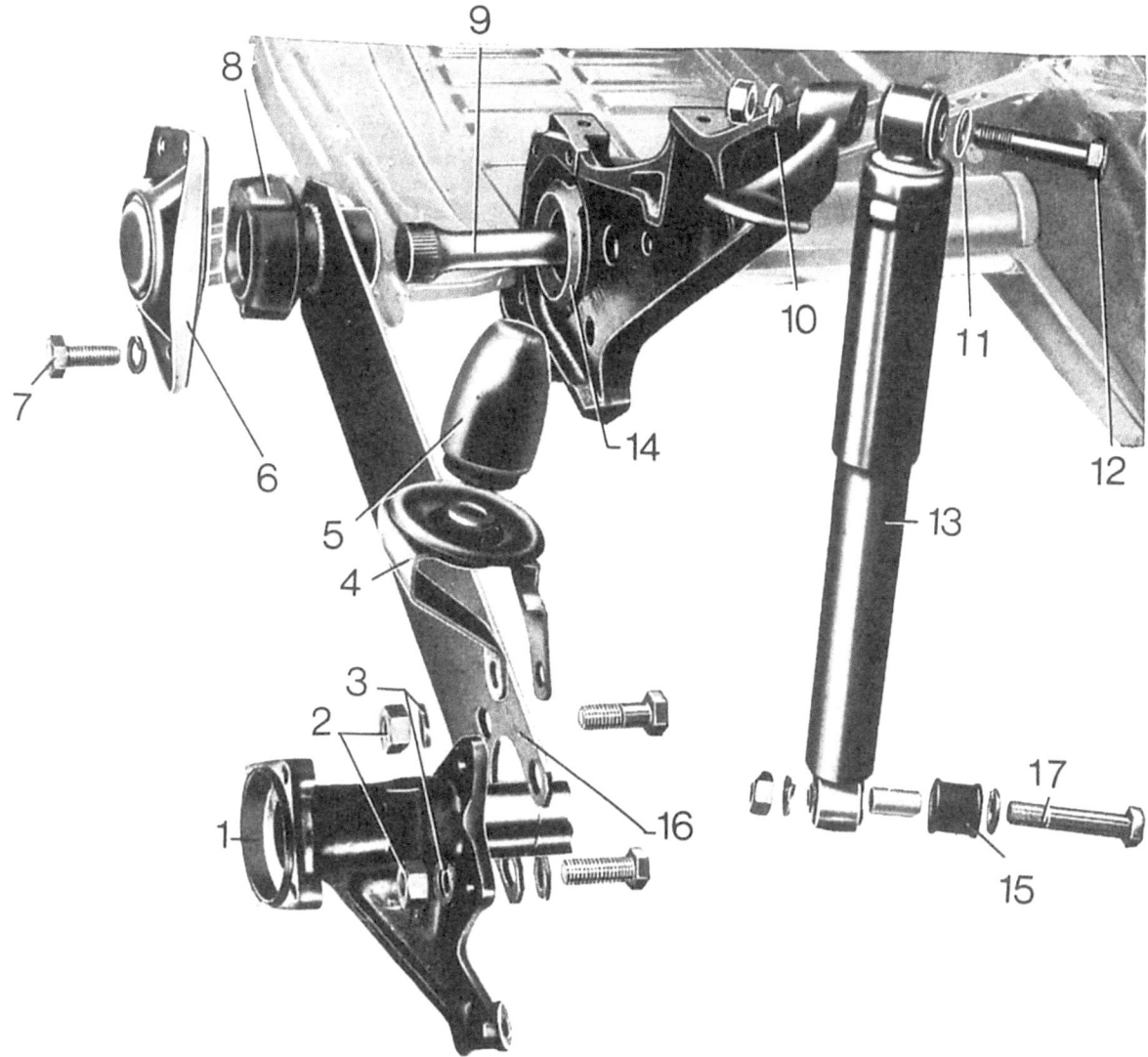

Fig. 13.61. Details of rear suspension

1 Bearing flange	6 Cover for hub	11 Washer	15 Rubber bush
2 Nuts	7 Bolt	12 Top shock absorber	16 Trailing arm
3 Spring washers	8 Outer rubber bush	anchor bolt	17 Lower shock absorber
4 Buffer bracket	9 Torsion bar	13 Shock absorber	anchor/bolt
5 Buffer	10 Nut and washer	14 Inner rubber bush	

for the tube to the mounting plate and connect the column to the flexible coupling; do not tighten the clamp bolt for the coupling. Fit the contact ring into the steering column bearing from below (see Chapter 11 for details of steering column bearing).

14 Fit the steering column switch but do not tighten the screws. Now fit the circlip to the steering column tube. The steering must be in the centre position (the marking ring on the steering worm must align with the joint on the housing). Tighten the clip holding the column to the coupling at the bottom and clamp the nut; use a new lock plate. Connect the earth cable for the horn.

15 Fit the new support plate to the steering column tube on the bulkhead and bend the tabs over to lock the bolts.

16 Check that the turn signal lever is in the central position and install the steering wheel so that the cancelling mechanism is in the correct position. If it is not then the cams will be damaged by the cancelling ring tongue. Torque the steering wheel nut to the specified torque. Now move the column switch so that the gap between the top of the switch housing and the underside of the wheel boss is 2 to 4 mm (0.08 to 0.16 in). Details of fitting the

switch are given in Section 12. Tighten the switch housing screws. They move in the elongated holes of the bracket on the column tube.

17 Now check that the column and tube are aligned. There must not be any strain on the lattice type part of the column. If necessary slacken the various bolts and ease the column tube. Finally tighten the holding bolts to the specified torque.

18 It is essential that the steering geometry be checked once this repair is done.

19 Refit the tank and the hardboard cover. Do not forget the fuel gauge sender unit connections. Refit the battery earth strap.

Shock absorbers (dampers) - heavy duty type

20 If the car is to be used on rough terrain or for towing, it may be advantageous to fit heavy duty shock absorbers. The local VW dealer will be able to provide advice on the type to be fitted.

21 Removal and refitting of the heavy duty type is as for the standard shock absorber. If it is decided to fit the heavy duty type, they should be fitted as a complete set of four.

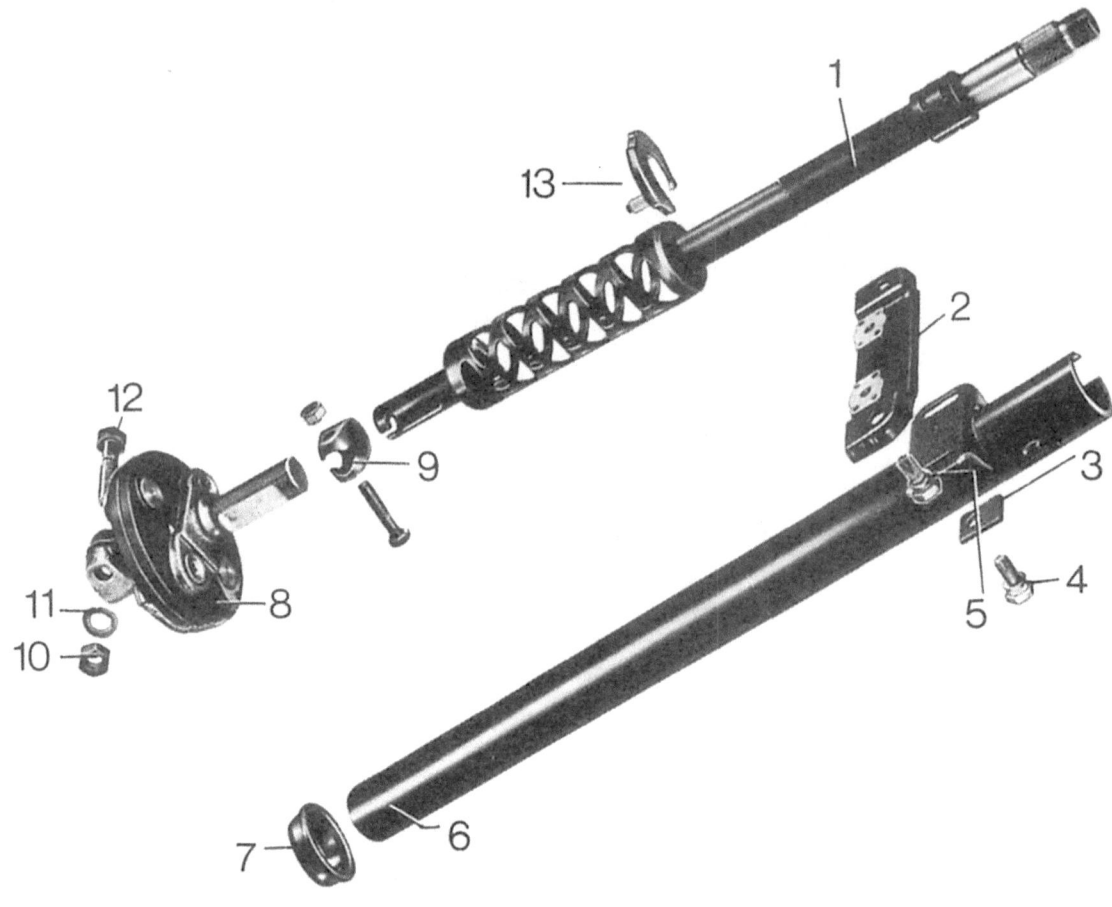

Fig. 13.62. Safety type steering column

1	Steering column	4	Shear bolt
2	Column mounting	5	Shear bolt
	plate	6	Column tube
3	Packing	7	Bush

8	Flexible coupling disc	12	Bolt
9	Clamp	13	Column support ring
10	Nut		
11	Washer		

22 For towing, a special type of shock absorber known as 'Load-a-Juster' may be fitted to the rear only. These consist of, in effect, coil springs fitted around standard shock absorbers. Removal and refitting is quite simple and it is possible to fit the 'Load-a-Justers' for a limited period (eg whilst towing a caravan on holiday) and to remove them afterwards for normal use. For more extensive towing, an uprated version of this unit may be used. However, this requires correct adjustment or handling may be adversely affected.
23 It is not recommended that the 'Load-a-Justers' are left on the car for normal use, as the handling can be adversely affected when the car is running light.
24 For fitment of any of the above devices, it is recommended that you seek the advice of the local dealer first.

Tyres - general
25 Tyres should be kept inflated at the correct pressures, and inspected regularly for abnormal tread wear patterns and damage.
26 With regard to mixing radial and crossply tyres, there are two important rules to observe. Firstly, never mix radial and crossply tyres on the same axle. And secondly, if using two radial tyres and two crossply tyres, the radials must be on the rear axle.
27 Having given these rules, it must be emphasised that for preference it is much more satisfactory to fit four tyres (and the spare) of the same type of construction. The handling of the car can be adversely affected by mixing tyres of different construction.

14 Bodywork and underframe

General description of modifications
1 The 1200 and 1200L have gradually acquired most of the bodywork improvements made for the more expensive VW models.
2 The details in the rest of this Section point out where these fitments differ from earlier models and give revised methods of fitting and adjustments.

Door trim panels (later models) - removal and refitting
3 First remove the window winder and door latch lever. The winder.handle has a plastic cover which should be prised off at the spindle end. A crosshead screw is then accessible and should be removed (photo). The recessed finger plate behind the inner door handle lever can be prised out also with a screwdriver (photo). The crosshead screw behind it can then be removed to release the assembly (photo).
4 The door is modified and the arm rest is bolted to the frame. Remove these screws (photo). Now use a wooden or plastic strip to go between the panel and the door and ease out the retaining clips. Be careful not to tear them from the trim panel. The trim panel may now be lifted from the door (photo).
5 Refitting is the reverse of removal. Remember to fit the

14.3a Prise the plastic cover off and remove the screw from the centre of the winder handle

14.3b Remove the recess plate from the inner door handle . . .

14.3c . . . and remove the screw

14.4a Take out the screws holding the door pull . . .

14.4b . . . and the trim may be lifted away as the clips are eased out of the door

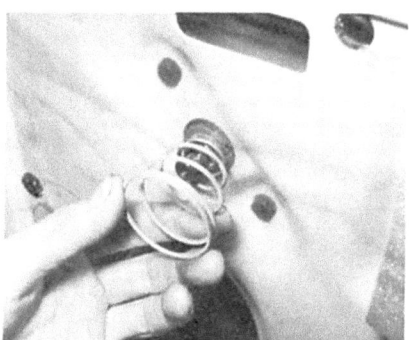

14.5a Do not forget the tension spring on the winder handle . . .

14.5b . . . or the rubbing washer

14.7 Undo the screws holding the window support to the winding mechanism

14.8 Removing the glass

tension spring behind the trim panel over the window regulator spindle (photo) and the rubbing washer behind the window handle (photo).

Window regulator mechanism and window (later models) - removal and refitting

6 Remove the door trim and the plastic sheet. If care is used the plastic sheet will come away in one piece and can be used again, otherwise it is a rather tedious job cutting out another one.

7 Lower the window and undo the screws holding the window frame to the winding mechanism (photo).

8 Undo the screws holding the winder to the door, ease the winder forwards and the glass may be drawn out downwards (photo).

9 Now undo the screws holding the winding handle mechanism to the door (photo) and the winder mechanism may be eased out downwards (photo). A photograph of the winder mechanism held against the door is given. Note the plastic bushes.

10 It is not possible to repair the winder mechanism. Do not grease the drive spiral, a little light oil is all that is required. If there are tight spots it may be possible to straighten the tube. Should this not cure the trouble a new mechanism is required.

11 The refitting is quite a struggle. Get someone with patience to help you. Fit the winder in through the slot with the front location (winder hub) first. Wriggle the winder mechanism until you can pick up all the securing bolts thread holes but do not put the bolts in yet. This is where a second pair of hands helps a lot. Insert the glass behind the winder from the bottom and ease it gently into the door channels.

12 Holding the glass in position fit the screws which hold the glass carrier (the plated piece) to the winder. Fasten the winder to the bottom of the door and refit the winder fixing screws (3) and then the two bolts which hold the nut.

13 Tighten all the screws gently and try the mechanism. It may be necessary to slacken the screws holding the window to the winder and reposition them a little.

This sequence of photographs deals with the repair of the dent and paintwork damage shown in this photo. The procedure will be similar for the repair of a hole. It should be noted that the procedures given here are simplified – more explicit instructions will be found in the text

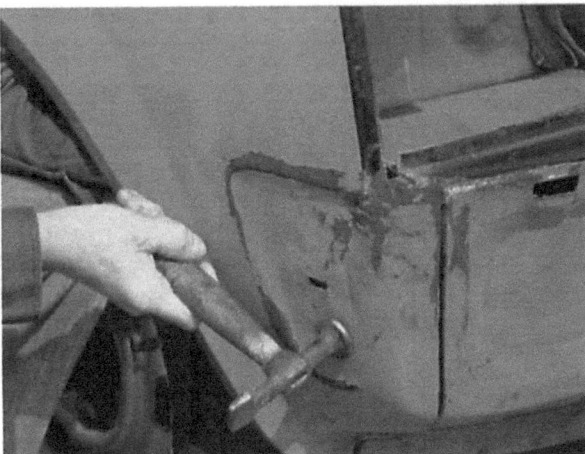

In the case of a dent the first job – after removing surrounding trim – is to hammer out the dent where access is possible. This will minimise filling. Here, the large dent having been hammered out, the damaged area is being made slightly concave

Now all paint must be removed from the damaged area, by rubbing with coarse abrasive paper. Alternatively, a wire brush or abrasive pad can be used in a power drill. Where the repair area meets good paintwork, the edge of the paintwork should be 'feathered', using a finer grade of abrasive paper

In the case of a hole caused by rusting, all damaged sheet-metal should be cut away before proceeding to this stage. Here, the damaged area is being treated with rust remover and inhibitor before being filled

Mix the body filler according to its manufacturer's instructions. In the case of corrosion damage, it will be necessary to block off any large holes before filling – this can be done with aluminium or plastic mesh, or aluminium tape. Make sure the area is absolutely clean before ...

... applying the filler. Filler should be applied with a flexible applicator, as shown, for best results; the wooden spatula being used for confined areas. Apply thin layers of filler at 20-minute intervals, until the surface of the filler is slightly proud of the surrounding bodywork

Initial shaping can be done with a Surform plane or Dreadnought file. Then, using progressively finer grades of wet-and-dry paper, wrapped around a sanding block, and copious amounts of clean water, rub down the filler until really smooth and flat. Again, feather the edges of adjoining paintwork

The whole repair area can now be sprayed or brush-painted with primer. If spraying, ensure adjoining areas are protected from over-spray. Note that at least one inch of the surrounding sound paintwork should be coated with primer. Primer has a 'thick' consistency, so will find small imperfections

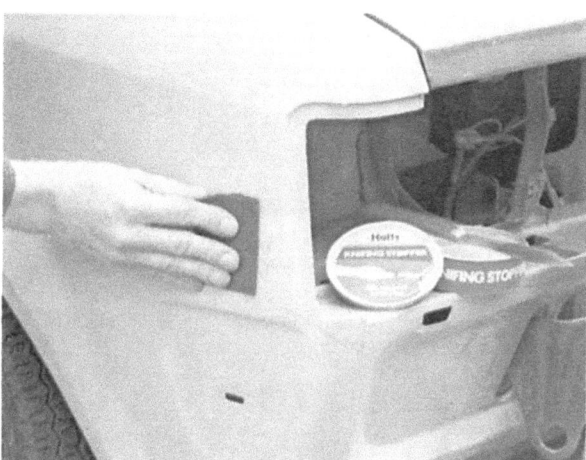

Again, using plenty of water, rub down the primer with a fine grade wet-and-dry paper (400 grade is probably best) until it is really smooth and well blended into the surrounding paintwork. Any remaining imperfections can now be filled by carefully applied knifing stopper paste

When the stopper has hardened, rub down the repair area again before applying the final coat of primer. Before rubbing down this last coat of primer, ensure the repair area is blemish-free – use more stopper if necessary. To ensure that the surface of the primer is really smooth use some finishing compound

The top coat can now be applied. When working out of doors, pick a dry, warm and wind-free day. Ensure surrounding areas are protected from over-spray. Agitate the aerosol thoroughly, then spray the centre of the repair area, working outwards with a circular motion. Apply the paint as several thin coats

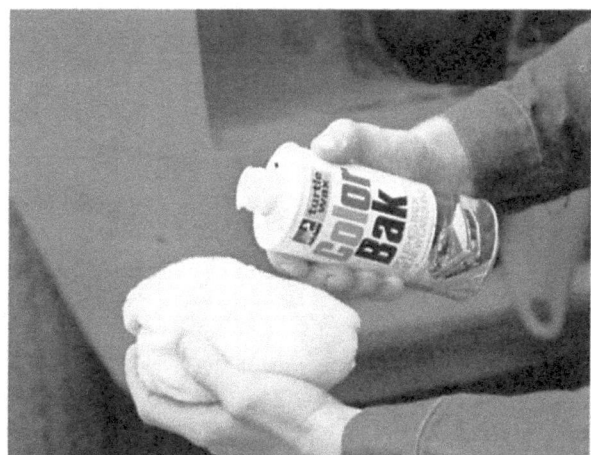

After a period of about two weeks, which the paint needs to harden fully, the surface of the repaired area can be 'cut' with a mild cutting compound prior to wax polishing. When carrying out bodywork repairs, remember that the quality of the finished job is proportional to the time and effort expended

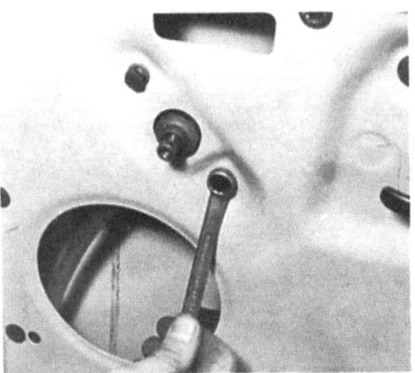

14.9a The bolts holding the winder handle mechanism

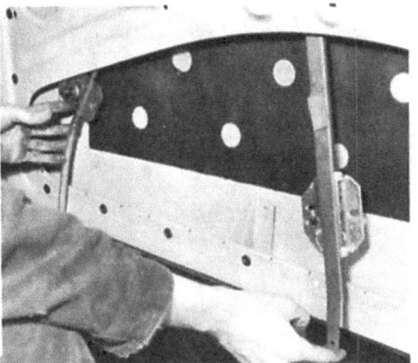

14.9b Remove the winder mechanism

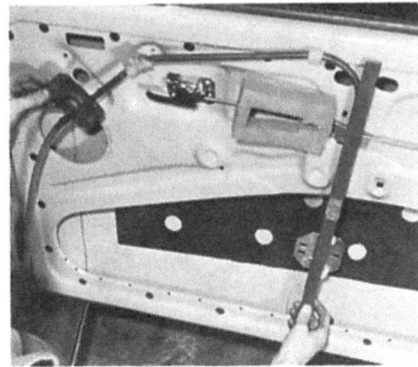

14.9c The mechanism ready for refitting

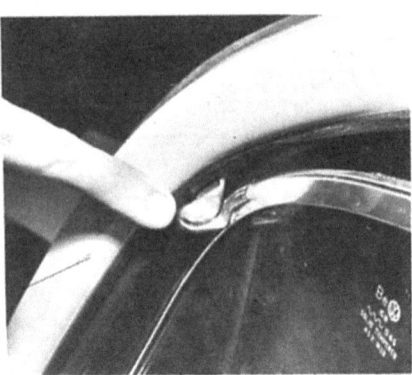

14.16 Quarterlight upper pivot

14.21 Remove the bolts holding the inner handle . . .

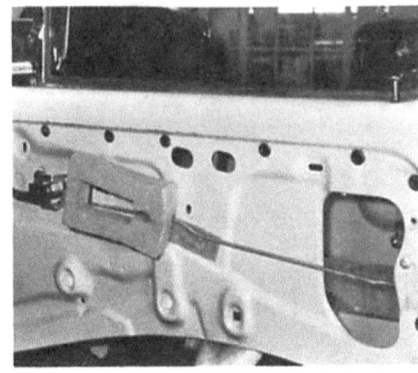

14.22 . . . and take it away with the remote control lever

14.23 Unclip the inside lock control

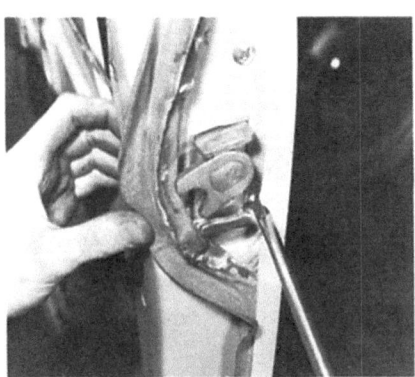

14.24a Undo the screws holding the lock in the door edge . . .

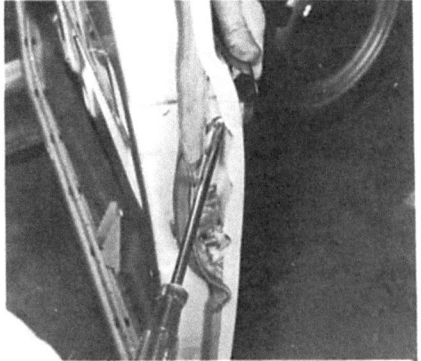

14.24b . . . and the one holding the handle

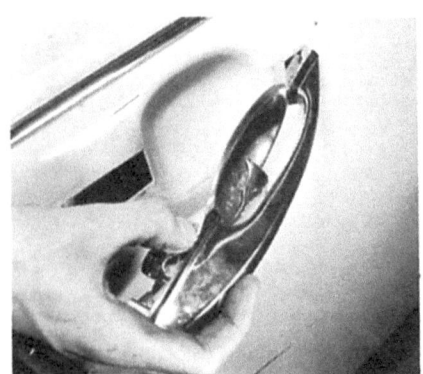

14.24c The handle may now be removed · · ·

14.25 . . . and the lock removed from the inside

14.33 The removable disc for an extra mirror

14 Above all do not rush the job or force things.

15 Refit the plastic sheet and the trim.

Quarterlight (later models) - removal and refitting

16 If only the glass is being renewed the top pivot pin must be drilled out (photo). The glass may then be lifted up and out.

17 When fitting a new glass the upper pin should be properly riveted and hard material used, otherwise the car security is jeopardised.

18 If the lower pivot is giving trouble it will be necessary to remove the main window and lifter and take out the whole main frame channel to get to it. This involves removing all the weatherstrips and undoing the securing bolts at the rear edge of the door frame. The channel strip is then taken out complete with the window dividing strip.

Door latch mechanism (later models) - removal and refitting

19 Remove the door trim.

20 The latch mechanism is divided into three sections:

  a) The inside handle
  b) The locking mechanism worked from inside the car
  c) The latch proper and the outside handle

21 The inside handle may be removed by undoing two bolts (photo).

22 The remote control rod with its packing may then be removed (photo).

23 The inside lock mechanism may now be disconnected (photo).

24 Ease the sealing strip away from the door (photo) and remove the screws holding the lock, and the handle (photo). The lock handle may now be taken off the door (photo).

25 The lock is quite complicated and if it does not work properly then it should be replaced (photo) by a new one.

26 Reassembly is straightforward. Refit the inside (remote control) handle. The lock should be in the locked position. Do not forget the foam rubber packing. Fit the lock to the door, make sure it works from inside, and finally refit the interior locking pin. Refit the trim.

Door latch striker plate (later models) - adjustment

27 Rattles in doors are usually due to an incorrect striker plate position.

28 First check that the door fits the aperture properly by seeing that the gaps are more or less equal all round and that it fits flush with the side panel of the bodywork. There should be no rubbing and all the weatherstrip should show signs of equal compression.

29 Then make sure that the latch on the door is working properly.

30 If the door will shut and latch only when slammed it means that the rubber wedge at the top of the striker plate is too far out thus preventing the corresponding wedge on the door from moving right in. If the door can be rattled in and out when latched the wedge on the striker plate is too far in. To remedy either of these conditions slacken the striker plate fixing screws and move the upper end in or out as required.

31 If adjustment still fails to prevent any looseness when the door is shut then it is in order to put some packing between the wedge and the bracket, to which it is held by two screws.

Extra rear view mirror and radio aerial - provision for fitting

32 VW make vehicles for many countries so a thoughtful designer has made provision for a rear view mirror fixing on either side of the vehicle.

33 A small disc is fitted into the door on the opposite side to the provided mirror and this may be removed to fit an extra mirror (photo).

34 It is obviously best to get the extra mirror from VW, as it fits the hole. It may be necessary to open the hole a little with a round file and to cut a small slot for the fixing tab, and bend it in.

35 File off the triangular tab on the mirror locknut, and screw the nut onto the mirror arm about two turns, making sure the flat sides of the lugs are towards the mirror. Fit the mirror arm and nut through the panel and turn it until the locknut contacts the bent-in tab. Pull the mirror towards you and screw the arm into the nut, tightening the nut and at the same time adjusting the mirror.

36 In the same photo will be seen the existing hole for the radio aerial. Remove the plug and fit the aerial according to the instructions provided with it.

Front seats (later models) - removal, refitting and repair

37 Later models are fitted with three point seats. To remove this type proceed as follows.

38 Push the seat back to the last but one position. Take the covers off the runners, then insert a screwdriver into the bracket from the front and push the locking plate down.

39 Pull the longitudinal position adjusting lever on the frame tunnel and slide the seat out to the rear.

40 Before refitting the seat, check the friction pads and spring clips. If the clips are not pressed into the upper friction pads, the seat will rattle.

41 Insert the seat into the runners at the rear first, and then into the front bracket. The positional lever on the frame tunnel should be pulled to the rear. Refit the covers to the runners.

42 The seat upholstery is liable to sag with age causing creasing of the seat surface. This may be remedied as follows.

43 Remove the seat and lay it upside down on the clean surface so that the springs are visible. It will be seen that there are round helical springs and flat springs. These are connected with wire clips. Remove the rear three clips and shorten them about ¾ inch (20 mm). Refit them, and then join the flat springs together with clips made out of welding wire or similar.

44 Remove the seat cover, smooth out the wadding and insert sufficient extra to fill the seat.

Minor body damage - repair

See photo sequences on pages 246 and 247.

Repair of minor scratches in the vehicle's bodywork

If the scratch is very superficial, and does not penetrate to the metal of the bodywork - repair is very simple. Lightly rub the area of the scratch with a paintwork renovator or a very fine cutting paste, to remove the loose paint from the scratch and to clear the surrounding bodywork of wax polish. Rinse the area with clean water.

Apply touch-up paint to the scratch using a thin paintbrush; continue to apply thin layers of paint until the surface of the paint in the scratch is level with the surrounding paintwork. Allow the new paint at least two weeks to harden, then, blend it into the surrounding paintwork by rubbing the paintwork in the scratch area with a paintwork renovator, or a very fine cutting paste. Finally apply wax polish.

An alternative to painting over the scratch is to use a paint transfer. Use the same preparation for the affected area, then simply pick a patch of a suitable size to cover the scratch completely. Hold the patch against the scratch and burnish its backing paper, the paper will adhere to the paintwork, freeing itself from the backing paper at the same time. Polish the affected area to blend the patch into the surrounding paintwork.

Where a scratch has penetrated right through to the metal of the bodywork, causing the metal to rust, a different repair technique is required. Remove any loose rust from the bottom of the scratch with a penknife; then apply rust inhibiting paint to prevent the formation of rust in the future. Using a rubber or nylon applicator, fill the scratch with bodystopper paste. If required, this paste can be mixed with cellulose thinners to provide a very thin paste which is ideal for filling narrow scratches. Before the stopper paste on the scratch hardens, wrap a piece of smooth cotton rag around the top of a finger. Dip the finger in cellulose thinners and then quickly sweep it across the surface of the stopper paste in the scratch; this will ensure that the surface of the stopper paste is slightly hollowed. The scratch can now be painted over as described earlier in this Section.

Repair of dents in the vehicle's bodywork

When deep denting of the vehicle's bodywork has taken place the first task is to pull the dent out, until the affected bodywork almost attains its original shape. There is little point in trying to restore the original shape completely, as the metal in the damaged area will have stretched on impact and cannot be reshaped fully to its original contour. It is better to bring the level of the dent up to a point which is about 1/8 inch (3 mm) below the level of the surrounding bodywork. In cases where the dent is very shallow anyway, it is not worth trying to pull it all out.

If the underside of the dent is accessible, it can be hammered out gently from behind, using a mallet with a wooden or plastic head. Whilst doing this, hold a suitable block of wood firmly against the outside of the dent. This block will absorb the impact from the hammer blows and thus prevent a large area of bodywork being 'belled-out'.

Should the dent be in a section of the bodywork which has a double skin or some other factor making it inaccessible from behind, a different technique is called for. Drill several small holes through the metal inside the dent area - particularly in the deeper sections. Then screw long self-tapping screws into the holes just sufficiently for them to gain a good purchase in the metal. Now the dent can be pulled out by pulling on the protruding heads of the screws with a pair of pliers.

The next stage of the repair is the removal of the paint from the damaged area, and from an inch or so of the surrounding 'sound' bodywork. This is accomplished more easily by using a wire brush or abrasive pad on a power drill, although it can be done just as effectively by hand using sheets of abrasive paper. To complete the preparations for filling, score the surface of the bare metal with a screwdriver or the tang of a file, or alternatively, drill small holes in the affected area. This will provide a really good 'key' for the filler paste. To complete the repair see the Section on filling and re-spraying.

Repair of rust holes or gashes in the vehicle's bodywork

Remove all paint from the affected area and from an inch or so of the surrounding 'sound' bodywork, using an abrasive pad or a wire brush on a power drill. If these are not available a few sheets of abrasive paper will do the job just as effectively. With the paint removed you will be able to gauge the severity of the corrosion and therefore decide whether to renew the whole panel (if this is possible) or to repair the affected area. New body panels are not as expensive as most people think and it is often quicker and more satisfactory to fit a new panel than to attempt to repair large areas of corrosion.

Remove all fittings from the affected area except those which will act as a guide to the original shape of the damaged bodywork (eg headlamp shells etc). Then, using tin snips or a hacksaw blade, remove all loose metal and any other metal badly affected by corrosion. Hammer the edges of the hole inwards in order to create a slight depression for the filler paste.

Wire brush the affected area to remove the powdery rust from the surface of the remaining metal. Paint the affected area with rust inhibiting paint; if the back of the rusted area is accessible treat this also.

Before filling can take place it will be necessary to block the hole in some way. This can be achieved by the use of one of the following materials: zinc gauze, aluminium tape or polyurethane foam.

Zinc gauze is probably the best material to use for a large hole. Cut a piece to the approximate size and shape of the hole to be filled, then position it in the hole so that its edges are below the level of the surrounding bodywork. It can be retained in position by several blobs of filler paste around its periphery.

Aluminium tape should be used for small or very narrow holes. Pull a piece off the roll and trim it to the approximate size and shape required, then pull off the backing paper (if used) and stick the tape over the hole; it can be overlapped if the thickness of one piece is insufficient. Burnish down the edges of the tape with the handle of a screwdriver, or similar, to ensure that the tape is securely attached to the metal underneath.

Polyurethane foam is best used where the hole is situated in a section of bodywork of complex shape, backed by a small box section (eg where the sill panel meets the rear wheel arch — most vehicles). The usual mixing procedure for this foam is as follows: put equal amounts of fluid from each of the two cans provided in the kit, into one container. Stir until the mixture begins to thicken, then quickly pour this mixture into the hole, and hold a piece of cardboard over the larger apertures. Almost immediately the polyurethane will begin to expand, gushing frantically out of any small holes left unblocked. When the foam hardens it can be cut back to just below the level of the surrounding bodywork with a hacksaw blade.

Having blocked off the hole the affected area must now be filled and sprayed - see Section on bodywork filling and re-spraying.

Bodywork repairs - filling and re-spraying

Before using this Section, see Sections on dent, deep scratch, rust hole and gash repairs.

Many types of bodyfiller are available, but generally speaking those proprietary kits which contain a tin of filler paste and a tube of resin hardener are best for this type of repair. A wide, flexible plastic or nylon applicator will be found invaluable for imparting a smooth and well contoured finish to the surface of the filler.

Mix up a little filler on a clean piece of card or board - use the hardener sparingly (follow the maker's instructions on the packet) otherwise the filler will set very rapidly.

Using the applicator, apply the filler paste to the prepared area; draw the applicator across the surface of the filler to achieve the correct contour and to level the filler surface. As soon as a contour that approximates the correct one is achieved, stop working the paste - if you carry on too long the paste will become sticky and begin to 'pick-up' on the applicator.

Continue to add thin layers of filler paste at twenty-minute intervals until the level of the filler is just 'proud' of the surrounding bodywork.

Once the filler has hardened, excess can be removed using a plane or file. From then on, progressively finer grades of abrasive paper should be used, starting with a 40 grade 'wet or dry' paper. Always wrap the abrasive paper around a flat rubber cork or wooden block - otherwise the surface of the filler will not be completely flat. During the smoothing of the filler surface the 'wet or dry' paper should be periodically rinsed in water - this will ensure that a very smooth finish is imparted to the filler at the final stage.

At this stage the 'dent' should be surrounded by a ring of bare metal, which in turn should be encircled by the finely 'feathered' edge of the good paintwork. Rinse the repair area with clean water, until all of the dust produced by the rubbing-down operation is gone.

Spray the whole repair area with a light coat of grey primer; this will show up any imperfections in the surface of the filler. Repair these imperfections with fresh filler paste or bodystopper, and once more smooth the surface with abrasive paper. If bodystopper is used, it can be mixed with cellulose thinners to form a really thin paste which is ideal for filling small holes. Repeat this spray and repair procedure until you are satisfied that the surface of the filler, and the feathered edge of the paintwork are perfect. Clean the repair area with clean water and allow to dry fully.

The repair area is now ready for spraying. Paint spraying must be carried out in a warm, dry, windless and dust free atmosphere. This condition can be created artificially if you have access to a large indoor working area, but if you are forced to work in the open, you will have to pick your day very carefully. If you are working indoors, dousing the floor in the work area with water will 'lay' the dust which would otherwise be in the atmosphere. If the repair area is confined to one body panel, mask off the surrounding panels; this will help to minimise the effects of a slight mismatching in paint colours. Bodywork fittings (eg chrome strips, door handles etc) will also need to be masked off. Use genuine masking tape and several thicknesses of newspapers for the masking operation.

Before commencing to spray, agitate the aerosol can thoroughly, then spray a test area (an old tin, or similar) until the technique is mastered. Cover the repair area with a thick coat of primer; the thickness should be built up using several thin layers of paint rather than one thick one. Using 400 grade 'wet or dry' paper, rub down the surface of the primer until it is really smooth. While doing this, the work area should be thoroughly doused with water. Allow to dry before spraying on more paint.

Spray on the top coat, again building up the thickness by using several thin layers of paint. Start spraying in the centre of the repair area and then, using a circular motion, work outwards until the whole repair area and about 2 inches of the surrounding original paintwork is covered. Remove all masking material 10 to 15 minutes after spraying on the final coat of paint. Allow the new paint at least two weeks to harden fully; then, using a paintwork renovator or a very fine cutting paste, blend the edges of the new paint into the existing paintwork. Finally, apply wax polish.

Major body damage - repair

Where serious damage has occurred or large areas need renewal due to neglect, it means certainly that completely new sections or panels will need welding in and this is best left to professionals. If the damage is due to impact it will also be necessary to completely check the alignment of the bodyshell structure. Due to the principle of construction the strength and shape of the whole can be affected by damage to a part. In such instances the services of the official agent with specialist checking jigs are essential. If a body is left misaligned it is first of all dangerous as the car will not handle properly, and secondly, uneven stresses will be imposed on the steering, engine and transmission, causing abnormal wear or complete failure.

Safety first!

Professional motor mechanics are trained in safe working procedures. However enthusiastic you may be about getting on with the job in hand, do take the time to ensure that your safety is not put at risk. A moment's lack of attention can result in an accident, as can failure to observe certain elementary precautions.

There will always be new ways of having accidents, and the following points do not pretend to be a comprehensive list of all dangers; they are intended rather to make you aware of the risks and to encourage a safety-conscious approach to all work you carry out on your vehicle.

Essential DOs and DON'Ts

DON'T rely on a single jack when working underneath the vehicle. Always use reliable additional means of support, such as axle stands, securely placed under a part of the vehicle that you know will not give way.

DON'T attempt to loosen or tighten high-torque nuts (e.g. wheel hub nuts) while the vehicle is on a jack; it may be pulled off.

DON'T start the engine without first ascertaining that the transmission is in neutral (or 'Park' where applicable) and the parking brake applied.

DON'T suddenly remove the filler cap from a hot cooling system – cover it with a cloth and release the pressure gradually first, or you may get scalded by escaping coolant.

DON'T attempt to drain oil until you are sure it has cooled sufficiently to avoid scalding you.

DON'T grasp any part of the engine, exhaust or catalytic converter without first ascertaining that it is sufficiently cool to avoid burning you.

DON'T allow brake fluid or antifreeze to contact vehicle paintwork.

DON'T syphon toxic liquids such as fuel, brake fluid or antifreeze by mouth, or allow them to remain on your skin.

DON'T inhale dust – it may be injurious to health (see *Asbestos* below).

DON'T allow any spilt oil or grease to remain on the floor – wipe it up straight away, before someone slips on it.

DON'T use ill-fitting spanners or other tools which may slip and cause injury.

DON'T attempt to lift a heavy component which may be beyond your capability – get assistance.

DON'T rush to finish a job, or take unverified short cuts.

DON'T allow children or animals in or around an unattended vehicle.

DO wear eye protection when using power tools such as drill, sander, bench grinder etc, and when working under the vehicle.

DO use a barrier cream on your hands prior to undertaking dirty jobs – it will protect your skin from infection as well as making the dirt easier to remove afterwards; but make sure your hands aren't left slippery. Note that long-term contact with used engine oil can be a health hazard.

DO keep loose clothing (cuffs, tie etc) and long hair well out of the way of moving mechanical parts.

DO remove rings, wristwatch etc, before working on the vehicle – especially the electrical system.

DO ensure that any lifting tackle used has a safe working load rating adequate for the job.

DO keep your work area tidy – it is only too easy to fall over articles left lying around.

DO get someone to check periodically that all is well, when working alone on the vehicle.

DO carry out work in a logical sequence and check that everything is correctly assembled and tightened afterwards.

DO remember that your vehicle's safety affects that of yourself and others. If in doubt on any point, get specialist advice.

IF, in spite of following these precautions, you are unfortunate enough to injure yourself, seek medical attention as soon as possible.

Asbestos

Certain friction, insulating, sealing, and other products – such as brake linings, brake bands, clutch linings, torque converters, gaskets, etc – contain asbestos. *Extreme care must be taken to avoid inhalation of dust from such products since it is hazardous to health.* If in doubt, assume that they *do* contain asbestos.

Fire

Remember at all times that petrol (gasoline) is highly flammable. Never smoke, or have any kind of naked flame around, when working on the vehicle. But the risk does not end there – a spark caused by an electrical short-circuit, by two metal surfaces contacting each other, by careless use of tools, or even by static electricity built up in your body under certain conditions, can ignite petrol vapour, which in a confined space is highly explosive.

Always disconnect the battery earth (ground) terminal before working on any part of the fuel or electrical system, and never risk spilling fuel on to a hot engine or exhaust.

It is recommended that a fire extinguisher of a type suitable for fuel and electrical fires is kept handy in the garage or workplace at all times. Never try to extinguish a fuel or electrical fire with water.

Note: *Any reference to a 'torch' appearing in this manual should always be taken to mean a hand-held battery-operated electric lamp or flashlight. It does NOT mean a welding/gas torch or blowlamp.*

Fumes

Certain fumes are highly toxic and can quickly cause unconsciousness and even death if inhaled to any extent. Petrol (gasoline) vapour comes into this category, as do the vapours from certain solvents such as trichloroethylene. Any draining or pouring of such volatile fluids should be done in a well ventilated area.

When using cleaning fluids and solvents, read the instructions carefully. Never use materials from unmarked containers – they may give off poisonous vapours.

Never run the engine of a motor vehicle in an enclosed space such as a garage. Exhaust fumes contain carbon monoxide which is extremely poisonous; if you need to run the engine, always do so in the open air or at least have the rear of the vehicle outside the workplace.

If you are fortunate enough to have the use of an inspection pit, never drain or pour petrol, and never run the engine, while the vehicle is standing over it; the fumes, being heavier than air, will concentrate in the pit with possibly lethal results.

The battery

Never cause a spark, or allow a naked light, near the vehicle's battery. It will normally be giving off a certain amount of hydrogen gas, which is highly explosive.

Always disconnect the battery earth (ground) terminal before working on the fuel or electrical systems.

If possible, loosen the filler plugs or cover when charging the battery from an external source. Do not charge at an excessive rate or the battery may burst.

Take care when topping up and when carrying the battery. The acid electrolyte, even when diluted, is very corrosive and should not be allowed to contact the eyes or skin.

If you ever need to prepare electrolyte yourself, always add the acid slowly to the water, and never the other way round. Protect against splashes by wearing rubber gloves and goggles.

When jump starting a car using a booster battery, for negative earth (ground) vehicles, connect the jump leads in the following sequence: First connect one jump lead between the positive (+) terminals of the two batteries. Then connect the other jump lead first to the negative (–) terminal of the booster battery, and then to a good earthing (ground) point on the vehicle to be started, at least 18 in (45 cm) from the battery if possible. Ensure that hands and jump leads are clear of any moving parts, and that the two vehicles do not touch. Disconnect the leads in the reverse order.

Mains electricity

When using an electric power tool, inspection light etc, which works from the mains, always ensure that the appliance is correctly connected to its plug and that, where necessary, it is properly earthed (grounded). Do not use such appliances in damp conditions and, again, beware of creating a spark or applying excessive heat in the vicinity of fuel or fuel vapour.

Ignition HT voltage

A severe electric shock can result from touching certain parts of the ignition system, such as the HT leads, when the engine is running or being cranked, particularly if components are damp or the insulation is defective. Where an electronic ignition system is fitted, the HT voltage is much higher and could prove fatal.

Index

Zeitfracht Medien GmbH
Ferdinand-Jühlke-Straße 7
99095 Erfurt, Deutschland
produktsicherheit@kolibri360.de